W9-CEQ-623

PUBLIC FINANCE

The McGraw-Hill Series Economics

PUBLIC FINANCE

NINTH EDITION

Harvey S. Rosen
Princeton University

Ted Gayer
Georgetown University

McGraw Hill **Higher Education**

The McGraw·Hill Companies

Mc Graw Hill Higher Education

PUBLIC FINANCE

Published by McGraw-Hill/Irwin, a business unit of The McGraw-Hill Companies, Inc., 1221 Avenue of the Americas, New York, NY, 10020. Copyright © 2010, 2008, 2005, 2002, 1999, 1995, 1992, 1988, 1984 by The McGraw-Hill Companies, Inc. All rights reserved. No part of this publication may be reproduced or distributed in any form or by any means, or stored in a database or retrieval system, without the prior written consent of The McGraw-Hill Companies, Inc., including, but not limited to, in any network or other electronic storage or transmission, or broadcast for distance learning.

Some ancillaries, including electronic and print components, may not be available to customers outside the United States.

This book is printed on acid-free paper.

1 2 3 4 5 6 7 8 9 0 QWD/QWD 0 9

ISBN   978-0-07-351135-1
MHID   0-07-351135-8

Vice president and editor-in-chief: *Brent Gordon*
Publisher: *Douglas Reiner*
Director of development: *Ann Torbert*
Development editor: *Anne E. Hilbert*
Editorial coordinator: *Marianne L. Magday*
Vice president and director of marketing: *Robin J. Zwettler*
Marketing director: *Rhonda Seelinger*
Associate marketing manager: *Dean Karampelas*
Vice president of editing, design and production: *Sesha Bolisetty*
Project manager: *Dana M. Pauley*
Production supervisor: *Gina Hangos*
Design coordinator: *Joanne Mennemeier*
Senior photo research coordinator: *Jeremy Cheshareck*
Media project manager: *Balaji Sundararaman, Hurix Systems Pvt. Ltd.*
Typeface: *10.5/12 Times Roman*
Compositor: *Glyph International*
Printer: *Quebecor World Dubuque Inc.*

Library of Congress Cataloging-in-Publication Data

Rosen, Harvey S.
    Public finance / Harvey S. Rosen, Ted Gayer.—9th ed.
        p. cm.—(The McGraw-Hill series economics)
    Includes index.
    ISBN-13: 978-0-07-351135-1 (alk. paper)
    ISBN-10: 0-07-351135-8 (alk. paper)
        1. Finance, Public—United States.   I. Gayer, Ted, 1970-   II. Title.
HJ257.2.R67 2010
336.73—dc22

2009029678

www.mhhe.com

To our children

HARVEY S. ROSEN

Harvey S. Rosen is the John L. Weinberg Professor of Economics and Business Policy at Princeton University. Professor Rosen, a Fellow of the Econometric Society and a Research Associate of the National Bureau of Economic Research, is well known for his contributions to the fields of Public Finance, Labor Economics, and Applied Microeconomics. From 1989 to 1991, he served as Deputy Assistant Secretary (Tax Analysis) at the US Treasury. During a second stint in Washington from 2003 to 2005, he served on the President's Council of Economic Advisers, first as a Member and then as Chairman. In this capacity, he provided advice to the White House on a wide variety of policy issues, including tax reform, Social Security, health care, energy, the federal budget, and financial market regulation. In 2007 he received from the National Tax Association its most prestigious award, the Daniel M. Holland medal for distinguished lifetime contributions to the study and practice of public finance.

TED GAYER

Ted Gayer is an associate professor at Georgetown University's Public Policy Institute. He is also an adjunct fellow at the Public Policy Institute of California and an adjunct scholar at the American Enterprise Institute. Professor Gayer has published research in environmental economics, regulation, and education policy. From 2003 to 2004, he served as a Senior Economist on the President's Council of Economic Advisers, where he worked primarily on environmental and regulatory policy. He is currently a member of the Environmental Protection Agency's Science Advisory Board. From 2007 to 2008, he served as Deputy Assistant Secretary (Microeconomic Analysis) at the US Treasury. In this capacity, he helped develop policies relating to a wide variety of issues, including housing, credit markets, agriculture, health care, energy, insurance, and the environment. He was also responsible for guiding the Treasury's participation in the Social Security and Medicare Trustees working groups.

The British philosopher and mathematician Bertrand Russell wrote, "Change is one thing, progress is another." In this Ninth edition, we continue to make substantive changes that reflect progress made in the field of public finance. Yet we have been careful to stay focused on the central mission of the book, which is to explain as clearly as possible how the tools of economics can be used to analyze government expenditure and tax policies.

The field of public finance is constantly developing. There are new applications of experimental and quasi-experimental techniques to measure the impact of public policies, and there are new insights provided by fundamental economic theory into the roles of government spending and taxation.

This book incorporates recent developments and along the way takes its readers to the frontiers of current research and policy. While the information presented is cutting edge and reflects the work of economists currently active in the field, our approach makes it accessible to undergraduates whose only prior exposure to economics is at the introductory level.

Each chapter of this Ninth edition has something new. Rather than provide a long list of changes, we will instead highlight some of the key innovations.

NEW WORLDS TO EXPLORE

Financial Crisis Coverage

The current generation of students will long remember the financial crisis of 2008 and 2009. Some commentators believe that government policies toward housing may have contributed to the crisis, and at various places throughout the book, we discuss these arguments. For example, the political economy chapter (Chapter 6) discusses some of the consequences when financial firms are operated privately but their debt is, in effect, viewed as backed by the federal government. Similary, Chapters 5, 15, and 18 highlight examples of how the government subsidized housing, possibly contributing to overconsumption in this sector.

Expanded Climate Change Coverage

We have expanded our coverage of climate change policy. For example, the chapter on externalities (Chapter 5) includes a new discussion focusing on the choice between a carbon tax and a cap-and-trade program to regulate greenhouse gases. The cost-benefit analysis chapter (Chapter 8) discusses how the choice of a discount rate dramatically affects the scale of the policies needed to deal efficiently with the challenges of climate change.

Health Care

The chapter on government and the market for health care (Chapter 10) expands considerably the material on reform options. It now includes a discussion of the individual mandate program recently instituted in the state of Massachusetts, as well as a new discussion of international experiences with single-payer health care systems.

Tax Issues

The chapters on the US revenue system (Part V)—especially Chapter 17 on the personal income tax—provide numerous updates on tax policies stemming from recent legislation and from proposals made by President Obama.

Expanded End-of-Chapter Material

We have also expanded the discussion questions at the end of each chapter, in order to provide students with further opportunities to master the tools of public finance.

All of the changes in this Ninth edition were made to further our goal of providing students with a clear and coherent view of the role of government spending and taxation. Our years of policy experience have convinced us that modern public finance provides a practical and invaluable framework for thinking about policy issues. In this textbook, we have tried to do just what we did when we worked in Washington—to emphasize the links between sound economics and the analysis of real-world policy problems.

Harvey S. Rosen and Ted Gayer

UP-TO-DATE TOOLS
AND SUPPLEMENTS

Animated PowerPoint Slides

The Ninth edition includes revised, in-depth, comprehensive PowerPoint slides with animated graphs and figures that appear as if drawn line by line to clarify difficult concepts for students.

Test Bank

Public Finance has been known for its strong, rigorous test bank questions, and the Ninth edition continues this tradition. The test bank has been expertly updated to reflect the cutting-edge changes in the text. New questions in every chapter provide additional opportunities to test student knowledge.

Instructor's Manual and Online Learning Center

Like the test bank, the instructor's manual has been updated in both content and structure.

www.mhhe.com/rosen9e

In the Online Learning Center, students can access PowerPoint slides and interesting Web links, while instructors can also access a downloadable version of the Instructor's Manual and the Test Bank.

CourseSmart

CourseSmart is a new way for faculty to find and review eTextbooks. It's also a great option for students who are interested in accessing their course materials digitally. CourseSmart offers thousands of the most commonly adopted textbooks across hundreds of courses from a wide variety of higher education publishers. It is the only place for faculty to review and compare the full text of a textbook online. At Course-Smart, students can save up to 50% off the cost of a print book, reduce their impact on the environment, and gain access to powerful Web tools for learning including full text search, notes and highlighting, and e-mail tools for sharing notes between classmates. Complete tech support is also available for each title.

Finding your eBook is easy. Visit www.CourseSmart.com and search by title, author, or ISBN.

Acknowledgments

It is a pleasure to acknowledge the people who have helped in the preparation of *Public Finance*. Across all the editions of this book, nearly 400 academic colleagues who teach public finance have responded to surveys that provided useful material on how they focus their courses. The input afforded insights about their needs and those of their students.

We have been the beneficiaries of numerous suggestions for improvements over the previous edition. We are very thankful to Lucas Adin (Georgetown University) and Michael Barker (Georgetown University) for their research support, and Jennifer Lee (Georgetown University) for her keen eye. In addition, a number of people helped with particular issues in this edition. They include:

Donna Anderson
University of Wisconsin, La Crosse

Thomas Barthold
Joint Committee on Taxation

Robert Brown
California State University, San Marcos

Leonard Burman
Urban Institute

Bradley Childs
Belmont University

Robert Chirinko
Emory University

Gary Galles
Pepperdine University

Haynes Goddard
University of Cincinnati

Winston Harrington
Resources for the Future

Randall Holcombe
Florida State University

John K. Horowitz
University of Maryland

Valerie Kepner
King's College

Tori Knight
Carson-Newman College

Peng Li
Huazhong University of Science and Technology

Pirudas Lwamugira
Fitchburg State College

Simon Medcalfe
Brenau University

Farshid Mojaver
University of California, Davis

Adele Morris
Brookings Institute

Peter Norman
University of North Carolina, Chapel Hill

Uwe E. Reinhardt
Princeton University

Jose Daniel Rodriguez-Delgado
University of Minnesota

Carol Rosenberg
Urban Institute

Helen Schneider
University of Texas at Austin

Mark Showalter
Brigham Young University

Jonathan Skinner
Dartmouth College

Amy Taylor
US Center for Health Services Research

Kiertisak Toh
Radford University

We also appreciate the people who reviewed and made useful suggestions to earlier editions of this text. They include:

Roy D. Adams
Iowa State University

James Alm
University of Colorado

Gary M. Anderson
California State University, Northridge

Gerald Auten
US Treasury

Charles L. Ballard
Michigan State University

Marco Bassetto
University of Minnesota, Minneapolis

Anne Louise Berry
Stanford University

Douglas Blair
Rutgers University

Rebecca Blank
University of Michigan

Serguey Braguinsky
SUNY Buffalo

Alex M. Brill
House Ways and Means Committee

Eleanor Brown
Pomona College

Neil Bruce
Queens University

Lawrence P. Brunner
Central Michigan University

Rachel Burton
Georgetown University

Stuart Butler
Heritage Foundation

Donald E. Campbell
College of William and Mary

Adam Carasso
The Urban Institute

Kai Chan
Princeton University

Sewin Chan
New York University

Howard Chernick
Hunter College

John A. Christianson
University of San Diego

Edward Coulson
Pennsylvania State University

Steven G. Craig
University of Houston

Susan Dadres
Southern Methodist University

Bev Dahlby
University of Alberta

Robert A. Dickler
Bowie State University

Avinash Dixit
Princeton University

Kevin T. Duffy-Deno
Southeastern Massachusetts University

Nada Eissa
Georgetown University

Eric Engen
Federal Reserve Board

O. Homer Erekson
Miami University, Ohio

Judy Feder
Georgetown University

Allan M. Feldman
Brown University

Lee Fennell
University of Texas

John Fitzgerald
Bowdoin College

Fred E. Foldvary
Virginia Tech

Jane G. Fortson
Princeton University

Ken Fortson
Princeton University

Don Fullerton
University of Texas

William Gale
Brookings Institution

Malcolm Getz
Vanderbilt University

J. Fred Giertz
University of Illinois

Amihai Glazer
University of California, Irvine

Roy T. Gobin
Loyola University of Chicago

William T. Gormley
Georgetown University

Joshua Graff Zivin
Columbia University

Jane Gravelle
Congressional Research Service

Gordon Gray
American Enterprise Institute

Michael Greenstone
Massachusetts Institute of Technology

Timothy J. Gronberg
Texas A & M University

Simon Hakim
Temple University

Jonathan H. Hamilton
University of Florida

Rich Hanson
University of California, Irvine

Kevin Hassett
American Enterprise Institute

L. Jay Helms
University of California, Davis

Eric Helland
Claremont McKenna College

Roger S. Hewett
Drake University

James Hines
University of Michigan

Janet Holtzblatt
US Treasury

Douglas Holtz-Eakin
Syracuse University

Gary A. Hoover
University of Alabama

Hilary Hoynes
University of California, Davis

Paul Hughes-Cromwick
Henry Ford Health System

Robert Inman
University of Pennsylvania

Micah Jensen
Georgetown University

Rebecca Kalmus
Harvard University

Robert Kelly
Fairfield University

Edward Kienzle
Boston College

Bruce R. Kingman
SUNY, Albany

Jeffrey Kling
Brookings Institution

Helen Ladd
Duke University

Charles G. Leathers
University of Alabama

Gary D. Lemon
De Pauw University

Al Lerman
US Treasury

Steve Lile
Western Kentucky University

Alessandro Lizzeri
Princeton University

Bradley S. Loomis
Rochester Institute of Technology

Edward Lopez
University of North Texas

Jens Ludwig
Georgetown University

Robin Lumsdaine
Brown University

Molly K. Macauley
Resources for the Future

Brigitte Madrian
University of Pennsylvania

N. Gregory Mankiw
Harvard University

Randall Mariger
University of Washington

Jim Marton
University of Kentucky

Jonathan Meer
Stanford University

Philip Meguire
University of Canterbury

Roger P. Mendels
University of Windsor

Fanus van der Merwe
Potchefstroom University for Christian Higher Education, South Africa

Olivia Mitchell
University of Pennsylvania

Robert Moore
Occidental College

James J. Murphy
University of Massachusetts

John Murray
Bank of Canada

Noelwah Netusil
Reed College

Pia M. Orrenius
Federal Reserve Bank of Dallas

Susan Parks
University of Wisconsin, Whitewater

Anthony Pellechio
World Bank

Alfredo M. Pereira
University of California, San Diego

Wade Pfau
National Graduate Institute of Policy Studies

Florenz Plassmann
Binghamton University (SUNY)

Paul Portney
University of Arizona

James Poterba
Massachusetts Institute of Technology

B. Michael Pritchett
Brigham Young University

Christopher J. Rempel
Reed College

Mark Rider
US Treasury

Robert Rider
University of Southern California

Stephen Rubb
Bentley College

Steven R. Sachs
University of Connecticut

Efraim Sadka
Tel-Aviv University

Gian S. Sahota
Vanderbilt University

Robert C. Sahr
Oregon State University

Andrew Samwick
Dartmouth College

Benjamin Scafidi
Georgia State University

James K. Self
Indiana University

Albert J. Shamash
Trenton State College

Daniel Shaviro
New York University

Eytan Sheshinski
Hebrew University

Kenneth Small
University of California, Irvine

John L. Solow
University of Iowa

John Sondey
South Dakota State University

Richard Steinberg
Virginia Polytechnic Institute and State University

C. Eugene Steuerle
The Urban Institute

Thomas F. Stinson
University of Minnesota

John Straub
Tufts University

Paul Styger
Potchefstroom University for Christian Higher Education, South Africa

Phillip Swagel
US Treasury

Gregory A. Trandel
University of Georgia

Alan Viard
American Enterprise Institute

Lennard van Vuren
Potchefstroom University for Christian Higher Education, South Africa

Marianne Vigneault
Bishop's University

Michael Wasylenko
Syracuse University

Kristen Willard
Columbia University

Clifford Winston
Brookings Institution

Mark L. Wilson
West Virginia University-Tech

Valerie Yates
University of Pennsylvania College of General Studies

Aaron Yelowitz
University of Kentucky

James Young
Northern Illinois University

Sajid Zaidi
Princeton University

George Zodrow
Rice University

Finally, we both would like to thank our families for their support. Longtime readers of this book might recall that the first edition was written when Lynne Rosen and Jonathan Rosen were babies. Now they are college graduates, and have been delighted to welcome Zachary Gayer and Jacob Gayer into the *Public Finance* family.

Harvey S. Rosen and Ted Gayer

Brief Table of Contents

Table of Contents

Part One

GETTING STARTED

People's views on how the government should conduct its financial operations are heavily influenced by their political philosophies. Some people's top priority is individual freedom; others place more emphasis on promoting the well-being of the community as a whole. Philosophical differences can and do lead to disagreements on the appropriate scope for government economic activity.

However, forming intelligent opinions about public policy requires not only a political philosophy but also an understanding of what government actually does. Who has the legal power to conduct economic policy? What does government spend money on, and how does it raise revenue? Chapter 1 discusses how political views affect attitudes toward public finance, and outlines the operation of the US system of public finance. It provides a broad framework for thinking about the details of the public finance system that are discussed in subsequent chapters.

Chapters 2 and 3 present the analytical tools used by public finance economists. Chapter 2 focuses on the tools of positive analysis, which deals with statements of cause and effect. The question here is how economists try to assess the impacts of various government policies. However, we want to determine not only the effects of government policies, but whether or not they produce results that are in some sense good. This is the role of normative analysis, which requires an explicit ethical framework, because without one, it is impossible to say what is good. This ethical framework is covered in Chapter 3.

Chapter One

INTRODUCTION

Public Finance is nothing else than a sophisticated discussion of the relationship between the individual and the state. There is no better school of training than public finance.
—FORMER CZECH PRIME MINISTER VACLAV KLAUS

The year is 1030 BC. For decades, the Israelite tribes have been living without a central government. The Bible records that the people have asked the prophet Samuel to "make us a king to judge us like all the nations" [1 Samuel 8:5]. Samuel tries to discourage the Israelites by describing what life will be like under a monarchy:

> This will be the manner of the king that shall reign over you; he will take your sons, and appoint them unto him, for his chariots, and to be his horsemen; and they shall run before his chariots . . . And he will take your daughters to be perfumers, and to be cooks, and to be bakers. And he will take your fields, and your vineyards, and your oliveyards, even the best of them, and give them to his servants . . . He will take the tenth of your flocks; and ye shall be his servants. And ye shall cry out in that day because of your king whom ye shall have chosen [1 Samuel 8:11–18].

The Israelites are undeterred by this depressing scenario: "The people refused to hearken unto the voice of Samuel; and they said: 'Nay; but there shall be a king over us; that we also may be like all the nations; and that our king may judge us, and go out before us, and fight our battles'" [1 Samuel 8:19–20].

This biblical episode illustrates an age-old ambivalence about government. Government is a necessity—"all the nations" have it, after all—but at the same time it has undesirable aspects. These mixed feelings toward government are inextricably bound up with its taxing and spending activities. The king will provide things that the people want (in this case, an army), but only at a cost. The resources for all government expenditures ultimately must come from the private sector. As Samuel so graphically explains, taxes can be burdensome.

Centuries have passed, mixed feelings about government remain, and much of the controversy still centers around its financial behavior. This book is about the taxing and spending activities of government, a subject usually called **public finance.**

This term is something of a misnomer, because the fundamental issues are not financial (that is, relating to money). Rather, the key problems relate to the use of real resources. For this reason, some authors prefer the label **public sector economics** or simply **public economics.**

We focus on the microeconomic functions of government—the way government affects the allocation of resources and the distribution of income. Nowadays, the macroeconomic roles of government—the use of taxing, spending, and monetary policies to affect the overall level of unemployment and the price level—are usually taught in separate courses.

The boundaries of public finance are sometimes unclear. Governmental regulatory policies have important effects on resource allocation. Such policies have goals that sometimes can also be achieved by government spending or taxation. For example,

public finance

The field of economics that analyzes government taxation and spending.

public sector economics

See public finance.

public economics

See public finance.

if the government wishes to limit the size of corporations, one possible policy is to impose large taxes on big corporations. Another is to issue regulations making firms that exceed a particular size illegal. However, while corporate taxation is a subject of intense study in public finance, antitrust issues receive only tangential treatment in public finance texts and are covered instead in courses on industrial organization. While this practice seems arbitrary, it is necessary to limit the scope of the field. This book follows tradition by focusing on governmental spending and revenue-raising activities, only occasionally touching on government regulatory policies.

▶ PUBLIC FINANCE AND IDEOLOGY

Public finance economists analyze not only the effects of actual government taxing and spending activities but also what these activities ought to be. Opinions on how government should function in the economic sphere are influenced by ideological views concerning the relationship between the individual and the state. Political philosophers have distinguished two major approaches.

Organic View of Government

In this view, society is conceived of as a natural organism. Each individual is a part of this organism, and the government can be thought of as its heart. Yang Chang-chi, Mao Tse-tung's ethics teacher in Beijing, held that "a country is an organic whole, just as the human body is an organic whole. It is not like a machine which can be taken apart and put together again" (quoted in Johnson [1983, p. 197]). The individual has significance only as part of the community, and the good of the individual is defined with respect to the good of the whole. Thus, the community is stressed above the individual. For example, in the *Republic* of Plato, an activity of a citizen is desirable only if it leads to a just society. Perhaps the most infamous instance of an organic conception of government is provided by Nazism: "National Socialism does not recognize a separate individual sphere which, apart from the community, is to be painstakingly protected from any interference by the State. . . . Every activity of daily life has meaning and value only as a service to the whole."[1]

The goals of the society are set by the state, which attempts to lead society toward their realization. Of course, the choice of goals differs considerably. Plato conceived of a state whose goal was the achievement of a golden age in which human activities would be guided by perfect rationality. On the other hand, Adolf Hitler [1971/1925, p. 393] viewed the state's purpose as the achievement of racial purity: "The state is a means to an end. Its end lies in the preservation and advancement of a community of physically and psychically homogeneous creatures." More recently, the Iranian Ayatollah Khomeini argued that "only a good society can create good believers." He wrote that "Man is half-angel, half-devil," and the goal of government should be to "combat [the devil part] through laws and suitable punishments" (quoted in Taheri [2003]).

---

[1] Stuckart and Globke [1968, p. 330]. (Wilhelm Stuckart and Hans Globke were ranking members of the Nazi Ministry of the Interior.)

Because societal goals can differ, a crucial question is how they are to be selected. Proponents of the organic view usually argue that certain goals are *natural* for the societal organism. Pursuit of sovereignty over some geographical area is an example of such a natural goal. (Think of the Nazi drive for domination over Europe.) However, although philosophers have struggled for centuries to explain what natural means, the answer is far from clear.

Mechanistic View of Government

In this view, government is not an organic part of society. Rather, it is a contrivance created by individuals to better achieve their individual goals. As the American statesman Henry Clay said in 1829, "Government is a trust, and the officers of the government are trustees; and both the trust and the trustees are created for the benefit of the people." The individual rather than the group is at center stage.

Accepting that government exists for the good of the people, we are still left with the problem of defining just what *good* is and how the government should promote it. Virtually everyone agrees that it is good for individuals when government protects them from violence. To do so government must have a monopoly on coercive power. Otherwise, anarchy develops, and as the 17th-century philosopher Thomas Hobbes [1963/1651, p. 143] noted, "The life of man [becomes] solitary, poor, nasty, brutish and short." The example of Somalia, in which no effective national government exists and violence is widespread, confirms Hobbes's observation. Similarly, in *The Wealth of Nations*, Adam Smith argued that government should protect "the society from the violence and invasion of other independent societies," and protect "as far as possible every member of the society from the injustice or oppression of every other member of it" [1977/1776, Book V, pp. 182, 198].

The most limited government, then, has but one function—to protect its members from physical coercion. Beyond that, Smith argued that government should have responsibility for "creating and maintaining certain public works and certain public institutions, which it can never be for the interest of any individual, or small number of individuals, to erect and maintain" [1977/1776, Book V, pp. 210–211]. Here one thinks of items like roads, bridges, and sewers—the infrastructure required for society to function.[2]

At this point, opinions within the mechanistic tradition diverge. Libertarians, who believe in a very limited government, argue against any further economic role for the government. In Smith's words, "Every man, as long as he does not violate the laws of justice, is left perfectly free to pursue his own interest his own way" [1977/1776, Book V, p. 180]. Libertarians are extremely skeptical about the ability of governments to improve social welfare. As Thomas Jefferson pungently put it in his first inaugural address,

> Sometimes it is said that man cannot be trusted with the government of himself. Can he, then, be trusted with the government of others? Or have we found angels in the forms of kings to govern him? Let history answer this question.

In contrast, those whom we might call social democrats believe that substantial government intervention is required for the good of individuals. These interventions can take such diverse forms as safety regulations for the workplace, laws banning

---

[2] Some argue that even these items should be provided by private entrepreneurs. Problems that might arise in doing so are discussed in Chapter 4.

racial and sexual discrimination in housing, or welfare payments to the poor. When social democrats are confronted with the objection that such interventions impinge on individual freedom, they are apt to respond that freedom is more than the absence of physical coercion. An impoverished individual may be free to spend his income as he pleases, but the scope of that freedom is quite limited. Between the libertarian and social democratic positions there is a continuum of views with respect to the appropriate amount of government intervention.

Viewpoint of This Book

The notion that the individual rather than the group is paramount is relatively new. Historian Lawrence Stone [1977, pp. 4–5] notes that before the modern period,

> It was generally agreed that the interests of the group, whether that of kin, the village, or later the state, took priority over the wishes of the individual and the achievement of his particular ends. "Life, liberty and the pursuit of happiness" were personal ideals which the average, educated 16th-century man would certainly have rejected as the prime goals of a good society.

Since then, however, the mechanistic view of government has come to dominate Anglo-American political thought. However, its dominance is not total. Anyone who claims that something must be done in the "national interest," without reference to the welfare of some individual or group of individuals, is implicitly taking an organic point of view. More generally, even in highly individualistic societies, people sometimes feel it necessary to act on behalf of, or even sacrifice their lives for, the nation.

Not surprisingly, Anglo-American economic thought has also developed along individualistic lines. Individuals and their wants are the main focus in mainstream economics, a view reflected in this text. However, as stressed earlier, within the individualistic tradition there is much controversy with respect to how active government should be. Thus, adopting a mechanistic point of view does not by itself provide us with an ideology that tells us whether any particular economic intervention should be undertaken.[3]

This point is important because economic policy is not based on economic analysis alone. The desirability of a given course of government action (or inaction) inevitably depends in part on ethical and political judgments. As this country's ongoing debate over public finance illustrates, reasonable people can disagree on these matters. We attempt to reflect different points of view as fairly as possible.

▶ GOVERNMENT AT A GLANCE

We have shown how ideology can affect one's views of the appropriate scope for governmental activity. However, to form sensible views about public policy requires more than ideology. One also needs information about how the government actually functions. What legal constraints are imposed on the public sector? What does the government spend money on, and how are these expenditures financed? Before delving into the details of the US system of public finance, we provide a brief overview of these issues.

---

[3] This question really makes no sense in the context of an organic view of government in which the government is above the people, and there is an assumption that it should guide every aspect of life.

The Legal Framework

The Constitution reflects the Founding Fathers' concerns about governmental intervention in the economy. We first discuss constitutional provisions relating to the spending and taxing activities of the federal government and then turn to the states.

Federal Government   Article 1, Section 8, of the Constitution empowers Congress "to pay the Debts and provide for the common Defense and general Welfare of the United States." Over the years, the notion of "general welfare" has been interpreted very broadly by Congress and the courts, and now this clause effectively puts no constraints on government spending.[4] The Constitution does not limit the size of federal expenditure, either absolutely or relative to the size of the economy. Bills to appropriate expenditures (like practically all other laws) can originate in either house of Congress. An appropriations bill becomes law when it receives a majority vote in both houses and the president signs it. If the president vetoes an expenditure bill, it can still become law if it subsequently receives a two-thirds majority vote in each house.

How does Congress finance these expenditures? Federal taxing powers are authorized in Article 1, Section 8: "The Congress shall have Power to lay and collect Taxes, Duties, Imposts and Excises." Unlike expenditure bills, "All Bills for raising Revenue shall originate in the House of Representatives" [Article 1, Section 7].

In light of the enormous dissatisfaction with British tax policy during the colonial period, it is no surprise that considerable care was taken to constrain governmental taxing power, as described in the following paragraphs:

1. "[A]ll Duties, Imposts and Excises shall be uniform throughout the United States" [Article 1, Section 8]. Congress cannot discriminate among states when it sets tax rates. If the federal government levies a tax on gasoline, the *rate* must be the same in every state. This does not imply that the per capita *amount* collected will be the same in each state. Presumably, states in which individuals drive more than average have higher tax liabilities, other things being the same. Thus, it is still possible (and indeed likely) that various taxes make some states worse off than others.[5]

2. "No . . . direct Tax shall be laid, unless in Proportion to the Census or Enumeration herein before directed to be taken" [Article 1, Section 9]. A direct tax is a tax levied on a *person* as opposed to a *commodity*. Essentially, this provision says that if State A has twice the population of State B, then any direct tax levied by Congress must yield twice as much revenue from State A as from State B.

In the late 19th century, attempts to introduce a federal tax on income were declared unconstitutional by the Supreme Court because income taxation leads to state tax burdens that are not proportional to population. Given this decision, the only way to introduce an income tax was via a constitutional amendment. The 16th Amendment, ratified in 1913, states, "Congress shall have power to levy and collect taxes on incomes, from whatever source derived, without apportionment among the several states, and without regard to census or enumeration." Today the individual income tax is one of the mainstays of the federal revenue system.

3. "No person shall be . . . deprived of life, liberty, or property, without due process of law; nor shall private property be taken for public use, without just compensation"

---

[4] Article 1 also mandates that certain specific expenditures be made. For example, Congress has to appropriate funds to maintain both an army and a court system.

[5] No tax law in history has ever been struck down for violating this clause. However, a close call occurred in the early 1980s. Congress passed a tax on oil that exempted oil from the North Slope of Alaska. A federal district court ruled that the tax was unconstitutional, but this decision was ultimately reversed by the Supreme Court.

[Fifth Amendment]. From the point of view of tax policy, this clause means distinctions created by the tax law must be reasonable. However, it is not always simple to determine which distinctions are "reasonable" and doing so is an ongoing part of the legislative and judicial processes.

4. "No Tax or Duty shall be laid on Articles exported from any State" [Article 1, Section 9]. This provision was included to assure the southern states that their exports of tobacco and other commodities would not be jeopardized by the central government.

The federal government is not required to finance all its expenditures by taxation. If expenditures exceed revenues, it is empowered "to borrow Money on the credit of the United States" [Article 1, Section 8]. At various times over the past few decades, a constitutional amendment to require a balanced federal budget has received some support, but so far it has not passed.

State and Local Governments According to the 10th Amendment, "The powers not delegated to the United States by the Constitution, nor prohibited by it to the States, are reserved to the States respectively, or to the people." Thus, explicit authorization for states to spend and tax is not required. However, the Constitution does limit states' economic activities. Article 1, Section 10, states, "No State shall, without the Consent of the Congress, lay any Imposts or Duties on Imports or Exports." Thus, the federal government controls international economic policy. In addition, various constitutional provisions have been interpreted as requiring that the states not levy taxes arbitrarily, discriminate against outside residents, or levy taxes on imports from other states. For example, in 2005, the Supreme Court declared unconstitutional laws in Michigan and New York that granted in-state wineries a competitive advantage over out-of-state wineries.

States can impose spending and taxing restrictions on themselves in their own constitutions. State constitutions differ substantially with respect to the types of economic issues with which they deal. In recent years, one of the most interesting developments in public finance has been the movement of some states to amend their constitutions to limit the size of public sector spending.

From a legal point of view, the power of local governments to tax and spend is granted by the states. As a 19th-century judge put it:

> Municipal corporations owe their origin to, and derive their powers and rights wholly from, the [state] legislature. It breathes into them the breath of life, without which they cannot exist. As it creates, so it may destroy. If it may destroy, it may abridge and control [*City of Clinton v. Cedar Rapids*, 1868].

It would be a mistake, however, to view localities as lacking in fiscal autonomy. Many towns and cities have substantial political power and do not respond passively to the wishes of state and federal governments. An interesting development in recent years has been the competition of states and cities for federal funds. The cities often are more successful in their lobbying activities than the states!

The Size of Government

In a famous line from his State of the Union address in 1996, President Bill Clinton declared: "The era of big government is over." Such a statement presupposes that there is some way to determine whether or not the government is "big." Just how does one measure the size of government?

One measure often used by politicians and journalists is the number of workers in the public sector. However, inferences about the size of government drawn from the number of workers it employs can be misleading. Imagine a country where a few public servants operate a powerful computer that guides all economic decisions. In this country, the number of government employees certainly underestimates the importance of government. Similarly, it would be easy to construct a scenario in which a large number of workers is associated with a relatively weak public sector. The number of public sector employees is useful information, for some purposes, but it does not cast light on the central issue—the extent to which society's resources are subject to control by government.

A more sensible (and common) approach is to measure the size of government by the volume of its annual expenditures, of which there are basically three types:

1. Purchases of goods and services. The government buys a wide variety of items, everything from missiles to services provided by ecologists.
2. Transfers of income to people, businesses, or other governments. The government takes income from some individuals or organizations and gives it to others. Examples are welfare programs such as food stamps and subsidies paid to farmers for production (or nonproduction) of certain commodities.
3. Interest payments. The government often borrows to finance its activities and, like any borrower, must pay interest for the privilege of doing so.

The federal government itemizes its expenditures in a document referred to as the **unified budget.**[6] In 2008, federal expenditures (excluding grants made to state and local governments) were about $2,707 billion. Adding state and local government expenditures made that year gives us a total of $4,723 billion [*Economic Report of the President, 2009*, p. 381].[7] Figures on government expenditures are easily available and widely quoted. Typically when expenditures go up, people conclude that government has grown. However, some government activities have substantial effects on resource allocation even though they involve minimal explicit outlays. For example, issuing regulations per se is not very expensive, but compliance with the rules can be very costly. Air bag requirements raise the cost of cars. Various permit and inspection fees increase the price of housing. Labor market regulations such as the minimum wage may create unemployment, and regulation of the drug industry may slow the pace of scientific development.

Some have suggested that the costs imposed on the economy by government regulations be published in an annual **regulatory budget.** In this way, an explicit accounting for the costs of regulation would be available. Unfortunately, computing such costs is exceedingly difficult. For example, pharmaceutical experts disagree on what new cures would have been developed in the absence of drug regulation. Similarly, it is hard to estimate the impact of government-mandated safety procedures in the workplace on production costs. In view of such problems, it is unlikely there will ever be an official regulatory budget.[8] Unofficial estimates, however, suggest that the annual costs of federal regulations may be quite high, perhaps over $1 trillion annually [Crane, 2005].

[6] The publication of a budget document is constitutionally mandated: "a regular Statement and Account of the Receipts and Expenditures of all public Money shall be published from time to time" [Article 1, Section 9].
[7] Federal grants to state and local governments were $384 billion in 2008.
[8] Regulation is not necessarily undesirable just because it creates costs. Like any other government activity, it can be evaluated only by assessing the benefits as well as the costs. (Cost-benefit analysis is discussed in Chapter 8.)

Some Numbers   We reluctantly conclude that it is infeasible to summarize in a single number the magnitude of government's impact on the economy. That said, we are still left with the practical problem of finding some reasonable indicator of the government's size that can be used to estimate trends in its growth. Most economists are willing to accept conventionally defined government expenditure as a rough but useful measure. Like many other imperfect measures, it yields useful insights as long as its limitations are understood.

With all the appropriate caveats in mind, we present in Table 1.1 data on expenditures made by all levels of US government over time. The first column indicates that annual expenditures have increased by a factor of over 38 since 1960. This figure is a misleading indicator of the growth of government for several reasons:

1. Because of inflation, the dollar has decreased in value over time. In column 2, the expenditure figures are expressed in 2008 dollars. In real terms, government expenditure in 2008 was about 6.6 times the level in 1960.

2. The population has also grown over time. An increasing population by itself creates demands for a larger public sector. (For example, more roads and sewers are required to accommodate more people.) Column 3 shows real government expenditure per capita. Now the increase from 1960 to 2008 is a factor of about 3.9.

3. It is sometimes useful to examine government expenditure compared to the size of the economy. If government doubles in size but at the same time the economy triples, then in a relative sense, government has shrunk. Column 4 shows government expenditure as a percentage of Gross Domestic Product (GDP)—the market value of goods and services produced by the economy during the year. In 1960, the figure was 23.3 percent, and in 2008, it was 33.1 percent.

Table 1.1   **State, Local, and Federal Government Expenditures**
(Selected years)

	(1) **Total Expenditures** **(billions)**	(2) **2008 Dollars** **(billions)***	(3) **2008 Dollars** **per Capita**	(4) **Percent of** **GDP**
1960	$ 123	$ 714	$ 3,950	23.3%
1970	295	1,308	6,379	28.4
1980	843	1,905	8,367	30.2
1990	1,873	2,804	11,210	32.3
2000	2,887	3,527	12,487	29.4
2008	4,723	4,723	15,488	33.1

*Conversion to 2008 dollars done using the GDP deflator.

Source: Calculations based on *Economic Report of the President, 2009* [pp. 282, 286, 325, 381].

Total government expenditures have increased by a factor of 38.4 since 1960. Real expenditures have increased by a factor of 6.6, and per capita real expenditures have increased by a factor of 3.9. In 1960, government expenditures were 23.3 percent of Gross Domestic Product; in 2008 they were 33.1 percent.

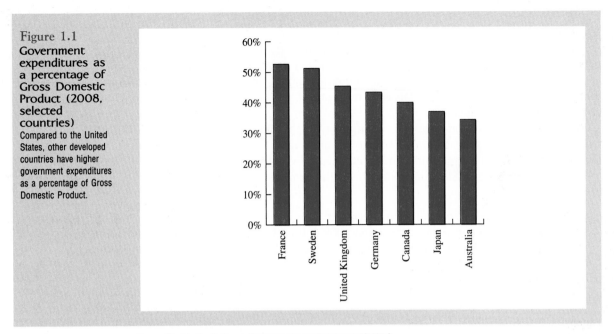

Figure 1.1

Government expenditures as a percentage of Gross Domestic Product (2008, selected countries)
Compared to the United States, other developed countries have higher government expenditures as a percentage of Gross Domestic Product.

Source: Organization for Economic Cooperation and Development [2008a].

In light of our previous discussion, the figures in Table 1.1 convey a false sense of precision. Still, there is no doubt that in the long run the economic role of government has grown. With almost a third of GDP going through the public sector, government is an enormous economic force.

Some international comparisons can help put the US data in perspective. Figure 1.1 shows figures on government expenditure relative to GDP for several developed countries. The data indicate that the United States is not alone in having an important public sector. Indeed, compared to countries such as France and Sweden, the US public sector is quite small. While relative public-sector sizes differ across nations for many reasons, the ideological considerations discussed earlier in this chapter probably play an important role.

One explanation for the large public sector in Sweden, for example, is that the government pays for most of health care, which is thought of as a community responsibility. In the United States, on the other hand, health care is viewed as more of an individual responsibility, so a substantial share of health care expenditures are made in the private sector.

Expenditures

We now turn from the overall magnitude of government expenditures to their composition. It is impossible to reflect the enormous scope of government spending activity in a brief table. In the federal budget for fiscal year 2009, the list of programs and their descriptions required over 1,300 pages! (Details are provided at the Web site: http://www.gpoaccess.gov/usbudget/.)

The major categories of federal government expenditure in 1965 and the present are depicted in Figure 1.2; the state and local expenditure data are in Figure 1.3.

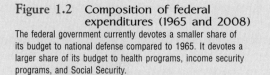

Figure 1.2 Composition of federal expenditures (1965 and 2008)

The federal government currently devotes a smaller share of its budget to national defense compared to 1965. It devotes a larger share of its budget to health programs, income security programs, and Social Security.

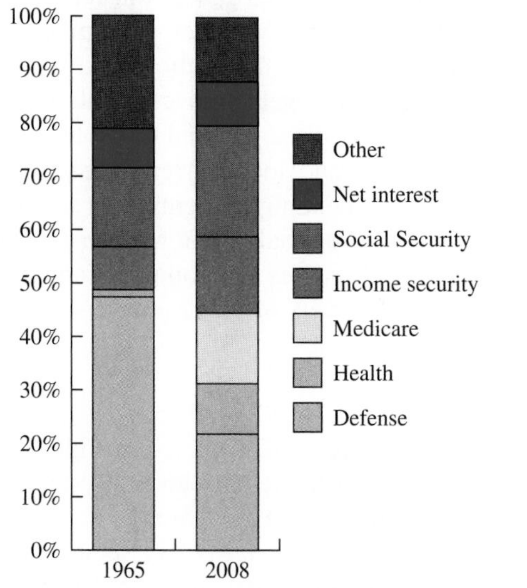

Legend:
- Other
- Net interest
- Social Security
- Income security
- Medicare
- Health
- Defense

Source: *Economic Report of the President, 2009* [p. 379].

Figure 1.3 Composition of state and local expenditures (1965 and 2005)

State and local governments currently devote a smaller share of their budgets to highways compared to 1965. They devote a larger share of their budgets to public welfare programs.

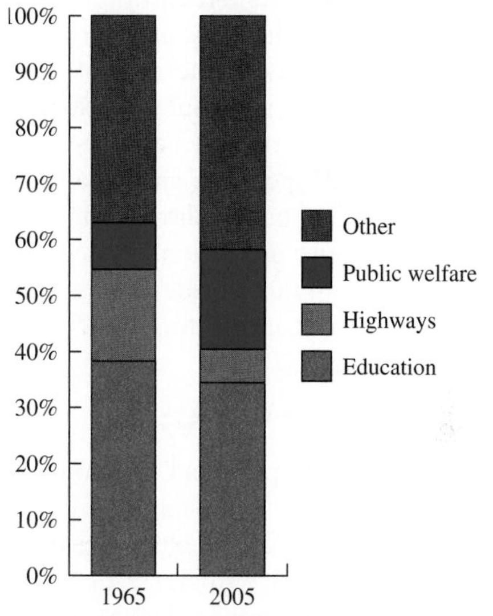

Legend:
- Other
- Public welfare
- Highways
- Education

Source: *Economic Report of the President, 2009* [p. 385].

The following aspects of the figures are noteworthy:

- National defense is an important component of government expenditure, but its relative importance has decreased over time. In 1965, it was 47 percent of the federal budget; this figure is now down to 22 percent.
- Social Security has grown enormously. Among other things, this program transfers income to individuals who are retired. It is now virtually tied with defense spending as the single largest spending item in the federal budget.
- Medicare, a health insurance system for the elderly, did not even exist in 1965; it now absorbs 13.1 percent of the federal budget.
- Public welfare activities have increased. As shown in Figure 1.3, between 1965 and 2005, their share of state and local budgets more than doubled from 8.5 to 17.6 percent. At the same time, the share of state and local spending devoted to highways has fallen considerably.
- Payments of interest on debt have remained roughly constant as a proportion of federal expenditures since 1965. They now account for about 8.4 percent of federal expenditures.

Note that fast-growing areas such as Social Security and interest payments are relatively fixed in the sense that they are determined by previous decisions. Indeed, much of the government budget consists of so-called **entitlement programs**—programs with cost determined not by fixed dollar amounts but by

entitlement programs

Programs whose expenditures are determined by the number of people who qualify, rather than pre-set budget allocations.

the number of people who qualify. The laws governing Social Security, many public welfare programs, and farm price supports include rules that determine who is entitled to benefits and the magnitude of the benefits. Expenditures on entitlement programs are, therefore, out of the hands of the current government, unless it changes the rules. Similarly, debt payments are determined by interest rates and previous deficits, again mostly out of the control of current decision makers. According to most estimates, about three-quarters of the federal budget is relatively uncontrollable. In Chapter 6, we discuss whether government spending is in fact out of control and if so, what can be done about it.

It is useful to break down total expenditures by level of government. The federal government accounts for about 45 percent of all direct expenditures, the states for 25 percent, and localities for 30 percent. State and local governments are clearly important players. They account for the bulk of spending on items such as police and fire protection, education, and transportation. Substantial public welfare expenditures are also made through the states. Chapter 22 discusses the complications that arise in coordinating the fiscal activities of different levels of government.

Revenues

The principal components of the federal tax system are depicted in Figure 1.4; the state and local tax information is in Figure 1.5. At the federal level, personal income taxation is currently the single most important source of revenue, accounting for about 45 percent of tax collections. Note the importance of the "Social Insurance" category in Figure 1.4. These are payroll tax collections used to finance Social Security and Medicare. They now account for more than a third of federal revenue collections. The fall in the importance of the federal corporate income tax is also of some interest. In 1965 it accounted for about 22 percent of federal revenues; the figure is now only 12 percent. In the state and local sector, the two most striking changes over time are the decreased importance of the property tax and the increased reliance on individual income taxes.

Changes in the Real Value of Debt   In popular discussions, taxes are usually viewed as the only source of government revenue. However, when the government is a debtor and prices increase, changes in the real value of the debt may be an important source of revenue. To see why, suppose that at the beginning of the year you owe a creditor $1,000, which does not have to be repaid until the end of the year. Suppose further that during the year, prices rise by 10 percent. The dollars you use to repay your creditor are worth 10 percent less than those you borrowed from her. In effect, inflation has reduced the real value of your debt by $100 (10 percent of $1,000). Alternatively, your real income has increased by $100 as a consequence of inflation. Of course, at the same time, your creditor's real income has fallen by $100.[9]

At the beginning of fiscal year 2008, the federal government's outstanding debt was about $5.4 trillion. During 2008, the inflation rate was about 2.7 percent. Applying the same logic as previously, inflation reduced the real value of the

---

[9] If the inflation is anticipated by borrowers and lenders, one expects that the interest rate will increase to take inflation into account. This phenomenon is discussed in Chapter 17 under "Taxes and Inflation."

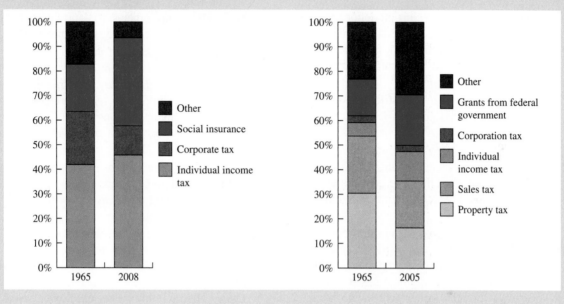

Figure 1.4   Composition of federal taxes (1965 and 2008)

Compared to 1965, the federal government currently relies more on the individual income tax, which at 45% of the total makes it the largest source of federal revenue. Tax payments for social insurance (which includes Social Security and Medicare) also make up a larger share of total tax revenue, currently amounting to 36% of total federal revenue. The share of revenue from the corporate tax has decreased over this period, and is currently at 12% of total federal revenue.

Legend (Figure 1.4):
- Other
- Social insurance
- Corporate tax
- Individual income tax

Source: *Economic Report of the President, 2009* [p. 379].

Figure 1.5   Composition of state and local taxes (1965 and 2005)

Compared to 1965, state and local governments currently rely more on the individual income tax and much less on the property tax.

Legend (Figure 1.5):
- Other
- Grants from federal government
- Corporation tax
- Individual income tax
- Sales tax
- Property tax

Source: *Economic Report of the President, 2009* [p. 385].

federal debt by \$146 billion (\$5.4 trillion $\times$ 0.027). In effect, this is as much a receipt for the government as any of the taxes listed in Figure 1.4. However, the government's accounting procedures exclude gains due to inflationary erosion of the debt on the revenue side of the account. We defer to Chapter 20 further discussion of issues related to the measurement of the debt and its economic significance.

Our Agenda

This section has set forth a collection of basic "facts"—facts on governmental fiscal institutions, on the size and scope of government spending, and on the methods used by government to finance itself. Parts of the rest of this book are devoted to presenting more facts—filling in the rather sketchy picture of how our fiscal system operates. Just as important, we explore the significance of these facts, asking whether the status quo has led to desirable outcomes, and if not, how it can be improved.

Summary

- Public finance, also known as public sector economics or public economics, focuses on the taxing and spending of government and their influence on the allocation of resources and distribution of income.
- Public finance economists both analyze actual policies and develop guidelines for government activities. In the latter role, economists are influenced by their attitudes toward the role of government in society.
- In an organic view of society, individuals are valued only by their contribution to the realization of social goals. These goals are determined by the government.
- In a mechanistic view of society, government is a contrivance erected to further individual goals. It is not clear how the government can reconcile sometimes conflicting individual goals.
- Individual decision making is the focus of much economics and is consistent with the mechanistic view of society adopted in this book. This does not eliminate much controversy over the appropriate role of the government in our economy.
- The Constitution embodies constraints on federal and state government economic activity.
- The federal government may effectively undertake any expenditures it wishes and may use debt and taxes to finance them. The federal government may not discriminate among states when choosing tax rates and may not place a levy on state exports. The 16th Amendment empowers the federal government to tax personal income.
- State governments are forbidden to levy tariffs on imports, discriminate against outside residents, or tax other states' products. Most states have balanced budget requirements.
- All common measures of the size of government—employees, expenditures, revenues, etc.—have some deficiency. In particular, these items miss the impact of regulatory costs. Nonetheless, there is strong evidence that the impact of the government on the allocation of national resources has increased over time.
- Government expenditures have increased in both nominal and real absolute terms, in per capita terms, and as a percentage of Gross Domestic Product.
- The share of defense spending in federal expenditure has fallen over time, while Social Security, public welfare, and payments on outstanding debt have increased in importance. The combination of entitlement programs and interest payments reduces yearly control over the level of expenditures.
- Personal income and Social Security payroll taxes are currently the largest sources of federal government revenue.

Discussion Questions

1. Indicate whether each of the following statements is consistent with an organic or mechanistic view of government:
   a. "If you want to believe in a national purpose that is greater than our individual interests, join us" [Senator John McCain].
   b. "Freedom of men under government is to have a standing rule to live by, common to every one of that society, and made by the legislative power vested in it; a liberty to follow my own will in all things, when the rule prescribes not, and not to be subject to the inconstant, unknown, arbitrary will of another man" [British Philosopher John Locke].
   c. "The old values of individualism, capitalism and egoism must be demolished" [Venezuelan President Hugo Chavez].
2. Explain how you would expect a libertarian, a social democrat, and someone with an organic conception of the state to react to the following laws:

a. A law prohibiting receiving compensation for organ donation.

b. A law mandating helmet use for motorcyclists.

c. A law mandating child safety seats.

d. A law prohibiting prostitution.

e. A law prohibiting polygamy.

f. A law barring the use of trans fats in restaurants.

3. Obesity is perceived to be a national health problem in the United States. One suggestion to deal with this problem is a "fat tax." The idea is to levy a tax on foods containing more than a government prescribed percentage of the daily minimal fat intake. Is such a tax consistent with a mechanistic view of government?

4. In each of the following circumstances, decide whether the impact of government on the economy increases or decreases and why. In each case, how does your answer compare to that given by standard measures of the size of government?

a. Normally, when employers offer health insurance benefits to their workers, these benefits extend to the spouses of the workers as well. Several years ago, San Francisco passed a law requiring firms that do business with the city to offer health and other benefits to both same- and opposite-sex unwed partners.

b. The federal government bans the use of incandescent light bulbs.

c. The ratio of government purchases of goods and services to Gross Domestic Product falls.

d. The federal budget is brought into balance by reducing grants-in-aid to state and local governments.

5. During 2007, the inflation rate in the United Kingdom was about 2.1 percent. At the beginning of that year, the national debt of the United Kingdom was about £502 billion. Discuss the implications of these facts for measuring government revenues in that country during 2007.

6. As noted in the text, in 1996 President Clinton declared that the era of big government is over. Has the size of government fallen since then? Provide an answer based on the following data: In 1996, federal government spending was $1.56 trillion and Gross Domestic Product (GDP) was $7.82 trillion. In 2007, federal spending was $2.73 trillion and GDP was $13.76 trillion. During this period, prices increased by about 34 percent. What additional data would you seek to provide a more complete answer to this question?

7. From 1981 to 1985, the US federal government increased defense spending from $153.9 billion to $245.1 billion per year, while over the same period Gross Domestic Product rose from $3.128 trillion to $4.220 trillion. From 2001 to 2005, the US federal government increased defense spending from $290.3 billion to $474.2 billion, while over the same period Gross Domestic Product rose from $10.128 trillion to $12.479 trillion. Which increase in defense spending was larger relative to Gross Domestic Product?

8. The following table shows the composition of US federal expenditures in 1993, 1997, 2001, and 2005.

	Federal Expenditures ($ billions)			
	1993	**1997**	**2001**	**2005**
Defense	$ 308.3	$ 285.7	$ 321.3	$ 529.9
Health	99.4	123.8	172.3	250.6
Medicare	130.6	190.0	217.4	298.6
Income security	210.0	235.0	269.8	345.8
Social Security	304.6	365.3	433.0	523.3
Net interest	198.7	244.0	206.2	184.0
Other	158.0	157.4	243.4	339.9
Total	$1,409.6	$1,601.2	$1,863.4	$2,472.1

From 1993 to 1997, GDP went from $6.6574 trillion to $8.3043 trillion, the GDP price deflator (used to calculate inflation) went from 88.381 to 95.414, and the population went from 260.255 million to 272.912 million. From 2001 to 2005, GDP went from $10.128 trillion to $13.1947 trillion, the GDP price deflator went from 102.399 to 113.000, and the population went from 285.454 million to 296.940 million.

a. For the years 1993 to 1997 and 2001 to 2005, calculate the absolute change in federal expenditures, the change in federal expenditures in real (i.e., inflation-adjusted) terms, the change in real government expenditures per capita, and the change in expenditures per GDP.

b. Which components of the budget had the largest relative increases from 1993 to 1997 and from 2001 to 2005? Which had the largest relative decreases?

9. The following table shows the composition of US federal tax revenues in 1993, 1997, 2001, and 2005.

Federal Taxes ($ billions)				
	1993	1997	2001	2005
Individual income tax	$ 509.7	$ 737.5	$ 994.3	$ 927.2
Coporate tax	117.5	182.3	151.1	278.3
Social insurance	428.3	539.4	694.0	794.1
Excise tax	99.0	120.3	152.0	154.2
Total	$1,154.5	$1,579.5	$1,991.4	$2,153.8

a. Using the information provided in question 8, for the years 1993 to 1997 and 2001 to 2005, calculate the absolute change in federal tax revenues, the change in federal tax revenues in real (i.e., inflation-adjusted) terms, the change in real tax revenues per capita, and the change in tax revenues per GDP.

b. Which components of federal taxes had the largest relative increases from 1993 to 1997 and from 2001 to 2005? Which had the largest relative decreases?

Appendix: Doing Research in Public Finance

Throughout the text, we cite many books and articles. These references are useful for those who want to delve into the various subjects in more detail. Students interested in writing term papers or theses on subjects in public finance should also consult the following journals that specialize in the field:

International Tax and Public Finance
Journal of Public Economics
National Tax Journal

Public Finance
Public Finance Quarterly

In addition, all the major general-interest economics journals frequently publish articles that deal with public finance issues. These include, but are not limited to:

American Economic Review
Journal of Economic Perspectives
Journal of Political Economy
Quarterly Journal of Economics
Review of Economics and Statistics

Articles on public finance in these and many other journals are indexed in the *Journal of Economic Literature* and can be searched on the Internet.

In addition, students should consult the volumes included in the Brookings Institution's series *Studies of Government Finance*. These books include careful and up-to-date discussions of important public finance issues. The Congressional Budget Office also provides useful reports on current policy controversies. A list of documents is provided at its Web site, http://www.cbo.gov.

The working paper series of the National Bureau of Economic Research, available through university libraries, is another good source of recent research on public finance. The technical difficulty of these papers is sometimes considerable, however. Papers can be downloaded at its Web site, http://www.nber.org.

Vast amounts of data are available on government spending and taxing activities. The following useful sources of information are published by the US Government Printing Office and are available online as indicated:

Statistical Abstract of the United States
(http://www.census.gov/compendia/statab/)
Economic Report of the President (http://www.gpoaccess.gov/eop/)
Budget of the United States (http://www.gpoaccess.gov/usbudget)
US Census of Governments (http://www.census.gov/govs/www/)

All the preceding are published annually, except for the *US Census of Governments*, which appears every five years. *Facts and Figures on Government Finance*, published annually by the Tax Foundation, is another compendium of data on government taxing and spending activities. For those who desire a long-run perspective, data going back to the 18th century are available in *Historical Statistics of the United States from Colonial Times to 1970* [US Government Printing Office]. Readers with a special interest in state and local public finance will want to read the reports issued by the US Advisory Commission on Intergovernmental Relations.

A great deal of public finance data is available on the Internet. A particularly useful site is *Resources for Economists on the Internet* (http://www.rfe.org). It lists and describes more than 900 Internet resources. The home page of the US Census Bureau (http://www.census.gov) is also very useful. Finally, for up-to-date information on tax policy issues, consult the Web site of the University of Michigan's Office of Tax Policy Research (http://www.otpr.org) and the Urban-Brookings Tax Policy Center (http://www.taxpolicycenter.org/).

Chapter Two

TOOLS OF POSITIVE ANALYSIS

Numbers live. Numbers take on vitality.

—JESSE JACKSON

A good subtitle for this chapter is "Why Is It So Hard to Tell What's Going On?" We constantly hear economists—and politicians—disagree vehemently about the likely consequences of various government actions. For example, in the 2008 presidential campaign, a hotly contested issue was whether the Bush administration's reduction in income tax rates for high earners should be retained. John McCain supported keeping the rate cuts, and Barack Obama did not. Many conservatives argued that lower tax rates create incentives for people to work harder. Many liberals were skeptical, arguing that taxes have little effect on work effort. Each side had economists testifying that their opinion was correct.

This kind of discussion occurs virtually whenever economists and policymakers consider the impact of a government program. Economists debate whether environmental regulations improve health outcomes, whether government-provided health insurance decreases mortality, whether school vouchers improve test scores, whether tax reductions for corporations generate more investment, whether unemployment insurance leads to longer unemployment spells, and a slew of other important issues. This chapter discusses the tools that economists use to estimate the impact of government programs on individuals' behavior.

▶ THE ROLE OF THEORY

Economic theory is a useful starting point for analyzing the impact of government policy because it provides a framework for thinking about the factors that might influence the behavior of interest. Consider again the lower tax rates endorsed by Senator McCain, and suppose we are interested in their effect on annual hours of work. The theory of labor supply posits that the work decision is based on the rational allocation of time.[1] Suppose Mr. Rogers has only a certain number of hours in the day: How many hours should he devote to work in the market, and how many hours to leisure? Rogers derives satisfaction ("utility") from leisure, but to earn income he must work and thereby surrender leisure time. Rogers's problem is to find the combination of income and leisure that maximizes his utility.

---

[1] A graphical exposition of the theory of labor supply appears in Chapter 18 under "Labor Supply."

Suppose Rogers's wage rate is $10 per hour. The wage is the cost of Rogers's time. For every hour he spends at leisure, Rogers gives up $10 in wages—time is literally money. However, a "rational" individual generally does not work every possible hour, even though leisure is costly. People spend time on leisure to the extent that leisure's benefits exceed its costs.

This model may seem unrealistic. It ignores the possibility that an individual's labor supply behavior can depend on the work decisions of other family members. Neither does the model consider whether the individual can work as many hours as desired. Indeed, the entire notion that people make their decisions by rationally considering costs and benefits may appear unrealistic.

However, the whole point of model building is to simplify as much as possible, so one can reduce a problem to its essentials. A model should not be judged on the basis of whether or not it is 100 percent accurate, but on whether it is plausible, informative, and offers testable implications. Most work in modern economics is based on the assumption that utility maximization is a good working hypothesis. This point of view is taken throughout the book.

Imagine that Mr. Rogers has found his utility-maximizing combination of income and leisure based on his wage rate of $10. Now the government imposes a tax on earnings of 20 percent. Then Rogers's after-tax or *net* wage is $8. How does a rational individual react—work more, work less, or not change? In public debate, arguments for all three possibilities are made with great assurance. In fact, however, the impact of an earnings tax on hours of work *cannot* be predicted on theoretical grounds.

To see why, first observe that the wage tax lowers the effective price of leisure. Before the tax, consumption of an hour of leisure cost Rogers $10. Under the earnings tax, Rogers's net wage is lower, and an hour of leisure costs him only $8. Since leisure has become cheaper, he will tend to consume more of it—to work less. This is called the **substitution effect.**

Another effect occurs simultaneously when the tax is imposed. If Rogers works the same number of hours after the tax, he receives only $8 for each of these hours, while before it was $10. In a real sense, Rogers has suffered a loss of income. To the extent that leisure is a **normal good**—consumption increases when income increases, and consumption decreases when income decreases—this income loss leads to less consumption of leisure. But less leisure means more work. Because the earnings tax makes Rogers poorer, it induces him to work more. This is called the **income effect.**

Thus, the tax simultaneously produces two effects: It induces substitution toward the cheaper activity (leisure), and it reduces real income. Since the substitution and income effects work in opposite directions, theory alone cannot determine the impact of an earnings tax.

The importance of the ambiguity caused by the conflict of income and substitution effects cannot be overemphasized. The theoretical model helps understand the relationship between income taxes and labor supply, but only empirical work—analysis based on observation and experience as opposed to theory—can tell us how labor force behavior is affected by changes in the tax system. Even intense armchair speculation on this matter must be regarded with considerable skepticism. Here, then, we see one major role for economic theory: to make us aware of the areas of our ignorance.

In other contexts, economic theory can be the reason for thinking that a research question is important in the first place. Consider a government policy of mandating safety-design features (such as seat belts, air bags, and antilock brakes) in automobiles.

substitution effect

The tendency of an individual to consume more of one good and less of another because of a decrease in the price of the former relative to the latter.

normal good

A good for which demand increases as income increases and demand decreases as income decreases, other things being the same.

income effect

The effect of a price change on the quantity demanded due exclusively to the fact that the consumer's income has changed.

The goal of such measures is to improve public safety. Yet, as pointed out by Peltzman [1975], economic theory suggests that this measure might actually backfire and increase fatalities. The basic logic is simple—economic theory says that, in general, when the cost of some activity goes down, people are more likely to engage in that activity. In this case, the safety-design features reduce the "cost" of driving fast and recklessly, because in the event of an accident, the injuries may be less severe. By this logic, then, mandating safety features could lead to more reckless driving and more associated accidents.

Empirical work is required to determine whether the reduction in fatalities from the additional safety-design features more than offsets the increase in fatalities due to more reckless driving. An additional testable proposition stemming from theory is that safety-design features would induce a disproportionate increase in pedestrian fatalities because pedestrians are exposed to the increase in reckless driving but do not experience the countervailing protection of the safety devices. Here we see another important function of economic theory: to generate hypotheses whose validity can be assessed through empirical work.

▶ CAUSATION VERSUS CORRELATION

The examples we have cited so far point to the importance of establishing a causal relationship between a certain government policy and an outcome of interest. In order for us to infer that government action X causes societal effect Y, three conditions must hold:

1. The cause (X) must precede the effect (Y). This makes sense, because a causal relationship is only possible if the cause leads to (that is, precedes) the effect.

correlation

A measure of the extent to which two events move together.

2. The cause and effect must be **correlated.** Two events are correlated if they move together. The correlation may be positive (X and Y move in the same direction) or negative (X and Y move in opposite directions). If Y does not change when X does, then X cannot be causing Y.

3. Other explanations for any observed correlation must be eliminated.

The last condition is tricky. It requires that other influences of Y (which we call factor Z) get ruled out before attributing X as the cause. Consider, for example, unemployment insurance (UI), a program under which the government makes payments to people who are out of work. An important question is whether increasing the payments leads to longer spells of unemployment. Suppose we can collect data on UI benefits from a group of individuals, some of whom received "high" levels of benefits and some of whom received "low" levels of benefits. We refer to those who received high benefits as the **treatment group,** because they received the "treatment" that we are evaluating. The workers who received low benefits did not receive the treatment and are referred to as the **control group.**

treatment group

The group of individuals who are subject to the intervention being studied.

Suppose we find that the treatment group of workers subsequently had shorter spells of unemployment on average than the control group. This suggests that the first two criteria for causation are met, but in order to infer that the higher UI benefits caused shorter unemployment duration, we must consider whether other explanations exist for the observed relationship between the two events. One possible explanation is that the people in the treatment group were different in other ways from those in the control group. For example, UI benefits are typically higher for those who

control group

The comparison group of individuals who are not subject to the intervention being studied.

had higher earnings in their previous jobs. Higher previous earnings, in turn, might reflect a greater motivation for work. Hence, higher motivation might lead to higher unemployment benefits *and* to a greater eagerness to find work. This suggests that factor Z (higher motivation) leads both to higher UI benefits when out of work and to shorter unemployment duration, so one cannot conclude that the higher benefits caused the shorter unemployment spells. In short, the fact that there is a correlation does not prove causation.

"Do you think all these film crews brought on global warming or did global warming bring on all these film crews?" Carole Cable. The Wall Street Journal.

The importance of distinguishing between correlation and causation arises in a variety of contexts. For example, there is a positive correlation between whether a man is married and his wages. On this basis, some pundits and policymakers have suggested that the government should institute financial incentives for people to marry. The problem is that there are other possible explanations for the correlation between men's marital status and their wages. It could be that men with better personalities do better in the job market and are more likely to find a spouse. One must rule out other explanations before promoting a policy that encourages marriage as a means of boosting wages.

▶ EXPERIMENTAL STUDIES

In our hypothetical example we saw that the observed relationship between UI benefits and unemployment duration was due to a third influence—motivation level. The problem is that the characteristics of the control group workers differed from the characteristics of the treatment group workers. As a result, the lower unemployment duration for the treatment group relative to the control was a **biased estimate** of the true causal impact of the higher benefits. A biased estimate is one that conflates the true causal impact with the impact of outside factors. In order to be compelling, empirical economics should eliminate bias when estimating the causal relationship between two events.

In order to rule out other factors, we would like to know the **counterfactual,** which is what would have happened to members of the treatment group had they not received the treatment. Of course, in our UI example it is impossible to know the true counterfactual because the treatment workers did indeed receive the higher benefits. In order to make things interesting, let's momentarily leave the real world for the world of science fiction in which time travel is possible. First, we form a control group of unemployed people who receive "low" UI benefits, and we measure how long it takes them to find a new job. Then we go back in time, grant the same unemployed people "high" UI benefits, and we measure how long it takes them to find a new job. In this scenario, our treatment group consists of the exact same people as our control group. The only difference is that the latter received high benefits and the former (in an alternative timeline) received low benefits. In other words, our control group *is* the counterfactual. Any difference in the treatment group's unemployment duration relative to the control group's unemployment duration can therefore reliably be attributed to the causal effect of receiving higher UI benefits.

In a world without time travel it is impossible to use the same people for both the control group and the treatment group. Luckily, there is a good alternative, which is to use an **experimental (or randomized) study,** in which subjects are *randomly* assigned to either the treatment group or the control group. With random assignment, the people in the control group are not literally the same people as those in the treatment group, but they have similar characteristics on average. Importantly, because selection into the treatment group is outside the individual's control, it is less likely that other factors (like motivation level) can lead the investigator to confuse correlation for causation.

Experimental studies are considered the gold standard of empirical studies because of this potential to eliminate bias. They are frequently used in the natural sciences such as medicine. For example, in order to test the effectiveness of a drug, researchers can randomly assign people to either a treatment group (in which case they receive the drug treatment) or to a control group (in which case they receive a placebo instead of the drug). Any observed differences in their medical outcomes can therefore be attributed to the drug rather than differences in other characteristics. It was on this basis that, several years ago, scientists determined that the antibiotic drug streptomycin was an effective treatment for tuberculosis.

Conducting an Experimental Study

In an experimental study of the effect of UI benefits on unemployment duration, the first step is to randomly assign a sample of unemployed people to receive either "high" or "low" weekly benefits. If we start with a small sample of people, then it is still possible that there will be large differences in the average characteristics of those in the control and treatment groups. But as our sample size increases, the characteristics of both groups will be the same on average. With random assignment, not only do we expect the two groups' observed characteristics (such as education) to be the same on average, but we also expect their unobserved characteristics (such as motivation level) to be the same on average. The final step is to compare the subsequent average unemployment duration across the two groups. Because the two groups have the same characteristics at the start of the study, any difference in unemployment duration between the two groups can be attributed to the level of UI benefits.

Pitfalls of Experimental Studies

It is hard for economists to conduct controlled experimental studies. Sometimes the difficulty is due to ethical issues. Suppose, for example, that policymakers want to know how many fewer illnesses would result from a given reduction in pollution. An experimental study would randomly assign people to different groups, some of which would be exposed to low levels of pollution and others to very high levels. While this would yield unbiased estimates of the effect of pollution reduction on health, most people would agree that such experiments are unethical.

Technical problems arise as well. Consider a hypothetical experiment to test the impact of a job-training program on subsequent wages. Workers are randomly selected to enroll or not enroll in a job-training program, which ensures that the treatment and control groups have similar characteristics on average. But what if some of the treatment group workers who were enrolled in the job-training program do not actually attend the program? When we later compare wages between the treatment and control groups, we might draw misleading inferences if we don't know which workers in the treatment group failed to attend. In the same way, members of the control group may find ways to get into the treatment group or obtain an experience similar to the treatment group, such as enrolling in substitute programs. In short, people in an experiment are not passive objects, and their behavior may undo the effects of randomization.

Another problem can arise when some workers involved in the experiment fail to respond to follow-up surveys requesting their wage information. For example, suppose that the job-training program actually does increase wages. However, suppose also that low-wage workers are less likely to report their future wages to the researcher. In this case, the average post-treatment wages of the control group are artificially high, because the low-wage people are not included in the computation of the average. We might then erroneously conclude that the treatment and control groups have the same wages. The basic problem is that even though the experiment started with random samples, when the final data are collected, the control group has been contaminated by the nonrandom disappearance of certain of its members.

A final problem is that people in an experiment may not behave the same way as they would if the entire society were subjected to the policy, especially if the experiment has limited duration. For example, suppose we conducted an experiment to estimate how much more frequently people go to the doctor when they have generous health insurance. We can randomly select some people to receive generous health insurance for a year and others to receive less generous health insurance for the same year. The problem is that the treatment group subjects might go to the doctor very frequently because they know the experiment will only last one year, after which health care will become much more expensive for them. The measured effect of the treatment will be a biased estimate of the impact of a government policy that provides generous health insurance indefinitely.

This leads to a more general concern with experiments. They are adept at achieving unbiased estimates of a causal relationship in a particular context. However, it is not clear whether the causal inferences from one context can be generalized to other populations, settings, and even to related treatments. For example, in the mid-1980s the state of Illinois conducted a controlled experiment in which a random sample of unemployed people was told they would receive a $500 bonus if they found a job within 11 weeks. (See Woodbury and Spiegelman [1987].) The findings suggested that the bonus reduced the time a person remained unemployed. Given the careful design of the study, this finding is likely unbiased. But what could a public official in California in 2009 learn from this experiment, which relied on a different population and took place in a different time period? In short, to what extent do the experimental results generalize? In the same way, suppose that one were back in Illinois in the 1980s, and the government could afford a bonus of only $250 rather than $500. How would that policy affect time spent unemployed? Presumably a bonus of $250 would have less of an impact than $500, but how much less is entirely unclear. The experimental results by themselves do not provide much guidance.

This example illustrates how experiments provide reliable estimates of the impact of a very specific policy on behavior, but they do not provide in-depth understanding (i.e., what goes on inside the black box) of why any changes have occurred. Consequently, we don't learn much about the likely impacts if the policy is applied in other contexts or if it is configured in a somewhat different fashion. This returns us to our discussion of the role of theory. By making assumptions on how people behave, in particular that they rationally maximize utility, theory can help us generalize particular experimental results to other populations or policies.

Thus, although experimental studies offer a credible way to evaluate the impact of a policy, they are not foolproof. In particular, researchers must carefully track the subjects in the control and treatment groups to maintain the original random assignment, and they must be cautious about generalizing the results to other settings or policies.

▶ OBSERVATIONAL STUDIES

Experimental studies are simply out of the question for many important issues. For example, as mentioned earlier, knowing the impact of tax reductions on labor supply is of major interest. An experimental study of this issue would require randomly giving some people tax cuts and others not. Even if this were legally and politically possible, we would still face the problem that the people in the tax cut group would know that they were part of an experiment, and this could affect their behavior. Under these circumstances, instead of experiments, economists rely on **observational studies,** which use data obtained by observing and measuring actual behavior outside of an experimental setting.

observational study

An empirical study that relies on observed data that are not obtained from an experimental setting.

Observational data come from a variety of sources. Some are collected by surveying people, such as telephone surveys of consumers or written surveys submitted by households every 10 years for the census. Other observational data come from administrative records, including historical records of births and deaths, or government data on national economic performance.

econometrics

The statistical tools for analyzing economic data.

Without randomization, observational studies must rely on other techniques to rule out factors that might contaminate causal inferences. **Econometrics** is the use of statistical analysis of economic data in order to estimate causal relationships. Specifically, econometrics uses *regression analysis* to estimate the relationship between two variables while holding other factors constant. We next explain how this technique works.

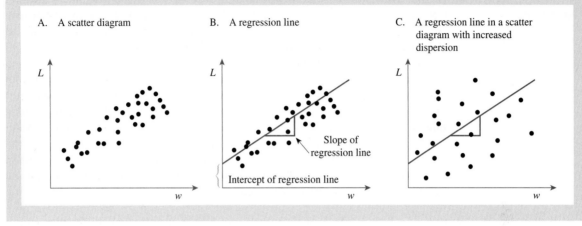

Figure 2.1   **Regression analysis**
Panel A shows there is a positive correlation between hours of work and after-tax wages. Panel B shows the regression line that fits through these data points, which yields an estimate of the magnitude of the relationship between the two variables. The estimated relationship between the two variables is more reliable in Panel B than in Panel C, because the data points in Panel C are more scattered.

A.   A scatter diagram

B.   A regression line

C.   A regression line in a scatter diagram with increased dispersion

Conducting an Observational Study

Suppose we are interested in estimating the effect of a reduction of the income tax on annual hours of work (which we denote as L, for labor supply). A change in the income tax changes the net wage rate (w) that a person receives. So we can state the problem as: If the tax rate is changed, is there an observed correlation between changes in W and changes in L, and can we rule out other Z-factors that can explain this correlation? In observational studies, variables that are thought to be causal (such as the net wage here) are referred to as *independent variables*. A variable that is thought to be an outcome (such as labor supply here) is referred to as the *dependent variable*.

To see how observational studies work, suppose we have information on the hours of work and on the after-tax wages for a sample of people for a given year. We can plot these data points, as shown in Figure 2.1A. This figure indicates a positive correlation between after-tax wages and labor supply—labor supply is higher when after-tax wages are higher. We are interested in estimating the magnitude of this relationship. This is the task of regression analysis, which fits a **regression line** through the observed data points. Obviously, no single straight line can cross through all these points. The purpose of regression analysis is to find the line that best fits this relationship, as shown in Figure 2.1B.[2] The slope of this line, known as the regression coefficient, is an estimate of the relationship between after-tax wages and labor supply. Suppose, for example, that the regression coefficient is 1.5. This suggests that an increase in the net wage by $10 is associated with an increase in labor supply by 15 hours per year.

regression line

The line that provides the best fit through a scatter of data points.

---

[2] In this example, we are assuming a linear relationship between the two variables. The "best" line minimizes the sum of the squared vertical distances between the points on the line and the points in the scatter. (See Wooldridge [2009].) Econometrics also allows for a nonlinear relationship between variables, which is frequently a preferable approach.

The reliability of the estimated regression coefficient depends on the distribution of the data in the scatter plot. To see why, suppose our scatter of points looked like those in Figure 2.1C. The regression line is identical to that in Figure 2.1B, but the scatter of points is more diffuse. Even though the estimated regression coefficient is the same, one has less faith in its reliability. Econometricians calculate a measure called the **standard error,** which indicates the reliability of the estimated coefficient. When the standard error is small in relation to the size of the estimated parameter, the coefficient is said to be statistically significant.

This example assumed there is only one explanatory variable, the net wage. Suppose that instead there were two independent variables: the net wage and nonlabor income (such as dividends and interest). Multiple regression analysis estimates the relationship between each independent variable and the dependent variable, holding all other independent variables constant. Multiple regression analysis is a very valuable tool, because in virtually all interesting problems, more than one independent variable can causally affect the dependent variable. If we can control for all factors that explain the dependent variable, this technique allows us to find the independent causal effect of whatever variable is under consideration.

Types of Data   Regression analysis can be conducted using different types of data. Figure 2.1 relied on data on after-tax wages and labor supply for a sample of people in a given year. Data that contain information on individual entities (for example, workers, consumers, firms, states, or countries) at a given point in time are known as **cross-sectional data.** A cross-sectional regression analysis relies on variation across different individual entities in order to estimate the regression line.

While cross-sectional data contain information on a group of individual entities at one point in time, **time-series data** include information on a single entity at different points in time. For example, we might have information on after-tax wages and labor supply for each year of one person's adult life. A time-series regression analysis relies on variation across time for one entity in order to estimate the regression line.

Finally, **panel data** (also called *longitudinal data*) combine the features of cross-sectional data and time-series data. That is, a panel data set contains information on individual entities at different points in time. You can think of panel data as a time series of cross-sectional data. For example, a panel data set might have information on thousands of different people from a variety of different years. We'll argue below that panel data have some unique advantages when it comes to doing empirical work in public finance.

Pitfalls of Observational Studies

Because observational studies rely on data collected in a nonexperimental setting, it is difficult to ensure that the control group forms a valid counterfactual. While the estimated regression coefficient provides a measure of the correlation between the independent and dependent variables, one cannot assume a causal relationship because outside factors could affect both of these variables.

Consider the hypothetical labor supply example above. Our regression analysis used cross-sectional data, in which some people had high after-tax wage rates and some had low after-tax wage rates. The analysis suggested that there is a positive correlation between after-tax wages and work hours. But remember, correlation does not necessarily imply causation. It could be that other factors influence both after-tax

standard error

A statistical measure of how much an estimated regression coefficient might vary from its true value.

cross-sectional data

Data that contain information on entities at a given point in time.

time-series data

Data that contain information on an entity at different points in time.

panel data

Data that contain information on individual entities at different points of time.

wages and hours worked, in which case the observed relationship is biased. Perhaps, for example, highly ambitious people have higher wages and also work longer hours. If so, then our observed positive correlation between after-tax wage rates and hours of work is at least partly due to differences in ambition.

As already noted, one way to address the bias in observational studies is to include other independent variables, which are referred to as control variables. Regression analysis allows us to estimate the independent effect of the variable we care about while taking into account the control variables. In our labor supply example, one might include variables such as age, nonlabor income, and gender, all of which might affect labor supply but could also be related to after-tax wage rates. But there are two problems. First, we might not think of all the control variables that should be included or all the relevant control variables may not be available in the data set. Second, some variables are very hard to measure, even in principle. Ambition is a good example. If either reason leads us to omit a control variable that is correlated with after-tax wages and influences labor supply, we will obtain biased estimates.

Despite the limitations of observational studies, they can provide useful information about the possible impacts of different government programs. The key point is that these studies must be interpreted with care, recognizing the possibility that outside factors might bias any causal inferences.

▶ QUASI-EXPERIMENTAL STUDIES

Experimental studies have excellent properties when it comes to eliminating bias, but they may be difficult or impossible to perform. Observational studies have knotty problems with bias, but the data are relatively easy to obtain. Can one obtain some of the advantages of each? A class of observational studies known as **quasi-experimental studies** (also known as *natural experiments*) are used by empirical economists to estimate a causal relationship. These studies identify situations in which outside circumstances in effect randomly assign people to control and treatment groups. The difference between an experiment and a quasi-experiment is that an experiment explicitly randomizes people into a treatment or control group, whereas a quasi-experiment uses observational data but relies on circumstances outside of the researcher's control that naturally lead to random assignment.

quasi-experimental study

An observational study that relies on circumstances outside of the researcher's control to mimic random assignment.

A clever early example of a quasi-experiment comes from the work of John Snow, a 19th-century physician. At the time it wasn't known that germs cause diseases, and there were many competing theories to explain outbreaks of cholera. Snow wanted to find out whether cholera was caused by exposure to contaminated water.[3] He discovered that two water companies served much of London. One company had its intake point upstream from the sewage discharges along the Thames and so had fairly pure water, while the other company had its intake point downstream from the sewage discharges and so provided contaminated water. A natural strategy would be to compare the households who received water from one company to the households who received water from the other company. However, a potential problem arises. What if the people who received the polluted water were systematically different from the others? If they lived in poorer neighborhoods, for example, a different incidence of cholera could be attributed to factors other than dirty water. Snow indeed considered

---

[3] This example comes from Freedman [1991].

this important issue, and demonstrated that the assignment of water companies to different houses was essentially random:

> The pipes of each Company go down all the streets, and into nearly all the courts and alleys. A few houses are supplied by one Company and a few by the other, according to the decision of the owner or occupier at that time when the Water Companies were in active competition. In many cases a single house has a supply different from that on either side. Each company supplies both rich and poor, both large houses and small; there is no difference either in the condition or occupation of the persons receiving the water of the different Companies [Snow 1855].

In effect, Snow convincingly showed that his observational study virtually replicated a randomized study, because the treatment and control groups had similar characteristics. This randomization enabled him to rule out other factors, so he could safely conclude that the substantially higher number of cholera victims in houses receiving the contaminated water was due to the sewage.

Conducting a Quasi-Experimental Study

A successful quasi-experiment hinges critically on whether the researcher has identified a situation in which assignment to the treatment group is random. We now discuss a few approaches to establishing a valid quasi-experimental research design.

Difference-in-Difference Quasi-Experiments From time to time, policymakers suggest raising the state tax on beer in order to reduce teen traffic fatalities. Does it work? An ideal experiment would randomly assign different beer taxes to different states and then measure whether teen traffic fatalities decline in the high-tax states relative to the low-tax states. Obviously, such a study is not possible.

Now, suppose we learned that between 1989 and 1992 a group of states substantially increased their tax rates on beer, and that following the tax increases, teen traffic fatalities in these states declined by 5.2 per 100,000 teens. Could we infer that the tax increase for beer caused the reduction in teen traffic fatalities? No, because it could be that teen fatality reductions would have occurred even without the tax increase.

We would therefore want to examine what happened to a control group of states. A sensible control group would consist of those states that did not increase their beer taxes between 1989 and 1992. If the control group of states serves as a reasonable counterfactual, then we can assume a similar reduction would have occurred for the treatment states had they not increased their beer tax.

Therefore, in order to estimate the effect of the beer tax, it would make sense to compute the *change* in teen traffic fatalities in the treatment states and compute the difference between it and the *change* in the control group states. As it happens, in the control group states, teen traffic fatalities declined by 8.1 per 100,000 teens. That is, there was actually a relative increase in teen traffic fatalities in the states that raised their beer tax. Hence, contrary to the view one might obtain looking simply at the data from the treatment states, it appears that the tax increases did not accomplish the goal of reducing teen traffic deaths.

This example, based on actual estimates obtained by Dee [1999],[4] is typical of a technique known as **difference-in-difference analysis.** The reason for the name is that it compares the difference in a treatment group's outcome after receiving the treatment

---

difference-in-difference analysis

An analysis that compares changes over time in an outcome of the treatment group to changes over the same time period in the outcome of the control group.

---

[4] The treatment states were California, Delaware, New Jersey, New York, and Rhode Island.

to the difference in the outcome of the control group over the same period. This technique achieves unbiased results if one can safely assume that the changes that occurred to the control group form a valid counterfactual; that is, that they reflect what would have happened to the treatment group had it not been treated. Note that a difference-in-difference analysis is only possible if one has panel data, because the computation requires knowing how the behavior of a given group of individuals changes over time (which is the time-series part) and then comparing it to the change over the same time period for another group of individuals (which is the cross-sectional part).

Instrumental Variables Quasi-Experiments   Sometimes an investigator suspects that assignment into a treatment group may not be random, thus violating a requirement for obtaining an unbiased estimate. One approach to dealing with the problem is called **instrumental variables analysis.** The idea behind instrumental variables analysis is to find some third variable that may have affected entry into the treatment group but in itself is not correlated with the outcome variable.

An important issue that many local governments face is whether to reduce kindergarten class sizes. Proponents argue that such a policy leads to higher student test scores. An experiment to investigate this issue would randomly assign kindergarten students to different class sizes and then measure differences in test scores between those in large versus small classes. In fact, such experiments have been conducted. (See Krueger [1999].) As discussed earlier, one possible drawback of such an experiment is that the temporary nature of the experiment might influence the outcome.

An observational study might rely on regression analysis to estimate whether students in smaller classes score higher than students in larger classes. However, such a study would likely yield biased results because the treatment and control groups differ in many ways that can influence both class size and test score. For example, parents who are relatively more concerned about educating their children might choose schools or school districts with smaller class sizes. Such parents might also engage in other activities (such as reading with their children) that help their children attain high test scores. Therefore, an observed negative correlation between class size and test scores is misleading because both are caused by the third variable, parental concern.

Hoxby [2000] developed a quasi-experiment in order to address this potential bias. She observed that the timings of births in any given school area fluctuate randomly. Because of these fluctuations, kindergarten classes are larger in some years than in others. While many factors determine whether a child attends a large or small kindergarten class, the variation in births from year to year represents a random component of this outcome. Hoxby therefore relied on the instrumental variables method, which takes advantage of the random determinant of class size to identify the effect on test scores. She used random fluctuations in enrollment year-to-year as an instrumental variable. This measure is correlated with class size, but does not directly influence test scores. Hoxby found that class size does not have a discernible effect on test scores.

Regression-Discontinuity Quasi-Experiments   Eligibility for some policy programs is determined by whether a measurable characteristic of a person is above or below a specific cut-off point. For example, the government might make public health insurance available only to households whose annual incomes are below $20,000. An observational study that compared health outcomes of those who received the public health insurance to those who did not would likely be biased

instrumental variables analysis

An analysis that relies on finding some variable that affects entry into the treatment group, but in itself is not correlated with the outcome variable.

because the two groups differ in many ways. Suppose, though, that instead of comparing the health of everyone above $20,000 with the health of everyone below $20,000, we compare the outcomes for those who were *just barely* eligible to those who *just barely* missed being eligible for the program. This is an attractive strategy, because while households that make substantially above and below $20,000 differ a lot from each other, households that make $20,001 are likely quite similar to those that make $19,999. This approach is called **regression-discontinuity analysis.** The fundamental assumption that must be met for this approach to replicate an experiment is that the characteristics of those who just barely missed eligibility are the same on average as those who just barely made it.

Suppose that a city is trying to decide whether to make summer school mandatory for its poorly performing students. It first wants to determine whether this step would improve academic performance. An ideal experiment would randomly assign some poorly performing students to summer school and then measure differences in future test scores between them and a control group of poorly performing students who did not attend summer school. However, political constraints probably would not permit such randomization. Instead, the city might rely on regression analysis to estimate whether students who attended summer school have higher future scores than those who did not. Unfortunately, such a study would likely yield biased results because the students who attend summer school tend to be poorer academic performers in the first place, so we would expect their future scores to be lower than those of other students even if summer school actually helped them.

Jacob and Lefgren [2004] developed a regression-discontinuity quasi-experiment to address this potential bias. In 1996, the Chicago Public Schools instituted a policy that tied summer school attendance to performance on standardized tests. Students who scored below a certain cut-off on the test were required to attend summer school; otherwise, they were not. Jacob and Lefgren focused on the subsequent test scores of students who just barely qualified for summer school relative to those who just barely missed qualifying. They found a jump in follow-up reading and math scores for third graders (but not sixth graders), suggesting the existence of a positive causal effect, at least for some grade levels.

Pitfalls of Quasi-Experimental Studies

Quasi-experimental studies attempt to estimate causal relationships using observational data. The biggest pitfall is that the natural experiment may not truly mimic random assignment to the treatment group. If the underlying trends in teen fatalities were fundamentally different in states that increased beer taxes from those in states that did not, then the differences-in-differences estimate of the impact on teen traffic fatalities would be biased. If the fluctuations in births in a school area were not random or did not play a significant role in determining whether a child was in a small or large kindergarten class, then the estimated test impacts would be biased. And if students who just barely qualified for summer school eligibility were different from those who just barely missed qualifying, then the estimates of impacts on future test scores would be biased. Studies based on quasi-experiments look for situations that replicate randomization, but it can be difficult to find quasi-experiments that are as straightforward as a pure randomized experiment.

Another concern is that quasi-experiments can only be applied to a limited number of research questions. Many interesting and important economic questions simply

regression-discontinuity analysis

An analysis that relies on a strict cut-off criterion for eligibility of the intervention under study in order to approximate an experimental design.

do not lend themselves to natural experiments. For example, as we'll discuss in Chapter 11, the government provides guaranteed retirement income to people through the Social Security program. A critical question is whether people save less on their own when they know that they will receive Social Security payments when they retire. The problem is that Social Security was introduced to the entire nation at the same time—*everyone* received the same "treatment." Hence, there are only very limited opportunities to identify natural experiments. One economist noted that if natural experiments were required in all areas of empirical work, it "would effectively stop estimation" [Hurd, 1990].

Quasi-experiments also share with experiments the concern about how to generalize the results to other settings and treatments. As discussed earlier, these studies provide reliable evidence of the response to a very specific change in policy, but they are limited in explaining why the changes have occurred. Thus, it is difficult to use the results to predict the impact of other policies.

▶ CONCLUSIONS

Economic theory plays a crucial role in empirical research by framing the research question and helping isolate a set of variables that may influence the behavior of interest. Empirical work then tests whether the causal relationship between a policy and an outcome suggested by the theory is consistent with real-world phenomena.

A randomized experiment is the cleanest way to establish a causal relationship between a policy and some type of behavior. However, it is not always clear whether the results of such experiments can be generalized to other contexts. In any case, economic researchers frequently must rely on observational data, which do not have the randomized feature of a controlled experiment. In these cases, the most reliable empirical analyses exploit natural experiments that mimic random assignment to the treatment or control groups.

It is not easy to conduct reliable empirical research. Different researchers may rely on different theoretical models, examine the behavior of different samples of people, and use different statistical techniques. Therefore, honest researchers will frequently come to very different conclusions about the implications of a policy. Do we therefore have to abandon all hope of learning about the factors that influence economic behavior? Definitely not. In many cases one can reconcile the different empirical findings and construct a coherent picture of the phenomenon under discussion. Feldstein [1982, p. 830] has likened the economist who undertakes such a task to the maharajah in the children's fable about the five blind men who examined an elephant:

> The important lesson in that story is not the fact that each blind man came away with a partial and "incorrect" piece of evidence. The lesson is rather that an intelligent maharajah who studied the findings of these five men could probably piece together a good judgmental picture of an elephant, especially if he had previously seen some other four-footed animal.

We will refer to empirical results throughout this book, and explain the pros and cons of the research designs that generated them. In cases where the profession has failed to achieve consensus, we will draw upon this chapter to explain why. More generally, it is hoped that this introduction to empirical methodology induces a healthy skepticism concerning claims about economic behavior that occur in public debate. Beware any argument that begins with the magic words "studies have proved."

Summary

- One goal of the field of public finance is to estimate how various government policies affect individuals' behavior.

- Economic theory provides a framework for thinking about the factors that might influence the behavior of interest, and helps generate hypotheses that can be tested through empirical research. However, theory alone cannot say how important any particular factor is.

- An important purpose of empirical work in public finance is to estimate the causal relationship between a government policy and some kind of behavior. Three conditions must hold in order to infer a causal relationship between a government program and an outcome: (1) the program precedes the outcome, (2) the program and outcome are correlated, and (3) other explanations of the observed correlation are eliminated.

- One must not confuse correlation with causation. The fact that two variables are correlated does not prove that one causes the other.

- Experimental studies randomly assign subjects to either a treatment group or control group. Random assignment reduces the likelihood that outside factors will lead the researcher to confuse correlation with causation.

- Experimental studies offer a credible way to evaluate the impact of government programs, but they are not foolproof. In particular, researchers must make sure the assignment remains random over time and be careful about generalizing the results.

- Because experimental studies are often impossible to conduct, public finance economists rely on observational studies that use data obtained from real-world economic settings.

- Econometrics is the use of statistical analysis of economic data in order to estimate causal relationships. An important econometric tool is regression analysis, which estimates the relationship between two variables while holding other factors constant.

- Observational data can be cross-sectional, time-series, or panel. Observational data are collected in nonexperimental settings. Therefore, the possible influence of outside factors can make it difficult to estimate causal relationships.

- A quasi-experiment uses observational data but relies on outside circumstances to replicate a randomized experiment.

- Quasi-experiments can be structured in several ways, such as a difference-in-difference analysis, instrumental variables analysis, and regression-discontinuity analysis.

Discussion Questions

1. In 2008, presidential candidate John McCain proposed extending the cut in marginal income tax rates passed during the Bush administration. Explain why theory alone cannot predict how labor supply would be affected if this proposal were implemented. If there were no political or legal impediments to doing so, how could you design an experimental study to estimate the impact of lower marginal tax rates on labor supply?

2. In an article on how exercise improves health, the *New York Times* reported on an observational study that found that each hour spent running added two hours to a person's life expectancy [Brody, 2006]. A week later, a letter to the editor questioned whether the results really proved anything about the impact of exercise on health, and suggested that the study could just as well be showing that "those with a strong heart and good health are otherwise more likely to enjoy running and do it more regularly." How does this challenge to the exercise study relate to the problems faced by economists trying to assess

the causal effects of economic policy? How could you design an experimental study to estimate the impact of running on life expectancy?

3. A researcher conducts a cross-sectional analysis of workers and finds a positive correlation between time spent on a computer at work and wages. The researcher concludes that computer use increases wages and advocates a policy of computer training for all children. What is a possible problem with this analysis?

4. In the 1970s, researchers at the RAND Corporation conducted a famous social experiment to investigate the relationship between health insurance coverage and health care utilization. In this experiment, samples of individuals were induced to trade their normal insurance policies for new RAND policies that offered different rates at which the insurance would reimburse the individual for health care expenses. In 1993, the Clinton administration used the results of the RAND experiment to predict how health care utilization would increase if insurance coverage were made universal. What problems might arise in using the social experimentation results to predict the impact of universal coverage?

5. In New York State, an individual's unemployment benefits depend on her previous earnings—the higher the earnings, the higher the benefits, up until a maximum benefit level is reached. In 1989, the state legislature and governor unexpectedly increased the maximum benefit level. This led to an increase in benefits for high earners, but no change in benefits for low earners [Meyer and Mok, 2007]. How might a researcher take advantage of this scenario to conduct a difference-in-difference quasi-experiment to estimate the effect of unemployment benefits on unemployment duration? Be sure to describe both the treatment group and the control group. What is the key assumption required for this quasi-experiment to generate unbiased estimates of the effect of unemployment insurance on unemployment duration?

6. Suppose that five states reduce income taxes in a given year. You are interested in estimating whether the tax cut has increased saving, and you find that the saving rate for residents of these five states increased by 2 percent in the year after it was introduced. Can you reasonably conclude that the tax cut caused the increase in saving? How would you conduct a difference-in-difference analysis to estimate the impact on saving? What assumption must hold for the difference-in-difference analysis to be valid?

7. In the run-up to the 2008 presidential campaign, Senator John McCain said, "Tax cuts, starting with Kennedy, as we all know, increase revenues. So what's the argument for increasing taxes? If you get the opposite effect out of tax cuts?" Why might the correlation between lower tax rates and higher tax revenues not be indicative of a causal relationship?

8. A perennial debate is whether federal budget deficits lead to higher interest rates. The following table gives some historical data on deficits and interest rates. For each year, the deficit is the difference between revenues and expenditures measured in current dollars; a negative figure is a deficit, and a positive figure is a surplus.

Year	Deficit	Interest Rate
1980	$ –73.8	15.3%
1985	–212.3	9.9
1990	–221.0	10.0
1995	–164.0	8.8
2000	236.4	9.2
2005	–318.3	6.2
2007	–162.0	8.1

On the basis of these data, what inference could you make about the relationship between federal deficits and interest rates? Explain why inferences based on these data alone might be problematic.

Chapter Three

TOOLS OF NORMATIVE ANALYSIS

The object of government is the welfare of the people. The material progress and prosperity of a nation are desirable chiefly so far as they lead to the moral and material welfare of all good citizens.

—PRESIDENT THEODORE ROOSEVELT

Pick up a newspaper any day and you are sure to find a story about a debate concerning the government's role in the economy. Should income taxes be cut? Do we need to subsidize the purchase of medicine for the elderly? Is using public land in Alaska for oil exploration a good idea? The list is virtually endless. Given the enormous diversity of the government's economic activities, some kind of general framework is needed to assess the desirability of various government actions. Without such a systematic framework, each government program ends up being evaluated on an ad hoc basis, and achieving a coherent economic policy becomes impossible.

▶ WELFARE ECONOMICS

welfare economics

The branch of economic theory concerned with the social desirability of alternative economic states.

The framework used by most public finance specialists is **welfare economics,** the branch of economic theory concerned with the social desirability of alternative economic states.[1] This chapter sketches the fundamentals of welfare economics. The theory is used to distinguish the circumstances under which markets can be expected to perform well from those under which markets fail to produce desirable results.

Pure Economy Exchange

We begin by considering a very simple economy. It consists of two people who consume two commodities with fixed supplies. The only economic problem here is to allocate amounts of the two goods between the two people. As simple as this model is, all the important results from the two good–two person case hold in economies with many people and commodities.[2] The two-by-two case is analyzed because of its simplicity.

---

[1] Welfare economics relies heavily on certain basic economic tools, particularly indifference curves. For a review, see the appendix at the end of the book.

[2] See Chapter 11 of Henderson and Quandt [1980] where the results are derived using calculus.

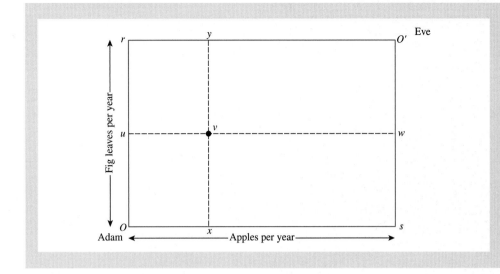

Figure 3.1
Edgeworth Box
The Edgeworth Box depicts the possible distributions of two commodities—in this case, apples and fig leaves—between Adam and Eve. The length of the box (*Os*) represents the number of apples that are available each year, and the height of the box (*Or*) represents the number of fig leaves that are available each year. At point *v*, Adam consumes *Ou* fig leaves and *Ox* apples, while Eve consumes *O'y* apples and *O'w* fig leaves.

The two people are Adam and Eve, and the two commodities are apples (food) and fig leaves (clothing). An analytical device known as the **Edgeworth Box** depicts the distribution of apples and fig leaves between Adam and Eve.[3] In Figure 3.1, the length of the Edgeworth Box, *Os*, represents the total number of apples available in the economy; the height, *Or*, is the total number of fig leaves. The amounts of the goods consumed by Adam are measured by distances from point *O*; the quantities consumed by Eve are measured by distances from *O'*. For example, at point *v*, Adam consumes *Ou* fig leaves and *Ox* apples, while Eve consumes *O'y* apples and *O'w* fig leaves. Thus, any point within the Edgeworth Box represents some allocation of apples and fig leaves between Adam and Eve.

Now assume Adam and Eve each have conventionally shaped indifference curves that represent their preferences for apples and fig leaves. In Figure 3.2, both sets of indifference curves are superimposed onto the Edgeworth Box. Adam's are labeled with *A*'s; Eve's are labeled with *E*'s. Indifference curves with greater numbers represent higher levels of happiness (utility). Adam is happier on indifference curve A_3 than on A_2 or A_1, and Eve is happier on indifference curve E_3 than on E_2 or E_1. In general, Eve's utility increases as her position moves toward the southwest, while Adam's utility increases as he moves toward the northeast.

Suppose some arbitrary distribution of apples and fig leaves is selected—say, point *g* in Figure 3.3. A_g is Adam's indifference curve that runs through point *g*, and E_g is Eve's. Now pose the following question: Is it possible to reallocate apples and fig leaves between Adam and Eve in such a way that Adam is made better off, while Eve is made no worse off? A moment's thought suggests such an allocation, at point *h*, for example, Adam is better off at this point because indifference curve A_h represents a higher utility level for him than A_g. On the other hand, Eve is no worse off at *h* because she is on her original indifference curve, E_g.

Can Adam's welfare be further increased without doing any harm to Eve? As long as Adam can be moved to indifference curves farther to the northeast while still

Edgeworth Box

A device used to depict the distribution of goods in a two good–two person world.

---

[3] Named after the 19th-century economist F. Y. Edgeworth.

Figure 3.2

Indifference curves in an Edgeworth Box
Adam and Eve each have a set of indifference curves that reflect their preferences for fig leaves and apples. Adam is happier the farther he can move toward the northeast of the box. Eve is happier the farther she can move toward the southwest of the box.

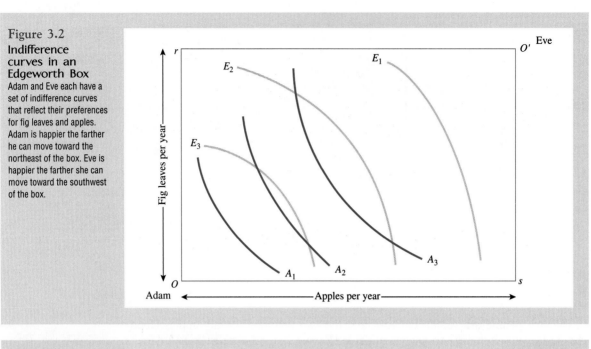

Figure 3.3

Making Adam better off without Eve becoming worse off
Moving from point g to point h to point p leaves Eve's utility unchanged but improves Adam's utility. At point p, it is impossible to make one of them better off without hurting the other. Therefore, point p is a Pareto efficient allocation.

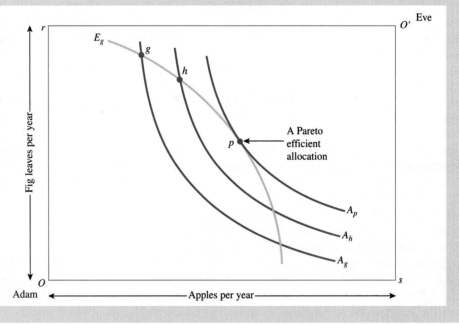

Pareto efficient

An allocation of resources such that no person can be made better off without making another person worse off.

remaining on E_g, it is possible. This process can be continued until Adam's indifference curve is just touching E_g, which occurs at point p in Figure 3.3. At this point, the only way to put Adam on a higher indifference curve than A_p would be to put Eve on a lower one. An allocation such as point p, at which the only way to make one person better off is to make another person worse off, is called **Pareto efficient.**[4] Pareto efficiency is

---

[4] Named after the 19th-century economist Vilfredo Pareto.

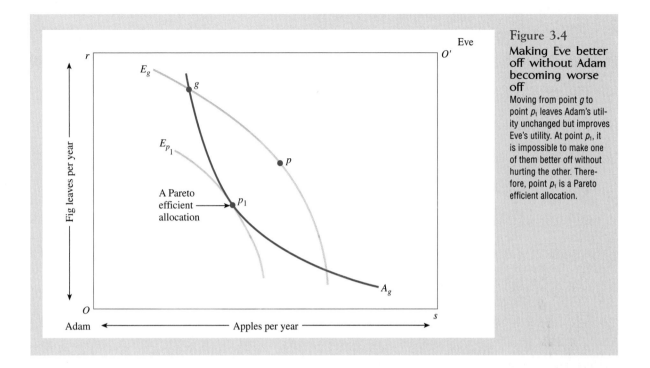

Figure 3.4
**Making Eve better
off without Adam
becoming worse
off**
Moving from point *g* to
point p_1 leaves Adam's utility unchanged but improves
Eve's utility. At point p_1, it
is impossible to make one
of them better off without
hurting the other. There-
fore, point p_1 is a Pareto
efficient allocation.

often used as the standard for evaluating the desirability of an allocation of resources. If the allocation is not Pareto efficient, it is "wasteful" in the sense that it is possible to make someone better off without hurting anybody else. When economists use the word *efficient*, they usually have Pareto efficiency in mind.

A related notion is that of a **Pareto improvement**—a reallocation of resources that makes one person better off without making anyone else worse off. In Figure 3.3, the move from *g* to *h* is a Pareto improvement, as is the move from *h* to *p*.

Point *p* is not the only Pareto efficient allocation that could have been reached by starting at point *g*. Figure 3.4 examines whether we can make Eve better off without lowering the utility of Adam. Logic similar to that surrounding Figure 3.3 suggests moving Eve to indifference curves farther to the southwest, provided that the allocation remains on indifference curve A_g. In doing so, we isolate point p_1. At p_1, the only way to improve Eve's welfare is to move Adam to a lower indifference curve. Then, by definition, p_1 is a Pareto efficient allocation.

So far, we have been looking at moves that make one person better off and leave the other at the same level of utility. Figure 3.5 shows reallocations from point *g* that make *both* Adam and Eve better off. At p_2, for example, Adam is better off than at point *g* (A_{p_2} is further to the northeast than A_g) and so is Eve (E_{p_2} is further to the southwest than E_g). Point p_2 is Pareto efficient, because at that point it is impossible to make either individual better off without making the other worse off. It should now be clear that starting at point *g*, a whole set of Pareto efficient points can be found. They differ with respect to how much each of the parties gains from the reallocation of resources.

Recall that the initial point *g* was selected arbitrarily. We can repeat the procedure for finding Pareto efficient allocations with any starting point. Had point *k* in Figure 3.6 been the original allocation, Pareto efficient allocations p_3 and p_4 could have been isolated. This exercise reveals a whole set of Pareto efficient points in the

Pareto improvement

**A reallocation of
resources that makes
at least one person
better off without making
anyone else worse off.**

Figure 3.5
Making both Adam and Eve better off
Moving from point g to point p_2 makes both Adam and Eve better off. At point p_2 it is impossible to make one of them better off without hurting the other. Therefore, point p_2 is a Pareto efficient allocation.

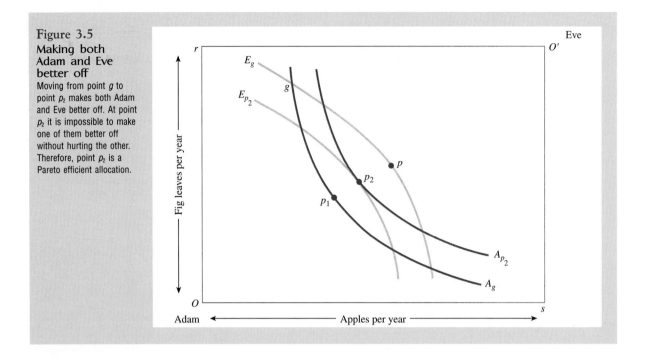

Figure 3.6
Starting from a different initial point
If instead we started at point k, we again would be able to reallocate the goods to make one person better off without hurting the other. A movement to either p_3 or to p_4 would represent a Pareto improvement.

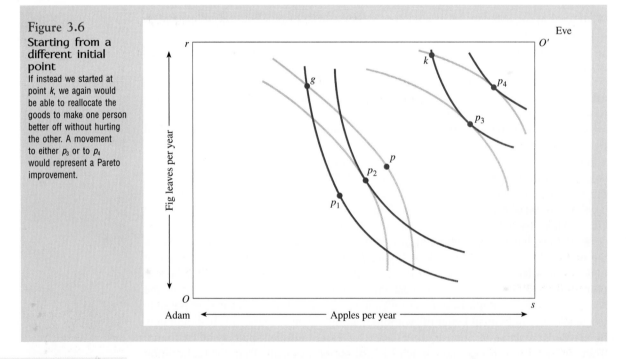

contract curve

The locus of all Pareto efficient points.

Edgeworth Box. The locus of all the Pareto efficient points is called the **contract curve,** and is denoted mm in Figure 3.7. Note that for an allocation to be Pareto efficient (to be on mm), it must be a point at which the indifference curves of Adam and Eve are barely touching. In mathematical terms, the indifference curves are tangent—the slopes of the indifference curves are equal.

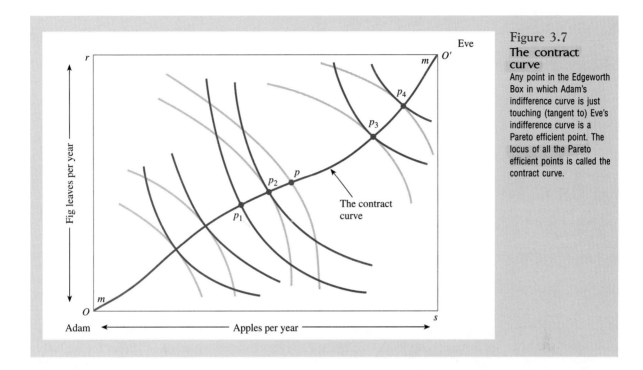

Figure 3.7
The contract curve
Any point in the Edgeworth Box in which Adam's indifference curve is just touching (tangent to) Eve's indifference curve is a Pareto efficient point. The locus of all the Pareto efficient points is called the contract curve.

In economic terms, the absolute value of the slope of the indifference curve indicates the rate at which the individual is willing to trade one good for an additional amount of another, called the *marginal rate of substitution (MRS)*.[5] Hence, Pareto efficiency requires that marginal rates of substitution be equal for all consumers:

$$MRS_{af}^{\text{Adam}} = MRS_{af}^{\text{Eve}} \tag{3.1}$$

where MRS_{af}^{Adam} is Adam's marginal rate of substitution of apples for fig leaves, and MRS_{af}^{Eve} is Eve's.

Production Economy

The Production Possibilities Curve   So far we have assumed that supplies of all the commodities are fixed. Consider what happens when productive inputs can shift between the production of apples and fig leaves, so the quantities of the two goods can change. Provided the inputs are efficiently used, if more apples are produced, then fig leaf production must necessarily fall and vice versa. The **production possibilities curve** shows the maximum quantity of fig leaves that can be produced along with any given quantity of apples.[6] A typical production possibilities curve is depicted as *CC* in Figure 3.8. As shown in Figure 3.8, one option available to the economy is to produce *Ow* fig leaves and *Ox* apples. The economy can increase apple production from *Ox* to *Oz*, distance *xz*. To do this, inputs have to be removed from the production of fig leaves and devoted to apples. Fig leaf production must

production possibilities curve

A graph that shows the maximum quantity of one output that can be produced, given the amount of the other output.

---

[5] The marginal rate of substitution is defined more carefully in the appendix at the end of this book.

[6] The production possibilities curve can be derived from an Edgeworth Box whose dimensions represent the quantities of inputs available for production.

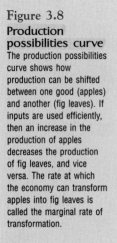

Figure 3.8
Production possibilities curve
The production possibilities curve shows how production can be shifted between one good (apples) and another (fig leaves). If inputs are used efficiently, then an increase in the production of apples decreases the production of fig leaves, and vice versa. The rate at which the economy can transform apples into fig leaves is called the marginal rate of transformation.

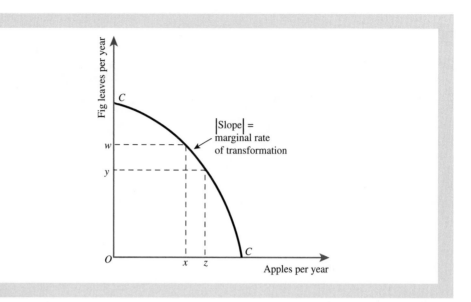

marginal rate of transformation

The rate at which the economy can transform one good into another good; it is the absolute value of the slope of the production possibilities frontier.

marginal cost

The incremental cost of producing one more unit of output.

fall by distance *wy* if apple production is to increase by *xz*. The ratio of distance *wy* to distance *xz* is called the **marginal rate of transformation** of apples for fig leaves (MRT_{af}) because it shows the rate at which the economy can transform apples into fig leaves. Just as MRS_{af} is the absolute value of the slope of an indifference curve, MRT_{af} is the absolute value of the slope of the production possibilities curve.

It is useful to express the marginal rate of transformation in terms of **marginal cost** *(MC)*—the incremental production cost of one more unit of output. To do so, recall that society can increase apple production by *xz* only by giving up *wy* fig leaves. In effect, then, the distance *wy* represents the incremental cost of producing apples, which we denote MC_a. Similarly, the distance *xz* is the incremental cost of producing fig leaves, MC_f. By definition, the absolute value of the slope of the production possibilities curve is distance *wy* divided by *xz*, or MC_a/MC_f. But also by definition, the slope of the production possibilities curve is the marginal rate of transformation. Hence, we have shown that

$$MRT_{af} = \frac{MC_a}{MC_f} \qquad (3.2)$$

Efficiency Conditions with Variable Production When the supplies of apples and fig leaves are variable, the condition for Pareto efficiency in Equation (3.1) must be extended. The condition becomes

$$MRT_{af} = MRS_{af}^{\text{Adam}} = MRS_{af}^{\text{Eve}} \qquad (3.3)$$

An arithmetic example shows why. Suppose that at a given allocation Adam's MRS_{af} is $^1/_3$, and the MRT_{af} is $^2/_3$. By the definition of MRT_{af}, at this allocation two additional fig leaves could be produced by giving up three apples. By the definition of MRS_{af}, if Adam lost three extra apples, he would require only *one* fig leaf to maintain his original utility level. Therefore, Adam could be made better off by giving up three apples and transforming them into *two* fig leaves, and no one else would be made worse off in the process. Such a trade is *always* possible as long as the marginal rate of substitution does not equal the marginal rate of transformation. Only when the slopes of the curves for each are equal is it impossible to make a Pareto improvement. Hence, $MRT_{af} = MRS_{af}$ is a necessary condition for Pareto efficiency. The rate at which apples can be transformed into fig leaves (MRT_{af}) must equal the rate at which consumers are willing to trade apples for fig leaves (MRS_{af}).

Using Equation (3.2), the conditions for Pareto efficiency can be reinterpreted in terms of marginal cost. Just substitute (3.2) into (3.3), which gives us

$$\frac{MC_a}{MC_f} = MRS_{af}^{\text{Adam}} = MRS_{af}^{\text{Eve}} \tag{3.4}$$

as a necessary condition for Pareto efficiency.

▶ THE FIRST FUNDAMENTAL THEOREM OF WELFARE ECONOMICS

Now that we have described the necessary conditions for Pareto efficiency, we may ask whether a given economy will achieve this apparently desirable state. It depends on what assumptions we make about the operations of that economy. Assume that: (1) All producers and consumers are perfect competitors; that is, no one has any market power. (2) A market exists for each and every commodity. Under these assumptions, the so-called *First Fundamental Theorem of Welfare Economics* states that a Pareto efficient allocation of resources emerges. In effect, this stunning result tells us that a competitive economy "automatically" allocates resources efficiently, without any need for centralized direction. (Think of Adam Smith's "invisible hand.") In a way, the First Welfare Theorem merely formalizes an insight that has long been recognized: When it comes to providing goods and services, free-enterprise systems are amazingly productive.[7]

A rigorous proof of the theorem requires fairly sophisticated mathematics, but the intuition isn't difficult. The essence of competition is that all people face the same prices—each consumer and producer is so small relative to the market that his or her actions alone cannot affect prices. In our example, this means Adam and Eve both pay the same prices for fig leaves (P_f) and apples (P_a). A basic result from the theory of consumer choice[8] is that a necessary condition for Adam to maximize utility is

$$MRS_{af}^{\text{Adam}} = \frac{P_a}{P_f} \tag{3.5}$$

Similarly, Eve's utility-maximizing bundle satisfies

$$MRS_{af}^{\text{Eve}} = \frac{P_a}{P_f} \tag{3.6}$$

Equations (3.5) and (3.6) together imply that

$$MRS_{af}^{\text{Adam}} = MRS_{af}^{\text{Eve}}$$

---

[7] "The bourgeoisie, during its rule of scarce 100 years, has created more massive and more colossal productive forces than have all preceding generations together," according to Karl Marx and Friedrich Engels in *The Communist Manifesto*, Part I [Tucker, 1978, p. 477].

[8] This result is derived in the appendix at the end of this book.

This condition, though, is identical to Equation (3.1), one of the necessary conditions for Pareto efficiency.

However, as emphasized in the preceding section, we must consider the production side as well. A basic result from economic theory is that a profit-maximizing competitive firm produces output up to the point at which marginal cost and price are equal. In our example, this means $P_a = MC_a$ and $P_f = MC_f$, or

$$\frac{MC_a}{MC_f} = \frac{P_a}{P_f} \tag{3.7}$$

But recall from Equation (3.2) that MC_a/MC_f is just the marginal rate of transformation. Thus, we can rewrite (3.7) as

$$MRT_{af} = \frac{P_a}{P_f} \tag{3.8}$$

Now consider Equations (3.5), (3.6), and (3.8), and notice that P_a/P_f appears on the right-hand side of each. Hence, these three equations together imply that $MRS_{af}^{\text{Adam}} = MRS_{af}^{\text{Eve}} = MRT_{af}$, which is the necessary condition for Pareto efficiency. Competition, along with maximizing behavior on the part of all individuals, leads to an efficient outcome.

Finally, we can take advantage of Equation (3.4) to write the conditions for Pareto efficiency in terms of marginal cost. Simply substitute (3.5) or (3.6) into (3.4) to find

$$\frac{P_a}{P_f} = \frac{MC_a}{MC_f} \tag{3.9}$$

Pareto efficiency requires that prices be in the same ratios as marginal costs, and competition guarantees this condition is met. The marginal cost of a commodity is the additional cost to society of providing it. According to Equation (3.9), efficiency requires that the additional cost of each commodity be reflected in its price.

▶ FAIRNESS AND THE SECOND FUNDAMENTAL THEOREM OF WELFARE ECONOMICS

If properly functioning competitive markets allocate resources efficiently, what economic role does the government have to play? Only a very small government would appear to be appropriate. Its main function would be to protect property rights so that markets can work. Government provides law and order, a court system, and national defense. Anything more is superfluous. However, such reasoning is based on a superficial understanding of the First Welfare Theorem. For one thing, it has implicitly been assumed that efficiency is the only criterion for deciding if a given allocation of resources is good. It is not obvious, however, that Pareto efficiency by itself is desirable.

To see why, let us return to the simple model in which the total quantity of each good is fixed. Consider Figure 3.9, which reproduces the contract curve mm derived in Figure 3.7. Compare the two allocations p_5 (at the lower left-hand corner of the box) and q (located near the center). Because p_5 lies on the contract curve, by definition it

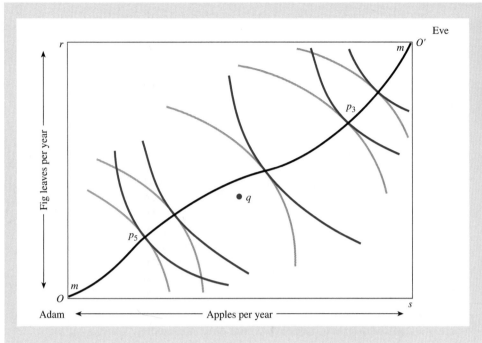

Figure 3.9
Efficiency versus equity
Point p_5 is Pareto efficient and point q is not. However, society might prefer point q because it provides a more equal distribution of the two goods.

is Pareto efficient. On the other hand, q is inefficient. Is allocation p_5 therefore better? That depends on what is meant by better. To the extent that society prefers a relatively equal distribution of real income, q might be preferred to p_5, even though q is not Pareto efficient. On the other hand, society might not care about distribution at all, or perhaps care more about Eve than Adam. In this case, p_5 would be preferred to q.

The key point is that the criterion of Pareto efficiency by itself is not enough to rank alternative allocations of resources. Rather, explicit value judgments are required on the fairness of the distribution of utility. To formalize this notion, note that the contract curve implicitly defines a relationship between the maximum amount of utility that Adam can attain for each level of Eve's utility. In Figure 3.10, Eve's utility is plotted on the horizontal axis, and Adam's utility is recorded on the vertical axis. Curve UU is the **utility possibilities curve** derived from the contract curve.[9] It shows the maximum amount of one person's utility given the other individual's utility level. Point $\tilde{p}_5$ corresponds to point p_5 on the contract curve in Figure 3.9. Here, Eve's utility is relatively high compared to Adam's. Point $\tilde{p}_3$ in Figure 3.10, which corresponds to p_3 in Figure 3.9, is just the opposite. Point $\tilde{q}$ corresponds to point q in Figure 3.9. Because q is off the contract curve, $\tilde{q}$ must be inside the utility possibilities curve, reflecting the fact that it is possible to increase one person's utility without decreasing the other's.

All points on or below the utility possibilities curve are attainable by society; all points above it are not attainable. By definition, all points on UU are Pareto efficient, but they represent very different distributions of real income between Adam

utility possibilities curve

A graph showing the maximum amount of one person's utility given each level of utility attained by the other person.

---

[9] The production possibilities curve in Figure 3.8 is drawn on the reasonable assumption that the absolute value of its slope continually increases as we move downward along it. The more apples produced, the more fig leaves given up to produce an apple. However, there is no reason to assume this holds for the trade-off between individuals' utilities. This is why UU in Figure 3.10 is wavy rather than smooth.

Figure 3.10
Utility possibilities curve
The utility possibilities curve shows the maximum feasible amount of one person's utility given the other person's utility level. Points on the curve are Pareto efficient, while points within the curve are not.

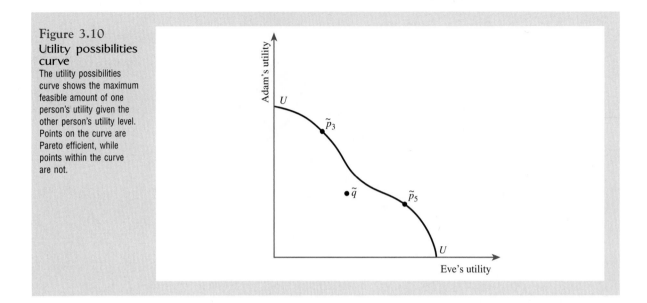

and Eve. Which point is best? The conventional way to answer this question is to postulate a **social welfare function,** which embodies society's views on the relative deservedness of Adam and Eve. A social welfare function is simply a statement of how society's well-being relates to the well-being of its members. Think of it this way: Just as an *individual's* welfare depends on the quantities of commodities she consumes, *society's* welfare depends on the utilities of each of its members. Algebraically, social welfare (W) is some function $F(\ )$ of each individual's utility:

$$W = F(U^{\text{Adam}}, U^{\text{Eve}}) \tag{3.10}$$

We assume the value of social welfare increases as either U^{Adam} or U^{Eve} increases—society is better off when any of its members becomes better off. Note that we have said nothing about how society manifests these preferences. Under some conditions, members of society may not be able to agree on how to rank each other's utilities, and the social welfare function does not even exist. For the moment, we simply assume it does exist.

Just as an individual's utility function for commodities leads to a set of indifference curves for those commodities, so does a social welfare function lead to a set of indifference curves between people's utilities. Figure 3.11 depicts a typical set of social indifference curves. Their downward slope indicates that if Eve's utility decreases, the only way to maintain a given level of social welfare is to increase Adam's utility, and vice versa. The level of social welfare increases as we move toward the northeast, reflecting the fact that an increase in any individual's utility increases social welfare, other things being the same.

In Figure 3.12, the social indifference curves are superimposed on the utility possibilities curve from Figure 3.10. Point *i* is not as desirable as point *ii* (point *ii* is on a higher social indifference curve than point *i*) even though point *i* is Pareto efficient and point *ii* is not. Here, society's value judgments, embodied in the social welfare function, favor a more equal distribution of real income, inefficient though it may be. Of course, point *iii* is preferred to either of these. It is both efficient and "fair."

Now, the First Welfare Theorem indicates that a properly working competitive system leads to some allocation on the utility possibilities curve. However, even

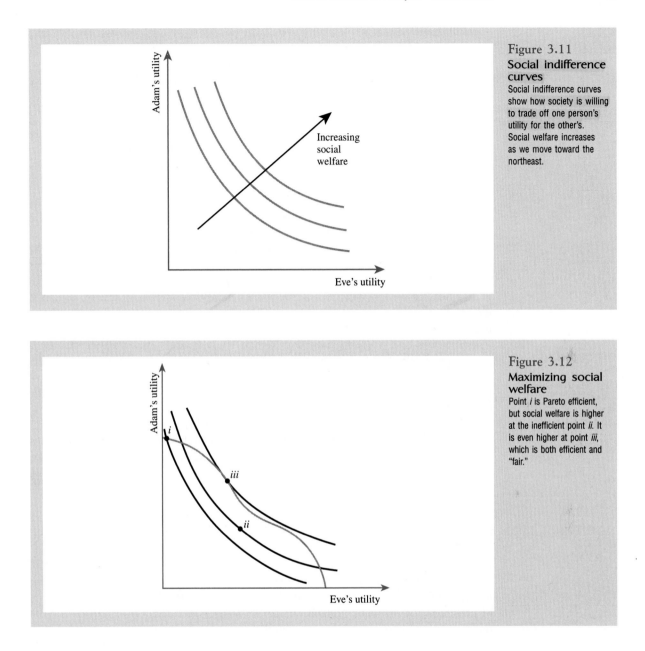

Figure 3.11

Social indifference curves

Social indifference curves show how society is willing to trade off one person's utility for the other's. Social welfare increases as we move toward the northeast.

Figure 3.12

Maximizing social welfare

Point *i* is Pareto efficient, but social welfare is higher at the inefficient point *ii*. It is even higher at point *iii*, which is both efficient and "fair."

though it is efficient, there is no reason that this particular allocation maximizes social welfare. We conclude that, even if the economy generates a Pareto efficient allocation of resources, government intervention may be necessary to achieve a "fair" distribution of utility.

Does the government have to intervene directly in markets in order to move the economy to the welfare-maximizing point? For example, does it have to impose ceilings on the prices of commodities consumed by the poor? The answer is no. According to the *Second Fundamental Theorem of Welfare Economics*, society can attain any Pareto efficient allocation of resources by making a suitable assignment of initial endowments and then letting people freely trade with each other as in our

Edgeworth Box model.[10] Roughly speaking, by redistributing income suitably and then getting out of the way and letting markets work, the government can attain any point on the utility possibilities frontier.

Author Tim Harford [2006] explains the *Second Fundamental Theorem of Welfare Economics* by using the analogy of a 100-meter race. He writes:

> If your goal is to have all the sprinters cross the line together, you could just change the rules of the race, ordering the fast runners to slow down and everyone to hold hands as they crossed the line. A waste of talent. Or you could move some starting blocks forward and some back, so that although each sprinter was running as fast as he could . . . the fastest had to cover enough extra ground that he would end up breaking the tape neck-and-neck with the slowest [pp. 73–74].

Achieving equity through such things as a tax on income is similar to requiring the fast runners to slow down, because it punishes income-enhancing behavior. But a reassignment of initial endowments (for example, simply taking away some apples from Adam and giving them to Eve) is similar to moving the starting blocks of the runners. The *Second Fundamental Theorem of Welfare Economics* shows that this can achieve equity without inhibiting efficiency.

The Second Welfare Theorem is important because it shows that, at least in theory, the issues of efficiency and distributional fairness can be separated. If society determines that the current distribution of resources is unfair, it need not interfere with market prices and impair efficiency. Rather, society need only transfer resources among people in a way deemed to be fair. Of course, the government needs some way to reallocate resources, and problems arise if the only available mechanisms for doing so (such as taxes) themselves induce inefficiences. We discuss further the relationship between efficiency and fairness in Chapter 16.

In addition to distributional issues, there is another reason why the First Welfare Theorem need not imply a minimal government. This is because the conditions required for its validity may not be satisfied by real-world markets. As we now show, when these conditions are absent, the free-market allocation of resources may be inefficient as well as unfair.

▶ MARKET FAILURE

In the famous film *Casablanca*, whenever something seems amiss, the police chief gives an order to "round up the usual suspects." Similarly, whenever markets appear to be failing to allocate resources efficiently, economists round up the same group of possible causes for the alleged failure. As suggested earlier, an economy may be inefficient for two general reasons—market power and nonexistence of markets.

Market Power

The First Welfare Theorem holds only if all consumers and firms are price takers. If some individuals or firms are price makers (they have the power to affect prices), then the allocation of resources is generally inefficient. Why? A firm with market power may be able to raise price above marginal cost by supplying less output than a competitor would. Thus, Equation (3.9), one of the necessary conditions for

---

[10] The proof requires that several technical conditions be satisfied. For example, all indifference curves have the standard (convex to the origin) shape.

Pareto efficiency, is violated. An insufficient quantity of resources is devoted to the commodity.

Price-making behavior can arise in several contexts. An extreme case is a **monopoly,** where there is only one firm in the market, and entry is blocked. Even in the less extreme case of oligopoly (a few sellers), the firms in an industry may be able to increase price above marginal cost. Finally, some industries have many firms, but each firm has some market power because the firms produce differentiated products. For example, a lot of firms produce running shoes, yet many consumers view Reeboks, Nikes, and Adidas as distinct commodities.

Nonexistence of Markets

The proof behind the First Welfare Theorem assumes a market exists for every commodity. After all, if a market for a commodity does not exist, then we can hardly expect the market to allocate it efficiently. In reality, markets for certain commodities may fail to emerge. Consider, for instance, insurance, a very important commodity in a world of uncertainty. Despite the existence of firms such as Aetna and Allstate, there are certain events for which insurance simply cannot be purchased on the private market. For example, suppose you wanted to purchase insurance against the possibility of becoming poor. Would a firm in a competitive market ever find it profitable to supply "poverty insurance"? The answer is no, because if you purchased such insurance, you might decide not to work very hard. To discourage such behavior, the insurance firm would have to monitor your behavior to determine whether your low income was due to bad luck or to goofing off. However, to perform such monitoring would be very difficult or impossible. Hence, there is no market for poverty insurance—it simply cannot be purchased.

Basically, the problem here is **asymmetric information**—one party in a transaction has information that is not available to another. One rationalization for governmental income support programs is that they provide poverty insurance that is unavailable privately. The premium on this "insurance policy" is the taxes you pay when you are able to earn income. In the event of poverty, your benefit comes in the form of welfare payments.

Another type of inefficiency associated with the nonexistence of a market is an **externality,** which is a situation in which one person's behavior affects the welfare of another in a way that is outside existing markets. For example, suppose your roommate begins smoking large cigars, polluting the air and making you worse off. Why is this an efficiency problem? Your roommate consumes a scarce resource, clean air, when he smokes cigars. However, there is no market for clean air that forces him to pay for it. In effect, he pays a price of zero for the clean air and therefore "overuses" it. The price system fails to provide correct signals about the opportunity cost of a commodity.

Welfare economics provides a useful framework for thinking about externalities. The derivation of Equation (3.9) implicitly assumed marginal cost meant *social* marginal cost—it embodied the incremental value of all of society's resources used in production. In our cigar example, however, your roommate's private marginal cost of smoking is less than the social marginal cost because he does not have to pay for the clean air he uses. The price of a cigar, which reflects its private marginal cost, does not correctly reflect its social marginal cost. Hence, Equation (3.9) is not satisfied, and the allocation of resources is inefficient. Incidentally, an externality can be positive—confer a benefit—as well as negative. Think of a molecular biologist

monopoly

A market with only one seller of a good.

asymmetric information

A situation in which one party engaged in an economic transaction has better information about the good or service traded than the other party.

externality

A cost or benefit that occurs when the activity of one entity directly affects the welfare of another in a way that is outside the market mechanism.

who publishes a paper about a novel gene-splicing technique that can be used by pharmaceutical firms. When a positive externality exists, the market generates an inefficiently low amount of the beneficial activity.

Closely related to an externality is a **public good,** a commodity that is *nonrival and nonexcludable in consumption*. Nonrival means that the fact that one person consumes it does not prevent anyone else from doing so as well. Nonexcludable means that it is either very expensive or impossible to prevent anyone from consuming it. The classic example of a public good is a lighthouse. When the lighthouse turns on its beacon, all ships in the vicinity benefit. The fact that one person takes advantage of the lighthouse's services does not keep anyone else from doing so simultaneously, and it is very difficult to prevent others from using the lighthouse.

People may have an incentive to hide how much they value a public good. Suppose that the lighthouse is beneficial to you. You know, however, that once the beacon is lit, you can enjoy its services, whether you pay for them or not. Therefore, you may claim the lighthouse means nothing to you, hoping to get a "free ride" after other people pay for it. Unfortunately, everyone has the same incentive, so the lighthouse may not get built, even though its construction could be very beneficial. The market mechanism may fail to force people to reveal their preferences for public goods, and possibly result in insufficient resources being devoted to them.

Overview

The First Welfare Theorem states that a properly working competitive economy generates a Pareto efficient allocation of resources without any government intervention. However, it is not obvious that an efficient allocation of resources in itself is socially desirable; many argue that distributional fairness must also be considered. Moreover, we have just shown that in real-world economies, competition may not hold and some markets may not exist. Hence, the market-determined allocation of resources is unlikely to be efficient. There are, then, opportunities for government to intervene and enhance economic efficiency.

It must be emphasized that while efficiency problems provide opportunities for government intervention in the economy, they do not necessarily justify it. The fact that the market-generated allocation of resources is imperfect does not necessarily mean the government can do better. For example, in certain cases, the costs of setting up a government agency to deal with an externality could exceed the cost of the externality itself. Moreover, governments, like people, can make mistakes. Some argue that government is inherently incapable of acting efficiently, so while in theory it can improve on the status quo, in practice it never will. While this argument is extreme, it highlights the fact that the fundamental theorem is helpful only in identifying situations in which intervention *may* lead to greater efficiency.

▶ BUYING INTO WELFARE ECONOMICS

These days, vigorous debates over how to organize an economy are occurring in countries as diverse as India, China, and Iraq. Nevertheless, the same issues arise in developed nations as well: How much of national output should be devoted to the public sector, and how should public expenditures be financed? The theory of welfare economics introduced in this chapter provides the standard framework for thinking about these issues. There are, however, some controversies surrounding the theory.

First, the underlying outlook is highly individualistic, with a focus on people's utilities and how to maximize them. This is brought out starkly in the formulation of the social welfare function, Equation (3.10). The view expressed in that equation is that a good society is one whose members are happy. As suggested in Chapter 1, however, other societal goals are possible—to maximize the power of the state, to glorify God, and so on. Welfare economics does not have much to say to people with such goals. It is no surprise that Iran's Ayatollah Khomeini used to say that economics is for donkeys.

Because welfare economics puts people's preferences at center stage, it requires that these preferences be taken seriously. People know best what gives them satisfaction. A contrary view, once nicely summarized by Thomas O'Neill, former speaker of the House of Representatives, is, "Often what the American people want is not good for them." If one believes that individuals' preferences are ill formed or corrupt, a theory that shows how to maximize their utility is essentially irrelevant.

Musgrave [1959] developed the concept of **merit goods** to describe commodities that ought to be provided even if the members of society do not demand them. Government support of the fine arts is often justified on this basis. Operas and concerts should be provided publicly if individuals are unwilling to pay enough to meet their costs. But as Baumol and Baumol [1981] have noted,

> The term *merit good* merely becomes a formal designation for the unadorned value judgment that the arts are good for society and therefore deserve financial support . . . [the] merit good approach is not really a justification for support—it merely invents a bit of terminology to designate the desire to do so [pp. 426–427].

merit good

A commodity that ought to be provided even if people do not demand it.

Another possible problem with the welfare economics framework is its concern with *results*. Situations are evaluated in terms of the allocation of resources, and not of *how* the allocation was determined. Perhaps a society should be judged by the *processes* used to arrive at the allocation, not the actual results. Are people free to enter contracts? Are public processes democratic? If this view is taken, welfare economics loses its normative significance.

On the other hand, welfare economics has a great advantage: it provides a coherent framework for assessing public policy. Every government intervention, after all, involves a reallocation of resources, and the whole purpose of welfare economics is to evaluate alternative allocations. The framework of welfare economics impels us to ask three key questions whenever a government activity is proposed:

- Will it have desirable distributional consequences?
- Will it enhance efficiency?
- Can it be done at a reasonable cost?

If the answer to these questions is no, the market should probably be left alone. Of course, answering these questions may require substantial research and, in the case of the first question, value judgments as well. But just asking the right questions provides an invaluable structure for the decision-making process. It forces people to make their ethical values explicit, and facilitates the detection of frivolous or self-serving programs.

Summary

- Welfare economics is the study of the desirability of alternative economic states.

- A Pareto efficient allocation occurs when no person can be made better off without making another person worse off. Pareto efficiency requires that each person's marginal rate of substitution between two commodities equal the marginal rate of transformation. Pareto efficiency is the economist's benchmark of efficient performance for an economy.

- The *First Fundamental Theorem of Welfare Economics* states that, under certain conditions, competitive market mechanisms lead to Pareto efficient outcomes.

- Despite its appeal, Pareto efficiency has no obvious claim as an ethical norm. Society may prefer an inefficient allocation on the basis of equity or some other criterion. This provides one possible reason for government intervention in the economy.

- A social welfare function summarizes society's preferences concerning the utility of each of its members. It may be used to find the allocation of resources that maximizes social welfare.

- The *Second Fundamental Theorem of Welfare Economics* states that society can attain any Pareto efficient allocation of resources by making a suitable assignment of initial endowments and then letting people freely trade with each other.

- A second reason for government intervention is market failure, which may occur in the presence of market power or when markets do not exist.

- The fact that the market does not allocate resources perfectly does not necessarily mean the government can do better. Each case must be evaluated on its own merits.

- Welfare economics is based on an individualistic social philosophy. It does not pay much attention to the processes used to achieve results. Thus, although it provides a coherent and useful framework for analyzing policy, welfare economics is not universally accepted.

Discussion Questions

1. In which of the following markets do you expect efficient outcomes? Why?
   a. Hurricane insurance for beach houses
   b. Medical care
   c. Stock market
   d. MP3 players
   e. Loans for students who wish to attend college
   f. Housing

2. In his commencement address at Wesleyan University in 2008, then-Senator Barack Obama told the students that "our individual salvation depends on collective salvation." Is this view consistent with the social welfare function defined in Equation (3.10)?

3. Certain market transactions, such as selling one's kidneys, seem morally repugnant to many people. At a conference discussion on what makes certain transactions morally repugnant, a professor of psychology said, "The problem is not that economists are unreasonable people, it's that they're evil people. . . . They work in a different moral universe." The psychologist argued that the burden of proof should be "on someone who wants to include a transaction in the marketplace." Contrast this view with the view inherent in the *First Fundamental Theorem of Welfare Economics*.

4. Many controversial issues in public finance concern when a central authority should allow markets to work and when it should intervene. Generally we think of the government as the central authority, but it could be a university

as well. For example, according to Princeton University's student newspaper, the *Daily Princetonian* (April 16, 2007), there was "a flourishing market of graduation ticket buyers and sellers on [the Internet]." However, the dean of students shut down the market, arguing that "[s]elling tickets undermines that spirit of community, and undermines the sense of class unity that seniors have worked hard to create."

To analyze this policy, assume that a typical senior's utility depends *only* on two commodities, graduation tickets and a composite of all other goods. Assume there are two students, Angelo and Bahn, each of whom starts out with three tickets. However, Angelo is "rich" and has twice the amount of all other goods as Bahn. For simplicity, you may assume that graduation tickets are infinitely divisible.

a. Draw an Edgeworth Box showing the initial allocation, assuming conventionally shaped indifference curves for both students.

b. Using the Edgeworth Box, explain how the ban on selling tickets can lead to an inefficient outcome.

c. Using the Edgeworth Box, represent a situation in which the ban on selling tickets does not reduce efficiency for these two students.

5. Recently, the California insurance commissioner proposed a regulation that would reduce the ability of insurers to use geographic location in determining automobile insurance rates. The change would raise the insurance rates of rural and suburban residents, and lower the rates of urban residents. Is such a policy efficient? Is it likely to improve social welfare?

6. Imagine a simple economy with only two people, Augustus and Livia.

a. Let the social welfare function be

$$W = U_L + U_A$$

where U_L and U_A are the utilities of Livia and Augustus, respectively. Graph the social indifference curves. How would you describe the relative importance assigned to their respective well-being?

b. Repeat part *a* when

$$W = U_L + 2U_A$$

c. Assume that the utility possibilities curve is as follows:

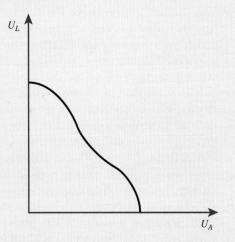

Graphically show how the optimal solution differs between the welfare functions given in parts *a* and *b*.

7. In recent years, a number of states have instituted taxes on patrons of nude and topless dance bars. Such taxes are known as "sin taxes," because they target behavior that is believed to be sinful. How do sin taxes relate to the notion of merit goods?

8. In each case listed below, can you rationalize the government policy on the basis of welfare economics?

a. In Los Angeles, the police respond to 127,000 burglar alarm calls per year. There is no charge. (Ninety-seven percent of the alarms are false.)

b. Legislation passed in 2008 provides some families that cannot meet their mortgage payments with government-subsidized mortgages.

c. The federal government regulates cherry frozen fruit pies, requiring that at least 25 percent of each pie by weight contain cherries and that no more than 15 percent of the cherries be blemished. There are no such regulations for apple, blueberry, or peach frozen pies.

d. Legislation passed in 2008 guarantees American sugar producers 85 percent of the domestic sugar market.

e. The National Energy Policy Act requires that all new toilets flush with only 1.6 gallons of water. Most American homes have toilets that consume 5.5 to 7 gallons per flush.

f. The United States currently provides a 51 cent per gallon subsidy for ethanol.

9. Your airplane crashes in the Pacific Ocean. You land on a desert island with one other passenger. A box containing 100 little bags of peanuts also washes up on the island. The peanuts are the only thing to eat.

   In this economy with two people, one commodity, and no production, represent the possible allocations in a diagram, and explain why every allocation is Pareto efficient. Is every allocation fair?

10. [This problem is for readers who know some calculus.] Suppose that there are only two people in society, Mark and Judy, who must split a fixed amount of income of $300. Mark's utility function is U_M and his income is I_M. Judy's utility function is U_J and her income is I_J. Suppose that

$$U_M = 100 \times I_M^{1/2} \quad \text{and} \quad U_J = 200 \times I_J^{1/2}$$

Let the social welfare function be

$$W = U_M + U_J$$

What distribution of the total income between Mark and Judy maximizes social welfare?

11. Suppose that Tang and Wilson must split a fixed 400 pounds of food between them. Tang's utility function is $U_T = \text{sqrt}(F_1)$ and Wilson's utility function is $U_W = \frac{1}{2}\text{sqrt}(F_2)$, where F_1 and F_2 are pounds of food to Tang and Wilson, respectively.

   a. How much utility will Tang and Wilson receive if the food is distributed evenly between them?

   b. If the social welfare function is $U_T + U_w$, then what distribution of food between Tang and Wilson maximizes social welfare?

   c. If social welfare is maximized if they each obtain the same level of utility, then what is the distribution of food between Tang and Wilson that maximizes social welfare?

12. Consider an economy with two people, Victoria and Albert, and two commodities, tea and crumpets. Currently, Victoria and Albert would both be willing to substitute two cups of tea for one crumpet. Further, if the economy were to produce one less cup of tea, the resources released from tea production could be used to produce three more crumpets. Is the allocation of resources in this economy Pareto efficient? If not, should there be more tea or more crumpets?

13. Suppose that Hannah's utility function is $U_H = 3T + 4C$ and that Jose's utility function is $U_J = 4T + 3C$, where T is pounds of tea per year and C is pounds of coffee per year. Suppose there are fixed amounts of 28 pounds of coffee per year and 21 pounds of tea per year. Suppose also that the initial allocation is 15 pounds of coffee to Hannah (leaving 13 pounds to Jose) and 10 pounds of tea to Hannah (leaving 11 pounds of tea to Jose).

   a. What do the utility functions say about the marginal rates of substitution of coffee for tea?

   b. Draw the Edgeworth Box showing indifference curves and the initial allocation.

   c. Draw the contract curve on the Edgeworth Box. Explain why it looks different from the contract curves depicted in the text.

   d. Is the initial allocation of coffee and tea Pareto efficient?

14. Indicate whether each of the following statements is true, false, or uncertain, and justify your answer.

   a. If everyone has the same marginal rate of substitution, then the allocation of resources is Pareto efficient.

   b. If the allocation of resources is Pareto efficient, then everyone has the same marginal rate of substitution.

   c. A policy change increases social welfare if, and only if, it represents a Pareto improvement.

   d. A reallocation from a point within the utility possibilities curve to a point on the utility possibilities curve results in a Pareto improvement.

Part Two

PUBLIC EXPENDITURE: PUBLIC GOODS AND EXTERNALITIES

The theory of welfare economics focused our attention on market failure and distributional considerations as reasons for considering government intervention. The chapters in this section examine the implications for government policy with respect to public goods and externalities. Chapter 4 introduces public goods. Chapter 5 deals with externalities, with special emphasis on environmental issues. In Chapter 6, we discuss whether our political institutions are likely to respond to market failures with the efficiency-enhancing policies derived in Chapters 4 and 5. Chapter 7 applies our analytical framework to the important issue of education policy. This part concludes with Chapter 8 on cost-benefit analysis, a theory-based set of practical rules for evaluating public expenditure.

Chapter Four

PUBLIC GOODS

> *There is no higher religion than human service. To work for the common good is the greatest creed.*
> —PRESIDENT WOODROW WILSON
>
> *I have never known much good done by those who affected to trade for the public good.*
> —ADAM SMITH

In the aftermath of the terrorist attacks on the United States on September 11, 2001, all Americans agreed that the government had to take steps to prevent future attacks. Although there was (and continues to be) a vigorous debate about just what those steps should be, everyone took for granted that providing defense was a proper function for government. What characteristic of national defense makes it an appropriate government responsibility? Are there other goods and services that partake of this characteristic, and should the government provide them as well? These questions lie at the heart of some of the most important controversies in public policy. In this chapter, we discuss the conditions under which public provision of commodities is appropriate. Special attention is devoted to understanding why markets may fail to provide particular goods at Pareto efficient levels.

▶ PUBLIC GOODS DEFINED

What's the difference between national defense and pizza? The question seems silly, but thinking about it leads to a useful framework for determining whether public or private provision of various commodities makes sense. To begin, one big difference between the two commodities is that two people cannot consume a pizza simultaneously—if I eat a piece, you can't. In contrast, your consumption of the protective services provided by the army does nothing to diminish my consumption of the same services. A second major difference is that I can easily exclude you from consuming my pizza, but excluding you from the benefits of national defense is all but impossible. (It's hard to imagine a situation in which terrorists are allowed to overrun your home but not mine.)

pure public good

A commodity that is nonrival and nonexcludable in consumption.

National defense is an example of a **pure public good,** defined as follows:

- Consumption of the good is *nonrival*—once it is provided, the additional resource cost of another person consuming the good is zero.

- Consumption of the good is *nonexcludable*—to prevent anyone from consuming the good is either very expensive or impossible.

private good

A commodity that is rival and excludable in consumption.

In contrast, a **private good** like pizza is rival and excludable.

Several aspects of our definition of public good are worth noting.

Even Though Everyone Consumes the Same Quantity of the Good, It Need Not Be Valued Equally by All   Consider house cleaning in an apartment with many college roommates, which has a public good characteristic to it—everyone benefits from a clean bathroom, and it is hard to exclude anyone from these benefits. Yet some students care about cleanliness much more than others. Similarly, in our defense example, people who are deeply concerned about the intentions of hostile foreigners place a higher value on national defense than people who feel relatively safe, other things being the same. Indeed, people might differ over whether the value of certain public goods is positive or negative. Each person has no choice but to consume the services of a new missile system. For those who believe the system enhances their safety, the value is positive. Others think additional missiles only lead to arms races and decrease national security. Such individuals value an additional missile negatively. They would be willing to pay not to have it around.

Classification as a Public Good Is Not an Absolute; It Depends on Market Conditions and the State of Technology   Think about a lighthouse. Once the beacon is lit, one ship can take advantage of it without impinging on another ship's ability to do the same. Moreover, no particular vessel can be excluded from taking advantage of the signal. Under these conditions, the lighthouse is a pure public good. But suppose that a jamming device were invented that made it possible to prevent ships from obtaining the lighthouse signal unless they purchased a special receiver. In this case, the nonexcludability criterion does not hold, and the lighthouse is no longer a pure public good. A scenic view is a pure public good when not many people are involved. But as the number of sightseers increases, the area may become congested. The same "quantity" of the scenic view is being "consumed" by each person, but its quality decreases with the number of people. Hence, the nonrivalness criterion is no longer satisfied.

In many cases, then, it makes sense to think of "publicness" as a matter of degree. A pure public good satisfies the definition exactly. Consumption of an **impure public good** is to some extent rival or excludable. There are not many examples of pure public goods. However, just as analysis of pure competition yields important insights into the operation of actual markets, so the analysis of pure public goods helps us to understand problems confronting public decision makers.

impure public good

A good that is rival and/or excludable to some extent.

A Commodity Can Satisfy One Part of the Definition of a Public Good and Not the Other   That is, nonexcludability and nonrivalness do not have to go together. Consider the streets of a downtown urban area during rush hour. Nonexcludability generally holds, because it is not feasible to set up enough toll booths to monitor traffic. But consumption is certainly rival, as anyone who has ever been caught in a traffic jam can testify. On the other hand, many people can enjoy a huge seashore area without diminishing the pleasure of others. Despite the fact that individuals do not rival each other in consumption, exclusion is easy if there are only a few access roads. Again, the characterization of a commodity depends on the state of technology and on legal arrangements. Consider road congestion again. Windshield-mounted transponders like E-ZPasses use radio waves to identify passing cars and automatically charge tolls to drivers' charge accounts. For example, the Melbourne CityLink highway in Australia does not require any toll plazas—drivers either pay by transponder or call in and register their license-plate number for the days they plan to use the road. Some toll roads vary their rates to reflect periods of higher and lower demand. One can imagine someday using such technology to charge cars as they enter congested city streets. The streets would become excludable.

Some Things That Are Not Conventionally Thought of as Commodities Have Public Good Characteristics   An important example is honesty. If each citizen is honest in commercial transactions, all of society benefits because the costs of doing business are lower. Such cost reductions are both nonexcludable and nonrival. Similarly, the income distribution is a public good. If income is distributed "fairly," each person gains satisfaction from living in a good society, and no one can be excluded from having that satisfaction. Of course, because of disagreements over notions of fairness, people may differ over how a given income distribution should be valued. Nevertheless, consumption of the income distribution is nonrival and nonexcludable, and therefore it is a public good. Certain types of information are also public goods. In Los Angeles, restaurants are now forced by the local government to display a hygiene rating—either "A" (clean), "B" (dirty), or "C" (disgusting). This information exhibits public good characteristics—it is nonrival in consumption in the sense that everyone can costlessly learn about the restaurant's hygiene by going to the Internet, newspaper, or simply glancing in the restaurant's window, and it is nonexcludable.

Private Goods Are Not Necessarily Provided Exclusively by the Private Sector   There are many **publicly provided private goods**—rival and excludable commodities that are provided by governments. Medical services and housing are two examples of private goods sometimes provided publicly. Similarly, as we will see later, public goods can be provided privately. (Think of individuals donating money to maintain public spaces, which is how Central Park in New York City manages to have such beautiful flowers.) In short, the label *private* or *public* does not by itself tell us anything about which sector provides the item.

> **publicly provided private goods**
>
> **Rival and excludable commodities that are provided by governments.**

Public Provision of a Good Does Not Necessarily Mean That It Is Also *Produced* by the Public Sector   Consider garbage collection. Some communities produce this service themselves—public sector managers purchase garbage trucks, hire workers, and arrange schedules. In other communities, the local government hires a private firm for the job and does not organize production itself. Some states even contract out their litigation to the private sector. For example, Oklahoma's attorney general hired private law firms to bring suit against poultry companies that allegedly polluted the state's waterways [Liptak, 2007].

▶ EFFICIENT PROVISION OF PUBLIC GOODS

What is the efficient amount of defense or of any other public good? To derive the conditions for efficient provision of a public good, we begin by reexamining private goods from a slightly different perspective than that in Chapter 3. Assume again a society populated by two people, Adam and Eve. There are two private goods,

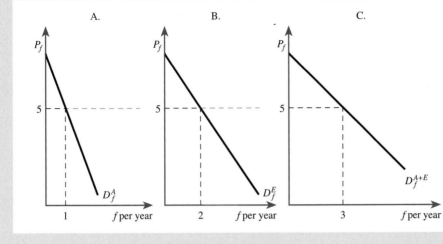

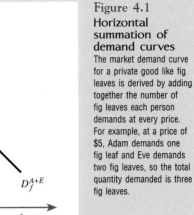

Figure 4.1
Horizontal summation of demand curves
The market demand curve for a private good like fig leaves is derived by adding together the number of fig leaves each person demands at every price. For example, at a price of $5, Adam demands one fig leaf and Eve demands two fig leaves, so the total quantity demanded is three fig leaves.

apples and fig leaves. In Figure 4.1A, the quantity of fig leaves (f) is measured on the horizontal axis, and the price per fig leaf (P_f) is on the vertical. Adam's demand curve for fig leaves is denoted by D_f^A. The demand curve shows the quantity of fig leaves that Adam would be willing to consume at each price, other things being the same.[1] Similarly, D_f^E in Figure 4.1B is Eve's demand curve for fig leaves. Each person's demand curve also shows how much he or she would be willing to pay for a particular quantity.

Suppose we want to derive the market demand curve for fig leaves. To do so, we simply add together the number of fig leaves each person demands at every price. In Figure 4.1A, at a price of $5, Adam demands one fig leaf, the horizontal distance between the vertical axis and D_f^A. Figure 4.1B indicates that at the same price, Eve demands two fig leaves. The total quantity demanded at a price of $5 is therefore three leaves. The market demand curve for fig leaves is labeled D_f^{A+E} in Figure 4.1C. As we have just shown, the point at which price is $5 and quantity is 3 lies on the market demand curve. Similarly, to find the market demand at any given price, sum the horizontal distance between each of the private demand curves and the vertical axis at that price. This process is called **horizontal summation.**

Figure 4.2 reproduces the information from Figure 4.1. Figure 4.2C then superimposes the market supply curve, labeled S_f, on the market demand curve D_f^{A+E}. Equilibrium in the market is where supply and demand are equal. This occurs at a price of $4 in Figure 4.2C. At this price, Adam consumes 1½ fig leaves and Eve consumes 3. Note that there is no reason to expect Adam and Eve to consume the same amounts. Because of different tastes, incomes, and other characteristics, they demand different quantities of fig leaves. This is possible because fig leaves are private goods.

The equilibrium in Figure 4.2C has a significant property: The allocation of fig leaves is Pareto efficient. In consumer theory, a utility-maximizing individual sets the marginal rate of substitution of fig leaves for apples (MRS_{fa}) equal to the price of fig

horizontal summation

The process of creating a market demand curve by summing the quantities demanded by each individual at every price.

---

[1] Demand curves are explained in the appendix to this book.

Figure 4.2
Efficient provision of a private good
The market is in equilibrium when supply and demand are equal.

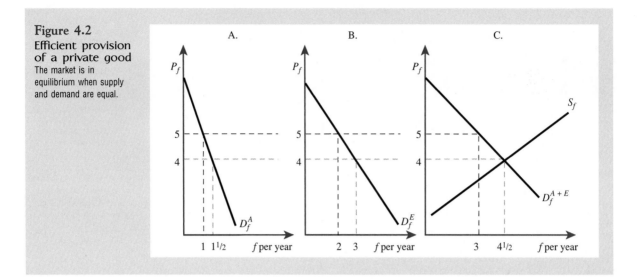

leaves (P_f) divided by the price of apples (P_a): $MRS_{fa} = P_f/P_a$.[2] Because only relative prices matter for rational choice, the price of apples can be arbitrarily set at any value. For convenience, set $P_a = \$1$. Thus, the condition for utility maximization reduces to $MRS_{fa} = P_f$. The price of fig leaves thus measures the rate at which an individual is willing to substitute fig leaves for apples. Now, Adam's demand curve for fig leaves (D_f^A) shows the maximum price per fig leaf that he would pay at each level of fig leaf consumption. Therefore, the demand curve also shows the MRS_{fa} at each level of fig leaf consumption. Similarly, D_f^E can be interpreted as Eve's MRS_{fa} schedule. In the same way, the supply curve S_f in Figure 4.2C shows how the marginal rate of transformation of fig leaves for apples (MRT_{fa}) varies with fig leaf production.[3]

At the equilibrium in Figure 4.2C, Adam and Eve both set MRS_{fa} equal to four, and the producer also sets MRT_{fa} equal to four. Hence, at equilibrium

$$MRS_{fa}^{\text{Adam}} = MRS_{fa}^{\text{Eve}} = MRT_{fa} \tag{4.1}$$

Equation (4.1) is the necessary condition for Pareto efficiency derived in Chapter 3. As long as the market is competitive and functions properly, the First Welfare Theorem guarantees that this condition holds.

Deriving the Efficiency Condition

Having now reinterpreted the condition for efficient provision of a private good, we turn to the case of a public good. Let's develop the condition intuitively before turning to a formal derivation. Suppose Adam and Eve both enjoy displays of fireworks. Eve's enjoyment of fireworks does not diminish Adam's and vice versa, and it is impossible for one person to exclude the other from watching the display. Hence, a fireworks display is a public good. The size of the fireworks display can be varied,

---

[2] See the appendix to this book for a proof.
[3] To demonstrate this, note that under competition, firms produce up to the point where price equals marginal cost. Hence, the supply curve S_f shows the marginal cost of each level of fig leaf production. As noted in Chapter 3 under "Welfare Economics," $MRT_{fa} = MC_f/MC_a$. Because $P_a = \$1$ and price equals marginal cost, then $MC_a = \$1$ and $MRT_{fa} = MC_f$. We can therefore identify the marginal rate of transformation with marginal cost, and hence with the supply curve.

and both Adam and Eve prefer bigger to smaller shows, other things being the same. Suppose that the display currently consists of 19 rockets and can be expanded at a cost of $5 per rocket, that Adam would be willing to pay $6 to expand the display by another rocket, and that Eve would be willing to pay $4. Is it efficient to increase the size of the display by one rocket? As usual, we must compare the additional value associated with that rocket (the "marginal benefit") to the cost of providing that rocket (the "marginal cost").[4] To compute the marginal benefit, note that because consumption of the display is nonrival, the 20th rocket is consumed by *both* Adam and Eve. Hence, the marginal benefit of the 20th rocket is the *sum* of what they are willing to pay, which is $10. Because the marginal cost is only $5, it pays to acquire the 20th rocket. More generally, if the sum of individuals' willingness to pay for an additional unit of a public good exceeds its marginal cost, efficiency requires that the unit be purchased; otherwise, it should not. Hence, *efficiency requires that provision of a public good be expanded until the point at which the sum of each person's marginal benefit for the last unit just equals the marginal cost.*

To derive this result graphically, consider panel A of Figure 4.3 in which Adam's consumption of rockets (r) is measured on the horizontal axis, and the price per rocket (P_r) is on the vertical axis. Adam's demand curve for rockets is D_r^A. Similarly, Eve's demand curve for rockets is D_r^E in Figure 4.3B. How do we derive the group willingness to pay for rockets? To find the group demand curve for fig leaves—a private good—we horizontally summed the individual demand curves. That procedure allowed Adam and Eve to consume different quantities of fig leaves at the same price. For a private good, this is fine. However, the services produced by the rockets—a public good—*must* be consumed in *equal* amounts. If Adam consumes a 20-rocket fireworks display, Eve must also consume a 20-rocket fireworks display. It makes no sense to try to sum the quantities of a public good that the individuals would consume at a given price.

Instead, to find the group willingness to pay for rockets, we add the *prices* that each would be willing to pay for a given quantity. The demand curve in Figure 4.3A tells us that Adam is willing to pay $6 for the 20th rocket. Eve is willing to pay $4 for the 20th rocket. Their group willingness to pay for the 20th rocket is therefore $10. Thus, if we define D_r^{A+E} in Figure 4.3C to be the group willingness to pay schedule, then the vertical distance between D_r^{A+E} and the point $r = 20$ must be 10.[5] Other points on D_r^{A+E} are determined by repeating this procedure for each output level. For a public good, then, the group willingness to pay is found by **vertical summation** of the individual demand curves.

Note the symmetry between private and public goods. With a private good, everyone has the same *MRS,* but people can consume different quantities. Therefore, demands are summed horizontally over the differing quantities. For public goods, everyone consumes the same quantity, but people can have different *MRS*s. Vertical summation is required to find the group willingness to pay. Put another way, for standard private goods, everyone sees the same price and then people decide what quantity they want. For public goods, everyone sees the same quantity and people decide what price they are willing to pay.

The efficient quantity of rockets is found where the sum of Adam's and Eve's willingness to pay for an additional unit just equals the marginal cost of producing

vertical summation

The process of creating an aggregate demand curve for a public good by adding the prices each individual is willing to pay for a given quantity of the good.

---

[4] This is a typical example of marginal analysis in economics. See the appendix at the end of the book for further discussion.
[5] D_r^{A+E} is not a conventional demand schedule because it does not show the quantity that would be demanded at each price. However, this notation highlights the similarities to the private good case.

Figure 4.3
Vertical summation of demand curves
The total demand curve for a public good like rockets is derived by adding the prices that each person is willing to pay for a given quantity. For example, Adam is willing to pay $6 for the 20th rocket and Eve is willing to pay $4 for the 20th rocket, so the total willingness to pay for the 20th rocket is $10.

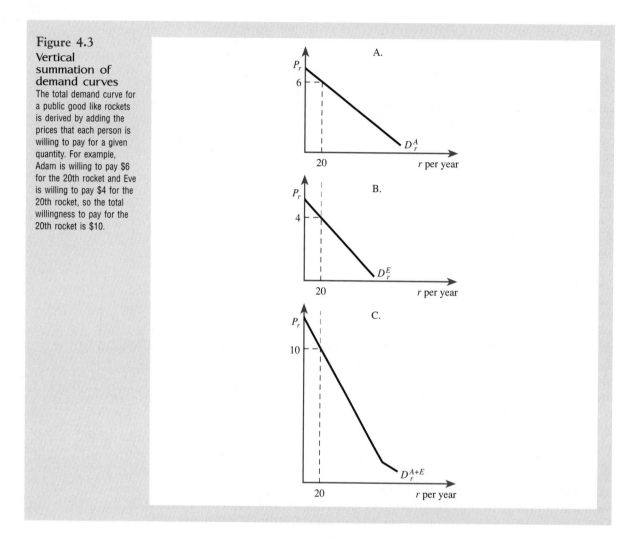

a unit. In Figure 4.4C, the marginal cost schedule, S_r, is superimposed on the group willingness to pay curve D_r^{A+E}.[6] The intersection occurs at output 45, where the marginal cost is $6.

Once again, prices can be interpreted in terms of marginal rates of substitution. Reasoning as before, Adam's marginal willingness to pay for rockets is his marginal rate of substitution (MRS_{ra}^{Adam}), and Eve's marginal willingness to pay for rockets is her marginal rate of substitution (MRS_{ra}^{Eve}). Therefore, the sum of the prices they are willing to pay equals $MRS_{ra}^{Adam} + MRS_{ra}^{Eve}$. From the production standpoint, price still represents the marginal rate of transformation, MRT_{ra}. Hence, the equilibrium in Figure 4.4C is characterized by the condition

$$MRS_{ra}^{Adam} + MRS_{ra}^{Eve} = MRT_{ra} \tag{4.2}$$

Contrast this with the conditions for efficiently providing a private good in Equation (4.1). For a private good, efficiency requires that each individual have the same

---

[6] This analysis does not consider explicitly the production possibilities frontier that lies behind this supply curve. See Samuelson [1955].

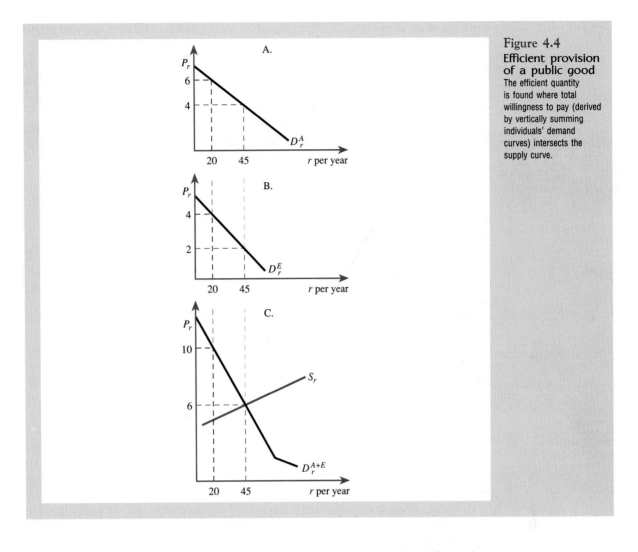

Figure 4.4
**Efficient provision
of a public good**
The efficient quantity
is found where total
willingness to pay (derived
by vertically summing
individuals' demand
curves) intersects the
supply curve.

marginal rate of substitution, and that this equal the marginal rate of transformation. For a pure public good, the sum of the marginal rates of substitution must equal the marginal rate of transformation.[7] Because everybody must consume the same amount of the public good, its efficient provision requires that the *total* valuation they place on the last unit provided—the sum of the *MRS*s—equal the incremental cost to society of providing it—the *MRT*.

Problems in Achieving Efficiency

As stressed in Chapter 3, under a reasonably general set of conditions, a decentralized market system provides private goods efficiently. Do market forces lead to the efficient level of public goods ($r = 45$) in Figure 4.4? The answer depends in part on the extent to which Adam and Eve reveal their true preferences for fireworks. When

---

[7] This analysis assumes the taxes required to finance the public good can be raised without distorting economic decisions in the private sector. When this is not the case, the efficiency condition changes. See Kaplow [2008b].

a private good is exchanged in a competitive market, an individual has no incentive to lie about how much he or she values it. If Eve is willing to pay the going price for a fig leaf, then she has nothing to gain by failing to buy one.

However, people may have incentives to hide their true preferences for a public good. Adam may falsely claim that fireworks mean nothing to him. If he can get Eve to foot the entire bill, he can still enjoy the show and yet have more money to spend on apples and fig leaves. Someone who lets other people pay while enjoying the benefits himself is known as a **free rider.** Of course, Eve also would like to be a free rider. Hence, the market may fall short of providing the efficient amount of the public good. No automatic tendency exists for markets to attain the efficient allocation in Figure 4.4.

Even if consumption is excludable, market provision of a nonrival good is likely to be inefficient. Suppose now that the fireworks display is excludable; people cannot see the show without purchasing an admission ticket to a very large coliseum. A profit-maximizing entrepreneur sells tickets. For a fireworks display of a particular size, the additional cost of another person viewing it is zero (because the display is nonrival). Efficiency requires that every person be admitted who values the display at more than zero; that is, people should be admitted as long as the benefit to them exceeds the incremental cost of zero. Hence, efficiency requires a price of zero. But if the entrepreneur charges everyone a price of zero, then she cannot stay in business.

Is there a way out? Suppose the following two conditions hold: (1) the entrepreneur knows each person's demand curve for the public good; and (2) it is difficult or impossible to transfer the good from one person to another. Under these two conditions, the entrepreneur could charge each person an individual price based on his or her willingness to pay, a procedure known as **perfect price discrimination.** People who valued the rocket display at only a penny would pay exactly that amount; even they would not be excluded. Thus, everyone who put any positive value on the show would attend, which is an efficient outcome.[8] However, because those who valued the display a lot would pay a very high price, the entrepreneur would be able to stay in business.

Perfect price discrimination may seem to be the solution until we recall that the first condition requires knowledge of everybody's preferences. But if individuals' demand curves were known, there would be no problem in determining the optimum provision in the first place.[9] We conclude that even if a nonrival commodity is excludable, private provision is unlikely to be efficient.

---

free rider

The incentive to let other people pay for a public good while you enjoy the benefits.

---

perfect price discrimination

When a producer charges each person the maximum he or she is willing to pay for the good.

POLICY PERSPECTIVE

Global Positioning System

The Global Positioning System (GPS), a satellite navigation system developed by the US Department of Defense, is another example of a nonrival, yet excludable, good. GPS satellites send radio signals that can be picked up by receivers, allowing their users to determine their precise location. These receivers are sold on the private market. GPS is used to aid navigation, mapmaking and land surveying, earthquake

---

[8] The outcome is efficient because the price paid by the *marginal* consumer equals marginal cost.

[9] Several mechanisms have been designed to induce people to reveal their true preferences to a government agency. See the appendix to this chapter.

research, and military targeting, among other functions. The GPS signal is a nonrival good, because people can take advantage of the radio signal without diminishing others' ability to use it. Because the marginal cost of letting another person receive the signal is zero, efficiency requires that every person who values the GPS signal should be allowed to receive it.

In the case of GPS, though, security objectives have at times dominated efficiency concerns. The US military, which operates the satellites, originally excluded users by intentionally introducing errors in the location information sent to receivers held by the private individuals. The accurate signals were encrypted and thus only available to the US military and its allies. While this may have enhanced security, it was clearly inefficient because it denied the benefits of GPS to many users who valued it above its zero marginal cost. Therefore, in 2000, President Clinton made accurate GPS signals available to civilians. Since then, the military has developed the ability to deny the GPS signal to hostile forces in specific areas without affecting the signal to the rest of the world.

The Free Rider Problem

Some suggest that the free rider problem necessarily leads to inefficient levels of public goods; therefore, efficiency requires government provision of such goods. The argument is that the government can somehow find out everyone's true preferences, and then, using its coercive power, force everybody to pay for public goods. If all this is possible, the government can prevent the free rider problem and ensure that public goods are optimally provided.

It must be emphasized that free ridership is not a given; it is an implication of the *hypothesis* that people maximize a utility function that depends only on their own consumption of goods. To be sure, one can find examples in which public goods are not provided because people fail to reveal their preferences. On the other hand, in many instances individuals can and do act collectively without government coercion. Fund drives spearheaded by volunteers have led to the establishment and maintenance of churches, music halls, libraries, scientific laboratories, art museums, hospitals, and other such facilities. There is even some evidence of successful private provision of that classic public good, the lighthouse [Coase, 1974]. One prominent economist has argued, "I do not know of many historical records or other empirical evidence which show convincingly that the problem of correct revelation of preferences has been of any practical significance."[10]

These observations do not prove that free ridership is irrelevant. Although some goods that appear to have public characteristics are privately provided, others that "ought" to be provided (on grounds of efficiency) may not be. Moreover, the quantity of those public goods that are privately provided may be insufficient. The key point is that the importance of the free rider problem is an empirical question whose answer should not be taken for granted.

Several laboratory experiments have been conducted to investigate the importance of free rider behavior. In a typical experiment, each of several subjects is given a

---

[10] Johansen [1977, p. 147] provides further discussion along these lines.

number of tokens that he or she can either keep or donate to a "group exchange." For each token he keeps, a subject receives some payoff, say $4. Further, every time someone in the group donates to the group exchange, *everyone* in the group collects some amount of money, say $3, including the person who makes the donation. Clearly, all the subjects would be better off if everyone donated all their tokens to the group exchange. Note, however, that donations to the group exchange provide a nonrival and nonexcludable payoff. The free rider theory suggests that the subjects therefore might very well decide to make no contributions to the group exchange, so that they could benefit from everyone else's donations while putting nothing in themselves.

What do the results show? The findings vary from experiment to experiment, but there are some consistent findings.[11] On average, people contribute roughly 50 percent of their resources to the provision of the public good. Some free riding therefore is present in the sense that the subjects fail to contribute all their tokens to the group exchange. On the other hand, the results contradict the notion that free riding leads to zero or trivial amounts of a public good. Some other important results are that (1) the more people repeat the game, the less likely they are to contribute; (2) when players have the opportunity to communicate prior to the game, cooperation is fostered; and (3) the contribution rates decline when the opportunity cost of giving goes up (i.e., when the reward for keeping a token increases).

Although caution must be exercised in interpreting the results of laboratory experiments, the results suggest that people may derive a "warm glow" feeling of satisfaction from giving that works counter to the pursuit of the narrow self-interest of free riding.

▶ THE PRIVATIZATION DEBATE

privatization

Countries throughout the world are debating the virtues of privatizing governmental functions. **Privatization** means taking services that are supplied by the government and turning them over to the private sector for provision and/or production. In this section, we first discuss issues relating to *provision* and then turn to *production*.

The process of turning services that are supplied by the government over to the private sector for provision and/or production.

Public versus Private Provision

Sometimes the services provided by publicly provided goods can be obtained privately. The commodity "protection" can be obtained from a publicly provided police force. Alternatively, to some extent, protection can also be gained by purchasing strong locks, burglar alarms, and bodyguards, which are obtained privately. Indeed, in countries such as Kenya—where crime rates are very high—many workers hire private all-night guards for protection [*Economist*, 2007c, p. 50]. A large backyard can serve many of the functions of a public park. Even substitutes for services provided by public courts of law can be obtained privately. Because of the enormous costs of using the government's judicial system, companies sometimes bypass the courts and instead settle their disputes before mutually agreed-upon neutral advisers.

Over time, the mix between public and private provision has changed substantially. During the 19th century, there was much greater private responsibility for education, police protection, libraries, and other functions than there is now. However, there

---

[11] Cinyabuguma, Page, and Putterman [2005] provide a review of the experimental findings.

appears to be a trend back to the private sector for provision of what we have come to consider publicly provided goods and services. For example, as a result of budget cuts that reduce sanitation collections, businesspeople in several cities band together and hire their own refuse collectors to keep their streets clean. In some communities, individual homeowners contract with private companies to provide protection against fires. Indeed, in Denmark about two-thirds of the country's fire service is provided by a private firm.

What is the right mix of public and private provision? To approach this question, think of publicly and privately provided goods as inputs into the production of some output that people desire. Teachers, classrooms, textbooks, and private tutors are inputs into the production of an output we might call educational quality. Assume that what ultimately matters to people is the level of output, educational quality, not the particular inputs used to produce it. What criteria should be used to select the amount of each input? There are several considerations.

Relative Wage and Materials Costs If the public and private sectors pay different amounts for labor and materials, then the less expensive sector is to be preferred on efficiency grounds, all other things equal. For example, the input costs faced by public schools exceed those in private schools when public sector teachers are unionized while their private sector counterparts are not.

Administrative Costs Under public provision, any fixed administrative costs can be spread over a large group of people. Instead of everyone spending time negotiating an arrangement for garbage collection, the negotiation is done by one office for everybody. The larger the community, the greater the advantage to being able to spread these costs. Similarly, a public school system that provides the same education in every school saves parents the time and effort involved in researching schools to figure out which are the good ones.

Diversity of Tastes Households with and without children have very different views about the desirability of high-quality education. People who store jewels in their homes may value property protection more than people who do not. To the extent such diversity is present, private provision is more efficient because people can tailor their consumption to their own tastes. As President Reagan put it, "Such a strategy ensures production of services that are demanded by consumers, not those chosen by government bureaucrats." Clearly, the benefits of diversity must be weighed against any possible increases in administrative costs.

Distributional Issues The community's notions of fairness may require that some commodities be made available to everybody, an idea sometimes referred to as **commodity egalitarianism.** Commodity egalitarianism may help explain the wide appeal of publicly provided education—people believe everyone should have access to at least some minimum level of schooling. This notion also arises in the ongoing debate over medical care.

commodity egalitarianism

The idea that some commodities ought to be made available to everybody.

Public versus Private Production

Airport security became a major object of concern after September 11. While there was a consensus that the security system had failed miserably and had to be upgraded, there was a contentious debate on how to accomplish this. Some argued that airport security workers should be federalized; that is, they should be employees of the federal government. Others argued that while the government should pay for airport security, it would best be left to private firms, which would be monitored and held accountable for mistakes.

This debate highlights the fact that people can agree that certain items should be provided by the public sector, but still disagree over whether they should be produced publicly or privately. Part of the controversy stems from fundamental differences regarding the extent to which government should intervene in the economy (see Chapter 1). Part is due to differences of opinions about the relative costs of public and private production. Some argue that public sector managers, unlike their private sector counterparts, do not have to worry about making profits or becoming the victims of takeovers or bankruptcy. Hence, public sector managers have little incentive to monitor the activities of their enterprises carefully. This notion has an ancient pedigree. In 1776 Adam Smith argued:

> In every great monarchy in Europe the sale of the crown lands would produce a very large sum of money which, if applied to the payments of the public debts, would deliver from mortgage a much greater revenue than any which those lands have ever afforded to the crown. . . . When the crown lands had become private property, they would, in the course of a few years, become well improved and well cultivated.[12]

Anecdotal evidence for this viewpoint abounds. For example, Hurricane Katrina destroyed both a government-owned car bridge and a privately owned train bridge in Bay St. Louis, Mississippi. The private owners of the train bridge started reconstructing it within weeks, and the bridge was rebuilt within six months. The government-owned car bridge was little more than pilings 16 months after Katrina [Cooper, 2007]. When Chicago replaced city crews with private towing companies to haul away abandoned cars, the net annual savings were estimated at $2.5 million. In 1998, a private company took over the South Florida State Psychiatric Hospital, which had long been viewed as a dumping ground where patients were treated poorly. While advocates for the mentally ill were initially horrified at this development, a year later they agreed that conditions at the hospital had improved. Further, the company said that it was making a profit.

Opponents of privatization respond that these examples overstate the cost savings of private production. In fact, there is surprisingly little systematic evidence on the cost differences between private and public production. An important reason for this is that the *quality* of the services provided in the two modes may be different, which makes comparisons difficult. Perhaps, for example, private hospitals have lower costs than their public counterparts because the former refuse to admit patients with illnesses that are expensive to treat. This brings us to the central argument of opponents of private production: Private contractors produce inferior products.

Incomplete Contracts   A possible response to this criticism is that the government can simply write a contract with the private provider, completely specifying the quality of the service that the government wants. However, as Hart, Shleifer, and Vishny [1997] note, it is sometimes impossible to write a contract that is anywhere near being complete because one cannot specify in advance every possible

---

[12] Quoted in Sheshinski and Lopez-Calva [1999].

contingency. For example, a "government would not contract out the conduct of its foreign policy because unforeseen contingencies are a key part of foreign policy, and a private contractor would have enormous power to maximize its own wealth (by, for instance, refusing to send troops somewhere) without violating the letter of the contract" (p. 3). On the other hand, for certain relatively routine activities (garbage collection, snow removal), incomplete contracts are not a serious impediment to private production. In short, when the private sector cost is lower than that in the public sector and relatively complete contracts can be written, a strong case can be made for private production.

Advocates of privatization believe that, even if it is impossible to write a complete contract, there are other mechanisms for getting private firms to refrain from engaging in inefficient cost reductions. To the extent consumers buy the good themselves and there are a number of suppliers, then they can switch if their current supplier provides shoddy service. Nursing homes are one example. In addition, reputation building may be important—a private supplier who wants more contracts in the future has an incentive to avoid inefficient cost reductions in the present. Shleifer [1998] argues that the desire to build a good reputation has been of some importance among private producers of prisons.

POLICY PERSPECTIVE

Should Airport Security Be Produced Publicly or Privately?

The contracting framework provides a nice vehicle for thinking about airport security, an issue that was mentioned earlier. Those who favored private production of airport security argued that it is quite possible to write complete contracts for routine tasks such as screening luggage. The government could set standards and monitor performance. Profit-maximizing private firms would have an incentive to take advantage of technology to keep labor costs down. Further, they argued that a private system run by local firms would be more accountable than a federal system. They noted that Israel, which has some of the best airport security in the world, replaced its government employees with private ones under contract to the airport authority. The Israeli government sets and enforces standards for security, but the airport operator is in charge of operations and accountable for mistakes (see Tierney [2001]).

On the other hand, those who believed that airport security should be publicly produced argued that it is impossible to write a contract to cover all eventualities and that private firms would skimp on training for their workers in order to increase profits. They point to the system in place on September 11, 2001, in which airport security was funded by airlines and security personnel received low pay and little training [Krugman, 2001]. An additional criticism was that a privatized system would lead to different airports having different levels of security [Uchitelle, 2001, p. WK3].

Ultimately, the debate was won by those who favored public production of airport security. In November of 2001, airport security was put under the supervision of a new federal agency, the Transportation Security Administration (TSA), and security screeners became members of the federal workforce. The new law did permit five US airports to keep private security personnel, and it allowed other airports to apply to TSA to switch from a federal to a private screener workforce. While only a few studies have examined the effectiveness of publicly provided airport security, the Government Accountability Office [2007] found that private and federal workers performed similarly on covert testing of screening for threats. On the cost side, the inspector general for the Homeland Security Department found that the TSA engaged in wasteful spending, such as over $250,000 for artwork and over $30,000 for silk plants for its new crisis management center.

Market Environment   A final issue that is important in the privatization debate is the market environment in which the public or private enterprise operates. A privately owned monopoly may produce very inefficient results from society's standpoint, while a publicly owned operation that has a lot of competition may produce quite efficiently. With respect to this latter possibility, consider the case of Phoenix, Arizona. Dissatisfaction with the cost and performance of its public works department led Phoenix to allow private companies to bid for contracts to collect garbage in various neighborhoods. The public works department was allowed to bid as well. At first, the public works department was unsuccessful, because the private firms were able to do the job better and more cheaply. But over time, it tried various experiments such as having drivers redesign garbage collection routes, and eventually it was able to win back the contracts.

The Phoenix story suggests that public versus private ownership is less important than whether competition is present. Along the same lines, in their study of international data on privatization, Dewenter and Malatesta [2001] found that while government firms are less profitable than private firms, there is not much evidence that privatization per se improves profitability. Rather, profitability begins improving a few years before privatization—substantial restructuring occurs before the firms are sold to the private sector. To explain this finding, Dewenter and Malatesta suggest that although governments are capable of improving efficiency, over time such gains can be dissipated because governments do not face competitive pressures to maintain them. If this is the case, then the real benefit of privatization is to perpetuate the gains.

▶ PUBLIC GOODS AND PUBLIC CHOICE

The use of the word *public* to describe commodities that are nonrival and nonexcludable almost seems to prejudge the question of whether they ought to be provided by the public sector. Indeed, we have shown that private markets are unlikely to generate pure public goods in Pareto efficient quantities. Some collective decision must be made regarding the quantity to be supplied. However, in contrast to a pure public good like national defense, sometimes there may be private substitutes for a publicly provided good. But community decision making is also needed in these cases, this time to choose the extent to which public provision will be used. Thus, the subjects of public goods and public choice are closely linked. In Chapter 6 we discuss and evaluate a number of mechanisms for making collective decisions.

Summary

- Public goods are characterized by nonrivalness and nonexcludability in consumption. Thus, each person consumes the same amount, but not necessarily the preferred amount, of the public good.
- Efficient provision of public goods requires that the sum of the individual *MRS*s equal the *MRT*, unlike private goods where each *MRS* equals the *MRT*.
- Market mechanisms are unlikely to provide nonrival goods efficiently, even if they are excludable.
- Casual observation and laboratory studies indicate that people do not fully exploit

free-riding possibilities. Nonetheless, in certain cases, free riding is a significant problem.
- Public goods can be provided privately, and private goods can be provided publicly.
- Even in cases where public provision of a good is selected, a choice between public and private production must be made. A key factor in determining whether public or private production will be more efficient is the market environment. Another important question is the extent to which complete contracts can be written with private sector service providers.

Discussion Questions

1. Which of the following do you consider pure public goods? Private goods? Why?
   a. Wilderness areas
   b. Satellite television
   c. Medical school education
   d. Public television programs
   e. Automated teller machine (ATM)

2. Indicate whether each of the following statements is true, false, or uncertain, and justify your answer.
   a. Efficient provision of a public good occurs at the level at which each member of society places the same value on the last unit.
   b. If a good is nonrival and excludable, it will never be produced by the private sector.
   c. A road is nonrival because one person's use of it does not reduce another person's use of it.
   d. Larger communities tend to consume greater quantities of a nonrival good than smaller communities.

3. Tarzan and Jane live alone in the jungle and have trained Cheetah both to patrol the perimeter of their clearing and to harvest tropical fruits. Cheetah can collect 3 pounds of fruit an hour and currently spends 6 hours patrolling, 8 hours picking, and 10 hours sleeping.

   a. What are the public and private goods in this example?
   b. If Tarzan and Jane are each currently willing to give up one hour of patrol for 2 pounds of fruit, is the current allocation of Cheetah's time Pareto efficient? Should he patrol more or less?

4. In 2008, the US government spent about $1.6 million on the search for extraterrestrial intelligence (SETI). Is such research a public good? Is it sensible for the government to pay for such research?

5. The aircraft company Airbus receives much of its funding from European governments. Airbus recently decided to build a new 550-seat megajetliner, with duty-free shopping courts and restaurants on board. The project has experienced production delays as well as cost overruns, and it now appears that there will be very few buyers. An industry expert says the idea from the start was "nonsense" [Aboulafia, 2006]. Is public sector production of aircrafts ever justified? Explain why it could lead to the apparently ill-advised decision to build the mega-jetliner.

6. Although Mexico has vast reserves of oil, in recent years its production of oil has been

falling. In order to reverse this decline, President Felipe Calderon recently attempted to privatize the state-run oil company Pemex [Luhnow, 2008]. Many opponents of the proposal argued that privatization of Mexico's telephone company Telmex had led to a monopoly, which was charging exorbitant prices. Would you expect something similar to happen if Pemex were privatized? Relate your answer to our discussion of the role of market environment when assessing the consequences of privatization.

7. It has been estimated that private prisons are about 5 to 15 percent cheaper, on a per prisoner basis, than public prisons [*Economist*, 2007b]. On this basis, would you recommend that prisons be privatized? If not, what other information would you require?

8. Several years ago, some citizens of the town of Manchester, Vermont, decided to launch a school fund-raising campaign. A private group of citizens decided how much every household and business should contribute, and there was a good deal of social pressure to pay the full amount. One flier urged, "We cannot sit back and wait for our neighbors to carry the load" [Tomsho, 2001, p. A1]. Use the experimental results on free riding discussed in this chapter to predict the outcome of this campaign.

9. In order to respond to the tastes of its patrons, Fairfax County Public Library discards books that have not been checked out in two years in order to make space for more popular books [Miller, 2007]. This policy led them to pull classic works by William Faulkner and Thomas Hardy, freeing up space for popular works by John Grisham and James Patterson. Given that it has become easier and cheaper to find books in retail and online stores in recent years, do libraries provide a public good? Is the public good aspect of libraries met by providing books with mass-market appeal or by providing a cultural storehouse of classic books?

10. Private military firms provided much of the logistical support to American troops in Afghanistan and Iraq, and some people have advocated using such troops to help stop the genocide being carried out in Darfur, Sudan. Critics of these mercenary troops argue that they charge too much,

act irresponsibly, and fail to provide long-term fixes. As one opponent stated, "There's no reason to assume that a private company hired to perform a public service will do better than people employed directly by the government" [Krugman, 2006b, p. A27]. Relate this debate to our discussion of the role that contracts play in deciding whether to produce a public good privately.

11. Suppose that there are only two fishermen, Zach and Jacob, who fish along a certain coast. They would each benefit if lighthouses were built along the coast where they fish. The marginal cost of building each additional lighthouse is $100. The marginal benefit to Zach of each additional lighthouse is $90 - Q$, and the marginal benefit to Jacob is $40 - Q$, where Q equals the number of lighthouses.

   a. Explain why we might not expect to find the efficient number of lighthouses along this coast.

   b. What is the efficient number of lighthouses? What would be the net benefits to Zach and Jacob if the efficient number were provided?

12. A lone person fishing at a lake can catch 10 fish per day. Each additional person fishing at the lake reduces the catch per person by one fish per day. If a person would rather stay home than catch fewer than four fish (i.e., the opportunity cost of going to the lake is four fish), how many people will show up each day to fish at the lake? What are the net benefits to society of this outcome? What is the efficient number of people fishing to show up at the lake? Is access to the lake a public good?

13. Britney and Paris are neighbors. During the winter, it is impossible for a snowplow to clear the street in front of Britney's house without clearing the front of Paris's. Britney's marginal benefit from snowplowing services is $12 - Z$, where Z is the number of times the street is plowed. Paris's marginal benefit is $8 - 2Z$. The marginal cost of getting the street plowed is $16.

   Sketch the two marginal benefit schedules and the aggregate marginal benefit schedule. Draw in the marginal cost schedule, and find the efficient level of provision for snowplowing services.

Appendix

▶ PREFERENCE REVELATION MECHANISMS

Markets generally fail to induce individuals to reveal their true preferences for nonexcludable public goods, and, hence, a price system fails to provide them in efficient amounts. Is there some way, short of forcing everyone to take a lie detector test, to get people to tell the truth? Several procedures have been suggested for inducing people to reveal their true preferences. We now describe one based on the work of Groves and Loeb [1975].[13]

Imagine a government agent approaches Eve and says, "Please tell me your demand curve for rocket displays. I will use this information plus the information I receive from Adam to select a Pareto efficient quantity of rockets and to assign each of you a tax. But before you give me your answer, I want you to realize that you will be taxed in the following way: Whenever the level of public good provision increases by a unit, the change in your tax bill will be the incremental cost of that unit, minus the value that everyone else puts on the increase."

After the agent departs, the first thing Eve does is to represent the tax structure algebraically. If ΔT^{Eve} is the change in her tax bill when provision of the public good is expanded by one unit, MRT_{ra} is the incremental resource cost of the one unit, MRS_{ra}^{Total} is the marginal value of one more unit to Adam and Eve, and MRS_{ra}^{Eve} is the marginal value to Eve alone, then

$$\Delta T^{\text{Eve}} = MRT_{ra} - (MRS_{ra}^{\text{Total}} - MRS_{ra}^{\text{Eve}}) \qquad (4A.1)$$

Faced with Equation (4A.1), Eve has to decide whether or not to tell the truth, that is, to reveal her true marginal valuation for every level of rocket display provision. She knows that from her selfish point of view, production should continue up to the point where the marginal benefit of consuming one more unit, MRS_{ra}^{Eve}, equals the marginal cost to her, which is just the increase in her tax bill. Thus, Eve would like to see the public good provided in an amount such that

$$\Delta T^{\text{Eve}} = MRS_{ra}^{\text{Eve}} \qquad (4A.2)$$

Substituting from Equation (4A.1) for ΔT^{Eve} gives us

$$MRT_{ra} - (MRS_{ra}^{\text{Total}} - MRS_{ra}^{\text{Eve}}) = MRS_{ra}^{\text{Eve}}$$

Adding $(MRS_{ra}^{\text{Total}} - MRS_{ra}^{\text{Eve}})$ to both sides of the equation yields

$$MRT_{ra} = MRS_{ra}^{\text{Total}} \qquad (4A.3)$$

Because conditions (4A.2) and (4A.3) are equivalent, it would be in Eve's interest to tell the truth if she knew the government would use her information to achieve the allocation corresponding to Equation (4A.3).

But then she realizes this is exactly what the government agent will do. Why? Remember the agent promised to select a Pareto efficient provision given the information he receives. Such a provision is characterized by Equation (4.2) in the text. Since, by definition, $MRS_{ra}^{\text{Total}} = MRS_{ra}^{\text{Adam}} + MRS_{ra}^{\text{Eve}}$, Equations (4A.3) and (4.2) are identical. Thus, the government's provision of rocket displays will satisfy Equation (4A.3),

---

[13] See also Tideman and Tullock [1976].

and Eve has an incentive to tell the truth. Provided that Adam is confronted with the same kind of tax structure, he too has an incentive to be truthful. The free rider problem appears to have been solved.

To see intuitively why the system works, consider the right-hand side of Equation (4A.1), which shows how Eve's tax bill is determined. Note that $(MRS_{ra}^{Total} - MRS_{ra}^{Eve})$ is the sum of everyone's marginal benefit but Eve's. Hence, the increase in Eve's tax bill when output expands does not depend on her own marginal benefit, and therefore she has no incentive to lie about it.

There are several problems with this mechanism, many of which are shared by other devices to solve the free rider problem. First, taxpayers may not be able to understand the system. (If you don't think this is a problem, try to explain it to a friend who has not had any economics courses.) Second, even if the scheme can be made comprehensible, taxpayers have to be willing to make the effort to compute their entire demand curves and report them to the government. People may feel it is not worth their time. Third, given that millions of people are involved in governmental decisions, the costs of gathering and assimilating all the information would be prohibitive.[14] (For relatively small groups like social clubs, this would not be as much of a problem.) We conclude that although preference revelation mechanisms of this kind provide interesting insights into the structure of the free rider problem, they are not a practical way for resolving it, at least for public sector decision making.

---

[14] There are some additional technical problems. The taxes collected may not balance the budget, and coalitions can form and thwart the system. See Tideman and Tullock [1976].

Chapter Five

EXTERNALITIES

> *We should tax what we burn, not what we earn.*
>
> —AL GORE

As a by-product of their activities, paper mills produce the chemical dioxin. It forms when the chlorine used for bleaching wood pulp combines with a substance in the pulp. Once dioxin is released into the environment, it ends up in everyone's fat tissue and in the milk of nursing mothers. According to some scientists, dioxin is responsible for birth defects and cancer, among other health problems.

Economists often claim that markets allocate resources efficiently (see Chapter 3). Dioxin is the outcome of the operation of markets. Does this mean that having dioxin in the environment is efficient? To answer this question, it helps to distinguish different ways in which people can affect each other's welfare.

Suppose large numbers of suburbanites decide they want to live in an urban setting. As they move to the city, the price of urban land increases. Urban property owners are better off, but renters are worse off. Merchants in the city benefit from increased demand for their products, while their suburban counterparts lose business. By the time the economy settles into a new equilibrium, the distribution of real income has changed substantially.

In this migration example, all the effects are transmitted *via changes in market prices*. Suppose that before the change in tastes, the allocation of resources was Pareto efficient. The shifts in supply and demand curves change relative prices, but competition guarantees that the relevant marginal rates of substitution will all be equal to the marginal rate of transformation. Thus, while the behavior of some people affects the welfare of others, there is no market failure. As long as the effects are transmitted via prices, markets are efficient.[1]

The dioxin case embodies a different type of interaction from the urban land example. The decrease in welfare of the dioxin victims is not a result of price changes. Rather, the output choices of the paper mill factories directly affect the utilities of the neighboring people. When the activity of one entity (a person or a firm) directly affects the welfare of another in a way that is not reflected in the market price, that effect is called an **externality** (because one entity directly affects the welfare of another entity that is "external" to the market). Unlike effects that are transmitted through market prices, externalities reduce economic efficiency.

externality

A cost or benefit that occurs when the activity of one entity directly affects the welfare of another in a way that is outside the market mechanism.

---

[1] Of course, the new pattern of prices may be more or less desirable from a distributional point of view, depending on one's ethical judgments as embodied in the social welfare function. Effects on welfare that are transmitted via prices are sometimes referred to as pecuniary externalities. Mishan [1971] argues convincingly that because such effects are part of the normal functioning of the market, this is a confusing appellation. It is mentioned here only for the sake of completeness and is ignored henceforth.

In this chapter, we analyze these inefficiencies and possible remedies for them. One of the most important applications of externality theory arises in the debate over environmental quality, and much of the discussion focuses on this issue.

▶ THE NATURE OF EXTERNALITIES

Suppose Bart operates a factory that dumps its waste into a river nobody owns. Lisa makes her living by fishing from the river. Bart's activities impose costs on Lisa that are not reflected in market prices, so the harm done to Lisa is not incorporated into Bart's market decision. In this example, clean water is an input to Bart's production process. It gets used up just like all other inputs: land, labor, capital, and materials. Clean water is also a scarce resource with alternative uses, such as fishing by Lisa. As such, efficiency requires that for the water he uses, Bart should pay a price that reflects the water's value as a scarce resource that can be used for other activities. Instead, Bart pays a zero price and, as a consequence, uses the water in inefficiently large quantities.

Posing the externality problem this way exposes its source. Bart uses his other inputs efficiently because he must pay their owners prices that reflect their value in alternative uses. Otherwise, the owners of the inputs simply sell them elsewhere. However, if no one owns the river, there is no market for its use and everyone can use it for free. An externality, then, is a consequence of the failure or inability to establish property rights. If someone owned the river, people would have to pay for its use, and no externality would materialize.

Suppose Lisa owned the river. She could charge Bart a fee for polluting that reflected the damage done to her catch. Bart would take these charges into account when making his production decisions and would no longer use the water inefficiently. On the other hand, if Bart owned the river, he could make money by charging Lisa for the privilege of fishing in it. The amount of money that Lisa would be willing to pay Bart for the right to fish in the river would depend on the amount of pollution present. Hence, Bart would have an incentive not to pollute excessively. Otherwise, he could not make as much money from Lisa.

As long as someone owns a resource, its price reflects the value for alternative uses, and the resource is therefore used efficiently (at least in the absence of any other market failures). In contrast, resources that are owned in common are overused because no one has an incentive to economize.

To expand on the subject, note the following characteristics of externalities.

Externalities Can Be Produced by Consumers as Well as Firms   Not all externalities are produced by firms. Just think of the person who smokes a cigar in a crowded room, lowering others' utility by using up the common resource, fresh air.

Externalities Are Reciprocal in Nature   In our example, it seems natural to refer to Bart as the "polluter." However, we could just as well think of Lisa as "polluting" the river with fishermen, increasing the social cost of Bart's production. As an alternative to fishing, using the river for waste disposal is not obviously worse

"We make clouds, clouds make rain, and rain spoils ball games. That's why people don't like smokers!"   © 2000 Randy Glasbergen.

from a social point of view. As we show later, it depends on the costs of alternatives for both activities.

Externalities Can Be Positive   Suppose that in response to a terrorist threat you were to get yourself vaccinated against smallpox. You would incur some costs: the price of the vaccination, the associated discomfort, and the slight risk that it would induce a case of the disease. There would be a benefit to you in terms of a reduced probability of being stricken by the disease in the event of a bioterrorism attack. However, you would also help other members of your community, who would be less likely to come down with the disease because they could not catch it from you. But neither you nor other people take into account such external benefits when weighing the benefits and costs of getting vaccinated, and hence not enough people are vaccinated in the absence of some public intervention.

Public Goods Can Be Viewed as a Special Kind of Externality   Specifically, when an individual creates a positive externality with full effects felt by every person in the economy, the externality is a pure public good. At times, the boundary between public goods and externalities is a bit fuzzy. Suppose that I install in my backyard a device for electrocuting mosquitoes. If I kill the whole community's mosquitoes, then I have, in effect, created a pure public good. If only a few neighbors are affected, then it is an externality. Although positive externalities and public goods are quite similar from a formal point of view, in practice it is useful to distinguish between them.

Figure 5.1

An externality problem

The marginal social cost of production is the marginal private cost to Bart plus the marginal damage done to Lisa. Bart produces where his marginal private cost equals marginal benefit, output Q_1. However, the efficient output is Q^*, where marginal social cost equals marginal benefit.

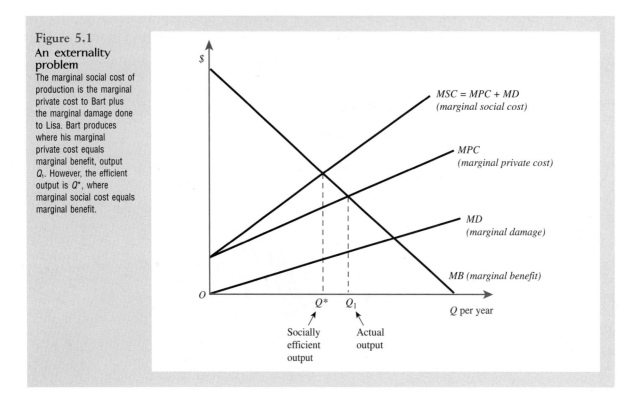

▶ GRAPHICAL ANALYSIS

Figure 5.1 analyzes the Bart-Lisa example described earlier. The horizontal axis measures the amount of output, Q, produced by Bart's factory, and the vertical axis measures dollars. The curve *MB* shows the marginal benefit to Bart of each level of output; it is assumed to decline as output increases.[2] Also associated with each level of output is some marginal private cost, *MPC*. Marginal private cost reflects payments made by Bart for inputs and is assumed here to increase with output. As a by-product of its activities, the factory produces pollution that makes Lisa worse off. Assume that there is a fixed amount of pollution per unit of output, so as the factory's output increases, so does the amount of pollution it creates. The marginal damage inflicted on Lisa by the pollution at each level of output is denoted by *MD*. *MD* is drawn sloping upward, reflecting the assumption that as Lisa is subjected to additional pollution, she becomes worse off at an increasing rate.

If Bart wants to maximize profits, he produces each unit of output for which the marginal benefit *to him* exceeds the marginal cost *to him*. In Figure 5.1, he produces all levels of output for which *MB* exceeds *MPC* but does not produce where *MPC* exceeds *MB*. Thus, he produces up to output level Q_1, at which *MPC* intersects *MB*.

---

[2] If Bart consumes all the output of his factory, then the declining *MB* reflects the diminishing marginal utility of output. If Bart sells his output in a competitive market, *MB* is constant at the market price.

From society's point of view, production should occur as long as the marginal benefit *to society* exceeds the marginal cost *to society*. The marginal cost to society has two components: First are the inputs purchased by Bart. Their value is reflected in *MPC*. Second is the marginal damage done to Lisa as reflected in *MD*. Hence, marginal social cost is *MPC plus MD*. Graphically, we find the marginal social cost schedule by adding together the heights of *MPC* and *MD* at each level of output. It is depicted in Figure 5.1 as *MSC*. Note that, by construction, the vertical distance between *MSC* and *MPC* is *MD*. (Because *MSC* = *MPC* + *MD*, it follows that *MSC* − *MPC* = *MD*.)

Efficiency from a social point of view requires production of only those units of output for which *MB* exceeds *MSC*. Thus, output should be at Q^*, where the two schedules intersect.

Implications

This analysis suggests the following observations: First, when externalities exist, private markets do not produce the socially efficient output level. In particular, when a good generates a negative externality, a free market produces more than the efficient output.[3]

Second, the model not only shows that efficiency would be enhanced by a move from Q_1 to Q^*, but it also provides a way to measure the benefits of doing so. Figure 5.2 replicates from Figure 5.1 the marginal benefit (*MB*), marginal private cost (*MPC*), marginal damage (*MD*), and marginal social cost (*MSC*) schedules. When output is cut from Q_1 to Q^*, Bart loses profits. To calculate the size of his loss, recall that Bart's marginal profit from each unit of output is the difference between marginal benefit and marginal private cost. If the marginal private cost of the eighth unit is $10 and its marginal benefit is $12, the marginal profit is $2. Geometrically, the marginal profit on a given unit of output is the vertical distance between *MB* and *MPC*. If Bart is forced to cut back from Q_1 to Q^*, he therefore loses the difference between the *MB* and *MPC* curves for each unit of production between Q_1 and Q^*. This is area *dcg* in Figure 5.2.

At the same time, however, Lisa becomes better off because as Bart's output falls, so do the damages to her fishery. For each unit decline in Bart's output, Lisa gains an amount equal to the marginal damage associated with that unit of output. In Figure 5.2, Lisa's gain for each unit of output reduction is the vertical distance between *MD* and the horizontal axis. Therefore, Lisa's gain when output is reduced from Q_1 to Q^* is the area under the marginal damage curve between Q^* and Q_1, *abfe*. Now note that *abfe* equals area *cdhg*. This is by construction—the vertical distance between *MSC* and *MPC* is *MD*, which is the same as the vertical distance between *MD* and the horizontal axis.

In sum, if output were reduced from Q_1 to Q^*, Bart would lose area *dcg* and Lisa would gain area *cdhg*. Provided that society views a dollar to Bart as equivalent to a dollar to Lisa, then moving from Q_1 to Q^* yields a net gain to society equal to the difference between *cdhg* and *dcg*, which is *dhg*.

---

[3] This model assumes the only way to reduce pollution is to reduce output. If antipollution technology is available, it may be possible to maintain output and still reduce pollution. Later in the chapter we examine such approaches to pollution reduction. However, for now it is enough to point out that the analysis is basically the same, because the adoption of new technologies requires the use of resources.

Figure 5.2

Gains and losses from moving to an efficient level of output
When output falls from Q_1 to Q^*, Bart loses area *dcg* in profits. However, the reduction in Bart's output increases Lisa's welfare by area *cdhg*. Thus, the net gain to society is area *dhg*.

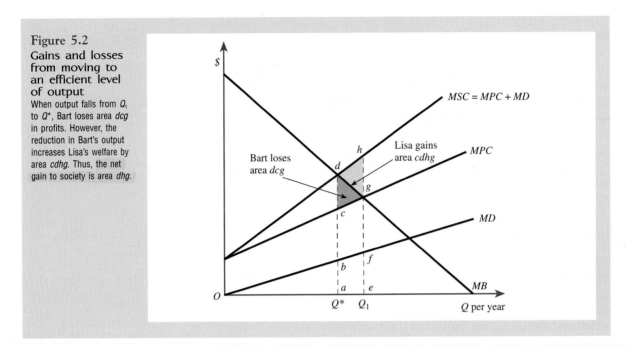

Third, the analysis implies that, in general, zero pollution is not socially desirable. Finding the right amount of pollution requires trading off its benefits and costs, and the optimum generally occurs at some positive level of pollution. Because virtually all productive activity involves some pollution, requiring pollution to be set at zero is equivalent to banning all production, clearly an inefficient solution. If all this seems only like common sense, it is. But note that Congress once set as a national goal that "the discharge of pollutants into the navigable waters be eliminated by 1985."

Finally, implementing the framework of Figure 5.2 requires more than drawing hypothetical marginal damage and benefit curves. Their actual locations and shapes must be determined, at least approximately. However, difficult practical questions arise when it comes to identifying and valuing pollution damage.

Which Pollutants Do Harm?   In our earlier example, it was entirely clear that Bart's factory caused harm to Lisa by reducing the number of fish she caught. However, in the real world, it is typically difficult to determine which pollutants cause harm and by how much. We now discuss some empirical approaches to this problem.

EMPIRICAL EVIDENCE

What Is the Effect of Pollution on Health?

Total suspended particles (TSPs) are widely considered to be the most damaging air pollutant to health. Several studies have established a correlation between TSPs and mortality rates. However, it is difficult to establish the size of the causal impact. The difficulty arises because scientists cannot perform randomized studies on the effects of pollution. Instead, investigators must rely on cross-sectional or time-series observational evidence. These studies could have biased results if other factors that differ across location or time affect both air pollution and mortality. For example, polluted industrialized areas might have higher mortality rates because they attract lower-income, less healthy residents. Therefore, the observed correlation between air pollution and mortality might not be entirely causal.

A further complication is that these studies are unable to measure the *lifetime* exposure of adults to air pollution. Because people move in and out of cities, it is difficult to measure lifetime exposure to pollution and its link to health outcomes.

Chay and Greenstone [2003] study the impact of air pollution on mortality. They focus on infants, because unlike adults, one can measure an infant's lifetime exposure to pollution. They also conduct a quasi-experimental analysis by taking advantage of the fact that the economic recession of the early 1980s led to sharp reductions in TSPs in some areas of the United States but not others. Importantly, the changes in air pollution appear to have been virtually random—the areas that experienced substantial TSP reductions had similar overall characteristics to those that did not. By comparing the two types of areas, Chay and Greenstone found that a 1 percent reduction in TSPs led to a 0.35 percent reduction in the infant mortality rate. This implies that the TSP reductions, induced by the 1980–1982 recession, led to 2,500 fewer infants deaths than otherwise would have been the case.

Even once a pollutant has been identified as causing harm, policymakers must consider the possibility that reducing the pollutant will have unanticipated negative consequences. For example, in order to make gasoline burn more cleanly and thus reduce air pollution, policymakers required oil companies to add a chemical ingredient called M.T.B.E. to gasoline. However, in 1999 the Environmental Protection Agency stopped this requirement because scientists discovered that, when it leaked, M.T.B.E. was a potentially dangerous source of *water* pollution.

What Activities Produce Pollutants?   Once a harmful pollutant is identified, policymakers must identify which production processes generate it. Consider acid rain, a phenomenon of widespread concern. Scientists have shown that acid rain forms when sulfur oxides and nitrogen oxides emitted into the air react with water vapor to create acids. These acids fall to earth in rain and snow, increasing the general level of acidity with potentially harmful effects on plant and animal life.

However, it is not known just how much acid rain is associated with factory production and how much with natural activities such as plant decay and volcanic eruptions. Moreover, it is difficult to determine what amount of nitrogen and sulfur emissions generated in a given region eventually become acid rain. It depends in part on local weather conditions and on the extent to which other pollutants such as nonmethane hydrocarbons are present. This highlights the difficulty of assessing which production activities cause acid rain and should thus be subject to government intervention.

What Is the Value of the Damage Done?   The marginal damage schedule shows the dollar value of the external costs imposed by each additional unit of output. Therefore, once the physical damage a pollutant creates is determined, the dollar value of that damage must be calculated. When economists think about measuring the value of something, typically they think of people's willingness to pay for it. If you are willing to pay $210 for a bicycle, that is its value to you.

Unlike bicycles, pollution reduction is generally not bought and sold in explicit markets. (Some exceptions are discussed shortly.) How, then, can people's marginal willingness to pay for pollution removal be measured? One approach is to infer it indirectly by studying housing prices. When people shop for houses, they consider both the quality of the house itself and the characteristics of the neighborhood, such as cleanliness of the streets and quality of schools. Families also care about the level of air pollution in the neighborhoods. Consider two identical houses situated in two identical neighborhoods, except that the first is in an unpolluted area and the second is in a polluted area. We expect the house in the unpolluted area to have a higher price. This price differential approximates people's willingness to pay for clean air.

These observations suggest a natural strategy for estimating people's willingness to pay for clean air. Using multiple regression analysis (see Chapter 2), researchers can estimate the relationship between housing prices and air quality using a sample of houses in a given area or areas. We now highlight one of the studies that have followed this strategy.

EMPIRICAL EVIDENCE

The Effect of Air Pollution on Housing Values

Using regression analysis, a researcher can estimate the correlation between air quality and housing prices, holding all other measured characteristics constant. However, it is difficult to establish whether this is a causal relationship because other unmeasured characteristics could affect both air quality and housing prices. For example, highly industrialized neighborhoods might have lower housing prices because they are visually less attractive and also have lower air quality, but this does not mean that air quality causes the lower prices.

Chay and Greenstone [2005] conduct a quasi-experiment to estimate the causal relationship between TSPs and the average housing values in a county. For their analysis, they rely on legislation in the 1970s that set a limit on TSP emissions. Counties that were above this limit were subject to strict regulation, while those below the limit (no matter how close) were not subject to the same strict regulations. In effect, then, the counties just above the limit were the treatment group and those just below the limit were the control group. Chay and Greenstone found that the counties in the treatment group experienced a large drop in TSPs due to the regulations, which led to an increase in housing prices. According to their estimates, the improvements in air quality stemming from the regulation led to a $45 billion aggregate increase in housing values between 1970 and 1980.

A fundamental concern with studies of this kind is the validity of a willingness-to-pay measure for cleaner air. People may be unaware of the effects of air pollution on their health, and hence underestimate the value of reducing it. Also, the willingness-to-pay measure ignores equity concerns. In sum, the econometric approach to valuation is promising, but it does not definitively determine the value of damage done.

Conclusion

Implementing the framework of Figure 5.2 requires the skills of biologists, engineers, ecologists, and health practitioners, among others, in order to estimate the marginal damages associated with pollution. Investigating a pollution problem requires a resolutely interdisciplinary approach. Having said this, however, we emphasize that even with superb engineering and biological data, one simply cannot make efficient decisions without applying the economist's tool of marginal analysis.

▶ PRIVATE RESPONSES

In the presence of externalities, markets can lead to inefficient outcomes. This section discusses the circumstances under which private individuals, acting on their own, can avoid externality problems.

Bargaining and the Coase Theorem

Recall our earlier argument that the root cause of the inefficiencies associated with externalities is the absence of property rights. When property rights are assigned, individuals may respond to the externality by bargaining with each other. To see how, suppose property rights to the river are assigned to Bart. Assume further that it is costless for Lisa and Bart to bargain with each other. Is it possible for the two parties to strike a bargain that results in output being reduced from Q_1?

Bart would be willing to not produce a given unit of output as long as he received a payment that exceeded his net incremental gain from producing that unit ($MB - MPC$). On the other hand, Lisa would be willing to pay Bart not to produce a given unit as long as the payment was less than the marginal damage done to her, MD. As long as the amount that Lisa is willing to pay Bart exceeds the cost to Bart of not producing, the opportunity for a bargain exists. Algebraically, the requirement is that $MD > (MB - MPC)$. Figure 5.3 (which reproduces the information from Figure 5.1) indicates that at output Q_1, $MB - MPC$ is zero, while MD is positive. Hence, MD exceeds $MB - MPC$, and there is scope for a bargain.

Similar reasoning indicates that the payment Lisa would be willing to make exceeds $MB - MPC$ at every output level to the right of Q^*. In contrast, to the left of Q^*, the amount of money Bart would demand to reduce his output would exceed what Lisa would be willing to pay. Hence, Lisa pays Bart to reduce output just to Q^*, the efficient level. We cannot tell without more information exactly how much Lisa ends up paying Bart, although the total payment will be at least *dcg* (the amount Bart loses by decreasing output to Q^*) and no greater than *cdhg* (the amount that Lisa gains by having Bart decrease output to Q^*). The exact amount depends on the relative bargaining strengths of the two parties. Regardless of how the gains from the bargain are divided, however, production ends up at Q^*.

Now suppose the shoe is on the other foot, and Lisa is assigned the property rights to the river. Bart cannot produce any output without first gaining Lisa's permission. The bargaining process now consists of Bart paying for Lisa's consent to pollute. Lisa is willing to accept some pollution as long as the payment she receives from Bart for each unit of his output exceeds the marginal damage (MD) caused by that output to her fishing enterprise. Bart finds it worthwhile to pay for the privilege of producing as long as the amount is less than the value of $MB - MPC$ for that unit of output. Notice that for the first unit of output Bart produces, his marginal profit

Figure 5.3
Coase Theorem
If Bart has property rights to the river, he will reduce output by one unit as long as he receives a payment that exceeds the incremental profit he would have received from producing that unit (*MB – MPC*). Lisa is willing to pay Bart to reduce a unit of production as long as the payment is less than the damage the output causes her, *MD*. There is room for them to bargain at any level of output greater than *Q**.

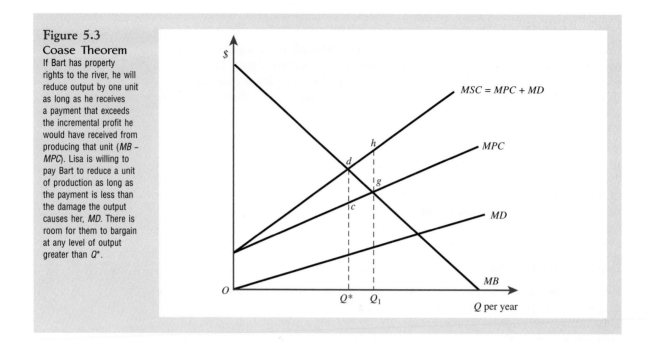

($MB - MPC$) far exceeds the marginal damage (MD) to Lisa, so there is ample room to bargain and allow Bart to produce this unit. Applying this reasoning to each additional unit of production shows that they have every incentive to reach an agreement whereby Lisa sells Bart the right to produce at $Q*$.

Two important assumptions played a key role in the preceding analysis:

1. The costs to the parties of bargaining are low.
2. The owners of resources can identify the source of damages to their property and legally prevent damages.

The implication of the discussion surrounding Figure 5.3 is that, under these two assumptions, the efficient solution will be achieved *independently* of who is assigned the property rights, as long as *someone* is assigned those rights. This result, known as the **Coase Theorem** (after Nobel laureate Ronald Coase), implies that once property rights are established, government intervention is not required to deal with externalities [Coase, 1960].

The two assumptions do not always hold. For example, externalities such as air pollution involve millions of people (both polluters and pollutees). It is difficult to imagine them getting together for negotiations at a sufficiently low cost.[4] Further, even if property rights to air were established, it is not clear how owners would be able to identify which of thousands of potential polluters was responsible for dirtying their airspace and for what proportion of the damage each was liable.

The Coase Theorem is most relevant for cases in which only a few parties are involved and the sources of the externality are well defined. Even when these conditions hold, the assignment of property rights *is* relevant from the point of view

Coase Theorem

Provided that transaction costs are negligible, an efficient solution to an externality problem is achieved as long as someone is assigned property rights, independent of who is assigned those rights.

---

[4] Although transaction costs might make an efficient outcome unlikely through bargaining, the transaction costs of implementing a government solution might not be less.

of income distribution. Property rights are valuable; if Lisa owns the river, it will increase her income relative to Bart's, and vice versa.

Assigning property rights along Coasian lines could help solve some significant problems, such as reversing the extinction of species. For example, in order to conserve elephant populations in Africa, one approach is simply to ban hunting. However, the local villagers have no incentive to obey the ban; they hunt anyway (the law is hard to enforce), and the marginal cost to them of each animal killed is effectively zero. A price of zero leads to substantial overhunting. Another approach is to assign property rights to the animals. In this case, the villagers have an incentive to conserve the herds, because they can make money by selling permission to hunt them. According to Sugg [1996], Kenya banned all hunting in 1977, and its elephant population fell from 167,000 to 16,000 by 1989. In contrast, in 1982, Zimbabwe granted landowners property rights over wildlife; between that time and 1995 its elephant population grew from 40,000 to 68,000. The idea of giving individuals property rights to wild animals on their land has apparently caught on. In southern Africa, many farmers have found it profitable to stop growing food, let their land revert to its natural state, and then charge tourists to view the animals. About 18 percent of the land in the southern third of Africa is now devoted to such ecotourism [Heal, 2003].

Mergers

One way to deal with an externality is to "internalize" it by combining the involved parties. For simplicity, imagine there is only one polluter and one pollutee, as in the Bart-Lisa scenario from earlier in the chapter. As stressed already, if Bart took into account the damages he imposed on Lisa's fishery, then a net gain would be possible. (Refer back to the discussion surrounding Figure 5.2.) In other words, if Bart and Lisa coordinated their activities, then the profit of the joint enterprise would be higher than the sum of their individual profits when they don't coordinate. In effect, by failing to act together, Bart and Lisa are just throwing away money!

The market, then, provides a strong incentive for the two firms to merge—Lisa can buy the factory, Bart can buy the fishery, or some third party can buy them both. Once the two firms merge, the externality is internalized—it is taken into account by the party that generates the externality. For instance, if Bart purchased the fishery, he would willingly produce less output than before, because at the margin doing so would increase the profits of his fishery subsidiary more than it decreased the profits from his factory subsidiary. Consequently, the external effects would not exist, and the market would not be inefficient. Indeed, an outside observer would not even characterize the situation as an "externality" because all decisions would be made within a single firm.

Social Conventions

Unlike firms, individuals cannot merge to internalize externalities. However, certain social conventions can be viewed as attempts to force people to take into account the externalities they generate. Schoolchildren are taught that littering is irresponsible and not "nice." If this teaching is effective, a child learns that even though she bears a small cost by holding on to a candy wrapper until she finds a garbage can, she should incur this cost because it is less than the cost imposed on other people by having to view her unsightly garbage. Think about the golden rule, "Do unto others as you would have others do unto you." A (much) less elegant way of expressing this sentiment is, "Before you undertake some activity, take into account its external marginal benefits and costs." The same notion is embodied in the Talmudic precept, "If a person desires to open a shop in the courtyard, his neighbor may stop him because he will be kept awake by the noise of people going in and out of the shop." Some moral precepts, then, induce people to empathize with others, and hence internalize the externalities their behavior may create. In effect, these precepts correct for the absence of missing markets.

▶ PUBLIC RESPONSES TO EXTERNALITIES: TAXES AND SUBSIDIES

In cases where individuals acting on their own cannot attain an efficient solution, government can intervene by levying taxes and subsidies on certain market activities.[5]

Taxes

Pigouvian tax

A tax levied on each unit of an externality-generator's output in an amount equal to the marginal damage at the efficient level of output.

Bart produces inefficiently because the prices he pays for inputs are below social costs. Specifically, because his input prices are too low, the price of his output is too low. A natural solution, suggested by the British economist A. C. Pigou in the 1930s, is to levy a tax on the polluter that makes up for the fact that some of his inputs are priced too low. A **Pigouvian tax** is a tax levied on each unit of a polluter's output in an amount just equal to the marginal damage it inflicts *at the efficient level of output*. Figure 5.4 reproduces the example of Figure 5.1. In this case, the marginal damage at the efficient output Q^* is distance cd. This is the Pigouvian tax. (Remember that the vertical distance between MSC and MPC is MD.)

How does Bart react to the imposition of a tax of cd dollars per unit? The tax raises Bart's effective marginal cost. For each unit he produces, Bart has to make payments both to the suppliers of his inputs (measured by MPC) *and* to the tax collector (measured by cd). Geometrically, Bart's new marginal cost schedule is found by adding cd to MPC at each level of output. This involves shifting up MPC by the vertical distance cd.

Profit maximization requires that Bart produce where marginal benefit equals his marginal cost. This now occurs at the intersection of MB and $MPC + cd$, which is at the efficient output Q^*. In effect, the tax forces Bart to take into account the costs of the externality that he generates and induces him to produce efficiently. Note that the tax generates revenue of cd dollars for each of the id units produced ($id = OQ^*$). Hence, tax revenue is $cd \times id$, which is the area of rectangle $ijcd$ in Figure 5.4. It would be tempting to use these revenues to compensate Lisa, who still is being hurt by Bart's activities, although to a lesser extent than before the tax. However, caution must be exercised. If it becomes known that anyone who fishes along the river receives a payment, then some people may choose to fish there who otherwise would not have done so. Recall the reciprocal nature of externalities. Compensation would

---

[5] In this and the next section we explore a number of ways in which the government can intervene to address externalities. However, the list of possibilities considered is by no means exhaustive. See Stavins [2003] for a careful discussion of several alternatives.

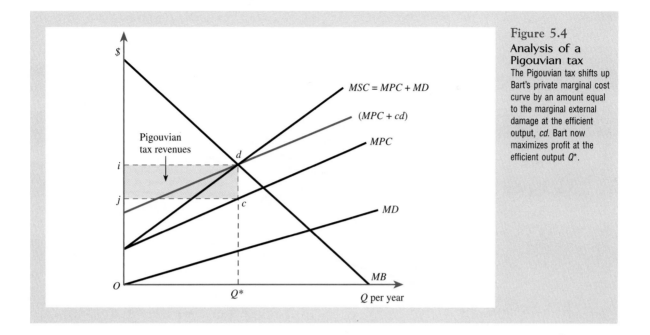

Figure 5.4
Analysis of a Pigouvian tax
The Pigouvian tax shifts up Bart's private marginal cost curve by an amount equal to the marginal external damage at the efficient output, *cd*. Bart now maximizes profit at the efficient output Q^*.

lead those who fish to ignore the costs they impose on Bart's production. The result is an inefficiently large amount of fishing done in the river. The key point is that compensation to the victim of the pollution is not necessary to achieve efficiency, and indeed will likely lead to inefficiency.

Practical problems arise in implementing a Pigouvian tax system. In light of the previously mentioned difficulties in estimating the marginal damage function, finding the correct tax rate is bound to be hard. Still, sensible compromises can be made. Consider the externality of harmful emissions from automobiles. In theory, a tax based on the number of miles driven enhances efficiency. Even more efficient would be a tax on the number of miles driven that also varies by location and time of day, since the pollution is more harmful when emitted in populated areas and when emitted during times of high traffic congestion. But a per-mile tax that varies by time and place could be prohibitively expensive to administer. The government might instead levy a gasoline tax, even though it is not gasoline use per se that determines the size of the externality. The gasoline tax would not lead to the most efficient outcome, but it still might be a substantial improvement over the status quo.

Subsidies

Assuming a fixed number of polluting firms, the efficient level of production can be obtained by paying the polluter not to pollute. Although this notion may at first seem peculiar, it works much like the tax. This is because a subsidy for not polluting is simply another method of raising the polluter's effective production cost.

Suppose the government announces that it will pay Bart a subsidy of *cd* for each unit of output below Q_1 he does *not* produce. What will Bart do? In Figure 5.5, Bart's marginal benefit at output level Q_1 is the distance between *MB* and the horizontal axis, *ge*. The marginal cost of producing at Q_1 is the sum of the amount Bart pays for his inputs (which we read off the *MPC* curve) *and* the subsidy of *cd* that

Figure 5.5
Analysis of a Pigouvian subsidy
A Pigouvian subsidy for each unit Bart does *not* produce shifts up his private marginal cost curve by the amount of the per-unit subsidy, *cd*, and induces him to produce at the efficient level of output.

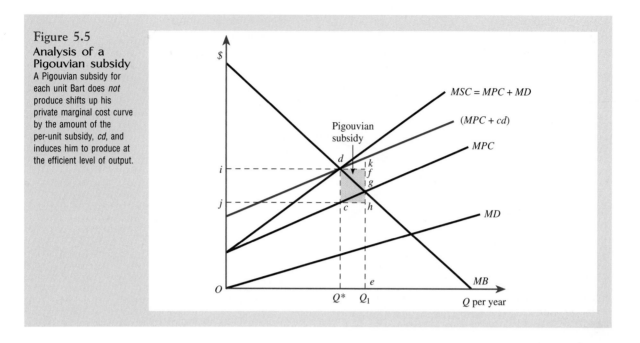

he forgoes by producing. Once again, then, the perceived marginal cost schedule is $MPC + cd$. At output Q_1, this is distance *ek* ($= eg + gk$).

But *ek* exceeds the marginal benefit, *ge*. As long as the marginal cost exceeds the marginal benefit at Q_1, it is not sensible for Bart to produce this last unit of output. Instead, he should forgo its production and accept the subsidy. The same line of reasoning indicates that Bart does not produce any output in excess of Q^*. At all output levels to the right of Q^*, the sum of the marginal private cost and the subsidy exceeds the marginal benefit. On the other hand, at all points to the left of Q^*, it is worthwhile for Bart to produce even though he has to give up the subsidy. For these output levels, the total opportunity cost, $MPC + cd$, is less than the marginal benefit. Hence, the subsidy induces Bart to produce just to Q^*, the efficient output.[6]

The distributional consequences of the tax and subsidy schemes differ dramatically. Instead of having to pay the tax of *ijcd*, Bart receives a payment equal to the number of units of forgone production, *ch*, times the subsidy per unit, *cd*, which equals rectangle *dfhc* in Figure 5.5. That an efficient solution can be associated with different income distributions is no surprise. It is analogous to the result from Chapter 3—there are an infinite number of efficient allocations in the Edgeworth Box, each of which is associated with its own distribution of real income.

In addition to the problems associated with the Pigouvian tax scheme, the subsidy program has a few of its own. First, recall that the analysis of Figure 5.5 assumes

---

[6] In Figure 5.5, Q_1 is the baseline from which Bart's reduction in output is measured. In principle, any baseline to the right of Q^* would do. The choice of baseline does affect the $MPC + cd$ schedule in the figure. At any point to the right of the chosen baseline, the subsidy equals zero, which means that *cd* equals zero and the $MPC + cd$ schedule is the same as the MPC schedule. One potential problem with Piouvian subsidies is that firms might game the system by undertaking inefficient actions that increase their assigned baselines.

a fixed number of firms. The subsidy leads to higher profits, so in the long run, more firms may be induced to locate along the river. The subsidy may cause so many new firms to relocate on the river that total pollution actually increases.

Second, subsidies may be ethically undesirable. As Mishan [1971, p. 25] notes:

> It may be argued [that] the freedom to operate noisy vehicles, or pollutive plant, does incidentally damage the welfare of others, while the freedom desired by members of the public to live in clean and quiet surroundings does not, of itself, reduce the welfare of others. If such arguments can be sustained, there is a case . . . for making polluters legally liable.

▶ PUBLIC RESPONSES TO EXTERNALITIES: EMISSIONS FEES AND CAP-AND-TRADE PROGRAMS

The previous section demonstrated how a tax on each unit of Bart's output can lead to the socially efficient outcome. One problem with this approach is that it might not give Bart the proper incentives to search for ways to reduce pollution other than reducing output. Why should Bart install pollution control technology that reduces his emissions per unit of output if doing so won't change his tax bill?

One way to address this problem is to levy a Pigouvian tax on each unit of emissions rather than on each unit of output. This tax is called an **emissions fee.** To examine such a tax, consider Figure 5.6, which shows Bart's annual level of pollution reduction on the horizontal axis. In this diagram the curve labeled *MSB* shows the marginal social benefit to Lisa of each unit of pollution Bart reduces. In other words, *MSB* shows the fall in Lisa's costs for each unit reduction in Bart's pollution. This curve is drawn downward sloping, reflecting our assumption that Lisa becomes

emissions fee

A tax levied on each unit of pollution.

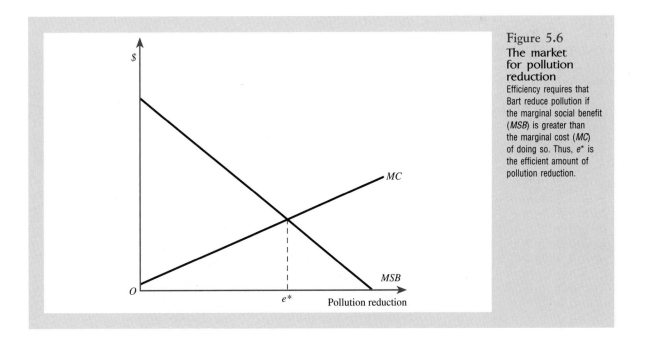

Figure 5.6
The market for pollution reduction
Efficiency requires that Bart reduce pollution if the marginal social benefit (*MSB*) is greater than the marginal cost (*MC*) of doing so. Thus, *e** is the efficient amount of pollution reduction.

worse off at an increasing rate for each additional unit of pollution. The curve labeled *MC* shows the marginal cost to Bart of reducing each unit of pollution. Bart's costs for reducing pollution can stem from reducing output, shifting to cleaner inputs, or installing a new technology to control pollution. We assume this curve is upward sloping, suggesting that the cost to Bart of reducing pollution increases at an increasing rate.

If Coasian bargaining does not occur and the government does not intervene, then Bart has no incentive to reduce pollution and will be at point *O*. However, the efficient outcome is where the marginal cost to Bart of cutting pollution equals the marginal benefit to Lisa of the pollution reduction, which occurs at point *e**. At any point to the left of *e**, the benefit of further pollution reduction outweighs the cost, so more reduction improves efficiency. At any point to the right of *e**, the benefit of the last unit of pollution reduced is not worth the cost of doing so, so less reduction improves efficiency.

What can the government do to attain *e**, the efficient amount of pollution reduction? We will examine three different approaches: emissions fee, cap-and-trade, and command-and-control regulation.

Emissions Fee

An emissions fee works much the same way as the tax we considered earlier. The only difference is that in this case a tax is levied on each unit of pollution rather than on each unit of output. Figure 5.7 replicates the curves from Figure 5.6. Recall that with no government intervention, Bart does not reduce emissions, so he is at point *O*. Now assume that the government levies an emissions fee that charges *f** for each unit of pollution, where *f** is the marginal social benefit of pollution reduction at the efficient level *e**. How does Bart respond?

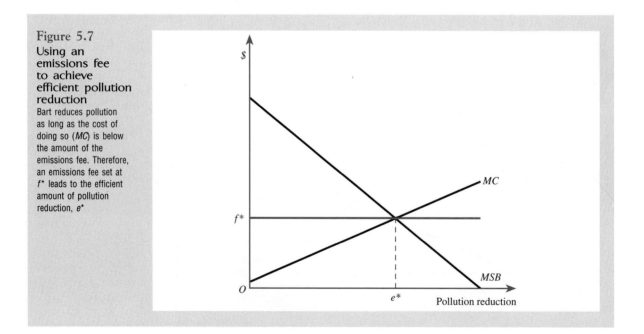

Figure 5.7

Using an emissions fee to achieve efficient pollution reduction

Bart reduces pollution as long as the cost of doing so (*MC*) is below the amount of the emissions fee. Therefore, an emissions fee set at *f** leads to the efficient amount of pollution reduction, *e**

Figure 5.8 Uniform pollution reductions across polluters are not cost effective
If each polluter cuts his pollution by 50 units, Bart's marginal cost is lower than Homer's. Therefore, requiring Bart to reduce more and Homer to reduce less achieves the same reduction goal at a lower total cost. The cost of cutting a given amount of pollution is minimized when the marginal costs of reducing are equal across all polluters.

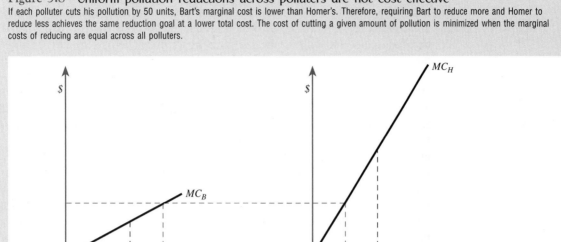

Bart incurs a cost of *MC* for each unit he reduces emissions. However, with the emissions fee in place, his tax bill goes down by *f** for each unit of pollution he cuts. If the amount he saves in taxes per unit exceeds the cost of reducing pollution by another unit, Bart pollutes less. Algebraically, if $f^* > MC$, he reduces pollution. Figure 5.7 indicates that this condition holds at all points to the left of *e**, so Bart will cut back on polluting until the efficient point. He won't reduce pollution further because the marginal cost of doing so exceeds his reduction in taxes.

This example demonstrates that the government can achieve the desired amount of pollution reduction with an emissions fee. Of course, the government could have obtained the same outcome simply by requiring Bart to cut his pollution by *e**. However, the emissions fee has some distinct advantages when there is more than one polluter.

Let's assume that, in addition to Bart, Homer also pollutes the river in which Lisa fishes. Assume also that it is more costly for Homer to reduce pollution than it is for Bart, so his marginal cost curve is higher. Figure 5.8 shows the marginal cost curves for both Bart (labeled MC_B) and for Homer (labeled MC_H). Suppose that initially they each emit 90 units of pollution per year and that the government has estimated that the efficient amount of pollution reduction is 100 units per year between the two of them. That is, total pollution needs to be reduced from 180 to 80 units per year.

How should this reduction in pollution be allocated between Bart and Homer? One idea is for the government to require each of them to reduce pollution by 50 units per year (meaning each is allowed to pollute 40 rather than 90 units per year). While this would achieve the desired reduction, it would do so at a higher cost than is necessary. To see why, notice in Figure 5.8 that the marginal cost to Homer of reducing the 50th unit is higher than the marginal cost to Bart of reducing the 50th unit (that is, $MC_H > MC_B$). Suppose instead we required Bart to reduce one more unit and allowed Homer to reduce one fewer unit. The total emissions reduction would still be 100 units. However, because the savings to Homer outweighs the increase in cost to Bart, this shift would reduce the overall cost of achieving the 100-unit reduction. As long as the marginal costs differ across the two polluters, one can redistribute the burden so that total costs are reduced. In other words, *the total cost of emissions reduction is minimized only when the marginal costs are equal across all polluters.* An outcome is called **cost effective** if it is achieved at the lowest cost possible. In Figure 5.8, the cost-effective means of achieving the 100-unit reduction is for Bart to cut his pollution by 75 units and for Homer to reduce his by 25 units.

Some might find the cost-effective outcome inequitable because it requires different levels of responsibility for pollution reduction. After all, why should Homer have a lower burden just because he finds it expensive to reduce pollution? However, with an emissions fee it is possible to achieve the cost-effective outcome *and* reward those who reduce more pollution. To see how, consider Figure 5.9, which replicates the curves from Figure 5.8. Now consider an emissions fee set at f'. For simplicity, let's assume that f' corresponds to a fee of $50 per unit of pollution. Recall that with an emissions fee, a polluter reduces emissions if the tax savings exceeds the marginal cost of cutting pollution (that is, if $f' > MC$). With this emissions fee, Bart reduces 75 units and Homer reduces 25 units, which is the cost-effective result because at this allocation the marginal costs are equal. From an equity standpoint, Homer is not being rewarded because he has to pay $50 for each unit of pollution he continues to produce. After cutting his pollution by 25 units, Homer still pollutes 65 units annually and must therefore pay annual taxes equal to $3,250 (= $50 × 65). Because Bart reduces his pollution by 75 units, his annual tax liability is only $750 (= $50 × 15). In short, the firm that cuts back pollution less isn't really getting away with anything because it has a larger tax liability than if it were to cut back more.

cost effective

A policy that achieves a given outcome at the lowest cost possible.

Figure 5.9   An emissions fee is cost effective
An emissions fee induces each polluter to reduce pollution up to the point where the marginal cost of reducing equals the level of the fee. This results in equal marginal costs across polluters, which is cost effective.

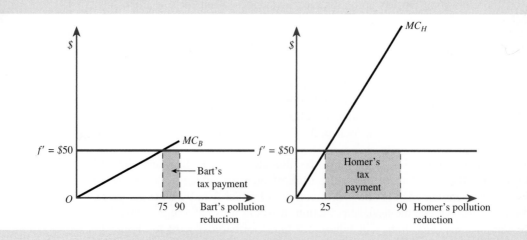

The key advantage of an emissions fee is that it achieves pollution reduction at the lowest possible cost. Notice in Figure 5.9 that for *any* emissions fee, the marginal cost of reduction is the same for Bart and Homer (that is, $MC_B = MC_H$), so we obtain a cost-effective outcome. To be sure, a fee higher than \$50 would lead to more than a 100-unit reduction per year and a fee lower than \$50 would lead to less than a 100-unit annual reduction. But whatever the reduction, the fee achieves it at the lowest cost possible.

Although we have been discussing emissions fees in the context of pollution, it is equally relevant for dealing with other kinds of externalities. We now discuss one such case.

POLICY PERSPECTIVE

Congestion Pricing

On crowded roads and highways, every motorist imposes costs on other motorists by increasing congestion. Parry, Walls, and Harrington [2007] estimate that the external costs of driving are approximately 20 cents per mile driven. However, no one is forced to take these costs into account, so this situation is a classic externality. Efficiency could be enhanced by an "emissions fee" on driving equal to the marginal congestion costs (wasted gasoline, time, and so on) imposed on other drivers. In order to be efficient, the fee would be adjusted for time and place. Motorists driving through city rush-hour traffic would pay more than those driving in rural settings or in off-peak hours. A policy of **congestion pricing** would internalize these costs, resulting in a substantial welfare gain for the United States.

Some cities have experimented with congestion pricing. Singapore, for example, has electronic tolls that vary according to the time of day. Trondheim, Norway, imposes charges for access to the city center, with the charges varying by the time of day. Single drivers in San Diego can use high-occupation-vehicle lanes for a price that depends on how congested the highway is at the moment.

London recently implemented a form of congestion pricing to deal with its notorious traffic problem. In 2003, the city began levying a fee of £5 (about \$9) for the privilege of driving into the center of the city during peak hours. Compliance is monitored by video cameras that identify the license plates of drivers who fail to pay the fee. Such drivers are then charged a substantial fine. Congestion pricing has reduced the number of vehicles on London streets by approximately 16 percent [Transport for London, 2007].

congestion pricing

A tax levied on driving equal to the marginal congestion costs imposed on other drivers.

Cap-and-Trade

An alternative policy to an emissions fee is for the government to require Bart and Homer to submit one government-issued permit for each unit of pollution they emit. In terms of our example, in order to cut pollution from 180 units down to 80 units, the government would issue 80 permits each year. The level of pollution reduction that Bart and Homer achieve individually depends strictly on the number of permits they each own. What's the best way to allocate the permits between Bart

Figure 5.10   A cap-and-trade system is cost effective
Bart receives all 80 permits, but there is scope for a bargain between Homer and Bart. Bart sells permits to Homer until their marginal costs are equal, which is cost effective.

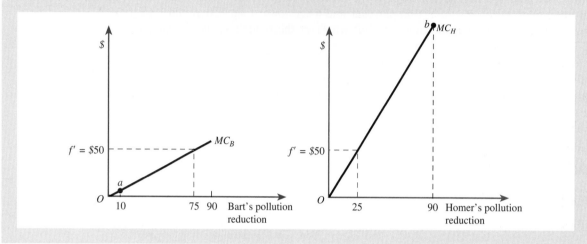

and Homer? From an efficiency standpoint, the initial allocation of permits among the polluters does not matter at all.[7] Given our discussion of the Coase Theorem, this should come as no surprise. By allocating permits the government establishes property rights for the air; the assignment of property rights has distributional, not efficiency, consequences. As long as Bart and Homer are allowed to trade the permits with each other, the ultimate outcome is cost effective. A system of tradable pollution permits is known as **cap-and-trade.**

To see why cap-and-trade is cost effective regardless of the initial allocation of permits, consider Figure 5.10, which replicates the marginal cost curves from Figure 5.8. For simplicity, let's assume that Bart receives all 80 permits issued by the government. Because Bart was originally emitting 90 units each year, with 80 permits he now has to reduce emissions by only 10 units, which puts him at point a on Figure 5.10. On the other hand, because Homer doesn't have any permits, he must eliminate his pollution. This amounts to a reduction of 90 units, which puts him at point b on Figure 5.10. At this outcome, MC_H far exceeds MC_B, so total costs are much higher than they need be—the allocation is not cost effective.

How does trading change this outcome? If Bart sold one of his permits to Homer, Bart would have to reduce another unit of pollution. Therefore, he would only sell a permit if the amount he received for it at least covered his cost of reducing the additional unit of pollution. By buying a permit, Homer would be able to pollute one more unit. Therefore, he would only buy a permit if it cost less than the savings he obtained from polluting one more unit. Because the marginal cost to Bart at point a is less than the marginal cost to Homer at point b, there is scope for a bargain, and Bart sells Homer one of his permits. By the same logic, Bart continues to sell permits to Homer until $MC_B = MC_H$. But recall that $MC_B = MC_H$ defines the cost-effective outcome. We have shown, then, that cap-and-trade is a cost-effective policy.

cap-and-trade

A policy of granting permits to pollute, with the number of permits set at the desired pollution level, and allowing polluters to trade the permits.

---

[7] This only holds if the market for permits is a competitive market (see Hahn [1984]).

Note also that at this point, the market price for the permits is f' (= \$50), which is the same as the emissions fee discussed earlier.

Notice that the same pollution reduction would occur no matter how the government initially allocated the permits between Bart and Homer. Of course, the allocation of permits does affect income distribution, as each of them would like to be sellers of permits rather than buyers of permits. This should come as no surprise—according to the Second Welfare Theorem from Chapter 3, a given efficient outcome can arise from a variety of initial income distributions.

Emissions fees and cap-and-trade systems are symmetrical policies. In our example, an emissions fee set at f' achieves the same pollution reduction from Bart and Homer as a cap-and-trade program in which the government issues 80 permits each year. More generally, for every emissions fee, in theory there is a cap-and-trade system that achieves just the same outcome, and vice versa. However, in practice, there are some differences in how the two systems perform.

Emissions Fee versus Cap-and-Trade

We now examine several practical differences between an emissions fee and a cap-and-trade system.[8]

Responsiveness to Inflation   Recall our earlier example in which the government established an emissions fee set at \$50 per unit of pollution. Suppose that the economy is experiencing inflation. If the fee is not adjusted for changes in the price level each year, then in real terms, its cost to Bart and Homer falls over time. In other words, inflation lowers the real emissions fee, which leads to less pollution reduction. In contrast, the cap-and-trade system leads to the same amount of pollution regardless of inflation—with an annual cap of 80 units of pollution, that's the amount of pollution. True, the emissions fee could yield the same result if its level were adjusted each year for inflation. The advantage of cap-and-trade is that no legislative or regulatory action is needed; the adjustment takes place automatically.

Responsiveness to Cost Changes   The marginal cost of reducing pollution is likely to change from year to year. The costs might increase if, for example, the demand for the goods being made by the polluting firms increases, thus increasing the opportunity cost of scaling back production. On the other hand, the costs might decrease if firms learn to use their inputs more efficiently. To analyze the consequences of cost changes, suppose that a \$50 emissions fee is levied on Bart and Homer. Now assume that both Bart's and Homer's marginal costs happen to increase after the imposition of the emissions fee. According to Figure 5.9, with a \$50 emissions fee, an increase in the marginal cost curves leads to less pollution reduction (or more pollution). Note that under the emissions fee, Bart and Homer are guaranteed to never pay more than \$50 to reduce a unit of pollution. No matter how high the cost of reduction gets, they can always opt to pay \$50 per unit of pollution instead of reducing another unit of pollution. With the emissions fee, pollution reduction decreases as marginal costs increase.

---

[8] The list is not exhaustive. For more details, see Gayer and Horowitz [2006].

Assume instead that the government institutes a cap-and-trade program. If Bart's and Homer's marginal costs increase, Figure 5.10 tells us that the level of pollution reduction stays the same. As mentioned earlier, a cap-and-trade system sets a strict limit on pollution, which does not vary as economic conditions change. However, unlike the emissions fee, the cost of achieving the pollution reduction target can become very high as marginal costs increase. As the marginal cost curves shift up, the market price for permits increases, thus imposing higher costs on Bart and Homer. With cap-and-trade, pollution reduction is constant as marginal costs increase.

In sum, an emissions fee limits the cost of reducing pollution but leads to changes in emissions as economic circumstances change, whereas a cap-and-trade system limits the amount of emissions but leads to changes in the cost of reducing pollution as the economy changes. Neither system automatically leads to an efficient outcome when the costs of pollution reductions change.

One interesting option is to combine the cap-and-trade system with the emissions fee. In this hybrid approach, the government sets up a cap-and-trade system that fixes the amount of allowable pollution. However, the government also makes it known that it will sell as many additional permits as is demanded at a preestablished price. This price, known as the **safety valve price,** can be set rather high so it will only be used if the cost of pollution reduction is much higher than expected. In effect, the safety valve relaxes the pollution cap if the marginal cost of reduction increases beyond a level that policymakers deem acceptable.

safety valve price

Within a cap-and-trade system, a price set by government at which polluters can purchase additional permits beyond the cap.

Responsiveness to Uncertainty   The costs of addressing many important environmental problems are highly uncertain. When such uncertainty exists, an emissions fee and a cap-and-trade program can lead to different results.[9]

For simplicity, let's consider an example with only one polluter. The government is deciding between instituting an emissions fee and a cap-and-trade system. We will consider two cases: one in which the marginal social benefit schedule of reducing pollution is inelastic and one in which it is elastic. With an inelastic schedule, the first units of pollution reduction are highly valuable, but as more reductions occur, their incremental benefit falls off rapidly. With an elastic schedule, the marginal value of each unit of pollution reduction remains fairly constant.

Inelastic Marginal Social Benefit Schedule Figure 5.11 shows an inelastic marginal social benefits schedule. Suppose now that the government is uncertain about the marginal cost of reducing this pollutant. The government's best guess is that the marginal cost schedule is MC^*. However, it could be as high as MC'.

Relying on its best-guess estimate of MC^*, if the government were to use a cap-and-trade system, it would issue enough permits to achieve a reduction of e^*. If MC^* turns out to represent the true costs, then this outcome is efficient. Recall that with a cap-and-trade system, the level of pollution (and thus pollution reduction) is fixed no matter what happens to costs. However, if it turns out that the true marginal cost curve is MC', then the efficient outcome is e', so the cap-and-trade leads to too much pollution reduction (that is, $e^* > e'$). Notice that while the cap-and-trade outcome is inefficient if costs are higher than anticipated, it is not too bad from an efficiency standpoint, because e^* is fairly close to e'.

---

[9] This issue was first explored by Weitzman [1974].

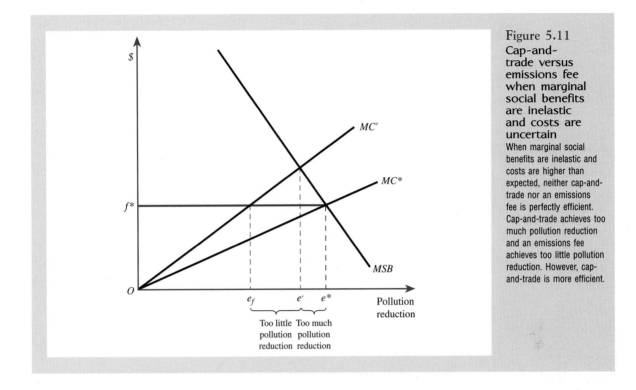

Figure 5.11
Cap-and-trade versus emissions fee when marginal social benefits are inelastic and costs are uncertain
When marginal social benefits are inelastic and costs are higher than expected, neither cap-and-trade nor an emissions fee is perfectly efficient. Cap-and-trade achieves too much pollution reduction and an emissions fee achieves too little pollution reduction. However, cap-and-trade is more efficient.

What happens if the government uses an emissions fee under these circumstances? Consider again Figure 5.11. Relying on its best-guess estimate of MC^*, the government would set the fee at f^* in order to achieve a reduction of e^*. As before, if MC^* turns out to represent the true costs, then this outcome is efficient. Recall that with an emissions fee, the level of pollution (and thus pollution reduction) changes as the cost curves change. If it turns out that the true marginal cost curve is MC', then the emissions fee leads to a reduction of e_f, whereas e' is the efficient outcome.

Importantly, while the cap-and-trade outcome in Figure 5.11 was only mildly inefficient if the costs were higher than expected, the emissions fee outcome is highly inefficient because e_f is much smaller than e'. We conclude that *a cap-and-trade system is preferable to an emissions fee when marginal social benefits are inelastic and costs are uncertain.* Intuitively, when marginal social benefits are inelastic, a change in cost has very little effect on the optimal amount of pollution reduction. Therefore, a cap-and-trade system (which fixes the amount of allowable pollution) won't deviate much from the new efficient level. While this analysis has focused on the case where the marginal costs of pollution reduction are higher than expected, similar results can be derived when they are lower than expected. (See Discussion Question 14 at the end of the chapter.)

Elastic Marginal Social Benefit Schedule Figure 5.12 replicates the marginal cost curves from Figure 5.11. However, in this diagram the marginal social benefits of pollution reduction are assumed to be relatively elastic. Just as in the previous example, if the government were to use a cap-and-trade system, it would issue enough permits to achieve a reduction of e^*. If it turns out that the true marginal cost curve

Figure 5.12
Cap-and-trade versus emissions fee when marginal social benefits are elastic and costs are uncertain
When marginal social benefits are elastic and costs are higher than expected, neither cap-and-trade nor an emissions fee is perfectly efficient. Cap-and-trade achieves too much pollution reduction, and an emissions fee achieves too little pollution reduction. However, an emissions fee is more efficient.

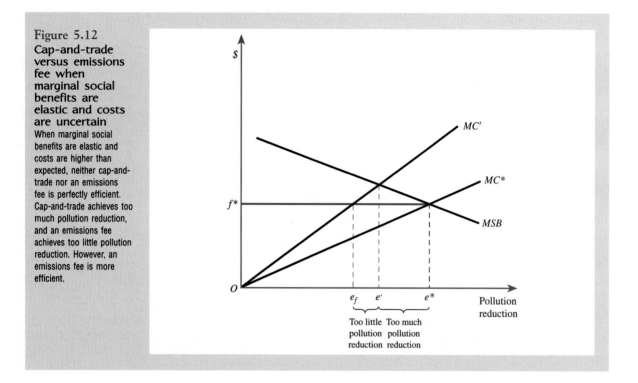

is MC', then the efficient outcome is at e', so the cap-and-trade leads to too much pollution reduction (that is, $e^* > e'$).

Figure 5.12 also shows the consequences of an emissions fee. As before, the government would set the fee at f^* in order to reduce emissions by e^*. If MC^* turns out to represent the true costs, then this outcome is efficient. If it turns out that the true marginal cost curve is MC', then the emissions fee leads to a reduction of e_f, whereas e' is the efficient outcome. However, unlike the example with inelastic marginal social benefits, in this case e_f is closer to the efficient outcome than is e^*, the reduction achieved by the cap-and-trade. We conclude that *an emissions fee is preferable to a cap-and-trade system when marginal social benefits are elastic and costs are uncertain.* Intuitively, when marginal social benefits are elastic, a change in cost has a big effect on the optimal amount of pollution reduction. Therefore, a cap-and-trade system (which fixes the amount of allowable pollution) deviates substantially from the new efficient level.

Where does all of this leave us? In a world of uncertainty, we cannot know for sure whether emissions fees or cap-and-trade systems are more efficient. Among other things, it depends on how fast the marginal social benefits of reducing pollution fall with the amount of cleanup. This brings us back to a recurring theme in this chapter. Formulating sensible environmental policy requires an interdisciplinary effort—information from a variety of fields is needed to determine various technical relationships, including the shape of the marginal social benefit schedule. The tools of economics then allow us to use this information to find efficient solutions.

Distributional Effects   Even in the certainty case when cap-and-trade and emissions fees are equivalent from an efficiency standpoint, they can have different distributional consequences. With an emissions fee, polluters pay taxes for each unit of pollution and the revenue goes to the government. With a cap-and-trade system, if the permits are allocated directly to the polluters for free, then the government receives no revenue. On the other hand, a cap-and-trade system can generate government revenues if the permits are sold directly by the government to polluters rather than allocated for free.

POLICY PERSPECTIVE

Addressing Climate Change

The most prominent externality issue on the public policy agenda is climate change. Many economic activities release greenhouse gases—such as carbon dioxide, nitrous oxide, and methane—that trap solar energy within the earth's atmosphere. The extra heat warms the climate, creating economic, health, and ecological impacts. Because our climate is a complex system and the impacts are global, it is difficult to estimate precisely the magnitude of the contribution of greenhouse gas emissions on the climate. An international panel of scientists predicts an increase in global temperature of 1.1 to 6.3 degrees Celsius by 2100 [Intergovernmental Panel on Climate Change, 2007]. The precise magnitudes of the associated economic, health, and ecological effects are also difficult to know.

Although the issues involved in assessing the causes and consequences of climate change are complicated, the basic framework developed in this chapter provides a sensible guide for policy: reduce greenhouse gas emissions up to the point that the marginal benefits equal the marginal costs. Using this framework, one economist estimates that the optimal climate policy would reduce global greenhouse gas emissions 15 percent by 2015, 25 percent by 2050, and 45 percent by 2100. These emission levels correspond to an optimal emissions fee (in 2005 dollars) per ton of carbon of approximately $42 in 2015, $98 in 2050, and $215 in 2100 [Nordhaus, 2008].

As our theory indicates, the optimal reductions can be achieved through either an emissions fee (that is, a tax on carbon emissions) or a cap-and-trade program. Which approach is more efficient? Most research suggests that the marginal social benefits of emission reductions are more elastic than the marginal costs. In light of the uncertainty surrounding the costs of reducing emissions, this suggests that a carbon tax that establishes a fixed annual price is more efficient than a cap that establishes a fixed annual emissions level [Congressional Budget Office, 2008b]. That said, the efficiency of a cap-and-trade can be enhanced if it includes certain flexibility features, such as allowing polluters to bank unused permits for future use or borrow future permits for current use. Also, including a safety valve increases the efficiency of a cap-and-trade program by making it more like a carbon tax.

Command-and-Control Regulation

Emissions fees and cap-and-trade systems are called **incentive-based regulations** because they provide polluters with market incentives to reduce pollution. Basically, each approach increases the opportunity cost of polluting, forcing polluters to take

incentive-based regulations

Policies that provide polluters with financial incentives to reduce pollution.

into account the marginal external damages associated with their behavior. Incentive-based regulations allow polluters great flexibility in how to reduce their emissions. Bart might find it cheaper to reduce pollution by cutting his output, while Homer might find it costs less to buy a technology that reduces pollution. Both options are allowed under an incentive-based regulation, because the idea is to find the cheapest feasible way to reduce pollution. In addition to flexibility about how to reduce pollution, there is also flexibility about who should reduce pollution. For example, if the cost of reducing the marginal unit of pollution is cheaper for Bart than for Homer, under a cap-and-trade system Homer buys a permit from Bart. In effect, the built-in flexibility allows Homer to pay Bart to reduce pollution for him. Similarly, under an emissions fee, Bart reduces pollution more than Homer, who instead opts to pay more in taxes.

In contrast to these flexible approaches, the traditional approach to environmental regulation has relied on **command-and-control regulations.** Command-and-control regulations take a variety of forms, but they all are less flexible than incentive-based regulations. A **technology standard** is a command-and-control regulation that requires polluters to install a certain technology to clean up their emissions. Polluters are violating the law if they reduce pollution through any other means, no matter how effective these other means might be. For example, legislation passed several years ago required all new power plants to install "scrubbers" rather than allow them to clean up emissions by switching to cleaner fuels. Unlike incentive-based regulation, a technology standard provides firms no incentive to look for cheaper ways to reduce pollution. Why invest in developing a new cleanup technology when the law won't allow you to use it? Therefore, technology standards are unlikely to be cost effective.

A **performance standard** is a type of command-and-control regulation that sets an emissions goal for each polluter. The polluter frequently has the flexibility to meet this standard in any way it chooses, so this type of regulation is more cost effective than a technology standard. However, because the performance standard sets a fixed emissions goal for each individual firm, the burden of reducing pollution cannot be shifted to firms that can achieve it more cheaply. As a result, performance standards are unlikely to be cost effective.

Several empirical studies have compared the costs of using cost-effective versus command-and-control approaches to obtaining a given reduction in pollution. The particular results depend on the type of pollution being considered and the site of the pollution. One summary of these findings shows that command-and-control regulations are 1.07 to 22 times more expensive than the cost-effective approach [*Economic Report of the President, 2003*].

A good example of an inefficient command-and-control approach is the federal government's corporate average fuel economy (CAFE) standards for all new passenger vehicles. These standards dictate the average gasoline mileage that vehicle fleets must attain (27.5 miles per gallon for cars and 22.2 miles per gallon for light trucks such as SUVs). The goal of the policy is to reduce gasoline consumption. CAFE standards have limited flexibility because manufacturers cannot shift the burden among each other to lower overall cost. An alternative approach to reducing gasoline consumption would be to levy a tax on gasoline, which is a form of emissions fee. The Congressional Budget Office compared an increase in CAFE standards to an increase in the gasoline tax that would achieve the same reduction in gasoline consumption and found that CAFE costs about $700 million more per year [Congressional Budget Office, 2004b].

---

command-and-control regulations

Policies that require a given amount of pollution reduction with limited or no flexibility with respect to how it may be achieved.

technology standard

A type of command-and-control regulation that requires firms to use a particular technology to reduce their pollution.

performance standard

A command-and-control regulation that sets an emissions goal for each individual polluter and allows some flexibility in meeting the goal.

Is Command-and-Control Ever Better?   A command-and-control approach is preferable to an incentive-based approach under certain conditions. The functioning of an incentive-based approach is possible only if the emissions can be monitored. If it is impossible or very expensive to monitor emissions, then the government won't be able to charge a per-unit emissions fee or establish whether a polluter has enough permits to cover its emissions. Some forms of pollution are relatively easy to monitor, such as emissions of sulfur dioxide from power plants. It is more difficult to keep track of other forms, such as agricultural runoff of chemicals, sediment, and nutrients. In such cases, a technology standard might be more efficient, because it is relatively easy to monitor whether a firm has installed the technology.

Another potential problem with incentive-based regulations is that they can lead to high concentrations of pollution in certain local areas. Because an incentive-based system limits total emissions from all sources, it is possible that there will be higher emissions in some areas than others. If emissions concentrate in a localized area, they might cause much higher damages than if they were more diffuse. Localized concentrations of emissions are known as **hot spots.** A command-and-control standard can avoid hot spots by restricting emissions from each individual pollution source.[10]

hot spots

Localized concentrations of emissions.

▶ THE US RESPONSE

How do real-world responses to externality problems compare to the solutions suggested by theory? In the case of air pollution, the main federal law is the Clean Air Act, which has been amended a number of times.[11] In the 1970 Amendments to the Clean Air Act, Congress charged the Environmental Protection Agency (EPA) with establishing national air quality standards. Congress mandated that the standards were to be uniform across the country and to be set at a level that would "provide an adequate margin of safety." Neither of these conditions is based on concerns with efficiency. Efficient policy would allow standards to vary geographically as costs and benefits vary and would attempt to set standards at the level that maximizes net benefits. In contrast, the courts have ruled that the law prohibits the EPA from even considering costs in setting the standards.

The major environmental regulations of the 1970s relied on the command-and-control approach. For example, the 1970 Amendments to the Clean Air Act established technology standards and performance standards for new sources of air pollution and mandated emission standards for cars, trucks, and buses. The requirement to ignore costs when setting standards and the reliance on command-and-control regulations has undoubtedly increased the costs of achieving our environmental goals.

Has clean air legislation accomplished its goals? The six main air pollutants regulated under the Clean Air Act have all decreased since 1970. However, one must be cautious in attributing such decreases entirely to environmental regulation. Perhaps, for example, the improvement was due in part to technological advances that allow firms to use their inputs more efficiently, thus generating less pollution. Indeed, Goklany [1999] provides evidence that air pollution in the US was declining well before the Clean Air Act. Nonetheless, a variety of analyses indicate that the Clean

---

[10] An incentive-based approach can also address hot spots. For example, an emissions fee can charge different tax levels depending on the source of the pollution. Similarly, a cap-and-trade system can require some sources to "cash in" more permits per unit of emissions than other sources. Nonetheless, this does add complexity to the incentive-based approaches.

[11] Excellent summaries of the act's provisions are in Portney [2000].

Air Act has been instrumental in reducing pollution below levels that otherwise would have occurred [Freeman, 2002, p. 127]. As already stressed, though, this finding does not mean that the reductions in pollution were achieved in an efficient manner.

In certain contexts, the command-and-control approach has not only been inefficient, but also ineffectual. Why might this be the case? Baumol [1976] emphasizes how the efficacy of regulation depends on the vigilance of the regulator, that is:

> the promptness with which orders are issued, the severity of their provisions, the strength of the regulator's resistance to demands for modifications, his effectiveness in detecting and documenting violations, his vigor and success in prosecuting them, and the severity of the penalties imposed by the judicial mechanism [p. 445].

This is a tall order, especially considering the political pressures under which the regulator is likely to be acting. In contrast, emissions fees "depend not on the watchfulness of the regulator but on the reliable tenacity of the tax collector. They work by inviting the polluter to avoid his payments through the loophole deliberately left to him—the reduction of his emissions" [Baumol, 1976, p. 446].

In addition, the "or else" approach of regulation often backfires. The ultimate threat is to close the polluting facility. In many cases, however, such closure would create major dislocations among workers and/or consumers and is therefore politically difficult. The Texas state legislature once decided that complying with EPA rules for testing cars and trucks for excessive emissions would be too costly. The legislature simply defied the EPA's orders to set up a new system. In the same spirit, when a court in India ordered authorities in Delhi to replace its fleet of 10,000 buses that run on diesel fuel with cleaner natural gas buses, nothing happened. The city authorities simply were not willing to go up against the bus owners, who promised, among other things, to protest by a hunger strike to the death. Indeed, two years after the court's decision, Delhi continued licensing new diesel buses [Dugger, 2001, p. A3].

This is not to say command-and-control regulation is never useful. As discussed earlier, when pollutants are difficult to monitor, it might be the best solution. But in general, command-and-control is probably the source of much of the problems with environmental policy.

Progress with Incentive-based Approaches

Although the command-and-control approach has dominated US environmental policy, economists' arguments in favor of incentive-based approaches are gaining ground. In particular, several important cap-and-trade programs have been implemented. This section discusses one of them.

POLICY PERSPECTIVE

Cap-and-Trade for Sulfur Dioxide

Acid rain forms when sulfur oxides and nitrogen oxides emitted into the air react with water vapor to create acids. The Acid Rain Trading Program, created as part of the 1990 Amendments to the Clean Air Act, is the most notable US example of an incentive-based approach. It sets a national annual cap on sulfur dioxide emissions. All electric utilities (the main producers of sulfur dioxide) must have an "emissions allowance" for each ton of sulfur dioxide they emit into the atmosphere. The total number of allowances equals the cap. The allowances are initially distributed among existing electric-generating units for free, after which they can be bought and sold, just as in our theoretical model (Figure 5.10).[12] Currently, there are allowances for about 9 million tons per year [Burtraw, 2002, p. 140].

The trading market for the allowances is very active. The price per allowance ranges between $150 and $200. Interestingly, this is substantially below the price that was originally predicted, implying that hitting the target amount of sulfur dioxide emissions cost less than most people anticipated. Indeed, some estimates suggest that the program saves between $0.9 billion and $1.8 billion per year relative to the costs of a conventional regulatory approach [*Economic Report of the President, 2004*, p. 185]. Our theory predicts that cap-and-trade approaches provide financial incentives for firms to find new technologies for reducing pollution, and this prediction has been borne out. For example, some firms reduced their emissions by combining coals with various sulfur contents to attain intermediate results. Prior to the emissions trading program, such blending was not considered to be technologically practical, but the program gave firms incentives to figure out ways to make it work [Burtraw, 2002, p. 144]. In short, the sulfur dioxide emissions trading experiment has been a success.

Sulfur dioxide trading is widely seen as a success story. Nevertheless, incentive-based approaches are far from replacing command-and-control regulation for dealing with environmental issues. As the costs of traditional environmental programs continue to increase—it is estimated they already amount to more than 2 percent of GDP—the efficiency of incentive-based approaches may make them more attractive to policymakers.

▶ IMPLICATIONS FOR INCOME DISTRIBUTION

Our main focus so far has been on the efficiency aspects of externalities. Welfare economics indicates that we must also take distributional considerations into account. However, attempts to assess the distributional implications of environmental improvement raise a number of difficult questions.

Who Benefits?

In our simple model, the distribution of benefits is a trivial issue because there is only one type of pollution and one pollution victim. In reality, individuals suffer differently from various externalities. Some evidence suggests that poor neighborhoods tend to have more exposure to air pollution than high-income neighborhoods [Gayer, 2000]. If this is true, lowering the level of air pollution might make the

---

[12] The program sets aside 2.8 percent of allowances each year that are auctioned off. The auction revenue is transferred back pro rata to the electric utilities from which the auction pool was created.

distribution of real income more equal, other things being the same. On the other hand, the benefits of environmental programs that improve recreational areas such as national parks probably benefit mainly high-income families, who tend to be their main users.

Even knowing who suffers from some externality does not tell us how much they value removing it. Suppose a high-income family would be willing to pay more for a given improvement in air quality than a low-income family. Then even if a cleanup program reduces more of the *physical* amount of pollution for low- than for high-income families, in *dollar* terms the program can end up favoring those with high incomes.

Who Bears the Cost?

Suppose that large numbers of polluting firms are induced to reduce output by government policy. As these firms contract, the demand for the inputs they employ falls, making the owners of these inputs worse off.[13] Some of the polluters' former workers may suffer unemployment in the short run and be forced to work at lower wages in the long run. If these workers have low incomes, environmental cleanup increases income inequality.

The extent to which the poor bear the costs of environmental protection is a source of bitter controversy. Critics of environmentalism argue that efforts to prevent factories from operating in inner cities have "worsened the economic woes of the mostly poor" people who live there [Ross, 1999, p. A26]. Environmentalists label such assertions "job blackmail" and believe there is no good evidence that the poor are really hurt.

Another consideration is that if polluting firms are forced to take into account marginal social costs, their products tend to become more expensive. From an efficiency point of view, this is entirely desirable, because otherwise prices give incorrect signals concerning full resource costs. Nevertheless, buyers of these commodities are generally made worse off. If the commodities so affected are consumed primarily by high-income groups, the distribution of real income becomes more equal. Thus, to assess the distributional implications of reducing pollution, we also need to know the demand patterns of the goods produced by polluting companies.

It is obviously a formidable task to determine the distribution of the costs of pollution control. In one study, Hassett, Mathur, and Metcalf [2007] find that a carbon tax would place a higher proportional burden on lower-income households. However, the relative burden on low earners is greatly reduced when considering households' lifetime (rather than annual) income. This finding alleviates, but does not eliminate, the concern that a carbon tax or a cap-and-trade climate policy would place a disproportionate burden on low earners.

▶ POSITIVE EXTERNALITIES

Most of the focus so far has been on negative externalities. We did observe, however, that spillover effects could also be positive. The analysis of this case is symmetrical. Suppose that when a firm does research and development (R&D), the marginal private

---

[13] More specifically, under certain conditions, those inputs used relatively intensively in the production of the polluting good fall in price. See Chapter 14 under "General Equilibrium Models."

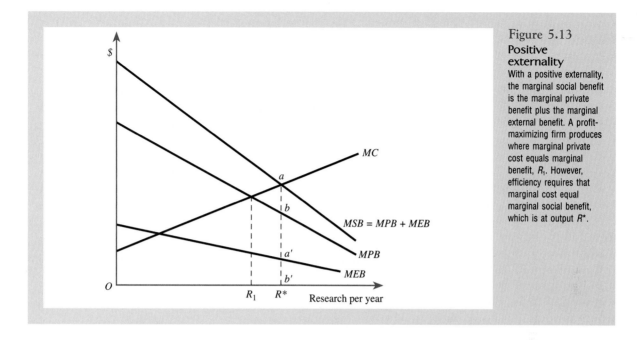

Figure 5.13
Positive externality
With a positive externality, the marginal social benefit is the marginal private benefit plus the marginal external benefit. A profit-maximizing firm produces where marginal private cost equals marginal benefit, R_1. However, efficiency requires that marginal cost equal marginal social benefit, which is at output R^*.

benefit (*MPB*) and marginal cost (*MC*) schedules are as depicted in Figure 5.13. The firm chooses R&D level R_1, where $MC = MPB$. Assume further that the firm's R&D enables other firms to produce their outputs more cheaply, but that these firms do not have to pay for using scientific results because they become part of general knowledge.[14] In Figure 5.13, the marginal benefit to other firms of each quantity of research is denoted *MEB* (for marginal external benefit). The marginal *social* benefit of research is the sum of *MPB* and *MEB*, and is denoted *MSB*.

Efficiency requires the equality of marginal cost and marginal *social* benefit, which occurs at R^*. Hence, R&D is underprovided. Just as a negative externality can be corrected by a Pigouvian tax, a positive externality can be corrected by a Pigouvian subsidy. Specifically, if the R&D-conducting firm is given a subsidy equal to the marginal external benefit at the optimum—distance *ab* in Figure 5.13—it will produce efficiently.[15] The lesson is clear: When an individual or firm produces positive externalities, the market underprovides the activity or good, but an appropriate subsidy can remedy the situation. Of course, all the difficulties in measuring the quantity and value of the externality still remain. Some research concludes that the private rate of return to R&D is about 10 percent, while the social rate of return is about 50 percent. If these figures are correct, then the positive externalities associated with R&D are substantial.

A Cautionary Note

Many people who have never heard the term *positive externality* nevertheless have a good intuitive grasp of the concept and its policy implications. They understand that if they can convince the government their activities create beneficial spillovers,

---

[14] Sometimes this type of situation can partially be avoided by patent laws. But in many cases, the results of pure research are not patentable, even though they may be used for commercial purposes.
[15] Note that by construction, $ab = a'b'$.

they may be able to dip into the treasury for a subsidy. Requests for such subsidies must be viewed cautiously for two reasons:

- One way or another, the subsidy has to come from resources extracted from taxpayers. Hence, every subsidy embodies a redistribution of income from taxpayers as a whole to the recipients. Even if the subsidy has good efficiency consequences, its distributional implications may not be desirable. This depends on the value judgments embodied in the social welfare function.
- The fact that an activity is beneficial per se does *not* mean that a subsidy is required for efficiency. A subsidy is appropriate only if the market does not allow those performing the activity to capture the full marginal return. For example, a brilliant surgeon who does much good for humanity creates no positive externality as long as the surgeon's salary reflects the incremental value of his or her services.

We next discuss these points in the context of public policy aimed at increasing homeownership rates. Some commentators have argued that these policies contributed to the housing and financial crisis of 2008 and 2009.

POLICY PERSPECTIVE

Owner-Occupied Housing

Through a variety of provisions in the US federal income tax code, owner-occupied housing receives a substantial subsidy. (These provisions are detailed in Chapter 17.) This subsidy is currently worth over $110 billion annually [Joint Committee on Taxation, 2008, pp. 51–52]. Can this subsidy be justified? Arguments usually boil down to an assertion that homeownership creates positive externalities. Homeowners take good care of their property and keep it clean, which makes their neighbors better off; hence, the externality. In addition, homeownership provides an individual with a stake in the nation. This increases social stability, another desirable spillover effect.

Careful maintenance of property certainly creates positive externalities, and homeowners are more likely than renters to take care of their property, to garden, and so on [Glaeser and Shapiro, 2003]. But is it homeownership as such that induces this desirable behavior? The beneficial side effects associated with homeownership might just as well be a consequence of the fact that the 66 percent of American families who are homeowners tend to have relatively high incomes. (The median income of homeowners is almost twice that of renters.) Neither is there any evidence that low ownership rates necessarily contribute to social instability. In Switzerland, a nation not known for its revolutionary tendencies, only about a third of the dwellings are owner occupied.

Of course, even if the subsidy does not contribute to correcting an inefficiency, it might be justifiable on equity grounds. But as just noted, homeowners tend to have higher incomes than renters. Thus, only if the distributional objective is to increase income inequality does a subsidy for homeownership make sense from this standpoint.

Summary

- An externality occurs when the activity of one person affects another person outside the market mechanism. Externalities may generally be traced to the absence of enforceable property rights.

- Externalities cause market price to diverge from social cost, bringing about an inefficient allocation of resources.

- The Coase Theorem indicates that private parties may bargain toward the efficient output if property rights are established. However, bargaining costs must be low and the source of the externality easily identified.

- A Pigouvian tax is a tax levied on pollution in an amount equal to the marginal social damage at the efficient level. Such a tax gives the producer a private incentive to pollute the efficient amount.

- A subsidy for pollution not produced can induce producers to pollute at the efficient level. However, subsidies can lead to too much production, are administratively difficult, and are regarded by some as ethically unappealing.

- An emissions fee (a tax levied on each unit of pollution) achieves a given amount of pollution reduction at the lowest feasible cost.

- A cap-and-trade system grants permits to pollute, but allows the permits to be traded. It achieves a given amount of pollution reduction at the lowest feasible cost.

- Command-and-control regulations are less flexible than incentive-based regulations, and are therefore likely to be costlier.

- Positive externalities generally lead to under-provision of an activity. A subsidy can correct the problem, but care must be taken to avoid wasteful subsidies.

Discussion Questions

1. According to former Vice President Al Gore, "Classical economics defines productivity narrowly and encourages us to equate gains in productivity with economic progress. But the Holy Grail of progress is so alluring that economists tend to overlook the bad side effects that often accompany improvements" [Miller, 1997, p. A22]. Discuss whether or not this is a fair characterization of "classical economics." Gore also stated that we need to take "bold and unequivocal action . . . [to] make the rescue of the environment the central organizing principle for civilization." Suppose that you were a policymaker trying to decide what to do about automobile emissions. How might you use Gore's dictum as a framework for making your decision?

2. After finding a plastic container in her dormitory trash can, a Princeton undergraduate circulated an e-mail reminding students that "recycling is always a good thing!" Use the theory of externalities to evaluate this statement.

3. During the Democratic presidential primary campaign in 2008, Governor Bill Richardson said he favored a cap-and-trade approach for carbon regulation rather than a carbon tax because the latter is "passed on to consumers" and so is "a bad idea." Senator Barack Obama disagreed, saying that both the carbon tax and the cap-and-trade program lead to higher costs for consumers. Which candidate was correct about the distributional impacts of the two policies?

4. In the following figure, the number of parties that Cassanova gives per month is measured on the horizontal axis, and dollars are measured on the vertical. MC_p is the marginal cost of providing parties and MB_p is Cassanova's marginal benefit schedule from having parties.

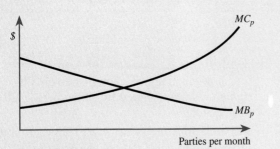

Parties per month

a. Graphically, show how many parties Cassanova will host.

b. Suppose there is a fixed marginal external benefit, $$b, per party to Cassanova's friends. Illustrate this on your graph.

c. What is the socially (no pun intended) optimal level of parties? How could the Social Committee induce Cassanova to throw this number?

d. On your graph, show the optimal subsidy per party and the total amount paid to Cassanova. Who gains and loses under this plan?

5. Suppose that the conditions for the Coase Theorem hold; that is, property rights for a resource are clearly established and bargaining costs are low. If so, what are the efficiency consequences if the government imposes a Pigouvian tax equal to the marginal external damage of production?

6. For each of the following situations, is the Coase Theorem applicable? Why or why not?

a. A farmer who grows organic corn is at risk of having his crop contaminated by genetically modified corn grown by his neighbors.

b. In Brazil it is illegal to catch and sell certain tropical fish. Nevertheless, in some remote parts of the Amazon River, hundreds of divers come to capture exotic fish for sale on the international black market. The presence of so many divers is depleting the stock of exotic fish.

c. In the state of Washington, many farmers burn their fields to clear the wheat stubble and prepare for the next planting season. Nearby city dwellers complain about the pollution.

d. Users of the Internet generally incur a zero incremental cost for transmitting information. As a consequence, congestion occurs, and users are frustrated by delays.

7. Some observers have argued that importing oil makes the United States hostage to the policies of Saudi Arabia and other countries in the Middle East. This complicates US foreign policy.

a. Explain why an externality is present in this situation.

b. Propose a Pigouvian tax to deal with the externality.

c. Some economists want to curb domestic gasoline consumption but are wary of giving the government substantially more revenues than it already has. As an alternative, Feldstein [2006b, p. A10] suggested a system of tradable gasoline rights (TGR):

"In a system of tradable gasoline rights, the government would give each adult a TGR debit card. The gasoline pumps at service stations that now read credit cards and debit cards would be modified to read these new TGR debit cards as well. Buying a gallon of gasoline would require using up one tradable gasoline right as well as paying money. The government would decide how many gallons of gasoline should be consumed per year and would give out that total number of TGRs. In 2006, Americans will buy about 110 billion gallons of gasoline. . . . To reduce total consumption by 5%, [government] would cut the number of TGRs to 104.5 billion."

Draw a diagram to illustrate how the price of the tradable gasoline rights would be determined. Suppose that the market price per voucher were 75 cents. How would this change the opportunity cost of buying a gallon of gasoline?

8. In India, a drug used to treat sick cows is leading to the death of many vultures that feed off of dead cattle. Before the decrease in the number of vultures, they sometimes used to smash into the engines of jets taking off from New Delhi's airports, posing a serious threat to air travelers. However, the decline of the vulture population has led to a sharp increase in the populations of rats and feral dogs, which are now the main scavengers of rotting meat [Gentleman, 2006, p. A4]. There have been calls for a ban on the drug used to treat the cows.

Identify the externalities that are present in this situation. Comment on the efficiency of banning the drug. How would you design an incentive-based regulation to attain an efficient outcome?

9. In California, drivers of hybrid cars are permitted to use the dedicated high-occupancy-vehicle (HOV) lanes on the highways. Given the recent increase in purchases of hybrids, these HOV lanes are becoming increasingly clogged, which leads to an increase in gasoline use and in harmful emissions. Describe an alternative policy for addressing problems with traffic congestion.

10. American suburbs are expanding to more rural areas at the same time as pig farms are expanding in size [*Economist*, 2007d, p. 36]. The smells emanating from the massive amounts of pig manure adversely affect property values. Imagine that the Little Pigs (LP) hog farm is situated near 100 houses. The following table shows, for each level of LP's output, the marginal cost (*MC*) of a hog, the marginal benefit (*MB*) to LP, and the marginal damage (*MD*) done to property values:

Output	MC	MB	MD
1	400	1,600	400
2	800	1,600	800
3	1,200	1,600	900
4	1,600	1,600	1,000
5	3,200	1,600	1,200
6	6,400	1,600	1,400

a. How many hogs does LP produce?
b. What is the efficient number of hogs?
c. Suppose the owner of LP can reduce the marginal damages of hog smells by two-thirds by modifying the hogs' diet. The modified diet increases the marginal cost of each hog by $100. What is the efficient number of hogs?

11. The private marginal benefit for commodity X is given by $10 - X$, where X is the number of units consumed. The private marginal cost of producing X is constant at $5. For each unit of X produced, an external cost of $2 is imposed on members of society. In the absence of any government intervention, how much X is produced? What is the efficient level of production of X? What is the gain to society involved in moving from the inefficient to the efficient level of production? Suggest a Pigouvian tax that would lead to the efficient level. How much revenue would the tax raise?

12. Suppose that two firms emit a certain pollutant. The marginal cost of reducing pollution for each firm is as follows: $MC_1 = 300e_1$ and $MC_2 = 100e_2$, where e_1 and e_2 are the amounts (in tons) of emissions reduced by the first and second firms, respectively. Assume that in the absence of government intervention, Firm 1 generates 100 units of emissions and Firm 2 generates 80 units of emissions.

a. Suppose regulators decide to reduce total pollution by 40 units. In order to be cost effective, how much should each firm cut its pollution?
b. What emissions fee should be imposed to achieve the cost-effective outcome? How much would each firm pay in taxes?
c. Suppose that instead of an emissions fee, the regulatory agency introduces a tradable permit system and issues 140 permits, each of which allows the emission of one ton of pollution. Firm 1 uses its political influence to convince the regulatory agency to issue 100 permits to itself and only 40 permits to Firm 2. How many, if any, permits are traded between the firms? What is the minimum amount of money that must be paid (total) for these permits? By how many tons does each firm end up reducing its pollution?

13. Figure 5.11 demonstrates the efficiency implications of using cap-and-trade versus an emissions fee when costs are higher than expected and marginal social benefits are inelastic. Figure 5.12 does the same thing under the assumption of elastic marginal social benefits. Now consider the case where marginal costs turn out to be *lower* than anticipated. For both cap-and-trade and an emissions fee, show whether there is too much or too little emissions reduction. Which approach is more efficient when marginal social benefits are inelastic and when they are elastic?

Chapter Six

POLITICAL ECONOMY

I always like to win. I don't get hung up on ideology. Whatever it takes, I will do.
—GOVERNOR ARNOLD SCHWARZENEGGER

Textbook discussions of market failures and their remedies tend to convey a rather rosy view of government. With a tax here, an expenditure there, the state readily corrects all market imperfections, meanwhile seeing to it that incomes are distributed in an ethically desirable way. Such a view is at variance with apparent widespread public dissatisfaction with government performance. Public opinion polls, for example, consistently report that fewer than 30 percent of the people approve of the way Congress handles its job. Humorist P. J. O'Rourke probably summarized the sentiments of many when he quipped, "Feeling good about government is like looking on the bright side of any catastrophe. When you quit looking on the bright side, the catastrophe is still there."

Perhaps this is merely gratuitous whining. As a matter of definition, in a democracy we get the government we want. Another possibility, however, is that it is inherently difficult for even democratically elected governments to respond to the national interest. This chapter applies economic principles to the analysis of political decision making, a field known as **political economy.** Political economy models assume that individuals view government as a mechanism for maximizing their self-interest. Two points are important regarding this assumption:

political economy

The field that applies economic principles to the analysis of political decision making.

- The pursuit of self-interest does not necessarily lead to inefficient outcomes. As we saw in Chapter 3, under certain conditions the marketplace harnesses self-interest to serve a social end. The question is, "What, if anything, performs that role in the 'political market'?"
- While the maximization assumption may not be totally accurate, just as in more conventional settings, it provides a good starting point for analysis.

At the outset, we examine direct democracies and how well they translate the preferences of their members into collective action. We then turn to the complications that arise when decisions are made not by individuals themselves but by their elected representatives.

▶ DIRECT DEMOCRACY

Democratic societies use various voting procedures to decide on public expenditures. This section looks at some of these procedures.

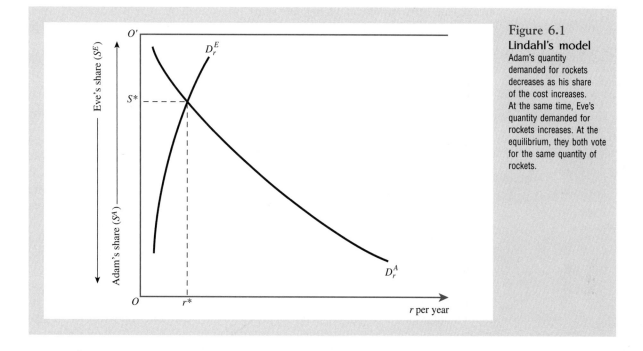

Figure 6.1
Lindahl's model
Adam's quantity demanded for rockets decreases as his share of the cost increases. At the same time, Eve's quantity demanded for rockets increases. At the equilibrium, they both vote for the same quantity of rockets.

Unanimity Rules

Recall from Chapter 4 how the free rider problem can lead to a disturbing situation—because people are selfish, public goods are underprovided, even though everyone could be made better off if they were provided in efficient amounts. This suggests that, in principle, if a vote were taken on whether to provide an efficient quantity of the good, consent would be unanimous as long as there was a suitable tax system to finance it. A procedure designed to elicit unanimous agreement was proposed in the early 20th century by Erik Lindahl [1958/1919].

To understand Lindahl's procedure, assume again there are two individuals, Adam and Eve, and one public good, rockets for fireworks (r). Suppose Adam is told that his share of the cost of rocket provision will be 30 percent. Then if the market price per rocket is P_r, Adam's price per rocket is $0.30 \times P_r$. Given this price, the prices of other goods, his tastes, and his income, there is some quantity of rockets that Adam wants to consume. More generally, let S^A denote Adam's share of the cost of rocket provision. For any particular value of S^A, Adam demands some quantity of rockets. As his tax share increases and rockets become more expensive for him, he demands a smaller quantity.

In Figure 6.1, the horizontal axis measures the quantity of rockets. Adam's tax share is measured by the vertical distance from point O. The curve D_r^A shows how the quantity of rockets demanded by Adam decreases as his tax share increases.

In the same way, define S^E as Eve's share of the cost of rockets. (By definition, $S^A + S^E = 1$.) When S^E goes up, the quantity demanded by Eve decreases. In Figure 6.1, Eve's tax share increases as we move down along the vertical axis from O'. (Thus, the distance OO' is 1.) Her demand schedule is denoted D_r^E. It slopes upward because upward movements along the vertical axis represent a lower price to her.

An obvious similarity exists between the role of tax shares in the Lindahl model and market prices in the usual theory of demand. But there is an important difference.

Instead of each individual facing the same price, each faces a personalized price per unit of public good, which depends on his or her tax share. The tax shares are referred to as **Lindahl prices.**

An equilibrium is a set of Lindahl prices such that at those prices each person votes for the same quantity of the public good. In Figure 6.1, Adam's equilibrium tax share is OS^* and Eve's is $O'S^*$. At these Lindahl prices, both parties agree that r^* rockets should be provided.

Feasibility of Unanimity Rules   The Lindahl model shows the tax shares and level of public good provision to which everyone agrees. The big question is how to reach the equilibrium. Imagine that an auctioneer announces some initial set of tax shares. On the basis of their respective demand schedules, Adam and Eve vote for the number of rockets they want. If agreement is not unanimous, the auctioneer announces another set of tax shares. The process continues until Adam and Eve unanimously agree on the quantity of rockets (r^* in Figure 6.1). The determination of the quantity of public goods, then, is quite similar to the market process. Like the market outcome, one can prove that the allocation is Pareto efficient.[1]

As a practical method for providing public goods, Lindahl's procedure has two main problems. First, it assumes people vote sincerely. If Adam can guess the maximum amount that Eve would spend for rockets rather than do without them, he can try to force her to that allocation. Eve has the same incentives. Strategic behavior may prevent Adam and Eve from reaching the Lindahl equilibrium.

Second, finding the mutually agreeable tax shares may take a lot of time. In this example, there are only two parties. In most important cases, many people are involved. Getting everyone's consent involves enormous decision-making costs. Indeed, although unanimity rules guarantee that no one will be "exploited," they often lead to situations in which *no* decisions are made. For example, the World Trade Organization (WTO), which sets rules for coordinating trade among its 144 member nations, operates on a unanimity rule. A journalist reporting on a WTO meeting once noted that the only shocking thing that might happen would be "if they manage[d] to agree on anything at all" [Kahn, 2001, p. A3].

Majority Voting Rules

Because unanimity is difficult to attain, voting systems not requiring it may be desirable. With a **majority voting rule,** one more than half of the voters must favor a measure to gain approval.

Although the mechanics of majority voting are familiar, it is useful to review them carefully. Consider a community with three voters, Brad, Jen, and Angelina, who have to choose among three levels of missile provision, A, B, and C. Level A is small, level B is moderate, and level C is large. The voters' preferences are depicted in Table 6.1. Each column shows how the voter ranks the choices. For example, Jen most prefers level C, but given a choice between B and A, would prefer B.

Suppose an election were held on whether to adopt A or B. Brad would vote for A, while Jen and Angelina would vote for B. Hence, B would win by a vote of 2 to 1. Similarly, if an election were held between B and C, B would win by a vote

---

[1] Intuitively, assume $P_r = 1$. Then Eve sets $S^E P_r = MRS_{ra}^{Eve}$, and Adam sets $S^A P_r = MRS_{ra}^{Adam}$. Therefore, $MRS_{ra}^{Eve} + MRS_{ra}^{Adam} = S^E P_r + S^A P_r = P_r(S^E + S^A) = P_r$. But P_r represents MRT_{ra}, so $MRS_{ra}^{Eve} + MRS_{ra}^{Adam} = MRT_{ra}$, which is the necessary condition for Pareto efficiency of Equation (4.2).

Table 6.1   **Voter Preferences That Lead to an Equilibrium**

	Voter		
Choice	Brad	Jen	Angelina
First	A	C	B
Second	B	B	C
Third	C	A	A

Given these voter preferences, in an election between A and B, B would win. In an election between B and C, B would again win. Because B wins any election against its opposition, it is the option selected by majority rule.

of 2 to 1. Level B wins any election against its opposition, and thus is the option selected by majority rule. Note that the selection of B is independent of the order in which the votes are taken.

Majority decision rules do not always yield such clear-cut results. Consider the preferences depicted in Table 6.2. Again, imagine a series of paired elections to determine the most preferred level. In an election between A and B, A would win by a vote of 2 to 1. If an election were held between B and C, B would win by a vote of 2 to 1. Finally, in an election between A and C, C would win by the same margin. This result is disconcerting. The first election suggests that A is preferred to B; the second that B is preferred to C. Conventional notions of consistency suggest that A should therefore be preferred to C. But in the third election, just the opposite occurs. Although each individual voter's preferences are consistent, the community's are not. This phenomenon is referred to as the **voting paradox.**

Moreover, with the preferences in Table 6.2, the ultimate outcome depends crucially on the order in which the votes are taken. If the first election is between propositions A and B and the winner (A) runs against C, then C is the ultimate choice. On the other hand, if the first election is B versus C, and the winner (B) runs against A, then A is chosen. Under such circumstances, the ability to control the order of voting—the agenda—confers great power. **Agenda manipulation** is the process of organizing the order of votes to ensure a favorable outcome.

A related problem is that paired voting can go on forever without reaching a decision. After the election between A and B, A wins. If C challenges A, then C wins. If B then challenges C, B wins. The process can continue indefinitely, a phenomenon called **cycling.** A good historical example of cycling concerns the 17th Amendment to the US Constitution, which provides for direct election of US senators. Adoption of the amendment was delayed for many years due to voting cycling.

voting paradox

With majority voting, community preferences can be inconsistent even though each individual's preferences are consistent.

agenda manipulation

The process of organizing the order in which votes are taken to ensure a favorable outcome.

cycling

When paired majority voting on more than two possibilities goes on indefinitely without a conclusion ever being reached.

Table 6.2   **Voter Preferences That Lead to Cycling**

	Voter		
Choice	Brad	Jen	Angelina
First	A	C	B
Second	B	A	C
Third	C	B	A

Given these voter preferences, in an election between A and B, A would win. In an election between B and C, B would win. And in an election between A and C, C would win. Thus, we have a voting paradox: group preferences are inconsistent even though each individual's preferences are consistent.

Figure 6.2
Graphing the preferences from Table 6.2
Brad and Angelina have single-peaked preferences. However, Jen has double-peaked preferences.

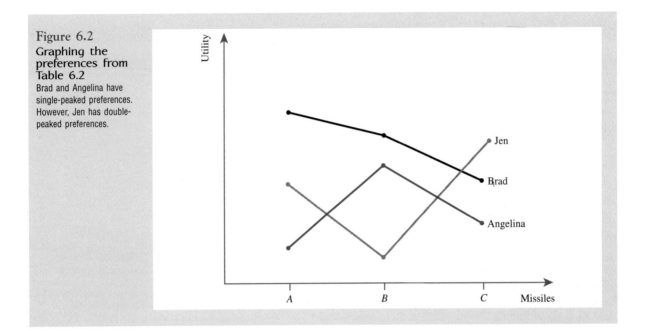

peak

A point on the graph of an individual's preferences at which all the neighboring points have lower utility.

single-peaked preferences

Utility consistently falls as a voter moves away from his or her most preferred outcome.

double-peaked preferences

If, as a voter moves away from his or her most preferred outcome, utility goes down, but then goes back up again.

Clearly, majority voting need not lead to these problems. After all, the elections associated with Table 6.1 went smoothly. Why the difference? It turns on the structure of individual preferences for various levels of missile procurement. Consider again the people in Table 6.2. Because Brad prefers A to B to C, it follows that A gives Brad more utility than B, and B more than C. The schedule denoted Brad in Figure 6.2 depicts this relationship. The schedules labeled Jen and Angelina do the same for the other voters.

We define a **peak** in an individual's preferences as a point at which all the neighboring points are lower.[2] A voter has **single-peaked preferences** if, as she moves away from her most preferred outcome in any and all directions, her utility consistently falls. She has **double-peaked preferences** if, as she moves away from the most preferred outcome, utility goes down, but then goes up again. Thus, Brad has a single peak at point A; Angelina has a single peak at point B; and Jen has two peaks, one at A and one at C. It turns out that Jen's preferences are the ones that lead to the voting paradox. If Jen had *any* set of single-peaked preferences, majority voting would lead to a consistent decision. This is why no voting paradox emerges from Table 6.1. There, each voter has single-peaked preferences. More generally, if all voters' preferences are single peaked, no voting paradox occurs.

Because multipeaked preferences can throw a wrench into majority voting, it is important to know whether they are likely to be important as a practical matter. Consider again Jen's two-peaked preferences in Table 6.2. She prefers either very large or very small missile expenditures to a quantity in the middle. Although such preferences are not necessarily irrational, they do seem a bit peculiar. Perhaps Jen believes that moderate numbers of missiles provide little if any real protection, so that unless expenditures are large, they might as well be close to nothing.

[2] For this analysis, the absolute amount of utility associated with each alternative is irrelevant. The vertical distances could change, but as long as the pattern of peaks stays unchanged, so does the election's outcome.

Table 6.3 **Preferred Level of Party Expenditure**

Voter	Expenditure
Donald	$ 5
Daisy	100
Huey	150
Dewey	160
Louie	700

If all voters have single-peaked preferences, then majority voting leads to an outcome that reflects the preference of the median voter. In this case, majority voting leads to a $150 expenditure on the party.

Suppose, however, that instead of missiles, voters are choosing among expenditure levels for a public park—a good for which there are private substitutes. Assume that in the presence of small or medium public park expenditures, voter Vince will join a private country club, but given large expenditures, he will use the public park. Provided that Vince's tax burden increases with park expenditure, he prefers a small to a medium park—since neither of these options benefits Vince, he prefers the one with the smaller tax burden. But his most preferred outcome might be the large expenditure public park. (This depends in part on the associated tax burden compared to the country club membership fee.) In short, Vince may prefer either the small or large public park to the medium-sized one. Thus, when there are private substitutes for a publicly provided good, a multipeaked pattern like Jen's in Figure 6.2 can easily emerge.

Moreover, when issues cannot be ranked along a single dimension, multipeaked preferences are also a serious possibility.[3] Suppose that a community is trying to decide how to use a vacant building. Choice A is an abortion clinic, choice B is an adult bookstore, and choice C is an Army recruitment office. Unlike the choice among different levels of missile expenditure, here the alternatives do not represent more or less of a single characteristic. Multipeaked preferences can easily emerge.

The Median Voter Theorem Let us now return to the simple case in which all alternatives being considered represent smaller or greater amounts of a characteristic. People rank each alternative on the basis of this characteristic. An example is how much of some public good to acquire. Define the **median voter** as the voter whose preferences lie in the middle of the set of all voters' preferences; half the voters want more of the good than the median voter, and half want less. The **median voter theorem** states that as long as all preferences are single peaked, the outcome of majority voting reflects the preferences of the median voter. (With an even number of voters, there may be a tie between two median voters, which must be broken arbitrarily.)

To demonstrate the theorem, assume there are five voters: Donald, Daisy, Huey, Dewey, and Louie. They are deciding how large a party to give together, and each of them has single-peaked preferences over party sizes. The most preferred level for each voter is noted in Table 6.3. *Because preferences are single peaked*, the closer an expenditure level is to a given voter's peak, the more he or she prefers it. A movement from zero party expenditure to $5 would be preferred to no money by all voters. A movement from $5 to $100 would be approved by Daisy, Huey, Dewey, and Louie, and from $100 to $150 by Huey, Dewey, and Louie. Any increase beyond

median voter

The voter whose preferences lie in the middle of the set of all voters' preferences; half the voters want more of the item selected and half want less.

median voter theorem

As long as all preferences are single peaked and several other conditions are satisfied, the outcome of majority voting reflects the preferences of the median voter.

---

[3] Atkinson and Stiglitz [1980, p. 306] explain how the notion of a "peak" is generalized to a multidimensional setting.

$150, however, would be blocked by at least three voters: Donald, Daisy, and Huey. Hence, the majority votes for $150. But this is just the amount preferred by Huey, the median voter. The election results mirror the median voter's preferences.

To summarize: When all preferences are single peaked, majority voting yields a stable result, and the choice selected reflects the preferences of the median voter. However, when some voters' preferences are multipeaked, a voting paradox can emerge.[4] Because multipeaked preferences may be important in many realistic situations, majority voting cannot be depended on to yield consistent public choices. Moreover, as we shall discuss shortly, even when majority voting leads to consistent decisions, it may not be efficient in the sense that overall benefits exceed costs.

Logrolling

logrolling

The trading of votes to obtain passage of a package of legislative proposals.

A possible problem with simple majority voting is that it does not allow people to register how strongly they feel about the issues. Whether a particular voter just barely prefers A to B or has an enormous preference for A has no influence on the outcome. **Logrolling** systems allow people to trade votes and hence register how strongly they feel about various issues. Suppose that voters Smith and Jones prefer not to have more missiles, but they don't care all that much. Brown, on the other hand, definitely wants more missiles. With a logrolling system, Brown may be able to convince Jones to vote for more missiles if Brown promises to vote for a new road to go by Jones's factory.

Vote trading is controversial. Its proponents argue that trading votes leads to efficient provision of public goods, just as trading commodities leads to efficient provision of private goods. Proponents also emphasize its potential for revealing the intensity of preferences and establishing a stable equilibrium. Moreover, the compromises implicit in vote trading are necessary for a democratic system to function. As sociologist James Q. Wilson [2000] has noted, "Vote trades are called pork barrels or logrolling, but such trades are essential to finding some way to balance competing interests, each of which is defended by a legislator who owes little to any other legislator. Vote trades and pork-barrel projects are an essential way of achieving what force and language cannot produce."

A numerical example helps illustrate these advantages. Suppose a community is considering three projects, a hospital, a library, and a swimming pool. The community has three voters, Melanie, Rhett, and Scarlet. Table 6.4 shows their benefits for each project. (A minus sign indicates a net loss; that is, the costs exceed the benefits.)

The first thing to notice about the table is that the total net benefit for each project is positive. Thus, by definition, the community as a whole would be better off if each project were adopted.[5] But what happens if the projects are voted on *one at a time?* Melanie votes for the hospital because her net benefit is positive, but Rhett and Scarlet vote against it because their benefits are negative. The hospital therefore loses. Similarly, the library and the swimming pool go down in defeat.

Vote trading can help remedy this situation. Suppose Melanie agrees to vote for the library if Rhett consents to vote for the hospital. Melanie comes out ahead by

---

[4] The presence of one or more voters with multipeaked preferences does not *necessarily* lead to a voting paradox. It depends on the number of voters and the structure of their preferences. See Discussion Question 1 at the end of this chapter.

[5] We assume the absence of externalities or any other factors that would make private costs and benefits unequal to their social counterparts.

Table 6.4 **Logrolling Can Improve Welfare**

| Project | Voter | | | Total Net Benefits |
	Melanie	Rhett	Scarlet	
Hospital	200	−50	−55	95
Library	−40	150	−30	80
Pool	−120	−60	400	220

If each project is voted on separately, none is adopted even though each yields positive net benefits. However, with vote trading social welfare is improved.

160 (= 200 − 40) with the trade; Rhett comes out ahead by 100 (= 150 − 50). They therefore strike the deal, and the hospital and library pass. This improves social welfare. Alternatively, Melanie can make a deal in which she gives her support for the pool in return for Scarlet's vote for the hospital. This would also improve social welfare.

On the other hand, opponents of logrolling stress that it is likely to result in special-interest gains not sufficient to outweigh general losses. Large amounts of waste can be incurred. For example, an agriculture bill passed by Congress in 2007 spent over $300 billion "on wealthy farm households" and "guaranteed already well-off farmers high incomes" [*Economist*, 2008, p. 46]. Most economists viewed this expenditure as both wasteful and unfair. Why did it pass? One important reason is that members of Congress from agricultural states were able to get the support of urban members in return for supporting spending on food stamps [*Economist*, 2008, p. 46].

Table 6.5 illustrates a situation in which logrolling leads to such undesirable outcomes. Here we have the same three voters and three projects under consideration as in Table 6.4, but with a different set of net benefits. Every project has a negative net benefit. Each should therefore be rejected, as would be the case if the projects were voted on one at a time.

However, with logrolling, some or all of these inefficient projects could pass. Suppose Melanie offers to support the library in return for Rhett's vote for the hospital. The deal is consummated because both of them come out ahead—Melanie by 160 (= 200 − 40) and Rhett by 40 (= 150 − 110). With the support of Melanie and Rhett together, both projects pass. Alternatively, Rhett and Scarlet can trade votes for the pool and the library, so both of those projects would be adopted.

To understand the source of this outcome, think about Melanie and Rhett's vote trading over the hospital and the library. Note that Scarlet comes out behind on

Table 6.5 **Logrolling Can also Lower Welfare**

| Project | Voter | | | Total Net Benefits |
	Melanie	Rhett	Scarlet	
Hospital	200	−110	−105	−15
Library	−40	150	−120	−10
Pool	−270	−140	400	−10

If each project is voted on separately, none is adopted. This is efficient because each yields negative net benefits. However, with vote trading, some or all of the projects will pass, which is inefficient.

both projects. This demonstrates how with logrolling, a majority of voters can form a coalition to vote for projects that serve their interests, but whose costs are borne mainly by the minority. Hence, although the benefits of the projects to the majority exceed the costs, this is not true for society as a whole. We conclude that while logrolling can sometimes improve on the results from simple majority voting, this is not necessarily the case.

Arrow's Impossibility Theorem

We have shown that neither simple majority voting nor logrolling has entirely desirable properties. Many other voting schemes have also been considered, and they, too, are flawed.[6] An important question is whether *any* ethically acceptable method for translating individual preferences into collective preferences is free of difficulties. It depends on what you mean by "ethically acceptable." Nobel laureate Kenneth Arrow [1951] proposed that in a democratic society, a collective decision-making rule should satisfy the following criteria:[7]

1. It can produce a decision whatever the configuration of voters' preferences. Thus, for example, the procedure must not fall apart if some people have multipeaked preferences.
2. It must be able to rank all possible outcomes.
3. It must be responsive to individuals' preferences. Specifically, if every individual prefers A to B, then society's ranking must prefer A to B.
4. It must be consistent in the sense that if A is preferred to B and B is preferred to C, then A is preferred to C.[8]
5. Society's ranking of A and B must depend only on individuals' rankings of A and B. Thus, the collective ranking of manned space travel and foreign aid does not depend on how individuals rank either of them relative to research on a cure for AIDS. This assumption is sometimes called the **independence of irrelevant alternatives.**
6. Dictatorship is ruled out. Social preferences must not reflect the preferences of only a single individual.

Taken together, these criteria seem quite reasonable. Basically, they say that society's choice mechanism should be logical and respect individuals' preferences. Unfortunately, the stunning conclusion of Arrow's analysis is that in general it is *impossible* to find a rule that satisfies all these criteria.[9] A democratic society cannot be expected to make consistent decisions.

This result, called Arrow's Impossibility Theorem, thus casts doubt on the very ability of democracies to function. Naturally, the theorem has generated debate, much of which has focused on whether other sets of criteria might allow formation of a

independence of irrelevant alternatives

Society's ranking of two different projects depends only on individuals' rankings of the two projects, not on how individuals rank the two projects relative to other alternatives.

---

[6] These include point voting (each person is given a fixed number of points that are cast for the different alternatives), plurality voting (the alternative with the most votes wins), Borda counts (each alternative is ranked by each voter, and the ranks are totaled to choose), Condorcet elections (the alternative that defeats the rest in paired elections wins), and exhaustive voting (the proposal favored least by the largest number of voters is repeatedly removed until only one remains). See Levin and Nalebuff [1995] for further details.

[7] Arrow's requirements have been stated in a number of different ways. This treatment follows Blair and Pollak [1983].

[8] More precisely, in this context *preferred to* means *better than* or *just as good as*.

[9] The proof involves fairly sophisticated mathematics. The procedure of proof is to show that if all six conditions are imposed, phenomena like the voting paradox can arise.

social decision-making rule. It turns out that if any of the six criteria is dropped, a decision-making rule that satisfies the other five *can* be constructed. But whether or not it is permissible to drop any of the criteria depends on one's views of their ethical validity.

Arrow's theorem does not state that it is *necessarily* impossible to find a consistent decision-making rule. Rather, the theorem only says one cannot guarantee that society will be able to do so. For certain patterns of individual preferences, no problems arise. An obvious example is when members of society have identical preferences. Some have suggested that the real significance of Arrow's theorem is that it shows the need for a virtual uniformity of tastes if a democracy is to work. They then argue that many institutions have the express purpose of molding people's tastes to make sure that uniformity emerges. An example is mandatory public education. This observation is consistent with the view of the British statesman Benjamin Disraeli: "Whenever is found what is called a paternal government, there is found state education. It has been discovered that the best way to ensure implicit obedience is to commence tyranny in the nursery." Lott [1999] analyzed the pattern of expenditures on education across countries and found a result similar in spirit to Disraeli's assertion—more totalitarian governments tend to make greater investments in public education, other things being the same.

A very different view is that Arrow's theorem does not really have much to say about the viability of democratic processes. Another Nobel prize winner, James Buchanan [1960], believes that the inconsistencies of majority voting have beneficial aspects:

> Majority rule is acceptable in a free society precisely because it allows a sort of jockeying back and forth among alternatives, upon none of which relative unanimity can be obtained. . . . It serves to insure that competing alternatives may be experimentally and provisionally adopted, tested, and replaced by new compromise alternatives approved by a majority group of ever-changing composition. This is [the] democratic choice process [p. 83].

Another important question raised by Arrow's theorem concerns the use of social welfare functions. Recall from Chapter 3 that a social welfare function is a rule that evaluates the desirability of any given set of individuals' utilities. In a democratic society, the social welfare function must be chosen collectively. But Arrow's theorem says that it may be impossible to make such decisions, and hence we cannot assume that a social welfare function really exists. However, if it does not exist, how can economists use the social welfare function to rank alternative states? Some economists therefore reject the function's use. They argue that it is merely a way of introducing value judgments and not a representation of "society's" preferences. As such, a social welfare function does not isolate the correct allocation of resources. However, most economists believe that the function is an important tool. It may not provide "the" answer, but it can be used to draw out the implications of alternative sets of value judgments. With this interpretation, the social welfare function provides valuable insights.

▶ REPRESENTATIVE DEMOCRACY

Although the discussion of public decision making thus far sheds light on some important questions, it is based on an unrealistic view of government: It is essentially a big computer that elicits from citizens their preferences and uses this information to produce social decisions. The state has no interests of its own; it is neutral and benign.

In fact, of course, governing is done by people—politicians, judges, bureaucrats, and others. Realistic political economy models must study the goals and behavior of the people who govern. This section discusses a few such models. They assume that people in government, like other individuals, attempt to maximize their self-interest.

Elected Politicians

Our earlier discussion of direct democracy led to the median voter theorem: If individual preferences are single peaked and can be represented along a single dimension, the outcome of majority voting reflects the preferences of the median voter. In reality, direct referenda on fiscal matters are most unusual. More commonly, citizens elect representatives who make decisions on their behalf. Nevertheless, under certain assumptions, the median voter theorem helps explain how these representatives set their positions.

Consider an election between two candidates, Smith and Jones. Assume voters have single-peaked preferences along the spectrum of political views. Voters cast ballots to maximize their own utility, and candidates seek to maximize the number of votes received.

What happens? Under these conditions, a vote-maximizing politician adopts the preferred program of the *median voter*—the voter whose preferences are exactly in the middle of the distribution of preferences. To see why, assume voters rank all positions on the basis of whether they are "conservative" or "liberal." Figure 6.3 shows a hypothetical distribution of voters who most prefer each point in the political spectrum. Suppose that Candidate Jones adopts position M, at the median, and Candidate Smith chooses position S, to the right of center. Because all voters have single-peaked preferences and want to maximize utility, each supports the candidate whose views lie closest to his or her own. Smith will win all the votes to the right of S, as well as some of the votes between S and M. Because M is the median, one-half of the voters lie to the left of M. Jones will receive all of these votes and some of those to the right of M, guaranteeing him a majority. The only way for Smith to prevent himself from being "outflanked" is to move to position M himself. Therefore, it pays both candidates to place themselves as close as possible to the position of the median voter.

Figure 6.3
Median voter theorem for elections
The candidate who adopts the median position (M) will defeat the candidate who adopts the position away from the median (S), because the former candidate wins all the votes to the left of M (which is half of the votes) plus some of the votes between M and S.

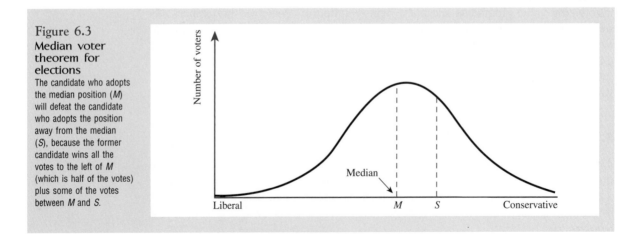

"Perhaps Your Majesty should try governing from the center." © The New Yorker Collection 1997 J. B. Handelsman from cartoonbank.com. All Rights Reserved.

This model has a striking implication: Two-party systems tend to be stable in the sense that both parties stake out positions near the "center." In some respects, this is a good description of American political life. It appears, for example, that presidential candidates who are perceived as too far from the middle-of-the-road (Barry Goldwater in 1964 and George McGovern in 1972) fare poorly with the electorate.[10] During the 2008 presidential election, a journalist suggested that then-Senator Obama "was talking toward the center with John McCain" [Davis, 2008]. According to the median voter model, there is nothing at all surprising about such a phenomenon. As suggested by the cartoon, departing from the center can be hazardous for a politician!

Before taking this rather optimistic result too much to heart, however, several issues require careful examination.

Single-Dimensional Rankings   If all political beliefs cannot be ranked along a single spectrum, the median voter theorem falls apart because the identity of the median voter depends on the issue being considered. The median voter with respect to affirmative action questions may not be the same person as the median voter on

---

[10] One of Goldwater's campaign slogans was "A choice, not an echo." The median voter theorem helps to explain why echoes are so prevalent.

defense issues. Similarly, just as in the case of direct referenda, if preferences are not single peaked, there may not be a stable voting equilibrium at all.

Ideology   The model assumes that politicians are simple vote maximizers, but they may care about more than just winning elections. Ideology can play an important role. After all, in 1850 Henry Clay said, "Sir, I would rather be right than be president."

Personality   The assumption that voters' decisions depend only on issues may be unrealistic. Personalities may sometimes be more important. Some have argued, for example, that much of President Ronald Reagan's appeal was his fatherly personality.

Leadership   In the model, politicians passively respond to voters' preferences. But these preferences may be influenced by the politicians themselves. This is just another way of saying that politicians provide leadership. An interesting extreme case of how leadership can change election outcomes occurs when the actions of a politician actually change the composition of his or her constituency. For example, a mayor whose support comes primarily from the poor could implement policies that tend to drive high-income people out of the jurisdiction, thus changing the identity of the median voter. There is some evidence that such a phenomenon occurred in Boston during the first half of the 20th century and in Detroit during the second [Glaeser and Shleifer, 2005].

Decision to Vote   The analysis assumes every eligible citizen chooses to exercise his or her franchise. If the candidates' positions are too close, however, some people may not vote out of boredom. Individuals with extreme views may feel too alienated to vote. The model also ignores the costs of acquiring information and voting. A fully informed voter makes a determination on the suitability of a candidate's platform, the probability that the candidate will be able and willing to keep his or her promises, and so forth. The fact that these costs may be high, together with the perception that a single vote will not influence the outcome anyway, may induce a self-interested citizen to abstain from voting. A free rider problem emerges—each individual has an incentive not to vote, but unless a sizable number of people do so, a democracy cannot function. Although low voter participation rates are often bemoaned (for example, only 62 percent of the voting-age population cast a vote in the 2008 presidential election, which is actually higher than in most recent elections), the real puzzle may be why the percentage is so *high*. Part of the answer may be the success with which the educational system instills the idea that a citizen's obligation to vote transcends narrow self-interest.

Public Employees

The next group we consider is public employees, also referred to as bureaucrats. To understand their role, note that the legislation enacted by elected politicians is often vague. The precise way a program is run is largely in the hands of public employees. For example, the Clean Air Act stipulates that the government must set standards "requisite to protect the public health with an adequate margin of safety" [Clean Air Act, Section 104(b)(1)]. How is health status to be measured? What scientific standard is to be used to determine what an "adequate margin" is? The law was silent on these issues. The task of filling these gaps fell to the bureaucrats in the Environmental Protection Agency, giving them enormous latitude and power.

Bureaucrats receive a lot of bitter criticism. They are blamed for being unresponsive, creating excessive red tape, and intruding too much into the private affairs of citizens. Even a rock group joined in the attack:

> Red tape, I can see can't you see
> Red tape, do'in to you, do'in to me
> Red tape, bureaucracy in D.C.
> Red tape, killing you and killing me.
> Tax this, tax that, tax this, tax that.
> NO MORE RED TAPE.[11]

However, a modern government simply cannot function without bureaucracy. Bureaucrats provide valuable technical expertise in the design and execution of programs. The fact that their tenures in office often exceed those of elected officials provides a vital "institutional memory." Another important function of bureaucrats is to provide accurate documentation of public sector transactions to ensure that all eligible citizens receive equal treatment from a particular publicly provided service, and to prevent various forms of corruption.

On the other hand, it would be naive to assume a bureaucrat's only aim is to interpret and passively fulfill the wishes of the electorate and its representatives. Having said this, we are still left with the problem of specifying the bureaucrat's goals. Niskanen [1971] argued that in the market-oriented private sector, an individual who wants to "get ahead" does so by making his or her company as profitable as possible. The individual's salary rises with the firm's profits. In contrast, bureaucrats tend to focus on such items as perquisites of office, public reputation, power, and patronage because opportunities for monetary gains are minimal.[12] Niskanen suggested that power, status, and so on are positively correlated with the size of the bureaucrat's budget and concluded that the bureaucrat's objective is to maximize his or her budget.

To assess the implications of this hypothesis, consider Figure 6.4. The output of a bureaucracy, Q, is measured on the horizontal axis. Q might represent the number of units of public housing managed by the Department of Housing and Urban Development or the quantity of Abrams tanks stockpiled by the Department of Defense. Dollars are measured on the vertical axis. The curve V represents the total value placed on each level of Q by the legislative sponsor who controls the budget. The slope of V is the marginal social benefit of the output; it is drawn on the reasonable assumption of diminishing marginal benefit. The total cost of providing each output level is C. Its slope measures the marginal cost of each unit of output. C is drawn on the assumption of increasing marginal cost.

Suppose the bureaucrat knows that the sponsor will accept any project whose total benefits exceed total costs. Then the bureaucrat proposes Q_{bc}, the output level that maximizes the size of the bureau subject to the constraint that C not be above V. However, Q_{bc} is an inefficient level of output. Efficiency requires that a unit of output be produced only as long as the *additional* benefit from that output exceeds the *additional* cost. Hence, the efficient output is where marginal cost equals marginal

---

[11] From "Red Tape," words and music by Keith Morris and Greg Hetson of the Circle Jerks. © 1980, Irving Music, Inc., and Plagued Music (BMI). All rights reserved. International copyright secured.

[12] Obviously, this distinction is blurred in the real world. Firm executives care about power and job perks as well as money. Nevertheless, the distinction is useful for analytical purposes.

Figure 6.4
Niskanen's model of bureaucracy
The efficient output of this bureaucracy is at Q^*, where society's net benefits are maximized. However, a government official who seeks to maximize the size of the bureaucracy prefers output Q_{bc}, which is inefficiently high.

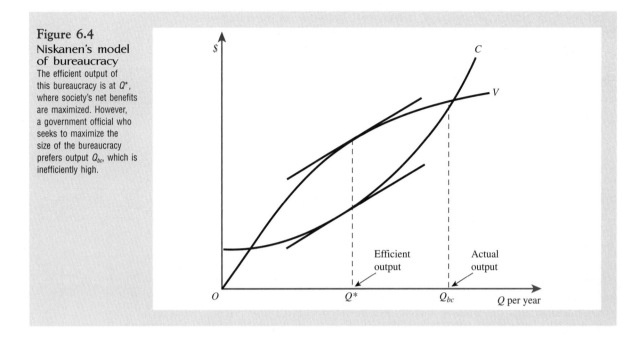

benefit, *not* total cost equals total benefit. In Figure 6.4, the efficient level is Q^*, where the *slopes* of V and C are equal. Thus, the bureaucrat's desire to build as large an "empire" as possible leads to an inefficiently large bureaucracy.

An important implication of Niskanen's model is that bureaucrats have incentives to expend effort on promotional activities to increase the sponsor's perceptions of the bureau's benefits—to shift up the V curve. This is analogous to the use of advertising in the private sector. If such efforts succeed, the equilibrium value of Q_{bc} moves to the right. Hence, Defense Department officials emphasize security threats, and their counterparts in Health and Human Services promote awareness of the poverty problem.

In essence, Niskanen assumes that the bureaucrat can present his or her output to the sponsor as an all-or-nothing proposition: Take Q_{bc} or none at all. An obvious question is why the sponsor doesn't simply overrule the bureaucrat. The bureaucrat's informational advantage is critical here. The process of producing the bureaucratic output is likely to be highly complex and require specialized information that is not easily obtainable by the sponsor. Can a typical member of Congress really be expected to know about the intricacies of nuclear submarines or the benefits and costs of alternative job-training programs for welfare recipients? A particularly striking example of the importance of information comes from South Africa. Even after the fall of apartheid, the white bureaucrats who had administered that regime continued to play a predominant role in running the country. Why? "[T]he bureaucrats alone know the secrets of running the state" [Keller, 1994, p. A1].

Special Interests

We have been assuming so far that citizens who seek to influence government policy can act only as individual voters. In fact, people with common interests can exercise disproportionate power by acting together. The source of the group's power might be that its members tend to have higher voter participation rates than the population as a whole. Alternatively, members might be willing to make campaign contributions and/or pay bribes. As an example, a billion dollars in campaign contributions were made to the presidential campaigns in 2008.

On what bases are these interest groups established? There are many possibilities.

Source of Income: Capital or Labor   According to orthodox Marxism, people's political interests are determined by whether they are capitalists or laborers. This view is too simple to explain interest-group formation in the contemporary United States. Even though individuals with high incomes tend to receive a disproportionate share of their income from capital, much of the income of the rich is also derived from labor. Thus, it is difficult even to tell who is a "capitalist" and who a "laborer." Indeed, studies of the distribution of income in the United States and other Western nations indicate that the driving force behind inequality in total income is the inequality in labor income [Lee, 2005].

Size of Income   The rich and the poor disagree on many economic policy issues. For example, they may hold different views on the merits of redistributive spending programs. Similarly, each group supports implicit or explicit subsidies for goods they consume intensively. Hence, the rich support subsidies for owner-occupied housing, while the poor favor special treatment for rental housing.

Source of Income: Industry of Employment   Both workers and owners have a common interest in government support for their industry. In the steel, textile, and automobile industries, for example, unions and management work shoulder to shoulder in order to lobby the government for protection against foreign competition.

Region   Residents of geographical regions often share common interests. Citizens of the Sun Belt are interested in favorable tax treatment of oil; midwesterners care about agricultural subsidies; and northeasterners lobby for expenditures on urban development.

Demographic and Personal Characteristics   The elderly favor subsidized health care and generous retirement programs; young married couples are interested in good schools and low payroll taxes. Religious beliefs play a major role in debates over the funding of abortion and state aid to private schools. Ethnic groups differ on the propriety of government expenditure for bilingual education programs. Gender is an important basis for interest-group formation; in the 2008 elections, women voted in disproportionately large numbers for Democrats, and Republicans expressed much concern over the gender gap.

The list could go on indefinitely. Given the numerous bases on which interest groups can be established, it is no surprise that people who are in opposition on one issue may be in agreement on another; "politics makes strange bedfellows" is more or less the order of the day.

This discussion has ignored the question of how individuals with common interests actually manage to organize themselves. Belonging to a group may require membership fees, donation of time, and so forth. Each individual has an incentive to let others do the work while he or she reaps the benefits, becoming a free rider. The

Figure 6.5
Rent-seeking
If the peanut industry succeeds in getting the government to enforce a cartel (perhaps by requiring a permit to grow peanuts or establishing a peanut quota), then the incumbent firms can maintain an artificially high price and receive rents.

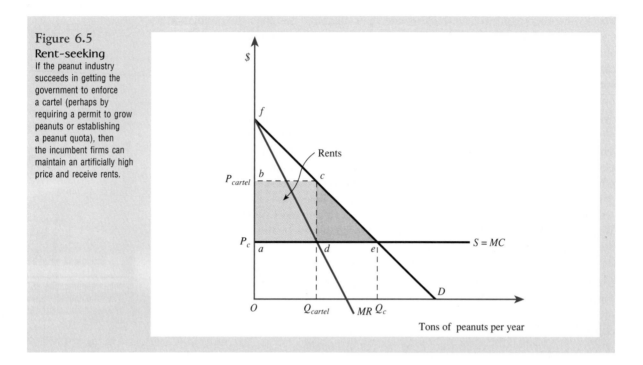

probability that a group will actually form increases when the number of individuals is small, and it is possible to levy sanctions against nonjoiners. But in some cases, rational financial self-interest is probably not the explanation. The debate over the public funding of abortion illustrates the influence of ideology and emotion on the decision to join a group.

Rent-Seeking   We have noted that groups of citizens can manipulate the political system to redistribute income toward themselves. Generically, such activity is called **rent-seeking**—using the government to obtain higher than normal returns ("rents"). Rent-seeking takes a variety of forms. An important variant is when a group of producers induces the government to restrict the output in their industry. Restricting output leads to higher prices for producers, allowing them to earn rents. For example, for many years in the United States, you could grow peanuts only if you had a government license, and the licenses allowed for just 1.5 million acres of land to be devoted to peanut production. By restricting the amount of land that could be used to grow peanuts, the government reduced peanut production and generated rents for the producers.

To analyze rent-seeking, consider Figure 6.5, which depicts the peanut market. The demand curve is D. For simplicity, we assume that the supply of peanuts, S, is horizontal. In the absence of government intervention, the equilibrium is at the intersection of supply and demand, where output is Q_c and price is P_c. (The subscript c reminds us that it is the competitive outcome.) It would be in the peanut producers' interest if they could all agree to reduce their respective outputs and thereby force up the market price. More precisely, they would be better off if they jointly acted to maximize industry profits and split them up—in effect to form a **cartel,** an arrangement under which suppliers band together to restrict output and raise price.

rent-seeking

Using the government to obtain higher than normal returns ("rents").

cartel

An arrangement under which suppliers band together to restrict output and raise price.

Why don't they just do it? Because even though *collectively* they would benefit by being part of a cartel, this does not mean that it is in any *individual's* self-interest. When the cartel raises its price, any individual farm has an incentive to cheat, that is, to increase its production beyond its agreed-upon quota. But all farms face this incentive, and as they all increase their outputs, the price falls back to the competitive equilibrium. This is where the government comes in. If the producers can get the government to enforce the cartel, then they can maintain the high price without having to worry about cheating. In the case of the peanut industry, for many decades the government had a simple way to enforce the cartel—it made growing peanuts without a license a federal crime! Further, even if you had a license, the quantity of peanuts you could grow was determined by a government quota. The program was very successful from the farmers' point of view. Domestic peanut prices were twice as high as world prices, leading to huge rents for the owners of licenses. When peanut licenses were eliminated by Congress in 2002, they were replaced with a multibillion dollar direct subsidy [Riedl, 2002].

What is the best price from the cartel's standpoint? To maximize industry profits, the cartel needs to produce the output at which industry marginal cost (the incremental cost of producing a ton of peanuts) equals industry marginal revenue (the incremental revenue from selling a ton of peanuts). The supply curve represents the marginal cost (MC) of production, and the marginal revenue curve is depicted as MR. The cartel output, Q_{cartel}, is determined by their intersection, and the associated price is P_{cartel}. By virtue of the higher price they receive per ton of peanuts (distance ab) on each of the ad units they sell, the peanut farmers earn rents equal to area $abcd$.

It costs money for the producers to maintain the system of licenses. Presumably, they have to make campaign contributions to key members of Congress, hire lobbyists, and so on. What is the maximal amount that they would be willing to pay to maintain the system? Because rents are a payment above the ordinary return, the *most* that the firms would be willing to pay for their favored position is the total amount of the rents, *abcd*.

So far, it would seem that the rent-seeking behavior simply leads to a transfer from consumers (who pay a higher price) to the producers (who receive rents). But more is at stake. Recall that consumer surplus is the area above the price and below the demand curve. (See the appendix at the end of this book.) Hence, prior to the licenses, consumer surplus was area *fae*. Similar reasoning suggests that consumer surplus after the licenses is area *fbc*. Hence, consumers are worse off by the difference between the two areas, *abce*. Recall that of this, *abcd* goes to the producers. Who gets the rest of the lost surplus, *dce*? The answer is nobody—it is a **deadweight loss** to society, a pure waste with no accompanying gain. The deadweight loss occurs because the increase in peanut prices distorts consumers' choices between peanuts and all other goods, leading to fewer peanuts being produced than is efficient.

In standard treatments of monopoly, area *dce* is the only deadweight loss. But in our rent-seeking model, the deadweight loss might actually be larger. As already suggested, rent-seeking can use up resources—lobbyists spend their time influencing legislators, consultants testify before regulatory panels, and advertisers conduct public relations campaigns. Such resources, which could have been used to produce new goods and services, are instead consumed in a struggle over the distribution of existing goods and services. Hence, area *abcd* does not represent a mere lump-sum transfer; it is a measure of real resources used up to maintain a position of market

deadweight loss

The pure waste created when the marginal budget of a commodity differs from its marginal cost.

power. In short, according to this view, the deadweight loss associated with rent-seeking is the *sum* of *abcd* and *dce*, or *abce*.

We cannot conclude that area *abce* is always the loss, however. In many cases, this area may overstate the efficiency cost of rent-seeking. For example, some rent-seeking takes the form of campaign contributions and bribes, and these are simply transfers—they do not "use up" real resources. Nevertheless, an important contribution of the rent-seeking model is that it focuses our attention on the potential size of the waste generated by the government's power to create rents.

A final question is why rent-seeking is allowed to exist. After all, Figure 6.5 shows that the losses to consumers are greater than the gains to the producers. Why don't the consumers prevent the introduction of such licenses?

One reason is that interest groups may be well organized and armed with information, while those who will bear the costs are not organized and may not even be aware of what is going on. Even if those citizens who will bear the costs are well informed, it may not be worth their while to fight back. Because the costs of the program are spread over the population as a whole, any given peanut consumer's share is low, and it is not worth the time and effort to organize opposition. In contrast, the benefits are relatively concentrated, making political organization worthwhile for potential beneficiaries.

Other Actors

Without attempting to be exhaustive, we list a few other parties that affect government fiscal decisions.

Through court decisions, the judiciary has major effects on government spending. Judges have mandated public expenditures on items as diverse as bilingual education in the public schools and prison remodeling. A striking example occurred when a California court ruled that an additional $2.5 billion had to be spent on California's prison health care system. This is only part of the court-ordered $7 billion plan to improve health care facilities for inmates [White, 2008, p. A3].

Journalists can affect fiscal outcomes by bringing certain issues to public attention. For example, the widespread publicity given to crumbling bridges and roads has induced a number of jurisdictions to increase spending on infrastructure. A study by Gerber, Karlan, and Bergan [2006] examined whether newspapers influence the way people vote. They randomly assigned people to receive either the *Washington Post* (generally considered to be a liberal newspaper), the *Washington Times* (generally considered to be conservative), and no newspaper at all. They found that those receiving the *Washington Post* were 8 percentage points more likely to vote for a Democratic candidate for governor than those who did not receive a paper, suggesting that the media indeed can influence voting behavior.

Finally, given that information is potentially an important source of power, experts can influence public sector decisions. Legislative aides who gain expertise on certain programs often play important roles in drafting statutes. There are also experts outside the government. Academic social scientists, environmental engineers, and others seek to use their expertise to influence economic policy. Economists love to quote John Maynard Keynes's [1965/1936, p. 383] famous dictum "the ideas of economists and political philosophers, both when they are right and when they are wrong, are more powerful than is commonly understood. Indeed, the world is ruled by little else." However, it is extremely difficult to determine whether social science research influences policy, and if so, through what channels this influence operates.

Table 6.6   **Ratio of Government Expenditures to Gross Domestic Product in Selected Countries** *(selected years)*

Year	Canada	Switzerland	United Kingdom
1900	9.5	n.a.	14.4
1910	11.4	n.a.	12.7
1920	16.1	n.a.	26.2
1930	18.9	15.9	26.1
1940	23.1	19.2	30.0
1950	22.1	19.9	39.0
1960	29.7	17.7	31.9
1970	36.0	21.3	41.8
1980	41.6	29.3	45.2
1990	48.8	30.3	41.1
2000	41.1	35.1	39.1
2007	39.1	33.7	44.4

Sources: Years before 1970 from Pommerehne [1977]. Subsequent years computed from Organization for Economic Cooperation and Development [2007b].

Note: Switzerland data are not available for 2007, so the value supplied is from 2006. n.a. = not available.

▶ EXPLAINING GOVERNMENT GROWTH

Much of the concern about political economy issues has been stimulated by the growth of government. As documented in Chapter 1, public expenditures in the United States have grown enormously over the long run, both in absolute terms and proportionately. A growing public sector is not unique to the United States, as the figures for a few other Western countries in Table 6.6 indicate. Thus, as we seek explanations for the growth of government, care must be taken not to rely too heavily on events and institutions that are peculiar to the US experience. Some of the most prominent theories follow. They are not necessarily mutually exclusive. No single theory accounts for the whole phenomenon. Indeed, even taken together, they still leave much unexplained.

Citizen Preferences   One view is that growth in government expenditure is an expression of the preferences of the citizenry. Suppose the median voter's demand for public sector goods and services (G) is some function (f) of the relative price of public sector goods and services (P) and income (I):

$$G = f(P, I) \qquad (6.1)$$

There are many different ways such a demand function can lead to an increasing proportion of income devoted to the public sector. Suppose that when income increases by a given percentage, the quantity demanded of public goods and services increases by a greater percentage—the income elasticity of demand is greater than one. If so, the process of income growth by itself leads to an ever-increasing share of income going to the public sector, other things being the same.[13] Similarly, if the price elasticity of

---

[13] The hypothesis that government services rise at a faster rate than income is often called Wagner's Law, after Adolph Wagner, the 19th-century economist who formulated it.

demand for G is less than one and P increases over time, the government's share of income can increase.

The important point is that the increase in the relative size of the public sector does not necessarily imply something is "wrong" with the political process. Government growth could well be a consequence of the wishes of voters, who rationally take into account its opportunity cost in terms of forgone consumption in the private sector. The question then becomes whether the actual changes in P and I over time could have accounted for the observed historical changes in G. To answer this question, a natural approach is to begin by computing the actual percentage changes in P and I that have occurred over time. Then multiply the percentage change in P by an econometric estimate of the elasticity of G with respect to P, and the percentage change in I by the elasticity with respect to I. This calculation yields the percentage change in G attributable solely to changes in P and I. Next compare this figure with the actual change in G. One estimate based on this approach suggests that only about 40 percent of the growth in US public budgets can be explained by Equation (6.1). (See Holsey and Borcherding [1997].) While this is an admittedly rough calculation, it does suggest that more is going on than a simple median voter story can explain.

Marxist View   Some Marxist theories view the rise of state expenditure as inherent to the political-economic system. In the Marxist model, the private sector tends to overproduce, so the capitalist-controlled government must expand expenditures to absorb this production. Typically, this is accomplished by augmenting military spending. At the same time, the state attempts to decrease worker discontent by increasing spending for social services. Eventually, rising expenditures outpace tax revenue capacity, and the government collapses.

The historical facts seem to contradict this analysis. For example, it is noteworthy that in Western Europe, the enormous increase in the size and scope of government in the post–World War II era has been accompanied by anything but a resurgence in militarism. The main contribution of this Marxist analysis is its explicit recognition of the links between the economic and political systems as sources of government growth.

Chance Events   In contrast to the theories that view government growth as inevitable are those that consider it to be the consequence of chance events. In "normal" periods there is only moderate growth in public expenditure. Occasionally, however, external shocks to the economic and social system "require" higher levels of government expenditure and novel methods of financing. Even after the shock disappears, higher levels continue to prevail because of inertia. Examples of shocks are the Great Depression, World War II, the Great Society, and the Vietnam War.

Changes in Social Attitudes   Popular discussions sometimes suggest that social trends encouraging personal self-assertiveness lead people to make extravagant demands on the political system. At the same time, widespread television advertising creates unrealistically high expectations, leading to a "Santa Claus mentality" that causes people to lose track of the fact that government programs do have an opportunity cost.

However, one could just as well argue that people undervalue the benefits of government projects instead of their costs. In this case, the public sector is too small, not too big. More generally, although recent social phenomena might account for some movement in the growth of government expenditure, it has been going on for too many years and in too many places for this explanation to have much credibility.

Income Redistribution   Government grows because low-income individuals use the political system to redistribute income toward themselves. The idea is that politicians can attract voters whose incomes are at or below the median by offering benefits that impose a net cost on those whose incomes are above the median. As long as average income exceeds the median, and the mechanisms used to bring about redistribution are not too detrimental to incentives, politicians can gain votes by increasing the scope of government-sponsored income distribution. Suppose, for example, that there are five voters whose incomes are $5,000; $10,000; $15,000; $25,000; and $40,000. The median income is $15,000 and the average income is $19,000. A politician who supports government programs that transfer income to those with less than $25,000 will win in majority voting. Consistent with this story is the notion that as the difference between the median and average income grows, so too does the amount of government-sponsored redistribution—the more that income is concentrated at the top, the greater the potential benefits to the median voter of redistributive transfers. According to the literature surveyed by Persson and Tabellini [1999], this is indeed a reasonable characterization of income transfer policy in developed nations.

A possible problem with this theory is that it does not explain why the share of public expenditures increases *gradually* (as in Table 1.1). Why not a huge once-and-for-all transfer as the poor confiscate the incomes of the rich? Because in Western countries, property and/or status requirements for voting have *gradually* been abolished during the last century. In the United States, many of the remaining barriers to voting were removed by civil rights laws passed in the 1960s. Extension of the right to vote to those at the bottom of the income scale increases the proportion of voters likely to support politicians promising redistribution. Hence, the gradual extension of the franchise leads to continuous growth in government, rather than a once-and-for-all increase. This conjecture is consistent with Husted and Kenny's [1997] analysis of state spending patterns from 1950 to 1958. During this period, a number of states eliminated poll taxes and literacy tests, which led to higher voter turnout, particularly among the poor. In such states, there was "a sharp rise in welfare spending but no change in other spending" [p. 54].

A limitation of this theory is that it fails to explain the methods used by government to redistribute income. If it is correct, most income transfers should go to the poor and should take the form that would maximize their welfare, that is, direct cash transfers. Instead, as we see in Chapter 12, transfers in the United States are often given in kind (that is, in the form of goods and services rather than cash) and many benefit those in the middle- and upper-income classes.

An alternative view is that income redistribution favors primarily middle-income individuals: "Public expenditures are made for the benefit primarily of the middle classes, and financed by taxes which are borne in considerable part by the poor and the rich."[14] But there are also government transfer programs with rich beneficiaries; see, for example, the discussion of Medicare in Chapter 10.

Transfer programs that benefit different income classes can exist simultaneously, so these various views of government redistribution are not necessarily mutually exclusive.

---

[14] This proposition is known as Director's Law, after the economist Aaron Director.

The important point here is their common theme. Politicians, rent-seeking special-interest groups, and bureaucrats vote themselves programs of ever-increasing size.

Controlling Government Growth

As already noted, substantial growth in the public sector need not imply that anything is wrong with the budgetary process. For those who believe that public sector fiscal behavior is more or less dictated by the preferences of the median voter, bringing government under control is a nonissue. On the other hand, for those who perceive growth in government as a symptom of flaws in the political process, constraining the government is very much a problem.

Two types of argument are made in the controllability debate. One view is that the basic problem results from commitments made by government in the past, so there is very little current politicians can do to change the rate of growth or composition of government expenditures. Entitlement programs that provide benefits to the retired, disabled, unemployed, sick, and others are the largest category of uncontrollable expenditures. When we add other items such as payments on the national debt, farm support programs, and certain defense expenditures, about 75 percent of the federal budget is uncontrollable.

Are these expenditures really uncontrollable? If legislation created entitlement programs, it can take them away. In theory, then, many of the programs can be reduced or even eliminated. In reality, both moral and political considerations work against reneging on past promises to various groups in the population. Any serious reductions are likely to be scheduled far in the future, so that people who have made commitments based on current programs will not be affected.

According to the second argument, our political institutions are fundamentally flawed, and bringing things under control is more than just a matter of changing the entitlement programs. A number of remedies have been proposed.

Change Bureaucratic Incentives   Niskanen, who views bureaucracy as a cause of unwarranted government growth, suggests that financial incentives be created to mitigate bureaucrats' empire-building tendencies. For example, the salary of a government manager could be made to depend negatively on changes in the size of his or her agency. A bureaucrat who cut the agency's budget would get a raise. (Similar rewards could be offered to budget-cutting legislators.) However, such a system could lead to undesirable results. To increase his or her salary, the bureaucrat might reduce the budget beyond the point at which marginal benefits equal marginal costs. Do we really want a social worker's salary to increase every time he or she cuts the number of families deemed eligible to receive welfare payments?

Niskanen also suggests expanding the use of private firms to produce public goods and services, although the public sector would continue to finance them. The issues surrounding privatization were already discussed in Chapter 4.

Change Fiscal Institutions   Most of the focus on bringing government spending under control has been on the budget-making process. Over the years, critics of the process have argued that federal budget making is undisciplined.

Beginning in the 1980s, Congress passed several pieces of legislation whose goal was to impose some discipline by establishing spending and revenue targets. For example, the budget passed in 1997 put a cap on discretionary spending for each year from 1998 to 2002. (Discretionary spending refers to spending that Congress actually votes on, everything from building tanks to paying civil servants.) An elaborate set of parliamentary rules determined circumstances under which the cap could be exceeded.

The problem is that Congress has shown more than a little creativity when it comes to circumventing rules. For example, congressional spending caps allowed exemptions for unforeseen emergencies. In 1999, $4.5 billion to pay for the decennial census was categorized this way. But given that the census is mandated by the Constitution, the need to pay for the year 2000 census arguably could have been predicted over 200 years ago! More recently, expenditures of nearly $90 billion for the wars in Afghanistan and Iraq were classified as emergencies and thus not counted against the caps.

Given such anecdotes, it is natural to ask whether fiscal institutions matter at all. If the president and Congress both want to spend a certain amount of money, won't they simply collude to get around whatever rules prevail? Indeed, it took only one year for Congress to violate its "pay-as-you-go" rule (adopted in 2007) that requires new spending or tax cuts to be offset by other spending decreases or tax increases. The Economic Stimulus Act of 2008 increased the budget deficit by $152 billion and offered no pay-as-you-go offsets [*Wall Street Journal*, 2008, p. A14]. That said, one cannot rule out the possibility that congressional budget rules have reduced the deficit, because one doesn't know what spending would have looked like in the absence of such rules.

Another way to try to study the importance of fiscal institutions is to look at the experience of the states, most of which have rules in their constitutions that forbid deficits in their operating budgets. (The operating budget pays for current expenses, as opposed to the capital budget, which finances long-term investments like roads and buildings.) Importantly, the rules differ in their scope and severity. In some states, the only requirement is for the governor to submit a balanced budget. If it turns out that the governor's projections are incorrect and a deficit results, there is no requirement that the state raise taxes or cut spending—the state can borrow to finance the deficit and carry it into the next year. Other states do not allow such behavior—deficits cannot be carried forward. Accounting tricks of the kind described above are sometimes used to deal with the presence of deficits in these states. For example, the governor of Colorado once reduced his state's deficit by $268 million by delaying payments of a month's worth of wages to state employees by one day, pushing them from the last day of the current fiscal year into the first day of the next. Nevertheless, such gambits are generally not employed.

A natural research strategy is to investigate whether states with strict budgetary rules have smaller deficits and react more quickly to unanticipated shortfalls in revenue than states with lenient rules. There is some evidence that, in fact, this is what happens. It is a bit tricky to interpret this evidence, because we do not know if the outcomes in the states with strict rules really are due to the rules themselves. It could be, for example, that strict rules are passed by fiscally conservative legislators, who would deal aggressively with deficits even without legal compulsion. Several econometric studies have concluded that, even after taking such complications into account, fiscal institutions matter. In an analysis of federal budget rules, economist Alan Auerbach found that "the rules did have some effects, rather than simply being statements of policy intentions. The rules may also have had some success at deficit control" [Auerbach, 2008].

Institute Constitutional Limitations   The problems with budget rules passed by Congress is that they are simply pieces of legislation and as such can readily be amended, suspended, or repealed by a majority vote of both houses of Congress. Some would go further and put budgetary rules into the Constitution itself. Several constitutional amendments have been proposed; the provisions of the following variant are typical.

1. Congress must adopt a budget statement "in which total outlays are no greater than total receipts."
2. Total receipts may not increase "by a rate greater than the rate of increase in national income."
3. "The Congress and President shall . . . ensure that actual outlays do not exceed the outlays set forth in the budget statement."
4. The provisions can be overridden in times of war.

Most economists—both liberals and conservatives—believe a balanced budget amendment is an ill-conceived idea for several reasons.[15]

First, adopting a statement of outlays and revenues requires making forecasts about how the economy will perform. This problem is sufficiently difficult that forecasters with complete integrity can produce very different estimates. How does the Congress choose among forecasts? If an incorrect forecast is chosen, Congress may be in violation of the law without realizing it! Things become even murkier when one realizes that some forecasts will be biased by political considerations. Those who want to expand expenditures, for example, would encourage forecasts that overestimated tax revenues during the coming year and vice versa.

Second, the amendment fails to define "outlays" and "receipts." By using suitable accounting methods, Congress could easily circumvent the law. One way to do this is to create corporations that are authorized to make expenditures and borrow but are not officially part of the government. For example, before 1968 the Federal National Mortgage Association (Fannie Mae) was a government entity that bought mortgages, bundled them into "mortgage-backed securities," and resold them to the private sector. Fannie Mae was privatized in 1968 in part to get its debts off the federal budget and make it politically easier for the administration to increase expenditures for the Vietnam War. During the financial crisis of 2008, Fannie Mae collapsed, and as soon as it did, the government took it back over. Hence, Fannie might have been "privatized" in the accounting sense, but in a real sense, its spending and borrowing activities were part of the federal budget. Such off-budget activity remains an important way of concealing the actual size of the budget, and it would likely increase if there were a balanced budget amendment. Alternatively, legislators might try to accomplish with regulation goals what they might otherwise have attained by increased expenditure. For example, instead of spending more on health care, Congress could mandate that employers provide insurance for their workers.

Finally, legal scholars have noted some important questions. What happens if there is a deficit? Is the entire Congress put in jail? Could Congress be sued for spending too much? Would federal judges wind up making economic policy? Could a single citizen go to court and obtain an injunction to stop all government activity in the event of a deficit? The experience with Congressional spending caps is informative. When the consequences of complying with the law seemed worse than ignoring the law, the law was ignored.

Nevertheless, constitutional limitations on spending and deficits remain popular. A balanced budget amendment was narrowly defeated in the Congress in 1997. But the proposal is likely to be raised again in the future.

---

[15] See Schultze [1995] for arguments against an amendment, and Buchanan [1995] for arguments in favor.

Conclusions

Public decision making is complicated and not well understood. Contrary to simple models of democracy, there appear to be forces pulling government expenditures away from levels that would be preferred by the median voter. However, critics of the current budgetary process have not come up with a satisfactory alternative. The formulation of meaningful rules and constraints for the budgetary process, either at the constitutional or statutory level, is an important item on both the academic and political agendas for the years ahead.

Finally, it should be stressed that a judgment that the current system of public finance is inequitable or inefficient does not necessarily imply that government as an institution is "bad." People who like market-oriented approaches to resource allocation can nevertheless seek to improve markets. The same goes for government.

Summary

- Political economy applies economic principles to the analysis of political decision making.
- Economists have studied several methods for choosing levels of public goods in a direct democracy.

  Lindahl pricing results in a unanimous decision to provide an efficient quantity of public goods, but relies on honest revelation of preferences.

  Majority voting may lead to inconsistent decisions regarding public goods if some people's preferences are not single peaked.

  Logrolling allows voters to express the intensity of their preferences by trading votes. However, minority gains may come at the expense of greater general losses.

- Arrow's Impossibility Theorem states that, in general, it is impossible to find a decision-making rule that simultaneously satisfies a number of apparently reasonable criteria. The implication is that democracies are inherently prone to make inconsistent decisions.
- Explanations of government behavior in a representative democracy require studying the interaction of elected officials, public employees, and special-interest groups.
- Under restrictive assumptions, the actions of elected officials mimic the wishes of the median voter.

- Public employees have an important impact on the development and implementation of economic policy. One theory predicts that bureaucrats attempt to maximize the size of their agencies' budgets, resulting in oversupply of the service.
- Rent-seeking private citizens form groups to influence government activity. Special interests can form on the basis of income source, income size, industry, region, or personal characteristics.
- The growth of government has been rapid by any measure. Explanations of this phenomenon include:

  Citizens simply want a larger government.

  The public sector must expand to absorb private excess production.

  Random events (such as wars) increase the growth of government, while inertia prevents a return to previous levels.

  Unrealistic expectations have resulted in increasing demands that ignore the opportunity costs of public programs.

  Certain groups use the government to redistribute income to themselves.

- Proposals to control the growth in government include encouraging private sector competition, reforming the budget process, and constitutional amendments.

Discussion Questions

1. Suppose there are five people—1, 2, 3, 4, and 5—who rank projects A, B, C, and D as follows:

1	2	3	4	5
A	A	D	C	B
D	C	B	B	C
C	B	C	D	D
B	D	A	A	A

   a. Sketch the preferences, as in Figure 6.2.
   b. Will any project be chosen by a majority vote rule? If so, which one? If not, explain why.

2. The 2005 transportation bill listed over 5,000 "high-priority projects" to be funded through the Department of Transportation. These included the money for "safe access to streets for bicyclists and pedestrians" in Covina, California, and money for expanding a state road in Robbins, Tennessee. Which of our models of political decision making best explains this scenario in which particular projects are funded in each of the states?

3. Three voters, A, B, and C, will decide by majority rule whether to pass bills on issues X and Y. *Each of the two issues will be voted on separately.* The change in net benefits (in dollars) that would result from passage of each bill is as follows:

	Issue	
Voter	**X**	**Y**
A	+6	−3
B	−1	+4
C	−2	−3

   a. Which issues (if any) would pass if decided by majority rule? Is this the efficient outcome?
   b. Which issues (if any) would pass if logrolling were allowed? Would logrolling improve efficiency? Would it result in the efficient outcome?
   c. Suppose that it were legal for one voter to pay another to vote a certain way. Would allowing such side payments improve efficiency from part b? Would it result in the efficient outcome?
   d. What amount of side payments would take place if paying for votes were allowed?

4. The Free City of Christiania is a community of about 800 adults and 250 children within the city of Copenhagen. It was set up by "hippies and others" and is not subject to the same laws as the rest of Denmark. "There is no governing council or other administrative body, and everything is decided by consensus. . . . In practice, this means that many decisions are never made. . . . [T]ensions are rising among different groups of residents over how to share and pay for communal responsibilities" [Kinzer, 1996, p. A3]. Is this outcome consistent with our theories of voting in a direct democracy? What voting procedures would you recommend for Christiania?

5. In 2005, Kuwaiti women won the right to vote in parliamentary elections. Indeed, women voters now outnumber men voters in Kuwait because women are automatically registered while men have to register on their own. One woman noted, "The Ministers of Parliament used to vote against us; now they are wooing us to vote for them" [Fattah, 2006]. What does this tell us about the validity of the predictions of the median voter theorem?

6. In 1998, the people of Puerto Rico held a referendum in which there were five choices—retain commonwealth status, become a state, become independent, "free association" (a type of independence that would delegate certain powers to the United States), and "none of the above." Discuss the problems that can arise when people vote over five options.

7. Members of the European Union (EU) are required to keep their deficits below 3 percent of Gross Domestic Product. Countries that violate the rule can face huge fines. Nonetheless, many European countries have not met the 3 percent deficit target, and no fines have actually been imposed. On the basis of the US experience with congressional budget rules, how effective

would you predict the EU deficit limits to be? What kind of behavior would you expect to see EU countries exhibit?

8. The discussion of rent-seeking in this chapter noted that peanuts could not be grown without licenses. The licenses could be sold to nonfarmers, and in fact, many of them were owned by firms that had nothing to do with farming, such as insurance companies. Does this fact affect your view of whether or not it would be fair to eliminate the system of licenses for peanut farming? Include in your answer a discussion of the price that owners of the licenses have to pay for them.

9. Assume that the demand curve for milk is given by $Q = 100 - 10P$, where P is the price per gallon and Q is the quantity demanded per year. The supply curve is horizontal at a price of 2.

   a. Assuming that the market is competitive, what is the price per gallon of milk and the number of gallons sold?

   b. With the connivance of some politicians, the dairy farmers are able to form and maintain a cartel. (Such a cartel actually operates in the northeastern United States.) What is the cartel price, and how many gallons of milk are purchased? [Hint: The marginal revenue curve (MR) is given by $MR = 10 - Q/5$. Also, remember that the supply curve shows the marginal cost associated with each level of output.]

   c. What are the rents associated with the cartel?

   d. Suppose that in order to maintain the cartel, the dairy farmers simply give lump-sum campaign contributions to the relevant politicians. What is the maximum contribution they would be willing to make? What is the deadweight loss of the cartel?

   e. Suppose that instead of lump-sum contributions to politicians, the dairy farmers hire lobbyists and lawyers to make their case in Congress. How does this change your estimate of the deadweight loss associated with this rent-seeking activity?

10. In the aftermath of September 11 there were fears that terrorists would attempt to sabotage the country's food supply. Food safety is under the jurisdiction of the Food and Drug Administration (FDA). Use the Niskanen model of bureaucracy (Figure 6.4) to predict how new concerns over food safety would affect the optimal number of FDA employees and the actual number of employees.

11. Consider a society with three people (John, Eleanor, and Abigail) who use majority rule to decide how much money to spend on schools. There are three options for spending on a public park: H (high), M (medium), and L (low). These individuals rank the three options in the following way:

Rank	John	Eleanor	Abigail
1	M	L	H
2	L	M	M
3	H	H	L

   a. Consider all possible pairwise elections: M versus H, H versus L, and L versus M. What is the outcome of each election? Does it appear, in this case, that majority rule would lead to a stable outcome on spending on the public park? If so, what is that choice? Would giving one person the ability to set the agenda affect the outcome? Explain.

   b. Now suppose that Eleanor's preference ordering changed to the following: first choice = L, second choice = H, and third choice = M. Would majority rule lead to a stable outcome? If so, what is that choice? Would giving one person the ability to set the agenda affect the outcome? Explain.

EDUCATION

The foundation of every state is the education of its youth.

—DIOGENES LAERTIUS

The previous chapters have presented the approach that economists use to determine when government intervention is justified in the market economy. We now put this approach into action by applying it to the area of education. In addition to being an excellent case study for the application of the tools of public finance, education is of independent interest if for no other reason than the enormous amount of money that governments spend on it. In the United States, the combined spending of local, state, and federal governments on elementary and secondary education exceeds $521 billion [US Bureau of the Census, 2009, p. 151].[1] As Table 7.1 indicates, since 1980, real per-pupil expenditures on elementary and secondary education have increased by about 81 percent. Nevertheless, for many years Americans have considered the nation's public schools to be operating at a substandard level [Phi Delta Kappa/Gallup, 2005]. These facts underscore the importance of carefully evaluating education policy using the public finance skills we have acquired.

Table 7.1 Real Annual Expenditure per Pupil in Public Elementary and Secondary Schools *(selected years)*

School Year	Expenditure per Pupil (2006 dollars)
1980	$5,016
1985	6,057
1990	7,102
1995	7,322
2000	8,068
2005	8,998
2006	9,100

Source: US Bureau of the Census [2009, p. 151].

Real per-pupil expenditures on elementary and secondary public education have increased by 81 percent since 1980.

---

[1] Chapter 22 examines the rationale for the division of education spending across the different levels of government.

▶ JUSTIFYING GOVERNMENT INTERVENTION IN EDUCATION

The framework of welfare economics suggests that we begin with a fundamental question: Why should the government involve itself so extensively in education, rather than leave its provision to the market? As seen in previous chapters, markets fail to provide a good efficiently when it is a public good or when it generates externalities, so we consider whether education falls into either of these categories.

Is Education a Public Good?

Recall that a public good is nonrival and nonexcludable. Education does not fit either of these criteria. It is rival in consumption, at least to some extent, because as the number of students in a classroom increases past some point, each student receives less individualized attention from the teacher, the classroom becomes more congested, and there are other strains on educational resources. Unlike a nonrival good, adding another "consumer" of education imposes a cost on other consumers. Education is excludable because one can easily prevent a student from obtaining the services provided by a school. In short, education is primarily a private good, improving students' welfare by enhancing their ability to earn a living and, more generally, to deal with life.

Does Education Generate Positive Externalities?

Even though education is primarily a private good, many argue that educating a child provides benefits to other people in society.

One possible positive externality derives from the fact that education serves as a powerful force for socialization. As the Greek historian Plutarch wrote in his *Morals,* "The very spring and root of honesty and virtue lie in good education." And in democratic governments, education gives voters perspective on which to base their political choices. As George Washington wrote, "In proportion as the structure of a government gives force to public opinion, it is essential that public opinion should be enlightened." Both of these views suggest that education helps to make an informed and cohesive citizenry, which serves an especially important function within a democracy. Indeed, Glaeser, Ponzetto, and Shleifer [2006] find a high empirical correlation between the levels of education and democratic government across countries.

However, there have recently been some challenges to this conventional wisdom. Acemoglu et al. [2005] consider how years of education are correlated with democracy across countries. (The extent of democracy is measured by a numerical index based on a checklist of questions, including items such as whether the country has fair elections, whether those who are elected actually govern, whether there are competitive political parties, and so on.) As one might expect, they find a positive correlation—countries with higher average years of schooling also are more democratic. They note, however, that countries vary so much in their cultures, histories, and social institutions that it would be misleading to ascribe a causal relationship to this cross-sectional correlation. Therefore, they focus on how *changes* in years of education *within* a country change the index of democracy. In effect, by focusing on changes within countries, they control for the differences in characteristics across countries that are difficult or impossible to measure. Their analysis of the data suggests that once one looks within countries, the correlation between education and democracy disappears. Their controversial conclusion is that the evidence does not support the notion that increases in education make a country more democratic. One must be cautious about this finding. It might be because other things were changing within various countries, and these changes masked the impact of education. In any case, this study reminds us that many propositions that we take for granted can be very difficult to verify empirically.

The Case of Higher Education   The magnitude of the external benefits of education likely varies by education level. For example, if the socialization benefits of education exhibit diminishing marginal returns, then elementary and secondary schooling generate higher external benefits than higher education, suggesting that government should intervene less in higher education than in earlier levels.

Indeed, the federal government subsidizes higher education less than primary and secondary education. Nonetheless, the federal government has been supporting higher education on a large scale since the mid-1960s.[2] In 2008, the federal government spent approximately $17 billion on direct grants and work-study programs for college students. Student federal aid also came in the form of $74 billion worth of loans. More than 23 million awards of federal grants or loans were made in 2008 [US Bureau of the Census, 2009, p. 178]. In addition, several subsidies for higher education are included in the personal income tax system. These include the HOPE tax credit and the Lifetime Learning tax credit (which in 2008 amounted to approximately a $6 billion government subsidy) and the deductibility of interest on student loans, some educational expenses, and scholarship and fellowship income (which in 2008 cost the Treasury approximately $4 billion) [US Office of Management and Budget, 2008, p. 290].

Some argue that college education should be subsidized because it increases productivity. That college increases productivity may be true, but *as long as the earnings of college graduates reflect their higher productivity, there is no externality*. We will examine later the question of whether education does in fact lead to higher earnings. For now, the key point is that for the externality argument to be convincing, one must show that there are productivity gains due to higher education that are not reflected in students' future earnings.

Even if higher education provides positive externalities, this would not provide an efficiency justification for current government programs, which subsidize all eligible students at the same rate. Are the external benefits of all kinds of college training equal? Do art history, accounting, and premedical courses all produce the same externalities? If not, efficiency would require that they be subsidized differentially.

Proponents of subsidies argue that if they were removed, fewer people would attend college. This is probably true, because removing the subsidies would

---

[2] For further details, see Kane [1998]. State and local governments also provide substantial support, amounting to over $65 billion annually [US Department of Education, 2007, Tables 340, 341, and 342].

increase private costs for individuals. However, by itself this does not justify subsidies. If subsidies were granted to young people who wanted to open auto repair shops and these were cut, then the number of auto repair shops would also decline. Why should a potential car mechanic be treated differently from a potential classicist?

Some argue that this reasoning ignores imperfections in the private sector market for loans. It is very difficult to provide collateral for loans for **human capital**—investments that people make in themselves to increase their productivity—so these lending markets might not materialize. In that case, some students for whom the benefits of higher education exceed the costs might nevertheless not go to college due to a lack of funds, which is an inefficient outcome. One possible remedy for this market failure is for the government to make loans available to any student at the market rate of interest. Opponents of this policy believe that students should not have to borrow to attend college because the burden of debt distorts their career choices: young people should "choose careers based on their real interests, not on their interest rates" [Zimmerman, 2007]. A contrary view is that "the prospect of heavy debt after graduation would no doubt discourage some students from borrowing. But that may be the wisest form of restraint. Someone finally has to pay the bill, and it is hard to see why that should be the taxpayers rather than the direct beneficiary of the schooling" [Passell, 1985].

human capital

The investments that individuals make in education, training, and health care that raise their productive capacity.

Is the Education Market Inequitable?

The preceding arguments for and against government intervention in education focus on economic efficiency. As we discussed in Chapter 3, welfare economics also requires us to consider equity, and here, too, arguments can be made for public education and for subsidized higher education.

Recall from Chapter 4 the notion of commodity egalitarianism, which suggests that fairness requires that certain goods be available to everyone. If education is a normal good, then we would expect a free market for education to lead to different levels of education for different income classes, with some lower-income people perhaps winding up with little or no education. The commodity egalitarianism view suggests that it should be made available to all citizens regardless of the benefits and costs. This view is especially prevalent with respect to elementary and secondary education.

But does the equity argument also justify government subsidies for higher education? Subsidies for college students represent a transfer from taxpayers as a whole to college students. Looking at the student as part of the family he or she has grown up in, it seems that educational aid programs do indeed enhance income equality. The likelihood of receiving federal aid decreases as family income increases. Remember, though, that most college students are individuals about to form their own households, and the lifetime incomes of college graduates are higher than those of the population as a whole. Therefore to the extent that those receiving the subsidies would have gone to college anyway, the subsidies could lead to greater income inequality. Indeed, Cameron and Heckman [2001] find that family income in itself does not affect college attendance. Rather, income is a measure of the long-term environment in which children are raised. When measures of ability are included in their statistical analyses of college enrollment, tuition and family income diminish greatly in importance.

▶ WHAT CAN GOVERNMENT INTERVENTION IN EDUCATION ACCOMPLISH?

If education produces positive externalities, it follows that government should subsidize it. We go beyond subsidization, however, when we make public elementary and secondary education both free (taxpayer financed) and compulsory. Such a system, which is common in many countries, cannot be rationalized on efficiency grounds alone. Because students obtain private benefits of education, an efficient policy would pay only part of their education costs. A notion like commodity egalitarianism must be introduced to rationalize a policy that provides a certain level of education, without regard to cost or external benefits.

Another feature of our system is that in addition to financing education, government produces it as well. Why should this be the case? One theory is that government needs to produce education in order for society to obtain certain positive externalities. Education improves productivity and makes one a more informed and socialized citizen. The productivity gains are likely taken into account in the decision to get an education, because they lead to higher wages. However, the private benefits of being a more informed citizen are relatively small to each individual student. According to this theory, if the government funded but did not produce education, then private schools in competition for students would devote all their resources to teaching productivity-enhancing skills, not citizenry skills. The conclusion is that the development of a common commitment to established democratic processes is more easily carried out in a system of public schools protected from private competition. The validity of this theory, however, is very difficult to assess.

Does Government Intervention Crowd Out Private Education?

Whatever the rationale for providing free public schools, a surprising result of economic theory is that such a system does not necessarily induce everyone to consume more schooling than they would have in a private market. Consider the case of Gepetto, who is deciding how much education his son Pinocchio should consume. In Figure 7.1A, the amount of education is measured on the horizontal axis, and the quantity of all other goods consumed by the family on the vertical. (For simplicity, think of the amount of education as hours spent in the classroom. A more complicated model would also include aspects of the education that enhance its quality.) In the absence of a public school system, Gepetto can purchase as much education in the private market as he chooses at the going price, and his options are summarized by budget constraint AB. Subject to this constraint, he purchases e_o hours of education for Pinocchio; c_o is left over for expenditure on other goods.

Now suppose a public school opens. Gepetto can send Pinocchio to the public school for e_p hours per week at no cost to himself.[3] This option is represented not by a line but by the single point x, where education consumption is e_p and Gepetto can

---

[3] We realistically assume Gepetto's tax payments are independent of whether he has children enrolled in public school.

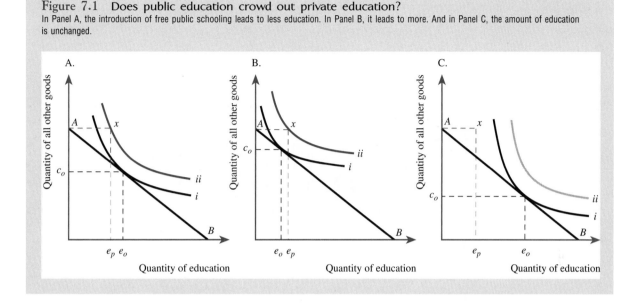

Figure 7.1   Does public education crowd out private education?
In Panel A, the introduction of free public schooling leads to less education. In Panel B, it leads to more. And in Panel C, the amount of education is unchanged.

spend his entire income on all other goods. Because indifference curve *ii*, which passes through *x*, is higher than indifference curve *i*, Gepetto takes Pinocchio out of private school and enrolls him in the public system. Importantly, e_p is less than e_o. Pinocchio's consumption of education falls. Intuitively, the existence of public education leads to a large increase in the opportunity cost of private education, inducing Gepetto to opt out of the private system, reducing Pinocchio's consumption of education as he does so. In this way, the public school system **crowds out** education. Note, however, that Figure 7.1A views public schooling as a "take-it-or-leave-it" option. To the extent that the amount of education offered through public schools can be supplemented by private lessons, it is less likely that public schooling will crowd out education consumed.

Of course, for a different set of indifference curves, public education could have induced Gepetto to increase his household's consumption of education. This is shown in Figure 7.1B, where the opening of the public school increases Pinocchio's consumption of education from e_o to e_p. Figure 7.1C shows a set of indifference curves in which there is no change in consumption of education after the introduction of public school. This analysis demonstrates that one cannot take for granted that the government provision of free education (or any other commodity, for that matter) leads to an increase in its consumption.

crowd out

When public provision of a good substitutes for private provision of the good.

Does Government Spending Improve Educational Outcomes?

Suppose that we accept the arguments in favor of government intervention in education, and in particular, that the government should run public schools. This leaves open the question of whether higher expenditures actually lead to better education. This is an inherently difficult question because it is not clear exactly what a "better education" is. Education has many goals, including improving students' cognitive skills, teaching them responsibility and how to get along with others, helping them

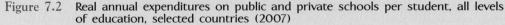

Figure 7.2   Real annual expenditures on public and private schools per student, all levels of education, selected countries (2007)

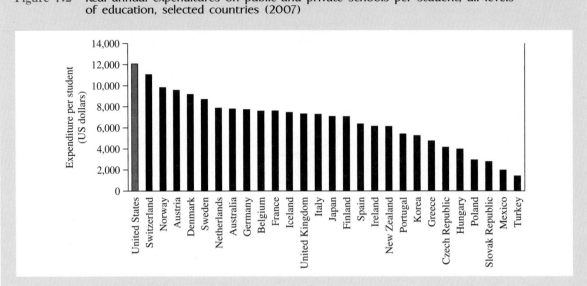

Source: Organization for Economic Cooperation and Development [2007a].

become informed and well-adjusted citizens, and improving the quality of their lives, both economically and socially. It is hard to quantify any of these things, let alone summarize them all in a single, precise measure. Therefore, most studies instead focus on a narrow set of outcome measures that at least have the virtue of being measurable. These include test scores, attendance records, dropout rates, continuation rates to higher levels of schooling, and earnings. Let's start by taking a look at test scores.

Figure 7.2 shows that the United States spends more per pupil than all other developed nations. Yet the test scores of US students are far from the top of this group. For example, in a test given to 15-year-olds in 29 developed nations, the United States placed fifteenth in reading literacy, nineteenth in science literacy, and twenty-fourth in mathematics literacy [Organization for Economic Cooperation and Development, 2004]. Numbers such as these have convinced some observers that increased spending has little impact on test scores. We now examine the empirical literature related to this issue.

EMPIRICAL EVIDENCE

Does Spending on Education Improve Student Test Scores?

Attempts to evaluate the effect of expenditures on student outcomes started with the Coleman Report [Coleman et al., 1966], which found that family background and peer effects—not the amount of public funding of schooling—explain student performance. However, this was an observational study and, as stressed in Chapter 2, such an approach makes it very difficult to assess causal effects. For example, if more educational resources were devoted to remedial classes, then there could be a negative correlation between expenditures and student outcomes even if expenditures helped students.

A better approach would be to run an experiment that randomly assigns students into high- and low-spending school districts, and then measure the differences in test outcomes. While a few randomized studies have been done (we discuss some later), they are difficult to conduct and are therefore rare.

Several recent studies instead use quasi-experiments that take advantage of changes in state laws that have increased funding to some school districts relative to others. Because public education has traditionally been financed by local taxes, wealthier school districts tend to spend more than other school districts. In order to equalize spending, some states started giving larger grants for education to low-income jurisdictions than to high-income jurisdictions. Massachusetts implemented such an approach in the early 1990s. By isolating the component of the funding changes due to the redistribution plan, Guryan [2003] found that increases in per-pupil spending led to significant increases in math, reading, science, and social studies test scores for fourth- and eighth-grade students.

Nonetheless, the issue is not settled. Hanushek [2002] surveyed a large number of previous studies and found that in most cases the data do not support a relationship between student expenditure and student performance. One contentious question regarding this claim is how to account for expenditures on a relatively small group of disabled students—should the expenditure numbers be corrected so that only money spent on "regular" students is taken into account? Without such a correction, a cross-sectional analysis of the relationship between expenditures and student outcomes could be misleading if schools spend more money on low-performing remedial or disabled students.

Even if we grant that expenditures have little effect on achievement, the implications are not clear. As Hanushek [2002, p. 46] notes, "The evidence does not say that money and resources never matter. Nor does it say that money and resources could not matter. . . . Indeed, a plausible interpretation of the evidence is that some schools in fact use resources effectively but that these schools are counterbalanced by others that do not." This gives rise to the question of whether some types of educational expenditures have a bigger impact on educational quality than others. For example, Figlio and Kenny [2006] find a positive correlation between student test scores and merit pay for teachers, suggesting that spending money to reward excellent teachers might be an effective way to improve educational outcomes.

Public Spending and the Quality of Education

Ultimately, the goal is not to increase educational expenditures per se; rather, it is to improve students' academic performance. Therefore, it is important to evaluate the efficacy of various kinds of spending. For example, is it more effective to reduce the student-to-teacher ratio, hire teachers with greater levels of teacher experience and education, increase teacher salaries, or provide newer books and facilities? Using the jargon of economics, which inputs have the greatest marginal effect on educational output? Several studies have estimated the contributions of various inputs to educational outcomes.[4] We will focus on one popular policy option, reducing class size.

---

[4] For example, Aaronson, Barrow, and Sander [2003] and Hanushek, Rivkin, and Kain [2005] find that teacher quality affects student outcomes. However, the research literature is less clear about what policy tools can improve teacher quality.

EMPIRICAL EVIDENCE

Does Reducing Class Size Improve Student Test Scores?

Reducing class sizes involves both costs and benefits. The costs arise because it requires hiring more teachers and providing more classrooms. These costs are relatively straightforward to measure: For the United States overall, the cost per pupil of lowering class size by 10 percent would be about $692 [authors' estimate, based on Hoxby, 2002a, p. 23]. Unfortunately, it is difficult to estimate the causal relationship between class size and student outcomes. Observational studies of the impact of class size are biased if students in smaller classes are different from students in larger classes, and if these differences contribute to differences in test scores. For example, if wealthier families locate in school districts with smaller classes and children from such families tend to get better test grades in any case, then we would overestimate the independent effect of smaller classes. On the other hand, the bias might be in the other direction if school districts provide smaller classes for remedial and special needs students.

A random experiment provides a better chance of assessing the causal relationship. The Tennessee Student/Teacher Achievement Ratio experiment (known as Project STAR), randomly assigned kindergarten students to small classes (13 to 17 students per teacher) and larger classes (22 to 25 students per teacher). Krueger [1999] found that students in the smaller classes tested higher than students in the larger classes. In a follow-up study, Krueger and Whitmore [2001] concluded that the students who were assigned to the smaller classes were more likely to take a college entrance exam and that this effect was greater for African-American students.

The results of Tennessee's Project STAR have reinforced many policymakers' beliefs that class size reductions are a good thing. Nevertheless one must be careful about assuming that the results of an experiment in one setting will hold in another setting. California presents a clear lesson in the dangers of ignoring this dictum. Partly on the basis of Project STAR, California passed a law in 1996 that reduced class sizes by roughly 10 students per class. So far, so good. But to accomplish this goal, the law required California schools to hire more teachers. Such an expansion in the teaching force was not a component of Project STAR, because the experiment did not involve a statewide reduction in class size. The only way for California to increase substantially the number of teachers was to hire teachers with relatively less experience and fewer credentials. Thus, the average quality of the teaching force fell. Remarkably, Jepsen and Rivkin [2002] found that the advantages of the smaller classes were offset by the deterioration of teacher quality. Thus, reducing class size did not improve the quality of public education in California.

Does Education Increase Earnings?

Although the impact of school expenditures and school quality on test scores is an important and interesting question, it tells us little about another critical variable—future earnings. Even if high educational expenditures do not increase test scores, we may not be very concerned if they increase people's earnings as adults. Likewise, if high educational expenditures increase test scores but have no effect on earnings, then we might question whether this is public money well spent.

It might seem obvious that more money spent on education leads to higher future earnings. If spending improves the quality of education, then the students will become more productive workers in the future. This increase in their "human capital" should translate into higher wages. However, given the previously discussed ambiguity about whether more spending actually improves educational outcomes (at least as represented by test outcomes), one cannot take for granted that such spending increases future incomes. For elementary and secondary education, it appears that increases on the margin in educational expenditure have little impact on subsequent earnings. The most optimistic estimates suggest that a 10 percent increase in educational expenditures generates increases of only about 1 or 2 percent in subsequent earnings [Heckman, 1999]. However, the efficacy of expenditures on education depends on the age and economic status of the students involved. In particular, Heckman [2008] suggests that investments made in early childhood to disadvantaged children have the highest returns.

Note also that this finding relates to spending *on the margin*. In other words, while another dollar spent on education might not affect future earnings much, this does not imply that earnings would be the same if we spent nothing on education and no one went to school. Indeed, a substantial empirical literature suggests that by augmenting human capital, additional schooling has substantially increased subsequent earnings.[5] Labor economists estimate each year of schooling increases annual earnings between 5 and 13 percent [Card, 1999].

▶ NEW DIRECTIONS FOR PUBLIC EDUCATION

The US public school system has been accused of producing a rising tide of mediocrity that puts our nation at economic and social risk. Like so much else in the area of education policy, this assertion is controversial. While SAT scores have been falling since the 1960s, this may be because the composition of the students taking the exam has changed over time—as college has grown more popular, more students toward the lower end of the ability distribution have been taking the test. The National Assessment of Educational Progress, administered by the US Department of Education, is less subject to such biases because it consistently tests a representative sample of US students. The results from this test suggest that over the past 30 years, math and reading scores for 4th, 8th, and 12th graders have improved slightly [US Department of Education, 2007b]. Such modest increases do not mollify critics, who believe that the improvements are not enough given the large increases in real per-pupil spending over time (see Table 7.1). Many of these critics believe that major structural changes in public education are needed. We now discuss a few options.

---

[5] However, another theory is that additional years of education (especially at the college level) serve primarily as a screening device that identifies for prospective employers those individuals with high ability. According to this theory, someone who is highly productive needs to signal this characteristic to prospective employers, and he or she can accomplish this by withstanding the rigors of the college admissions process and by obtaining a degree. The implication is that it isn't education per se that leads to higher productivity and thus higher wages; rather, education only serves as a signal of preexisting ability.

Charter Schools

If increasing spending on education is not the answer, how can the situation be improved? Economists are generally prone to consider whether any market in trouble might benefit from an infusion of competition. This is true in the debate over education policy. Some economists are convinced schools would improve if they were forced to compete with one another to attract students. This is part of the motivation for **charter schools,** which are public schools that operate under government charters that hold them to state standards, but have freedom to experiment and some independence in making their spending and hiring decisions. Forty-one states currently have laws that support charter schools. By making regular public schools compete for students with the charter schools, the hope is that the public schools will rethink their educational strategies and provide a higher-quality experience.

Anecdotal evidence from states like Arizona, which has the nation's most liberal charter law, suggests that charter schools increase diversity of choice. Some Arizona charter schools take a "back-to-basics" approach, some focus on the performing arts, some cater to pregnant students, and so on. Do these diverse options lead to improved student performance? Determining the causal relationship between attendance at a charter school and educational outcomes is difficult, because families choose whether to send their children to charter schools, so it is likely that family differences drive at least some of the differences in student outcomes.

However, some quasi-experimental research suggests that charter schools improve student outcomes. Hoxby and Rockoff [2004] examined the impact of attending a charter school on math and reading scores. They focused on data from Chicago, where any charter school that is oversubscribed uses a lottery to determine which students will attend the charter school. In effect, this process sets up an experiment in which students who randomly draw into a particular charter school can be compared to students who do not. Hoxby and Rockoff found that students who attended charter schools starting in elementary grades scored higher in both math and reading tests.

In a different study, Hoxby [2002b] examined what happened to regular public schools in Michigan when they were exposed to competition from the introduction of charter schools. She used a difference-in-difference strategy of the kind described in Chapter 2. Her analysis compared the change in student test scores for public schools located in districts that faced high competition from charter schools to the change in student test scores for public schools located in districts that faced little such competition. Hoxby found that regular public schools that faced competition from charters increased their students' achievement test scores relative to regular public schools that did not face such competition. And the schools appear to have done it without increasing spending per pupil.

Vouchers

Recently, much attention has been paid to plans to improve public school quality by increasing the scope of choice through a **school voucher** system. The basic approach is to provide financial support to students rather than directly to schools. Each student could be given a tuition voucher, for example, that could be redeemed at whatever qualified private school suited the student's family best. This is similar to a program in effect since 1992 in Sweden, where parents can use public money to pay

charter schools

Public schools that operate under special state government charters. Within limits established by their charters, these schools can experiment with a variety of approaches to education and have some independence in making spending and hiring decisions.

school voucher

A voucher given to a family to help pay for tuition at any qualified school. The school redeems the voucher for cash.

for any school that satisfies basic government rules [*Economist*, 2007e]. Proponents of school vouchers believe that the effects of competition would be as salutary in the education market as they are in other markets. Terrible public schools that do not reform would lose enrollees and be forced to close. According to this view, parents' and students' perceptions of teacher quality would become the basis for punishing bad teachers and poorly run public schools. Further, the availability of tuition vouchers would prompt entrepreneurs to establish new private schools in areas where the existing schools are poor.

Critics of vouchers offer a number of objections:

- Consumers in the education market may not be well informed, so the competitive outcome would be far from satisfactory. Supporters of this view point to the proliferation of vocational schools of dubious value that prey on students eligible for federal student loans and grants.

- Moving children to private schools might reduce the positive externalities of education. Greater competition among schools could lead them to focus on improving the private benefits to the students (such as increasing their wage-earning potential), while ignoring aspects of education that yield societal benefits (such as building a shared sense of national identity).

- Relatively good students might use vouchers to escape poorly performing public schools, leaving the weaker students behind. Because the quality of a student's education depends, in part, on the quality of his or her peers, the result would be an even worse education for the poor students than before the introduction of the vouchers. When Chile introduced a voucher system several years ago, it appears that the higher-ability students did in fact opt out of the public schools in disproportionately high numbers [Ladd, 2002, p. 19].

- A voucher system might be inequitable. The goal of the voucher system is to provide the opportunity for families to choose a private school should they wish. However, some families would opt for a private school even without a voucher, so providing them with a voucher would serve only to increase their incomes. To the extent such families have higher than average incomes, the end result would be to accentuate inequalities in the distribution of income.

Voucher enthusiasts argue that most of these objections can be dealt with by properly designing the program. For example, equity concerns could be addressed by targeting the vouchers primarily at low-income families. In any case, the debate focuses our attention on the importance of detailed design questions that would have to be addressed in implementing a national voucher system. How much latitude can schools have in designing their curricula? Can schools hire teachers who are not credentialed? What criteria can oversubscribed schools use to choose which students will be enrolled? Can church-run schools be included in the program? Can parents donate extra resources to the schools of their choice, or would this violate standards of equal education? How will students' families be informed about the different schooling choices available to them?

A number of communities have recently begun experimenting with voucher programs. In Milwaukee, for example, in 1990 about 1,000 low-income students began attending private schools using state-aid vouchers worth about $3,200 each. Rouse [1998] conducted an analysis of the results and found that students who attended the private schools had higher scores on mathematics achievement tests and about the same scores on reading tests. Further, Hoxby [2004] found evidence that the greater competition engendered by the Milwaukee voucher program led to test score improvements in public schools.

Other studies have evaluated privately funded voucher systems in Dayton, Ohio; Washington, DC; and New York City. These programs are attractive from a research standpoint because they randomly assigned the vouchers to eligible low-income families. Howell and Peterson [2002] evaluated the first three years of these programs and found that attending private school had no effect on the test scores of whites and Hispanics, but they did find positive math and reading test effects for African-American children.[6] The results of the Milwaukee program and the other experimental programs should help inform future debates over competition in the market for education.

School Accountability

In the 1990s, some states started experimenting with a different type of school reform known as **school accountability.** In order to make schools accountable for their performance, these states began requiring students to take standardized tests to monitor academic performance. While some states simply issued "report cards" on the performance of the schools, other states linked specific rewards and sanctions to the outcomes of the tests. By 2000, thirty-nine states had accountability systems, although there was great variation in the tests and the performance-based rewards and sanctions. For example, some states financially reward teachers in schools that test well, some states penalize teachers in schools that perform poorly, and other states allow school choice for students attending low-performing schools.

In 2002, President Bush signed the No Child Left Behind Act of 2001 (NCLB), which expanded school accountability to all states. NCLB mandates each state to introduce annual testing of all students from third through eighth grade, and it requires schools to issue report cards comparing their scores to those of other schools.[7] Schools that fail to show adequate progress for two years in a row must let students transfer to other public schools. A study examining one school district found that 16 percent of parents who received an NCLB notification chose to switch their child to a school with better test scores [Hastings and Weinstein, 2007]. Schools whose scores continue to stagnate or decline for three years must pay for tutoring or remedial classes for low-income students. After four years without progress, schools can be forced to replace certain staff or implement a new curriculum.

Proponents of school accountability believe that it provides an incentive for school administrators and teachers to reduce bureaucracy and to focus on providing core educational skills to students. Rouse, Hannaway, Goldhaber, and Figlio [2007] found that the schools that face accountability pressure change their instructional practices in meaningful ways. Hanushek and Raymond [2005] examined the introduction of school accountability in various states in the 1990s and concluded that it increased student achievement. Importantly, they found that the positive impacts occur only if the schools receive either rewards or sanctions that are tied to their performance. Issuing report cards on school performance by itself does not provide a sufficient incentive for improvement.

---

[6] Subsequent studies have called into question the robustness of these results. See, for example, Krueger and Zhu [2004].

[7] NCLB allows states to design the tests and cut-off standards used to calculate whether students are making progress.

The most common criticism of school accountability is that detrimental effects arise from focusing too much on standardized tests. The concern is that teachers don't have any incentive to foster creativity, problem-solving, and socialization skills, and instead focus on "teaching to the test." Jacob [2005] found that school accountability in Chicago did lead teachers to focus on skills emphasized on the tests that were tied to accountability. Interestingly, very similar concerns have been raised in some foreign countries whose students do much better on standardized tests than Americans. Specifically, some observers in countries such as Japan and Korea fear that their educational systems rely excessively on test performance, making them too regimented and neglectful of social and emotional development, creativity, and individuality [Lee, 2001].

Critics also contend that school accountability leads to strategic gaming that does not help students. For example, Jacob [2005] found evidence that school accountability in Chicago led some teachers to exclude low-ability students from the test-taking pool by placing them in special education. Figlio's [2005] research indicated that schools assign long suspensions to low-performing students subject to disciplinary action near the test-taking period. Jacob and Levitt [2003] found evidence that school accountability actually led some teachers in Chicago to cheat by changing answers to their students' standardized tests.

The economic literature demonstrates the trade-offs involved with designing a policy of school accountability. Tying rewards and sanctions to explicit performance standards provides incentives for schools to change; however, it also provides incentives for unintended behavior such as gaming the system and even cheating. This illustrates a more general proposition that arises again and again in public finance: people respond to incentives, and unless this fact is taken into account, even well-intentioned public policies may have unintended negative consequences.

Summary

- Real per-pupil government expenditures on elementary and secondary education in the United States have increased by about 81 percent since 1980.

- Although education is generally publicly provided, it is not a public good. However, many argue that education generates positive externalities.

- The presence of positive externalities does not justify the current structure of government programs for higher education, which subsidize all eligible students at the same rate.

- Equity concerns are often used to rationalize government subsidies for education. In the spirit of commodity egalitarianism, some suggest that education should be provided to everyone, regardless of their preferences.

- Public provision of education might crowd out private provision.

- The evidence on whether increasing expenditures on public education improves average test scores is mixed.

- The evidence suggests that marginal increases in education expenditures have very little impact on future earnings. The estimated effect is relatively large for additional spending on younger, disadvantaged children.

- Some economists argue that public schools would improve if they were subjected to competition. One proposal in this spirit is the use of charter schools, which are public schools that have greater freedom to experiment in their spending and hiring decisions.

- Another proposal is school vouchers, under which financial support for education goes to the family of the student, not directly to the school. The voucher can then be redeemed at whatever qualified school the family prefers.

- A recent reform effort is school accountability, under which school performance is monitored through standardized tests. The government then either issues "report cards" on performance or links financial incentives to the test outcomes.

Discussion Questions

1. What are the different rationales given for government provision of education? Explain whether the rationales have different implications for government provision of higher education versus primary and secondary education.

2. Many studies find that higher levels of education quality (as measured by test scores) increase growth rates of national income [Jamison, Jamison, and Hanushek, 2006]. What are the implications of this finding for whether or not education should be subsidized by the government?

3. It is inefficient if individuals who would derive positive net benefits from higher education are unable to obtain loans to finance their education. One commentator suggests that the government should give loans for higher education. These loans would be financed charging recipients "a lifelong flat-rate tithe on all earnings" so that "the future banker would end up paying more [than a future elementary school teacher]" [Zimmerman, 2007]. Discuss whether such a program would be efficient.

4. The analysis surrounding Figure 7.1 assumes that public schooling is a "take-it-or-leave-it" option. That is, individuals are not allowed to supplement public education with private lessons. Show how the diagram must be modified if, to the contrary, parents can purchase additional hours of education for their children who are enrolled in public school. Another assumption behind the model is that public education is "free" in the sense that parents do not pay any taxes for it. Show how the model must be modified if public school is financed by taxes levied on parents.

5. A deeply held belief in Europe is that university education should be financed almost entirely by the government. In France, undergraduates pay about $400 per year in tuition; in Germany, federal law explicitly forbids public universities to charge tuition. However, European governments typically don't provide much money for universities, leading to problems with maintaining quality. In response, some observers want to start charging students substantial amounts of tuition. One German official responded that "one of the prime rights of humanity is to have a free university education." In the same way, a Labor member of the British parliament argued, "Introducing a market into higher education is something the Labor Party should not be doing" [Lyall, 2003, p. A3]. Discuss the efficiency and equity consequences of a system of taxpayer-financed higher education.

6. Suppose a family (with only one child) earns $50,000 per year and lives in a community without publicly provided education.

   a. Draw the family's budget constraint showing the trade-off between quantity of education for the child and all other goods.

   b. Suppose now that an option of free public education worth $8,000 per student is introduced. Show how this changes the family's budget constraint.

   c. The family reduces its consumption of education after the introduction of free public education. Using part b, draw a set of indifference curves consistent with this outcome.

   d. Now show how a school voucher redeemable for $8,000 worth of education changes the family's budget constraint. What happens to the amount of education the family purchases for the child?

7. Suppose a state is considering whether to require that all public school teachers have a master's degree. Currently, only 40 percent of the teachers in the state have such a degree.

a. A researcher conducts a cross-sectional analysis that compares test scores of students in the state whose teachers have master's degrees to the test scores of students in the state whose teachers do not. The researcher finds that students whose teachers have master's degrees score significantly higher on the standardized tests. Why might such a study be biased?

b. Now suppose another state conducted an experiment in which 500 students were randomly selected to be either in a class taught by a teacher with a master's degree (treatment group) or a class with a teacher without a master's degree (control group). This experiment found that the treatment group scored significantly better than the control group. How useful is this experiment in informing the state's decision about whether to have a master's degree requirement?

Cost-Benefit Analysis

If you visited Boston during the last decade, you probably noticed that traffic downtown was particularly congested. The reason was the "Big Dig," a massive $14.6 billion public works project that involved the construction of new roads and another tunnel to Logan Airport. Many people have doubts that it was worth the money. How would one go about thinking about this issue? Infrastructure projects like the Big Dig are just one variety of the thousands of public projects that are under consideration at any given time, everything from breast cancer screening programs to space exploration. How should the government decide whether or not to pursue a particular project? The theory of welfare economics provides a framework for deciding: Evaluate the social welfare function before and after the project, and see whether social welfare increases. If it does, then do the project.

This method is correct, but not very useful. The amount of information required to specify and evaluate a social welfare function is enormous. While social welfare functions are valuable for thinking through certain conceptual problems, they are generally not much help for the day-to-day problems of project evaluation. However, welfare economics does provide the basis for **cost-benefit analysis**—a set of practical procedures for guiding public expenditure decisions.[1]

Most government projects and policies result in the private sector having more of some scarce commodities and less of others. At the core of cost-benefit analysis is a set of systematic procedures for valuing these commodities, which allows policy analysts to determine whether a project is, on balance, beneficial. Cost-benefit analysis allows policymakers to attempt to do what well-functioning markets do automatically—allocate resources to a project as long as the marginal social benefit exceeds the marginal social cost.

cost-benefit analysis

A set of procedures based on welfare economics for guiding public expenditure decisions.

▶ PRESENT VALUE

Project evaluation usually requires comparing costs and benefits from different time periods. For example, preschool education for poor children requires substantial expenditures in the present and then yields returns in the future. In this section we discuss issues that arise in comparing dollar amounts from different time periods. Initially, we assume that no price inflation occurs. We show later how to take inflation into account.

---

[1] Boardman et al. [2006] discuss the links between welfare economics and cost-benefit analysis.

Projecting Present Dollars into the Future

Suppose that you take $100 to the bank and deposit it in an account that yields 5 percent interest after taxes. At the end of one year, you will have $(1 + 0.05) \times $100 = 105—the $100 initially deposited, plus $5 in interest. Suppose further that you let the money sit in the account for another year. At the end of the second year, you will have $(1 + 0.05) \times $105 = 110.25. This can also be written as $(1 + 0.05) \times (1 + 0.05) \times 100 = (1 + 0.05)^2 \times 100$. Similarly, if the money is deposited for three years, it will be worth $(1 + 0.05)^3 \times 100 by the end of the third year. More generally, if R is invested for T years at an interest rate of r, at the end of T years, it will be worth $R \times (1 + r)^T$. This formula shows the future value of money invested in the present.

Projecting Future Dollars into the Present

Now suppose that someone offers a contract that promises to pay you $100 *one year from now*. The person is trustworthy, so you do not have to worry about default. (Also, remember there is no inflation.) What is the maximum amount that you should be willing to pay *today* for this promise? It is tempting to say that a promise to pay $100 is worth $100. But this neglects the fact that the promised $100 is not payable for a year, and in the meantime you are forgoing the interest that could be earned on the money. Why should you pay $100 today to receive $100 a year from now, if you can receive $105 a year from now simply by putting the $100 in the bank today? Thus, the value today of $100 payable one year from now is *less* than $100. The **present value** of a future amount of money is the maximum amount you would be willing to pay today for the right to receive the money in the future.

present value

The value today of a given amount of money to be paid or received in the future.

To find the very most you would be willing to give up now in exchange for $100 payable one year in the future, you must find the number that, when multiplied by $(1 + 0.05)$ just equals $100. By definition, this is $$100/(1 + 0.05)$ or approximately $95.24. Thus, when the interest rate is 5 percent, the present value of $100 payable one year from now is $$100/(1 + 0.05)$. Note the symmetry with the familiar problem of projecting money into the future that we just discussed. To find the value of money today one year in the future, you *multiply* by 1 plus the interest rate; to find the value of money one year in the future today, you *divide* by 1 plus the interest rate.

Next consider a promise to pay $100 *two* years from now. In this case, the calculation has to take into account the fact that if you invested $100 yourself for two years, at the end it would be worth $$100/(1 + 0.05)^2$. The most you would be willing to pay today for $100 in two years is the amount that when multiplied by $(1 + 0.05)^2$ yields exactly $100, that is, $$100/(1 + 0.05)^2$, or about $90.70.

In general, when the interest rate is r, the present value of a promise to pay R in T years is simply $R/(1 + r)^T$.[2] Thus, even in the absence of inflation, a dollar in the future is worth less than a dollar today and must be "discounted" by an amount that depends on the interest rate and when the money is receivable. For this reason, r is often referred to as the **discount rate.** Similarly, $(1 + r)^T$ is called

discount rate

The rate of interest used to compute present value.

---

[2] This assumes the interest rate is constant at r. Suppose that the interest rate changes over time, so in year 1 it is r_1, in year 2, r_2, and so on. Then the present value of a sum R_T payable T years from now is $R_T/[(1 + r_1) \times (1 + r_2) \times \cdots \times (1 + r_T)]$.

the **discount factor** for money T periods into the future. Note that the further into the future the promise is payable (the larger is T), the smaller is the present value. Intuitively, the longer you have to wait for a sum to be paid, the less you are willing to pay for it today, other things being the same.

Finally, consider a promise to pay $\$R_0$ today, *and* $\$R_1$ one year from now, *and* $\$R_2$ two years from now, and so on for T years. How much is this deal worth? By now, it is clear that the naive answer ($\$R_0 + \$R_1 + \cdots + \$R_T$) is wrong because it assumes that a dollar in the future is exactly equivalent to a dollar in the present. Without dividing by the discount factor, adding up dollars from different points in time is like adding apples and oranges. The correct approach is to convert each year's amount to its present value and *then* add them.

Table 8.1 shows the present value of each year's payment. To find the present value (PV) of the income stream, $\$R_0$, $\$R_1$, $\$R_2$, . . . , $\$R_T$ we simply add the figures in the last column:

$$PV = R_0 + \frac{R_1}{(1+r)} + \frac{R_2}{(1+r)^2} + \cdots + \frac{R_T}{(1+r)^T} \tag{8.1}$$

The importance of computing present value is hard to overestimate. Ignoring it can lead to serious errors. In particular, failure to discount makes ventures that yield returns in the future appear more valuable than they really are. For example, consider a project that yields a return of \$1 million 20 years from now. If the interest rate is 5 percent, the present value is \$376,889 [$=\$1,000,000/(1.05)^{20}$]. If $r = 10$ percent, the present value is only \$148,644 [$=\$1,000,000/(1.10)^{20}$].

Inflation

How do we modify the procedure when the price level is expected to increase in the future? To begin, consider a project that, in present prices, yields the same return each year. Call this return $\$R_0$. Now assume that inflation occurs at a rate of 3 percent per year, and the dollar value of the return increases along with all prices. Therefore, the dollar value of the return one year from now, $\$\tilde{R}_1$, is $(1.03) \times \$R_0$. Similarly, two years into the future, the dollar value is $\$\tilde{R}_2 = (1.03)^2 \times R_0$. In general, this same return has a dollar value in year T of $\$\tilde{R}_T = (1 + 0.03)^T \times R_0$.

The dollar values $\$\tilde{R}_0$, $\$\tilde{R}_1$, $\$\tilde{R}_2$, . . . , $\$\tilde{R}_T$ are referred to as **nominal amounts.** Nominal amounts are valued according to the level of prices in the year the return occurs. One can measure these returns in terms of the prices that exist in a single year. These are called **real amounts** because they do not reflect changes that are due

Table 8.1 Calculating Present Value

Dollars Payable	Years in Future	Discount Factor	Present Value
R_0	0	1	R_0
R_1	1	$(1 + r)$	$R_1 / (1 + r)$
R_2	2	$(1 + r)^2$	$R_2 / (1 + r)^2$
.	.	.	.
.	.	.	.
.	.	.	.
R_T	T	$(1 + r)^T$	$R_T / (1 + r)^T$

In order to compute the present value of an income stream, divide each year's amount by the corresponding discount factor and then sum these terms across all years.

merely to alterations in the price level. In our example, the real amount was assumed to be a constant $\$R_0$ measured in present prices. More generally, if the real returns in present year prices are $\$R_0$, $\$R_1$, $\$R_2$, . . . , $\$R_T$, and inflation occurs at a rate of π per year, then the nominal returns are $\$R_0$, $\$R_1 \times (1 + \pi)$, $\$R_2 \times (1 + \pi)^2$, . . . , $\$R_T \times (1 + \pi)^T$.

But this is not the end of the story. When prices are expected to rise, lenders are no longer willing to make loans at the interest rate r that prevailed when prices were stable. Lenders realize they are going to be paid back in depreciated dollars, and to keep even in real terms, their first year's payment must also be inflated by $(1 + \pi)$. Similarly, the second year's payment must be inflated by $(1 + \pi)^2$. In other words, the market interest rate increases by an amount approximately equal to the expected rate of inflation, from r percent to $r + \pi$ percent.[3]

We see, then, that when inflation is anticipated, *both* the stream of returns and the discount rate increase. When expressed in *nominal* terms, the present value of the income stream is thus

$$PV = R_0 + \frac{(1+\pi)R_1}{(1+\pi)(1+r)} + \frac{(1+\pi)^2 R_2}{(1+\pi)^2(1+r)^2} + \cdots + \frac{(1+\pi)^2 R_T}{(1+\pi)^T(1+r)^T} \qquad (8.2)$$

A glance at Equation (8.2) indicates that it is equivalent to Equation (8.1) because all the terms involving $(1 + \pi)$ cancel out. The moral of the story is that we obtain the *same* answer whether real or nominal magnitudes are used. It is crucial, however, that dollar magnitudes and discount rates be measured consistently. If real values are used for the Rs, the discount rate must also be measured in real terms—the market rate of interest *minus* the expected inflation rate. Alternatively, if we discount by the market rate of interest, returns should be measured in nominal terms.

▶ PRIVATE SECTOR PROJECT EVALUATION

As we noted at the beginning of the chapter, the central problem in cost-benefit analysis is valuing the inputs and outputs of government projects. A useful starting point is to consider the same problem from a private firm's point of view.

Suppose a firm is considering two mutually exclusive projects, X and Y. The real benefits and costs of project X are B^X and C^X, respectively; and those for project Y are B^Y and C^Y. For both projects, the benefits and costs are realized immediately. The firm must answer two questions: First, should either project be done at all; are the projects *admissible*? (The firm has the option of doing neither project.) Second, if both projects are admissible, which is *preferable*? Because both benefits and costs occur immediately, answering these questions is simple. Compute the net return to project X, $B^X - C^X$, and compare it to the net return to Y, $B^Y - C^Y$. A project is admissible only if its net return is positive, that is, if the benefits exceed the costs. If both projects are admissible and the firm can only adopt one of them, it should choose the project with the higher net return.

---

[3] The product of $(1 + r)$ and $(1 + \pi)$ is $1 + r + \pi + r\pi$. Thus, the nominal rate actually exceeds the real rate by $\pi + r\pi$. However, for numbers of reasonable magnitude, $r\pi$ is negligible in size, so $r + \pi$ is a good approximation. Under some circumstances, nominal interest rates may fail to rise by exactly the rate of inflation. See Chapter 17 under "Taxes and Inflation."

In reality, most projects involve a stream of real benefits and returns that occur over time rather than instantaneously. Suppose that the initial benefits and costs of project X are B_0^X and C_0^X, those at the end of the first year are B_1^X and C_1^X, and those at the end of the last year are B_T^X and C_T^X. We can characterize project X as a stream of net returns (some of which may be negative):

$$(B_0^X - C_0^X), (B_1^X - C_1^X), (B_2^X - C_2^X), \ldots, (B_T^X - C_T^X)$$

The present value of this income stream (PV^x) is

$$PV^X = B_0^X - C_0^X + \frac{B_1^X - C_1^X}{(1+r)} + \frac{B_2^X - C_2^X}{(1+r)^2} + \cdots + \frac{B_T^X - C_T^X}{(1+r)^T}$$

where r is the discount rate that is appropriate for a private sector project. (Selection of a discount rate is discussed shortly.)

Similarly, suppose that project Y generates streams of costs and benefits B^Y and C^Y over a period of T' years. (There is no reason for T and T' to be the same.) Project Y's present value is

$$PV^Y = B_0^Y - C_0^Y + \frac{B_1^Y - C_1^Y}{(1+r)} + \frac{B_2^Y - C_2^Y}{(1+r)^2} + \cdots + \frac{B_{T'}^Y - C_{T'}^Y}{(1+r)^{T'}}$$

present value criteria

Rules for evaluating projects stating that (1) only projects with positive net present value should be carried out; and (2) of two mutually exclusive projects, the preferred project is the one with the higher net present value.

Since both projects are now evaluated in present value terms, we can use the same rules that were applied to the instantaneous project described earlier. The **present value criteria** for project evaluation are that:

- A project is admissible only if its present value is positive.
- When two projects are mutually exclusive, the preferred project is the one with the higher present value.

The discount rate plays a key role in the analysis. Different values of r can lead to very different conclusions concerning the admissibility and comparability of projects.

Consider the two projects shown in Table 8.2, a research and development program (R&D) and an advertising campaign. Both require an initial outlay of $1,000. The R&D program produces a return of $600 at the end of the first year and $550 at the end of the third year. The advertising campaign, on the other hand, has a single large payoff of $1,200 in three years.

The calculations show that the discount rate chosen is important. For low values of r, the advertising is preferred to R&D. However, higher discount rates weigh against the advertising (where the returns are concentrated further into the future) and may even make the project inadmissible.

Thus, one must take considerable care that the value of r represents as closely as possible the firm's actual opportunity cost of funds. If the discount rate chosen is too high, it tends to discriminate against projects with returns that come in the relatively distant future and vice versa. The firm's tax situation is relevant in this context. If the going market rate of return is 10 percent, but the firm's tax rate is 25 percent, its after-tax return is only 7.5 percent. Because the after-tax return represents the firm's opportunity cost, it should be used for r.

Several criteria other than present value are often used for project evaluation. As we will see, they can sometimes give misleading answers, and therefore, the present value criteria are preferable. However, these other methods are popular, so it is necessary to understand them and to be aware of their problems.

Table 8.2   **Comparing the Present Value of Two Projects**

| Year | Annual Net Return | | $r =$ | PV | |
	R&D	Advertising		R&D	Advertising
0	−$1,000	−$1,000	0	$150	$200
1	600	0	0.01	128	165
2	0	0	0.03	86	98
3	550	1,200	0.05	46	37
			0.07	10	−21

The choice of the discount rate can affect which of two projects yields higher present value. In this example, a lower discount rate makes the advertising project relatively more attractive, while a higher discount rate makes the R&D project relatively more attractive.

Internal Rate of Return

A firm is considering the following project: It spends $1 million today on a new computer network and reaps a benefit of $1.04 million in increased profits a year from now. If you were asked to compute the computer network's "rate of return," you would probably respond, "4 percent." Implicitly, you calculated that figure by finding the value of ρ that solves the following equation:

$$-\$1,000,000 + \frac{\$1,040,000}{(1+\rho)} = 0$$

We can generalize this procedure as follows: If a project yields a stream of benefits (B) and costs (C) over T periods, the **internal rate of return** (ρ) is defined as the ρ that solves the equation

$$B_0 - C_0 + \frac{B_1 - C_1}{(1+\rho)} + \frac{B_2 - C_2}{(1+\rho)^2} + \cdots + \frac{B_T - C_T}{(1+\rho)^T} = 0 \qquad (8.3)$$

internal rate of return

The discount rate that would make a project's net present value zero.

The internal rate of return is the discount rate that would make the present value of the project just equal to zero.

An obvious admissibility criterion is to accept a project if ρ exceeds the firm's opportunity cost of funds, r. For example, if the project earns 4 percent while the firm can obtain 3 percent on other investments, the project should be undertaken. The corresponding comparability criterion is that if two mutually exclusive projects are both admissible, choose the one with the higher value of ρ.

Project selection using the internal rate of return can, however, lead to bad decisions. Consider project X that requires the expenditure of $100 today and yields $110 a year from now, so that its internal rate of return is 10 percent. Project Y requires $1,000 today and yields $1,080 in a year, generating an internal rate of return of 8 percent. (Neither project can be duplicated.) Assume that the firm can borrow and lend freely at a 6 percent rate of interest.

On the basis of internal rate of return, X is clearly preferred to Y. However, the firm makes only $4 profit on X ($10 minus $6 in interest costs), while it makes a $20 profit on Y ($80 minus $60 in interest costs). Contrary to the conclusion implied by the internal rate of return, the firm should prefer Y, the project with the higher profit. In short, when projects differ in size, the internal rate of return can give poor guidance.[4] In contrast, the present value rule gives correct answers even when the projects differ in scale. The present value of X is $-100 + 110/1.06 = 3.77$, while that of Y is $-1,000 + 1,080/1.06 = 18.87$. The present value criterion says that Y is preferable, as it should.

Benefit–Cost Ratio

Suppose that a project yields a stream of benefits $B_0, B_1, B_2, \ldots, B_T$, and a stream of costs $C_0, C_1, C_2, \ldots, C_T$. Then the present value of the benefits, B, is

$$B = B_0 + \frac{B_1}{(1+r)} + \frac{B_2}{(1+r)^2} + \cdots + \frac{B_T}{(1+r)^T}$$

and the present value of the costs, C, is

$$C = C_0 + \frac{C_1}{(1+r)} + \frac{C_2}{(1+r)^2} + \cdots + \frac{C_T}{(1+r)^T} \qquad (8.4)$$

benefit-cost ratio

The ratio of the present value of a stream of benefits to the present value of a stream of costs for a project.

The **benefit-cost ratio** is defined as B/C.

Admissibility requires that a project's benefit-cost ratio exceed 1. Application of this rule always gives correct guidance. To see why, note simply that $B/C > 1$ implies that $B - C > 0$, which is just the present value criterion for admissibility.

As a basis for comparing admissible projects, however, the benefit-cost ratio is virtually useless. Consider a state that is studying two methods for disposing of toxic wastes. Method I is a toxic waste dump with $B = \$250$ million, $C = \$100$ million, and therefore a benefit-cost ratio of 2.5. Method II involves sending the wastes in a rocket to Saturn, which has $B = \$200$ million, $C = \$100$ million, and therefore a benefit-cost ratio of 2. The state's leaders choose the dump because it has the higher value of B/C. Now suppose that in their analysis of the dump, the analysts inadvertently neglected to take into account seepage-induced crop damage of \$40 million. If the \$40 million is viewed as a reduction in the dump's benefits, its B/C becomes $\$210/\$100 = 2.1$, and the dump is still preferred to the rocket. However, the \$40 million can just as well be viewed as an increase in costs, in which case $B/C = \$250/\$140 = 1.79$. Now the rocket looks better than the dump!

We have illustrated that there is an inherent ambiguity in computing benefit-cost ratios because benefits can always be counted as "negative costs" and vice versa. Thus, by judicious classification of benefits and costs, any admissible project's benefit-cost ratio can be made arbitrarily high. In contrast, a glance at Equation (8.1) indicates that such shenanigans have no effect whatsoever on the present value criterion because it is based on the *difference* between benefits and costs rather than their *ratio*.

We conclude that the internal rate of return and the benefit-cost ratio can lead to incorrect inferences. The present value criterion is the most reliable guide.

---

[4] This result rests on the assumption that neither project can be duplicated. Otherwise, duplicating project X 10 times would yield a \$100 profit, which is greater than the \$80 profit of project Y.

▶ DISCOUNT RATE FOR GOVERNMENT PROJECTS

Sensible decision making by the government also requires present value calculations. However, the public sector should compute costs, benefits, and discount rates differently from the private sector. This section discusses problems in the selection of a public sector discount rate. We then turn to problems in evaluating costs and benefits.

As suggested previously, the discount rate chosen by private individuals should reflect the rate of return available on alternative investments. Although in practice pinpointing this rate may be difficult, from a conceptual point of view the firm's opportunity cost of funds gives the correct value of r.

There is less consensus on the conceptually appropriate discount rate for government projects. We now discuss several possibilities.[5]

Rates Based on Returns in the Private Sector

Suppose the last $1,000 of private investment in the economy yields an annual rate of return of 16 percent. If the government extracts $1,000 from the private sector for a project, and the $1,000 is entirely at the expense of private sector investment, society loses the $160 that would have been generated by the private sector project. Thus, the opportunity cost of the government project is the 16 percent rate of return in the private sector. Because it measures the opportunity cost, 16 percent is the appropriate discount rate. It is irrelevant whether or not this return is taxed. Whether it all stays with the investor or part goes to the government, the before-tax rate of return measures the value of output that the funds would have generated for society.

In practice, funds for a given project are collected from a variety of taxes, each of which has a different effect on consumption and investment. Hence, contrary to the assumption made earlier, it is likely that some of the funds for the government project would come at the expense of consumption as well as investment. What is the opportunity cost of funds that come at the expense of consumption? Consider Kenny, who is deciding how much to consume and how much to save this year. For each dollar Kenny consumes this year, he gives up one dollar of consumption next year *plus* the rate of return he would have earned on the dollar saved. Hence, the opportunity cost to Kenny of a dollar of consumption now is measured by the rate of return he would have received if he had saved the dollar. Suppose the before-tax yield on an investment opportunity available to Kenny is 16 percent, but he must pay 50 percent of the return to the government in the form of taxes. All that Kenny gives up when he consumes an additional dollar today is the *after*-tax rate of return of 8 percent. Because the after-tax rate of return measures what an *individual* loses when consumption is reduced, dollars that come at the expense of consumption should be discounted by the after-tax rate of return.

Because funds for the public sector reduce both private sector consumption and investment, a natural solution is to use a weighted average of the before- and after-tax rates of return, with the weight on the before-tax rate equal to the proportion of funds that comes from investment, and that on the after-tax rate the proportion that comes from consumption. In the preceding example, if one-quarter of the funds come

---

[5] See Tresch [2002, Chapter 24] for further discussion of the alternative views.

at the expense of investment and three-quarters at the expense of consumption, then the public sector discount rate is 10 percent ($\frac{1}{4} \times$ 16 percent + $\frac{3}{4} \times$ 8 percent). Unfortunately, in practice it is hard to determine what the proportions of sacrificed consumption and investment actually are for a given government project. And even with information on the impact of each tax on consumption and investment, it is difficult in practice to determine which tax is used to finance which project. The inability to determine reliably a set of weights lessens the usefulness of this approach as a practical guide to determining discount rates.

Social Discount Rate

social rate of discount

The rate at which society is willing to trade off present consumption for future consumption.

An alternative view is that public expenditure evaluation should involve a **social rate of discount,** which measures the valuation *society* places on consumption that is sacrificed in the present. But why should society's view of the opportunity cost of forgoing consumption differ from the opportunity cost revealed in market rates of return? The social discount rate may be lower for several reasons.

Paternalism   Even from the point of view of their own narrow self-interest, people may not be farsighted enough to weigh adequately benefits in the future; they therefore discount such benefits at too high a rate. The government should use the discount rate that individuals *would* use if they knew their own good. This is a paternalistic argument—government forces citizens to consume less in the present, and in return, they have more in the future, at which time they presumably thank the government for its foresight. Like all paternalistic arguments, it raises the fundamental philosophical question of when the government's preferences should be imposed on individuals.

Closely related is the notion that interest rates generated by the private sector do not take into account the interests of future generations; therefore, the government must apply a lower rate to projects that will affect people in the future. Skeptics believe that the idea of government as the unselfish guardian of the interests of future generations assumes an unrealistic degree of omniscience and benevolence. Moreover, even totally selfish individuals often engage in projects that benefit future generations. If future generations are expected to benefit from some project, the anticipated profitability is high, which encourages investment today. Private firms plant trees today in return for profits on wood sales that may not be realized for many years.[6]

Market Inefficiency   When a firm undertakes an investment, it generates knowledge and technological know-how that can benefit other firms. In a sense, then, investment creates positive externalities, and by the usual kinds of arguments, investment is underprovided by private markets (see Chapter 5 under "Positive Externalities"). By applying a discount rate lower than the market's, the government can correct this inefficiency. The enormous practical problem here is measuring the actual size of the externality. Moreover, the theory of externalities suggests that a more appropriate remedy would be to determine the size of the marginal external benefit at the optimum and grant a subsidy of that amount (see again Chapter 5).

---

[6] Why should people invest in a project whose returns may not be realized until after they are dead? Because investors can always sell the rights to future profits to members of the younger generation and hence consume their share of the anticipated profits during their lifetimes.

It appears, then, that none of the arguments against using market rates provides much specific guidance with respect to the choice of a public sector discount rate. Where does this leave us? It would be difficult to argue very strongly against any public rate of discount in a range between the before- and after-tax rates of return in the private sector. One practical procedure is to evaluate the present value of a project over a range of discount rates and see whether or not the present value stays positive for all reasonable values of r. If it does, the analyst can feel some confidence that the conclusion is not sensitive to the discount rate. *Sensitivity analysis* is the process of conducting a cost-benefit analysis under a set of alternative reasonable assumptions and seeing whether the substantive results change.

Discounting and the Economics of Climate Change

Proponents of the use of a social discount rate emphasize that discount rates based on the private sector are too high to mirror properly the interests of future generations. Opponents believe that private sector discount rates are adequate for this task. The debate on how to value the welfare of future generations is especially critical when considering policy for dealing with global climate change. For example, an influential report prepared for the British government by economist Nicholas Stern calculated that the present value of the cost of climate change in the future is enormous, and therefore societies today should be willing to spend huge amounts to reduce greenhouse gas emissions [Stern, 2006]. Implementing Stern's recommendations could cost about $27 trillion today [Nordhaus, 2008].

This figure is orders of magnitude higher than the findings from other reputable studies. Why? In doing the discounting to find the present value of future damages from climate change, Stern uses a social discount rate of almost zero. With such a low discount rate, Stern's result is not surprising, because it implies that the present value of the costs of *any* problem that persists indefinitely into the future—no matter how small—will have an enormous present value. If Stern had chosen a discount rate more closely related to market rates of return, his conclusions would have been radically different. As one economist noted:

> [I]t is not an exaggeration to say that the biggest uncertainty of all in the economics of climate change is the uncertainty about which interest rate to use for discounting. In one form or another, this little secret is known to insiders in the economics of climate change, but it needs to be more widely appreciated by economists at large [Weitzman, 2007, p. 705].

Government Discounting in Practice

Historically, the federal government has used a variety of discount rates, depending on the agency and the type of project. According to guidelines issued by the US Office of Management and Budget (OMB) [2003], federal agencies are now required to conduct two separate analyses when evaluating their projects: one using a real discount rate of 7 percent and another using a real discount rate of 3 percent. This convention is very much in line with the economic reasoning discussed earlier in this chapter. Seven percent is an estimate of the private return on investment, so it is the appropriate discount rate for projects that extract resources from private investment. Three percent is an estimate of the rate at which society discounts future consumption, so it is the appropriate discount rate for projects that primarily extract resources from private consumption. Because it is usually difficult to know whether a government project is taking resources from private investment or private consumption, OMB's recommendation of using both discount rates allows one to see whether the substantive results are sensitive to the difference. Further, for government projects that affect future generations, OMB recommends an additional sensitivity analysis using discount rates of 1 to 3 percent. This is consistent with the notion, also discussed earlier, that the social discount rate may be lower than the market rate of return.

In the context of federal budget planning, there are major inconsistencies in the conventions used for discounting. When a new tax or expenditure program is introduced, its effects over a five-year period must be reported to determine whether or not they will put the budget out of balance.[7] For these purposes, all that matters are the sums of the relevant taxes or expenditures; future flows are discounted at a rate of zero. Thus, for example, a policy that increased spending by a billion dollars today and was financed by a tax of a billion dollars five years from now would be viewed as having no effect on the deficit, while in present value terms, the package would lose money.

Beyond the five-year window, the fiscal consequences of fiscal proposals are ignored; in effect, they are discounted at a rate of infinity! Consider a policy that raises $5 billion within the first five years, but after 10 years loses $20 billion. Under current budgetary rules, such a policy is scored as creating a surplus, while with any reasonable discount rate, its long-run effect is to lose money for the government. There is, in fact, some evidence that this peculiar fashion of discounting has biased government decision making in favor of policies that increase revenue in the short term but reduce it in the long term [Bazelon and Smetters, 1999].

▶ VALUING PUBLIC BENEFITS AND COSTS

The next step in project evaluation is computing benefits and costs. From a private firm's point of view, this computation is relatively straightforward. The benefits from a project are the revenues received; the costs are the firm's payments for inputs; and both are measured by market prices. The evaluation problem is more complicated for the government because market prices may not reflect *social* benefits and costs. Consider, for example, a highway expansion that might do some damage to the environment. One can imagine both the private and public sectors undertaking this project, but the private and public cost-benefit analyses would be rather different, because the private sector would ignore social costs, which include externalities.

We now discuss several ways for measuring the benefits and costs of public sector projects.

Market Prices

As noted in Chapter 3, in a properly functioning competitive economy, the price of a good simultaneously reflects its marginal social cost of production and its marginal value to consumers. It would appear that if the government uses inputs and/or produces outputs that are traded in private markets, then market prices should be used for valuation.

---

[7] For some purposes, the Senate requires flows over a 10-year period.

The problem is that real-world markets have many imperfections, such as monopoly, externalities, and so on. Therefore, prices do not necessarily reflect marginal social costs and benefits. The relevant question, however, is not whether market prices are perfect, but whether they are likely to be superior to alternative measures of value. Such measures would either have to be made up or derived from highly complicated—and questionable—models of the economy. And, whatever their problems, market prices provide plenty of information at a low cost. Most economists believe that in the absence of any glaring imperfections, market prices should be used to compute public benefits and costs.

Adjusted Market Prices

The prices of goods traded in imperfect markets generally do not reflect their marginal social costs.[8] The **shadow price** of such a commodity is its underlying social marginal cost. Although market prices of goods in imperfect markets diverge from shadow prices, in some cases the market prices can be used to *estimate* the shadow prices. We discuss the relevant circumstances next. In each case, the key insight is that the shadow price depends on how the economy responds to the government intervention.

shadow price

The underlying social marginal cost of a good.

Monopoly   In the nation of South Africa, the production of beer is monopolized by the company South African Breweries, Ltd. Imagine that the Education Ministry is contemplating the purchase of some beer for a controlled experiment to determine the impact of beer consumption on the performance of college students. How should the project's cost-benefit analysis take into account the fact that this input is monopolistically produced?

In contrast to perfect competition, under which price is equal to marginal cost, a monopolist's price is above marginal cost (see Chapter 3). Should the government value the beer at its market price (which measures its value to consumers) or at its marginal production cost (which measures the incremental value of the resources used in its production)?

The answer depends on the impact of the government purchase on the market. If production of beer is expected to increase by the exact amount used by the project, the social opportunity cost is the value of the resources used in the extra production—the marginal production cost. On the other hand, if no more beer will be produced, the government's use comes at the expense of private consumers, who value the beer at its demand price. If some combination of the two responses is expected, a weighted average of price and marginal cost is appropriate. (Note the similarity to the previous discount rate problem.)

Taxes   If an input is subject to a sales tax, the price received by the producer of the input is less than the price paid by the purchaser. This is because some portion of the purchase price goes to the tax collector. When the government purchases an input subject to sales tax, should the producer's or purchaser's price be used in the cost calculations? The basic principle is the same as that for the monopoly case. If production is expected to expand, then the producer's supply price is appropriate. If production is expected to stay constant, the consumer's price should be used. A combination of responses requires a weighted average.

---

[8] For further details, see Boardman et al. [2006].

Unemployment   If a worker for a public sector project is hired away from a private job, then society's opportunity cost is the worker's wage rate in the private sector, because it reflects the value of the lost output that the worker had been producing. Things get trickier when the project employs someone who is currently involuntarily unemployed. Because hiring an unemployed worker does not lower output elsewhere in the economy, the wage the worker is paid by the government does not represent an opportunity cost. All that is forgone when the worker is hired is the leisure he or she was consuming, the value of which is presumably low if the unemployment is involuntary. There are two complications, however: (1) If the government is running its stabilization policy to maintain a constant rate of employment, hiring an unemployed worker may mean reducing employment and output elsewhere in the economy. In this case, the social cost of the worker is his or her wage. (2) Even if the worker is involuntarily unemployed when the project begins, he or she may not necessarily be so during its entire duration. But forecasting an individual's future employment prospects is difficult. In light of the current lack of consensus on the causes and nature of unemployment, the pricing of unemployed resources remains a problem with no agreed-on solution. In the absence of a major depression, valuation of unemployed labor at the going wage is probably a good approximation for practical purposes.

Consumer Surplus

A private firm is generally small relative to the economy, so changes in its output do not affect the market price of its product. In contrast, public sector projects can be so large that they change market prices, and this affects the way in which benefits should be calculated. For example, a government irrigation project could lower the marginal cost of agricultural production so much that the market price of food falls. But if the market price changes, how should the additional amount of food be valued—at its original price, at its price after the project, or at some price in between?

The situation for a hypothetical avocado-growing region is depicted in Figure 8.1. Pounds of avocados are measured on the horizontal axis, the price per pound is measured on the vertical, and D_a is the demand schedule for avocados. Before the irrigation project, the supply curve is labeled S_a, and market price and quantity are $2.89 and A_0, respectively. (The supply curve is drawn horizontally for convenience. The main points would still hold even if it sloped upward.)

Suppose that after more land is brought into production by the irrigation project, the supply curve for avocados shifts to S_a'. At the new equilibrium, the price falls to $1.35, and avocado consumption increases to A_1. How much better off are consumers? Another way of stating this question is, "How much would consumers be willing to pay for the privilege of consuming A_1 pounds of avocados at price $1.35 rather than A_0 pounds at price $2.89?"

The economic tool for answering this question is **consumer surplus**—the amount by which the sum that individuals would have been willing to pay exceeds the sum they actually have to pay. As shown in the appendix to this book, consumer surplus is measured by the area under the demand curve and above a horizontal line at the market price. Thus, when the price is $2.89, consumer surplus is *ebd*.

When the price of avocados falls to $1.35 because of the irrigation project, consumer surplus is still the area under the demand curve and above a horizontal line at the going price, but because the price is now $1.35, the relevant area is *ecg*. Consumer surplus has increased by the difference between areas *ecg* and *ebd*—area *bcgd*. Thus,

---

consumer surplus

The amount by which consumers' willingness to pay for a commodity exceeds the sum they actually have to pay.

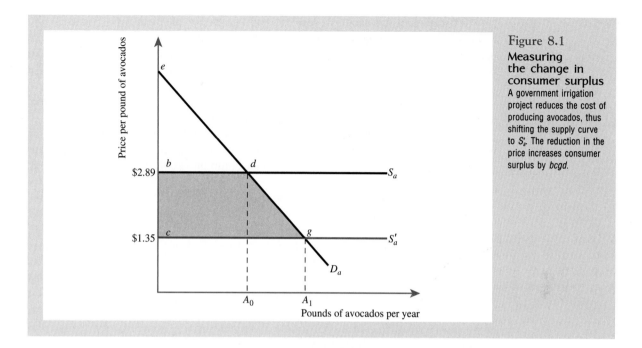

Figure 8.1

Measuring the change in consumer surplus
A government irrigation project reduces the cost of producing avocados, thus shifting the supply curve to S'_a. The reduction in the price increases consumer surplus by *bcgd*.

the area behind the demand curve between the two prices measures the value to consumers of being able to purchase avocados at the lower price. Provided the planner can estimate the shape of the demand curve, the project's benefit can be measured.

If the supply curve of the commodity under consideration is upward sloping, then changes in producer surplus (also explained in the appendix at the end of the book) can be brought into play. For example, in the cost-benefit analysis of rent controls, the change in landlords' surplus could be estimated given information on the shape of the supply curve of rental housing.

Inferences from Economic Behavior

So far we have been dealing with cases in which market data can serve as a starting point for valuing social costs and benefits. Sometimes the good in question is not explicitly traded, so no market price exists. We discuss two examples of how people's willingness to pay for such commodities can be estimated.

The Value of Time   One important component of Boston's Big Dig project mentioned at the beginning of this chapter was a 3.5-mile stretch of highway that cost $6.5 billion. It was estimated that with the new highway in place, the ride from downtown to the airport would be reduced from 45 minutes to 8 minutes. Was this a good deal? While it is true that "time is money," to do cost-benefit analysis we need to know *how much* money. A common way to estimate the value of time is to take advantage of the theory of leisure-income choice. People who have control over the amount they work do so up to the point where the subjective value of leisure is equal to the income they gain from one more hour of work—the after-tax wage rate. Thus, the after-tax wage can be used to value the time that is saved.[9]

---

[9] For further details, see Chapter 18 under "Labor Supply."

Although this approach is useful, it has two major problems: (1) Some people cannot choose their hours of work. Involuntary unemployment represents an extreme case. (2) Not all uses of time away from the job are equivalent. For example, to avoid spending time on the road, a person who hated driving might be willing to pay at a rate exceeding his wage. On the other hand, a person who used the road for pleasure drives on weekends might not care very much about the opportunity cost of time, particularly if she could not work on weekends anyway.

Several investigators have estimated the value of time by looking at people's choices between modes of transportation that involve different traveling times. Suppose that in a given community people can commute to work either by bus or by train. The train takes less time, but it is more expensive. By seeing how much extra money people are willing to pay for the train, we can infer how much they are willing to pay to reduce their commuting time, and hence how they value that time. Of course, other characteristics of people, such as their incomes, affect their choice of travel mode. Statistical techniques like those described in Chapter 2 can be used to take these variables into account. On the basis of several such studies, a reasonable estimate of the effective cost of traveling time is about 50 percent of the after-tax wage rate (see von Wartburg and Waters [2004]).

The Value of Life   In a 2007 article about determining compensation for the victims of the September 11 terrorist attacks, the *New York Times* noted that "assigning a dollar value to a person's life might seem impossible, not to mention unthinkable" [Marsh, 2007]. Indeed, our religious and cultural values suggest that life is priceless. Consider the events that transpired a few years ago when a 22-month-old boy fell into an abandoned well. A rescue team with special training worked for 13 hours through the night to dig a separate hole to reach the trapped baby. A camera was dropped into the well to monitor the boy, and paramedics and a doctor were also on hand through the night to give medical advice. In the news accounts of this story, not a single person questioned whether saving the child's life was worth the cost. Arguing that any price was too high for saving his life would have been unthinkable. Similarly, if you were asked to value your own life, it would not be surprising if only the sky was the limit.

Such a position presents obvious difficulties for cost-benefit analysis. If the value of life is infinite, any project that leads even to a single life being saved has an infinitely high present value. *This leaves no sensible way to determine the admissibility of projects.* If *every* road in America were a divided four-lane highway, traffic fatalities would doubtless decrease. Would this be a good project? Similarly, any project that cost even one life would have an infinitely low value. In this context, consider the fact that to meet government mandated fuel efficiency standards, automobile manufacturers produce lighter cars than would otherwise be the case. But lighter cars are associated with higher fatality rates in accidents. Do fuel standards therefore automatically fail cost-benefit tests?

Economists have considered two methods for assigning finite values to human life, one based on lost earnings and the other on the probability of death.

Lost Earnings   Under the lost earnings method, the value of life is the present value of the individual's net earnings over a lifetime. If an individual dies as a consequence of a given project, the cost to society is just the expected present value of the output that person would have produced. This approach is often used in law courts to determine how much compensation the relatives of accident fatalities should receive. However, taken literally, this approach means that society would suffer no loss if the aged, infirm, or severely handicapped were summarily executed. This implication is sufficiently bizarre that the method is rejected by economists.

Probability of Death A second approach has as its starting point the notion that most projects do not actually affect with *certainty* a given individual's prospects for living. Rather, it is more typical for a change in the *probability* of a person's death to be involved. For example, you do not know that cancer research will save *your* life. All that can be determined is that it may reduce the *probability* of your death. The reason this distinction is so important is that even if people view their lives as having infinite value, they continually accept increases in the probability of death for finite amounts of money. An individual driving a light car is subject to a greater probability of death in an auto accident than someone in a heavy car, other things being the same. People are willing to accept the increased risk of death because of the money they save by purchasing lighter cars.

Another way that people reveal their risk preferences is by their occupational choices. Some jobs involve a higher probability of death than others. Suppose we compare two workers who have identical job qualifications and job characteristics, except that one has a riskier job than the other. The individual in the riskier job is expected to have a higher wage to compensate for the higher probability of death. The difference between the two wages provides an estimate of the value that people place on a decreased probability of death.[10]

In the same spirit, there have been many studies of the amounts that people are willing to pay for safety devices, such as smoke alarms, that reduce the probability of death by a given amount. Different studies come up with quite different results, but a rough guess on the basis of such research is that the value of life is between $4 million and $10 million [Viscusi, 2006]. Now, you might think that this range is so great as to be useless. However, these estimates can be very useful in weeding out senseless projects. For example, the regulations relating to the emergency floor lights on commercial planes cost about $900,000 per life saved. These regulations clearly pass the admissibility criterion. On the other hand, governmental asbestos removal rules cost more than $100 million per life saved.

An appealing aspect of this approach to valuing life is that it puts the analysis on the same willingness-to-pay basis that is so fruitful in other contexts. It remains highly controversial, however. Critics have argued that the probabilistic approach is irrelevant once it is conceded that *some* people's lives are *certainly* going to be at stake. The fact that we happen to be ignorant of just who will die is beside the point. This position leads us back to where we started, with no way to value projects that involve human life.

This academic controversy has become a matter of public concern because of various proposals to subject government safety and environmental regulations to cost-benefit analysis. Some object to valuing lives in cost-benefit analyses, stating, "There is no price for life because its value is immeasurable" [Ackerman and Heinzerling, 2004]. Unfortunately, in a world of scarce resources, we have no choice in the matter. The only question is whether or not sensible ways for setting the price are used.

---

[10] See Viscusi and Aldy [2003] for further discussion of such estimates.

Valuing Intangibles

No matter how ingenious the investigator, some benefits and costs are impossible to value: One of the benefits of the space shuttle program is increased national prestige. Indeed, President George W. Bush argued that space exploration "is a desire written in the human heart." Creating national parks gives people the thrill of enjoying beautiful scenery. The mind boggles at putting a dollar value on these "commodities." Three points must be kept in mind when intangible items might be important.

First, intangibles can subvert the entire cost-benefit exercise. By claiming that they are large enough, *any* project can be made admissible. For example, the administrator of NASA said that the "most important" reasons justifying the US space program are "emotional or value-driven" and "can't be captured on a spreadsheet" [Griffin, 2007]. However, presumably anyone who favors a particular project can make a case on the basis of its "emotional" impact. How does one then choose among projects?

Second, the tools of cost-benefit analysis can be used to force planners to reveal limits on how they value intangibles. Suppose the space shuttle's measurable costs and benefits are C and B, respectively, and its intangible benefits, such as national prestige, are an unknown amount X. Then if the measured costs are greater than measured benefits, X must exceed $(C - B)$ for the program to be admissible. Such information may reveal that the intangible is not valuable enough to merit doing the project. If $(C - B)$ for the space shuttle were $10 million per year, people might agree that its contribution to national prestige was worth it. But if the figure were $10 billion, a different conclusion might emerge.

Finally, even if measuring certain benefits is impossible, there may be alternative methods of attaining them. Systematic study of the costs of various alternatives should be done to find the cheapest way possible to achieve a given end. This is sometimes called **cost-effectiveness analysis.** Thus, while one cannot put a dollar value on national security, it still may be feasible to subject the costs of alternative weapons systems to scrutiny.

cost-effectiveness analysis

Comparing the costs of the various alternatives that attain similar benefits to determine which one is the cheapest.

▶ GAMES COST-BENEFIT ANALYSTS PLAY

In addition to the problems we have already discussed, Tresch [2002] has noted a number of common errors in cost-benefit analysis.

The Chain-Reaction Game

An advocate for a proposal can make it look especially attractive by counting secondary profits arising from it as part of the benefits. If the government builds a road, the primary benefits are the reductions in transportation costs for individuals and firms. At the same time, though, profits of local restaurants, motels, and gas stations increase. This leads to increased profits in the local food, bed-linen, and gasoline-production industries. If enough secondary effects are added to the benefit side, eventually a positive present value can be obtained for practically any project.

This procedure ignores the fact that the project may induce losses as well as profits. After the road is built, the profits of train operators decrease as some of their customers turn to cars for transportation. Increased auto use may bid up the price of gasoline, decreasing the welfare of many gasoline consumers.

In short, the problem with the chain-reaction game is that it counts as benefits changes that are merely transfers. The increase in the price of gasoline, for example, transfers income from gasoline consumers to gasoline producers, but it does not represent a net benefit of the project. As noted later, distributional considerations may indeed be relevant to the decision maker. But if so, consistency requires that if secondary benefits are counted, so should secondary losses.

The Labor Game

During the 2008 campaign, then-Senator Obama frequently argued that his plan to invest in clean energy technology would "create 5 million green collar jobs." His statement is a typical example of the argument that some project should be implemented because of all the employment it "creates." Essentially, the wages of the workers employed are viewed as *benefits* of the project. This line of reasoning is problematic because wages belong on the cost, not the benefit, side of the calculation. Of course, as already suggested, it is true that if workers are involuntarily unemployed, their social cost is less than their wage. Even in an area with high unemployment, it is unlikely that all the labor used in the project would have been unemployed, or that all those who were unemployed would have remained so for a long time.

The Double-Counting Game

Suppose that the government is considering irrigating some land that currently cannot be cultivated. It counts as the project's benefits the sum of (1) the increase in value of the land *and* (2) the present value of the stream of net income obtained from farming it. The problem here is that a farmer can *either* farm the land and take as gains the net income stream *or* sell the land to someone else. Under competition, the sale price of the land just equals the present value of the net income from farming it. Because the farmer cannot do both simultaneously, counting both (1) and (2) represents a doubling of the true benefits.

This error may seem so silly that no one would ever commit it. However, Tresch [2002, p. 825] points out that at one time double counting was the official policy of the Bureau of Reclamation within the US Department of the Interior. The bureau's instructions for cost-benefit analysts stipulated that the benefits of land irrigation be computed as the *sum* of the increase in land value and the present value of the net income from farming it.

▶ DISTRIBUTIONAL CONSIDERATIONS

In the private sector, normally no consideration is given to the question of who receives the benefits and bears the costs of a project. A dollar is a dollar, regardless of who is involved. Some economists argue that the same view be taken in public project analysis. If the present value of a project is positive, it should be undertaken regardless of who gains and loses. This is because as long as the present value is positive, the gainers *could* compensate the losers and still enjoy a net increase in utility. This notion, sometimes called the **Hicks-Kaldor criterion,**[11] thus bases project selection on whether there is a *potential* Pareto improvement. The actual compensation does

Hicks-Kaldor criterion

A project should be undertaken if it has a positive net present value, regardless of the distributional consequences.

---

[11] Named after the economists John Hicks and Nicholas Kaldor.

not have to take place. That is, it is permissible to impose costs on some members of society if that provides greater benefits to other individuals.

Others believe that because the goal of government is to maximize social welfare, the distributional implications of a project should be taken into account. Moreover, because it is the actual pattern of benefits and costs that really matters, the Hicks-Kaldor criterion does not provide a satisfactory escape from grappling with distributional issues.

One way to avoid the distributional problem is to assume the government can and will costlessly correct any undesirable distributional aspects of a project by making the appropriate transfers between gainers and losers.[12] The government works continually in the background to ensure that income stays optimally distributed, so the cost-benefit analyst need be concerned only with computing present values. Again, reality gets in the way. The government may have neither the power nor the ability to distribute income optimally.[13] (See Chapter 12.)

Suppose the policymaker believes that some group in the population is especially deserving. This distributional preference can be taken into account by assuming that a dollar benefit to a member of this group is worth more than a dollar going to others in the population. This, of course, tends to bias the selection of projects in favor of those that especially benefit the preferred group. Although much of the discussion of distributional issues has focused on income as the basis for classifying people, presumably characteristics such as race, ethnicity, and gender can be used as well.

After the analyst is given the criteria for membership in the preferred group, she must face the question of precisely how to weight benefits to members of that group relative to the rest of society. Is a dollar to a poor person counted twice as much as a dollar to a rich person, or 50 times as much? The resolution of such issues depends on value judgments. All the analyst can do is induce the policymaker to state explicitly his value judgments and understand their implications.

A potential hazard of introducing distributional considerations is that political concerns may come to dominate the cost-benefit exercise. Depending on how weights are chosen, any project can generate a positive present value, regardless of how inefficient it is. In addition, incorporating distributional considerations substantially increases the information requirements of cost-benefit analysis. The analyst needs to estimate not only benefits and costs but also how they are distributed across the population. As we discuss in Chapter 12, it is difficult to assess the distributional implications of government fiscal activities.

► UNCERTAINTY

In 2005, the levees protecting New Orleans were breached during Hurricane Katrina, leading to disastrous flooding. This catastrophe serves as a grim reminder of the fact that the outcomes of public projects are uncertain. Many important debates over project proposals center around the fact that no one knows how they will turn out. How much will a job-training program increase the earnings of welfare recipients? Will a high-tech weapons system function properly under combat conditions?

---

[12] *Costlessly* in this context means that the transfer system costs nothing to administer, and the transfers are done in such a way that they do not distort people's behavior (see Chapter 15).

[13] Moreover, as the government works behind the scenes to modify the income distribution, relative prices probably change. But as relative prices change, so do the benefit and cost calculations. Hence, efficiency and equity issues cannot be separated as neatly as suggested here.

Suppose that two projects are being considered. They have identical costs, and both affect only one citizen, Kyle. Project X guarantees a benefit of $1,000 with certainty. Project Y creates a benefit of zero dollars with a probability of one-half, and a benefit of $2,000 with a probability of one-half. Which project does Kyle prefer?

Note that *on average*, X and Y have the same benefit. This is because the expected benefit from Y is $(\frac{1}{2} \times \$0) + (\frac{1}{2} \times \$2,000) = \$1,000$. Nevertheless, if Kyle is risk averse, he prefers X to Y.[14] This is because project Y subjects Kyle to risk, while X is a sure thing. In other words, if Kyle is risk averse, he would be willing to trade project Y for a *certain* amount of money less than $1,000—he would give up some income in return for gaining some security. The most obvious evidence that people are in fact willing to pay to avoid risk is the widespread holding of insurance policies of various kinds. (See Chapter 9.) Therefore, when the benefits or costs of a project are risky, they must be converted into **certainty equivalents**—the amount of *certain* income the individual would be willing to trade for the set of uncertain outcomes generated by the project. The computation of certainty equivalents requires information on both the distribution of returns from the project and how risk averse the people involved are. The method of calculation is described in the appendix to this chapter.

The calculation of certainty equivalents presupposes that the random distribution of costs and benefits is known in advance. In some cases, this is a reasonable assumption. For example, engineering and weather data could be used to estimate how a proposed dam would reduce the probability of flood destruction. In many important cases, however, it is hard to assign probabilities to various outcomes. There is not enough experience with nuclear reactors to gauge the likelihood of various malfunctions. Similarly, how do you estimate the probability that a new AIDS vaccine will be effective? As usual, the best the analyst can do is to make explicit his or her assumptions and determine the extent to which substantive findings change when these assumptions are modified.

certainty equivalent

The value of an uncertain project measured in terms of how much certain income an individual would be willing to give up for the set of uncertain outcomes generated by the project.

▶ AN APPLICATION: ARE REDUCTIONS IN CLASS SIZE WORTH IT?

In Chapter 7 we discussed research on the effect of class size on students' test scores. A related literature examines whether children in smaller classes have higher earnings as adults, other things being the same. In one econometric analysis of the relationship between class size and earnings, Card and Krueger [1996] estimated that a 10 percent reduction in class size is associated with future annual earnings increases of 0.4 to 1.1 percent. If it is correct, this estimate suggests that decreasing class size does produce monetary benefits.

By itself, though, this does not tell us whether implementing reductions in class size would be a sensible policy. After all, making classes smaller is costly—more teachers need to be hired, additional classrooms built, and so on. Do the benefits outweigh the costs? Peltzman [1997] employs the tools of cost-benefit analysis to address this question. His analysis illustrates several of the key issues raised in this chapter.

---

[14] We will discuss risk aversion in greater detail in Chapter 9.

Cost-benefit analysis entails selecting a discount rate and specifying the costs and benefits for each year. We now discuss in turn how Peltzman deals with each of these problems.

Discount Rate

Theoretical considerations do not pin down a particular discount rate, so Peltzman follows the sensible practice of selecting a couple and seeing whether the substantive results are sensitive to the difference. The (real) rates he chooses are 3 percent and 7 percent.

Costs

Peltzman assumes that a 10 percent reduction in class size would require 10 percent more of all inputs used in public school education—teachers, classroom space, equipment, and so on. Thus, a permanent reduction in class size of 10 percent would increase yearly costs by 10 percent. In 1994, the average cost per student in US public schools was about $6,500, so a 10 percent increase is $650. This cost is incurred for each of the 13 years that the student is in school. Because these costs are incurred over time, they must be discounted. Row (1) of Table 8.3 shows the present value of $650 over a 13-year period for both $r = 3$ percent and $r = 7$ percent. In our earlier notation, these figures represent C, the present value of the project's costs (per student), at each discount rate.

This calculation of C involves a variety of simplifications; one of the most important is that the costs per year of schooling are constant. In fact, per-student costs are typically higher in high school than in elementary school. Allocating a greater proportion of the costs to future years would tend to reduce their present value.

Benefits

As noted earlier, Card and Krueger [1996] estimate that the range of returns to an increase in class size is 0.4 to 1.1 percent. Peltzman takes the midpoint of this range, 0.75 percent. He assumes that individuals go to work immediately upon leaving school, and work for the next 50 years. Hence, earnings are increased by 0.75 percent for each of the next 50 years. In 1994 median annual earnings for male workers 25 and older were $30,000; increasing this sum by 0.75 percent implies a raise of $225

Table 8.3 Costs and Benefits of Reducing Class Sizes by 10 Percent	Present Value	
	$r = 7\%$	$r = 3\%$
(1) Costs ($650 annually for 1994 through 2006)	$5,813	$7,120
(2) Benefits ($225 annually for 2007 through 2056)	$1,379	$4,060
(3) Benefits minus costs	−$4,434	−$3,060

Source: Computations based on Peltzman [1997].

These estimates suggest that the costs of reducing class size by 10 percent outweigh the benefits, at either a 3 or 7 percent discount rate.

per year over a 50-year period. Just like the costs, the benefits must be discounted. Note that the first of these $225 flows occurs 13 years in the future; hence its present value is $225/(1 + r)^{13}$. The present values of the benefits per student (B) for both discount rates are recorded in row (2) of the table.

Just as was true on the cost side, the calculation of benefits involves a number of important simplifications. Men generally earn more than women, so that using median earnings for males imparts an upward bias to the estimate of the benefits. Another issue is that earnings typically increase over time instead of staying constant. Further, the analysis ignores nonmonetary returns to education, which might include a reduced likelihood to commit crime, better informed choices in elections, and so on. To the extent that such effects are present, Peltzman's estimates of the social benefits to education are too low.

The Bottom Line and Evaluation

Computation of the net present value of this project is now straightforward. For each discount rate, take the benefit figure in row (2) of Table 8.3 and subtract from it the cost in row (1). These computations, recorded in row (3), reveal that when r is 7 percent, costs exceed benefits by $4,434, and when r is 3 percent, costs exceed benefits by $3,060. Thus, with either discount rate, ($B − C$) is less than zero, and reducing class size by 10 percent fails the admissibility criterion. On this basis, Peltzman concludes, tongue-in-cheek, that students would be better off if class size were *raised* by 10 percent, and the savings used to give each student a bond that paid the market rate of interest [p. 226].

This analysis of class-size reductions illustrates some important aspects of practical cost-benefit analysis:

- The analysis is often interdisciplinary because economists alone do not have the expertise to evaluate all costs and benefits. Thus, for example, engineering studies would be required to determine what expenditures really would be needed to expand classroom capacity by 10 percent. Similarly, if one wanted to include crime reduction in the benefits, one would want to consult sociologists who study criminal behavior.

- Evaluation of costs and benefits, especially those arising in the future, is likely to require ad hoc assumptions. We noted earlier, for example, that Peltzman's simplifying assumption that earnings are constant over time is certainly not correct. But in order to do better, one needs an alternative assumption of how earnings will rise (or fall) over time, and it is not obvious how to do that.

- In situations characterized by so much uncertainty, it may overburden the analysis to include distributional considerations. For example, an investigator who cannot predict with much precision how class size affects earnings overall can hardly be expected to estimate the distribution of the benefits by income group.

- For all its limitations, cost-benefit analysis is a remarkably useful way to summarize information. It also forces analysts to make explicit their assumptions so that the reasons for their ultimate recommendation are clear. In the case of Peltzman's examination of class size reductions, for example, because some of the assumptions are questionable, the conclusions may ultimately be proved incorrect. Nevertheless, it is an extremely valuable exercise because it establishes a rational framework within which to conduct future discussions of this important issue.

▶ USE (AND NONUSE) BY GOVERNMENT

This chapter clearly indicates that cost-benefit analysis is not a panacea that provides a definitive "scientific" answer to every question. Nevertheless, it helps to ensure consistent decision making that focuses on the right issues. Have these methods been put to work by the government? The federal government has been ordering that various kinds of projects be subjected to cost-benefit analysis ever since the 1930s. Presidents Reagan, Bush, and Clinton each issued executive orders requiring cost-benefit analyses for all major regulations.

That said, both Democratic and Republican administrations often ignore or fudge orders to perform cost-benefit analyses, and the Congress has not been enthusiastic about getting them done either. Federal agencies generally do not comply with the directives that require them to perform cost-benefit analyses, and when cost-benefit analyses are done, the quality is often poor. Hahn and Dudley [2007] studied 74 cost-benefit analyses of federal environmental regulations and found that a significant portion of them did not report basic economic information, such as information on net benefits and policy alternatives.

Why hasn't cost-benefit analysis had more effect on the style of government decision making? Part of the answer lies in the many practical difficulties in implementing cost-benefit analysis, especially when there is no consensus as to what the government's objectives are. In addition, many bureaucrats lack either the ability or the temperament to perform the analysis—particularly when it comes to their own programs. And neither are politicians particularly interested in seeing their pet projects subjected to scrutiny.

The story gets even worse when we consider the fact that, in certain vital areas, cost-benefit analysis has actually been expressly forbidden:

- The Clean Air Act prohibits costs from being considered when air quality standards are being set. In 1997, when the president's chief environmental aide was confronted with the fact that the costs of some new environmental regulations would exceed the benefits by hundreds of billions of dollars, she replied, "It is not at all about the money. . . . These are health standards" [Cushman, 1997, p. 28]. Any other stance would have been illegal!

- The same act requires companies to install equipment that reduces pollution as much as is feasible, regardless of how small the benefits of the incremental reduction or how large the incremental costs of the equipment.

- The Endangered Species Act requires the Fish and Wildlife Service to protect every endangered species in the United States, regardless of the cost.

- The Food, Drug, and Cosmetic Act requires the Food and Drug Administration to ban any additive to food that may induce cancer in animals or humans, regardless of how tiny the risk or how important the benefits of the substance.

A 1995 attempt by several members of Congress to change some of these laws was defeated. Moreover, in 2001 the Supreme Court upheld the constitutionality of the Clean Air Act's prohibition of cost-benefit analysis. While this may have been the right decision from a legal perspective, it was unfortunate from a policy standpoint. Although cost-benefit analysis is surely an imperfect tool, it is the only analytical framework available for making consistent decisions. Forbidding cost-benefit analysis amounts to outlawing sensible decision making.

Summary

- Cost-benefit analysis is the practical use of welfare economics to evaluate potential projects.

- To make net benefits from different years comparable, their present value must be computed.

- Other methods—internal rate of return, benefit-cost ratio—can lead to incorrect decisions.

- Choosing the discount rate is critical in cost-benefit analyses. In public sector analyses, three possible measures are the before-tax private rate of return, a weighted average of before- and after-tax private rates of return, and the social discount rate. Choosing among them depends on the type of private activity displaced—investment or consumption—and the extent to which private markets reflect society's preferences.

- In practice, the US government applies discount rates inconsistently.

- The benefits and costs of public projects may be measured in several ways:

  Market prices serve well if there is no strong reason to believe they depart from social marginal costs.

  Shadow prices adjust market prices for deviations from social marginal costs due to market imperfections.

  If labor is currently unemployed and will remain so for the duration of the project, the opportunity cost is small.

  If large government projects change equilibrium prices, consumer surplus can be used to measure benefits.

For nonmarket commodities, the values can sometimes be inferred by observing people's behavior. Two examples are computing the benefits of saving time and the benefits of reducing the probability of death.

- Certain intangible benefits and costs simply cannot be measured. The safest approach is to exclude them in a cost-benefit analysis and then calculate how large they must be to reverse the decision.

- Cost-benefit analyses sometimes fall prey to several pitfalls:

  Chain-reaction game—secondary benefits are included to make a proposal appear more favorable, without including the corresponding secondary costs.

  Labor game—wages are viewed as *benefits* rather than *costs* of the project.

  Double-counting game—benefits are erroneously counted twice.

- Including distributional considerations in cost-benefit analysis is controversial. Some analysts count dollars equally for all persons, while others apply weights that favor projects for selected population groups.

- In uncertain situations, individuals favor less-risky projects, other things being the same. In general, the costs and benefits of uncertain projects must be converted to certainty equivalents.

Discussion Questions

1. "If you were running the government, would you ask whether it would be cost-effective to make children's pajamas flame-resistant, or would you just order the manufacturers to do it? Would you be moved by the pleas of crib manufacturers who told you it would cost them a bundle to move those slats closer together?" [Herbert, 1995]. How would you respond to these questions?

2. New Jersey recently instituted an enhanced auto emissions testing system at inspection sites throughout the state. According to news reports, the new tests increased waiting times from about 15 minutes to 2 hours. How should this observation be factored into a cost-benefit analysis of the emissions testing program?

3. A project yields an annual benefit of $25 a year, starting next year and continuing forever. What is the present value of the benefits if the interest rate is 10 percent? [Hint: The infinite sum $x + x^2 + x^3 + \cdots$ is equal to $x/(1 - x)$, where x is a number less than 1.] Generalize your answer to show that if the perpetual annual benefit is B and the interest rate is r, then the present value is B/r.

4. Suppose that you are planning to take a year vacation to bike across the United States. Someone is willing to sell you a new bicycle for $500. At the end of the year, you expect to resell the bicycle for $350. The benefit to you of using the bicycle is the equivalent of $170.

    a. What is the internal rate of return?

    b. If the discount rate is 5 percent, should you buy the bicycle?

5. Bill rides the subway at a cost of 75 cents per trip, but would switch if the price were any higher. His only alternative is a bus that takes five minutes longer, but costs only 50 cents. He makes 10 trips per year. The city is considering renovations of the subway system that would reduce the trip by 10 minutes, but fares would rise by 40 cents per trip to cover the costs. The fare increase and reduced travel time both take effect in one year and last forever. The interest rate is 25 percent.

    a. As far as Bill is concerned, what are the present values of the project's benefits and costs?

    b. The city's population consists of 55,000 middle-class people, all of whom are identical to Bill, and 5,000 poor people. Poor people are either unemployed or have jobs close to their homes, so they do not use any form of public transportation. What are the total benefits and costs of the project for the city as a whole? What is the net present value of the project?

    c. Some members of the city council propose an alternative project that consists of an immediate tax of $1.25 per middle-class person to provide "free" legal services for the poor in both of the following two years. The legal services are valued by the poor at a total of $62,500 per year. (Assume this amount is received at the end of each of the two years.) What is the present value of the project?

    d. If the city must choose between the subway project and the legal services project, which should it select?

    e. What is the "distributional weight" of each dollar received by a poor person that would make the present values of the two projects just equal? That is, how much must each dollar of income to a poor person be weighted relative to that of a middle-class person? Interpret your answer.

6. Suppose that the government is debating whether to spend $100 billion today to address climate change. It is estimated that $700 billion of damage will be averted, but these benefits will accrue 100 years from now. A critic of the proposal says that it would be far better to invest the $100 billion, earning an average real return of 5 percent per year, and then use the proceeds in 100 years to repair the damage from climate change. Is this critic correct?

7. Suppose that the city government is considering a law that requires everyone to have at least three people per vehicle while driving during rush hour. In debating the plan, the mayor says the law will generate benefits in terms of cleaner air and less traffic congestion. The mayor acknowledges that there might also be costs involved with the law, but states that these might actually be negative because car owners will experience less wear-and-tear on their automobiles, and hence spend less money on repairs. Comment on the mayor's reasoning. How would you determine if the proposed requirement on carpooling is a good idea?

8. An article in the *Economist* [2007f, p. 42] tells the story of an economist who once visited China during the rule of Mao Zedong. He sees hundreds of workers building a dam with shovels and asks, "Why don't they use a mechanical digger?" The foreman replies, "That would put people out of work." How does this comment relate to the "labor game" discussed in the chapter?

9. According to Viscusi and Gayer [2005], regulations in the United States vary greatly in the cost per each life they save. For example, the regulation to install passive restraints in vehicles has a cost per life saved of $600,000, whereas the regulation to remove asbestos in workplaces has a cost per life saved of $180 million. What does this information imply about whether the regulations pass a cost-benefit test? How might resources be shifted between these regulations in order to reduce cost or save more lives?

Appendix

▶ CALCULATING THE CERTAINTY EQUIVALENT VALUE

This appendix shows how to calculate the certainty equivalent value of an uncertain project. As such, it also serves as an introduction to the economics of uncertainty, which we will discuss in greater detail in Chapter 9.

Consider Jones, who currently earns E dollars. He enters a job-training program with an unpredictable effect on his future earnings. The program will leave his annual earnings unchanged with a probability of ½, or it will increase his earnings by y dollars, also with a probability of ½.[15] The benefit of the program is the amount that Jones would be willing to pay for it, so the key problem here is to determine that amount. A natural answer is $y/2$ dollars, the expected increase in his earnings.[16] However, this value is too high, because it neglects the fact that the outcome is uncertain and therefore subjects Jones to risk. As long as Jones dislikes risk, he would give up some income in return for gaining some security. When the benefits or costs of a project are risky, they must be converted into certainty equivalents, the amounts of *certain* income that the individual would be willing to trade for the set of uncertain outcomes generated by the project.

The notion of certainty equivalence is illustrated in Figure 8.A. The horizontal axis measures Jones's income, and the vertical axis indicates the amount of his utility. Schedule OU is Jones's utility function, which shows the total amount of utility associated with each income level. Algebraically, the amount of utility associated with a given income level, I, is $U(I)$. The shape of the schedule reflects the plausible assumption that as income increases, utility also increases, but at a declining rate—there is diminishing marginal utility of income.

To find the utility associated with any income level, simply go from the horizontal axis up to OU, and then off to the vertical axis. For example, if the training project yields no return so that Jones's income is E, then his utility is $U(E)$, as indicated on the vertical axis. Similarly, if the project succeeds so that Jones's income increases by y, his total income is $(E + y)$, and his utility is $U(E + y)$.

Because each outcome occurs with a probability of ½, Jones's average or expected *income* is $E + y/2$, which lies halfway between E and $(E + y)$ and is denoted $\bar{I}$. However, what Jones really cares about is not expected income, but expected *utility*.[17] Expected utility is just the average of the utilities of the two outcomes, or $½U(E) + ½U(E + y)$. Geometrically, expected utility is halfway between $U(E)$ and $U(E + y)$ and is denoted by $\bar{U}$.

We are now in a position to find out exactly how much certain money the job-training program is worth to Jones. All we have to do is find the amount of income that corresponds to utility level $\bar{U}$. This is shown on the horizontal axis as C, which is by definition the certainty equivalent. It is crucial to note that C is less than $\bar{I}$—the

---

[15] Probabilities of ½ are used for simplicity. The general results hold regardless of the probabilities chosen.

[16] Expected earnings are found by multiplying each possible outcome by the associated probability and then adding: $(½ \times 0) + (½ \times y) = y/2$.

[17] Those who are familiar with the theory of uncertainty will recognize the implicit assumption that individuals have "von Neumann–Morgenstern utility functions."

Figure 8.A
Computing
the certainty
equivalent of a
risky project

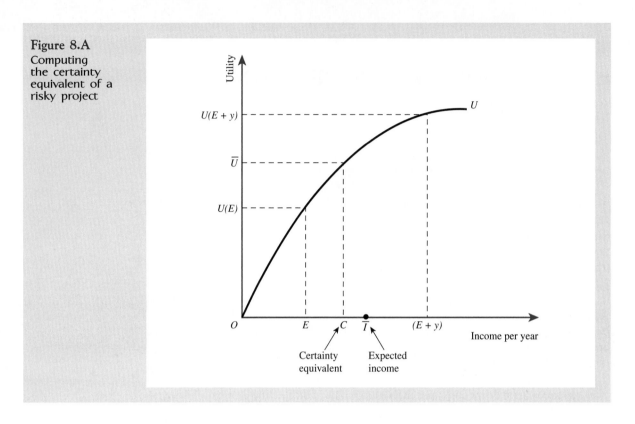

certainty equivalent of the job-training program is *less* than the expected income. This is consistent with the intuition developed earlier. Jones is willing to pay a premium of $(\overline{I} - C)$ in exchange for the security of a sure thing. We have shown, then, that proper evaluation of the costs and benefits of an uncertain project requires that the project's expected value be reduced by a risk premium that depends on the shape of the individual's utility function.

In a way, this is a disappointing outcome, because it is much simpler to compute an expected value than a certainty equivalent. Fortunately, it turns out that in many cases the expected value is enough. Suppose a new bomber is being considered, and because the technology is not completely understood, analysts are unsure of its eventual cost. The cost will be either $15 per family or $25, each with probability of ½. Although in the aggregate a large amount of money is at stake, on a per-*family* basis, the sums involved are quite small compared to income. In terms of Figure 8.A, the two outcomes are very close to each other on curve *OU*. As points on *OU* get closer and closer together, the expected value and certainty equivalent become virtually identical, other things being the same. Intuitively, people do not require a risk premium to accept a gamble that involves only a small amount of income.

Thus, for projects that spread risk over large numbers of people, expected values can provide good measures of uncertain benefits and costs. But for cases in which risks are large relative to individuals' incomes, certainty equivalents must be computed.

Part Three

PUBLIC EXPENDITURE: SOCIAL INSURANCE AND INCOME MAINTENANCE

Programs that provide various types of insurance comprise a large and growing share of the government budget. In this part of the book, we use the framework of welfare economics to study these programs, which are collectively referred to as social insurance. Chapter 9 uses the specific example of health care to illustrate how insurance markets work and why they may fail to generate efficient and fair outcomes. Chapter 10 then discusses and evaluates the role that government plays in health insurance markets. Chapter 11 deals with Social Security, a program for retirees that provides (among other things) insurance against the possibility that people may use up their resources before they die.

To some extent, government programs that redistribute income are also a form of insurance—they protect people against the risk of living in abject poverty. Chapter 12 uses the theory of welfare economics to discuss the conceptual basis for income redistribution, and Chapter 13 analyzes the major US antipoverty programs.

Chapter Nine

THE HEALTH CARE MARKET

We have reached a point in this country where the rising cost of health care has put too many families and businesses on a collision course with financial ruin and left too many without coverage at all; a course that Democrats and Republicans, small business owners, and CEOs have all come to agree is not sustainable or acceptable any longer.

—PRESIDENT BARACK OBAMA

For all Americans, we must confront the rising cost of care, strengthen the doctor-patient relationship, and help people afford the insurance coverage they need.

—PRESIDENT GEORGE W. BUSH

▶ WHAT'S SPECIAL ABOUT HEALTH CARE?

As the quotes from Presidents Obama and Bush indicate, health care occupies a very special place on the public policy agenda. This is due partly to the belief that health care is unique and that private markets alone cannot be trusted to determine health care outcomes. Health care, of course, is different from goods like digital cameras and MP3 players because receiving it can be a matter of life and death. On the other hand, food and shelter are also crucial for survival, but the nation is not debating whether private markets are a good way to provide these commodities.

Another reason why health care commands so much public attention is that we spend so much on it, and the amounts have been increasing rapidly over time. Figure 9.1 shows the rapid growth in US health expenditures as a percentage of Gross Domestic Product (GDP). Health care expenditures were 5 percent of GDP in 1960, and by 2007 they were over 16 percent of GDP. We now spend a larger percentage of our GDP on health care than we do on food, clothing, or housing.

But by itself, the fact that health care costs are increasing dramatically does not necessarily mean that there is a problem. Expenditures on organic food and cell phones have also grown dramatically in recent years, but no one is terribly upset about it. Indeed, Nobel laureate Robert Fogel has argued, "The increasing share of global income spent on healthcare expenditures is not a calamity; it is a sign of the remarkable economic and social progress of our age" [Fogel, 2004, p. 107].

So what unique attributes of health care might justify government involvement in this market?

The Role of Insurance

To understand the unique aspects of the health care market, we must first understand the general role of insurance. Understanding the theory of insurance will help us both

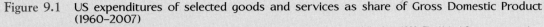

Figure 9.1   US expenditures of selected goods and services as share of Gross Domestic Product (1960–2007)

US health care expenditures as a percentage of Gross Domestic Product have increased substantially since 1960. The United States now spends a larger percentage of its Gross Domestic Product on health than on food, clothing, or housing.

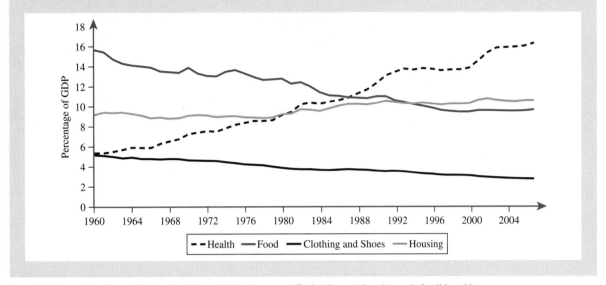

Source: US Bureau of the Census [2009, pp. 95, 425], and National Income and Product Accounts (www.bea.gov/national/nipaweb/index.asp).

to understand health care issues and to analyze government programs that protect people against a variety of adverse events. These programs, several of which are discussed in subsequent chapters, are collectively referred to as **social insurance.**

Basically, the way that health insurance works is that buyers pay money, called an **insurance premium,** to providers of insurance, which in turn agree to disburse some amount to the insured person should an adverse health event such as illness occur. Other things being the same, the greater the insurance premium, the more compensation the buyer receives in case of illness.

To think about why people are willing to pay for insurance, it helps to analyze a specific numerical example. Consider Emily, whose income is $50,000 per year. Suppose that there is a 1 in 10 chance that she will get sick in a given year and that the cost of the illness (in terms of medical bills and lost time at work) is $30,000, thus leaving her with only $20,000 in income for that year.

In order to evaluate the options to Emily, we need to understand the statistical concept of **expected value,** which is the amount that an individual can expect to receive "on average" when she faces uncertain outcomes. The expected value is computed by taking a weighted sum of each of the uncertain outcomes, with the weights being the probabilities of the respective outcomes. Algebraically,

Expected value (EV) = (Probability of outcome 1 × Payout in outcome 1)
+ (Probability of outcome 2 × Payout in outcome 2)

(9.1)

For example, suppose that you will receive $12 if a heart is drawn from a deck of cards, and that you will lose $4 if a spade, diamond, or club is drawn. The probability of drawing a heart is ¼ and the probability of drawing some other suit is ¾.

social insurance programs

Government programs that provide insurance to protect against adverse events.

insurance premium

Money paid to an insurance company in exchange for compensation if a specified adverse event occurs.

expected value

The average value over all possible uncertain outcomes, with each outcome weighted by its probability of occurring.

Table 9.1 Why Buy Insurance?

Insurance Options	Income	Probability of Staying Healthy	Probability of Getting Sick	Lost Income If She Gets Sick	(A) Income If She Stays Healthy	(B) Income If She Gets Sick	(C) Expected Value
Option 1: No insurance	$50,000	9 in 10	1 in 10	$30,000	$50,000	$20,000	$47,000
Option 2: Full insurance	$50,000	9 in 10	1 in 10	$30,000	$47,000	$47,000	$47,000

Buying a full insurance policy at the actuarially fair premium yields the same expected value for Emily as buying no insurance at all. However, if she is risk averse, having the insurance policy makes her better off.

Therefore, the expected value to you of this uncertain event is computed as $EV = (\frac{1}{4})(\$12) + (\frac{3}{4})(-\$4) = \$0$.

For this uncertain situation, the expected value is zero—on average, you would neither gain nor lose money.

Now let's return to the problem that is confronting Emily. Table 9.1 examines two options available to her each year. In option 1, she does not buy insurance. Thus, she keeps earning $50,000 and risks losing $30,000 if the illness happens. Emily faces two possible outcomes with option 1: either she does not get sick and has an income of $50,000 (column A), or she gets sick and has an income of $20,000 (column B). The probability of the first outcome is 9 in 10, and the probability of the second outcome is 1 in 10. Using Equation (9.1) we compute in column C the expected value (also known as her expected income) of this option as follows:

$$EV \text{ (Option 1)} = (\%_{10})(\$50,000) + (\frac{1}{10})(\$20,000) = \$47,000 \qquad (9.2)$$

Now consider option 2. Rather than accepting the risk of having only $20,000 if she becomes ill, Emily can instead pay an insurer an annual premium that will cover her expenses in case of illness. How much would this insurance policy cost? An **actuarially fair insurance premium** would charge just enough to cover the expected compensation for the expenses. In other words, an actuarially fair insurance premium would charge the expected value of the loss, so that, on average, the insurance company neither loses nor gains any money. (The insurance company would need to charge above the actuarially fair insurance premium in order to cover any overhead costs. But for simplicity, for now we assume that there are no such costs.) Given that there is a 9 in 10 chance of no loss in income and a 1 in 10 chance of a $30,000 loss, the expected value of the loss is $(\%_{10})(\$0) + (\frac{1}{10})(\$30,000) = \$3,000$. So the actuarially fair insurance premium would be $3,000 each year. Think of this from the insurer's point of view. By charging $3,000 to each of 10 people with a 1 in 10 risk of losing $30,000, the insurer can expect to receive $30,000 each year, which is just enough to cover the insurer's expected payouts for the year. As the following cartoon humorously suggests, when the risk of the adverse event increases, so does the premium that the company has to charge in order to break even.

actuarially fair insurance premium

An insurance premium for a given time period set equal to the expected payout for the same time period.

"For someone your age, the yearly premium on a $5,000 policy is $8,000." © Mike Baldwin. Reprinted with permission from www.CartoonStock.com.

In option 2, Emily pays the annual $3,000 premium whether she is sick or not. If she turns out to be healthy (column A), her income is therefore $47,000. If she gets sick (column B), she still pays the $3,000 premium, yet the $30,000 in lost income due to illness is fully compensated by her insurer. Therefore, her income is still $47,000. In short, with option 2 Emily receives $47,000 whether she is sick or healthy.

Given that options 1 and 2 both provide the same expected income, one might guess that Emily would be indifferent between them. However, such reasoning ignores the fact that option 2 gives Emily $47,000 with *certainty* (whether or not she is sick), whereas option 1 gives her $47,000 *on average*. We can show that in general, Emily prefers option 2, which provides the same expected income, but with certainty.[1]

To see why, recall that a standard assumption of economic theory is that people prefer more income to less, but that each additional unit of income contributes smaller and smaller gains in utility. Such "diminishing marginal utility" means that the pain of losing an incremental dollar is greater than the pleasure of gaining an incremental dollar.

Emily's problem is illustrated by Figure 9.2, which shows her utility measured on the vertical axis and her income on the horizontal axis. This function, which is labeled U, has a concave curvature, which reflects the assumption of diminishing marginal utility. If she is sick this year, then she is at point A, with utility U_A. If she turns out to be healthy this year, then she is at point B, with utility U_B. One

---

[1] We also discussed the value of certainty in the appendix to Chapter 8.

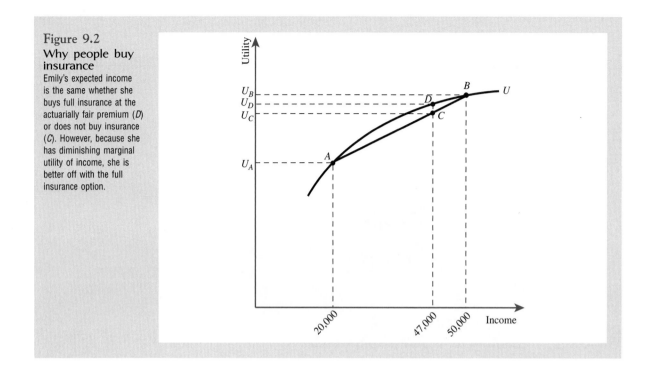

reasonable view of how a person behaves when confronted with such risk is that she uses the strategy that maximizes her utility on average, or her **expected utility.** To compute expected utility, we use the same logic behind the expected value formula and weight the utility level associated with each outcome by the probability of that outcome occurring. Thus,

$$\text{Expected utility } (EU) \text{ for Emily} = (\tfrac{9}{10})U(\$50{,}000) + (\tfrac{1}{10})U(\$20{,}000) \qquad (9.3)$$

where $U(\$50{,}000)$ is the utility of $50,000 and $U(\$20{,}000)$ is defined analogously.

Diagrammatically, Equation (9.3) is equivalent to moving 90 percent up from U_A to U_B along the vertical axis and 90 percent from $20,000 to $50,000 along the horizontal axis, which corresponds to point C that is located on the line that connects points A and B in Figure 9.2. So if Emily chooses option 1 and does not buy insurance, she is at point C, with utility U_C. But if Emily instead buys insurance so that she receives $47,000 for sure, then she is at point D, with utility U_D, which is higher than the utility she receives with no insurance. So while both options give the same expected value, the option with certainty gives higher expected utility. Thus, because people have diminishing marginal utility, they have a preference for **risk smoothing,** which entails reducing income in high-earning years in order to protect themselves against major drops in consumption in low-earning years.

This example illustrates a fundamental result: Under the standard assumption of diminishing marginal utility of income, when an individual is offered actuarially fair insurance, she insures fully against the possible loss of income from illness.[2]

---

[2] An important assumption is that the underlying utility function does not change when the individual is ill. If illness raises the marginal utility of income, then more than full income replacement is optimal. If being sick lowers the marginal utility of income, then less than full income replacement is optimal [Viscusi, 1992].

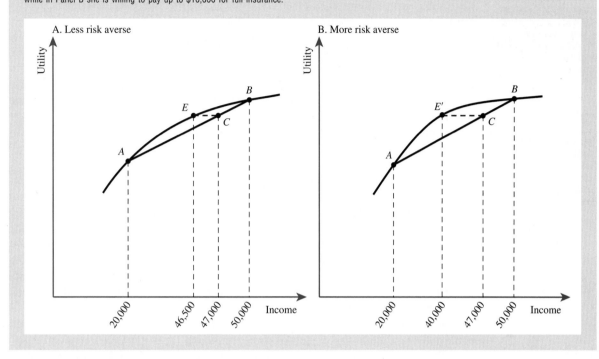

Figure 9.3   Do people buy insurance with loading fees?
The more risk averse Emily is, the more she is willing to pay for full insurance. In Panel A, she is only willing to pay up to $3,500 for full insurance, while in Panel B she is willing to pay up to $10,000 for full insurance.

But what if the insurance company does not offer an actuarially fair premium? Let's consider again the example in Figure 9.2, where we showed that the actuarially fair premium is $3,000. Suppose that instead the insurance company charges more than that to cover the same loss, say $4,000 per year in premiums? Will Emily stop buying insurance? Not necessarily.

Figure 9.3 shows that the answer depends on the shape of her utility function. If she has the utility function shown in Panel A, then she would rather not purchase this insurance. To see why, recall that if she does not buy insurance, her expected income is $47,000 (point *C*). Notice that she is indifferent between point *C* and point *E* on this diagram, because they both give the same expected utility. Point *E* corresponds to her receiving $46,500 with certainty; that is, it is achieved if she fully insures against the risk at a premium of $3,500. Therefore, she is willing to pay up to $3,500 for insurance rather than going without insurance. If the insurance company charges $4,000, she won't buy the plan.

If instead Emily has the utility function shown in Panel B, then she is willing to pay up to $10,000 for the insurance plan (which puts her at point *E'*). Because the insurance company only charges $4,000, she buys the coverage and achieves higher utility than if she goes uninsured.

The difference between Panels A and B is that the utility function in Panel B has more curvature. This demonstrates a general result: the demand for insurance depends on the curvature of the utility function, also known as the level of **risk aversion.** Someone who is relatively more risk averse (for example, the utility function in Panel B rather than the utility function in Panel A) is willing to pay a

risk aversion

A preference for paying more than the actuarially fair premium in order to guarantee compensation if an adverse event occurs.

risk premium

The amount above the actuarially fair premium that a risk-averse person is willing to pay to guarantee compensation if an adverse event occurs.

loading fee

The difference between the premium an insurance company charges and the actuarially fair premium level.

greater amount above the actuarially fair premium. This difference is called the **risk premium.** Intuitively, this makes perfect sense—the greater the curvature, the more rapid is the diminishing marginal utility of income. That is, greater risk aversion means a greater relative loss of utility from losing income, and therefore a greater willingness to pay to insure against the loss.

The fact that insurance companies can charge higher premiums than the actuarially fair rate suggests that people are in fact risk averse. Even in a competitive market, insurance companies charge higher than actuarially fair premiums to allow them to cover such items as administrative costs and taxes. The difference between the premium an insurance company charges and the actuarially fair premium is called the **loading fee.** One simple way to measure the loading fee is the ratio of market insurance premiums divided by benefits paid out. Today the average loading ratio for private insurance companies is about 1.20 [Phelps, 2003].

The Role of Risk Pooling

The previous example leads us to consider the highly important role that insurance companies play in pooling together people who face risks. To begin, consider the very unrealistic situation in which the insurance company insures only Emily, and no one else. By purchasing a policy from this company, Emily can eliminate the financial risks associated with illness. But now the insurance company is stuck with the risk. From a societal point of view, risk has not been reduced; it has simply been transferred from the individual to the insurance company.

Now suppose that the company has 10 customers instead of 1. If it charges an actuarially fair premium to each of them, and each faces a 1 in 10 chance of getting sick, then this would be enough to cover expenses should 1 of the 10 people get sick, as expected. No one knows which of the people will get sick, but the insurance company has a pretty good idea of what its payments will be. Risk has been substantially reduced. Still, it's conceivable that two people would get sick, leaving the insurance company with the risk of being 50 percent short on funds. If instead the insurance company covered 100,000 people instead of just 10, then the likelihood of having to deal with more than 1 in 10 sick people would decrease dramatically. Think of a roulette wheel in which the odds of landing on black versus red are 50 percent. You may get lucky and land on black two or three times in a row, but as the number of spins increases, the proportion of times one lands on black will converge to 50 percent. The same is true of the insurance company: The more people in its insurance pool, the more predictable its outlays. This greater predictability allows the insurance company to charge a premium that with some assurance will cover its costs and thus lower the risk it faces. In effect, then, by *pooling* the risk across individuals, the insurance company has actually lowered risk from a social point of view.[3]

Adverse Selection in the Health Insurance Market

With the basics of the health insurance market in hand, we are ready to return to the key question: What is special about it? After all, given that there is an incentive

---

[3] While a larger insurance pool helps to eliminate the risk, it only works if the risk is independent across the insured people. For example, the risk of an earthquake is not independent across residents of northern California. If one home in the area gets destroyed, then others in the area will likely get destroyed as well, and the insurance company won't have enough money to compensate everyone. With the important exception of contagious diseases, for the most part this isn't a problem with health insurance.

to provide health insurance (in a competitive market, loading fees allow insurers to make a normal profit), why is government intervention needed?

One problem stems from a market failure phenomenon that we first encountered in Chapter 3—**asymmetric information.** Asymmetric information exists when one party in a transaction has information that is not available to another party in the transaction. Asymmetric information is especially problematic in the market for health insurance. To illustrate, let's return to our previous example, where we showed that an insurance policy costing $3,000 would fully insure Emily.

Now assume that there are nine other people in addition to Emily, each of whom also faces a risk of losing $30,000 due to illness. However, while some of them face a 1 in 10 chance of illness like Emily, others face a 1 in 5 risk. Further, assume that only each individual knows whether he or she is at high or low risk for illness. (The individual has information about family medical history, health habits, stress at work, and so on, that the insurance company lacks.) We examine this situation in Table 9.2, which assumes that half of the 10 people face a 1 in 5 risk. As shown in column C of the table, the high-risk people have an expected income loss of $6,000, and the low-risk people have an expected income loss of $3,000. Now, if the insurance company knew who the high-risk individuals were, it could charge them a higher premium and cover its costs (column D). The problem is that it does not know—individuals in this example have more information about their health status than the company. Therefore, the insurer has no choice other than to charge everyone the same premium. If the insurer charges a $3,000 premium (column E), it is a great deal to the buyers who have a 1 in 5 risk of getting sick, because their expected compensation is $6,000 yet they only pay a $3,000 premium. However, the company would have expected annual net *losses* of $15,000, since it would not make enough

asymmetric information

A situation in which one party engaged in an economic transaction has better information about the good or service traded than the other party.

Table 9.2 **How Asymmetric Information can Cause Failure in the Insurance Market**

Insurance Buyer	(A) Probability of Getting Sick	(B) Lost Income if Sick	(C) Expected Lost Income	(D) Expected Benefit Minus Premium (Differential Premiums)	(E) Expected Benefit Minus Premium (Premium = $3,000)	(F) Expected Benefit Minus Premium (Premium = $4,500)
Emily	1 in 5 (high risk)	$30,000	$6,000	$0	$ 3,000	$ 1,500
Jacob	1 in 5 (high risk)	30,000	6,000	0	3,000	1,500
Emma	1 in 5 (high risk)	30,000	6,000	0	3,000	1,500
Michael	1 in 5 (high risk)	30,000	6,000	0	3,000	1,500
Madison	1 in 5 (high risk)	30,000	6,000	0	3,000	1,500
Joshua	1 in 10 (low risk)	30,000	3,000	0	0	-1,500
Olivia	1 in 10 (low risk)	30,000	3,000	0	0	-1,500
Matthew	1 in 10 (low risk)	30,000	3,000	0	0	-1,500
Hannah	1 in 10 (low risk)	30,000	3,000	0	0	-1,500
Ethan	1 in 10 (low risk)	30,000	3,000	0	0	-1,500
Insurer's net profits				0	-15,000	0

If the insurance company knew which people were high risk and which were low risk, it could charge the actuarially fair premium to each and just come out even (column D). However, if it can't distinguish the high-risk from the low-risk people, a uniform premium of $3,000 leads to losses for the company (column E). Charging a uniform premium equal to the average actuarially fair premium of the two groups enables the company to cover costs (column F), but the low-risk people have an incentive to drop out of the insurance pool, and the insurer ends up losing money.

in premiums to cover the expected payouts. An insurance company with expected annual losses would not stay in business for long.

In the presence of these losses, the insurer might instead decide to charge each of the 10 people a premium of $4,500, which is the average expected income loss across all 10 people (column F). These 10 people would pay a total of $45,000 in premiums, and the expected payout would also be $45,000. Thus, the insurer could stay in business (ignoring for simplicity the loading fees).

But there is a problem here as well. With a $4,500 premium, the insurance plan remains a good deal for the high-risk people. They can each expect to receive $6,000 in health care compensation, although they only pay $4,500 in premiums. However, the $4,500 premium is a bad deal for the low-risk people. Their expected health care compensation is $3,000, while they must pay $4,500 in premiums. Consequently, the high-risk people are attracted to this insurance plan while the healthier people may not purchase it. In short, because of the information asymmetry, the insurer gets customers who are, from its point of view, exactly the wrong people. This phenomenon is known as **adverse selection.** More generally, adverse selection occurs when an insurance provider sets a premium based on the average risk of a population, but the low-risk people do not purchase the insurance policy, leaving the insurer to lose money.

But the story is not over. If the five healthy people decide not to buy insurance, the $4,500 premium is no longer enough for the insurance company to recover its expected payouts to the remaining five people. The insurance company must raise its premium. If the risk of illness had differed among the remaining customers, the company would again expect to lose the relatively low-risk people. In short, if an insurance company has less information on the health risks faced by its customers than do the customers, any premium set to cover the average risk level may induce the lower-risk people to leave the market. People who could have benefited from insurance at an actuarially fair rate go without insurance, and indeed, the market may stop functioning altogether as more and more participants opt out. This phenomenon is sometimes described by the colorful term "death spiral."

We have shown that asymmetric information *can* kill off a market, not that it necessarily *will*. Recall from our discussion of Figure 9.3 that the more risk averse a person is, the more likely that person is to purchase an insurance policy that is not actuarially fair. If an insurance company charged a uniform premium that was actuarially fair for the high-risk people, this would be a bad deal for the low-risk people. However, given that most people are risk averse, the low-risk people might still want to buy the insurance coverage. In such a case, the market for insurance would not collapse, although it might underprovide coverage for some low-risk people. Ultimately, it is an empirical question whether asymmetric information is present in a given market, and if so, whether it actually leads to market failure.

adverse selection

The phenomenon under which the uninformed side of a deal gets exactly the wrong people trading with it (that is, it gets an adverse selection of the informed parties).

EMPIRICAL EVIDENCE

A Death Spiral at Harvard?

In the presence of adverse selection, relatively healthy people may decline insurance coverage if the premium is set based on the community's average health risk. This would lead to higher premiums and healthy people opting out. Such a "death spiral" could lead to a collapse of the market. But is this important as a real-world phenomenon?

Cutler and Reber [1998] examined a change in Harvard University's health insurance coverage for their employees. Before the change, Harvard employees could enroll in a more generous insurance plan for only a slightly larger premium than if they enrolled in a less generous plan. Thus, Harvard gave a large subsidy for the generous insurance plan. Motivated by budget problems, in 1995 Harvard changed to a system in which the university would contribute an equal amount to each insurance plan, regardless of which one an employee chose. Each employee would get an amount that could then be used for any of the insurance options. As a consequence, a person in the generous plan had to pay about $700 more per year than someone in the less generous plan.

Thus, suddenly people at Harvard had to pay more if they wanted the more generous insurance plan. As expected from standard economic theory, many people left the generous plan to enroll in a less generous plan. But the people who switched plans were not a random subsample of the original enrollees. Specifically, those who left the generous plan were younger (and presumably healthier) than those who decided to stay. This indicates sorting by health status as predicted by the theory of adverse selection. Sure enough, the premium for the generous plan increased substantially (it doubled!) one year later in order to cover the increased costs of insuring an older (and presumably less healthy) population. This again led to the relatively younger people leaving the generous plan. Rather than raise premiums even higher, the plan was dropped the following year. So within two years of the change, adverse selection eliminated the generous health plan.

Does Adverse Selection Justify Government Intervention?   Given that adverse selection can lead to inefficient provision of health insurance, a natural question is whether there is some way to eliminate the information asymmetry that leads to the problem in the first place. If the private market can do so, then government intervention is not needed. Private market insurers can, in fact, take some steps to reduce the information asymmetry. Indeed, research indicates that in some insurance markets, providers obtain enough information about their customers to avert the problem of adverse selection.[4]

In the health insurance context, insurance companies can screen their customers and charge different premiums to customers based on their risk profiles, a practice known as **experience rating.** Indeed, we observe insurers denying coverage (or offering only limited coverage) or charging higher premiums for people who are in bad health or who have bad health histories when they apply for insurance. The more information insurance companies can obtain about their customers' health risk, the more they can overcome the inefficiencies of adverse selection.

Yet improving efficiency in the insurance market by obtaining better data raises serious equity issues. A world without asymmetric information could be troubling because those who are genetically inclined toward a sickness would have to pay significantly more for insurance, and perhaps even be priced out of the market.

The government can address this fairness problem by providing health insurance coverage for the entire US population (or perhaps a subpopulation), making participation mandatory and setting a uniform rate for premiums. Employer-provider

experience rating

The practice of charging different insurance premiums based on the existing risk of the insurance buyers.

---

[4] Chiappori and Salanie [2000] find no evidence of adverse selection in the French market for automobile insurance. Neither do Cawley and Philipson [1999] in the life insurance market or Cardon and Hendel [2002] in the health insurance market.

coverage might also accomplish this, especially for large employers who pool many individuals with different risks into one insurance plan. Charging uniform premiums to a community made up of individuals with different health risks is called **community rating.** Community rating is inefficient because some people pay more for insurance than it is worth to them, while others would prefer to pay more money in order to buy more insurance. Nevertheless, community rating would eliminate the inequities associated with sorting by health risk. The question is whether the gains in fairness outweigh the losses in terms of efficiency.

Advocates of experience rating argue that community rating really isn't all that fair because it fails to reward people who have healthy lifestyles. And some research indicates that, in any case, experience rating is not of any practical importance in real-world private health care markets. A provocative study by Pauly and Herring [1999] questions whether private insurance companies actually succeed in their attempts to charge different premiums for different risk categories. They find that premiums for individual insurance coverage do not rise commensurately with anticipated medical expenses. Indeed, individuals with twice the expected health costs of other customers pay only about 20 to 40 percent higher premiums. Pauly and Herring conjecture that individual insurance buyers are able to shop around enough to find lower rates, and that they frequently choose to lock into long-term renewable policies. For both reasons, premiums need not rise in proportion to health risk.

Nonetheless, we see that a possible role of government is to find a balance between reducing the inefficiencies caused by adverse selection and addressing the equity concerns that arise when people with different health risks are charged different premiums.

Insurance and Moral Hazard

Adverse selection arises because insurers don't have complete knowledge of the health risks of those they insure. A different type of information asymmetry arises because having insurance may distort one's behavior in ways that are not precisely known by the insurer.

Consider again the simple case in which everyone faces the identical risk of being sick each year. There is thus a well-functioning market for health insurance with each person paying an actuarially fair premium (again, ignoring loading fees). People engage in risk smoothing in order to maximize expected utility.

But the benefit of risk smoothing can come at a cost to efficiency. Because the cost of illness will be fully compensated, the insured might be more likely to engage in risky behavior, such as eating a lot of junk food, not exercising much, and smoking. The incentive to increase risky behavior because the adverse outcomes of that behavior are covered by insurance is known as **moral hazard.** For example, a person with an insurance policy that compensates him for anything stolen from his home might be less likely to lock his doors. This problem arises because of asymmetric information: The insurance provider charges for coverage based on an assumed level of risky behavior by the insured, but cannot know how much the insured will increase risky behavior once she is covered. The existence of moral hazard introduces a fundamental tension into the design of insurance policies: The more that an insurance plan smoothes risk by covering health care costs, the more it leads to inefficient overuse of health care through an increase in risky behavior.

Another efficiency issue related to insurance markets arises because the policy pays some or all of the incremental cost of health care. This increases the incentive

community rating

The practice of charging uniform insurance premiums for people in different risk categories within a community, thus resulting in low-risk people subsidizing high-risk people.

moral hazard

When obtaining insurance against an adverse outcome leads to changes in behavior that increase the likelihood of the outcome.

for the insured to purchase more health care services (such as visits to the doctor). To explore the consequences of this observation, we first need to elaborate on the basic structure of health insurance plans. Insurance plans require people to pay a premium (usually monthly) in order to receive the guarantee of compensation should a certain adverse event occur. Most insurance policies also require individuals to pay for some of their health expenses out of their own pockets. The policy's **deductible** is the amount of health care costs the individual must pay each year before the insurance company starts paying compensation. For example, a $1,000 deductible means that the insured must pay the first $1,000 in health expenses each year before receiving any money from the insurance company.

In addition to the deductible, however, the insured person generally pays some portion of her medical bills. This amount paid by the insured person can take two forms. The first form, called a **copayment,** is a fixed amount paid for a medical service. For example, an insurance company may require a $20 copayment for each visit to one's primary care physician. The second form, called the **coinsurance** rate, is a percentage of the medical bill paid by the insured person. For example, with a 20 percent coinsurance rate, an insured person would have to pay $40 out of $200 charge (above the deductible).

We can now analyze the problem of overconsumption of health services using a conventional supply-and-demand diagram. In Figure 9.4, the market demand curve for medical services is label D_m. For simplicity, assume that the marginal cost of producing medical services is a constant, P_0. Hence, the supply curve, S_m, is a horizontal line at P_0. As usual, equilibrium is at the intersection of supply and demand; the price and quantity are P_0 and M_0, respectively. Total expenditure on medical services is the product of the price per unit times number of units, that is OP_0 times OM_0, or rectangle P_0OM_0a (the shaded area in the diagram).

deductible

The fixed amount of expenditures that must be incurred within a year before the insured is eligible to receive insurance compensation.

copayment

A fixed amount paid by the insured for a medical service.

coinsurance

A percentage of the cost of a medical service that the insured must pay.

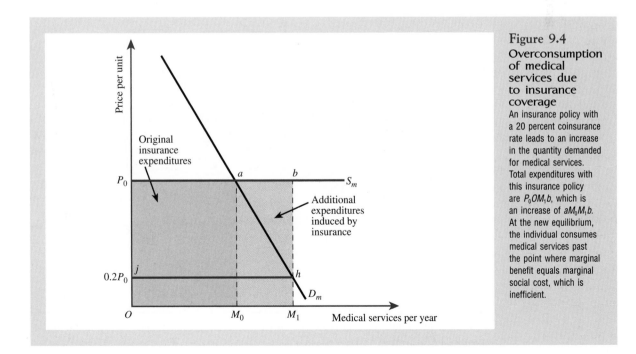

Figure 9.4
Overconsumption of medical services due to insurance coverage
An insurance policy with a 20 percent coinsurance rate leads to an increase in the quantity demanded for medical services. Total expenditures with this insurance policy are P_0OM_1b, which is an increase of aM_0M_1b. At the new equilibrium, the individual consumes medical services past the point where marginal benefit equals marginal social cost, which is inefficient.

How does the introduction of insurance affect the market? To keep things simple, assume that the policy has no deductible, but does have a 20 percent coinsurance rate. That is, the patients covered by this policy must pay only 20 percent of the cost of all medical services they receive in the year. Of course, these people had to pay the insurance premium in order to obtain coverage; however, once they pay this set fee they only face the marginal cost of 20 percent of the price of medical services.

The key to analyzing the impact of insurance is to realize that a 20 percent coinsurance rate is equivalent to an 80 percent reduction in the price facing the patient— if the incremental cost to the hospital for a day's stay is $800, then the patient pays only $160. In Figure 9.4, the patient no longer confronts price P_0, but instead only pays 0.2 times P_0. Given this lower price, the quantity demanded increases to M_1, and the patient spends area $OjhM_1$ on medical services.

At the new equilibrium, although the patient is paying $0.2P_0$ per unit, the marginal cost of providing health services is still P_0; the difference ($0.8 \times P_0$) is paid by the insurance company. Hence, *total* expenditures are OP_0 times OM_1, or the rectangle P_0OM_1b, with the insurance company paying P_0bhj. Thus, because of the insurance, health care expenditures increase from P_0OM_0a to P_0OM_1b, or the red area aM_0M_1b. The cartoon shows a comic take on the overconsumption of health care induced by insurance.

The problem here is that the individual consumes medical services past the point where the marginal benefit to the individual equals the marginal cost. This is inefficient, because for each medical service purchased after M_0, the additional cost (measured by the marginal cost) outweighs the additional benefit of the purchase (measured by the individual's marginal willingness to pay, which is the vertical

"First we'll do a whole series of tests. With a medical plan as good as yours we're bound to come up with something." © Elmer Parolini. Reprinted with permission from www.CartoonStock.com.

distance up to the demand curve).[5] We can measure the size of the inefficiency, known as **deadweight loss,** by summing the differences between the marginal cost and marginal benefit for each unit of medical services purchased from M_0 to M_1. The deadweight loss is therefore the triangle *abh*.

In this example, insurance coverage has led to M_1 medical services being purchased each year, but at this level the marginal benefit of the services is close to zero. At this point on the demand curve, the incremental benefit of additional provisions of medical services is very small. The notion that additional medical services have very small (i.e., flat) impacts on health is sometimes referred to as **flat-of-the-curve medicine.** Importantly, even if we are on the flat curve of medicine, it does not mean that medical care fails to confer important benefits. It means only that the *marginal* gain associated with *additional* health care is small.

Is the United States on the flat curve of medicine? Those who believe that it is point out that the United States spends more per capita on health care than other developed nations yet does not have better health outcomes. Per capita health care spending in the United States is nearly 2½ times higher than the average of the developed nations, and nearly 50 percent higher than the next highest country, yet the average life expectancy and infant mortality rate are about at the average of all developed countries. However, one must be careful about drawing inferences from this simple comparison. Expenditure differences across countries are attributable in part to how much a country spends on research and development for medical technology, which can generate health benefits to all countries. Also, health outcomes across countries might vary due to such factors as lifestyle, culture, and income distribution. For example, the greater life expectancy of Canadians relative to Americans is due in part to differences in cultural and behavioral factors, such as the higher rates of obesity, accidents, and homicides in the United States [O'Neill and O'Neill, 2007]. Finally, although life expectancy and infant mortality are important, ultimately they are crude measures of overall health status, because they don't account for the quality of health care. For example, if two countries have the same life expectancy but one of them fails to offer hip replacement surgery to its citizens, we would not want to say that the health care outcomes are the same.

The Elasticity of Demand for Medical Services   Figure 9.4 clearly indicates that the actual amount by which expenditures increase depends on the shape of the demand curve. In this context, note that by representing demand as downward sloping, the figure assumes that an increase in price induces people to reduce their consumption of health care. But when people are sick, don't they just follow the doctor's orders, regardless of price? Would you haggle with your surgeon in the midst of an appendicitis attack? If not, then the demand curve for medical services is perfectly vertical, and thus the existence of insurance does not lead to the inefficiencies of moral hazard. Such reasoning, however, ignores the fact that many medical procedures are in fact discretionary. For example, not everyone opts for diagnostic tests and cortisone treatment for their allergies. When patients must pay a price for services, they might not take every test or buy every prescription suggested by their physician.

Ultimately, the response of health care spending to changes in its price is an empirical question. How can we estimate this elasticity of demand? One way is to

deadweight loss

The pure waste created when the marginal benefit of a commodity differs from its marginal cost.

flat-of-the-curve medicine

The notion that at a certain point, the additional health gains of greater spending on health care are relatively limited.

---

[5] See the discussion of consumer surplus in the appendix at the end of the book.

compare the amount of medical services purchased by people in generous insurance plans to those in less generous plans. However, this is unlikely to provide credible results, because different types of people choose different plans. For example, people who have a high demand for medical services might opt into generous plans with low coinsurance rates, so it would be their intrinsic high demand that would lead to more services purchased, not the lower effective price associated with the plan.

In the late 1970s and early 1980s, the RAND Corporation employed a better way to estimate the elasticity of demand for medical services—a randomized experiment. It randomly assigned approximately 2,000 nonelderly families from six cities to 14 different insurance plans that varied the price of services to them. The plans varied by coinsurance rates (0, 25, 50, and 95 percent) and by the total cap on the families' out-of-pocket expenditures (5, 10, and 15 percent of family income, with a maximum of $1,000). Because assignment to each insurance plan was random, any differences in the amount of medical services consumed were attributable to the characteristics of the insurance plans, not the characteristics of the participants. The results suggested that a 10 percent increase in the price of medical services reduced the quantity demanded by about 2 percent [Newhouse et al., 1993]. Thus, the demand for medical services does in fact respond to their price, which tells us that moral hazard from insurance coverage can lead to considerable inefficiencies. Incidentally, the RAND study also found that the people in the experiment who received more medical services experienced only very slight health improvements relative to the others, which is consistent with the flat-of-the-curve hypothesis [Newhouse et al., 1993].

Does Moral Hazard Justify Government Intervention?

The implication of moral hazard is that we can expect inefficiently high health care spending if patients do not directly confront the cost of the services they purchase. However, as we discussed earlier, given that people are risk averse, there is a clear utility gain from purchasing insurance coverage to protect against medical costs. We therefore face a trade-off: The more generous the policy, the greater the protection from the financial risks of illness but the greater the moral hazard as well. Efficient insurance balances the gains from reducing risk against the losses associated with moral hazard by requiring high out-of-pocket payments for low-cost medical services and more generous benefits for expensive services.

Can the government improve the trade-off or eliminate moral hazard altogether? The efficiency problems caused by moral hazard are not unique to private health insurance markets. They arise whenever a **third party** pays for part or all of the marginal cost of medical services. In the preceding example, a private insurance company was the third party, covering 80 percent of the marginal cost. When insurance is provided publicly, then government is the third party, but the analysis of moral hazard is exactly the same. Table 9.3 shows that if we consider private and public provision of health care together, third-party payments have increased in importance over time. The percentage of total health care expenditures financed directly by consumers has dropped substantially over the years to the point where 12 percent of health expenditures today are paid out of pocket.

The key point is that government provision of health insurance leads to exactly the same moral hazard problem as private insurance, because it too reduces the price of medical services faced by the patients. As will be discussed in Chapter 10, both

third-party payment

Payment for services by someone other than the consumer.

Table 9.3   **Out-of-pocket Expenditures in the United States** *(selected years)*

Percent of Total Health Care Expenditures Paid out of Pocket *(Selected Years)*

1960	1970	1980	1990	1999	2000	2007
49.4%	34.2%	24.4%	19.7%	15.1%	14.7%	12.0%

Percent of Health Care Expenditure of Each Category Paid out of Pocket (2006)

Hospital care:	3.3%
Physician and clinical services:	10.3
Dental services:	44.4
Prescription drugs:	22.0
Nursing home care:	26.4

Sources: Data for 1990 through 2007 from the US Bureau of the Census [2009]. 2007 is an estimate. Data for 1960–1980 from Levit et al. [1994].

Out-of-pocket expenditures on health care have declined dramatically in the United States since 1960. Such expenditures are especially low for hospital care and physician and clinical services.

the private and public sectors have dealt with the moral hazard problem by trying to restrict consumers' choices. Neither has been very successful. Unlike the case of adverse selection, it is hard to argue even on theoretical grounds that the government is necessarily better at dealing with moral hazard than the private sector.

Other Information Problems in the Health Care Market

Another problem with the health care market is that people may not be well informed about the services that they purchase. In the market for MP3 players, consumers know what the item will be used for, and they can fairly easily learn and understand what features the different players provide. Medical care, however, is much more complicated. Figuring out the best treatment for lung cancer is a lot harder than choosing among MP3 players. Patients therefore have to rely on the expertise of their physician. It's hard to think of another market in which consumers rely so heavily on the advice of the person who is selling them the service. The problem is compounded because patients may lack good information even on whether their own doctor is competent.

Do Information Problems Justify Government Intervention?   Patients' lack of information is the rationale for a number of governmental regulations. For example, in order for doctors to obtain a license to practice medicine in a state, they must receive a medical degree from an accredited medical school, where the accreditation is granted by the American Medical Association. The idea is to make sure that patients, who might have difficulty distinguishing a good doctor from a bad one, don't have to worry about being treated by incompetents. Here, too, we face a trade-off. Allowing physicians to accredit medical schools, in effect, gives them control over the supply of doctors. By restricting supply, physicians can raise their own incomes above the competitive level, which leads to inefficiencies of its own. There is, in fact, some statistical evidence that health care providers take advantage of their ability to set standards to raise their own incomes. For example, Anderson et al. [2000] found that doctors' incomes are higher in states that restrict the use of alternative medicine, and Kleiner and Kudrle [2000] show that dentists earn more in states with tougher licensing requirements. In short, there is a trade-off. Health care providers have the best information about how to deliver health care, but if the government gives them the power to set standards, they may use it to increase their own incomes.

Externalities of Health Care

A free market for health insurance can lead to inefficiencies even in the absence of asymmetric information. Buying medical services can create externalities, both positive and negative. If you get a flu vaccination, there is a positive externality because it reduces the probability that others will become infected by the disease. On the other hand, if you overuse antibiotics so that new strains of immune bacteria develop, then others become worse off. According to the usual arguments (see Chapter 5), in the presence of externalities, government intervention can enhance efficiency. In many instances, however, health care confers no externalities. Getting treated for a broken arm improves your welfare, but does not increase the utility of others.

▶ DO WE WANT EFFICIENT PROVISION OF HEALTH CARE?

So far we have discussed the various reasons why a health care market might be inefficient. But even if the health market were efficient, society might deem the outcome to be inequitable. An efficient health care market would lead to differences in health insurance coverage and would lead to health care services that vary by income. Such differences evoke strong feelings of concern for those who cannot afford insurance or quality care. Below we discuss the different equity concerns that are used to justify government intervention in the health care market.

Paternalism

In an efficient health insurance market, people purchase different amounts of insurance, with some people undoubtedly carrying no coverage whatsoever. These people might not purchase health insurance because they believe (rightly or wrongly) that their risk of illness is low or because they are not very risk averse. Paternalistic arguments would suggest that such people either have the "wrong" tastes (they should be more risk averse) or they have "wrong" expectations (they should put a higher weight on the probability of a bad outcome). In either case, the paternalistic argument is that people should be forced into health insurance, and more generally, that health care decisions are too complicated to be left in people's own hands. Thus, for example, Krugman [2006a] argues that "people who are forced to pay for medical care out of pocket don't have the ability to make good decisions about what care to purchase."

The Problem of the Uninsured

Alternatively, some people may not purchase health insurance because their incomes are low, and the cost is too high for them. Note the difference between this phenomenon and the issues raised in our discussion of paternalism—people might have the "right" preferences and risk assessments, but still not purchase health insurance because it is so expensive. Given the dramatic rise in health care costs in recent years (as shown in Figure 9.1), this notion has received much attention. In the United States today, 16 percent of the population (about 47 million people) are without either public or private health insurance. As we will discuss in Chapter 10, the poor and elderly are covered by public programs. (However, about 14 million people who are eligible for federal or state health insurance assistance fail to enroll.) It is typically workers in low-paying jobs, workers without regular employment, and self-employed workers who are uninsured. Cutler [2003] finds that the recent dramatic rise in the uninsured population is due to the large increase in the premiums charged to individuals in employer-sponsored health insurance plans. In the late 1980s, the typical individual paid $150 annually to enroll in health insurance; by the late 1990s, the premium had more than doubled to $350 annually [Cutler, 2003].

Who Are the Uninsured?   The uninsured are a rather diverse group, varying by age, income, race, immigrant status, and employment status (among other things). Of children less than 18 years old 11.7 percent are uninsured, and 29.3 percent of 18- to 24-year-olds are uninsured. These two groups each make up 36.1 percent of the total uninsured population. Approximately 32 percent of people in households that earn below the poverty line are uninsured, but so are 8.5 percent of those who earn more than $75,000. People living in households that earn more than $50,000 make up nearly 38 percent of the total uninsured population. These people are in the top half of the income distribution, so presumably can afford insurance but decide against coverage. About 15 percent of whites, 21 percent of blacks, and 34 percent of Hispanics are uninsured [US Bureau of the Census, 2009, p. 105].

Approximately 21 percent of the uninsured are noncitizens, and so would probably not receive coverage under any proposed health care reform plan. With respect to employment status, about 22 percent of the uninsured are unemployed, yet approximately 13 percent work part-time and 46 percent work full-time [US Bureau of the Census, 2008a]. The probability of having health insurance rises with the size of the firm for which one works. Presumably, this difference is because the cost of insurance depends on firm size. As the number of employees increases, the per-employee administrative costs of running an insurance plan fall. Moreover, firms with many employees spread the risk of serious health care problems over a larger number of people, and hence can obtain better rates.

Clearly, much of the anxiety over the state of US health care is due to concern for the uninsured. It is crucial to realize, however, that the absence of health insurance and the absence of health care are not the same thing. Some people pay for their health care out of pocket, although on average, the uninsured pay for only 44 percent of the medical services they use. The free (to them) care is provided primarily through hospitals, which in itself can lead to inefficiency by channeling routine care into technologically advanced and expensive hospitals. In 2004, uninsured people received approximately $41 billion in uncompensated care, and US hospitals provided about 63 percent of this uncompensated care, which was financed by increasing the bills paid by other parties [Hadley and Holahan, 2004]. Nevertheless, people without health insurance generally consume fewer health care services than those with similar health problems who are insured. Surprisingly, however, it is not clear the extent to which the lack of health insurance translates into poor health outcomes.

EMPIRICAL EVIDENCE
Does Health Insurance Improve Health?

A major concern of the US health system is the absence of insurance for 47 million American residents. The reason for the concern is the belief that these people have worse health outcomes due to their lack of insurance coverage. While it seems straightforward that not having insurance diminishes one's health, in practice it is difficult to estimate the causal link between insurance coverage and health. Causality is difficult to establish because people who are uninsured are almost certainly different in many ways from those who are insured, and these differences could contribute to differences in health. For example, younger adults are more likely to be uninsured, and they also tend to be healthier. Studies that rely on observational data to estimate the link between health insurance and health outcomes have limited reliability because of the difficulty of controlling for factors that contribute to health and that differ for insured and uninsured people [Brown et al., 1998].

A better approach to estimating the causal relationship would rely on an experiment that randomly assigns some people into an insurance policy and others into being uninsured. Due to ethical concerns, such an experiment has never been conducted. However, the RAND experiment discussed earlier did randomize people into different levels of insurance coverage and found no impact of greater insurance coverage on a number of health outcomes, but did find some improvement for persons with poor vision and for persons with high blood pressure.

Given the difficulty of conducting a randomized experiment, several studies have instead used quasi-experiments that rely on changes in health insurance coverage due to changes in state or federal laws. For example, Lurie et al. [1986] took advantage of a policy change in California which involved some people losing their state-provided health insurance and others not. They find that those who lost the insurance experienced, on average, a statistically significant increase in diastolic blood pressure.

In another study, Finkelstein and McKnight [2005] estimate the change in the mortality rate for elderly people after government health insurance was made available to them. In order to control for other factors that might have affected health status, Finkelstein and McKnight compare changes in the health of the elderly to changes in the health of the near elderly (who did not receive the government insurance). Because the two groups are similar, one can reasonably attribute any difference in their health changes to the presence of the government insurance. Finkelstein and McKnight also compare mortality rates for elderly people in states that had a big increase in health insurance coverage due to the government program compared to states that had a smaller increase. In both cases, they find no evidence of a health effect.

Levy and Meltzer [2004] survey the literature on the impacts of health insurance on health, placing particular emphasis on whether each study uses an experiment or quasi-experiment to address the causality problem. They find that studies that examine small-scale changes in health insurance at the state or city level show weak evidence of an insurance effect on health. However, studies that examine larger-scale changes at the federal level show more consistent evidence of a link between insurance and health, although even some of these studies suggest that the link is weaker than one might guess. Levy and Meltzer conclude that "health insurance can improve health," but they state that there is no conclusive evidence on whether it is preferable to expand coverage or instead to focus public spending on other interventions (such as community health centers or advertising campaigns to improve nutrition) that can improve health.

High Health Care Costs

Figure 9.5 puts US expenditures in an international context. It shows that the United States has much higher health expenditures per GDP than Australia, Canada, France, Germany, Japan, and the United Kingdom. Interestingly, although the United States has a higher *level* of expenditure as a share of GDP than these countries, over the long term its rate of *growth* in these expenditures has not been much out of line with theirs. For the developed countries in Figure 9.5, health care expenditures went from an average of 4.2 percent of GDP in 1960 to 10.3 percent of GDP in 2006. The five other developed countries have very different systems for financing health care than the United States has.

Why have health care costs been growing so rapidly? Recall that market failures, such as moral hazard caused by third-party payments, can contribute to high costs.

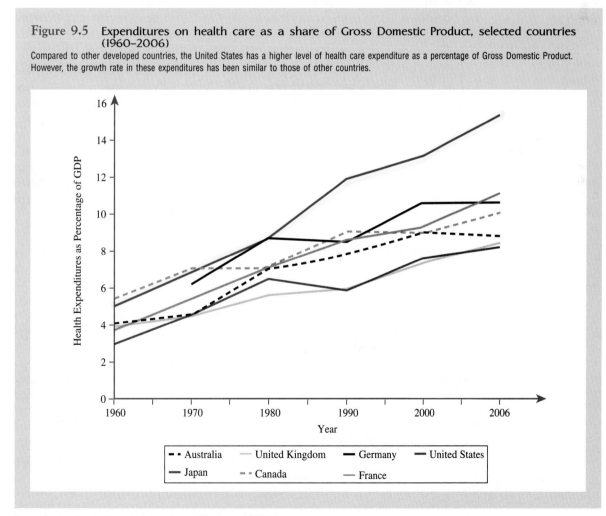

Figure 9.5 Expenditures on health care as a share of Gross Domestic Product, selected countries (1960–2006)

Compared to other developed countries, the United States has a higher level of health care expenditure as a percentage of Gross Domestic Product. However, the growth rate in these expenditures has been similar to those of other countries.

Source: Organization for Economic Cooperation and Development [2008a].

However, for third-party payments to explain the *growth* in health care expenditures, it is necessary for insurance coverage to have been *growing*. According to research by Newhouse [1992], there is little evidence that *changes* in the number of insured have been sufficiently large to account for the bulk of the growth in expenditures. Other factors must be at work. This section discusses several possibilities. In light of the fact that costs have been increasing throughout the world, as we evaluate these possibilities, we should not focus exclusively on factors that are idiosyncratic to the US system.

The Graying of America   In 1980, 11.3 percent of the US population was 65 and over; currently the figure is 12.6 percent. During the same period, the proportion of the population 85 and over increased from 1.0 to 1.8 percent [US Bureau of the Census, 2009, p. 10]. As the population ages, one expects health care expenditures to increase as well, since older people have a higher demand for health care services. To what extent can this phenomenon explain the rise in health care expenditures? To obtain a rough answer to this question, Newhouse [1992] calculated how much total spending would have changed if the per capita expenditures in each age group of the population had stayed the same between 1950 and 1987 and only the proportions of the population in each age group changed. He found that the change in age structure accounts for just a tiny fraction of the increase in expenditure.

Income Growth   Since 1960, per capita real income has nearly tripled in the United States. To the extent that the demand for medical care increases with income, then income growth may drive the increase in health care expenditures. On the basis of econometric analyses of medical demand, Newhouse estimated that the income elasticity of demand for medical care is between 0.2 and 0.4—a 10 percent increase in income leads to a 2 to 4 percent increase in the demand for health care. Multiplying this elasticity by the actual percentage increase in income over time, Newhouse concluded that increases in income account for less than 10 percent of the growth in health care expenditures. Richer societies want more health care, but not enough more to explain the increase in health expenditures.

Improvements in Quality   Newhouse argued that the most important reason for the increase in spending on health care in the United States is improvements in medical technology. Physician training, medical techniques, and equipment have all improved over time. The last several decades have witnessed breathtaking developments in medical technology. As a result, the quality of health care has improved—diagnostic techniques, surgical procedures, and therapies for a wide range of medical problems get better all the time.

Consider treatment of heart attacks, which is certainly much more expensive (in real terms) today than it was decades ago. However, treatment of a heart attack today is simply not the same "commodity" as treatment of a heart attack in 1950. Back then, the standard practice for heart attack treatment (which was given to President Eisenhower after his heart attack in 1955) was to prescribe rest, morphine for the pain, and oxygen [Cutler, 2004]. The treatment is now dramatically different, and since Eisenhower's time, cardiovascular mortality has declined by over half, and the probability of dying after a heart attack has fallen by nearly three-quarters [Cutler, 2004]. According to research by Cutler and Kadiyala [2001], this dramatic decline is due to three factors: (1) advances in intensive medical therapies that treat heart attacks and strokes; (2) advances in nonacute medications such as drugs to control blood pressure, diabetes, and cholesterol; and (3) improvements in behavioral factors, such as the reduction in smoking. Therefore, although innovations like coronary bypass surgery and cardiac catheterization have raised *expenditures* per heart patient, they have actually reduced the *prices* of obtaining various health outcomes, such as surviving hospitalization due to a heart attack [Newhouse, 2001].

Another example of an increase in the quality of health care that has been associated with increased expenditures is the amazing improvement in technologies for treating low-birth-weight infants [Cutler, 2004]. The mortality rate for neonatal infants (under 28 days old) fell from 20.5 per 1,000 live births in 1950 to 4.7 per 1,000 live births in 2002. For post-neonatal infants (between 28 days and 11 months old), mortality fell from 8.7 per 1,000 live births in 1950 to 2.3 per 1,000 live births in 2002 [US Centers for Disease Control and Prevention, 2005, Table 22].

This technology-based theory of the cost increase in health care also helps explain why countries with different health care financing and delivery systems have all experienced increases in health care expenditures (see Figure 9.5). While these countries have rather different health care delivery systems, they have at least one thing in common—they have all been exposed to the same expensive innovations in technology.

The point is that increases in expenditures on medical technologies have led to increases in health care quality and are not necessarily indicative of inefficiencies or market failures. This technology-based explanation puts the debate over cost containment in a new light. If costs are rising mostly because of quality improvements, is it a bad thing? A key question in this context is whether people value these innovations at their marginal social cost. Cutler and McClellan [2001] examine technological advances for five different medical conditions. They find that the benefits of technological advances have exceeded the costs for four of these conditions: heart attacks, low-birth-weight infants, depression, and cataracts. They find that benefits and costs of technological advances in the treatment of a fifth condition (breast cancer) are about equal. Cutler [2007] finds that bypass surgery or angioplasty used to treat heart attack patients are remarkably cost-effective, resulting in one year of additional life expectancy at a cost of $40,000. Newhouse [1992] offers a provocative insight into whether technological advances in medicine are worth the costs: "If many consumers felt that new technology wasn't worth the price, it seems odd that we do not observe some firms trying to enter and offer at least some aspects of 1960s medicine at 1960s prices" [p. 16].

Buttressing this argument is a calculation by Murphy and Topel [2000] that improvements in life expectancy added about $2.8 trillion (in 1992 dollars) per year to US national wealth between 1970 and 1990. Any such calculation must be regarded as just a rough approximation for several reasons. First, how does one put a dollar value on added years of life? Murphy and Topel use measures derived from statistical estimates of the increased wages that workers require in order to compensate them for taking jobs that require relatively high risks of dying on the job; this approach was described in Chapter 8. Second, it is not clear that all the improvement in life expectancy was due to changes in health care. They note, though, that "about $1.5 trillion of the overall $2.8 trillion annual increase was due to the reduction in mortality from heart disease—an area in which medical advances in both prevention and acute care have been significant" [p. 24]. Third, although increases in life expectancy are very important, advances in medical care have also improved the quality of life, and these are valuable as well. Just think of hip replacements, Viagra, ulcer-treating drugs such as Zantac, and arthroscopic surgery. While it is difficult or impossible to attach a dollar value to these improvements, the benefits must be substantial. Hence, even allowing for the roughness of the Murphy-Topel calculation, its basic message that there are enormous benefits to spending on health care is compelling.

The focus of this discussion has been on whether medical expenditure is driven by technological change. An intriguing possibility, however, is that at least to some extent causation runs in the other direction—increases in spending raise the profitability of medical innovations and therefore encourage technological change. This is a difficult proposition to test, but some evidence suggests that it is plausible. Blume-Kohout and Sood [2008] found that the introduction of prescription drug coverage by Medicare was associated with significant increases in pharmaceutical research and development.

To the extent that health care markets are efficient yet lead to such high prices that many people end up without health insurance, society has to decide how much efficiency to sacrifice in order to achieve greater equity. A **commodity egalitarianism** view (discussed in Chapters 4 and 7) holds that some special commodities should be distributed to everyone, no matter what their circumstances and no matter what the net benefits are to society. There does, in fact, appear to be a strong societal consensus that everyone should have access to at least basic medical services. In Chapter 10, we will discuss various government programs to enhance accessibility, and proposals to improve these programs.

commodity egalitarianism

The idea that some commodities ought to be made available to everybody.

Summary

- Government-provided insurance (known as social insurance) makes up a large and increasing proportion of the federal budget.

- For a risk-averse person, an insurance plan that charges an actuarially fair premium increases expected utility because it allows risk smoothing.

- The more risk averse an individual is, the more he or she is willing to pay for an insurance policy.

- By pooling individuals into one insurance program, an insurance company can lower risk from a societal point of view.

- Adverse selection arises when those being insured know more about their risk than the insurance company. This prevents the insurance company from charging premiums that are in line with each individual's expected losses. If the insurance company instead charges an average premium across all customers, the low-risk people will tend to drop out of the plan, leaving the insurer to lose money.

- Government can address adverse selection by providing universal health insurance coverage and charging uniform premiums. This is inefficient but would eliminate sorting by risk.

- Moral hazard arises when obtaining insurance leads to changes in behavior that increase the likelihood of the adverse outcome.

- There is a trade-off in providing insurance: The more generous the insurance policy, the greater the protection from the financial risks of illness but the greater the moral hazard as well. Efficient insurance balances the gains from reducing risk against the losses associated with moral hazard by requiring high out-of-pocket payments for low-cost medical services and more generous benefits for expensive services.

- About 16 percent of the US population at any given time lacks health insurance. The proportion of the uninsured population under 65 years old has been growing over time.

- US health care expenditures as a percentage of Gross Domestic Product have been growing rapidly over time. They currently make up 16 percent of GDP. Possible reasons include the aging of the population, growth in income, the prevalence of third-party payments, and technological change. The evidence points to technological change as a primary factor.

Discussion Questions

1. Consider carefully the following quotation: "[E]conomists seem always to talk about the cost of medical care, as if that kind of spending were a bad thing. After all, where does the money go? To doctors, nurses, and the makers of medical supplies. Don't they buy diapers and pasta and cars? Would the nation be better off with more boom boxes and less penicillin, more nail polish and less antibacterial ointment? What difference does it make how money is spent, as long as it changes hands and results in employment?" [*New York Times Magazine*, December 12, 1993, p. 28].

    a. Do economists view spending on health care as a "bad thing"?

    b. The last sentence in the quotation suggests a criterion for evaluating spending on health care. What criterion would an economist use?

2. In 2008, Congress considered a plan to introduce taxpayer-financed insurance for individuals who live in hurricane zones. The program would have amounted to a subsidy of approximately $500 to each Floridian. Discuss how such a program might induce inefficient behavior. Incorporate the notion of *moral hazard* into your answer.

3. After removing all its traffic lights, the Dutch town of Drachten saw a decline in traffic fatalities. With the traffic lights, there was one road death every three years, but since their removal seven years ago there have been no road deaths. A city traffic planner explained, "It works well because it is dangerous, which is exactly what we want" [Millward, 2006]. Use the concepts developed in this chapter to explain this phenomenon.

4. Suppose a certain pharmaceutical drug has only one use: It is 100 percent effective at saving the life of someone afflicted with a certain rare disease. Given its effectiveness, patients who need it would purchase the drug even if its price increased dramatically. What are the efficiency implications of providing this drug to patients through a third-party payer?

5. Tennessee provides insurance coverage for up to $25,000 in annual health expenses. Of the $25,000, the most that can be spent on hospital bills is $15,000. Expenses above these thresholds are not covered by the state plan. Is Tennessee consistent with the theory of efficient insurance?

6. Suppose that an individual's demand curve for doctor visits per year is given by the equation $P = 100 - 25Q$, where Q is the number of doctor visits per year and P is the price per visit. Suppose also that the marginal cost of each doctor visit is $50.

    a. How many visits per year would be efficient? What is the total cost of the efficient number of visits?

    b. Suppose that the individual obtains insurance. There is no deductible, and the coinsurance rate is 50 percent. How many visits to the doctor will occur now? What are the individual's out-of-pocket costs? How much does the insurance company pay for this individual's doctors' visits?

    c. What is the deadweight loss (if any) caused by this insurance policy?

    d. What happens to the size of the deadweight loss if it turns out that the marginal external benefit of visiting the doctor is $50?

7. To work this problem, you'll need a calculator that can take logarithms or a spreadsheet program. Suppose that your utility function is $U = \ln(4I)$, where I is the amount of income you make in a given year. Suppose that you typically make $30,000 per year, but there is

a 5 percent chance that, in the next year, you will get sick and lose $20,000 in income due to medical costs.

a. What is your expected utility if you do not have insurance to protect against this adverse event?

b. Suppose you can buy insurance that will cover your losses if you get sick. What would be the actuarially fair premium? What is your expected utility if you buy the insurance policy?

c. What is the most that you'd be willing to pay for this policy?

*8. Suppose that your city government is interested in reducing littering. Currently, there is a $100 fine for littering and there is a 10 percent prob-ability of being caught if you litter. The city is deciding between two different policies: (1) It can increase the number of police that moni-tor littering, which would make the probability of being caught if you litter 20 percent rather than 10 percent; or (2) it can keep the monitor-ing the same yet raise the fine for littering from $100 to $200. (Notice that both policies have the same expected cost of littering.) If litterers are risk averse, which policy would lead to a larger reduction in littering? What if litterers are risk loving (that is, they have a concave utility func-tion, and so prefer an uncertain outcome to the certain outcome with the same expected value)?

---

*Difficult

Chapter Ten

GOVERNMENT AND THE MARKET FOR HEALTH CARE

The health of the people is really the foundation upon which all their happiness and all their powers as a state depend.

—BENJAMIN DISRAELI

In Chapter 9 we applied the theory of welfare economics to health care markets and saw the various ways that a free market can lead to inefficient or inequitable outcomes. Given this background, we are now ready to discuss the key features of the US health care market and the government's intervention in it.

The US health care industry is massive. It includes hospitals, nursing homes, doctors, nurses, and dentists, as well as producers of eyeglasses, prescription and nonprescription drugs, artificial limbs, and other equipment. It employs about 11 million people and accounts for about $2.2 trillion in annual expenditures, which is 16 percent of GDP.

Figure 10.1 shows how this money is spent. The two largest categories by far are hospitals (31 percent) and physician and clinical services (21 percent). Figure 10.2 shows the sources of health care funding. Consumers pay only 12 percent of health expenses out of pocket. The rest are paid for by third parties—private health insurance and other private sources (such as philanthropy) pay for 42 percent and the government pays for 46 percent (primarily through the Medicare and Medicaid programs, which are described later in this chapter). The payments from private insurance companies and from government come from premiums paid by consumers and revenue collected from taxpayers, respectively. Nevertheless, these still count as third-party payments because at the time of purchase, consumers do not directly face the full cost of their health services.

In 2006, approximately 84 percent of the US population had some form of insurance coverage. Approximately 68 percent of the population had private health insurance and over 26 percent had government health insurance, consisting primarily of Medicare and Medicaid. Some people receive insurance coverage from multiple sources. We now examine the private and government health insurance markets in turn.

▶ PRIVATE HEALTH INSURANCE

An important peculiarity of private insurance in the United States is that most of it—about 91 percent for those under 65—is provided through employers as a benefit to their employees.

Figure 10.1
Uses of health care funds in the United States (2007)
Hospital care accounts for 31 percent of US health care expenditures, which makes it the largest component. Physician and clinical services account for 21 percent of US health care expenditures.

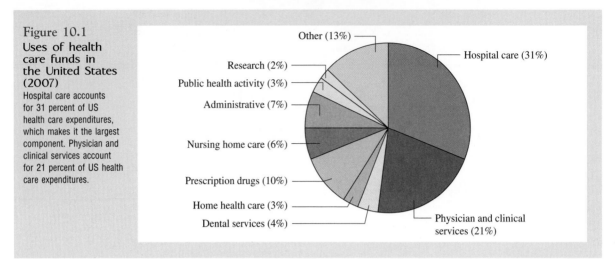

Source: Centers for Medicare and Medicaid Services [2008c].

Figure 10.2
Sources of health care funds in the United States (2007)
Consumers pay only 12 percent of health expenses out of pocket. The rest are paid for by third parties, mostly from private health insurance and government programs such as Medicare and Medicaid.

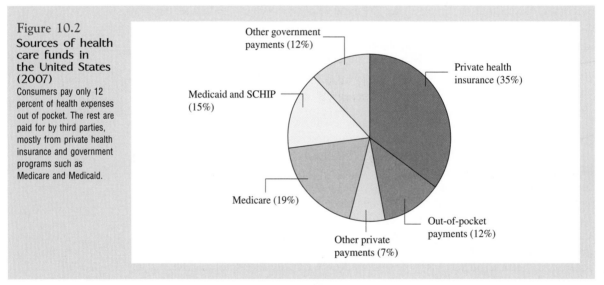

Source: Centers for Medicare and Medicaid Services [2008c].

The Implicit Subsidy for Employer-Provided Insurance

Why do so many Americans purchase health insurance through their employers? After all, we don't purchase food or clothing through our jobs. This phenomenon is in part an inadvertent by-product of government wage and price controls instituted during World War II. While these controls restricted how much an employer could pay in wages, they exempted other forms of compensation such as health care coverage. Predictably, employers started offering health insurance (and other nonwage benefits) to attract workers in a tight labor market. Between 1940 and 1950, the proportion of Americans with private health insurance coverage increased dramatically from 9.1 to 50.3 percent [Santerre and Neun, 2004, p. 314].

A key factor promoting employer-provided provision of health insurance is the federal tax system. Income in the form of wages is taxed, but income in the form of premiums paid by employers for health insurance is not. Consequently, the federal tax system effectively provides a subsidy to employer-provided health insurance. To see why, suppose that Marissa earns $50,000 per year in wages. Suppose also that her wages are taxed at 35 percent. Also assume that her employer does not provide any health insurance; instead, she purchases her own policy for $5,000 per year.

Now suppose that Marissa's employer offers to pay for her $5,000-per-year insurance policy by cutting her salary by the same amount. The employer is indifferent between paying the $5,000 in salary or in health insurance benefits. But Marissa is not indifferent. When her salary is cut by $5,000, she is not worse off by $5,000, because that $5,000 would have been taxed. Rather, she is worse off only by $5,000 minus the tax she would have owed on the $5,000. Since she would have paid $1,750 in taxes on the $5,000 in earnings (0.35 × $5,000), when her salary is cut by $5,000 she is only $3,250 (= $5,000 − $1,750) worse off. In short, in return for a $3,250 reduction in after-tax wages, Marissa saves $5,000 in health insurance payments. That's a good deal for her. In effect, the tax exemption for employer-provided health insurance lowers the opportunity cost of health insurance in terms of wages. This is the source of the subsidy. Other companies have the same incentive to offer health insurance; otherwise they risk losing their workers to a competitor.

The size of the implicit subsidy for employer-provided health insurance is very large. According to Burman, Garrett, and Khitatrakun [2008], it reduces the relative cost of employer-provided health insurance by about 30 percent. The exclusion of employer-provided health insurance and medical care from the income tax base costs the US Treasury about $117 billion per year in forgone tax revenues [Joint Committee on Taxation, 2008, p. 56].

Just like any other commodity, the quantity demanded for insurance increases when its price decreases. Thus, the implicit subsidy causes workers to want a larger share of their compensation paid in the form of health insurance than otherwise would have been the case. Consequently, health insurance packages become more generous—deductibles decrease, and insurance policies are more likely to include items such as vision, acupuncture, and routine dental benefits.

Nothing is wrong with buying insurance. As we discussed in Chapter 9, it plays a critical role in allowing people to protect themselves against the financial risks of illness. However, Chapter 9 also showed that insurance can lead to overconsumption of medical services. Likewise, by encouraging people to buy more insurance, the implicit subsidy can lead to overconsumption of health care. Many analysts therefore believe that employer-provided health benefits should be subject to taxation, just like other forms of income.

The Advantages of Employer-Provided Health Insurance

Increase the Risk Pool   Chapter 9 discussed how insurance companies reduce risk by pooling it across individuals. The more people in the insurance pool, the more predictable the outcome to the insurance company, and hence the lower the risk. One advantage of employer-provided health insurance, especially for large employers, is that it can provide a large pool of people under one insurance policy. Of course, an insurance company can increase the pool of insured by offering policies to individuals who do not work for the same employer; however, this could lead to adverse selection if low-risk people do not join the plan.

Reduce Adverse Selection   Group health insurance plans such as those provided by employers may also reduce the problem of adverse selection. Recall from Chapter 9 that community-rated health insurance markets can fail because some people with a lower than average risk of getting sick may drop out of the market. By selling a policy to all the workers in a firm, insurance companies don't have to worry as much about getting an adverse selection of customers. Thus, the insurance company can sell the insurance plan without having to devote much time and money to screening the people enrolling in the plan.

However, this works only if a worker's choice of employer is not based on her health status, a condition that may not hold. To see why, recall that health insurance is just one component of a worker's compensation. Other things being the same, a firm can pay its workers higher wages if it offers a less generous package of insurance benefits. Workers who have a lower than average risk of illness have an incentive to select employers whose packages include a high proportion of wages and little or no insurance. In the same way, firms with relatively generous insurance benefits will find themselves with a workforce that has higher risks than average. To pay the insurance premiums for this high-risk group, such employers have to lower the wage component of compensation, making the job attractive only to people with even higher risks. This is a typical adverse selection phenomenon, which may result in fewer firms offering insurance than is efficient. In short, while employer-provided insurance may reduce adverse selection, it does not eliminate it altogether.

Lower Administrative Costs   Another possible advantage of group plans over individual plans is that they have lower administrative costs. Developing and marketing an insurance plan involves fixed costs, and group plans can spread these costs over its members. Not surprisingly, then, group plans have lower loading fees than individual plans. In 2000, premiums for group insurance were approximately 19 percent higher than benefits, whereas they were approximately 50 percent higher than benefits for individual insurance plans. The ratio of premiums to benefits decreases as the number of employees in the group plan increases [Phelps, 2003, p. 343].

Employer-Provided Health Insurance and Job Lock

When a worker with employer-provided health insurance leaves her job, she also leaves behind her health insurance. This raises the possibility that our system reduces the likelihood that individuals will leave their jobs, a phenomenon known as **job lock.** Job lock could hurt economic efficiency if it discourages workers from moving to the jobs in which they could be the most productive.

Estimating the prevalence of job lock is challenging because people who select into jobs with health insurance coverage are likely different in many unobservable ways from those who select into jobs without health insurance coverage. Therefore, it would be misleading simply to compare job mobility across these two groups. An alternative approach takes advantage of the fact that some states have laws requiring employers to continue offering coverage to ex-employees (for a price), at least for a time. If mobility is higher in states with such laws, other things being the same, this

job lock

The tendency for workers to remain in their job in order to keep their employer-provided health insurance coverage.

is consistent with job lock. The evidence is mixed, but some studies indicate that job lock does exist, reducing job mobility by 25 to 50 percent [Madrian, 2006, p. 19].

In an attempt to address this problem, Congress passed the Health Insurance Policy Portability and Accountability Act of 1996 (known as the Kennedy-Kassenbaum Act, after its legislative sponsors). The act requires an employer to include a new employee (who previously had insurance) in the company's group insurance plan within 12 months at the same price as the insurance is available to other group members, even if the employee has a preexisting medical condition that will be quite expensive to treat and thereby increase the firm's insurance premiums. Further, the law requires insurance companies to make coverage available (at a price) to individuals who leave group plans, but it does not mandate a price for the nongroup coverage. Some policymakers believe that the law has been stymied because insurers charge individuals very high prices for nongroup policies.

Cost Control and Private Insurance

Until the early 1980s, most insurance policies provided for payments to health care providers on the basis of the actual costs of treating a patient, a system called **cost-based reimbursement** or **fee-for-service.** Recall from Chapter 9 that a third-party payment (such as fee-for-service) contributes to overconsumption of health services because it provides little incentive to economize; the more resources devoted to a patient, the more money the health care provider receives.

> **cost-based reimbursement or fee-for-service**
>
> A system under which health care providers receive payment for all services required.

In response to high and growing health care costs, employers turned to arrangements that limit utilization and keep prices down on the supply rather than demand side of the market. Under such arrangements, generically referred to as **managed care,** health care suppliers are given incentives to keep costs down. One example of such an incentive is **capitation-based reimbursement,** under which providers receive annual payments for each patient in their care, regardless of the services used by that patient.

> **managed care**
>
> Any of a variety of health care arrangements in which prices are kept down by supply-side control of services offered and prices charged.

> **capitation-based reimbursement**
>
> A system in which health care providers receive annual payments for each patient in their care, regardless of services actually used by that patient.

There are a variety of managed care arrangements. With **Health Maintenance Organizations** (HMOs), a group of physicians works only for a particular plan and patients can see doctors only in that plan. HMOs therefore combine the financing and delivery of health care into one organization by providing medical care to enrollees in exchange for their prepaid premiums. Within an HMO, a primary care provider serves as a gatekeeper who refers patients to specialists as deemed necessary.

> **Health Maintenance Organization**
>
> Organization that offers comprehensive health care from an established network of providers, often using capitation-based reimbursement.

With **Preferred Provider Organizations** (PPOs), a group of physicians accepts lower fees for access to a steady supply of patients provided by the network. Enrollees are given an incentive to obtain their health care from the network physicians because they must pay more (either through higher coinsurance or deductible) if they go outside the network. **Point-of-service** (POS) **plans** are similar to PPOs in that they give incentives to see physicians within the network; however, POS plans also assign each enrollee a primary care provider who serves as a gatekeeper who makes referrals to specialists.

> **Preferred Provider Organization**
>
> Organization that provides health care from providers who accept lower fees for access to the network and that give incentives to enrollees to obtain services from within the network of providers.

There are many variations on these themes. Today about 98 percent of insured Americans are in some kind of managed care arrangement, an increase from only 5 percent in 1980. Most of the increase has been in PPO plans and POS plans. PPO enrollment increased from 11 percent of covered workers in 1988 to 58 percent of covered workers in 2008; POS enrollment increased from 7 percent in 1993 to 24 percent in 1999, and then down to 12 percent in 2008 [Kaiser Family Foundation, 2008, Exhibit 5.1].

> **point-of-service plan**
>
> Similar to PPO, yet also assigns each enrollee a primary care provider to serve as a gatekeeper.

Has managed care helped to contain health costs? During much of the 1990s, this appeared to be the case. As we saw in Figure 9.1, the rate of increase in health care costs leveled off throughout much of the 1990s. But this phenomenon turned out to be short-lived, as costs have again risen in the 2000s. One explanation is that the shift toward managed care led to a one-time decrease in expenditures, but advances in medical technology continued, resulting in concomitant growth in expenditures.

The vexing problem with managed care arrangements is that by creating incentives to economize on costs, they simultaneously create incentives for health care providers to skimp on the quality of care. After all, the same payment is received regardless of the services provided. However, the work surveyed by Cutler [2002] suggests that health status is not worse for individuals in managed care arrangements, other things being the same.

► GOVERNMENT PROVISION OF HEALTH INSURANCE: MEDICARE AND MEDICAID

Government plays a large role in health care in the United States. It licenses physicians, monitors health threats in the environment, owns some hospitals, sponsors research on disease prevention, and runs childhood immunization programs, to name just a few activities. As we discussed previously, the government also implicitly subsidizes employer-provided health insurance. Our focus in this section is the federal government's programs that directly provide health insurance. The two key programs are Medicare and Medicaid.

Medicare

Federally funded government program that provides health insurance to people aged 65 and over and to the disabled.

Medicare: Overview

Eligibility   The **Medicare** program, enacted in 1965, provides health insurance for people aged 65 and older and to the disabled. Its primary purpose is to increase access to quality health care for the elderly. After Social Security, it is the largest domestic spending program. Figure 10.3 shows Medicare expenditures

Figure 10.3
Medicare expenditures (1966–2007)
Medicare is the second largest domestic spending program after Social Security. In 2007, expenditures for Medicare were $431 billion, which amounts to 3.1 percent of Gross Domestic Product.

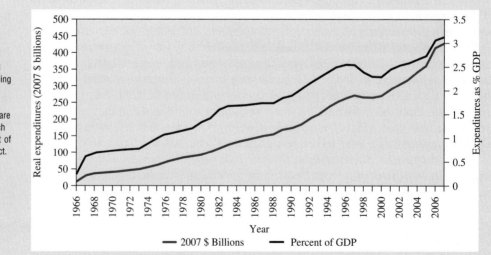

Year

— 2007 $ Billions   — Percent of GDP

Source: Centers for Medicare and Medicaid Services [2008c].

over time in real terms and as a share of Gross Domestic Product (GDP). In 2007, expenditures for Medicare were $431 billion, which amounts to 3.1 percent of GDP. Medicare expenditures are projected to grow rapidly, reaching 7.0 percent of GDP in 2035 and 10.8 percent of GDP in 2082 [Centers for Medicare and Medicaid Services, 2008b].

Medicare covers nearly the entire population aged 65 and older and is not means tested. The only requirement is that the person (or the person's spouse) has worked and paid payroll taxes for at least 10 years. Unlike Social Security, a person cannot receive Medicare benefits before the age of 65. Today there are about 37 million enrollees aged 65 and over [Centers for Medicare and Medicaid Services, 2008b].[1] The program is administered by the federal government, and eligibility standards are uniform across all states.

Benefits   Once a government decides to become involved in the medical sector, it must make a fundamental decision: Will health care services be produced by the government or by the private sector? Different countries have made quite different decisions. In the United Kingdom, for example, the government owns and runs hospitals. In contrast, in the United States health care is primarily provided by the private sector. Thus, Medicare is a system of government finance for health care, not government production of health care.

The largest components of the Medicare program are known as Part A and Part B (another part, D, will be discussed later). Part A, which accounted for about $203 billion in expenditures in 2007, is **hospital insurance** (HI) [Centers for Medicare and Medicaid Services, 2008b, p. 5]. Participation in HI is compulsory. It covers inpatient medical care. The patient must pay an inpatient hospital deductible of $1,024 for the first 60 days of care. HI covers all expenses above this amount during the first 60 days of care. For days 61 through 90, the patient must pay $256 per day. After 90 days, Medicare no longer covers hospital expenses. However, each enrollee is provided with an additional 60-day lifetime reserve, so for days 91 through 150 of the hospital stay the patient can receive HI coverage but must pay $512 per day. HI also covers up to 100 days of care in a skilled nursing facility per lifetime, with the patient paying $128 per day.[2]

Part B of Medicare, which accounted for about $179 billion in expenditures in 2007, is **supplementary medical insurance** (SMI) [Centers for Medicare and Medicaid Services, 2008b, p. 5]. It pays for physicians, supplies ordered by physicians, and medical services rendered outside the hospital. Unlike HI, SMI is voluntary. Enrollees must pay a monthly premium that varies over time and in 2008 was $96.40. Legislation passed in 2003 for the first time tied the required premium to income levels. Those making above $82,000 ($164,000 for couples) now have to pay higher premiums, with the size of the payment increasing with income. Patients must also pay a small ($135) annual deductible and a 20 percent coinsurance rate. About 99 percent of the eligible population chooses to enroll in SMI.

Financing   HI is financed by a payroll tax on the earnings of current workers. The rate is 1.45 percent on the employer and employee each, for a total of 2.90 percent.

hospital insurance

Part A component of Medicare that covers inpatient medical care and is funded through a payroll tax.

supplementary medical insurance

Part B component of Medicare that covers physician services and medical services rendered outside the hospital and is funded by a monthly premium and by general revenues.

---

[1] Medicare is also available to people who have been disabled for two years and to people with otherwise fatal kidney disease. There are about 7 million such enrollees.

[2] The deductible and copayments in this paragraph are for 2008.

As of 1994, the tax is applied to all earnings; there is no ceiling. The tax proceeds are deposited in the HI trust fund, from which disbursements to health care providers are made. Medicare therefore runs largely on a pay-as-you-go basis. About 86 percent of the HI expenditures of current retirees are paid by current workers.

HI faces severe fiscal challenges. Current projections indicate that HI expenditures will soon be higher than revenue collected through the payroll tax, and the gap will continue to grow over time. In the long run, then, Medicare HI faces large and increasing deficits.

Unlike HI, SMI relies primarily on general revenues for financing, not on a payroll tax.[3] Over the next 10 years, SMI benefit payments are expected to increase by 6.2 percent annually [Centers for Medicare and Medicaid Services, 2008b, p. 2]. Because of its general revenue financing, there is no issue of its trust fund becoming insolvent. But as we'll discuss in Chapter 11 on Social Security, entitlement trust funds are essentially accounting devices. Just like HI payments, money spent on the SMI program has an opportunity cost in terms of forgone uses of government revenue.

Prescription Drug Benefit   At the time of its inception in the 1960s, drugs were a relatively unimportant component of health care, and Medicare did not cover prescription drugs for its enrollees. Since then, pharmaceuticals have become ever more important in treating disease. In 2005, Americans spent about $200 billion on prescription drugs, filling over 3.3 billion prescriptions [Centers for Medicare and Medicaid Services, 2008c]. The Medicare Prescription Drug, Improvement, and Modernization Act of 2003 added a prescription drug benefit to Medicare (Part D), which began on January 1, 2006.

All Medicare beneficiaries are eligible for the drug coverage. Unlike the traditional Medicare programs, the enrollees obtain drug coverage either through a private stand-alone drug plan serving their geographic area or through a private plan that is integrated with Part A and Part B benefits under Medicare Part C (called Medicare Advantage).

Beneficiaries who join a private drug plan must pay a monthly premium that is set to cover approximately 25 percent of the cost of the standard drug benefit. The premium varies across plans and regions; in 2008 it averaged approximately $384 per year. (Low-income earners can qualify for reduced premiums and for support in covering out-of-pocket drug expenses.) The beneficiary must pay a $275 deductible, 25 percent of the cost from $275 to $2,510, and 100 percent of the cost from $2,510 to $5,726. After the $5,726 threshold is met, the enrollee must pay either $2.25 for generic drugs and $5.60 for brand drugs or 5 percent of the cost, whichever is greater. The deductibles and thresholds are indexed to rise each year with the growth in per capita Medicare drug benefit spending.

This structure is peculiar. After the relatively low deductible, the plan provides fairly generous benefits, and then provides no benefits for the intermediate range from $2,510 to $5,726 in costs, a range known as the "donut hole." It then provides very generous (though not full) coverage for amounts above $5,726. As we discussed in Chapter 9, efficient insurance would suggest a totally different approach—requiring out-of-pocket payment for the initial expenditures in order to mitigate the incentive for overconsumption of drugs, and then providing generous support for

---

[3] SMI also receives funds from the monthly premiums mentioned earlier, which are deducted directly from recipients' Social Security benefits. Originally, the goal was to have the premium cover about half of SMI's program costs. Currently, the premium covers about 25 percent of the cost of SMI, so the federal subsidy is large.

"Boy, I'm sure glad I got up here before Medicare started running low." © 2009 Mort Gergerg from cartoonbank.com. All Rights Reserved.

the high-cost expenditures in order to smooth risks. There is simply no economic rationale to justify the donut hole. Political considerations of the sort discussed in Chapter 6 might provide the best explanation. Because of the relatively low deductible, practically everyone in the Medicare population can enjoy some benefit from the drug plan. Spreading the benefits so widely helped garner the political support that was necessary to enact Part D.

In 2007, approximately 31 million seniors enrolled in the Medicare drug benefit, at a cost of $49.5 billion [Centers for Medicare and Medicaid Services, 2008b, pp. 24 and 36]. By 2017, it is expected that 44 million seniors will be enrolled, at a cost of $142.2 billion. Over the long run, expenditures on the Medicare drug benefit are projected to grow from 0.38 percent of GDP in 2008 to 1.93 percent of GDP in 2080 [Centers for Medicare and Medicaid Services, 2008b, p. 35]. This represents a significant commitment of the country's resources. Given its odd benefit structure and high expected costs, the Medicare drug benefit is controversial.

Cost Control under Medicare

Prospective Payment Systems (PPSs)   As we discussed in Chapter 9, health care costs have risen dramatically since the enactment of Medicare in 1965. The financial burden of rising health care costs was exacerbated by the **retrospective payment system** of compensation originally used by Medicare. Under the retrospective system, a hospital would provide care to the Medicare (Part A) recipient, and after the care was completed, the hospital would submit the bill to Medicare for reimbursement. This third-party payment system provided little incentive to economize on the costs of medical services.

retrospective payment system

Payment system, originally used by the Medicare Hospital Insurance program, in which compensation is paid after the care is completed and thus provides little incentive to economize on costs.

prospective payment system

Payment system, currently used by the Medicare Hospital Insurance program, in which the compensation level is set prior to the time that care is given.

diagnosis related groups

Classification system used to determine prospective compensation payments in the Medicare Hospital Insurance program.

Faced with rapidly increasing costs, in 1983 Medicare switched to a **prospective payment system** (PPS), which sets a fixed reimbursement level prior to the period for which care is given. Medicare's prospective payment system works through its classification of approximately 500 **diagnosis related groups** (DRGs). Each Medicare Part A patient is assigned to a DRG upon admission to the hospital, and the prospective payment is set according to the DRG classification. The payment for each DRG is determined by a national standard of the cost of treating the diagnosis, with adjustments made for factors that contribute to cost differences across hospitals.

Much like the private system's use of capitation payments, this provides an incentive for hospitals to conserve costs. If a hospital spends less on a patient than the amount covered by the prospective payment system, it gets to keep the difference. If instead it spends more on a patient's care than allotted by the prospective payment system, then it is not compensated for the difference. Indeed, there is evidence that the length of stay in hospitals declined after the introduction of the prospective payment system in the 1980s. The average length of stay for Medicare patients in short-stay hospitals was 10.5 days in 1981 (before PPS), 9.1 days in 1984 (while PPS was being phased in), and 8.5 days in 1985 (after PPS was fully phased in). This decline in the length of hospital stays appears not to have resulted in worse health outcomes. Neither hospital readmission rates nor patient mortality rates increased after the introduction of PPS [Phelps, 2003, p. 416].

While PPS initially diminished the rate of growth of Medicare hospital expenditures, over time expenditures began to grow again. This is exactly the same pattern that was observed with the introduction of managed care in the private sector—a temporary slowing of growth followed by a return to substantial increases. As in the case of managed care, part of the reason was the increase in costs due to changes in technology. Another was that the hospitals learned to game the system—they started classifying patients into costlier DRG categories, a practice known as "DRG creep." For example, a hospital receives greater compensation from Medicare simply by diagnosing "bacterial pneumonia" rather than "viral pneumonia."

resource-based relative value scale system

Set of values based on time and effort of physician labor used to determine physicians' fees in the supplementary medical insurance component of Medicare.

In order to constrain the cost of Medicare Part B, in 1989 Congress instituted a change in the payment for physician services. The system is based on the **resource-based relative value scale system,** which is a set of relative values based on time and effort of physician labor for various medical services. The system establishes physicians' fees based on these relative values, in an attempt to give physicians an incentive to keep costs down. While this system is a step in the direction of prospective payment, it still sets payment on a per-service, rather than a per-patient, basis. Thus, there is still a disincentive for physicians to economize on costs.

Note that, in effect, the resource-based relative value scale system is a price control—the government rather than the market sets a price for each service. Indeed, since the 1980s price controls on physicians who treat Medicare patients have been a key part of the government's strategy to contain Medicare costs. For example, Medicare Part B has frozen physicians' fees for extended periods and put in place volume performance standards that set an acceptable growth rate for spending on doctors' services each year, with penalties if the target is breached. Such price controls are complicated to administer (there are over 100,000 pages of Medicare regulations) and tend to have undesirable side effects. In this context, one major concern is that the controls make health care providers less disposed to treat Medicare patients. For example, after Medicare announced a 5.4 percent across-the-board reduction in physician reimbursements in 2002, a substantial number of medical practices simply stopped taking Medicare patients, including the Mayo Clinic's branch in Jacksonville,

Florida [Rosenberg, 2002, p. 11]. The use of price controls may also inhibit the development of new medical technology that improves the quality of health care. As discussed in Chapter 9, rising costs are not necessarily bad if they reflect improvements in health care for which patients would be willing to pay.

Medicare Managed Care   In another attempt to control Medicare costs, in 1985 Congress passed legislation that allowed Medicare beneficiaries to enroll in HMOs. Under this plan, the HMOs were paid a fixed amount per enrollee from Medicare, with the amount computed as 95 percent of the average annual medical costs of enrollees in the county who stayed in the traditional Medicare system. In order to entice people into the system, enrollees were covered for some services not included in traditional Medicare and faced lower out-of-pocket costs. Because the government payment was only 95 percent of the average amount in traditional Medicare, the hope was that the HMOs would save the government money.

This hope was not realized because the program neglected to take into account adverse selection. The cost savings for the program were based on the assumption that the individuals who opted into the HMOs would have received the average Medicare benefit if they had remained in Medicare. Instead, it was the healthier individuals who switched into the HMOs. Because coverage for these people cost less than the average, the payment to the HMO likely exceeded the cost savings when they left traditional Medicare. Finally recognizing this problem, Congress later reduced the per-person payment to HMOs and made them *risk-adjusted* (i.e., based on a beneficiary's age, sex, and health characteristics). This saved money, but also led to a reduction in Medicare HMO enrollment. Congress has since experimented with a variety of approaches to private plan coverage of Medicare recipients.

Medicare: Impacts on Spending and Health

We have shown that Medicare is an expensive government program and the growth continues even after many efforts to contain costs. What benefits has all this spending created?

To provide an answer, the first issue that has to be addressed is whether Medicare actually increased expenditures on health care for the elderly. A simple way to obtain an answer would be to compare health spending on the elderly before and after the introduction of Medicare. But this would not be very enlightening, because other things have changed over time that might cause such differences. For example, an increase in the rate of technological advancement during that time would contribute to higher medical expenses independent of Medicare.

To provide a more sophisticated answer, Finkelstein [2005] takes advantage of the fact that before the introduction of Medicare, there were substantial differences in private health insurance coverage across geographic regions. For example, in New England half of the elderly population had health insurance prior to Medicare, compared to only 12 percent of the elderly population in the southeast central United States. It follows that, for some regions, the enactment of Medicare led to big changes in insurance coverage for the elderly, whereas in others the changes were slight. Finkelstein uses this variation to estimate impacts on different types of medical expenditures. Specifically, if expenditures increased the most in regions where Medicare generated the largest increases in coverage, then one can reasonably attribute the differences to Medicare. She finds that, in fact, the introduction of Medicare led to substantial increases in spending. For example, during the first five years of Medicare total hospital spending increased by 23 percent.

Has this increase in health care spending led to better health outcomes? In a study that also relies on geographic variation in insurance coverage prior to Medicare, Finkelstein and McKnight [2005] come to the perhaps unexpected conclusion that the introduction of Medicare had no impact on mortality rates among the elderly. The conclusion may be less surprising when we recall from Chapter 9 that in other contexts, the link between health insurance coverage and health status is not as strong as one might guess. Finkelstein and McKnight support their finding by presenting evidence that elderly people with life-threatening illnesses received health care prior to Medicare, even if they did not have insurance. Skinner, Fisher, and Wennberg [2005] provide further evidence that the relationship between Medicare and health outcomes is tenuous. They find that there is substantial regional variation in Medicare expenditures, but that the areas that spend more do not experience better health outcomes for the elderly. Their results suggest that nearly 20 percent of Medicare expenditures appear to provide no benefit in terms of survival.

Does the fact that Medicare has produced little or no impact on health status mean that it has not provided any benefits? Not at all. Recall from Chapter 9 that the elimination or reduction of risk generates real improvements in welfare for people. Finkelstein and McKnight estimate that by reducing the risk of large out-of-pocket health expenses, Medicare generates an annual benefit of about $500 per beneficiary, or nearly $10 billion per year (2000 dollars). In a related study, McClellan and Skinner [2005] find that these risk-reduction benefits accrued disproportionately to low-income people, suggesting that the program serves a redistributive role. Taken together, this research suggests that the real benefit of Medicare has been in reducing risk for the elderly population, not improving their health per se.

Medicaid: Overview

Medicaid

Federal- and state-financed health insurance program for the poor.

Eligibility   Medicaid is by far the largest government spending program for low-income people. Administered jointly by the federal and state governments, Medicaid was established in 1965 to provide health insurance for recipients of cash welfare programs. However, legislation in the 1980s expanded eligibility for Medicaid. In addition to covering much of the welfare population, it now includes children in low-income two-parent families. Children and pregnant women in households that have incomes substantially above the poverty line also qualify, whether or not the families receive cash welfare.

State Children's Health Insurance Program (SCHIP)

Program that expanded Medicaid eligibility to some children with family incomes above Medicaid limits.

In 1997 Congress enacted the **State Children's Health Insurance Program (SCHIP),** which allowed states to expand further Medicaid eligibility to children with family incomes above the Medicaid limits. Each state is eligible for SCHIP funds so long as it adopts an approved plan to reduce the number of uninsured children. States have discretion either to expand coverage through its existing Medicaid program or develop a new, stand-alone insurance program for children.

The expansions of eligibility in the 1980s and 1990s have contributed to a large increase in the number of recipients. In 1990, there were 22.9 million recipients; by 2007, this figure had more than doubled to 50.0 million (including SCHIP), 48 percent of whom were children [Centers for Medicare and Medicaid Services, 2008a]. The growth in the number of recipients has been accompanied by increased program costs. Figure 10.4 shows combined federal and state Medicaid and SCHIP expenditures over time in real terms and as a share of Gross Domestic Product (GDP). In

Figure 10.4 Medicaid expenditures (1966–2007)

Medicaid has expanded over time, especially in the 1990s. In 2007, combined federal and state Medicaid and SCHIP expenditures were $338 billion, which amounts to 2.5 percent of Gross Domestic Product.

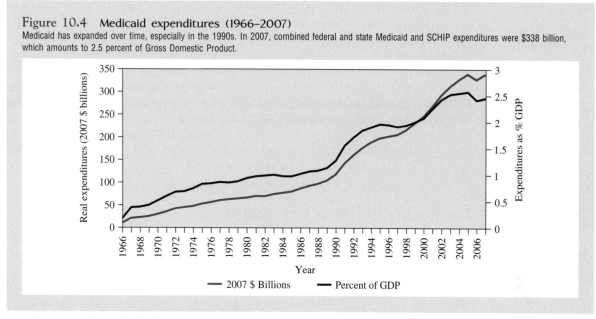

Source: Centers for Medicare and Medicaid Services [2008c].

2007, expenditures were $338 billion, which amounts to 2.5 percent of GDP [Centers for Medicare and Medicaid Services, 2008c].

Financing and Administration Medicaid is financed jointly by the federal and state governments. The federal government provides the state governments with a certain percentage of matching funds to cover the costs. These matching funds are higher for states with relatively low incomes, ranging from 50 percent federal coverage for high-income states to 83 percent federal coverage for low-income states. The federal government's contribution comes from general revenues, not from a payroll tax.

Medicaid is administered by the individual states. In order to receive the federal funds, each state must allow eligibility for certain groups, including most recipients of federal welfare payments, children under six or pregnant women who have a family income at or below 133 percent of the poverty line, and all children under 19 who are in families with incomes at or below the poverty line. However, states have the discretion to expand eligibility, which has led to variation across states.

Benefits Each state must also offer a minimum level of benefits that cover major medical services such as hospital and physician visits, prenatal care, and vaccines for children. States can offer more generous benefits, and most cover a wide range of medical services so that recipients end up with few or no out-of-pocket expenses.

The states have some flexibility with respect to how the program is administered. For example, they may institute capitation fee systems, under which medical care is provided for a particular individual or set of individuals by private managed care plans for a fixed monthly fee. One reason for such systems is to hold down costs. However, just as in the case of Medicare managed care, cost savings may not materialize if the capitation payment exceeds the amount that would have been spent on the beneficiary if he or she had remained in traditional Medicaid. Estimating the cost savings is difficult, because the people who choose Medicaid managed care likely differ in unobservable ways from those who don't, and these differences could drive differences in cost.

To address this problem, Duggan [2004] takes advantage of a natural experiment provided by the California Medicaid system. In some California counties, Medicaid recipients are *required* to enroll in managed care, so one need not be concerned that only relatively healthy people select into this option. Duggan compares per-person spending before and after beneficiaries were forced to enroll in Medicaid managed care. He finds that contracting out to managed care programs did not reduce government Medicaid costs. In fact, it increased costs.

Medicaid: Impacts on Health

We have shown that Medicaid has been expanding, both in terms of number of beneficiaries and cost. Has this translated into better health for the poor?

Take-Up Rate   In order for Medicaid to be effective, eligible people must enroll in the program. Despite the fact that the number of beneficiaries has increased over time, several studies suggest that the Medicaid eligibility expansions in the 1980s and 1990s led to only modest increases in enrollment. Only about 5 to 25 percent of the individuals who became eligible actually took up the benefit [Card and Shore-Sheppard, 2004]. This suggests that people are either not informed about their eligibility, or that some kind of stigma associated with receiving Medicaid leads people to forgo coverage.

Crowding Out   Even if more people decide to enroll in Medicaid, an increase in enrollees does not necessarily translate into a one-for-one increase in the number of low-income people insured. If a person gives up a private insurance plan because he or she becomes eligible for Medicaid, then the number of insured people is

crowd out

When public provision of a good substitutes for private provision of the good.

unchanged. In effect, public insurance **crowds out** private insurance. We demonstrate this in Figure 10.5, which examines the trade-off between health insurance and all other goods, where health insurance is measured by its level of generosity. Without publicly provided health insurance, the budget constraint is the line AC.

Now suppose the government provides health insurance for free, and it cannot be resold in the market. The government insurance plan provides M units of insurance coverage. Assume also that it is not possible for a person receiving the government insurance to purchase supplemental private insurance that is more generous. How does the introduction of the free public insurance change the budget constraint? Because Medicaid beneficiaries cannot purchase supplemental private insurance, anyone who accepts this public insurance must consume exactly M units of insurance. This option is represented by the single point F, where insurance consumption is M, and the recipients can spend their entire income on all other goods. If they want more insurance than M, they must forgo the government plan and return to the original budget constraint.

How does this government provision affect the total amount of insurance held by individuals? Panel A shows the indifference curves for someone who places a high value on private insurance, so she is willing to forgo a lot of other goods in order to obtain more generous insurance coverage. The introduction of public insurance has no

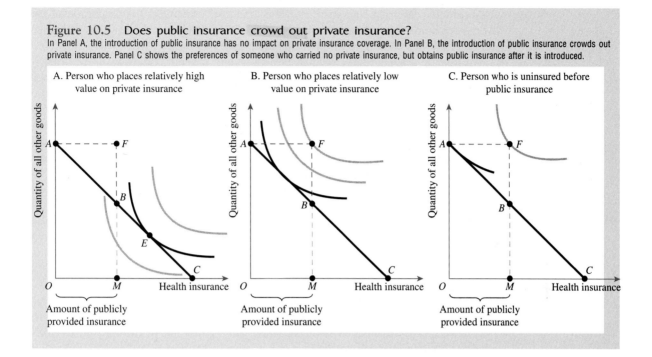

Figure 10.5   Does public insurance crowd out private insurance?
In Panel A, the introduction of public insurance has no impact on private insurance coverage. In Panel B, the introduction of public insurance crowds out private insurance. Panel C shows the preferences of someone who carried no private insurance, but obtains public insurance after it is introduced.

impact on this person, because she chooses point E whether or not government provides insurance. Panel B, on the other hand, shows the indifference curves for someone who places a lower value on private insurance. This person gives up private insurance coverage in order to obtain the free public insurance at level M. In this case, public insurance crowds out private insurance. Finally, Panel C shows someone who did not have any private insurance, but chooses the public insurance after it is made available.

Given that Medicaid is offered for free, we should expect *some* crowding out. The key question, then, is whether the situation depicted in Panel B is typical or not. When Medicaid started, the Panel B scenario was not at all typical. The Medicaid population was so poor that most beneficiaries did not have any private insurance to give up. But as Medicaid eligibility has expanded over the years, crowding out has become a very serious concern. Because the goal of expanding Medicaid is to increase insurance coverage for the poor or near poor, crowding out certainly needs to be taken into account by policymakers if they contemplate further expansions. That said, we should note that crowding out is not necessarily an entirely bad thing, because it frees up income for families to spend on other items, perhaps including better nutrition or safer housing, both of which could improve child health.

EMPIRICAL EVIDENCE
Are Medicaid Expansions Effective?

Is crowd out an important concern? During the expansions of the 1980s and 1990s, Medicaid enrollment increased, and private insurance coverage fell. While this is consistent with the crowding-out hypothesis, it is difficult to assess causality because there were other changes to the US economy at that time that could have led to rising

Medicaid and falling private insurance enrollment. For example, the proportion of the workforce in manufacturing (which traditionally provided relatively generous insurance benefit packages) was decreasing at the same time.

In order to estimate the extent of crowding out, several studies have used quasi-experimental research designs that take advantage of the changing eligibility requirements for children in the 1980s and 1990s. The natural experiment arises because states differed both with respect to when the eligibility requirements were changed as well as the ages at which children could receive benefits. Thus, for example, researchers can compare the change in incidence of private insurance in states that increased eligibility in a given year to those that did not. Using such quasi-experimental strategies, Gruber and Simon [2007] find that the crowd-out rate was approximately 60 percent—for every 100 people who enrolled in Medicaid due to the expansion, 60 of them gave up private insurance coverage.

Although there is still some debate on the degree of crowding out, the consensus is that the Medicaid expansions have led to smaller increases in insurance coverage than their designers intended.

This brings us to the important question of whether, on balance, Medicaid has actually improved the health status of low-income people. Most research concludes that, despite the issues associated with crowding out, at the end of the day, the various Medicaid expansions led to greater provision of health services and to improved health outcomes for the newly eligible [Currie and Gruber, 1996].

▸ HEALTH CARE REFORM

This chapter has discussed various efforts in the United States to attain the twin goals of expanding access to health insurance and controlling the costs of health care. We have demonstrated that these efforts frequently conflict with the goal of efficiency, therefore presenting society with difficult trade-offs. Despite the various policy changes, many commentators believe that costs are still growing too rapidly, not enough people have insurance, and that the entire system is inefficient and inequitable. One approach to increasing coverage is to expand existing programs. For example, one could expand Medicaid and SCHIP eligibility even further, and at the same time extend Medicare to people in their 50s. However, such an approach would likely lead to substantial crowding out of private insurance, thus limiting its effectiveness. Some critics of the status quo believe that these incremental reforms are not enough, and that more fundamental changes to the health care system are required. We now turn to some prominent reform proposals.

Mandates

Most states require their residents to purchase automobile insurance. Why not, then, similarly require every person to buy basic health insurance? One version of this idea has been proposed by the Heritage Foundation, a public policy institute in Washington, DC. Under the Heritage plan, the Medicare and Medicaid programs would be kept in place. However, the exclusion from taxation of employer-provided health care benefits would be ended. Instead, employers would be required to provide to their employees vouchers for health insurance, which the employees would use to purchase insurance on their own, or through some other organization, such as a church or fraternal group. Variants of this plan include government providing the vouchers or perhaps subsidizing the vouchers for low-income people.

According to its proponents, "Costs would be controlled by using the best device ever found to hold down costs without sacrificing quality and efficiency: consumer choice within a competitive market" [Butler, 1992, pp. 42–43]. The plan would require relatively little in the way of new bureaucracy, and it would preserve consumer choice. However, it is not clear that the vouchers would be large enough to induce most people to purchase insurance, and government subsidization of the vouchers could be costly and crowd out privately funded insurance. Further, like other market-driven approaches to reform, adverse selection might occur on the supply side of the market—insurers would have a tendency to reject high-risk customers. Either insurance companies would have to be allowed to charge higher premiums to such customers or some mechanism for forcing them to provide coverage would be needed.

One possible problem with requiring employers to provide health insurance to all workers is that it might reduce employment. One study estimated that 224,000 workers would lose their jobs if employers were required to provide health insurance similar to an existing average plan and to pay 80 percent of the premiums [Baicker and Levy, 2007]. There are also questions about how the mandate would be enforced. Would people who failed to buy insurance be thrown in jail? Is there any sufficiently large, yet feasible, financial penalty that would induce everyone to buy insurance?

The Massachusetts Plan   In April 2006, Massachusetts introduced an individual mandate in an attempt to achieve universal insurance coverage for its population. Individuals who do not have coverage face a financial penalty, as do employers with more than 10 employees who do not offer a health insurance plan. Health insurance premiums are subsidized for those with income less than three times the poverty line. The law also created a market in which individuals and small firms can purchase insurance. This market, called "The Connector," is regulated by the government, selects and approves insurance plans, and requires that premiums do not vary by any factor other than age. The Connector is supposed to allow individuals and firms to comply with the insurance mandate without facing unduly high administrative costs. It is too early to tell whether the Massachusetts plan will succeed in providing universal coverage at relatively low cost.

Health Savings Accounts

A recent market-oriented reform has sought to reduce the incentive to overconsume health services, which arises because today's third-party systems generally charge patients very little or nothing on the margin for covered medical expenses. One way to reduce this problem is to encourage people to buy **catastrophic insurance policies,** which entail individuals paying out of pocket for their health care expenses unless the expenses become large, at which point the insurer takes over. This provides the individual with an incentive to control routine costs, but still reduces the risk of high costs from a catastrophic illness.

Health Savings Accounts (HSAs), introduced by Congress in 2003, represent a move in this direction.[4] With an HSA, a person (or his employer on his behalf) purchases a catastrophic insurance policy. He then sets up a savings account out of which to pay the deductible and the copayments throughout the year. His employer

> **catastrophic insurance policy**
>
> An insurance policy that has a high deductible and generous coverage for high medical costs.
>
> **Health Savings Accounts (HSAs)**
>
> A type of insurance plan in which a person has a catastrophic insurance policy, and the person or the person's employer puts money in an account that can be used to pay for out-of-pocket medical expenses. The contributions to the account are tax deductible.

---

[4] As a precursor to HSAs, Congress introduced a similar approach, known as Medical Savings Accounts (MSAs) in 1996. However, these were only made available to a limited number of people and the legislation placed severe restrictions on who could enroll. In 1997, Congress also made MSAs available to Medicare recipients, but this too was only available to a limited number of people.

can likewise contribute funds to this account. The legislation provided an important tax incentive to adopt HSAs: All the money put into the account is excluded from the income tax, whether the deposit is made by the individual himself or the employer. Further, any money in the HSA not spent on out-of-pocket medical costs can roll over to the next year, and any interest earned on the account is not taxed. Upon retirement, all funds remaining in the account can be used for medical or non-health-related expenditures, but in the case of nonhealth expenditures, tax is due when the money is withdrawn.

Proponents of HSAs see them as an effective way for dealing with incentives to overconsume and bringing down the rate of growth of health expenditures [Feldstein, 2005]. Opponents believe that HSAs pose an adverse selection issue. They argue that HSAs are more attractive to people who are in relatively good health and therefore anticipate low expenses. This could leave the government or private group insurance to deal with the relatively ill (and expensive) patients. Additionally, while HSAs increase the incentive to buy high-deductible insurance, by lowering the relative price of health care, they may also increase expenditures. Ultimately, these are empirical questions. Baicker, Dow, and Wolfson [2006] estimate that the introduction of HSAs has led to a significant reduction in health care expenditures.

Single Payer

Another reform option would scrap the current health insurance market and replace it with a single provider of health insurance. The single-payer system would be funded by taxes and provide all citizens, regardless of income or health status, with a determined set of health care services, at no (or low) direct cost to the insured.

International Experiences   Variants of the single-payer approach are used in Canada and several European countries. In Canada, health care services are produced by the private sector, with the reimbursements negotiated by the government. In the United Kingdom, health services are produced by the public sector through the National Health Service. Perhaps the easiest way to think about implementing a single-payer system in the United States is extending Medicare to the entire population.

The fact that single-payer systems do not confront individuals with the incremental cost of their own care is a major virtue to its proponents and a major flaw to its critics. Proponents believe that market-driven approaches are unethical—sick people should not be forced to have to make cost-benefit decisions about receiving health care. Proponents also admire the universal-access feature of the program. This position embraces commodity egalitarianism, which holds that everyone should have access to medical services, no matter the cost.

Because patients pay little or nothing for care within single-payer systems, such systems must use other mechanisms to ration health services. In the United Kingdom and Canada, rationing is done by imposing constraints on the supply side of the system. In the United Kingdom, patients must go to their general practitioner, who is paid on a capitation basis by the government. The general practitioner serves as a gatekeeper to the health care system, deciding on whether to refer a patient to a hospital for more specialized care. The hospitals, in turn, decide how to allocate services to patients. In the United Kingdom, the allocation decisions are made in such a way that individuals have easy access to primary and emergency care, but long waiting times and limited access to specialty care and new technologies [Folland, Goodman, and Stano, 2006].

Health services in Canada are mostly provided by private practitioners who receive fee-for-service payments; however, prices are capped by regional governments. In effect, the Canadian single-payer system holds down costs through direct price controls on medical services. It appears, though, that neither the UK nor Canadian rationing systems have been fully effective in controlling costs: As we saw in Chapter 9, health care costs are increasing in those countries as well as in the United States.

Not surprisingly, the rationing of services by single-payer systems leads to the criticism that they allow the government—and not individual patients and doctors—to decide which health services to provide in a given situation. For example, the National Health Service in the UK sometimes denies patients access to certain cancer drugs, such as the kidney cancer pill Sutent, because of their high costs [Harris, 2008]. Deaton and Paxson [2001] note that decreases in mortality in the United States are mirrored by decreases in mortality in the United Kingdom, but only after four years. They speculate that this is because the centralized UK system impedes the adoption of expensive new technologies. Similarly, in Canada there are "growing complaints about long lines for diagnosis and surgery . . . [and] eroding public confidence in Canada's national health care system." As a consequence, there are "growing moves toward privately managed medical services and user fees in return for quicker service" [Krauss, 2003, p. A3]. Indeed, in 2005 the Canadian Supreme Court struck down the law banning private practitioners from offering health services covered by the government plan. The ruling stated that the waiting time for some medical services in Canada had become so long that it violated patients' "life and personal security, inviolability and freedom."

Some of the pros and cons of the single-payer systems of the United Kingdom and Canada relative to the US system can be seen in Table 10.1. Per capita health expenditures in the United States are about double those in Canada and the United Kingdom. Administrative costs are also considerably higher in the United States. However, the US system provides much greater access to innovative technologies. For example, magnetic resonance imagings (MRIs) are provided to patients at nearly five times the rate in the United States than in the United Kingdom or Canada. Similarly, only 4 percent of patients in the United States wait more than six months for elective surgery, compared to 15 percent and 14 percent for the United Kingdom and Canada, respectively.

Table 10.1   **Health Care Costs and Health Outcomes for Canada, United Kingdom, and United States**

	Canada	United Kingdom	United States
Health expenditures (dollars per capita)	$3,634	$2,820	$6,719
Administrative costs (dollars per capita)	$118	$69	$417
MRIs (per million people)	6.2	5.6	26.5
Wait > 6 months for elective surgery (percent in need of surgery)	14%	15%	4%
Life expectancy at birth (years)	80.4	79.1	77.8
Infant mortality rate (per 1,000 live births)	5.4	5.1	6.9

Sources: Organization for Economic Cooperation and Development 2008b and Commonwealth Fund [2007].

Note: All data are for 2005, 2006, or 2007, except the United Kingdom's administrative cost, which is for 1999. Dollar amounts are in 2006 dollars.

Per capita expenditures and administrative costs are considerably higher for the United States compared to Canada and the United Kingdom. However, the United States provides greater access to innovative technologies. Nonetheless, the United States has lower life expectancy and higher infant mortality.

Defenders of single-payer systems point out that while the relatively costly American system provides greater access to innovative medical technologies and short waiting times for specialty care, these features do not translate into better health outcomes in the United States. Indeed, as shown in Table 10.1, life expectancy is lower and infant mortality is higher in the United States than in the United Kingdom and Canada. Of course, as discussed in Chapter 9, health outcomes across countries depend on cultural and behavioral factors, in addition to health care spending. This makes it difficult to resolve the debate over the relative merits of the various health care systems.

Final Thoughts

As one contemplates the debate over the future of health care reform, several points are worth emphasizing:

- Developing a solution is bound to be difficult because of the same dilemma that arises in the design of *all* social insurance programs—the goal of providing security is likely to conflict with the goal of efficiency.
- There is no free lunch. The goals of universal coverage and cost containment are at odds with each other. We cannot bring millions of people into the health care system and expect costs to go down. In the same way, we cannot expect to achieve universal coverage without increasing regulation, because certain high-risk groups of people simply cannot obtain insurance in private markets. The only way one can imagine them getting insurance is a set of government rules that forces someone to insure them. This does not mean that universal coverage is an inappropriate goal, but one must be realistic about what is needed to achieve it.
- Although our focus has been primarily on health care expenditures, what we ultimately care about is people's health. The two are linked, although the statistical evidence on this matter is more tenuous than one might guess. Many commentators have argued that more spending on medical services in developed countries is unlikely to improve health, or at least the mortality rate. Lifestyle considerations such as smoking, diet, and exercise may be more important [Fuchs, 2000].

Summary

- US health care spending amounts to $2.2 trillion per year, which is 16 percent of Gross Domestic Product.
- Consumers pay only 12 percent of health expenses out of pocket. Private insurance and private sources pay 42 percent, and government pays 46 percent. Approximately 84 percent of the US population has some form of health insurance.
- Most private medical insurance in the United States is provided through employers as a benefit to the employees.

- Under federal tax law, employer-provided health insurance is not subject to taxation. This provides an implicit subsidy (worth about $152 billion per year in forgone tax revenues) for health insurance.
- The advantage of employer-provided health insurance rather than individual coverage is that it may increase the risk pool, reduce adverse selection, and lower administrative costs.
- Employer-provided health insurance might inhibit job mobility, a phenomenon known as job lock.

- Health Maintenance Organizations attempt to keep costs down by offering a comprehensive health care system in which patients choose from a network of providers working under a capitation-based reimbursement system.

- The Medicare program provides health insurance for people aged 65 and older. The major components of the system are hospital insurance (HI) and supplementary medical insurance (SMI), which pays for physicians and associated medical care.

- HI is financed by a payroll tax on the earnings of current workers at a rate of 1.45 percent on employers and employees each. SMI is financed out of general revenues. If current trends continue, Medicare expenditures are soon likely to outpace revenues.

- A prescription drug benefit was added to Medicare starting in 2006.

- Over the years, the government has attempted to control Medicare costs by switching from a retrospective to a prospective payment system and by introducing managed care to Medicare.

- The Medicare program has not improved the health status of the elderly very much, but it has led to significant benefits in the form of reducing the risk of facing major reductions in consumption due to medical expenses.

- The Medicaid program provides health insurance for the poor. In the past few decades, Medicaid eligibility has been expanded to include children in low-income two-parent families, and other children and pregnant women who are above the poverty line.

- The Medicaid expansions have induced crowding out of private insurance. However, on balance, Medicaid has improved the health of low-income people.

- Proposals to reform the health care system include individual mandates, which would require all people to purchase health insurance, and a single-payer system, under which all insurance would be provided by the government and financed by tax revenues.

Discussion Questions

1. In 1997, many Health Maintenance Organizations (HMOs) suffered a decline in the value of their stocks. One newspaper account stated, "Just when HMOs seemed to offer an answer to the intractable problem of soaring health-care costs, the bottom fell out. Some of the industry's biggest names are racking up losses, grappling with unexpected rises in medical bills, . . . , and squirming under a backlash from consumers, doctors and politicians" [Anders and Winslow, 1997]. Why do you think that HMOs were unable to keep their costs low? What is there about the structure of HMOs that would lead to consumer discontent?

2. In the Czech Republic, people are not directly charged for doctor visits or hospital stays. Indeed, the country's constitution says that "citizens have on the basis of public insurance the right to free medical care and free medical aids under the conditions defined by the law."

Nonetheless, the Czech government recently introduced a charge of $1.85 per doctor visit and $4.00 per day in the hospital [Kulish, 2008, p. A9]. How will this policy affect the efficiency of health care provision in the Czech Republic?

3. In Boca Raton, Florida, doctors frequently lock their doors at lunch in order to prevent Medicare patients from crowding into the office while they're away. One doctor commented that these patients have few serious medical problems. Rather, visiting the doctor has become a social activity, in which patients "bring their spouses and plan their days around their [doctors'] appointments" [Kolata, 2003]. What is there about the structure of Medicare that leads to such situations?

4. When the Medicare prescription drug benefit was under legislative consideration, some suggested that the program should require individuals to decide about whether to accept the

benefit when they enter the Medicare system, and to stick to that decision permanently. That is, individuals either accept the prescription benefit and begin paying premiums as soon as they become eligible, or they can never enter the program. Explain the efficiency rationale behind this proposal.

5. Medicare recipients can purchase supplemental private insurance (known as *Medigap insurance*) to fill the gap in coverage left by Medicare. This gap includes copayments, deductibles, and prescription drug expenses not covered by Medicare. Several years ago, the government enacted regulations that specify minimum standards for items that Medigap policies must cover. This made the policies more expensive, and as a consequence, about 25 percent of the elderly who would have purchased some Medigap insurance purchased none at all [Finkelstein, 2004].

   Consider an individual who consumes two goods, "insurance" and "all other goods." The cost of a unit of Medigap insurance is $1, as is the cost of a unit of all other goods. Sketch a budget constraint and set of indifference curves that are consistent with the following scenario: In an unregulated market, an individual with a $30,000 income purchases $5,000 worth of Medigap insurance. The government then puts mandates on Medigap policies that raise their minimum price to $8,000; that is, the individual must purchase at least $8,000 units of Medigap insurance or none at all. After considering the matter, the individual decides to go without Medigap insurance.

6. The analysis surrounding Figure 10.5 assumes that a person receiving government health insurance is not allowed to purchase supplemental private insurance. Show how the diagram must be modified if, to the contrary, individuals can purchase additional health insurance coverage. Another assumption behind the model is that government health insurance is "free" in the sense that individuals do not pay any taxes for it. Show how the model must be modified if government health insurance is financed by taxes.

7. The three panels in Figure 10.5 show instances in which health insurance either increases or stays the same with the introduction of government-provided insurance. Diagram a set of indifference curves that illustrates a situation where introducing government insurance leads to a reduction in total health insurance.

Chapter Eleven

SOCIAL SECURITY

Will you still need me, will you still feed me, when I'm sixty-four?
—JOHN LENNON AND PAUL MCCARTNEY

In his State of the Union address in 2005, President George W. Bush said, "We must join together to strengthen and save Social Security." Three years later, during the presidential campaign of 2008, then-Senator Barack Obama stated, "If we care about Social Security, which I do, and if we are firm in our commitment to make sure that it's going to be there for the next generation, and not just for our generation, then we have an obligation to figure out how to stabilize the system." Clearly, both Republicans and Democrats regard Social Security as being critically important. Indeed, it is the largest single domestic spending program. Figure 11.1 shows Social Security's growth, both in real dollars and as a share of Gross Domestic Product (GDP). In 2007, the program cost $594.5 billion, or 4.3 percent of GDP. The other point that emerges from both statements is that Social Security appears to be in trouble. This chapter describes the workings of Social Security and the challenges that it faces.

Figure 11.1   Social Security expenditures (1939–2007)
Social Security is the largest US domestic program. In 2007, Social Security expenditures were approximately $594.5 billion or about 4.3 percent of Gross Domestic Product.

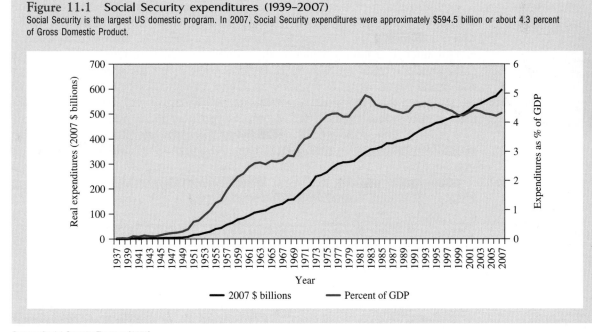

Source: Social Security Trustees [2008].

▶ WHY HAVE SOCIAL SECURITY?

We begin by examining Social Security—officially, Old Age Survivors, and Disability Insurance (OASDI)—through the lens of welfare economics. In this context, a critical question is whether there is some market failure that Social Security remedies.

Consumption Smoothing and the Annuity Market

In brief, Social Security works as follows: During their working lives, members of the system and their employers make contributions via a tax on payrolls. Upon retirement, members are eligible for monthly payments based in part on their contributions. The payments are fixed in real terms and last as long as the recipient lives. In effect, then, Social Security provides insurance against the possibility of living longer than expected and hence prematurely using up all the assets accumulated for retirement.[1] In order to understand the justifications for government provision of this kind of insurance, we need to discuss why people would want it in the first place.

Everyone realizes that there is a risk of dying too young and thus leaving one's family without adequate income. But perhaps less obviously, there is also a risk of living too long. For example, suppose that Darcy is 40 years old, and based on his medical history he expects to live to be 85 years old. He also expects to work until he is 65, saving enough along the way to maintain his standard of living during his 20-year retirement. A possible "problem" is that instead of dying at 85, Darcy may live to be 100. If so, Darcy faces dire financial consequences for the last 15 years of his life.

How can Darcy protect himself against the financial problems associated with living longer than he anticipated? He can buy a particular kind of insurance policy called an **annuity.** To purchase the annuity, Darcy pays the insurance company a certain amount of money, which is the policy's premium. In return, he receives a fixed annual income for as long as he lives.[2] The larger the premium, the larger the annual payments he receives in the future, other things being the same. Note the symmetry with life insurance. With life insurance, you pay the insurance company a given annual amount for as long as you live, and in return, the company pays a lump sum when you die. With an annuity, you pay the company a lump sum, and it provides you with a fixed annual amount for as long as you live. Life insurance policies and annuities serve the same basic function: They enable people to **consumption smooth,** that is, to reduce consumption in high-earning years in order to increase consumption in low-earning years. A risk-averse person is willing to reduce his consumption by buying life insurance in order to guarantee a certain consumption level for his family should he die. Similarly, he is willing to reduce his consumption by buying an annuity in return for a guaranteed income level throughout his retirement.[3]

annuity

Insurance plan that charges a premium and then pays a sum of money at some regular interval for as long as the policyholder lives.

consumption smoothing

Reducing consumption in high-earning years in order to increase consumption in low-earning years.

---

[1] Social Security also provides benefits for disabled workers and for dependents and survivors of disabled and retired workers.

[2] In reality, annuity contracts can be more complicated. For example, some annuities pay income for only a fixed number of years and some annuities pay a variable rate rather than a fixed amount each period.

[3] This discussion ignores the fact that, as pointed out in Chapter 8, a dollar of consumption today is worth more than a dollar in a later period because of the time value of money. Hence, a more precise statement of the result is that consumption smoothing implies a desire for equal present value of consumption across periods.

Adverse Selection and the Annuity Market

We can now restate the question posed at the beginning of this section as follows: "Social Security provides recipients with annuities, for which they pay with payroll taxes during their working years. Why can't the private market be relied upon to provide annuities instead?" One possible reason is that there is a failure in the annuities market because of **asymmetric information.** The annuity seller's profit depends on the buyer's life expectancy. The longer the buyer lives, the less money the seller makes. This means that the price that the seller charges has to take into account the buyer's life expectancy. The problem arises if the buyer of an annuity knows more about her life expectancy than the seller does. If the seller charges a premium based on the average life expectancy across buyers, this will be a bad deal for those with lower than average life expectancies and a good deal for those with higher than average life expectancies. If those with lower than average life expectancies choose not to buy annuities, then the seller is left with a pool of particularly healthy people, and must raise the premium in order to cover expected payouts. This, in turn, leads those with relatively short life expectancies within this pool to drop out, and so on. Because the seller gets an **adverse selection** of buyers, in theory the market may enter a "death spiral" of the kind we discussed in Chapter 9. Hence, one justification for Social Security is that it solves the adverse selection problem in the annuity market by forcing everyone to purchase the government annuity.

As stressed in Chapter 9, just because adverse selection can impede efficiency doesn't mean that it will. We must ask whether adverse selection in the annuity market is empirically important enough to justify government providing annuities through Social Security. This is a controversial issue. It is certainly true that the US market for annuities is small and underdeveloped, unlike the market for life insurance, which is thriving. Some see this as evidence of market failure, because risk-averse people should provide significant demand for annuities. But others argue that annuity markets shouldn't suffer from adverse selection any more than life insurance markets, because they both rely on the same assessment of mortality risk. Even though the market for annuities was small at the time of Social Security's founding, perhaps a more robust market has not developed because Social Security crowds out private annuities; that is, many potential buyers do not buy private annuities because, in effect, they already own a publicly provided annuity.

Other Justifications

Several considerations other than adverse selection may justify Social Security.

Lack of Foresight and Paternalism Some argue that if left to their own devices, most people would not accumulate enough assets to finance an adequate level of consumption during their retirement, even if they don't live longer than expected. This could be because people lack foresight to plan adequately for the future. Or it could be that people have a very clear view of the future, but given their preferences, they save less than society deems appropriate. In either case, the paternalistic argument is that people should be forced to save and thus the government must provide a mandatory annuity plan so that people will be adequately provided for in their retirement years.

This argument raises two issues. First, is it true that people would fail to provide for themselves adequately without Social Security? To find out requires estimating

asymmetric information

A situation in which one party engaged in an economic transaction has better information about the good or service traded than the other party.

adverse selection

The phenomenon under which the uninformed side of a deal gets exactly the wrong people trading with it (that is, it gets an adverse selection of the informed parties).

how people would behave in the absence of the program. As noted later, this is very difficult to do. Second, even if it is true, not everyone believes that the government should step in. Those with a highly individualistic philosophical framework believe that people should be left to make their own decisions, even if this occasionally results in mistakes. Others find it unacceptable for society to turn a blind eye to elderly people in poverty, even if it is a result of their own mistakes.

Moral Hazard   A related consideration is that individuals who do not save enough for their retirement years may believe that the government will feel obliged to come to their aid if they are in a sufficiently desperate situation. With this belief, younger individuals may purposely neglect to save adequately or fail to purchase an annuity during their working years, knowing that the government will bail them out in old age. Thus, the possibility of a government bail out leads to an inefficiently low amount of private saving. This is an example of **moral hazard,** which occurs when the existence (or expectation) of insurance increases the likelihood of the adverse outcome (see Chapter 9). One justification for the compulsory nature of Social Security is to address the inefficiently low saving caused by moral hazard.

moral hazard

When obtaining insurance against an adverse outcome leads to changes in behavior that increase the likelihood of the outcome.

Economize on Decision-Making and Administrative Costs   A person aiming to smooth consumption optimally needs to decide how much to save in preparation for retirement, which assets to invest in, and which annuity plan to purchase. In addition, each choice depends on one's life expectancy. These are complicated decisions and are likely to involve quite a bit of time and effort. If public decision makers can select an appropriate annuity program for everyone, individuals do not have to waste resources on making their own decisions. The counterpoint is that the government might not choose the right kind of policy for each person. After all, different people have different preferences, so it might be better to let people shop around on their own.

A related problem is the potential for high administrative costs on the supply side of the market. As discussed earlier, annuity providers need to obtain detailed information about buyers in order to estimate life expectancies in determining premiums. Also, annuities pay substantial commissions to their salespeople who find buyers for the plans. Both of these can contribute to high administrative costs. By requiring everyone to participate in Social Security, and by restricting the available options to participants, the government program could be cheaper to administer than private plans. The counterargument is basically the same as in the previous paragraph: To be sure, variety is costly, but that doesn't mean that variety is undesirable. It depends on the benefits derived from allowing people to tailor their policies to their own preferences.

Income Redistribution   Under Social Security, people with high lifetime earnings tend to receive proportionally smaller returns on their taxes than people with low lifetime earnings. To some extent, then, Social Security redistributes income, which isn't the case for private annuities. This helps explain why Social Security is compulsory. Otherwise, those who received smaller returns might opt out and purchase private annuities instead.

Improve the Economic Status of the Aged   One of the main purposes of Social Security is to maintain the incomes of the elderly. Has the program achieved this goal? The numbers tell a pretty upbeat story. The elderly used to be a relatively poor group. In 1970, about one in four elderly people was below the poverty line. Not only has the poverty rate for the elderly fallen, but it is now below the rate for the population as a whole. In 2006, 9.4 percent of the population over 65 was poor, while for the adult nonelderly population the rate was 10.8 percent, and for the child population the rate was 17.4 percent. In recent decades, the incomes of the elderly have increased at a faster rate than those of the rest of the population. Between 1974 and 2007, the real median income for all people over 15 increased by about 32 percent, while for the population over 65 it increased 48 percent.

A few caveats are in order. First, although Social Security has doubtless reduced poverty among the elderly, it has not eliminated it. Elderly females, particularly widows, are especially likely to experience economic distress. Second, it is difficult to estimate reliably the effect of Social Security on the living standards of the elderly. As just noted, the elderly poverty rate has dropped as Social Security spending has increased. However, one must always be cautious about inferring a causal relationship strictly on this type of time-series data. Given that Social Security was started for the entire country at the same time, setting up a quasi-experimental research design to assess whether there is a causal relationship is very difficult. Engelhardt and Gruber [2004] rely on certain sharp changes in Social Security benefits over time to estimate the impact on elderly poverty, and they find that Social Security does in fact seem to have lowered poverty levels.

Finally, although Social Security income makes up about 31 percent of all the income going to elderly households, these benefits do not necessarily represent a net increase of the resources available to retirees [Social Security Administration, 2008]. People may save less in anticipation of receiving Social Security, or they may leave the workforce to qualify for benefits. The question of how Social Security influences individuals' decisions is thus central to assessing the system's impact. We discuss this topic later in the chapter.

▶ STRUCTURE OF SOCIAL SECURITY

Whatever the controversies over the justification for Social Security, today virtually everyone who works in the United States is covered either by it or some other government retirement program. The system is rather complicated. The key provisions are explained below.[4]

Basic Components

Pay-As-You-Go Financing   When it was started in 1935, Social Security was broadly similar to a private pension system. During their working lives, individuals deposited some portion of their salaries into a fund. Over time, the fund would accumulate interest, and on retirement, the principal and accrued interest would be used to pay retirement benefits. This is known as a **fully funded** plan. This approach was scrapped almost immediately.

In 1939 the system was converted to a **pay-as-you-go** (or **unfunded**) plan, in which current retirees receive their benefits from the payments made by current

fully funded

A pension system in which an individual's benefits are paid out of deposits that have been made during his or her working life, plus accumulated interest.

pay-as-you-go (unfunded)

A pension system in which benefits paid to current retirees come from payments made by current workers.

---

[4] More details can be found at the Social Security Web site: www.ssa.gov.

workers. Each generation of retirees is therefore supported by payments made by the existing generation of workers, not from funds collected over the years through savings. An important reason for the switch to pay-as-you-go was the perception that the savings of many of the elderly had been wiped out by the Great Depression, and they deserved to be supported at a level higher than possible with only a few years of contributions collected in a fully funded system. Another reason for the switch to pay-as-you-go was the fear of some politicians at the time that the collection of funds in the fully funded system would be managed inefficiently by the government or perhaps even be spent on other government programs rather than the promised retirement benefits.

Because of changes to the system enacted in 1983, Social Security today is a partially funded system. That is, Social Security has accumulated some surplus revenue in a trust fund, so not every dollar collected in taxes is spent immediately on benefits to retirees. However, as we'll discuss later, the trust fund is essentially an accounting device. Hence, it is still largely accurate to characterize the system as pay-as-you-go.

Explicit Transfers   Another key change in the 1939 legislation was a broadening of the scope of the program. The 1935 act provided primarily for monthly retirement benefits for insured workers aged 65 and over. In 1939, monthly benefits for dependents and survivors of insured workers were introduced. Thus, Social Security not only provides insurance for outliving one's retirement savings, it also transfers income across individuals. The transfer function has grown in importance over time and culminated in the enactment of **Supplemental Security Income (SSI)** in 1972. SSI, although administered by the Social Security Administration, is not insurance by the conventional definition. It is a welfare program that provides a federal minimum income guarantee for the aged and disabled. SSI is discussed with other welfare programs in Chapter 13.

Supplemental Security Income (SSI)

A welfare program that provides a minimum income guarantee for the aged and disabled.

Benefit Structure   An individual's Social Security benefits depend on his or her earnings history, age, and other personal circumstances. The first step is to calculate the **average indexed monthly earnings (AIME),** which represents the individual's average monthly wages over the 35 highest years of earnings. In order to make wages earned over different years directly comparable, annual earnings are inflated by the increases in average wages in the economy since the earnings occurred.

Only annual wages up to a given ceiling are included in the AIME calculation. This ceiling is the same as the maximum amount of earnings subject to the Social Security payroll tax (discussed later).

The next step is to substitute the AIME into a benefit formula to find the individual's **primary insurance amount (PIA),** which is the basic benefit payable to a worker who retires at the normal retirement age or who becomes disabled. The benefit is an annuity payment to the retiree; that is, the recipient receives a monthly benefit (adjusted each year for inflation) until he or she dies.

average indexed monthly earnings

The top 35 years of wages in covered employment, indexed each year for average wage growth. The AIME is used to compute an individual's Social Security benefit.

primary insurance amount (PIA)

The basic Social Security benefit payable to a worker who retires at the normal retirement age or becomes disabled.

The benefit formula is structured so that the monthly benefit is proportionally higher for those with lower AIMEs. In 2008, the PIA was calculated as

90 percent of the first $711 of AIME, plus

32 percent of AIME between $711 and $4,288, plus

15 percent of AIME above $4,288.

Thus, for a 2008 retiree with an AIME of $200, the PIA was $180 (90 percent of AIME), while for a retiree with an AIME of $1,600, the PIA was about $924 (58 percent of AIME).[5] The dollar amounts of $711 and $4,288 in the formula are known as "bend points," and are adjusted each year for average wage growth. For a typical low earner (one receiving 45 percent of the national average wage) retiring at 65 in 2008, Social Security was about 52.6 percent of annual preretirement earnings; for an average earner it was 39.0 percent; and for a high earner (one at the maximum taxable limit), it was 26.9 percent [Social Security Trustees, 2008, pp. 193–194].

Upon retirement, the benefit is adjusted each year based on inflation, as measured by the Consumer Price Index. Very few financial assets offer this kind of protection against inflation.

Age at Which Benefit Is Drawn   The age at which an individual qualifies for full Social Security retirement benefits is called the **normal retirement age.**[6] For those born in 1937 or earlier, the normal retirement age was 65 years old. However, legislation passed in the 1980s required that the normal retirement age increase gradually over time. As a result, the retirement age was increased by two months per year for those born from 1938 to 1942. Those born from 1943 to 1954 have a normal retirement age of 66 years old. It then increases by two months per year, reaching 67 for workers born in 1960 or later.

> **normal retirement age**
>
> Age at which an individual qualifies for full Social Security retirement benefits. Historically, it was 65, but is now gradually being increased to 67.

A worker can begin receiving benefits as early as age 62, but doing so results in a permanent reduction in the monthly benefits. The benefit is reduced by $5/9$ of 1 percent a month for the first 36 months preceding the normal retirement age. For example, if a person retires at 62 rather than 65, his benefit is reduced 20 percent relative to retirement at the normal retirement age. Once the normal retirement age reaches 67, the benefit reduction of retiring at 62 will be 30 percent.[7] The reduction rate is set so that, for a person of average life expectancy, the reduction in monthly benefits just offsets the gain of receiving the benefits for more years.

In the same way, workers who don't start collecting benefits until after their normal retirement age receive a permanent increase in their monthly benefits. Each year delayed beyond the normal retirement age increases benefits by 8 percent.[8]

Recipient's Family Status   When a single worker retires at the normal retirement age, the actual monthly benefit is simply equal to the primary insurance amount (PIA). A worker with a dependent spouse or child can receive an additional 50 percent of the PIA. In other words, the spouse of a Social Security recipient is entitled either to his or her own PIA or 50 percent of his or her spouse's PIA, whichever is bigger. When recipients die, surviving spouses are entitled to either the deceased's or their own PIA, whichever is greater.

Earnings Test and Taxing Benefits   The benefits of Social Security recipients who have not reached the normal retirement age are reduced by one dollar for each two dollars they earn above $14,160 (adjusted each year by average wage growth).

---

[5] The law also specifies a special minimum benefit that provides long-term low-paid workers a higher benefit than the regular formula permits.

[6] To be eligible for Social Security benefits, a recipient must have paid the payroll tax for 40 quarters (10 years) over her lifetime.

[7] The reduction rate is $5/12$ of 1 percent a month for any additional months above 36 before the normal retirement age.

[8] There is no additional increase in benefits for delaying retirement after age 69.

Table 11.1   **Social Security Tax Rates** *(selected years)*

Year	Maximum Taxable Earnings (Dollars)	Combined Employer and Employee Tax (Percent)
1937	$ 3,000	2.00%
1950	3,000	3.00
1960	4,800	6.00
1970	7,800	8.40
1980	29,700	10.16
1990	51,300	12.40
2000	76,200	12.40
2008	102,000	12.40

Source: Office of the Chief Actuary, Social Security Administration [www.ssa.gov].

Note: These rates *do not* include the payroll tax used to finance Medicare, which is 1.45 percent each on employers and employees. There is no ceiling for that tax.

Payroll tax rates have grown over time. The current combined payroll tax rate is 12.4 percent, which is more than six times the original level. In 2008, the maximum taxable earnings level was $102,000.

This provision is known as the earnings test. However, individuals who lose benefits due to the earnings test may have their later benefits increased (with interest accrued). Thus, "the earnings test is not a tax at all: at a person's full retirement age, Social Security increases benefits to account for any lost to the earnings test in earlier years" [Biggs, 2008].

In addition, some people who get Social Security benefits have to pay income taxes on them. Up to 85 percent of the Social Security benefits received by people with combined incomes above a certain base amount are subject to the federal personal income tax.[9] The base amount is $25,000 for single taxpayers and $32,000 for married taxpayers.

Financing   Social Security is financed by a payroll tax. The tax is a fixed percentage of an employee's annual gross wages up to a certain amount. Half of the tax is levied on employers and half on employees. The legislative intention was apparently to split the cost of the program equally between workers and employers. However, some or all of the employers' share may be "shifted" to workers in the form of a lower pretax wage. Whether such shifting occurs is a complicated question discussed in Chapter 14. For now, we merely note that it is highly unlikely that the true division of the costs of the program is really 50–50.

As benefits have grown over time, so have payroll tax rates. As seen in Table 11.1, the current combined tax rate is 12.4 percent (i.e., 6.2 percent on the employer and employee each), which is more than six times the original level. Legislation passed in 1977 mandated that the maximum taxable earnings rise automatically each year with increases in average wages. In 2008, the maximum taxable earnings was $102,000.

The tax rates in Table 11.1 do not include the additional payroll tax that finances the Medicare hospital insurance program, which we discussed in Chapter 10. The

---

[9] The "combined income" is computed as adjusted gross income plus nontaxable interest plus one-half of the Social Security benefit.

Medicare payroll tax is currently 1.45 percent on the employee and the employer each, and since 1993 does not have a maximum taxable income limit. Thus, for an individual whose earnings are below the maximum taxable limit for Social Security, the combined payroll tax rate for Social Security and Medicare is 15.3 [$= 2 \times (6.2 + 1.45)$] percent.

A natural question is why Social Security is financed through a special payroll tax rather than from general revenues. Indeed, in 1999 President Clinton unsuccessfully proposed using general revenues in order to help infuse funds into the Social Security system. The reason for payroll tax financing is probably due to politics rather than economics. A link between taxes and benefits—no matter how tenuous—creates an obligation on the part of the government to maintain the system that promised the benefits. President Franklin Roosevelt articulated this position with typical eloquence:

> Those taxes were never a problem of economics. They are politics all the way through. We put those payroll contributions there so as to give the contributors a legal, moral, and political right to collect their pensions. With these taxes in there, no damn politician can ever scrap my Social Security Program.

Distributional Issues

Our description of Social Security indicates that it differs from a retirement insurance program. If providing retirement insurance were the only objective, all individuals would receive approximately the same return on their contributions. Specifically, each individual would receive an **actuarially fair return**—on average, the benefits received would equal the premiums paid. (The calculation must be made "on average" because total benefits depend on the individual's life span, which cannot be known in advance with certainty.) In fact, given the structure of the Social Security system, some types of people systematically receive higher returns than others. As we now show, Social Security redistributes income both across generations and also across different groups within a generation.

actuarially fair return

An insurance plan that on average pays out the same amount that it receives in contributions.

Intergenerational Redistribution   To understand how Social Security redistributes income across generations, recall that in a pure pay-as-you-go system, the benefits received by retirees in a given year equal the payments made by workers in the same year. If N_b is the number of beneficiaries and B is the average benefit per retiree, then total benefits are $N_b \times B$. The taxes paid by workers in a given year are the product of the tax rate (t), the number of covered workers (N_w), and the average covered wage per worker (w): $t \times N_w \times w$. Hence, equality between total benefits received in a year and total taxes paid in a year requires that

$$N_b \times B = t \times N_w \times w \qquad (11.1)$$

By rearranging terms, we see that the average benefit per retiree in a given year is

$$B = t \times \frac{N_w}{N_b} \times w \qquad (11.2)$$

Equation (11.2) has several important implications. First, if we assume that the tax rate is constant over time, then average benefits can increase only if wages increase or if the number of workers relative to retirees increases (that is, the population grows). If neither of these happens, then each year retirees receive an average benefit equal to exactly what they paid in taxes, so they earn an implicit rate of return of zero. (We refer to the return from a pay-as-you-go system as "implicit," to distinguish it from returns that accrue from investing in capital goods.) If, however, wages and population both increase at a constant rate, then retirees receive a positive return on the taxes they contributed to Social Security, with the return equal to the sum of wage growth and population growth. Thus, for example, if wages are increasing at 1.5 percent annually and the population is growing at 1 percent annually, then the return on taxes paid is 2.5 percent.[10] (Later in the chapter, we'll discuss the problems that arise when the ratio of workers to beneficiaries in a society falls.) The important point is that the implicit rate of return in a pay-as-you-go system is strictly determined by wage and population growth.

Equation (11.2) also suggests that one way to increase the average benefit to retirees is to increase the tax rate. But this does not lead to a *permanent* increase in the implicit rate of return. To be sure, the current generation of retirees would enjoy a higher return because they would receive higher average benefits although they paid into the system only at the old, lower tax rate during their working years. However, future generations of retirees are no better off; their implicit rate of return is not improved because they also have to pay higher taxes. This reinforces the point just made: Any sustainable increase in the return of a pay-as-you-go system can only be accomplished through some combination of population growth and wage growth.

A generation of retirees can receive extraordinarily high returns from a pay-as-you-go system when the system is just starting up. Specifically, when the system is launched, retirees receive an average benefit equal to the right-hand side of Equation (11.2), yet they never had to pay any payroll taxes during their working years. This amounts to an infinite return, which is indeed very generous. An example along these lines is that of Ida May Fuller, the first Social Security beneficiary. She worked for only three years after the establishment of Social Security and paid only $24.75 in payroll taxes. She started receiving benefits in 1940 at the age of 65, and lived to the age of 99, collecting $20,897 in benefits over her lifetime.

Just as retirees at the time the system was started received a windfall, if we were to end the pay-as-you-go system at some particular time, then the newly retired at that time would be in a bad position—they would have paid into the system during their working years but received no retirement benefits in return.

In practice, wage and population rates have varied over time, and so has the payroll tax, so it is difficult to make any simple statements about the intergenerational redistribution that has occurred due to Social Security. The most straightforward way to explore distributional issues is to compute **Social Security wealth** for several representative individuals. Social Security wealth is the expected lifetime net benefits from Social Security. It is computed as the difference between the present value of expected future benefit payments and the present value of expected payroll tax payments.[11]

Each frame in Figure 11.2 shows Social Security wealth estimates over time for four "representative" individuals: a "low earner" who always earned 45 percent of the average wage, an "average earner" who earned the average wage in the economy, a "high earner" who earned 160 percent of the average wage, and a "maximum earner" who always earned the maximum wage subject to the Social Security tax.

Social Security wealth

The present value of one's expected Social Security benefits minus expected payroll taxes paid.

---

[10] More precisely, the return on taxes paid is 2.515 percent, computed as $100 \times [(1.015 \times 1.01) - 1]$.

[11] Because Social Security benefits received depend on the length of life, the actual value is uncertain, and actuarial tables must be used to compute the value "on average," or the "expected" value. Because benefits and costs occur over time, lifetime benefits and costs must be computed as "present values," a concept we discussed in Chapter 8.

Figure 11.2   Social Security wealth for representative individuals

Currently, net lifetime Social Security transfers are higher for low earners than for high earners, are higher for one-earner couples than for two-earner couples, and are higher for females than for males. They have also tended to decrease over time.

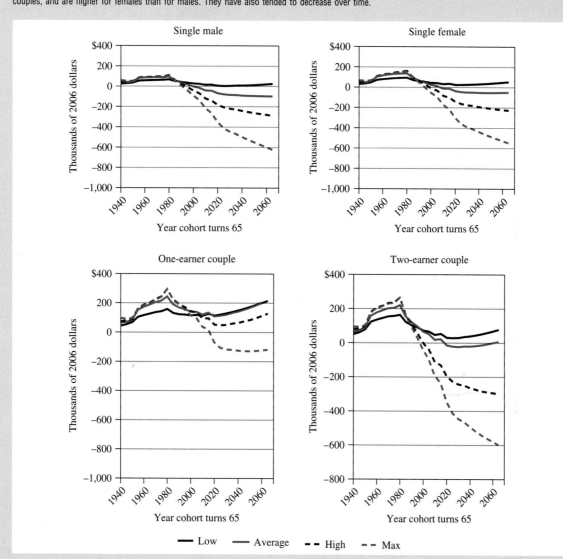

Source: Updated tables (for 2006) provided by C. Eugene Steuerle and Adam Carasso. See Steuerle and Bakija [1994] for original tables and methodology.
Note: All values expressed in 2006 dollars.

The four different frames correspond to a single male, a single female, a one-earner couple, and a two-earner couple. Taken together, the figures show that older generations have received more Social Security wealth than recent generations—Social Security redistributes income toward older generations. For example, consider two single men with average earnings, one who retired in 1980, and the other who will retire in 2015. For the first, the net benefit of Social Security is $94,104 while for the second it is negative $89,343. The cartoon cogently makes the point that Social Security redistributes wealth from younger to older generations.

"By the way, Sam, as someday you'll be paying for my entitlements, I'd like to thank you in advance." © The New Yorker Collection 1996 J. B. Handelsman from cartoonbank.com. All Rights Reserved.

Redistribution within a Generation   Figure 11.2 also reveals how Social Security redistributes income across income classes within a generation. For recent and future retirees, generally the higher the earnings, the smaller the gain from Social Security. For example, a high-earner single male who retires in the year 2015 is expected to lose $196,350 by virtue of his participation in Social Security, whereas a low-earner single male retiring at the same time is expected to lose only $8,605.

It does not follow, however, that all groups whose members tend to have low incomes benefit disproportionately from Social Security. This is because an individual's lifetime Social Security benefit depends not only on the benefit per year, but also the number of years he receives benefits. Hence, members of groups with relatively low expected life spans (such as African-Americans) tend to receive lower lifetime benefits, and vice versa. For example, Liebman [2001] calculates that among African-Americans who retired in the 1990s, the lifetime net benefit from Social Security was negative $2,514, as opposed to positive $250 for whites. However, if these African-Americans had the same expected life span and education as the rest of the population, their net benefit would have increased to a positive $18,259. To some extent, this reduces the overall progressivity of the Social Security system [Congressional Budget Office, 2006]. Taking into account life expectancies also leads to some interesting differences by gender. Women live longer than men, so their lifetime benefits are greater. According to Liebman's calculations, among people who retired in the 1990s, on average men came out behind by about $43,000 while women came out ahead by $37,000.

Social Security also redistributes income based on people's choices about living arrangements. Other things being the same, married people with uncovered spouses receive a higher implicit return than single people. For example, a single male with average earnings and retiring in 2015 can expect approximately $138,000 less in net benefits from Social Security than a single-earner couple with the same earnings and retiring the same year. This is because the married person receives an extra benefit for his or her spouse equal to 50 percent of his or her own benefit. Moreover, if the married person dies, the surviving spouse becomes entitled to the entire benefit.

Further, one-earner couples gain more from Social Security than two-earner couples. Consider a family in which the wife has higher lifetime covered earnings than the husband. If the benefit the husband would receive on the basis of his earnings history turns out to be less than 50 percent of his wife's benefit, the husband is entitled to *no more* than the 50 percent of his wife's benefit, which he would have received even without working. If his benefit is more than 50 percent of hers, he gains only the difference between his benefit and 50 percent of hers. Thus, even though the spouse with lower earnings is subject to the payroll tax during his or her working life, he or she gains little in Social Security benefits. A two-earner couple with average earnings and retiring in 2015 can expect approximately $114,000 less in net benefits from Social Security relative to a single-earner couple that earns the same amount and retires the same year.

Are these redistributive patterns desirable? As usual, the answer depends in part on value judgments. It could be argued, for example, that the people who suffered during the Great Depression and World War II were unfairly treated by fate, and therefore deserve to be compensated by younger generations. If so, the intergenerational transfers shown in Figure 11.2 might be appropriate. On the other hand, it is not clear what principle of equity would justify the distributions across different family types that were just described.

One is struck by how little public discussion there has been of the transfers implicit in Social Security. The sums involved are huge; if such amounts were being transferred via a direct expenditure program, there would probably be an ongoing major debate. However, the workings of the Social Security system are sufficiently obscure that public awareness of this situation is low.

The Trust Fund

In the 1980s the payroll tax rate was increased and benefits were cut. Since then, revenues have exceeded payments to beneficiaries, a situation that is expected to continue until around 2017. The motivation for the changes was to create surpluses in the short term that could be used to cover the benefits to retiring baby boomers in later years. Specifically, the surplus revenue is used to buy government bonds, which are "deposited" in the **Social Security Trust Fund.** The reason for the quotation marks is that it is misleading to think of the trust fund as a gigantic savings account that can be drawn upon to pay benefits in the future. Instead, the trust fund is largely an accounting device for keeping track of the annual surpluses generated by the Social Security portion of the federal budget. By itself, the trust fund does not contribute to the government's ability to pay benefits in the future.

To see why, we must recognize a fundamental fact—in any year in the future, the consumption of both retirees and workers must come out of that year's production. Hence, the trust fund can help finance future retirees' consumption only to the extent that it leads to an increase in economic output in the future. And the only way it can increase output in the future is by increasing the capital stock in the present, because a larger capital stock increases the productivity of future workers. Put another way,

Social Security Trust Fund

A fund in which Social Security surpluses are accumulated for the purpose of paying out benefits in the future.

unless the amounts accumulating in the trust fund are associated with more national saving, they do nothing to enhance the ability to pay future benefits.

Suppose the Social Security system runs a $10 billion surplus, which is "deposited" into the trust fund. If this $10 billion is devoted to savings, then it will increase productivity in the future, which generates wage growth, which generates more revenue out of which to make payments to future Social Security beneficiaries. Suppose instead that the $10 billion surplus leads Congress to spend $10 billion more on other government programs. There is still a $10 billion entry in the trust fund. This entry represents a $10 billion claim against the Treasury, which, when redeemed in the future, has to be financed by raising taxes, borrowing from the public, or reducing other expenditures. But this $10 billion has not increased national saving, since it was offset by an increase in government spending. So in a real sense, the ability of society to pay benefits in the future has not increased.

Thus, the pertinent question is whether or not the revenue in the trust fund amounts to new saving, or whether it is offset by increased government spending so there is no new saving. The law states that the trust fund is **off budget,** meaning that Congress should not consider it as available revenue when making spending decisions. However, the government also reports the **unified budget** each year, which includes the surplus revenue going into the trust fund. If policymakers think in terms of the unified budget when making their spending decisions, the likely result is that the trust fund revenue is not devoted to new saving—they think of Social Security as money to spend on various programs just like revenue from any other source. It turns out that although Social Security has run large surpluses since the mid-1980s, some econometric analyses suggest that these surpluses have been mostly (if not completely) offset by large deficits in the rest of the federal budget [Nataraj and Shoven, 2004]. However, it is difficult to sort out the independent effect of the trust fund on government spending, and this remains a controversial issue. We will return to this issue later in our discussion of proposals to reform Social Security.

> **off-budget items**
>
> Federal expenditures and revenues that are excluded by law from budget totals.

> **unified budget**
>
> The document that includes all the federal government's revenues and expenditures.

▶ EFFECTS OF SOCIAL SECURITY ON ECONOMIC BEHAVIOR

Some economists argue that the Social Security system distorts people's behavior and impairs economic efficiency. Most of the discussion has focused on saving behavior and labor supply decisions, to which we now turn.

Saving Behavior

> **life-cycle model**
>
> The theory that individuals' consumption and savings decisions during a given year are based on a planning process that considers lifetime circumstances.

The starting point for most work on Social Security and saving is the **life-cycle model,** which states that individuals' consumption and saving decisions are based on lifetime considerations. During their working lives, individuals save some portion of their incomes to accumulate wealth from which they can finance consumption during retirement.[12] Such funds are invested until they are needed, thus increasing society's capital stock. As we discussed earlier, a person with diminishing marginal utility prefers to smooth consumption over time, other things being the same. Saving provides a mechanism by which to achieve this goal, by moving consumption from

---

[12] Of course, savings are also accumulated for other reasons as well: to finance the purchase of durables or a child's higher education, for example. For a more complete discussion of the life-cycle theory, see Modigliani [1986].

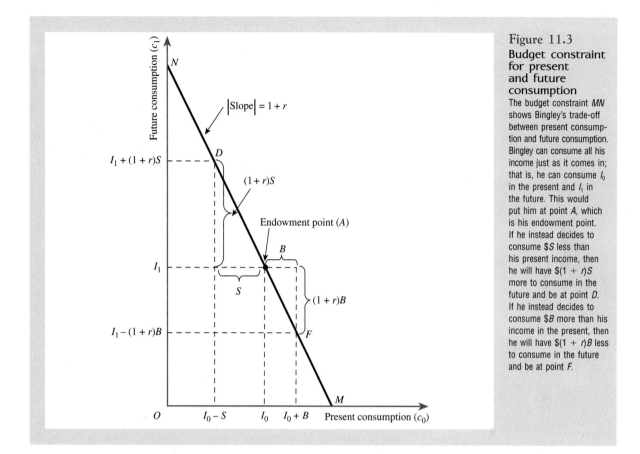

Figure 11.3
Budget constraint for present and future consumption
The budget constraint *MN* shows Bingley's trade-off between present consumption and future consumption. Bingley can consume all his income just as it comes in; that is, he can consume I_0 in the present and I_1 in the future. This would put him at point *A*, which is his endowment point. If he instead decides to consume $S less than his present income, then he will have $(1 + r)S$ more to consume in the future and be at point *D*. If he instead decides to consume $B more than his income in the present, then he will have $(1 + r)B$ less to consume in the future and be at point *F*.

working years to retirement years. The introduction of a Social Security system can substantially alter the amount of lifetime saving. Such changes are the consequences of three effects: (1) the wealth substitution effect, (2) the retirement effect, and (3) the bequest effect.

Wealth Substitution Effect   According to this theory, workers realize that in exchange for their Social Security contributions, they will receive a guaranteed retirement income. If they view Social Security taxes as a means of "saving" for these future benefits, they will tend to save less on their own. In effect, Social Security "crowds out" private saving. This phenomenon is referred to as the **wealth substitution effect.** As emphasized earlier, with a pay-as-you-go system the contributions are paid out to current beneficiaries. Thus, there is no increase in public saving to offset the decrease in private saving, which means a reduction in the total amount of capital accumulation.

Figure 11.3 analyzes the wealth substitution effect within the framework of the life-cycle model. Consider Bingley, who expects to live two periods: "now" (period 0) and the "future" (period 1). Bingley has an income of I_0 dollars now and knows that his income will be I_1 dollars in the future. (Think of "now" as "working years," when I_0 is labor earnings; and the "future" as retirement years, when I_1 is fixed pension income.) His problem is to decide how much to consume in each period. When Bingley decides how much to consume, he simultaneously decides how much to

wealth substitution effect

The crowding out of private savings due to the existence of Social Security.

save or borrow. If his consumption this period exceeds his current income, he must borrow. If his consumption is less than current income, he saves.

The first step in analyzing the saving decision is to depict the possible combinations of present and future consumption available to Bingley—his budget constraint. In Figure 11.3, the amount of current consumption, c_0, is measured on the horizontal axis, and future consumption, c_1, is measured on the vertical axis. One option available to Bingley is to consume all his income just as it comes in—to consume I_0 in the present and I_1 in the future. This bundle, called the **endowment point,** is denoted by A in Figure 11.3. At the endowment point, Bingley neither saves nor borrows.

Another option is to save out of current income in order to consume more in the future. Suppose that Bingley decides to save S dollars this period. If he invests his savings in an asset with a rate of return of r, he can increase his future consumption by $(1 + r)S$—the principal S plus the interest rS. By decreasing present consumption by S, Bingley can increase his future consumption by $(1 + r)S$. Graphically, this possibility is represented by moving S dollars to the left of the endowment point A, and $(1 + r)S$ dollars above it—point D in Figure 11.3.

Alternatively, Bingley can consume more than I_0 in the present if he can borrow against his future income. Assume that Bingley can borrow money at the same rate of interest, r, at which he can lend. If he borrows B dollars to add to his present consumption, by how much must he reduce his future consumption? When the future arrives, Bingley must pay back B *plus* interest of rB. Hence, Bingley can increase present consumption by B only if he is willing to reduce future consumption by $B + rB = (1 + r)B$. Graphically, this process involves moving B dollars to the right of the endowment point, and then $(1 + r)B$ dollars below it—point F in Figure 11.3.

By repeating this procedure for various values of S and B, we can determine how much future consumption is feasible given any amount of current consumption. In the process of doing so, we trace out budget line MN, which passes through the endowment point A, and has a slope in absolute value of $1 + r$. As always, the slope of a budget line represents the opportunity cost of one good in terms of the other. Its slope of $1 + r$ indicates that the cost of \$1 of consumption in the present is $1 + r$ dollars of forgone consumption in the future.[13] Because MN shows the trade-off between consumption across time, it is called the **intertemporal budget constraint.**

To determine the choice along MN, we introduce Bingley's preferences between future and present consumption, which are represented by conventionally shaped indifference curves in Figure 11.4. In this figure we reproduce Bingley's budget constraint, MN, and superimpose a few indifference curves labeled *i*, *ii*, and *iii*. Under the reasonable assumption that more consumption is preferred to less consumption, curves farther to the northeast represent higher levels of utility.

Subject to budget constraint MN, Bingley maximizes utility at point E_1, where he consumes $c_0{}^*$ in the present and $c_1{}^*$ in the future. With this information, it is easy to find how much Bingley saves. Because present income, I_0, exceeds present consumption, $c_0{}^*$, then by definition the difference, $I_0 - c_0{}^*$, is savings. Of course, this does not prove that it is always rational to save. If the highest feasible indifference

---

endowment point

The consumption bundle that is available if an individual neither borrows nor saves.

intertemporal budget constraint

The set of feasible consumption levels across time.

---

[13] To represent the budget line algebraically, note that the fundamental constraint facing Bingley is that the present value of his consumption equals the present value of his income. (See Chapter 8 for an explanation of present value.) The present value of his consumption is $c_0 + c_1/(1 + r)$, while the present value of his income stream is $I_0 + I_1/(1 + r)$. Thus, his selection of c_0 and c_1 must satisfy $c_0 + c_1/(1 + r) = I_0 + I_1/(1 + r)$. The reader can verify that viewed as a function of c_0 and c_1, this is a straight line whose slope is $-(1 + r)$ and that passes through the point (I_0, I_1).

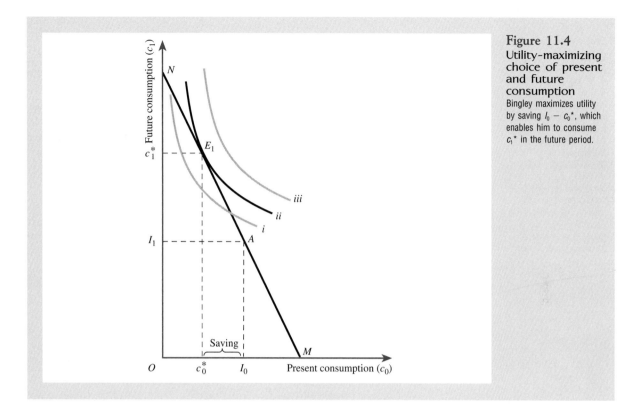

Figure 11.4
Utility-maximizing choice of present and future consumption
Bingley maximizes utility by saving $I_0 - c_0^*$, which enables him to consume c_1^* in the future period.

curve had been tangent to the budget line below point A, present consumption would have exceeded I_0, and Bingley would have borrowed.

We now consider how the introduction of Social Security might affect the saving decision. To simplify the analysis, we'll assume that the implicit return from Social Security just equals the market rate of interest. That is, if Bingley paid T in Social Security taxes during his working years, then his Social Security benefit when he retires is $(1 + r)T$. (An interesting and related analysis—which we provide as a discussion question at the end of the chapter—examines the consequences when the implicit rate of return from Social Security differs from the rate of return from private saving.)

How does the introduction of the Social Security program change Bingley's saving behavior? Figure 11.5 reproduces budget constraint MN from Figure 11.4. Starting at point A, the Social Security tax moves Bingley T units to the left—present consumption is reduced by the tax. But at the same time, the program moves him up by a distance of $(1 + r)T$, because his future consumption is increased by that amount. In short, the combination of the tax now together with the benefit in the future places Bingley on point R of the original budget constraint MN. In effect, R has replaced A as the endowment point. Therefore, as long as Bingley can continue to save and borrow at the market rate of interest, the budget constraint is still MN. And because the budget constraint is the same, so is Bingley's optimal bundle, E_1. However, even though his ultimate lifetime consumption pattern is the same, there is a critical difference in Bingley's behavior. In order to attain E_1, Bingley now only needs to save $I_0^T - c_0^*$, which is less than what he was saving before Social Security. In other words, Bingley views the taxes he pays to Social Security as part

Figure 11.5

Crowding out of private saving due to Social Security

The Social Security tax reduces Bingley's present consumption by T and increases his future consumption by $(1 + r)T$. Bingley now only needs to save $I_0^T - c_0^*$ to achieve his optimal consumption bundle. This is less than what he was saving before Social Security. Thus, Social Security crowds out some private saving.

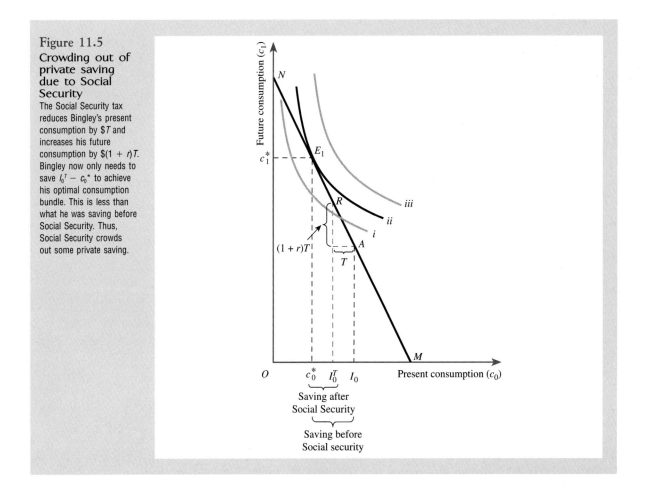

retirement effect

To the extent that Social Security induces people to retire earlier, people may save more in order to finance a longer retirement.

bequest effect

Theory that people may save more in order to finance a larger bequest to children in order to offset the intergenerational redistribution of income caused by Social Security.

of his savings, and therefore he saves less on his own. Thus, Social Security crowds out some private saving. This is the wealth substitution effect. In addition, because a pay-as-you-go system does not channel the taxes into capital accumulation, public saving does not compensate for this reduction in private saving.

Retirement Effect   The next effect of Social Security on saving stems from the observation that Social Security may lead people to retire earlier than they otherwise would. If the length of an individual's retirement period increases, she has more nonworking years during which consumption must be financed, but fewer working years to accumulate funds. This **retirement effect** tends to increase saving.

Bequest Effect   Suppose an important reason for saving is the bequest motive— people want to leave inheritances for their children. Now recall from Figure 11.2 that the Social Security system tends to shift income from children (worker/taxpayers) to parents (retiree/benefit recipients). Parents may therefore save more to increase bequests to their children to offset the distributional effect of Social Security. In essence, people increase their saving to undo the impact of Social Security on their children's incomes. This is referred to as the **bequest effect.**

EMPIRICAL EVIDENCE

Does Social Security Reduce Private Saving?

Given that the wealth substitution effect suggests a decrease in saving and the retirement and bequest effects suggest an increase in saving, theory alone cannot tell if and how Social Security affects saving. It is difficult to estimate empirically the impact of Social Security on saving because the program was started nationwide at the same time. One could examine changing patterns in private savings over time as the level of generosity of the program changed, but this would leave the concern that other factors changing over time were the cause of any changes in saving patterns. In a controversial study, Feldstein [1974] did such a time-series analysis of the relationship between saving and Social Security wealth (the expected present value of future Social Security benefits less the value of future payroll taxes) and found evidence of a negative effect on saving. In an updated version of the paper, Feldstein [1996] found that saving decreased by $2.80 for every $100 in Social Security wealth, which—given the current size of Social Security wealth—amounts to a sizable impact on capital accumulation in the United States.[14] However, other time-series studies find mixed results, with positive effects on saving in some cases [Leimer and Lesnoy, 1982].

Other studies instead rely on cross-sectional data to estimate personal savings as a function of Social Security wealth. Most of these studies find a negative relationship between Social Security wealth and saving, but a minority find a positive effect. It is not too surprising that the cross-sectional estimates vary substantially. As we discussed previously, Social Security wealth depends on individual characteristics such as gender and marital status. However, these same characteristics could themselves affect saving behavior. It is therefore difficult to sort out the independent effect of Social Security.[15]

Some recent studies have examined changes in government retirement programs in other countries. These studies have been able to rely on quasi-experiments, because the countries introduced reforms to their programs that led to sharp changes in expected net benefits to different people. For example, Attanasio and Brugiavini [2003] studied the impact of major reforms to Italy's social security system in 1992. The reforms substantially reduced retirement benefits; however, the size of the reduction varied across households. This allowed them to conduct a difference-in-difference analysis that compared changes in saving behavior for those greatly affected to those not significantly affected by the reforms. They found that social security wealth has a substantial effect on private saving—every $100 of social security wealth crowds out about $40 of private saving.[16] Taking all the empirical research together, it seems likely that Social Security has reduced saving, though the magnitude of the effect is unclear.

---

[14] Interestingly, when Social Security was introduced during the 1930s, the perception that it decreased saving was regarded as a virtue. Many believed that a major cause of the Great Depression was the failure of people to consume enough.

[15] Congressional Budget Office [1998] provides a review of the literature on the effect of Social Security on savings.

[16] Attanasio and Rohwedder [2003] conduct a similar difference-in-difference analysis based on social security reform in the United Kingdom and find even larger effects on private saving.

Retirement Decisions

In 1930, 54 percent of men over 65 participated in the labor force. By 1950, the participation rate for this group was 45.8 percent, and by 2008 it was down to 17 percent [Bureau of Labor Statistics, 2008, p. 17]. Several factors have doubtless contributed to this decline: rising incomes, changing life expectancies, and differences in occupations. Many investigators also believe that Social Security has played a key role in this dramatic change in retirement patterns.

To understand the retirement incentives associated with Social Security, we must return to the concept of Social Security wealth—the expected present value of net benefits to which an individual is entitled. Recall that a person first qualifies for Social Security benefits at age 62. Suppose that Kitty, a 62-year-old, is deciding whether or not to work another year. A key issue is what happens to her Social Security wealth if she puts off retirement for a year and works. If the change in her Social Security wealth is positive, then it adds to the (after-tax) wages she gets from work, and increases the incentive to work. If the change in Social Security wealth is negative, then it reduces the incentive to work another year.

By continuing to work and delaying Social Security benefits, Kitty would have to pay another year of the payroll tax and forgo a year of benefits, both of which reduce Social Security wealth. However, by working another year and forgoing Social Security benefits, she presumably gets to include an additional above-average year of earnings in the calculation of the 35-year average wages of the AIME, and—as discussed earlier—waiting another year also leads to an increase in the monthly benefits. These last two factors tend to increase Social Security wealth. Finally, the net benefits associated with waiting a year to claim benefits also depend on how long Kitty expects to live—the longer her life expectancy, the greater the incentive to wait and receive higher monthly benefits.

In short, from a theoretical standpoint, it is not clear whether Social Security provides positive or negative incentives for a 62-year-old to retire. One must explicitly calculate the various changes to Social Security wealth and see whether the net change is positive or negative. On the basis of such an exercise, Diamond and Gruber [1999] conclude that on average, there is neither an incentive nor a disincentive to retiring and collecting Social Security between the ages of 62 and 65. In other words, the adjustment to benefits for delaying retirement is actuarially fair in this age range. However, they find that there is a disincentive to continue working and forgoing Social Security benefits after 65, because the increase in monthly benefits after this point is not enough to make up for the lost years of benefits and the additional payroll taxes that must be paid.

How responsive are retirement decisions to this disincentive to work? Several econometric studies have assessed whether Social Security affects the age of retirement. For example, in a study of Social Security systems in 12 industrialized countries, Gruber and Wise [2004] find that the age at which benefits are first available has an important effect on the likelihood of retirement.

Implications

The available evidence is mixed, but suggests that Social Security likely depresses both saving and work effort. However, even if Social Security does distort economic decisions, this does not necessarily mean that it is a bad program. If society wants to achieve some level of income security for the elderly, and this protection is not available through private markets, then presumably it should be willing to pay for that security in terms of some loss of efficiency. On the other hand, if there are ways to obtain the same benefits to society with fewer inefficiencies, then reform of the system should be considered.

▶ LONG-TERM STRESSES ON SOCIAL SECURITY

As discussed previously, Social Security payroll taxes currently exceed the benefits that are paid out, and surpluses are expected to continue until approximately 2017, at which time the gap will be covered by redeeming the deposits in the trust fund. In order to obtain the money to redeem these deposits and pay promised benefits, the government will either have to raise taxes, cut other expenditures, or borrow from the public. Even if one mistakenly considers the trust fund as a gigantic savings account, the picture does not brighten very much: Recent estimates suggest that its funds will be exhausted in 2041 [Social Security Trustees, 2008].

The discrepancy between projected payroll tax revenues and payments to retirees is illustrated in Figure 11.6, which shows both measures as a percentage of Gross Domestic Product for the next 75 years. The shortfall that starts in 2017 persists indefinitely and widens over time. In short, given its current structure, Social Security is financially unstable.

To illuminate the source of the problem, let's return to Equation (11.1), which reflects the fact that under a pay-as-you-go system, the benefits received by current retirees equal the taxes paid by current workers. Rearranging this equation gives us

Figure 11.6   Projected revenues and payments of Social Security as share of Gross Domestic Product

The annual benefits paid by Social Security are expected to exceed annual tax revenue in 2017. The shortfall is predicted to widen and to persist indefinitely.

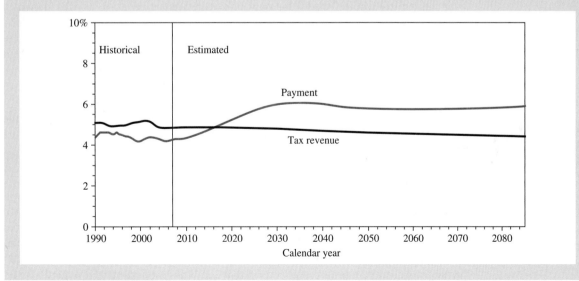

Source: Social Security Trustees [2008].

$$t = \frac{N_b}{N_w} \times \frac{B}{w} \tag{11.3}$$

dependency ratio

The ratio of Social Security beneficiaries to covered workers.

replacement ratio

The ratio of average Social Security benefits to average covered wages.

The first term on the right-hand side is the **dependency ratio,** the ratio of the number of beneficiaries (N_b) to the number of covered workers (N_w). The second term is the **replacement ratio,** the ratio of average benefits (B) to average covered wages (w). The long-term problems with the Social Security system arise because the United States has an aging population, which means that the dependency ratio is increasing over time. Currently, the dependency ratio is about 0.3, which means there are about 3.3 workers for every retiree. By 2030, when the baby boom generation hits normal retirement age, the ratio will be 0.45, which means there will be only about 2.2 workers supporting each retiree [Social Security Trustees, 2008, p. 9].

Equation (11.3) tells us that, with an increasing dependency ratio, there are several ways to keep a pay-as-you-go system solvent. One is to increase covered wages. However, the primary driver of wage increases is productivity growth stemming from increases in the capital stock. Given the current US saving rate, reasonable projections of wage growth suggest that it won't be nearly enough to cover the increasing dependency ratio. This leaves us with the unpleasant options of either increasing the tax rate or decreasing benefits. Many other countries face the same problem. Dependency ratios are increasing in China, Canada, Australia, and most nations in Western Europe, Latin America, and Asia [Congressional Budget Office, 2005a].

▶ SOCIAL SECURITY REFORM

Social Security's financial problems have received widespread attention. Given that the status quo is not sustainable over the long term, there has been a vigorous debate over how it should be changed.

Before discussing specific proposals, an important question must be addressed: Over what time horizon should financial solvency of the system be sought? Some have argued that it is sufficient to plan over a 75-year period. Is that long enough? While 75 years is indeed a long way off, a policy change that obtains solvency only over this period would "work" for only one year. That is because, as was shown in Figure 11.5, annual expenditures are expected to exceed annual revenues indefinitely into the future. Hence, when the 75-year window advances one year, the new 75th year (which was previously not counted in the solvency calculation) would put the system back into deficit for the new 75-year window. Therefore, many analysts advocate that any proposed reform of the Social Security program should achieve solvency over the indefinite future, a condition known as **sustainable solvency.**

sustainable solvency

Expected present values of revenues and expenditures are equal into the indefinite future.

In his satirical novel, *Boomsday,* author Christopher Buckley proposes to fix the problem with Social Security solvency by convincing one-fifth of the baby boomers to kill themselves. Happily, some less extreme options for reform are available.

Maintain the Current System

One view is that Social Security is not really having a "crisis." As Diamond and Orszag [2005, p. 11] note, "Social Security's long-term financial health can be restored through either minor adjustments or major surgery. In our view, major surgery is neither warranted nor desirable—sustainable solvency and improved social insurance can be accomplished by a progressive reform that combines modest benefit reductions and revenue increases." We now discuss a few approaches along these lines.

Raise the Payroll Tax   According to the Social Security Trustees [2008], sustainable solvency could be achieved with an increase in the payroll tax of 3.2 percentage points. Solvency over the 75-year window could be achieved with an increase in the payroll tax of 1.7 percentage points.

Raise the Maximum Taxable Earnings Level   Recall that earnings above $102,000 (adjusted each year for inflation) are not subject to the Social Security tax. If the earnings cap were lifted so that the payroll tax applied to all earnings, both revenues and benefits would increase. However, given the progressive nature of the benefit structure, future benefits would increase less than revenues, leading to a net reduction in the system's long-term deficit. Another idea along the same lines is to remove the cap on taxable income but retain it for the benefit calculation. This would increase tax revenues without changing benefits, and generate as much revenue as a 2.19 percentage point increase in the payroll tax.

Raise the Retirement Age   The long-run fiscal pressure on Social Security is due in part to the substantial increase in life expectancy since the start of the program. By living longer, people have more years of retirement and therefore collect more in benefits. As discussed earlier, the 1983 reforms recognized this problem and called for a gradual increase in the normal retirement age to 67 for those born in 1960 or later. Speeding up this increase so that the normal retirement age hit 67 for those born in 1947 (rather than 1960) and simultaneously increasing the normal retirement age by 1 month every 2 years until it reaches 68 would achieve the equivalent of a payroll tax increase of 0.46 percentage point.[17] While substantial, note that this falls far short of the 3.2 percentage point increase required to obtain sustainable solvency.

Reducing the Cost-of-Living Adjustment   Under the current system, a retiree's benefit is increased each year by the cost of living as measured by the Consumer Price Index (CPI). Reducing the cost-of-living adjustment would reduce benefits, thus moving the system toward solvency. For example, reducing the cost-of-living adjustment by 1 percentage point would be equivalent to a 1.43 percentage point increase in the payroll tax. Some economists have argued that the CPI overestimates the price increases faced by the elderly, so that if the goal is to maintain a constant real level of consumption, an adjustment less than the CPI is fully appropriate [Boskin et al., 1998].

Change the Benefit Formula   Benefits can be adjusted downward in a variety of ways. For example, recall that the AIME is computed as the average of a worker's top 35 years of earnings. If instead the top 38 years of earnings were used, average lifetime earnings would decrease, and so would average benefits. This change would be the equivalent of about a 0.31 percentage point increase in the payroll tax rate.

Recall that currently the 35 years of earnings are adjusted by average wage growth in order to make them comparable across years. Because prices tend to rise slower than wages, if the indexing instead relied on the Consumer Price Index, benefits would decrease and the fiscal outlook for the system would improve. Remarkably,

---

[17] These estimates and the others in this section are from the Chief Actuary of the Social Security Administration, and can be found at www.ssa.gov/OACT/solvency/provisions/index.html.

switching from wage indexing to price indexing *by itself* would lead to sustainable solvency. A variant of this idea is to continue using wage indexing for people with relatively low earnings (say the bottom 30 percent of the distribution of AIME) and use some combination of wage and price indexing for everyone else. In effect, this would reduce total benefits but do so in a way that left those at the bottom end of the earnings distribution no worse off [Pozen et al., 2004].

Comparing the Options   For those who want to maintain the current structure of Social Security, a variety of options are available for making the program solvent. Some care is required in comparing them, because options that have the same impact on the solvency of the system may have very different impacts on the economy. As we'll see in Chapter 15, for example, tax increases can distort the allocation of resources in a way that would not happen with a revenue-equivalent benefit cut. In the same way, options that raise the same amount of money can have different distributional effects. In short, the impact on solvency is only one criterion for evaluating Social Security reform proposals.

Privatize the System

In recent years, both policymakers and academics have given serious thought to the possibility of privatizing Social Security. The term *privatization* refers to a variety of plans that share a common feature: workers' and employers' Social Security contributions are earmarked into a **personal account.** Workers then invest these funds in various financial assets, particularly mutual funds (which are collections of assorted stocks and bonds). When the workers retire, they draw down the funds that have accumulated in their accounts. In principle, individuals could bequeath any unused funds in their accounts at the time of death. In effect, then, privatization moves Social Security in the direction of a fully funded pension system, as opposed to the current pay-as-you-go structure.

Just like incremental change under the status quo, there are many different ways to go about privatizing Social Security. Indeed, in recent years, a variety of approaches to privatization have been tried in several nations, including the United Kingdom, Sweden, Chile, Australia, Mexico, and Argentina.

We now consider some of the pros and cons of privatizing Social Security.

Effect on Solvency   Many people find privatization appealing because over the long term stocks tend to earn a substantially higher rate of return than the implicit rate of return that Social Security now pays on individuals' contributions into the system. If Social Security taxes were invested in the private market, the argument goes, these high rates of return would allow retirees to enjoy large benefits without imposing huge taxes on the current workforce. Solvency could be achieved painlessly.

To evaluate this argument, suppose that a partial privatization plan were enacted that allowed workers to divert part of their payroll taxes to their personal accounts. Workers who contribute money to their personal accounts will therefore pay less into traditional Social Security. Given the existing pay-as-you-go system, this means that there are fewer funds available to pay benefits to the current retirees. To compensate for this, the privatization plan would have to require that each dollar a worker diverts into a personal account be offset by a reduction in the worker's future benefits from the traditional Social Security program. Whether or not the overall fiscal situation of Social Security improves depends on whether the long-term benefit reduction is

personal accounts

Retirement savings accounts managed by individuals as part of a Social Security privatization plan. They are also known as "individual accounts" or "personal savings accounts."

enough to offset the immediate loss in tax revenue to the system. If the expected present value of the benefit reduction just equals the decrease in taxes, then the solvency of the system is unaffected. If the expected present value of the benefit reduction is less than the decrease in taxes, then Social Security's solvency would actually get worse.

Thus, there is no reason to believe that, by itself, privatization would improve the solvency situation. It depends on the rate at which future benefits are reduced, among other design features. Exactly the same logic suggests that critics of privatization who argue that it would necessarily impair the solvency of Social Security are also missing the point. The impact on solvency depends on how future benefits are treated under the specific proposal.

Effect on Saving   As we stressed earlier, consumption of both retirees and workers in a given year must come out of that year's production, so the only way to help finance future retirees' consumption is to increase future output. The only way to increase future output is to increase saving, which leads to the question of whether privatization would increase national saving. To think about this issue, note that the government has to finance its spending one way or another. Currently, part of the financing for the budget comes from borrowing money from the surplus in the trust fund. That is, the trust fund buys bonds, which are the same as loans to the government in exchange for payment with interest in future years. If personal accounts reduce the amount of money in the trust fund, the government still has to find money to finance its spending and therefore has to sell its bonds to private investors. In order to induce private investors to accept government bonds that would have been bought by the trust fund, their yield has to go up, or the yield on stocks must fall, or both. At the end of the day, all that takes place is a swap of public and private securities between the trust fund and private markets—privatization creates no new saving.

Some economists argue that this line of reasoning ignores important political economy considerations. They believe that when the realities of the budgetary process are taken into account, privatization probably would increase national saving. The key to this argument is that Social Security surpluses are included in the government's unified budget. Taking the Social Security surpluses away from the government and putting them in personal accounts would therefore lead to a larger deficit in the unified budget. To the extent that policymakers base their spending decisions on the size of the unified budget, they would reduce public spending, which would increase national saving, other things being the same. In effect, according to this view, private accounts "wall off" funds from the rest of government, reducing the ability of the government to borrow this money to finance expenditures. In fact, there is some evidence that, in the past, Social Security surpluses have led to increased government spending, so this view is not implausible [Nataraj and Shoven, 2004]. However, it is not clear whether the impact would be quantitatively significant.

Because increasing national saving is the key to providing the wherewithal to support future retirees, some privatization plans include provisions that require the money diverted from the payroll tax into the private account (known as a **carve out**) to be matched by an additional contribution out of the worker's pocket (known as an **add on**). For example, Liebman et al. [2005] propose the establishment of personal retirement accounts that would be funded by annual contributions equal to 3 percent of taxable earnings, ultimately half financed from payroll taxes and half from additional contributions from workers. Their argument is that out-of-pocket contributions are likely to be, at least in part, new saving, and that this new saving would lead to long-run increases in the capital stock and future output.

carve-out accounts

Personal accounts that are funded by diverting payroll tax revenues away from the traditional Social Security system.

add-on accounts

Personal accounts that are funded from workers' resources rather than by diverting money from the payroll tax.

Risk   As discussed earlier, most privatization plans would require that future benefits from traditional Social Security be reduced for every dollar diverted into one's personal account. Advocates of privatization argue that personal accounts will improve the benefits to recipients, because the money diverted into the accounts can be invested in stocks, which historically have earned a higher return than the implicit return from Social Security. However, these higher expected returns come at the price of higher risk. The crash in global stock markets in 2008 and 2009 vividly demonstrated that stocks can go down as well as up. Thus, one drawback of privatization is that it would expose individuals to more financial risk. In response, proponents of personal accounts argue that investing in diversified portfolios allows people to bring down risk to manageable levels. Indeed, some privatization proposals specifically require that personal accounts be invested in only a few broad-based mutual funds, guaranteeing a highly diversified portfolio.

Privatization proponents also argue that the apparent certitude of the status quo is illusory—individuals face the possibility that future legislators, confronting the inexorable consequences of Equation (11.3), will reduce retirement benefits. In fact, a number of countries, including the United States, have already made changes in their systems whose effect is to reduce benefits available to the current generation of young and middle-aged workers when they retire [Shoven and Slavov, 2006]. In effect, proponents of privatization turn the risk argument on its head—by reducing political risk, privatization leads to a safer, not a riskier, system.

Administration   No pension system can be administered for free. It costs money to hire people to collect funds, keep records, manage assets, calculate benefits, and so on. Some fear that such costs would be very high under privatization. A natural way to get a sense of whether this would be a problem is to examine the costs of institutions that currently offer retirement savings accounts or provide income to retirees. The result, not too surprisingly, is that the costs depend a lot on the details of the system. The more choices and services that are available to investors, the greater are the administrative costs. For example, the more often people can change their investments, the more expensive the program. Plans can cut administrative costs by restricting how often people can reallocate their assets, but at the cost of reducing flexibility. Administrative costs can also be kept down by restricting the choice of assets and by reducing the reporting information to investors, again at the expense of reducing flexibility. The key point is that with reasonable compromises regarding the services it provides, it appears that a privatized system can be administered at a relatively modest cost [Congressional Budget Office, 2004a].

Distribution   As already noted, although Social Security is called insurance, one of its important objectives is to redistribute income. The current system really has two distinct goals: to force individuals to insure themselves by reallocating income from their working years to their retirement years, and to distribute income to those elderly citizens who would otherwise lack an adequate level of support. Many of the problems with Social Security stem from the fact that it attempts to meet both objectives through a single structure of benefits and taxes.

Many privatization plans deal with these two objectives separately. The retirement finance objective is largely handled by the accumulations in individuals' personal accounts. Personal accounts generally do not lead to any redistribution, since each retiree receives payments based on how much was placed in the account and the rate of return earned. However, if one desired to accomplish some redistribution via the personal accounts, then the government could provide special matching funds for money placed in the accounts by low-income people [Feldstein and Samwick, 2002].

The redistribution objective can also be dealt with by a separate system of transfers to those whose personal accounts would not provide a level of support considered adequate by society. Supplemental Security Income (discussed in Chapter 13), which is funded out of general revenues, is a mechanism already in place for making such transfers. Presumably, it could be expanded to allow for as much redistribution to the elderly poor as society desired.

An important consequence of privatization is that family status would not have a major effect on the value of a person's Social Security wealth. If a one-earner couple and a two-earner couple paid the same amount into the same fund, they would receive the same benefits. The problem of supporting nonworking spouses could be dealt with by crediting each spouse with half of the total contributions made by the couple. In this way, even if divorce occurred, each spouse would carry a given balance on which retirement payments would be based.

Of course, general financing of the transfer part of Social Security would require it to compete openly with other government priorities. Policymakers and the public would have to determine explicitly the value of transfers to the elderly relative to other social objectives. Opponents of privatization argue that this would ultimately undermine the entire program [Munnell, 1999], but proponents disagree.

▶ CONCLUSIONS

Social Security is our largest single domestic spending program. From the standpoint of welfare economics, its main purpose is to provide insurance against the risk of outliving one's retirement savings. The program has likely significantly improved the living standards of the elderly. Nonetheless, it has also undoubtedly had unintended consequences. It is hard to imagine, for example, that the founders of Social Security really wanted to generate huge income redistributions based on marital status or on the number of earners in a family. The evidence also suggests that Social Security has reduced national savings, which hinders productivity growth.

Social Security currently faces financial problems because the ratio of retirees to workers is growing—the graying of America. Addressing this problem will require cutting benefits or increasing taxes, neither of which is politically popular. Such changes are particularly difficult because the current system, which dates back to the 1930s, has become almost sacrosanct. But the demographic trends are relentless, so policymakers have no choice but to confront the system's problems sooner or later. Hence, we can expect a lively debate to continue in the years to come.

Summary

- Social Security is the largest US domestic program. In 2007, Social Security expenditures were approximately $594.5 billion, about 4.3 percent of Gross Domestic Product.

- Social Security provides insurance against outliving one's retirement savings. In this way, it works as an annuity and improves welfare by helping people smooth their consumption.

- One justification for Social Security is that private annuity markets fail because of adverse selection. Another justification is that people lack foresight and save less than society deems appropriate.

- Social Security is largely a pay-as-you-go pension system in which an individual's benefits are paid out of the earnings of current workers. In contrast, in a fully funded pension system an individual's benefits are paid out of deposits that have been made during his or her working life, plus accumulated interest.

- Social Security benefits are calculated in two steps. Average indexed monthly earnings (AIME) are derived from the worker's earnings history and determine the primary insurance amount (PIA). To compute actual benefits, the PIA is adjusted by an amount depending on retirement age, family status, and other earnings.

- Social Security is financed by a payroll tax of 12.4 percent (up to earnings of $102,000), half of which is levied on employers and half on employees.

- Broadly speaking, Social Security redistributes incomes from high- to low-income individuals, from men to women, and from young to old. One-earner married couples tend to gain relative to either two-earner couples or single individuals.

- Currently, Social Security annual tax revenue exceeds annual benefit payments, with the difference going into the trust fund. The trust fund is essentially an accounting device, and by itself does not enhance society's ability to care for retirees in the future.

- Over time, the economic status of the elderly has improved. The evidence suggests that Social Security benefits have played an important role in this development.

- Social Security may reduce private saving due to the wealth substitution effect, or it may increase saving due to either the retirement effect or the bequest effect. A reasonable conclusion on the basis of the econometric results is that saving has been reduced, but by how much is not clear.

- The percentage of retired older workers has increased dramatically since the introduction of Social Security. There is some evidence that this is due in part to the Social Security system.

- Social Security taxes are projected to fall short of benefits starting about 2017. The shortfall is expected to continue indefinitely, which means that Social Security is financially unstable.

- One possible response to the financial problem is to maintain the current system, but to enact some combination of tax increases and benefit reductions in order to obtain solvency.

- Another possible response is to privatize the system—allow individuals to invest some or all of their Social Security contributions into a personal account. The impact of privatization on solvency depends on how much future benefits are reduced for each dollar redirected into a personal account.

- In order to help ease the burden of providing for the elderly in the future, a reform plan would have to lead to an increase in saving. Whether privatization would increase saving depends on the structure of the specific plan.

Discussion Questions

1. In a test for asymmetric information in the French auto insurance market, Chiappori and Salanié [2000] look at the relationship between the comprehensiveness of an individual's policy and the cost per unit coverage. Their argument is that, in the presence of asymmetric information, the more comprehensive the coverage, the greater the cost per franc of coverage. Explain the reasoning behind this argument. (By the way, they find no evidence for asymmetric information on this basis.)

2. As part of his privatization plan to reform Social Security, Nobel laureate Edward Prescott advocated that personal accounts be made mandatory in order to prevent rational individuals from deliberately undersaving [Prescott, 2004a].

Explain how moral hazard could lead people to undersave if Social Security were replaced with voluntary personal accounts.

3. In 1990, the ratio of people age 65 or older to people ages 20 to 64 in the United Kingdom was 26.7 percent. In the year 2050, this ratio is expected to be 45.8 percent. Assuming a pay-as-you-go social security system, what change in the payroll tax rate between 1990 and 2050 would be needed to maintain the 1990 ratio of benefits to wages? If the tax rate were kept constant, what would happen to the ratio of benefits to wages?

4. Does Social Security tend to benefit younger or older generations more, and why? Answer the same questions for men versus women, high-income versus low-income individuals, and two-earner versus one-earner married couples.

5. In her novel *Sense and Sensibility*, Jane Austen wrote, "If you observe, people always live forever when there is any annuity to be paid them." Relate this quotation to the issue of adverse selection in annuity markets.

6. The discussion surrounding Equation (11.1) noted that problems can arise in maintaining the same replacement ratio in a population in which the dependency ratio is growing. Suppose that instead of keeping the replacement ratio constant over time, the goal of public policy is to maintain a constant level of benefits. Explain how this changes one's views of the consequences of an increasing dependency ratio, especially if wages are increasing over time due to productivity gains.

7. Discuss: "Over the long term, the rate of return to stocks is greater than the rate of return to government bonds. Therefore, it would be easier to care for future retirees if the Social Security trust fund were invested in stocks rather than government bonds."

8. Consider a model in which an individual lives only two periods. The individual has diminishing marginal utility of consumption and receives an income of $20,000 in period 1 and an income of $5,000 in period 2. The private interest rate is 10 percent per period, and the person can borrow or lend money at this rate.

Assume also that the person intends to consume all of his income over his lifetime (that is, he won't leave any money for his heirs).

a. If there is no Social Security program, what is the individual's optimal consumption in each period?

b. Now assume there is a Social Security program that takes $3,000 from the individual in the first period and pays him this amount with interest in the second period. What is the impact of this system on the person's saving?

9. Figure 11.5 assumed that the implicit rate of return from Social Security was the same as the private rate of return available to Bingley from private savings. Assume now that Social Security has a lower implicit rate of return than the private return. How would the introduction of this Social Security system affect the budget constraint in Figure 11.5? What do you expect to happen to the amount Bingley saves?

10. It has been argued that the scheme for financing Social Security is unfair because people with low earnings are taxed at a higher rate than individuals with high earnings. Explain the basis for this contention. Opponents of this view argue that looking at the tax system by itself is misleading—when viewed as part of a tax-transfer system, Social Security gives proportionately larger increases to low-income individuals. Explain the basis for this contention as well.

11. Under one plan for Social Security reform, younger workers would be able to divert up to $1,000 of their payroll taxes into an individual account. However, this diversion of funds would be in exchange for lower defined benefits when they retire. The reduction in defined benefits would equal the amount diverted into the individual account, compounded at a given interest rate (known as the offset rate). Using the pay-as-you-go formula, explain the impact of this plan on Social Security solvency. What would the offset rate need to be in order for this plan to have no effect on solvency? What is the relationship between the offset rate chosen and the expected money's worth ratio for the younger workers?

Chapter Twelve

INCOME REDISTRIBUTION: CONCEPTUAL ISSUES

> *A decent provision for the poor is the true test of civilization.*
>
> —SAMUEL JOHNSON

"In general, the art of government consists in taking as much money as possible from one class of citizens to give to the other." While Voltaire's assertion is an overstatement, it is true that virtually every important political issue involves the distribution of income. Even when they are not explicit, questions of who will gain and who will lose lurk in the background of public policy debates. This chapter presents a framework for thinking about the normative and positive aspects of government redistribution policy. Chapter 13 then uses this framework to analyze major government programs for maintaining the incomes of the poor.

Before proceeding, we must discuss whether economists should consider distributional issues at all. Not everyone thinks so. Notions concerning the "right" income distribution are value judgments, and there is no "scientific" way to resolve differences on ethical matters. Therefore, some argue that discussing distributional issues is detrimental to objectivity in economics and economists should restrict themselves to analyzing only the efficiency aspects of social issues.

This view has two problems. First, as emphasized in Chapter 3, the theory of welfare economics indicates that efficiency by itself is an inadequate normative standard. Criteria other than efficiency must be considered when comparing alternative allocations of resources. Of course, one can assert that only efficiency matters, but this in itself is a value judgment.

Second, decision makers care about the distributional implications of policy. If economists ignore distribution, then policymakers will ignore economists. Policymakers may then end up focusing only on distributional issues and pay no attention at all to efficiency. The economist who systematically takes distribution into account can keep policymakers aware of both efficiency and distributional issues. Although training in economics certainly does not confer a superior ability to make ethical judgments, economists *are* skilled at drawing out the implications of alternative sets of values and measuring the costs of achieving various ethical goals.

A related question is whether government ought to be involved in changing the income distribution. As noted in Chapter 1, some important traditions of political philosophy suggest that government should play no redistributive role. However, even the most minimal government conceivable influences the income distribution. For example, when the government purchases materials for public goods, some firms receive contracts and others do not; presumably the owners of the firms receiving the contracts enjoy increases in their relative incomes. More generally, the government's taxing and spending activities are bound to change the distribution of real income.

▶ DISTRIBUTION OF INCOME

We begin by examining some information on the present distribution of income. Table 12.1 shows Census Bureau data on the US income distribution for selected years since the late 1960s. The table suggests the presence of a lot of inequality. In 2007, the richest fifth of the population received about 50 percent of total income, while the share of the poorest fifth was less than 4 percent. The table also suggests that inequality has increased over time. The share of income going to the poorest two-fifths of families is lower now than it was several decades ago. Interestingly, the increase in inequality has not been confined to the United States. It has occurred in all developed countries, although to a lesser degree [Glaeser, 2005].

Another way to assess the income distribution is to compute the number of people below the **poverty line,** a fixed level of real income considered enough to provide a minimally adequate standard of living.[1] While there is considerable arbitrariness in determining what is adequate, the notion of a poverty line still provides a useful benchmark. The poverty line for a family of four in 2007 was $21,200. During the same year, the median income—the level at which half the households were above and

poverty line

A fixed level of real income considered enough to provide a minimally adequate standard of living.

Table 12.1 **The Distribution of Money Income Among Households**
(*selected years*)

	Percentage Share					
Year	Lowest Fifth	Second Fifth	Middle Fifth	Fourth Fifth	Highest Fifth	Top 5 Percent
1967	4.0	10.8	17.3	24.2	43.6	17.2
1977	4.2	10.2	16.9	24.7	44.0	16.8
1982	4.0	10.0	16.5	24.5	45.0	17.0
1987	3.8	9.6	16.1	24.3	46.2	18.2
1992	3.8	9.4	15.8	24.2	46.9	18.6
1997	3.6	8.9	15.0	23.2	49.4	21.7
2002	3.5	8.8	14.8	23.3	49.7	21.7
2007	3.4	8.7	14.8	23.4	49.7	21.2

Source: US Bureau of the Census [2008b, Table H-2].

Note: These figures do not include the value of in-kind transfers.

Income inequality has increased over time. In 1967, the richest fifth of the population received 43.6 percent of total income, and the poorest fifth received 4.0 percent of total income. In 2007, the richest fifth of the population received 49.7 percent of total income, and the poorest fifth only 3.4 percent of the total.

---

[1] To compute the poverty line, the first step is to estimate the minimum cost of a diet that meets adequate nutritional standards. The second step is to find the proportion of income spent on food in families of different sizes. The poverty line is then found by multiplying the reciprocal of this proportion by the cost of the "adequate" diet.

Table 12.2   **Who is Poor?**

Group	Poverty Rate	Group	Poverty Rate
All persons	12.5%	Under 18 years	18.0%
White	8.2	65 years and older	9.7
Black	24.5	Female households,	
Hispanic origin	21.5	no husband present	28.3

Source: US Bureau of the Census [2008a].

Note: Figures are for 2007.

Poverty rates differ substantially across demographic groups.

half below—was $50,233. In 2007, 37.3 million people were below the poverty line, 12.5 percent of the population [US Bureau of the Census, 2009].

Table 12.2 shows the proportion of people below the poverty line for various demographic groups. Poverty is particularly widespread among female-headed households in which no husband is present—28.3 percent of such families are below the poverty line. Blacks and individuals of Hispanic origin also have poverty rates substantially above that for the population as a whole.

Figure 12.1 depicts changes in the poverty rate over time. The figures suggest that the incidence of poverty in the United States is considerably lower now than it was half a century ago. However, the trend has not been steadily downward.

The question of why there are large disparities in income has long occupied a central place in economics and is far from definitively settled.[2] In the United States and other Western countries, the most important reason for inequality in family incomes is differences in the earnings of family heads. Differences in property income (interest, dividends, etc.) account for only a small portion of income inequality. While very important, this observation does not really explain income inequality—one must still account for the large differences in earnings. Earned income depends on items as diverse as physical strength, intelligence, effort, health, education, marriage decisions, the existence of race and sex discrimination, the presence of public welfare programs, and luck. Many economists believe that the key factor driving the increase in inequality in recent years is an increase in the financial returns to education—because of changes in technology such as the widespread introduction of computers into the workplace, workers with college educations are now earning relatively more than their low-education counterparts. But no single item can account for every case of poverty. As we see later, this fact has bedeviled attempts to formulate sensible policies for redistributing income.

Interpreting the Distributional Data

The US Census data on the income distribution and the poverty rate receive an enormous amount of public discussion. It is therefore important to know the conventions used to construct these figures and their limitations.

Census Income Consists Only of the Family's Cash Receipts   A person's income during a given period is the sum of the amount consumed during that period

---

[2] Hoynes et al. [2006] investigate the various determinants of the income distribution.

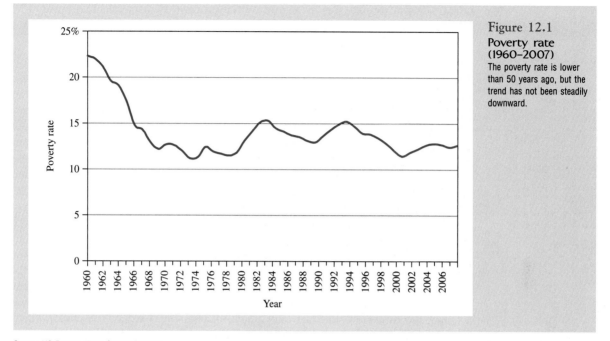

Figure 12.1
**Poverty rate
(1960–2007)**
The poverty rate is lower
than 50 years ago, but the
trend has not been steadily
downward.

Source: US Bureau of the Census [2008a].

and the amount saved. (A more detailed discussion of the definition of income is included in Chapter 17.) A family's income consists not only of the cash it receives but also **in-kind transfers**—payments in commodities or services as opposed to cash. The official definition's omission of in-kind income can lead to misleading estimates of the poverty rate. Imagine, for example, that your community provided poor people with vouchers that allowed them to live in the best hotel and eat in the fanciest restaurant in town. The official poverty rate would not change at all. While the government does not provide luxuries to the poor, it does provide food stamps, low-income housing programs, and subsidized medical care. According to the US Bureau of the Census [2007], including various noncash benefits from the government would reduce the official poverty rate from 12.5 percent to 10.3 percent.

> **in-kind transfer**
>
> **Payments from the government to individuals in the form of commodities or services rather than cash.**

One major form of in-kind income is the value of time adults devote to their households. The official data miss important differences in the levels of economic resources available to single-parent versus two-parent families and between two-parent families with both parents working versus those with one parent at home. In-kind income is also provided by durable goods. The most important example is a house, which provides its owner with a flow of housing services. The value of these services is the cost to the homeowner of renting a comparable dwelling. Thus, if a family owns a home that could rent for $5,000 per year, then this $5,000 should be included in its income. This observation is cogent given that more than 48 percent of households with incomes below $15,000 are homeowners.

Census Income Ignores Taxes All of the income data are *before* tax. Hence, the fact that the income tax system takes a larger share of income from high- than from low-income families is not reflected in the numbers. One of the most important programs for redistributing income to the poor, the earned income tax credit

(EITC), is run through the income tax. (The program is discussed in Chapter 13.) The EITC transfers over $39 billion annually to low-income families; these transfers are ignored in the poverty statistics.

Census Income Is Measured Annually   The concept of income makes sense only if it is measured over some time period. But it is not obvious what the time frame should be. A daily or weekly measure would be absurd, because even rich people could have zero incomes during some short period. It makes much more sense to measure the flow of income over a year, as the official figures do. However, even annual measures may not reflect a person's true economic position. After all, income can fluctuate substantially from year to year. From a theoretical point of view, lifetime income would be ideal, but the practical problems in estimating it are enormous.

Although distinguishing between different time periods may seem a mere academic quibble, it is really quite important. People tend to have low incomes when they are young, more when they are middle-aged, and less again when they are old and in retirement. Therefore, people who have *identical* lifetime incomes but are in different stages of the life cycle can show up in the annual data as having *unequal* incomes. Measures based on annual income, such as those in Tables 12.1 and 12.2, suggest more inequality than those constructed on the more appropriate lifetime basis. Using a longer-run measure of welfare than annual income could reduce the proportion of households in poverty by 3 or 4 percentage points [Jorgenson, 1998].

Consumption Data May Provide a Better Assessment of Well-Being   The official poverty rate and distribution data are all based on income. Some have argued that consumption-based measures are superior conceptually, because people's utility depends on consumption rather than income [Eberstadt, 2005]. Income and consumption need not move together. In years when income is temporarily low, for example, families can maintain their consumption level by dipping into their savings. Further, particularly at the low end of the distribution, income may come from sources, such as transfers from friends and family, which are hard to pick up in government surveys.

The issue is more than academic, because trends in consumption and income have differed historically. Consider, for example, Meyer and Sullivan's [2007] examination of the economic status of families headed by single mothers in the 1990s. They find that income dropped by about 15 percent for those who were in the lowest one-fifth of the income distribution and rose by about 15 percent for those in the highest one-fifth of the income distribution, suggesting that inequality increased. However, the trends in consumption showed a 5 percent *increase* for the bottom one-fifth of the income distribution, the same as for the top one-fifth.

It Is Unclear How to Define the Unit of Observation   Most people live with others, and at least to some extent make their economic decisions jointly. Should income distribution be measured over individuals or households? If economies are achieved by living together, should they be taken into account in computing an individual's income? For example, are the members of a two-person household with total income of $30,000 as well off as a single individual with $15,000? Although two may not be able to live as cheaply as one, they may be able to live as cheaply as 1.5. If so, the members of the couple are better off in real terms. But finding just the right adjustment factor is not easy. In this context, note from Table 12.2 that one of the categories is "female households, no husband present." However, according to Bauman's [1999] calculations, including the incomes of household members who are not legally members of a family (such as nonmarried cohabitors) would reclassify out of poverty about 55 percent of the people who are poor according to the official definition.

A related problem crops up when household structure changes over time. Consider what happens when increases in income allow a grandparent to move into an apartment of his or her own instead of sharing quarters with adult children. This creates a new economic unit, with a fairly low level of income. As measured by the official statistics, things have gotten worse—average income falls and economic inequality rises. But presumably the new living arrangements are making all the individuals involved better off.

We conclude that while the standard measures of income distribution and poverty levels provide some useful information, they should be interpreted cautiously. This is particularly true when making comparisons over time.

▶ RATIONALES FOR INCOME REDISTRIBUTION

While income is doubtless distributed unequally, people disagree about whether the government should undertake redistributional policies. This section discusses different views on this matter.

Simple Utilitarianism

Conventional welfare economics posits that society's welfare depends on the well-being of its members. Algebraically, if there are n individuals in society and the ith individual's utility is U_i, then social welfare, W, is some function $F(\cdot)$ of individuals' utilities:[3]

$$W = F(U_1, U_2, \ldots, U_n) \qquad (12.1)$$

Equation (12.1) is sometimes referred to as a **utilitarian social welfare function** because of its association with the utilitarian social philosophers of the 19th century.[4] It is assumed that an increase in any of the U_is, other things being the same, increases W. A change that makes someone better off without making anyone worse off increases social welfare.

utilitarian social welfare function

An equation stating that social welfare depends on individuals' utilities.

What does utilitarianism say about whether the government should redistribute income? The answer is straightforward but not terribly informative—redistribute income provided that it increases W. To obtain more specific guidance, let's consider an important special case of Equation (12.1):

$$W = U_1 + U_2 + \ldots + U_n \qquad (12.2)$$

Here social welfare is simply the sum of individuals' utilities. This is referred to as an **additive social welfare function.**

additive social welfare function

An equation defining social welfare as the sum of individuals' utilities.

---

[3] This discussion ignores the problems that arise if the members of society cannot agree on a social welfare function. See Chapter 6 under "Direct Democracy."

[4] Actually, the utilitarians postulated that social welfare was the sum of utilities, Equation (12.2), but the label is now often used to describe the more general formulation of Equation (12.1).

Suppose that the government's goal is to maximize the value of W given in Equation (12.2). This social welfare function, together with a few assumptions, allows us to obtain strong results. Assume:

1. Individuals have identical utility functions that depend only on their incomes.
2. These utility functions exhibit diminishing marginal utility of income—as individuals' incomes increase, they become better off, but at a decreasing rate.
3. The total amount of income available is fixed.

With these assumptions and an additive social welfare function, the government should redistribute income so as to obtain *complete equality*.

To prove this, assume that the society consists of only two people, Peter and Paul. (It is easy to generalize the argument to cases where there are more people.) In Figure 12.2, the horizontal distance OO' measures the total amount of income available in society. Paul's income is measured by the distance to the right of point O; Peter's income is measured by the distance to the left of point O'. Thus, any point along OO' represents some distribution of income between Paul and Peter. The problem is to find the "best" point.

Paul's marginal utility of income is measured vertically, beginning at point O. Following assumption 2, the schedule relating Paul's marginal utility of income to his level of income slopes downward. It is labeled MU_{Paul}. Peter's marginal utility of income is measured vertically, beginning at point O'. His marginal utility of income schedule is denoted MU_{Peter}. (Remember that movements to the left on the horizontal axis represent *increases* in Peter's income.) Because Peter and Paul have identical utility functions, MU_{Peter} is a mirror image of MU_{Paul}.

Assume that initially Paul's income is Oa and Peter's is $O'a$. Is social welfare as high as possible, or could the sum of utilities be increased if income were somehow redistributed between Paul and Peter? Suppose that ab dollars are taken from

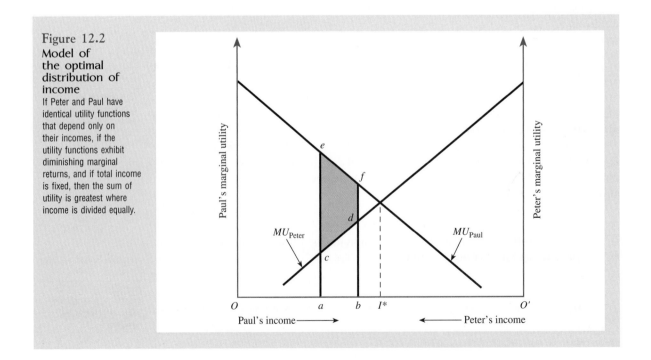

Figure 12.2
Model of the optimal distribution of income
If Peter and Paul have identical utility functions that depend only on their incomes, if the utility functions exhibit diminishing marginal returns, and if total income is fixed, then the sum of utility is greatest where income is divided equally.

Peter and given to Paul. Obviously, this makes Peter worse off and Paul better off. However, the crucial question is what happens to the *sum* of their utilities. Because Peter is richer than Paul, Peter's loss in utility is smaller than Paul's gain, so the sum of their utilities goes up. Geometrically, the area under each person's marginal utility of income schedule measures the change in his utility induced by the income change. Distributing *ab* dollars to Paul increases his utility by area *abfe*. Taking the *ab* dollars from Peter decreases his utility by area *abdc*. The sum of their utilities therefore increases by shaded area *cefd*.

Similar reasoning suggests that as long as incomes are unequal, marginal utilities are unequal, and the *sum* of utilities can be increased by distributing income to the poorer individual. Only at point *I**, where incomes and marginal utilities are equal, is social welfare maximized. Full income equality should be pursued.

The policy implications of this result are breathtaking, so the assumptions behind it require scrutiny.

Assumption 1   It is fundamentally impossible to determine whether individuals have identical utility functions. We simply cannot know whether individuals derive the same amount of satisfaction from the consumption of goods, because satisfaction cannot be objectively measured. There are, however, two possible defenses for the assumption.

First, although it cannot be *proved* that people derive the same utility from equal amounts of income, it is a reasonable guess. After all, if people generally do not vary wildly in their observable characteristics—weight, height, and so on—why should their utility functions differ? Further, as Nobel prize winner Amartya Sen [1999, p. 358] argued, "It is difficult to see how people can understand anything much about other people's minds and feelings, without making some comparisons with their own minds and feelings. Such comparisons may not be extremely precise, but . . . very precise interpersonal comparisons may not be needed to make systematic use of interpersonal comparisons."

Second, one can interpret the assumption not as a psychological statement, but as an *ethical* one. Specifically, in designing a redistributional policy, government ought to act *as if* all people have the same utility functions, whether they do or not.

Clearly, neither of these defenses would convince a skeptic, and the assumption remains troublesome.

Assumption 2   A more technical, but equally important, objection concerns the assumption of decreasing marginal utility of income. Although the marginal utility of any given *good* may decrease with its consumption, it is not clear that this is true for *income* as a whole. In Figure 12.2, the results change drastically if the marginal utility of income schedules fail to slope down. Suppose the marginal utility of income is instead constant at all levels of income. Then MU_{Peter} and MU_{Paul} are represented by an identical horizontal line. Whenever a dollar is taken from Peter, the loss in his utility is exactly equal to Paul's gain. Thus, the value of the sum of their utilities is independent of the income distribution. Government redistributive policy cannot change social welfare.

Assumption 3   This assumption means that the total amount of income in the society, distance OO', is fixed. The size of the pie does not change as the government redistributes its pieces. Suppose, however, that individuals' utilities depend not only on income but also on leisure. Each individual chooses how much leisure to surrender (how much to work) to maximize his or her utility. The taxes and subsidies enacted to redistribute income generally change people's work decisions and diminish total real income. Thus, a society whose goal is to maximize the sum of utilities faces an inescapable dilemma. On one hand, it prefers to equalize the distribution of income. However, in doing so, it reduces the total amount of income available. The optimal income distribution must take into account the costs (in lost real income) of achieving more equality. Some studies suggest these costs may be substantial. Cushing and McGarvey [2003] analyzed a hypothetical program of cash transfers from high- to low-income individuals, and estimated that the welfare losses for those who lose from the policy are from 1.11 to 10.97 times greater than the gains to the beneficiaries. However, research on this topic is still at a formative stage.

Thus, even the assumption of identical utility functions is not enough to guarantee that the goal of government distributional policy should be complete equality. The answer depends on the methods used to redistribute income and their effects on people's behavior.

The Maximin Criterion

In the utilitarian framework, the form of the social welfare function plays a crucial role in determining the appropriate governmental redistribution policy. So far, we have examined the simple additive social welfare function of Equation (12.2), according to which society is indifferent to the distribution of utilities. If a unit of utility (or "util") is taken away from one individual and given to another, the sum of utilities is unchanged, and by definition, so is social welfare.

Other utilitarian social welfare functions do not carry this implication, and hence yield different policy prescriptions. Consider the following social welfare function:

$$W = \text{Minimum}(U_1, U_2, \ldots, U_n) \tag{12.3}$$

maximin criterion

Social welfare depends on the utility of the individual who has the minimum utility in the society.

According to Equation (12.3), social welfare depends only on the utility of the person who has the lowest utility. This social objective is often called the **maximin criterion** because the objective is to maximize the utility of the person with the minimum utility. The maximin criterion implies that the income distribution should be perfectly equal, *except* to the extent that departures from equality increase the welfare of the worst-off person. Consider a society with a rich person, Peter, who employs a poor person, Paul. The government levies a tax on Peter, and distributes the proceeds to Paul. However, when Peter is taxed, he cuts production and fires Paul. Moreover, the income that Paul receives from the government is less than his job-related income loss. In this hypothetical economy, satisfaction of the maximin criterion would still allow for income disparities.

original position

An imaginary situation in which people have no knowledge of what their economic status in society will be.

The maximin criterion has received considerable attention, principally because of philosopher John Rawls's [1971] assertion that it has a special claim to ethical validity. Rawls's argument relies on his notion of the **original position,** an imaginary situation in which people have no knowledge of what their place in society is to be. Because people are ignorant of whether they will ultimately be rich or poor, Rawls believes that in the original position, everyone's opinions of distributional goals are impartial and fair. Rawls then argues that in the original position, people adopt the maximin social welfare function because of the insurance it provides against disastrous outcomes. People are frightened that they may end up at the bottom of the income distribution, and therefore want the level at the bottom as high as possible.

Rawls's analysis is controversial. One important issue is whether decisions that people would make in the original position have any superior claim to ethical validity. Why should individuals' amoral and selfish views in the original position be accorded special moral significance? Further, granted Rawls's view on the ethical validity of the original position, it is not obvious that rational self-interest would lead to the maximin criterion. Rawls's decision makers are so averse to risk that they are unwilling to take any chances. However, people might be willing to accept a small probability of being very poor in return for a good chance of receiving a high income.

Finally, critics have noted that the maximin criterion has some peculiar implications. Feldstein [1976, p. 84] considers the following scenario: "A new opportunity arises to raise the welfare of the least advantaged by a slight amount, but almost everyone else must be made substantially worse off, except for a few individuals who would become extremely wealthy." Because *all* that is relevant is the welfare of the worst-off person, the maximin criterion indicates that society should pursue this opportunity. Intuitively, however, such a course seems unappealing.

Pareto Efficient Income Redistribution

Our discussion of both additive and maximin social welfare functions assumed that redistribution makes some people better off and others worse off. Redistribution was never a Pareto improvement—a change that allowed all individuals to be at least as well off as under the status quo. This is a consequence of the assumption that each individual's utility depends on his or her income only. In contrast, imagine that high-income individuals are altruistic, so their utilities depend not only on their own incomes but those of the poor as well. Under such circumstances, redistribution can actually be a Pareto improvement.

Assume that if (rich) Peter were to give a dollar of income to (poor) Paul, then Peter's increase in satisfaction from doing a good deed would outweigh the loss of his own consumption. At the same time, assume that Paul's utility would increase if he received the dollar. Both individuals would be made better off by the transfer. Indeed, efficiency requires that income be redistributed until Peter's gain in utility from giving a dollar to Paul just equals the loss in Peter's utility caused by lower consumption. Suppose that it is difficult for Peter to bring about the income transfer on his own, perhaps because he lacks enough information to know just who is really poor. Then if the government costlessly does the transfer for Peter, efficiency is enhanced.

In a formal sense, this is just an externality problem. Paul's behavior (his consumption) affects Peter's welfare in a way that is external to the market. As usual in such cases, government may be able to increase efficiency. Pushing this line of reasoning to its logical extreme, one can regard the income distribution as a public good, because everyone's utility is affected by the degree of inequality. Suppose that each person would feel better off if the income distribution were more equal. No individual acting alone, however, is willing to transfer income to the poor. If the government uses its coercive power to force *everyone* who is wealthy to redistribute income to the poor, economic efficiency increases.

Although altruism doubtless plays an important part in human behavior, it does not follow that altruistic motives explain the majority of government income redistribution programs. This argument *assumes* that in the absence of coercion, people will contribute less than an efficient amount to the poor. Some argue, however, that if people really want to give to the poor, they do so—witness the billions of dollars in charitable contributions made each year.

There are other reasons self-interest might favor income redistribution. For one, there is always some chance that through circumstances beyond your control, you will become poor. An income distribution policy is a bit like insurance. When you are well off, you pay "premiums" in the form of tax payments to those who are currently poor. If bad times hit, the "policy" pays off, and you receive relief. The idea that government should provide a safety net is an old one. The 17th-century political philosopher Thomas Hobbes [1963/1651, pp. 303–304] noted, "And whereas many men, by *accident* become unable to maintain themselves by their labour; they ought not to be left to the charity of private persons; but to be provided for, as far forth as the necessities of nature require, by the laws of the Commonwealth" [emphasis added].

In addition, some believe that income distribution programs help purchase social stability. If poor people become *too* poor, they may engage in antisocial activities such as crime and rioting. A Norwegian businessman, commenting on his government's very large redistributional program, said, "It may be costly but there is social peace." The link between social stability and changes in income distribution is not totally clear, however. Some social commentators argue that in the United States, at least, the distribution of income has been of little political importance, perhaps because of an individualist strain in the characters of its citizens [Kristol, 1997].

Nonindividualistic Views

The views of income distribution discussed so far have quite different implications, but they share a utilitarian outlook. In each, social welfare is some function of individuals' utilities, and the properties of the optimal redistribution policy are *derived* from the social welfare function. Some thinkers have approached the problem by specifying what the income distribution should look like independent of individuals' tastes. For example, Plato argued that in a good society the ratio of the richest to the poorest person's income should be at the most four to one. Closely related is the idea that inequality *per se* is undesirable. Suppose, for example, that the incomes of high-income individuals increase without low-income individuals becoming any worse off. Standard utilitarian considerations suggest that this would be a good thing for society, while those who are averse to inequality would consider it a bad thing. Many in the latter group believe that, as a first principle, incomes should be distributed equally.[5]

commodity egalitarianism

The idea that some commodities ought to be made available to everybody.

A less extreme proposal is that only special commodities should be distributed equally, a position sometimes called **commodity egalitarianism.** In some cases, this view has considerable appeal. Most people believe that the right to vote should be distributed equally to all, as should the consumption of certain essential foodstuffs during times of war. Other types of commodity egalitarianism are more controversial. Should all American children consume the same quality of primary school education, or should some families be allowed to purchase more? Should everyone receive the same type of health care? Clearly, limiting the range of the "special" commodities is a difficult problem.

Interestingly, a position that bears at least a close resemblance to commodity egalitarianism can be rationalized on the basis of conventional welfare economics. Assume that Henry cares about Catherine's welfare. Specifically, Henry's utility depends on his own income as well as Catherine's level of *food consumption*, as

---

[5] This view is considerably stronger than that of Rawls, who allows inequality as long as it raises the welfare of the worst-off individual.

opposed to her *income*. (This might be due to the fact that Henry does not approve of the other commodities Catherine might consume.) In effect, then, Catherine's food consumption generates a positive externality. Following the logic developed in Chapter 5, efficiency may be enhanced if Catherine's food consumption is subsidized, or perhaps if food is provided to her directly. In short, when donors care about recipients' consumption of certain commodities, a policy of redistributing income via these commodities can be viewed as an attempt to correct an externality.

Other Considerations

Processes versus Outcomes   The positions discussed earlier take for granted that individuals' incomes are common property that can be redistributed as "society" sees fit. No attention is given to the fairness of either the processes by which the initial income distribution is determined or of the procedures used to redistribute it. In contrast, some argue that a just distribution of income is defined by the *process* that generated it. For example, a popular belief in the United States is that if "equal opportunity" (somehow defined) were available to all, then the ensuing outcome would be fair, *regardless* of the particular income distribution it happened to entail. Hence, if the process generating income is fair, there is no scope for government-sponsored income redistribution.

Arguing along these lines, the philosopher Robert Nozick [1974] has attacked the use of utilitarian principles to justify changes in the distribution of income. He argues that how "society" should redistribute its income is a meaningless question because "society" per se has no income to distribute. Only *people* receive income, and the sole possible justification for government redistributive activity is when the pattern of property holdings is somehow improper. Nozick's approach shifts emphasis from the search for a "good" social welfare function to a "good" set of rules to govern society's operation. The problem is how to evaluate social processes. It is hard to judge a process independent of the results generated. If a "good" set of rules consistently generates outcomes that are undesirable, how can the rules be considered good? That said, some argue that the distribution of income generated by the market does, in fact, accord with conventional notions of justice: "The market does reward hard work, diligence, honesty, thrift, and so on, and this accords well with most concepts of justice. . . . The point . . . is not that the market distribution is totally just but that over a broad range, it is likely to be closer to most people's conception of justice than the alternatives" [Browning, 2002, p. 511].

Mobility   An alternative argument against governmental redistributive policies is that, with sufficient social mobility, the distribution of income is of no particular ethical interest. Suppose that those at the bottom of the income distribution (or their children) will occupy higher rungs on the economic ladder in future years. At the same time, some other people will move down, at least in relative terms. Then, distributional statistics that remain relatively constant over time conceal quite a bit of churning *within* the income distribution. Even if people at the bottom are quite poor, it may not be a major social problem if the people who are there change over time. Interestingly, this notion seems to be consistent with survey information on people's attitudes toward income redistribution. To the extent that they perceive they have a chance to move upward in society, even relatively poor people say that they do not support income redistributive policies [Alesina and La Ferrara, 2005].

There have been several studies of income mobility. According to calculations by Gottschalk and Spolaore [2002], of those who were in the lowest one-fifth of the earnings distribution in 1984, only about 40 percent were there in 1993. There is also some evidence of income mobility across generations. Hertz [2006] found that of the children in households in the bottom one-fifth of income in the late 1960s, nearly 60 percent were in a higher-income category when they were adults in the 1990s. The United States is clearly not a stratified society. On the other hand, there is probably not sufficient mobility to convince utilitarians that income inequality is unimportant.

Corruption   An argument in favor of redistribution is that extreme inequality can lead to the subversion of legal, political, and regulatory institutions. A society cannot flourish economically unless property rights are secure. This is because growth requires investment, and people will not invest if they fear that their property will be taken from them, either by other individuals or by the government. Extreme inequality enters the story because if some people are much richer than others, they may be able to use some of their money to corrupt the courts and the political process so that they can steal from others with impunity. You and Khagram [2004] find a positive correlation between inequality and corruption across countries. Glaeser, Scheinkman, and Shleifer [2003] find some evidence that in countries where the rule of law is relatively weak (such as the transition economies of Eastern Europe), inequality does have a detrimental effect on economic growth.

▶ EXPENDITURE INCIDENCE

We turn now from a discussion of whether the government *ought* to redistribute income to analytical problems in assessing the effects of *actual* government redistributive programs. The impact of expenditure policy on the distribution of real income is referred to as **expenditure incidence.** The government influences income distribution through its taxation as well as its expenditure policies. (We defer a discussion of the tax side to Chapter 14.) Expenditure incidence is difficult to determine for several reasons, which follow.

expenditure incidence

The impact of government expenditures on the distribution of real income.

Relative Price Effects

Suppose that the government decides to subsidize the consumption of low-income housing. How does this affect the distribution of income? A first guess would be that the people who get the subsidy gain and those who pay the taxes lose. If those who pay the taxes have higher incomes than the subsidy recipients, the distribution of income becomes more equal.

Unfortunately, this simple story may be misleading. If the subsidy induces poor people to demand more housing, then the *pre*-subsidy cost of housing may rise. Therefore, the subsidy recipients do not benefit to the full extent of the subsidy; the landlords reap part of the gain. However, on theoretical grounds alone it cannot be determined how much, if at all, housing prices are bid up. As shown in Chapter 14, this depends on the shapes of the supply and demand curves for housing.

A housing subsidy program also affects the incomes of people who supply the inputs used in its construction. Thus, wages of workers in the building trades increase, as do prices of construction materials. If the owners of these inputs are middle and upper class, this will tend to make the distribution less equal.

More generally, any government program sets off a chain of price changes that affects the incomes of people both in their roles as consumers of goods and as suppliers of inputs. A spending program that raises the relative price of a good you consume makes you worse off, other things being the same. Similarly, a program that raises the relative price of a factor you supply makes you better off. The problem is that it is very hard to trace all the price changes generated by a particular policy. As a practical matter, economists usually assume that a given policy benefits only the recipients and the effects of other price changes on income distribution are minor. In many cases, this is probably a good assumption.

Public Goods

Substantial government expenditure is for public goods—goods that may be consumed simultaneously by more than one person. As noted in Chapter 4, the market does not force people to reveal how much they value public goods. But if we do not know how much each family values a public good, how can we determine its impact on the income distribution? The government spent over $650 billion on defense in 2008. How much in dollar terms did this increase the real income of each family? Did each benefit by the same amount? If not, did the poor benefit less than the rich, or vice versa?

It is impossible to answer questions like these definitively. Unfortunately, alternative answers based on equally plausible assumptions have very different implications. Chamberlain and Prante [2007] examined the distributional implications of expenditures on public goods such as defense using two different assumptions: (a) A household's share of the benefit is in proportion to its wealth, and (b) each household receives an equal share of the benefit. Under assumption (a), the top one-fifth of the population receives 27.0 percent of the government's total expenditure on public goods, while under assumption (b) it only receives 17.1 percent of public good expenditures. The results are clearly very sensitive to the assumptions.

Valuing In-Kind Transfers

Over the past several decades, the Agriculture Department has given away more than 3 billion pounds of surplus cheese, butter, and dried milk to poor Americans. The surplus food program is just one example of an in-kind transfer policy. We often think of in-kind transfers as being directed toward lower-income individuals: food stamps, Medicaid, and public housing come to mind. However, middle- and upper-income people also benefit from in-kind transfers. A prominent example is education.

Unlike pure public goods, in-kind transfers are not consumed by everyone. Nevertheless, estimating their value to beneficiaries is difficult. A convenient assumption is that a dollar spent by the government on an in-kind transfer is equivalent to a dollar increase in the recipient's income. Unfortunately, there is no reason to believe in-kind transfers are valued by beneficiaries on a dollar per dollar basis.

To see why, consider Jones, a typical welfare recipient who divides her monthly income of $300 between cheese and "all other goods." The market price of cheese is $2 per pound, and the units of "all other goods" are measured so that the price per unit is $1. In Figure 12.3, Jones's consumption of cheese is measured on the horizontal axis, and her consumption of all other goods on the vertical. Jones's budget constraint is line AB.[6] Assuming Jones maximizes her utility, she consumes bundle E_1, which consists of 260 units of all other goods and 20 pounds of cheese.

---

[6] For details on how to construct budget lines, see the appendix at the end of the book.

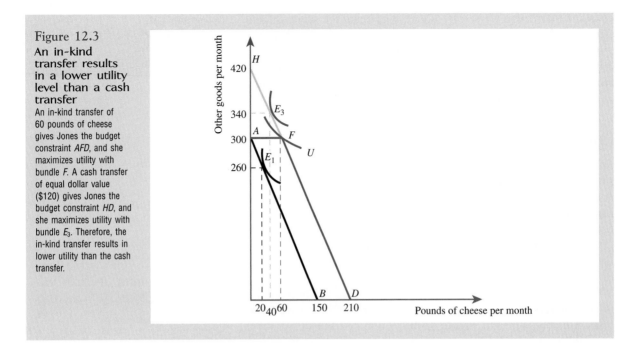

Figure 12.3

An in-kind transfer results in a lower utility level than a cash transfer

An in-kind transfer of 60 pounds of cheese gives Jones the budget constraint *AFD*, and she maximizes utility with bundle *F*. A cash transfer of equal dollar value ($120) gives Jones the budget constraint *HD*, and she maximizes utility with bundle E_3. Therefore, the in-kind transfer results in lower utility than the cash transfer.

Now suppose the government provides Jones with 60 pounds of cheese per month, which she is prohibited from reselling on the market. How does introduction of the cheese program change her situation? At any level of consumption of all other goods, Jones can now consume 60 more pounds of cheese than previously. Geometrically, her new budget constraint is found by moving 60 units to the right of each point on *AB*, yielding *AFD*. The highest indifference curve that she can reach subject to constraint *AFD* is curve *U* in Figure 12.3. It touches the constraint at its "corner"—at point *F*, where Jones's consumption of cheese is 60 and her consumption of all other goods is 300.

Compared to her original consumption bundle, Jones's consumption of both cheese and all other goods has gone up. Because the government provides her with free cheese, Jones can use money that would have been spent on cheese to buy more of all other goods.

Now suppose that instead of giving Jones 60 pounds of cheese, the government gives her cash equal to its market value, $120 (= 60 pounds × $2 per pound). An increase in income of $120 leads to a budget line that is exactly 120 units above *AB* at every point, represented in Figure 12.3 as line *HD*. Note that the cash transfer allows Jones to consume along segment *HF*. This opportunity was not available under the cheese program because Jones was not allowed to trade government cheese for any other goods.

Facing budget line *HD*, Jones maximizes utility at point E_3, where she consumes 340 of all other goods and 40 pounds of cheese. Comparing points E_3 and *F* we can conclude that (1) under the cash transfer program, Jones consumes less cheese and more of all other goods than under the cheese giveaway program; and (2) $120 worth of cheese does *not* make Jones as well off as $120 of income. Because E_3 is on a higher indifference curve than point *F*, the cash transfer makes her *better* off. Intuitively, the problem with the cheese program is that it forces Jones to consume the full 60 pounds of cheese. She would prefer to sell some of the cheese and spend the proceeds on other goods.

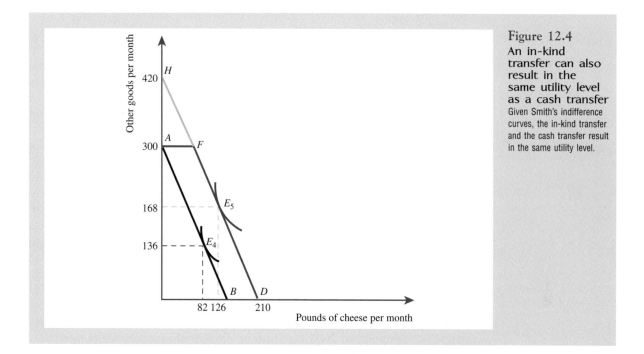

Figure 12.4
An in-kind
transfer can also
result in the
same utility level
as a cash transfer
Given Smith's indifference
curves, the in-kind transfer
and the cash transfer result
in the same utility level.

Is an in-kind transfer always worse than the cash equivalent? Not necessarily. Figure 12.4 depicts the situation of Smith, whose income is identical to Jones's, and who therefore faces exactly the same budget constraints (*AB* before the cheese program and *AFD* afterward). However, Smith has different tastes and thus a different set of indifference curves. Before the subsidy, he maximizes utility at point E_4, consuming 136 units of all other goods and 82 pounds of cheese. After the subsidy, he consumes 168 units of all other goods and 126 pounds of cheese. Smith would not be better off with a cash transfer because his most preferred point along *HD* is available under the cheese subsidy anyway. Because Smith is happy to consume more than 60 pounds of cheese, the restriction that he consume at least 60 pounds does him no harm.

Thus, we cannot know for certain whether an in-kind transfer is valued less than a direct income transfer. Ultimately, the answer has to be found by empirical analysis. For example, one study estimates that a dollar received in food stamps (vouchers that can only be used to purchase food) is worth only about 80 cents received in cash [Whitmore, 2002].

Another problem with in-kind transfer programs is that they often entail substantial administrative costs. In the cheese program just discussed, costs are incurred for storage, transportation, and distribution of the cheese. (The costs are so large that some communities choose not to participate.) Similarly, administrative costs of the food stamp program could be reduced if beneficiaries simply received checks instead of coupons redeemable for food.

Reasons for In-Kind Transfers

As we show in Chapter 13, in-kind transfers involving food, housing, and medical care play an important role in US income maintenance policy. If in-kind transfers are less beneficial than cash from the recipients' point of view *and* entail more administrative costs, how can we account for their presence? There are a number of possible explanations. Several relate to our earlier discussion of normative issues. In particular, commodity egalitarianism may play an important factor in distributional policy. For instance, the US Congress once explicitly set as a national goal "a decent home and a suitable living environment for every American family." Note the distinction between this goal and "enough income so that every American family can live in a decent home, if it chooses."

Moreover, in-kind transfers may also help curb welfare fraud. The discussion so far has assumed there are no problems in identifying who is eligible to receive a transfer and who is not. In reality, this is not the case, and people who do not qualify are sometimes able to obtain benefits. In-kind transfers may discourage ineligible persons from applying because some middle-class people may be quite willing to lie to receive cash, but less willing to lie to obtain a commodity they do not really want. This is especially true if the commodity is difficult to resell, like an apartment in a public housing project. In the same way, creating hassles for welfare recipients (waiting in line, filling out a lot of forms) may discourage those who are not "truly needy" from applying. Thus, there is a trade-off. On one hand, a poor person would prefer $500 in cash to $500 worth of public housing. But if the in-kind program leads to less fraud, more resources can be channeled to people who really need them. However, many would argue that the government has created far more than the optimal number of administrative hurdles for welfare recipients. For example, in 2003 the Bush administration proposed that to receive free school lunches, students would have to provide evidence, such as pay stubs, that their parents' incomes were sufficiently low. Some observers viewed this as an unfair burden on the children.

Finally, in-kind transfers are attractive politically because they help not only the beneficiary but also the producers of the favored commodity. A transfer program that increases the demand for housing benefits the building industry, which therefore is willing to lend its support to a political coalition in favor of the program. Similarly, the agricultural interests have always been avid supporters of food stamps. When the state of Oregon asked permission to convert food stamps into cash for welfare recipients several years ago, the idea was blocked by members of Congress from agricultural states. In the same way, the public employees who administer the various in-kind transfer programs put their political support behind them. For example, bureaucrats in the Department of Housing and Urban Development have traditionally registered vigorous opposition to proposals that subsidized housing be phased out and replaced with cash grants.

These explanations for in-kind transfers are not mutually exclusive, and they probably have all influenced policy design.

▶ CONCLUSION

We have surveyed a wide range of opinions concerning the desirability of explicit governmental policies to redistribute income. The views run the gamut from engineering complete equality to doing nothing. The scope of disagreement is not surprising. Setting a distributional objective is no less than formalizing one's views of what a good society should look like, and this is bound to be controversial. Theories on the optimal income distribution are normative rather than positive. As we will see in Chapter 13, it is not clear whether any coherent normative theory is consistent with actual US income distribution practices.

Summary

- Measuring the extent of poverty is difficult to do. Problems with the government's official poverty figures include (a) they count only cash receipts; (b) they ignore taxes; (c) they are based on annual income measures; (d) they ignore changes in household composition.

- If (1) social welfare is the sum of identical utility functions that depend only on income; (2) there is decreasing marginal utility of income; and (3) the total amount of income is fixed, then income should be equally distributed. These are strong assumptions, and weakening them gives radically different results.

- The maximin criterion states that the best income distribution maximizes the utility of the person who has the lowest utility. The ethical validity of this proposition is controversial.

- The income distribution may be like a public good—everyone derives utility from the fact that income is equitably distributed, but government coercion is needed to accomplish redistribution. Pareto efficient redistribution occurs when no one is made worse off as a result of a transfer.

- Other views of income distribution reject the utilitarian framework. Some believe it is a first principle that income, or at least certain goods, should be distributed equally. Others argue that the distribution of income is irrelevant as long as the distribution arises from a "fair" process.

- A government program can change relative prices, creating losses and gains for various individuals. It is difficult to trace all of these price changes, so economists generally focus only on the prices in the markets directly affected.

- Because people do not reveal how they value public goods, it is difficult to determine how these goods affect real incomes.

- Many government programs provide goods and services (in-kind transfers) instead of cash. Recipients are not legally allowed to sell the goods and services so received. If recipients would prefer to consume less, the value of the in-kind transfer is less than the market price.

- The prevalence of in-kind transfer programs may be due to paternalism, commodity egalitarianism, administrative feasibility, or political attractiveness

Discussion Questions

1. "I don't care how rich the very rich are. I care if they became rich in an unethical way, or if they use their riches in a particularly vulgar or revolting way. . . . I wouldn't mind if they lost [their wealth] or had it taxed away. But I don't mind if they keep it either. . . . But I do find poverty of the very poor unlovely. . . . That condition deserves, in my opinion, our most intensive care. I believe that the present focus on inequality of income diverts national attention from it" [Stein, 1996, p. A14]. Do you agree with this statement? Is it consistent with utilitarianism?

2. Suppose there are only two people, Simon and Charity, who must split a fixed income of $100. For Simon, the marginal utility of income is

$$MU_s = 400 - 2I_s$$

while for Charity, marginal utility is

$$MU_c = 400 - 6I_c$$

where I_c, I_s are the amounts of income to Charity and Simon, respectively.

a. What is the optimal distribution of income if the social welfare function is additive?

b. What is the optimal distribution if society values only the utility of Charity? What if the reverse is true? Comment on your answers.

c. Finally, comment on how your answers change if the marginal utility of income for both Simon and Charity is constant:

$$MU_c = 400 \quad MU_s = 400$$

3. President Vladimir Putin of Russia proposed replacing in-kind subsidies such as free public transportation and rent-free apartments for government workers with cash subsidies of between $20 and $120 per month. The proposal led to widespread complaints among Russian citizens that the cash subsidies were not large enough. One reportedly asked, "What is a perk worth?" [Chivers, 2004]. Use an indifference curve analysis to show how to convert an in-kind subsidy into a cash subsidy that leaves people equally well off.

4. The government of Mexico City recently began distributing the drug Viagra at a highly subsidized price to low-income elderly men. Suppose that the government gives each recipient six pills per month at a price of $1 per pill, and the market price is $10 per pill. Can we conclude that an individual participating in the program would be worse off if provided with a cash grant of $50 instead of the Viagra? (Hint: Analyze a model in which the individual chooses between two commodities, "Viagra pills" and "all other goods.")

5. Would a government program that transferred income from the middle class to both the poor and the rich be supported by someone with the maximin social welfare function?

6. An economy consists of two individuals, Lynne and Jonathan, whose utility levels are given by U_L and U_J, respectively.

   a. Suppose that the social welfare function is
   $$W = U_L + U_J$$

   True or false: Society is indifferent between giving a dollar to Lynne and a dollar to Jonathan.

   b. Now suppose that, instead, the social welfare function is
   $$W = U_L + 8U_J$$

   True or false: Society values Jonathan's happiness more than Lynne's.

   c. Now suppose that, instead, the social welfare function is
   $$W = \min[U_L, U_J]$$

   True or false: In this society, the optimal distribution of income is complete equality.

7. Consider the model of an in-kind transfer in Figure 12.3. Suppose that it is illegal for a recipient of the cheese to sell it. Nevertheless, there is a black market, where cheese can be sold for $1 per pound. Show how the existence of the black market affects the individual's budget constraint. Does it make her better off?

8. Sherry's utility is U_S and her income is Y_S. Marsha's utility is U_M and her income is Y_M. Suppose it is the case that:
$$U_S = 100Y_S^{1/2} \quad \text{and} \quad U_M = 100Y_M^{1/2} + 0.8U_S$$

Define the *Pareto efficient redistribution*, and explain why the concept is relevant in this situation. Suppose that initially Sherry and Marsha both have incomes of $100. Assuming that the social welfare function is additive, what happens to social welfare if $36 is taken away from Marsha and given to Sherry?

Chapter Thirteen

EXPENDITURE PROGRAMS FOR THE POOR

And distribution was made to each as had need.

—ACTS 4:35

While there is a strong consensus among Americans that government should help the poor, there is also enormous controversy over what form such help should take. This chapter discusses the major US expenditure programs aimed at helping the poor.

▶ A QUICK LOOK AT WELFARE SPENDING

"Welfare" in the United States is a patchwork of dozens of programs that provide benefits primarily to low-income individuals. These programs are **means-tested**—only individuals whose financial resources fall below a certain level can receive benefits. In 1968, government means-tested assistance accounted for about 1.8 percent of Gross Domestic Product (GDP). By 2004, the figure had grown to 5 percent. Most of the growth in government transfer programs has been in the form of in-kind assistance. In 1968, cash assistance was 48 percent of all means-tested benefits; it is now only about 19 percent of the total [Burke, 2006].

The importance of in-kind transfers is reflected in Table 13.1, which lists various categories of welfare spending. Although the table provides an adequate overview, it is not a comprehensive "poverty budget." This is because some programs that are not explicitly redistributional end up transferring considerable sums to the poor. Social Security is usually considered an insurance program rather than a distributional program (see Chapter 11). Yet Social Security payments are the only source of income for 20 percent of the beneficiaries. Similarly, the poor receive some unemployment insurance payments and veterans' pensions. In addition, many families that are not below the poverty line receive some sort of assistance from programs that are targeted to the poor. For example, over 12 percent of the households receiving food stamps are above the poverty level [US Department of Agriculture, 2008, p. 15].

means-tested

A spending program whose benefits flow only to those whose financial resources fall below a certain level.

Table 13.1   **Expenditures on Major Need-Tested Programs (2004)**

Program	Federal	State and Local
Medical care	$194.8	$127.8
Cash aid	94.0	18.1
Food benefits	45.5	2.7
Housing benefits	38.8	1.0
Education	27.4	1.8
Services	18.3	4.9
Jobs/training	6.1	0.9
Energy aid	2.1	0.1

Source: Burke [2006, p. 3].

Of the means-tested programs, Medicaid is by far the largest.

▶ TANF

From 1935 to 1996 the main government cash transfer program was **Aid to Families with Dependent Children (AFDC).** As the name implies, the program was focused on families with dependent children. Also, in general, only families in which one of the parents was missing were eligible. It was administered jointly by the federal government and the states. Each state determined its own benefit levels and eligibility standards, subject only to broad federal guidelines. Federal law required that an individual's AFDC grant be reduced by a dollar for each dollar the individual received in income, although certain small amounts of income were disregarded for this purpose.

In 1996 AFDC was superseded by the passage of the Personal Responsibility and Work Opportunity Reconciliation Act. This legislation created a new welfare program called **TANF—Temporary Assistance for Needy Families.** The major components of TANF are:[1]

- **No entitlement:** Under AFDC, anyone whose income was below a particular level and met certain other conditions was *entitled* to a cash benefit indefinitely. TANF ended AFDC and this cash entitlement. The *T* in TANF emphasizes that cash benefits are now available only on a *temporary* and provisional basis. About 4 million families receive TANF benefits each month.

- **Time limits:** In general, individuals cannot receive cash benefits for more than five years (although states can exempt up to 20 percent of their caseloads from this rule). States can set a shorter time limit if they choose.

- **Work requirement:** States face fiscal penalties if at least 50 percent of single-mother recipients and 90 percent of two-parent families are not working or in work preparation programs.

- **Block grants to states:** Under AFDC there was *no* fixed limit on federal spending. Under TANF each state is given a grant to finance welfare spending by the federal government; the size of the grant is fixed in advance. The state uses the grant (supplemented with its own funds) to run welfare as it sees fit, within broad limits. States now have virtually total control over the structure of their welfare

---

[1] For additional details, see Burke [2006].

systems, including which families to support. States can use their grants to pay for cash benefits, or job-training programs, or programs to eliminate teenage pregnancies and encourage marriage, and so forth. (But the states cannot loosen the work requirement and payment limits noted above.)

- **Benefit reduction rates:** As a corollary to the power to control the structure of their welfare programs, the states can decide how much to reduce benefits when welfare recipients earn income. Recall that, under AFDC, the reduction was (approximately) one-for-one—for each dollar of earnings, benefits were reduced by one dollar. Several states have continued this policy, while others have modified the rules.[2] Some have large benefit reduction rates. In Nebraska, for example, for each dollar of earnings, benefits are reduced by 80 cents. On the other hand, in Illinois, the reduction rate is only 33 cents on the dollar. California allows welfare recipients to earn $225 per month before reducing welfare payments, and then takes away 50 cents of benefits for each additional dollar of earnings. States vary not only in their effective tax rates, but also in the benefits they pay to a family with no earnings. For a single-parent family of three, for example, the figure is $215 in Alabama and $633 in Massachusetts. In short, welfare recipients' earnings are now subjected to a wide variety of policies.

▶ INCOME MAINTENANCE AND WORK INCENTIVES

The question of whether welfare reduces work effort and increases dependence on the government has dominated discussions of welfare policy for years. In this section we discuss how TANF affects recipients' work decisions.

The Basic Trade-offs

If we abstract from many of TANF's complexities, we can characterize a state's policy in terms of two variables. The first is a basic grant that the individual receives if she is not working, G. The second is the rate at which the grant is reduced when the recipient earns money, t. Suppose, for example, that a state provides $300 a month to welfare recipients, but that benefit is reduced by 25 cents for each dollar the individual earns. Then $G = 300$ and $t = 0.25$. If an individual earns $500, then her benefit is reduced by $125 (= 0.25 × 500), leaving her with a grant of $175 and with a total income of $675. Note that the benefit reduction rate is in effect a tax on earnings, which is why we denote it with a t. Note also that at some point, the recipient's earnings become high enough that she no longer receives any welfare at all. In this example, when she earns $1,200, the benefit reduction just equals her basic welfare payment. After that point, t no longer applies because her benefit is already zero.

Algebraically, the benefit received (B) is related to the basic grant, the tax rate, and level of earnings (E) by

$$B = G - tE$$

It follows that the benefit is zero ($B = 0$) when

$$E = \frac{G}{t}$$

or any higher level of E.

---

[2] For details, see Office of Family Assistance [2006].

These two equations highlight the fundamental dilemmas involved in designing an income maintenance system. The first equation shows us that, for a given program cost, the larger the basic grant, the larger must be the tax rate. That is, a system with good work incentives (a low value of t) might provide little money for those who are unable to work. The second equation shows us that, for a given basic grant, the lower the tax rate, the higher the breakeven level of earnings. But as the breakeven level of earnings increases, so does the number of people who are eligible for welfare, which also increases the costs of the system.

Analysis of Work Incentives

Indifference curve analysis of the individual's choice between leisure and income provides a useful way to see how TANF affects labor supply. Consider Marge, who is deciding how much time to devote each month to work and how much to nonmarket activity, which we call *leisure*. In Figure 13.1, the horizontal axis measures the number of hours of leisure. Even if Marge does not work, there is an upper limit to the amount of leisure she can consume, because there are just so many hours in a month. This number of hours, referred to as the **time endowment,** is distance OT in Figure 13.1. We assume all time not spent on leisure is devoted to work in the market. Any point on the horizontal axis therefore simultaneously indicates hours of leisure and hours of work. For example, at point a, Oa hours are devoted to leisure, and the difference between that and the time endowment, OT, represents time spent at work, aT.

Our first problem is to illustrate how Marge's income, which is measured on the vertical axis, varies with her hours of work. Assume that she can earn a wage of $\$w$ per hour. Also, for the moment, assume that no welfare is available. Then her income for any number of hours worked is just the product of $\$w$ and the number of hours. Suppose, for example, Marge does not work at all. If labor is her only source

time endowment

The maximum number of hours an individual can work during a given period.

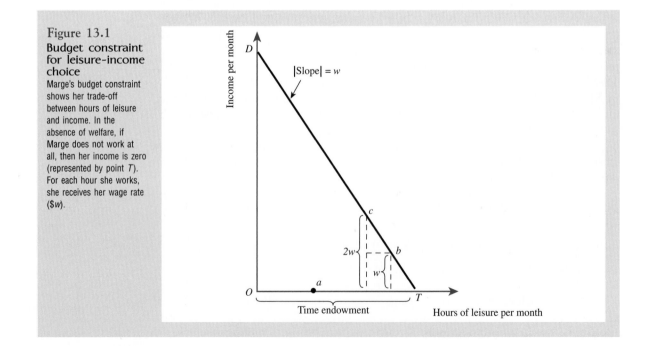

Figure 13.1
Budget constraint for leisure-income choice
Marge's budget constraint shows her trade-off between hours of leisure and income. In the absence of welfare, if Marge does not work at all, then her income is zero (represented by point T). For each hour she works, she receives her wage rate ($\$w$).

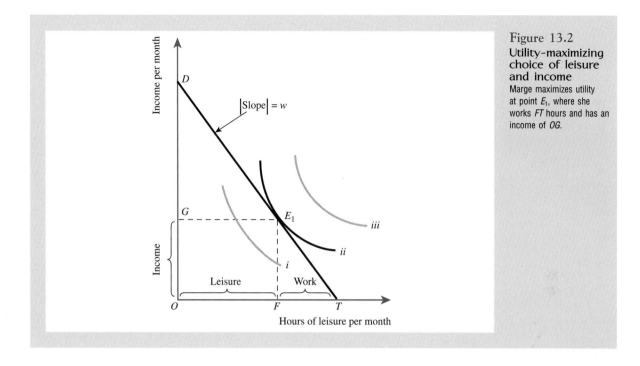

Figure 13.2
Utility–maximizing choice of leisure and income
Marge maximizes utility at point E_1, where she works *FT* hours and has an income of *OG*.

of income, her income is simply zero. This option of zero work and zero income is represented by point *T*.

If Marge works one hour each week, her consumption of leisure equals her time endowment minus one hour. This point is one hour to the left of *T* on the horizontal axis. Working one hour gives her a total of $w. The combination of one hour of work with a total income of $w is labeled point *b*. If Marge works two hours—moves two hours to the left of *T*—her total income is $2 \times w, which is labeled point *c*. Continuing to compute the income associated with each number of hours of work, we trace out all the leisure–income combinations available to Marge—straight line *TD*, whose slope, in absolute value, is the wage rate. *TD* is the analog of the budget constraint in the usual analysis of the choice between two goods. (See the appendix to the book.) Here, however, the goods are income and leisure. The price of an hour of leisure is its opportunity cost (the income forgone by not working that hour), which is just the wage.

To determine Marge's choice along *TD*, we need information on her tastes. In Figure 13.2 we reproduce the budget constraint *TD*. Assume that preferences for leisure and income can be represented by normal, convex-to-the-origin indifference curves. Three such curves are labeled *i*, *ii*, and *iii* in Figure 13.2. Marge maximizes utility at point E_1, where she devotes *OF* hours to leisure, works *FT* hours, and earns income *OG*.

Suppose now that Marge is eligible to participate in TANF, and that in her state the basic grant is $100 per month and the implicit tax rate is 25 percent. How does TANF change her budget constraint? Figure 13.3 illustrates the situation. As before, in the absence of welfare, Marge works *FT* hours and earns *OG*. In the presence of TANF, one option is point *Q*, where no labor is supplied and Marge receives $100 from welfare. If Marge works one hour, she receives *w* from her employer.

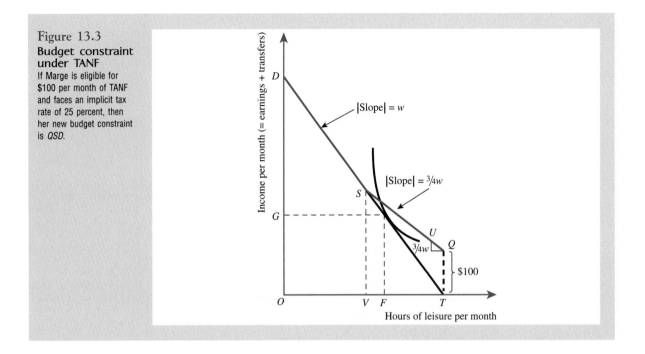

Figure 13.3

Budget constraint under TANF

If Marge is eligible for $100 per month of TANF and faces an implicit tax rate of 25 percent, then her new budget constraint is *QSD*.

Simultaneously, her grant is reduced by ¼*w*, still leaving her ahead by ¾*w*. Thus, another point on the budget constraint is *U*, which is one hour to the left of *Q*, and ¾*w* above it. Similarly, Marge continues to receive an effective hourly wage of ¾*w* until she works *VT* hours, at which point her earnings are high enough that she receives no welfare. Thus, the budget constraint is the kinked line *QSD*. Segment *QS* has a slope in absolute value of ¾*w*, segment *SD* a slope of *w*.

As usual, the ultimate work decision depends on the shapes of the individual's indifference curves. As drawn in Figure 13.4, Marge works less than she did before TANF (*KT* hours, as opposed to *FT* before).

As already noted, some states in effect impose a 100 percent tax rate on the earnings of welfare recipients. It is therefore of some interest to analyze the budget constraint and work incentives generated by this special case. Suppose, for concreteness, that an individual operating under such a system has a basic grant of $338.[3] In Figure 13.5, clearly one option that welfare makes available to Marge is point *P*, which is associated with zero hours of work and an income of $338 from welfare. Now suppose that Marge works one hour. Graphically, she moves one hour to the left from *P*. When Marge works one hour, she receives a wage of $*w* from her employer, *but* simultaneously her welfare is reduced by the same amount. The hour of work nets her nothing—her total income remains $338. This is represented by point *P*₁, where there is one hour of work and total income is $338. This continues until point *R*. Beyond *R*, each hour of work raises her income by $*w*.[4] Thus, the budget constraint is the kinked line *PRD*. Segment *PR* has zero slope, and segment *RD* has a slope whose absolute value is *w*.

How might Marge respond to such incentives? Figure 13.6 shows one distinct possibility: She maximizes utility at point *P*, where no labor is supplied. In no case

---

[3] This was the monthly benefit in 2003 for a single parent with two children and no income in the state of Delaware.

[4] For simplicity, we ignore the fact that Marge's earnings may be subject to payroll and income taxes.

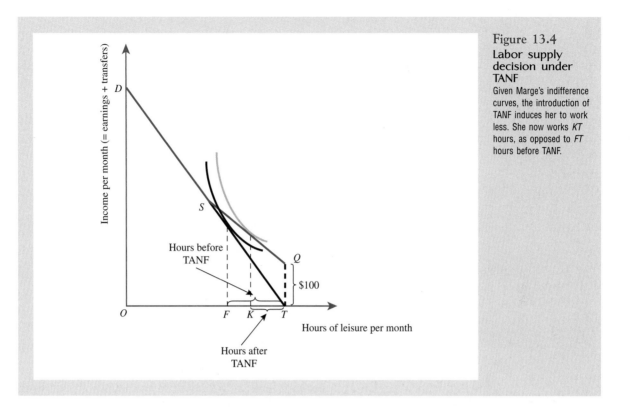

Figure 13.4
Labor supply decision under TANF
Given Marge's indifference curves, the introduction of TANF induces her to work less. She now works *KT* hours, as opposed to *FT* hours before TANF.

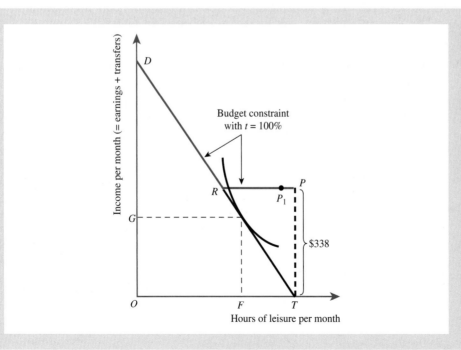

Figure 13.5
Budget constraint under a welfare system with a 100 percent tax rate on additional earnings
A welfare program with a 100 percent implicit marginal tax rate leads to budget constraint *PRD*.

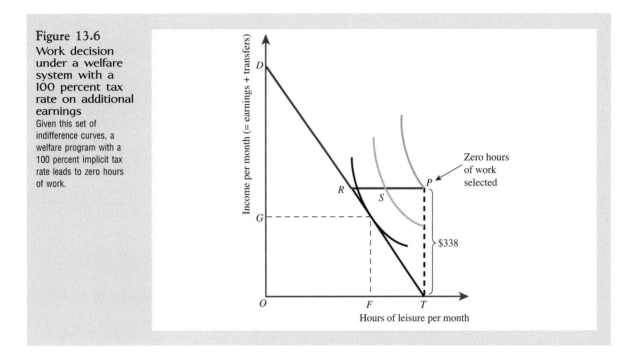

Figure 13.6
Work decision under a welfare system with a 100 percent tax rate on additional earnings
Given this set of indifference curves, a welfare program with a 100 percent implicit tax rate leads to zero hours of work.

will a rational person work between zero and PR hours. Why should someone work if she can receive the same income by not working?[5]

Of course, a welfare system with $t = 100$ percent does not necessarily induce an individual to stop working. Figure 13.7 depicts the leisure-income choice of Jones, who faces exactly the same budget constraint as Marge in Figure 13.5. However, Jones maximizes utility at point E_2, where she works MT hours per month.

The negative effect on work incentives embodied in Figure 13.6 was one of the major criticisms of AFDC. Indeed, there is considerable evidence that AFDC substantially reduced the labor supply of recipients. In his survey of the research in this area, Moffitt [2003] concluded that AFDC reduced labor supply by 10 to 50 percent among welfare recipients.

As noted above, although several states continued to impose implicit 100 percent tax rates after the passage of TANF in 1996, a number now have rates that are considerably smaller. Have these implicit tax rate reductions had an impact on the labor supply behavior of welfare recipients? Employment among the welfare population increased substantially after 1996. For example, although the labor force participation rates of single mothers did not change much from the 1980s into the mid-1990s, their labor force participation rose from 44 to 66 percent between 1994 and 2001. By 2001, the number of welfare cases was only 40 percent of its level in 1994 [Blank, 2005]. However, one must be cautious about ascribing this change to differences in implicit marginal tax rates. First, as already indicated, TANF changed other aspects of the welfare system, including work requirements. Second, the economy was experiencing an unprecedented boom in the late 1990s, and this by itself tended to increase employment among all groups. According to research surveyed by Blank

---

[5] In a more complicated model, an individual might select a point along segment PR to develop her skills or to signal her quality to future employers by maintaining a continuous work history.

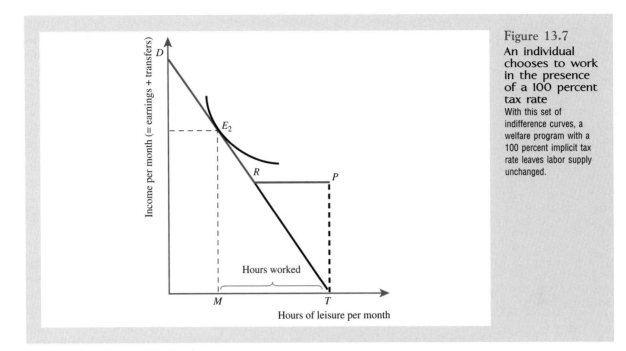

Figure 13.7
An individual chooses to work in the presence of a 100 percent tax rate
With this set of indifference curves, a welfare program with a 100 percent implicit tax rate leaves labor supply unchanged.

[2002], the marginal tax rate changes embodied in TANF did increase work effort, but there is not much consensus on the magnitude.

Work Requirements

The analysis so far assumes that the welfare recipient can choose her hours of work. If the individual chooses not to work after she goes on welfare, so be it. An alternative scheme is **workfare.** Able-bodied individuals receive transfer payments only if they agree to participate in a work-related activity and accept employment, if offered. Workfare can be easily interpreted in terms of our model of labor supply choice. Turn back to Figure 13.6, and recall how we demonstrated that an unconstrained individual would not voluntarily *choose* any point along segment *RP*. Workfare simply adds another constraint and says that if the individual does not choose a point like *S*, where she works *SP* hours, then she receives no welfare at all.

Under TANF, most recipients must in fact participate in some kind of work activity. How does mandated work affect welfare recipients? A number of states conducted randomized experiments to answer this question. Some recipients were assigned to workfare and others, the control group, were not. The research surveyed by Blank [2002] indicates that almost all of these programs produced significant increases in employment and earnings, and decreases in welfare usage. Unfortunately, the mandatory work programs did little to increase total incomes—beneficiaries' earnings increased, but only by a bit more than the decreases in their welfare benefits [Blank, 2006]. TANF did lead to a change in expenditure patterns, with recipients shifting toward buying items (such as transportation and clothing) that facilitate work outside the home [Kaushal, Gao, and Waldfogel, 2006].

This observation forces us to confront the question of whether public concern over how much welfare recipients work is somewhat misplaced. True, an important aspect

workfare

Able-bodied individuals who qualify for income support receive it only if they agree to participate in a work-related activity.

of any welfare system is the incentive structure it creates. And many people believe that special value should be placed upon work because it helps enhance individual dignity. That said, if the goal of welfare policy were only to maximize work effort, the government could simply force the poor into workhouses, as was done under the English Poor Law of 1834. Designing good transfer systems requires a careful balancing of incentive and equity considerations.

Time Limits

One of TANF's most dramatic innovations was the introduction of time limits—individuals can only receive five year's worth of benefits during their lifetimes. Did this policy succeed in getting people off of welfare? Any answer to this question must begin by noting perhaps the most dramatic statistic associated with TANF—the caseload dropped by over 60 percent between 1996 and 2007 [US Department of Health and Human Services, 2008]. We cannot attribute this drop in the caseload entirely to the time limits (or any other aspect of TANF) because during the 1990s, the economy was experiencing a boom, and this by itself tended to reduce the number of welfare recipients. Still, most analyses indicate that TANF and its time limits did play a role.

One interesting study along these lines was done by Grogger [2003], who noted that if time limits matter, they should have a bigger effect on welfare families having young children than families whose children are older. Why? Eligibility for TANF ends when the youngest child in the family turns 18. If your child is 13 or over, you may as well use up your benefits, because they will disappear in five years anyway. However, if your child is under 13, it makes sense to get off of welfare as soon as you can, so that you can "bank" your remaining quota of time and use it if you need the money at some later date. Grogger's analysis of the data suggests that time limits have, in fact, been important, accounting for about 12 percent of the decrease in welfare caseloads.

Family Structure

One of the main reasons for the passage of TANF in 1996 was the belief that AFDC had created incentives for low-income women to bear children out of wedlock. The basic idea was that an entitlement to welfare allowed low-income women to get by as single mothers. This tendency was reinforced by the fact that, in many states, women lost welfare benefits when they married. The hope was that the time limits on TANF would reverse this behavior. At the same time, a number of states developed specific programs to discourage teenage motherhood. An example is forcing a teen mother to live with her parents to be eligible for welfare.

Did TANF affect the structure of low-income families? The empirical results, unfortunately, are mixed. Some studies indicate positive effects of TANF (for example, more children were living with married parents after TANF than before), while others find no impact at all. It is unsurprising that the results are inconclusive. Marriage and childbearing patterns probably adjust only slowly over time. It is simply too soon to know if TANF has changed family structure.

National versus State Administration

During the debates over TANF, concerns were expressed that turning the system over to the states would lead to a "race to the bottom" because any state that enacted a generous welfare system would be flooded with poor individuals from other states, forcing it to reduce benefits. This is certainly possible, and there is indeed some statistical evidence that differences in TANF provisions have influenced the migration patterns of low-educated women across jurisdictions [Kaestner et al., 2003]. The preliminary evidence, though, is that there has not been a race to the bottom under TANF. Most states kept their basic benefits at about the same level; some actually increased them [Gallagher et al., 1998]. Of course, the usual caveats apply. In particular, TANF came into existence during a boom; during some future economic slowdown, the states might behave quite differently.

In any case, some commentators view the fact that the states can now design very different systems as a real advantage. "Any given state government may do no better than Washington, but the great variety of the former will make up for the deadening uniformity of the latter. And within the states, the operating agencies will be at the city and county level, where the task of improving lives . . . will be informed by the proximity of government to the voices of ordinary people" [Wilson, 1994, p. A10].

Of course, the well-being of the poor under TANF also depends on the other benefit programs that are available to them. We now turn to a discussion of these programs.

▶ THE EARNED INCOME TAX CREDIT

You may be surprised to learn that the largest program for making cash transfers to low-income individuals is administered not through the welfare bureaucracy but through the tax system. The **earned income tax credit (EITC)** is a subsidy to the earnings of low-income families. Only the working poor are eligible for the EITC; in this sense, it is thoroughly in sync with TANF's emphasis on linking welfare with work. As its name implies, the subsidy comes in the form of a tax credit, which is simply a reduction in tax liability. For example, if you owe the government $1,000 in income taxes but you also have a tax credit of $600, then you only have to pay $400. Importantly, if the EITC exceeds your tax liability, the difference is refunded to you—the government sends you a check. In effect, then, the credit is as good as cash.

> **earned income tax credit (EITC)**
>
> **A tax credit for low-income individuals.**

Although the EITC has been part of the tax system for a number of years, its scope was dramatically increased in 1993. The annual cost of the EITC is now over $39 billion.

The size of the subsidy depends on the number of children in the family; we consider here the case in which two or more children are present. In 2008, such a family is allowed a tax credit equal to 40 percent of all wage and salary income up to $12,060. Hence, the maximum credit is $4,824 (= 0.40 × $12,060). To help guarantee that only the poor benefit from the credit, it is phased out at incomes between $18,740 and $41,646. For each dollar of earnings in this phase-out range, the credit is reduced by 21.06 cents; at $41,646 of earnings, the credit is entirely exhausted. The system is summarized in Figure 13.8A, which shows the size of the credit for each level of earnings.[6]

One justification for the EITC is to improve work incentives for the poor. In the phase-in range, the federal government adds 40 cents to each dollar of earnings; in effect this is a negative marginal tax rate of 40 percent on earnings. (The tax rate is "marginal" because it is the rate that applies to an additional dollar of earnings.) However, the fact that the credit is taken away creates an implicit positive marginal

---

[6] Legislation passed in 2009 increased the EITC from 40 percent to 45 percent for families with three or more children, and it increased the phase-out range for joint filers. These changes applied to 2009 and 2010 only.

Figure 13.8

The Earned Income Tax Credit (EITC)

This example is for 2008 for a married couple with two or more children. Panel A shows the earned income tax credit for each level of earnings (for a family with two or more children in 2008). Panel B shows the implicit marginal tax rates associated with the earned income tax credit.

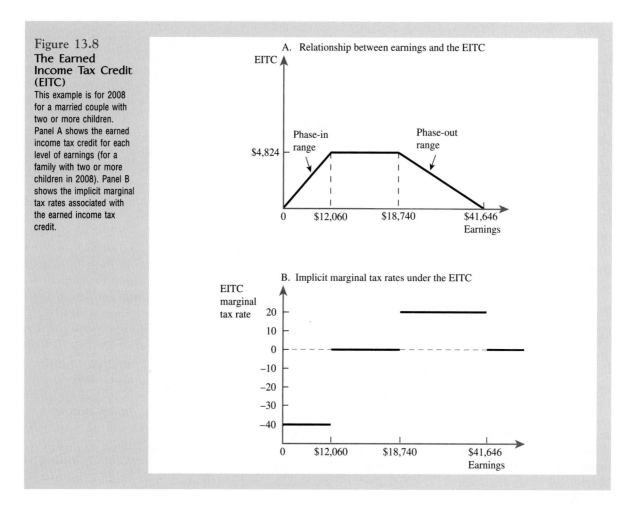

tax rate in the phase-out range—for each dollar of earnings, the credit goes down by 21.06 cents; in effect, this is a 21.06 percent marginal tax rate (see Figure 13.8B). This is higher than the ordinary income tax rate of 10 percent that applies to the lowest income bracket.

Thus, the EITC's incentives depend on the circumstances of the individual. A person who was not working before the EITC now faces a smaller marginal tax rate if she decides to enter the labor force, so the EITC improves her incentive to work. A low-income person who already worked and was in the phase-out range of EITC faces a higher marginal tax rate, which provides an incentive to work fewer hours. The incentive effects are a bit more complicated for a low-income person who already worked and was in the phase-in range of the EITC. The lower marginal tax rate increases the opportunity cost of leisure, which encourages her to substitute work for leisure. At the same time, though, the subsidy increases her income, and because leisure is a normal good, this encourages her to consume more leisure; that is, to work less. Without empirical work, we do not know which effect dominates, so for this person, the net effect of the EITC on work incentives is ambiguous.[7]

---

[7] In more technical terms, in the phase-in range of the EITC, the substitution effect moves the individual in the direction of more hours of work and the income effect moves her in the direction of fewer hours of work. See the appendix to the book for further discussion of income and substitution effects.

EMPIRICAL EVIDENCE

The Effect of the Earned Income Tax Credit on Labor Supply

A rich empirical literature studies the effect of the EITC on labor force participation and on hours worked by low-income people.[8] In order to estimate the effects of EITC, many of these studies take advantage of variation in EITC benefits based on individuals' characteristics (such as family status, family size, and income level). One can then estimate how labor supply behavior varies with the size of EITC benefits. In addition, policy changes in the 1990s generated a nice natural experiment: Benefit levels increased sharply, and by different amounts for different individuals. For example, families with two or more children receive a higher EITC subsidy than those with only one child, and this difference grew during the 1990s. This allows one to compute a difference-in-difference estimate. Specifically, one can look at the change in employment for families with two or more children before and after the policy change. Then compare it to the employment change for families with only one child. Such a calculation suggests that, after the policy change, employment rates increased by 1.2 to 3.2 percentage points for families with two or more children relative to families with only one child [Hotz et al., 2006].

The empirical literature consistently finds that the EITC encourages single women to enter the labor force, as theory predicts. For example, Meyer and Rosenbaum [2001] find that 60 percent of the 8.7 percentage point increase in employment of single mothers between 1984 and 1996 was due to the EITC. Further, 35 percent of the increase in participation between 1992 and 1996 was attributable to the EITC. On the other hand, the EITC appears to have had little impact on hours of work for low-income people who were already in the labor force. This finding is not hard to explain if the net effect of the EITC in the phase-in range is to encourage work. If so, this could approximately cancel the negative effect on work effort for those in the phase-out range, leaving the overall impact about zero.

Although the EITC provides an incentive for single women to participate in the labor force, it provides a *dis*incentive for married mothers. This is because the size of the EITC benefit depends on *family* earnings. If, for example, the husband is already in the labor force and the wife starts working, then the family's EITC benefit could decrease by pushing family earnings into the phase-out range. Eissa and Hoynes [2006] use data from before and after the 1993 expansion of the EITC to investigate this issue. They find that the expansion of EITC in the 1990s led to a 1 percentage point decrease in the participation rate of married mothers. Nonetheless, the empirical literature suggests that the EITC has succeeded in increasing employment overall, especially for low-income single mothers.

▶ SUPPLEMENTAL SECURITY INCOME

Supplemental Security Income (SSI), enacted in 1972, is a federal program that provides a basic monthly benefit for the aged, blind, or disabled. In 2006, the average monthly benefit payment for aged adults was $373 [US Bureau of the Census, 2009, p. 356]. Assets of SSI recipients cannot exceed certain limits: $2,000 for an

---

[8] See Hotz and Scholz [2003] for a review of the literature.

individual, $3,000 for a couple.[9] SSI recipients are allowed to earn $65 per month before there is any reduction in their payments. After that, benefits are reduced by 50 cents for each dollar earned.

A number of striking contrasts exist between SSI and the types of welfare available to those who are not blind, aged, or disabled. First, there is a uniform minimum federal guarantee for SSI and none for other programs.[10] Second, SSI benefits are considerably higher than the average in other programs. Third, work incentives under SSI are better than in many of the states. The implicit tax rate on additional earnings under SSI is only 50 percent. Further, there are no work mandates.

In recent years, there has been a perception that some recipients of SSI game the system; that is, they fake disabilities in order to receive payments. In response to these perceptions, the disability standards were tightened in 1996. At this point, there is not much evidence with respect to the impact of this change in eligibility rules.

▶ MEDICAID

Medicaid is by far the largest spending program for low-income individuals. Chapter 10 provides extensive details on the structure of Medicaid, as well as on the evidence of whether Medicaid crowds out private insurance. One issue not discussed in Chapter 10 is the effect of Medicaid on work incentives. Early in the chapter we noted that historically, when families earned enough money to get out of welfare, they immediately lost their Medicaid benefits. The potential loss of these benefits could lead to implicit marginal tax rates of greater than 100 percent, and was a major disincentive to leaving welfare. However, under TANF, families that earn enough to leave welfare remain eligible for Medicaid for 12 months. Further, the Medicaid expansions of the 1980s and 1990s extended coverage to low-income children and pregnant women who have no other ties to the welfare system. For example, a child under the age of six is eligible for Medicaid until his or her family has earnings that are 33 percent above the poverty line.

The possible loss of Medicaid benefits can create work disincentives, which we analyze using our model of leisure-income choice. In Figure 13.9, DT is Marge's budget constraint before Medicaid. Now assume that Medicaid is introduced; Marge has a three-year-old child who is eligible for Medicaid; and the value of the Medicaid policy to Marge is $1,000 per year. Assume further that when her income reaches Z dollars, her child loses eligibility for Medicaid. Ignoring for simplicity any transfers that Marge receives or taxes that she pays, how does Medicaid affect her budget constraint? One point on the new budget constraint is exactly $1,000 above point T—at zero hours of work she has an in-kind income of $1,000. This is represented by point N. Moving to the left from N, Marge's income increases by her wage rate for each dollar she earns. Medicaid does not change her wage rate, so the slope as she moves away from N is the same as the slope of DT. At XT hours of work, her earnings are Z. At this point, her child loses Medicaid eligibility, and, in effect, she has $1,000 taken away from her. That is, she moves from R to S. As she moves to the left of S, she again receives her wage rate for each hour of work and moves along segment DS.

Putting this all together, in the presence of Medicaid, Marge's budget constraint is $NRSD$. Looking at this constraint, you can see why the impact of Medicaid on

---

[9] This excludes small amounts for the value of home, automobile, and life insurance policies.

[10] However, at their option, states can supplement the federal benefits.

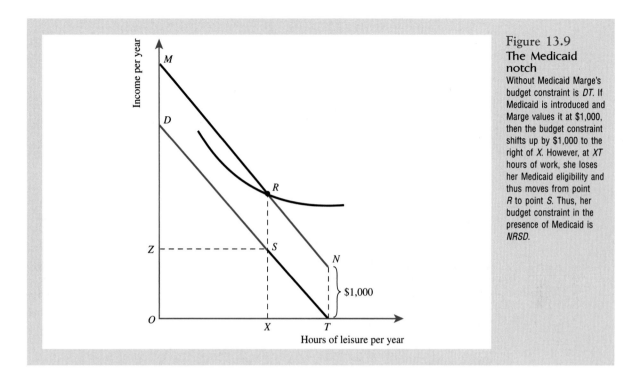

Figure 13.9
The Medicaid notch
Without Medicaid Marge's budget constraint is *DT*. If Medicaid is introduced and Marge values it at $1,000, then the budget constraint shifts up by $1,000 to the right of *X*. However, at *XT* hours of work, she loses her Medicaid eligibility and thus moves from point *R* to point *S*. Thus, her budget constraint in the presence of Medicaid is *NRSD*.

work incentives is characterized as a "notch." How much does Marge work? A strong possibility is that the highest indifference curve she can attain touches the budget constraint right at the notch, point *R*. This makes perfect sense—she earns just short of *Z* dollars, because if she earns one more dollar, she loses a thousand! Thus, Medicaid creates incentives to keep one's earnings below the cut-off level.

▶ UNEMPLOYMENT INSURANCE

Congress passed the legislation that led states to establish unemployment insurance (UI) programs in 1935, the same year as Social Security. The purpose of the program is to replace income lost due to unemployment. Virtually all wage earners are covered, and in 2005, 8 million individuals received first payments. The average weekly UI benefit was $288 [US Department of Labor, 2008].

Why should insurance against the possibility of unemployment be provided by the government? Recall from Chapter 9 that private markets can fail to provide adequate amounts of insurance in situations where adverse selection and moral hazard are important. Unemployment satisfies these conditions. Those workers who have the highest probability of becoming unemployed have the highest demand for unemployment insurance (adverse selection). Therefore, private firms that attempted to provide such insurance would have to charge relatively high premiums to make a profit, which would exclude many people from making purchases. At the same time, those workers who managed to obtain insurance might experience more unemployment than otherwise would have been the case (moral hazard). Because it is difficult for the insurer to determine whether or not a layoff is the fault of a worker, a private unemployment insurance company might find itself having to pay out large amounts of money for false claims. In short, it is hard to imagine that providing unemployment insurance would be a profitable venture for private insurance companies. Adverse selection would similarly discourage employers from providing UI benefits to their own employees, because offering UI as a fringe benefit might attract workers who were not interested in long-term employment relationships.

A compulsory government program avoids the adverse selection problem. Hence, government provision of UI has the potential to increase efficiency. However, government provision does *not* eliminate moral hazard. As we will see, this complicates the problem of designing a UI system. We now discuss how the UI program works.

Benefits

The number of weeks for which an individual can receive benefits is determined by a complicated formula that depends on work history and the state in which the person works. In most states, the regular maximum length of time is 26 weeks. However, this period can be extended if the state unemployment rate exceeds certain levels. For example, after September 11, 2001, it was extended by 13 weeks. In most states, the benefit formula is designed so that the gross replacement rate—the proportion of pretax earnings replaced by UI—is about 50 percent. (However, there is a maximum benefit level that cannot be exceeded.) UI benefits are subject to the federal personal income tax, but they are not subject to the Social Security payroll tax.[11]

Financing

UI is financed by a payroll tax. Unlike the Social Security system, in most states this tax is paid by employers only, not jointly by employers and employees.[12] The employer's UI tax liability for a given worker is the product of the employer's UI tax rate, t_u, and the worker's annual earnings up to the UI tax ceiling. Federal law dictates that the UI tax base include at least the first $7,000 of each covered worker's annual earnings. Forty-two states currently have UI tax bases above the federal base, with taxed earnings running as high as $35,300 in Hawaii.

An important feature of the payroll tax is that t_u differs across employers because UI is **experience rated**—t_u depends on the firm's layoff experience. Firms that lay off relatively large numbers of employees generate a lot of demands on the UI system. Therefore, such firms are assigned a relatively high t_u. However, if a worker is laid off, generally the increased costs to the employer due to the higher value of t_u are less than the UI benefits received by the worker. For this reason, the experience rating system is described as "imperfect."

experience rated

The practice of charging different insurance premiums based on the existing risk of the insurance buyers.

Effects on Unemployment

Since its inception, there have been concerns that UI increases unemployment. One possible reason is imperfect experience rating. To see why, suppose that the demand for a firm's product is temporarily slack, so the firm is considering temporary layoffs for some of its workers. With imperfect experience rating, the cost to the employer in increased UI taxes is less than the UI benefit to the worker. Hence, it

---

[11] Legislation passed in 2009 exempted up to $2,400 of unemployment insurance compensation for each beneficiary in that year.

[12] As we will discuss in Chapter 14, even though the tax is paid by employers, some or all of it may be shifted to employees.

may be mutually beneficial to lay the worker off temporarily. If the system were characterized by perfect experience rating, UI would provide no such incentive for temporary layoffs.

Much of the academic and political discussion of UI's incentives has focused on the impact of relatively high replacement rates on unemployment. As already suggested, an individual's employment status is often under his or her control. A worker's behavior on the job can influence the probability that he or she will lose it. Similarly, an unemployed worker can control the intensity with which he or she seeks a new job. The existence of UI may make workers more likely to accept employment in industries where the probability of future layoffs is great. In addition, UI may induce the unemployed to spend more time looking for work than they would have otherwise.

Is this moral hazard problem empirically important? This question has been the subject of many econometric studies, several of which adopt a quasi-experimental approach (see Chapter 2). These studies exploit differences in UI benefits across states, income groups, or time. For example, consider a large, unexpected increase in UI benefits for a certain income class but not for another within the same state. A difference-in-difference analysis would compare the change in unemployment duration for those who received the increase (the treatment group) to the change for those who did not (the control group). Meyer and Mok [2007] used this research design to examine the impact of a 36 percent increase in UI benefits to high earners in New York State and found that it led to a large increase in the number of unemployment insurance claims and to an increase in the length of time people stayed unemployed.

The fact that UI extends the duration of unemployment is not necessarily undesirable. If workers take more time to search, they may find jobs that are more appropriate for their skills, which enhances efficiency. This argument assumes that in the absence of UI, the amount of time devoted to searching would be suboptimal. Such might be the case if unemployed workers could not borrow to maintain their consumption levels while looking for jobs. More generally, a society that believes it is worthwhile to maintain consumption levels for the involuntarily unemployed may be willing to pay the price in terms of some increased voluntary unemployment.

Having said this, we can still ask if there are other ways to provide security with fewer disincentives. Several fascinating social experiments have been conducted to explore this issue. In an experiment in Illinois, members of a randomly selected group of unemployed individuals were offered a bonus of $500 if they found a job within 11 weeks and kept that job for four months. On average, people who were offered the bonus received UI for one week less than members of the control group, and the program saved more on UI benefits than it spent on bonuses [Woodbury and Spiegelman, 1987]. While the experiment was subject to many of the usual problems involved in social experimentation (see Chapter 2), this is a fruitful approach to future research.

▶ FOOD STAMPS AND CHILD NUTRITION

A food stamp is a government-issued voucher that can be used only for the purchase of food. (Animal food, alcohol, tobacco, and imported food are not allowed.) In 2007, during an average month 26.5 million people received food stamps, and total benefits were about $30.4 billion [US Department of Agriculture, 2008, p. xv]. The direct cost of the food stamps is paid by the federal government. However, the administration of the program, including distribution of the stamps, is done by the states.

Virtually all poor people are eligible to receive food stamps, including poor families without children and childless single men and women. A household's monthly food stamp allotment is based on its size and income. In 2007, the average monthly food stamp allotment per household was about $215 [US Department of Agriculture, 2008, p. xv]. The allotment is reduced when the household's income increases, but the implicit tax on food stamps is only 30 cents on the dollar.[13]

Because food stamps cannot be used to buy anything except food, we expect them to be worth less to individuals than the same amount of cash. Some evidence that this is true comes from a set of social experiments that were conducted several years ago. A group of food stamp recipients were given checks instead of food stamps, while a control group continued to receive food stamps. When the two groups were compared, it was found that between 20 and 30 percent of food stamp recipients reduced their spending on food when they were given cash instead [Whitmore, 2002].

Is the fact that food stamps induce recipients to consume more food than a cash grant good news or bad news? Our analysis of in-kind transfers from Chapter 12 suggests that this is an indication that the food stamp program is inefficient—recipients could be made better off without any additional expense if the program were cashed out. Indeed, Whitmore calculated that food stamp recipients valued their total benefits at only 80 percent of the value of the food stamps. On the other hand, to the extent that "society" believes that the poor, left to themselves, would not consume enough food, then inducing them to consume more is desirable. Additionally, from a political point of view, it may be easier to generate support for a program to "abolish hunger" than simply to pay cash. Interestingly, however, on the basis of data from food diaries, Whitmore found that replacing food stamps with cash, while reducing food consumption, appears to have had no negative consequences for nutrition. Much of the reduction in food spending was due to reduced consumption of soda and junk food.

An interesting feature of the food stamp program is that only about 70 percent of eligible households actually participate. Why do people fail to take advantage of the program? One possibility is that individuals are unaware they are eligible. Another is that there is some stigma associated with participation in the program; that is, the process of participation per se causes some reduction in utility. Indeed, the presence of stigma may be one reason why the government does not cash out food stamps. If enrolling in the program embarrasses people, then they may be less likely to participate, which keeps down costs. Nonetheless, the empirical evidence suggests that stigma is not a major cause of low take-up rates for the food stamp program [Currie, 2004].

▶ HOUSING ASSISTANCE

In the United States, subsidies for providing housing to the poor began in 1937. Until recently, the largest program was public housing. Public housing units are developed, owned, and run by local authorities that operate within a municipality, county, or several counties as a group. The federal government subsidizes both the costs of construction and a portion of the operating costs paid by the tenants. There are now about 1.2 million public housing units.

---

[13] In addition, the law allows certain deductions to be made before applying the 30 percent tax.

The average monthly value of public housing to a recipient has been estimated at about 90 percent of the cash value. The income limits for participation in public housing are locally established. Unlike other welfare programs, satisfying the means test does not automatically entitle a family to participate in public housing. As already noted, there are only 1.2 million public housing units, while there are about 37 million people whose incomes fall beneath the poverty line. Many more people want public housing than it is possible to accommodate. In short, public housing confers a relatively large value per recipient, but most poor people receive nothing from the program at all. Further, public housing has gained a reputation as a breeding ground for crime and other social pathologies. For this and other reasons, little federal public housing has been built since the early 1970s.

Many economists believe that if there are to be housing subsidies for the poor, their link to the public provision of housing should be broken. When subsidies are applied to private sector housing, the public sector no longer has to get involved in apartment construction and management. In addition, aid recipients are no longer geographically concentrated and marked publicly.

There are two federal housing programs organized somewhat along these lines, the so-called Section 8 certificate and voucher programs, founded in 1974 and 1983, respectively.[14] Under these programs, which serve nearly 2 million households, recipients search on the private market for housing units. If the dwelling meets certain quality standards and the rent is deemed fair by the government, it subsidizes the rent with payments directly to the landlord. (The tenant's rent payment is a fixed proportion of family income, currently set at 30 percent.) Unlike traditional public housing, Section 8 attempts to give the poor access to the existing stock of housing, instead of trying to add to the stock. However, Section 8 recipients are limited in their choice of dwellings, and cannot spend more than 30 percent of their incomes on rent.

Does publicly provided and subsidized low-income housing actually increase the stock of housing? To the extent that such housing merely replaces equivalent low-income housing that would have been supplied privately, then the housing programs may have little real effect on housing consumption among the poor. This is another version of the crowding-out phenomenon that we confronted earlier. Sinai and Waldfogel [2002] examined whether areas with more public and subsidized housing have more total housing, holding constant other variables that affect housing demand. They found that the government programs do increase the total stock of housing, but not on a one-for-one basis. Rather, for every three units of government subsidized housing there are two units less of housing that would have been provided by private markets. In short, some crowding out does occur. Sinai and Waldfogel find that crowding out is less important for programs such as Section 8 than for housing projects, which would seem to be another point in favor of the former.

One concern about public housing is that it reduces the economic self-sufficiency of its inhabitants. For example, because public housing is located far away from employment opportunities, tenants might have trouble getting jobs. Also, locating public housing in very poor neighborhoods might deprive young tenants of appropriate role models and contacts for jobs. And the physical environment provided by public housing may be detrimental to health.

If public housing generates such negative effects, then another benefit of voucher programs is simply getting low-income families into better environments. In an

---

[14] Details on the operation of the programs are provided in Olsen [2003].

interesting social experiment, a randomized group of public housing residents were given Section 8 housing vouchers and their subsequent social and economic status were compared to those who stayed behind in public housing. Four to seven years after random assignment, there were no statistically significant improvements in economic self-sufficiency, children's test scores, or physical health for the voucher recipients [Sanbonmatsu et al., 2006; Kling et al., 2007]. However, they did live in safer neighborhoods that had lower poverty rates than those who stayed in public housing [Kling et al., 2007]. Hence, the evidence on the overall effectiveness of voucher plans is mixed.

▶ PROGRAMS TO ENHANCE EARNINGS

Most expenditures for the poor are designed to increase their current consumption levels. In contrast, some programs have been designed to enhance their ability to support themselves in the future. These include educational and job-training programs.

Education

A popular view is that much poverty in the United States is due to poor development of cognitive and social skills in the children of disadvantaged families. Research by Nobel laureate James Heckman suggests that government interventions at a young age can improve these skills, improving the long-term economic and health outcomes of the recipients [Heckman, 2008]. Indeed, Heckman finds that programs targeted at young children in disadvantaged families have much higher economic returns than later interventions such as reduced student-to-teacher ratios or job-training programs. (See Chapter 7 for further discussion.)

Under legislation passed in 1965, the federal government provides funds to individual school districts for compensatory education at the elementary and secondary levels for disadvantaged students. The most famous example is the Head Start Program, which provides preschool activities for four- and five-year-old children from disadvantaged backgrounds. The idea is to ensure that by the time they start kindergarten, they can achieve at the same level as children from more affluent families. A survey of the literature on Head Start by Ludwig and Phillips [2007] concludes that the program offers long-term benefits to recipients and that these benefits outweigh the costs.

Employment and Job Training

Federal job-training programs address another possible cause of poverty—lack of job market skills. Suppose that poor people are not able to obtain jobs that provide good training because of discrimination, or because no such jobs are located in their neighborhoods. The goal of these programs is for the government to provide opportunities to develop marketable skills.

Do these programs work? According to the studies surveyed by Heckman [2000], they are not terribly effective. For adult females on welfare, the programs often produce earnings gains, and these gains exceed the costs of the programs. However, the impacts are not big enough to move many participants out of poverty. For males, programs that provide assistance with job search appear to be successful in the sense that the returns in terms of increased wages exceed the costs of the program, but these earnings increases are not large enough to make a significant difference in living standards. In short, "The best available evidence indicates that training programs are an inefficient transfer mechanism and an inefficient investment policy for low-skill adult workers" [Heckman, 2000].

▶ OVERVIEW

A reasonable way to begin an evaluation of the welfare system is to examine its impact on poverty rates. The impact is quite substantial. The various cash, food, and housing transfer programs reduce the poverty rate by about 48 percent.[15] This figure, of course, does not take into account the fact that in the absence of welfare, people's earnings might have been higher. Still, in terms of the popular metaphor of government welfare programs as a safety net, it appears that although many people have slipped through the holes, many others also have been caught. In this context, it is interesting to note that the introduction of TANF seems to have reduced the poverty rate among less-skilled women by about 2 percentage points [Blank, 2002, p. 1144]. This is significant because during the debate over TANF, there were many who feared that time limits and other provisions would lead to an increase in poverty.

An important question in this context is how work incentives have been affected in the process of redistributing all this income. It is a complicated question for several reasons. First, the earned income tax credit simultaneously subsidizes earnings for some workers and taxes them for others. Second, as stressed earlier, states have considerable autonomy in determining the implicit marginal tax rates associated with their programs, and these rates vary dramatically from state to state. Third, while our focus in this chapter has been on the implicit marginal tax rates associated with welfare, the explicit taxes levied on earnings by state and federal governments also affect incentives. In light of these considerations, the work incentives that confront an individual depend both on his or her state of residence and position in the earnings distribution.

While there is thus no "typical" welfare recipient, it is still useful to look at some illustrative calculations. Figure 13.10 shows Holt's [2005] computations of marginal tax rates on earnings for a single parent with two children in Wisconsin in 2000. It takes into account all federal and state taxes, as well as food stamps, TANF, Medicaid benefit reductions, and Wisconsin's subsidized child care and health insurance programs. The negative marginal tax rate at the very bottom of the income scale reflects the EITC subsidy. But the figure makes clear that this is soon overwhelmed by the various implicit and explicit marginal tax rates. Indeed, food stamp reductions in conjunction with the EITC phase-out contribute to marginal tax rates that, in some parts of the income distribution, reach 100 percent! We conclude that the cumulative effect of the various welfare programs and the tax system is not encouraging to work effort.

The US welfare system has been unpopular for years for reasons that go beyond work incentive issues. Academic economists—both liberals and conservatives—have focused much of their criticism on the messiness of the current system. It certainly is a hodgepodge. Some programs give cash assistance, and some are in-kind; some

---

[15] Personal communication from Dr. Wendell Primus, Joint Economic Committee, US Congress.

Figure 13.10

Estimated marginal tax rates for a one-parent, two-child household residing in Wisconsin (2000)
The cumulative effect of the various federal and state welfare programs and taxes can lead to high effective marginal tax rates.

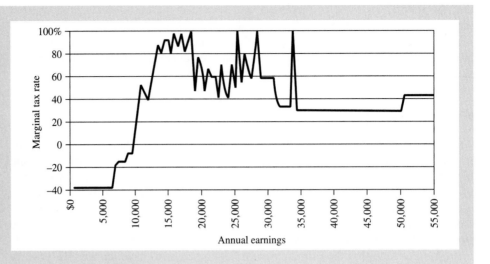

Source: Holt [2005, Part D, Figure 1].

are entitlements, and others are unavailable even to people with incomes far below the poverty line. Administrative responsibilities and financing are split haphazardly among federal, state, and local governments, and each program operates under its own rules.

Why not replace the various programs with a single cash assistance program? Murray [2006] offers such a plan to eliminate all transfer programs at the federal, state, and local levels, and instead substitute an annual cash grant of $10,000 for life starting at the age of 21. He argues that such a plan would be simpler to administer, effectively reduce poverty, and enhance efficiency.

Such proposals have several problems. First, as suggested earlier in the chapter, it appears to be infeasible politically. Second, from an efficiency point of view, a system of categorical programs may have some merit. If relatively large amounts of aid can be targeted at groups for whom labor supply incentives are not very important (for example, the disabled), then the overall efficiency of the system may be enhanced. Thus, while the current system is by no means ideal, its categorical structure is not necessarily a fatal flaw.

Perhaps the most controversial question associated with the current system is whether the benefits are high enough. Standard welfare economics indicates that the correct answer depends on the strength of one's preferences for income equality and the distortions in incentives induced by the system. A very different viewpoint is that poverty has moral and spiritual roots, and that conventional government programs are bound to fail because they fail to take this into account. In recent years, there has been some experimentation with faith-based social services, in which the government provides money to churches and other faith-based institutions, and they administer the programs. Indeed, increased federal support of faith-based programs was an important element of President George W. Bush's legislative agenda. There is some anecdotal evidence that such programs are effective, but not much in the way of systematic analysis.

An extreme critique of the current system, based in part on the fact that it ignores spiritual factors, is that "people cannot really be happy without self-respect, and it is difficult, if not impossible, to acquire self-respect living on the dole (at least if they are capable of supporting themselves)" [Browning, 2002, p. 527]. Proponents of transfers to the poor are quick to point out that they are not the only beneficiaries of public "charity." Numerous government expenditure and tax programs benefit middle- and upper-income people. Spending by the government on research and development increases the incomes of scientists [Goolsbee, 1998]; subsidies for the production of energy increase the incomes of the owners of oil wells; and defense programs increase the incomes of munitions manufacturers. Sometimes programs that are ostensibly for other purposes are actually nothing more than income distribution programs favoring special interests. For example, most economists believe that import quotas on various commodities such as sugar and peanuts serve no efficiency purpose and are only a veiled way of transferring income to the politically powerful agricultural industry, particularly the wealthy owners of large farms. However, "welfare to the rich" does not carry that label. Perhaps that is why no one worries about them losing *their* self-respect.

Summary

- Means-tested programs transfer income to people whose resources fall below a certain level. Government means-tested programs are about 5 percent of GDP.

- The current program of cash assistance, Temporary Assistance for Needy Families (TANF), was enacted in 1996. It removed the entitlement to cash benefits. In general, recipients cannot receive cash transfers for more than five years, and after two years they must take part in some work-related activity.

- Under TANF, the states have virtually total control over the structure of their welfare systems. States vary considerably in the rates at which they reduce benefits when recipients earn income.

- Any income maintenance system must deal with several issues, including the conflict between adequate support and good work incentives, welfare dependence, work requirements, and state versus federal administration.

- The earned income tax credit (EITC) provides a subsidy to the wages of qualified low-income individuals. The phase-out of the EITC after earnings exceed a certain threshold imposes a high implicit marginal tax rate on earnings. Although administered through the tax system, it is now the most important program for cash transfers to the poor.

- Supplemental Security Income (SSI) provides cash grants to the aged, blind, or disabled.

- Medicaid, the largest spending program for the poor, provides certain medical services at no charge.

- The unemployment insurance system has imperfect experience ratings for employers. Moreover, its benefits are frequently a substantial proportion of prior earnings. Both of these factors increase unemployment.

- A food stamp is a voucher that can be used only for the purchase of food. Food stamps appear to induce more food consumption than an equivalent amount of cash.

- In the past, housing assistance in the United States focused on the creation of public housing for the poor. The Section 8 program now provides a small number of recipients with housing vouchers to pay the rent on dwellings of their choice.

- The goal of education and job-training programs is to enhance the ability of the poor to support themselves in the future. The efficacy of job-training programs does not appear to be very substantial. However, compensatory education for children, such as Head Start, leads to long-term improvements in educational attainment and education.

Discussion Questions

1. In California, a welfare recipient can earn $225 per month without having her benefits reduced. Beyond $225, benefits are reduced by 50 cents for every dollar of earnings. Consider Elizabeth, a resident of California, who can earn $10 per hour. If she does not work at all, she is eligible for welfare benefits of $645.

   a. If she works 10 hours, how much are her earnings, how much is her welfare benefit, and how much is her income?

   b. After Elizabeth works a certain number of hours, she does not receive any benefit at all. What is that number of hours?

   c. Use your answer to parts *a* and *b* to plot her budget constraint.

   d. Sketch a set of indifference curves consistent with Elizabeth's participating in the labor market.

2. Suppose you wanted to conduct an econometric study of the impact of Head Start attendance on future earnings. You decide to define your treatment group as those children who attended Head Start and your control group as those with similar family backgrounds who did not attend Head Start. Why might such an analysis provide misleading results? What would be a more credible way of estimating the impact?

3. Suppose that the government introduces an income maintenance program for low-income people that offers a basic grant of $200 per month, but that for any earnings above $100, the grant is reduced dollar for dollar (that is, the marginal tax rate is 100 percent).

   a. Assume that Lois can earn $10 per hour and has no other income. Sketch her annual budget constraint with and without the program in effect. Carefully label the axes, intercepts, and all kink points. At how many hours of work is the grant reduced to zero?

   b. According to economic theory, what would happen to Lois's hours worked and *total* income if the government instituted this welfare plan?

   c. Suppose that the government decides to keep the monthly base grant at $200, but to lower the implicit marginal tax rate on

earnings to 66.67 percent. Draw the new budget constraint.

   d. Relative to the first plan, how will introduction of the new plan affect Lois's hours of work and total income?

4. Philip's demand curve for housing is shown in the following figure. (Assume that quantity of housing is measured simply by the number of square feet. Other aspects of quality are ignored.) The market price of housing is P_1; Philip can purchase as much housing as he desires at that price. Alternatively, Philip can live in public housing for a price of P_2 per square foot, but the only apartment available to him has H_2 square feet.

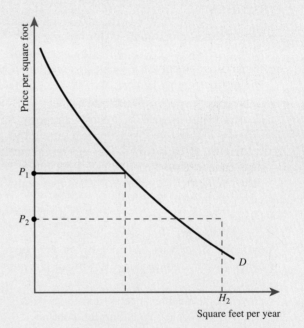

   Will Philip choose public housing or rent on the private market? Explain carefully. [Hint: Compare consumer surplus (see the appendix to the book) under both possibilities.]

5. Food stamp benefits are phased out in a complicated fashion that varies from state to state. However, at some point near the poverty line, food stamps worth about $1,250 are suddenly lost. Ignoring other aspects of the tax and transfer systems, sketch the income-leisure budget

constraint associated with this provision. (Don't worry about the specific slope and intercept of the constraint; just sketch the general shape.)

6. In the analysis of TANF's work incentives in Figure 13.4, the individual continues to work while receiving welfare. Reproduce the budget constraint from that figure, and sketch a set of indifference curves for an individual who would choose not to work while receiving welfare benefits.

7. The Section 8 program for housing assistance discussed in this chapter in effect shifts out the demand curve for low-income housing in a given community. Draw supply and demand diagrams that are consistent with the following outcomes:

   a. The price of low-income housing gets bid up, and there is no increase in the stock of low-income housing.

   b. There is no increase in the price of low-income housing, and there is an increase in the stock of low-income housing.

   c. There is an increase in the price of low-income housing, and there is an increase in the stock of low-income housing.

   Which of these scenarios is most consistent with the research by Sinai and Waldfogel that is discussed in the chapter?

8. Consider Eleanor, who qualifies for the earned income tax credit as depicted in Figure 13.8. Suppose that Eleanor can earn $8 per hour. Taking into account the EITC and ignoring other aspects of the tax and transfer systems:

   a. How much do her earnings increase when her labor supply increases from 0 to 1,000 hours per year?

   b. How much do her earnings increase when her labor supply increases from 1,000 to 1,500 hours per year?

   c. How much do her earnings increase when her labor supply increases from 1,500 to 2,000 hours per year?

   In each case, compute the incremental amount of earnings associated with the increase in work effort. Relate your answer to the implicit marginal tax rates embodied in the EITC.

9. Since the 1980s, individuals' UI benefits have been subject to the federal personal income tax (but not Social Security taxes). However, in 2009, the taxation of UI benefits for certain individuals was temporarily suspended. Suppose Wang's earnings are taxed at a rate of 15 percent by the personal income tax and at a combined rate of 7.45 percent by the Social Security and Medicare payroll taxes. Suppose that if Wang becomes unemployed, unemployment insurance replaces 50 percent of his before-tax earnings and benefits are available for two weeks.

   a. Prior to the 2009 legislation, what percent of Wang's *after*-tax income was replaced by UI? What happened to the replacement rate as a consequence of the 2009 legislation? What are the implications for the effects of UI on unemployment?

   b. Diagram Wang's budget constraint showing the trade-off between weekly income and hours of leisure per week, both when he is collecting UI and when he is off of UI. What are the consequences for hours worked if UI benefits are extended past their two-week limit?

10. In 2009, Congress considered a bill that would allow recipients of unemployment insurance to qualify for Medicaid, without being subject to means testing. Sketch the budget constraint for someone receiving UI benefits and Medicaid, assuming that the person would not qualify for Medicaid once employed.

Part Four

FRAMEWORK FOR TAX ANALYSIS

In 1899, the US Supreme Court declared: "The power to tax is the one great power upon which the whole national fabric is based. It is as necessary to the existence and prosperity of a nation as is the air he breathes to the natural man. It is not only the power to destroy but also the power to keep alive" [*Nicol v. Ames,* 1899]. Both politicians and economists have long realized the importance of taxation and have searched for a set of principles to guide tax policy. Centuries ago, the French statesman Jean-Baptiste Colbert suggested, "The art of taxation is the art of plucking the goose so as to get the largest possible amount of feathers with the least possible squealing" [Armitage-Smith, 1907, p. 36]. Modern economics takes a somewhat less cynical approach, emphasizing how taxes should be levied to enhance economic efficiency and to promote a "fair" distribution of income. These are the topics of the next three chapters. Our goal is to construct a theoretical framework for thinking about tax policy. A thorough discussion of actual US tax institutions is deferred to Part Five.

TAXATION AND INCOME DISTRIBUTION

Struggle and contrive as you will, lay your taxes as you please, the traders will shift it off from their own gain.

—JOHN LOCKE

American policy debates about the tax system are dominated by the question of whether its burden is distributed fairly. A sensible discussion of this normative issue requires some understanding of the positive question of how taxes affect the distribution of income. A simple way to determine how taxes change the income distribution would be to conduct a survey in which each person is asked how many dollars he or she pays to the tax collector each year. Simple—but usually wrong. An example demonstrates that assessing correctly the burden of taxation is much more complicated.

Suppose the price of a bottle of wine is $10. The government imposes a tax of $1 per bottle, to be collected in the following way: Every time a bottle is purchased, the tax collector (who is lurking about the store) takes a dollar out of the wine seller's hand before the money is put into the cash register. A casual observer might conclude that the wine seller is paying the tax.

However, suppose that a few weeks after its imposition, the tax induces a price rise to $11 per bottle. Clearly, the proprietor receives the same amount per bottle as he did before the tax. The tax has apparently made him no worse off. Consumers pay the entire tax in the form of higher prices. On the other hand, suppose that after the tax the price increases to only $10.30. In this case, the proprietor keeps only $9.30 for each bottle sold; he is worse off by 70 cents per bottle. Consumers are also worse off, however, because they have to pay 30 cents more per bottle.[1] In this case, producers and consumers share the burden of the tax. Yet another possibility is that after the tax is imposed, the price stays at $10. If this happens, the consumer is no worse off, while the seller bears the full burden of the tax.

The **statutory incidence** of a tax indicates who is legally responsible for the tax. All three cases in the preceding paragraph are identical in the sense that the statutory incidence is on the seller. But the situations differ drastically with respect to who really bears the burden. Because prices may change in response to the tax, knowledge of statutory incidence tells us *essentially nothing* about who really pays the tax. In contrast, the **economic incidence** of a tax is the change in the distribution of

---

statutory incidence

Indicates who is legally responsible for a tax.

economic incidence

The change in the distribution of real income induced by a tax.

---

[1] Actually, the change in the prices faced by consumers and producers is only part of the story. There is also a burden due to the tax-induced distortion of choice. See Chapter 15.

private real income induced by a tax. Our focus in this chapter is on the forces that determine the extent to which statutory and economic incidence differ—the amount of **tax shifting.**

tax shifting

The difference between statutory incidence and economic incidence.

▶ TAX INCIDENCE: GENERAL REMARKS

Several observations should be kept in mind in any discussion of how taxes affect the distribution of income.

Only People Can Bear Taxes

In a discussion of a tax bill that was once being considered by Congress, a *Wall Street Journal* columnist observed that "the Senate voted to approve a major tax-law revamp that focuses mainly on corporations, but lawmakers also approved important changes that will benefit many people" [Herman, 2004a]. By drawing a sharp distinction between "corporations" and "people," the statement reflects a common fallacy—that businesses have an independent ability to bear a tax. True, the US legal system treats certain institutions such as corporations as if they were people. Although for many purposes this is a convenient fiction, it sometimes creates confusion. From an economist's point of view, people—stockholders, workers, landlords, consumers—bear taxes. A corporation cannot.

Given that only people can bear taxes, how should they be classified for purposes of incidence analysis? Often their role in production—what inputs they supply to the production process—is used. (Inputs are often referred to as *factors of production*.) The focus is on how the tax system changes the distribution of income among capitalists, laborers, and landlords. This is referred to as the **functional distribution of income.**

functional distribution of income

The way income is distributed among people when they are classified according to the inputs they supply to the production process (for example, landlords, capitalists, laborers).

Framing the analysis this way seems a bit old-fashioned. Perhaps in 18th-century England property owners never worked and workers owned no property. But in the contemporary United States, many people who derive most of their income from labor also have savings accounts and/or common stocks. (Often, these assets are held for individuals in pensions.) Similarly, some people own huge amounts of capital and also work full-time. Thus, it seems more relevant to study how taxes affect the way in which total income is distributed among people: the **size distribution of income.** Given information on what proportion of people's income is from capital, land, and labor, changes in the functional distribution can be translated into changes in the size distribution. For example, a tax that lowers the relative return on capital tends to hurt those at the top of the income distribution because a relatively high proportion of the incomes of the rich is from capital.[2]

size distribution of income

The way that total income is distributed across income classes.

Other classification schemes might be interesting for particular problems. When increases in the federal tax on cigarettes are proposed, the incidence by region receives a great deal of attention. (Are people from tobacco-growing states going to

---

[2] However, some low-income retirees also derive the bulk of their income from capital.

suffer disproportionate harm?) Alternatively, when proposals are made to change the taxation of land in urban areas, analysts often look at incidence by race. It is easy to think of further examples based on sex, age, and so forth.

Both Sources and Uses of Income Should Be Considered

In the previous wine tax example, it is natural to assume that the distributional effects of the tax depend crucially on people's spending patterns. To the extent that the price of wine increases, the people who tend to consume a lot of wine are made worse off. However, if the tax reduces the demand for wine, the factors employed in wine production may suffer income losses. Thus, the tax can also change the income distribution by affecting the sources of income. Suppose that poor people spend a relatively large proportion of their incomes on wine, but that vineyards tend to be owned by the rich. Then on the uses of income side, the tax redistributes income away from the poor, but on the sources side, it redistributes income away from the rich. The overall incidence depends on how both the sources and uses of income are affected. This distinction is important for understanding the debate over former Vice President Gore's proposal to clean up the Florida Everglades. Because the ecology of the Everglades is harmed by the runoff from sugar fields, he argued that sugar products be subjected to a special tax and the proceeds used to finance a cleanup. Opposition came not only from consumer groups who were concerned about the price of products using sugar but also from Florida *workers,* who realized that by reducing the demand for sugar, this tax would hurt their incomes.

In practice, economists commonly ignore effects on the sources side when considering a tax on a commodity and ignore the uses side when analyzing a tax on an input. This procedure is appropriate if the most *systematic* effects of a commodity tax are on the uses of income and those of a factor tax on the sources of income. The assumption simplifies analyses, but its correctness must be considered for each case.

Incidence Depends on How Prices Are Determined

We have emphasized that the incidence problem is fundamentally one of determining how taxes change prices. Clearly, different models of price determination may give quite different answers to the question of who really bears a tax. This chapter considers several different models and compares the results.

A closely related issue is the time dimension of the analysis. Incidence depends on changes in prices, but change takes time. In most cases, responses are larger in the long run than the short run. Thus, the short- and long-run incidence of a tax may differ, and the time frame that is relevant for a given policy question must be specified.

Incidence Depends on the Disposition of Tax Revenues

Balanced-budget incidence computes the combined effects of levying taxes *and* government spending financed by those taxes. In general, the distributional effect of a tax depends on how the government spends the money. Expenditures on AIDS research have a very different distributional impact than spending on hot lunches for schoolchildren. Some studies assume the government spends the tax revenue exactly as the consumers would if they had received the money. This is equivalent to returning the revenue as a lump sum and letting consumers spend it.

Tax revenues are usually not earmarked for particular expenditures. It is then desirable to be able to abstract from the question of how the government spends the money. The idea is to examine how incidence differs when one tax is replaced with another, holding the government budget constant. This is called *differential tax incidence*. Because differential incidence looks at changes in taxes, a reference point is needed. The hypothetical "other tax" used as the basis of comparison is often assumed to be a **lump sum tax**—a tax for which the individual's liability does not depend upon behavior. (For example, a 10 percent income tax is *not* a lump sum tax because it depends on how much the individual earns. But a head tax of $500 independent of earnings *is* a lump sum tax.)

Finally, *absolute tax incidence* examines the effects of a tax when there is no change in either other taxes or government expenditure. Absolute incidence is of most interest for macroeconomic models in which tax levels are changed to achieve some stabilization goal.

Tax Progressiveness Can Be Measured in Several Ways

Suppose that an investigator has managed to calculate every person's real share of a particular tax—the economic incidence as defined previously. The bottom line of such an exercise is often a characterization of the tax as proportional, progressive, or regressive. The definition of **proportional** is straightforward; it describes a situation in which the ratio of taxes paid to income is constant regardless of income level.[3]

Defining progressive and regressive is not easy, and, unfortunately, ambiguities in definition sometimes confuse public debate. A natural way to define these words is in terms of the **average tax rate,** the ratio of taxes paid to income. If the average tax rate increases with income, the system is **progressive;** if it falls, the tax is **regressive.**

Confusion arises because some people think of progressiveness in terms of the **marginal tax rate**—the *change* in taxes paid with respect to a change in income. To illustrate the distinction, consider the following very simple income tax structure. Each individual computes her tax bill by subtracting $3,000 from income and paying an amount equal to 20 percent of the remainder. (If the difference is negative, the individual gets a subsidy equal to 20 percent of the figure.) Table 14.1 shows the amount of tax paid, the average tax rate, and the marginal tax rate for each of several income levels. The average rates increase with income. However, the marginal tax rate is constant at 0.2 because for each additional dollar earned, the individual pays an additional 20 cents, regardless of income level. People could disagree about the progressiveness of this tax system and each be right according to their own definitions. It is therefore very important to make the definition clear when using the terms *regressive* and *progressive*. From here on, we assume they are defined in terms of average tax rates.

lump sum tax

A tax whose value is independent of the individual's behavior.

proportional

A tax system under which an individual's average tax rate is the same at each level of income.

average tax rate

Ratio of taxes paid to income.

progressive

A tax system under which an individual's average tax rate increases with income.

regressive

A tax system under which an individual's average tax rate decreases with income.

marginal tax rate

The proportion of the last dollar of income taxed by the government.

---

[3] However, the definition of *income* is not straightforward; see Chapter 17.

Table 14.1 **Tax Liabilities under a Hypothetical Tax System**

Income	Tax Liability	Average Tax Rate	Marginal Tax Rate
$ 2,000	$ -200	-0.10	0.2
3,000	0	0	0.2
5,000	400	0.08	0.2
10,000	1,400	0.14	0.2
30,000	5,400	0.18	0.2

Under this hypothetical tax system, each individual computes her tax bill by subtracting $3,000 from income and paying an amount equal to 20 percent of the remainder. While the marginal tax rate is constant at 20 percent, the average tax rate is increasing as income increases, which means the tax is progressive.

Measuring *how* progressive a tax system is presents an even harder task than defining progressiveness. Many reasonable alternatives have been proposed, and we consider two simple ones. The first says that the greater the increase in average tax rates as income increases, the more progressive the system. Algebraically, let T_0 and T_1 be the true (as opposed to statutory) tax liabilities at income levels I_0 and I_1, respectively (I_1 is greater than I_0). The measurement of progressiveness, v_1, is

$$v_1 = \frac{\dfrac{T_1}{I_1} - \dfrac{T_0}{I_0}}{I_1 - I_0} \tag{14.1}$$

Once the analyst computes the values of T_1 and T_0 and substitutes into Equation (14.1), the tax system with the higher value of v_1 is said to be more progressive.

The second possibility is to say that one tax system is more progressive than another if its elasticity of tax revenues with respect to income (i.e., the percentage change in tax revenues divided by percentage change in income) is higher. Here the expression to be evaluated is v_2, defined as

$$v_2 = \frac{T_1 - T_0}{T_0} \div \frac{I_1 - I_0}{I_0} \tag{14.2}$$

Now consider the following proposal: Everyone's tax liability is to be increased by 20 percent of the amount of tax he or she currently pays. This proposal would increase the tax liability of a person who formerly paid T_0 to $1.2 \times T_0$, and the liability that was formerly T_1 to $1.2 \times T_1$. Member of Congress A says the proposal will make the tax system more progressive, while member of Congress B says it has no effect on progressiveness whatsoever. Who is right? It depends on the progressivity measure. Substituting the expressions $1.2 \times T_0$ and $1.2 \times T_1$ for T_0 and T_1, respectively, in Equation (14.1), v_1 increases by 20 percent. The proposal thus increases progressiveness. On the other hand, if the same substitution is done in Equation (14.2), the value of v_2 is unchanged. (Both the numerator and denominator are multiplied by 1.2, which cancels out the effect.) The lesson here is that even very intuitively appealing measures of progressiveness can give different answers.[4] Again, intelligent public debate requires that people make their definitions clear.

---

[4] Note also that v_1 and v_2, in general, depend on the level of income. That is, even a single tax system does not usually have a constant v_1 and v_2. This further complicates discussions of the degree of progressiveness.

▶ PARTIAL EQUILIBRIUM MODELS

With preliminaries out of the way, we turn now to the fundamental issue of this chapter: how taxes affect the income distribution. Recall that the essence of the problem is that taxes induce changes in relative prices. Knowing how prices are determined is therefore critical to the analysis. In this section we analyze **partial equilibrium models** of price determination—models that look only at the market in which the tax is imposed and ignore the ramifications in other markets. This kind of analysis is most appropriate when the market for the taxed commodity is relatively small compared to the economy as a whole. The vehicle for our analysis is the supply and demand model of perfect competition.

partial equilibrium models

Models that study only one market and ignore possible spillover effects in other markets.

Unit Taxes on Commodities

We study first the incidence of a **unit tax,** so named because it is levied as a fixed amount per unit of a commodity sold. For example, the federal government imposes a tax on champagne of $3.40 per wine gallon and a tax on cigarettes of $1.01 per pack. Suppose that the price and quantity of champagne are determined competitively by supply (S_c) and demand (D_c) as in Figure 14.1. Before imposition of the tax, the quantity demanded and price are Q_0 and P_0, respectively.

Now suppose that a unit tax of $u per gallon is imposed on each purchase, and the statutory incidence is on buyers. A key step in incidence analysis is to recognize that in the presence of a tax, the price paid by consumers and the price received by suppliers differ. Previously, we could use a supply-demand analysis to determine the *single* market price. Now, this analysis must be modified to accommodate two different prices, one for buyers and one for sellers.

We begin by determining how the tax affects the demand schedule. Consider an arbitrary point a on the demand curve. This point indicates that the *maximum* price

unit tax

A tax levied as a fixed amount per unit of commodity purchased.

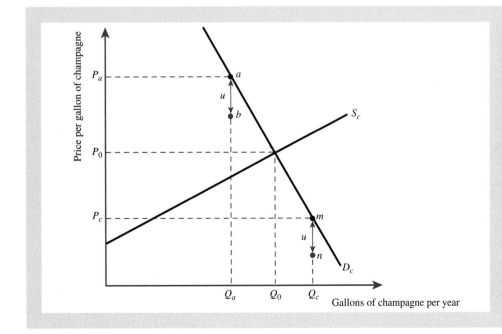

Figure 14.1
Price and quantity before taxation
A unit tax of $u per gallon changes the demand curve as perceived by suppliers. For example, the maximum price per gallon that people are willing to pay for Q_a is P_a. After the tax, when people pay P_a per gallon, producers only receive $P_a - u$ per gallon (which corresponds to point b). The new demand curve is located exactly u dollars below the old one.

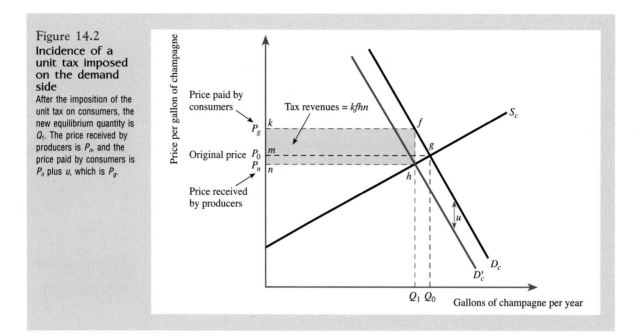

Figure 14.2

Incidence of a unit tax imposed on the demand side

After the imposition of the unit tax on consumers, the new equilibrium quantity is Q_1. The price received by producers is P_n, and the price paid by consumers is P_n plus u, which is P_g.

per gallon that people would be willing to pay for Q_a gallons is P_a. After the unit tax of u is imposed, the most that people would be willing to spend for Q_a is *still* P_a. There is no reason to believe the tax affects the underlying valuation people place on champagne. However, when people pay P_a per gallon, producers no longer receive the whole amount. Instead, they receive only $(P_a - u)$, an amount that is labeled point b in Figure 14.1. In other words, after the unit tax is imposed, a is no longer a point on the demand curve *as perceived by suppliers*. Point b is on the demand curve as perceived by suppliers, because they realize that if Q_a is supplied, they receive only $(P_a - u)$ per gallon. It is irrelevant to the suppliers how much consumers pay per gallon; all that matters to suppliers is the amount they receive per gallon.

Of course, point a was chosen arbitrarily. At any other point on the demand curve, the story is just the same. Thus, for example, after the tax is imposed, the price received by suppliers for output Q_c is at point n, which is found by subtracting the distance u from point m. Repeating this process at every point along the demand curve, we generate a new demand curve located exactly u dollars below the old one. In Figure 14.2, the demand curve so constructed is labeled D_c'. Schedule D_c' is relevant to suppliers because it shows how much they receive for each unit sold.

We are now in a position to find the equilibrium quantity of champagne after the unit tax is imposed. The equilibrium is where the supply equals demand as perceived by suppliers, output Q_1 in Figure 14.2. Thus, the tax lowers the quantity sold from Q_0 to Q_1.

The next step is to find the new equilibrium price. As noted earlier, there are really two prices at the new equilibrium: the price received by producers, and the price paid by consumers. The price received by producers is at the intersection of their effective demand and supply curves, which occurs at P_n. The price paid by consumers is P_n *plus* u, the unit tax. To find this price geometrically, we must go up from P_n a vertical distance exactly equal to u. But by construction, the distance between schedules D_c and D_c' is equal to u. Hence, to find the price paid by consumers, we simply go up from the intersection of D_c' and S_c to the original demand curve D_c.

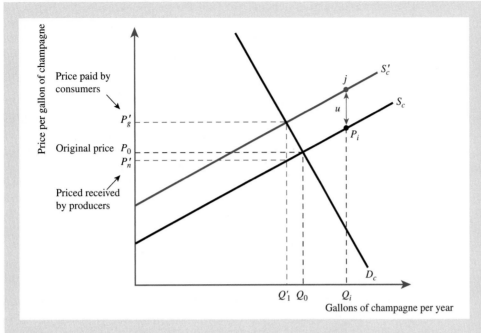

Figure 14.3
Incidence of a unit tax imposed on the supply side
A unit tax imposed on suppliers shifts up the supply curve by the amount of the tax. The posttax equilibrium quantity, price to consumers, and price to suppliers are the same as when the statutory incidence is on consumers.

The price so determined is P_g. Because P_g includes the tax, it is often referred to as the price *gross* of tax. On the other hand, P_n is the price *net* of tax.

The tax makes consumers worse off because P_g, the new price they face, is higher than the original price P_0. But the consumers' price does not increase by the full amount of the tax—$(P_g - P_0)$ is less than u. Producers also pay part of the tax in the form of a lower price received per gallon. Producers now receive only P_n, while before the tax they received P_0. Thus, the tax makes both producers and consumers worse off.[5] Notice that consumers and producers "split" the tax in the sense that the increase in the consumer price $(P_g - P_0)$ and the decrease in the producer price $(P_0 - P_n)$ just add up to $\$u$.

By definition, revenues collected are the product of the number of units purchased, Q_1, and the tax per unit, u. Geometrically, Q_1 is the width of rectangle *kfhn* and u is its height, so tax revenues are the area of this rectangle.

This analysis has two important implications.

The Incidence of a Unit Tax Is Independent of Whether It Is Levied on Consumers or Producers   Suppose the same tax u had been levied on the suppliers of champagne instead of the consumers. Consider an arbitrary price P_i on the original supply curve in Figure 14.3. The supply curve indicates that for suppliers to produce Q_i units, they must receive at least P_i per unit. After the unit tax, suppliers still need to receive P_i per unit. For them to do so, however, consumers must pay price $P_i + u$ per unit, which is shown geometrically as point j. It should now

---

[5] In terms of surplus measures, consumers are worse off by area *mkfg* and producers are worse off by *mghn*. The loss of total surplus exceeds the tax revenues by triangle *fhg;* this is the *excess burden* of the tax, as explained in Chapter 15. For a review of consumer and producer surplus, see the appendix at the end of this book.

be clear where the argument is heading. To find the supply curve as it is perceived by consumers, S_c must be shifted up by the amount of the unit tax. This new supply curve is labeled S_c'. The posttax equilibrium is at Q_1', where the schedules S_c' and D_c intersect. The price at the intersection, P_g', is the price paid by consumers. To find the price received by producers, we must subtract u from P_g', giving us P_n'. A glance at Figure 14.2 indicates that $Q_1' = Q_1$, $P_g' = P_g$, and $P_n' = P_n$. Thus, the incidence of the unit tax is independent of the side of the market on which it is levied.

This is the same as our statement that the statutory incidence of a tax tells us nothing of the economic incidence of the tax. It is irrelevant whether the tax collector (figuratively) stands next to consumers and takes u dollars every time they pay for a gallon of champagne or stands next to sellers and collects u dollars from them whenever they sell a gallon. Figures 14.2 and 14.3 prove that what matters is the size of the disparity the tax introduces between the price paid by consumers and the price received by producers, and not on which side of the market the disparity is introduced. The tax-induced difference between the price paid by consumers and the price received by producers is referred to as the **tax wedge.**

The Incidence of a Unit Tax Depends on the Elasticities of Supply and Demand

In Figure 14.2, consumers bear the brunt of the tax—the amount they pay goes up much more than the amount received by producers goes down. This result is strictly determined by the shapes of the demand and supply curves. In general, the more elastic the demand curve, the less the tax borne by consumers, other things being the same. Similarly, the more elastic the supply curve, the less the tax borne by producers, other things being the same. Intuitively, elasticity provides a rough measure of an economic agent's ability to escape the tax. The more elastic the demand, the easier it is for consumers to turn to other products when the price goes up, and therefore more of the tax must be borne by suppliers. Conversely, if consumers purchase the same amount regardless of price, the whole burden can be shifted to them. Similar considerations apply to the supply side.

Illustrations of extreme cases are provided in Figures 14.4 and 14.5. In Figure 14.4, commodity X is supplied perfectly inelastically. When a unit tax is imposed, the effective demand curve becomes D_X'. As before, the price received by producers (P_n) is at the intersection of S_X and D_X'. Note that P_n is exactly u less than P_0. Thus, the price received by producers falls by exactly the amount of the tax. At the same time, the price paid by consumers, P_g $(= P_n + u)$, remains at P_0. When supply is perfectly inelastic, producers bear the entire burden. Figure 14.5 represents an opposite extreme. The supply of commodity Z is perfectly elastic. Imposition of a unit tax leads to demand curve D_Z'. At the new equilibrium, quantity demanded is Z_1 and the price received by producers, P_n, is still P_0. The price paid by consumers, P_g, is therefore $P_0 + u$. In this case, consumers bear the entire burden of the tax.[6]

The Cigarette Tax Debate

Recently, the United States has been engaging in a policy debate regarding cigarette taxation. In 2009, the 39-cent-per-pack federal tax was raised to $1.01. Proponents of the higher tax seem to be interested primarily in discouraging smoking, and others care more about punishing tobacco producers. Those who want to discourage smoking are implicitly assuming that the tax will

---

[6] Note that as long as input costs are constant, the *long-run* supply curve for a competitive market is horizontal as in Figure 14.5. Hence, under these conditions, in the long run consumers bear the entire burden of the tax.

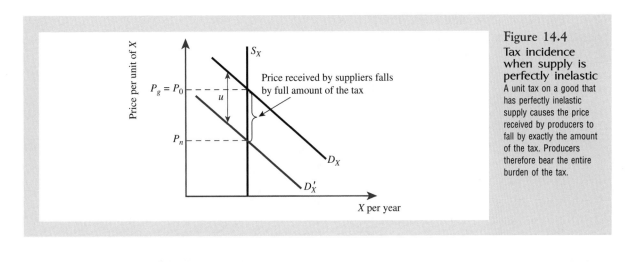

Figure 14.4
Tax incidence when supply is perfectly inelastic
A unit tax on a good that has perfectly inelastic supply causes the price received by producers to fall by exactly the amount of the tax. Producers therefore bear the entire burden of the tax.

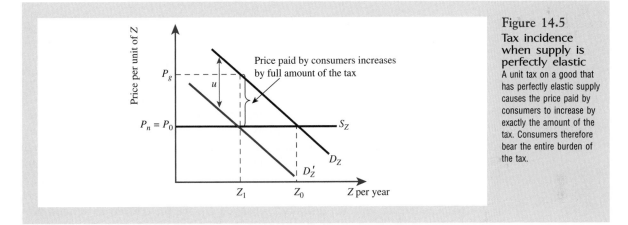

Figure 14.5
Tax incidence when supply is perfectly elastic
A unit tax on a good that has perfectly elastic supply causes the price paid by consumers to increase by exactly the amount of the tax. Consumers therefore bear the entire burden of the tax.

drive up the price paid by consumers, and those who want to punish the tobacco producers expect the price they receive to go down. How can one determine which effect would prevail? Our model of tax incidence tells us what we need to find out: the supply and demand elasticities in the cigarette market.

Ad Valorem Taxes

We now turn to the incidence of an **ad valorem tax,** a tax with a rate given as a *proportion* of the price. For example, the state of Tennessee levies a 5.5 percent tax on purchases of food. Virtually all state and local taxes on restaurant meals and clothing are ad valorem.

Luckily, the analysis of ad valorem taxes is very similar to that of unit taxes. The basic strategy is still to find out how the tax changes the effective demand curve and compute the new equilibrium. However, instead of moving the curve down by the same absolute amount for each quantity, the ad valorem tax lowers it by the same *proportion*. To show this, consider the demand (D_f) and supply (S_f) curves for food in Figure 14.6. In the absence of taxation, the equilibrium price and quantity are P_0 and

ad valorem tax

A tax computed as a percentage of the purchase value.

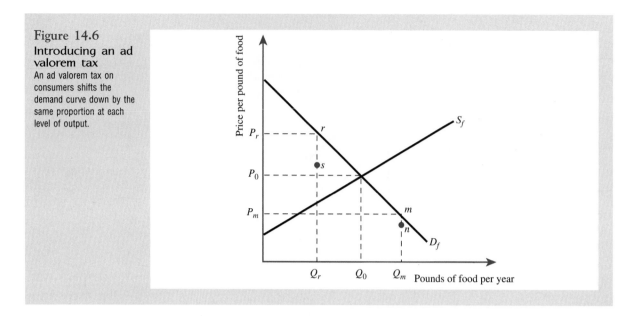

Figure 14.6
Introducing an ad valorem tax
An ad valorem tax on consumers shifts the demand curve down by the same proportion at each level of output.

Q_0, respectively. Now suppose that a tax of 25 percent of the gross price is levied on the consumption of food.[7] Consider point m on D_f. After the tax is imposed, P_m is still the most that consumers will pay for Q_m pounds of food; the amount producers will receive is 75 percent of the vertical distance between point m and the horizontal axis, which is labeled point n. Hence, point n is one point on the demand curve perceived by producers. Similarly, the price at point r migrates down one-quarter of the way between it and the horizontal axis to point s. Repeating this exercise for every point on D_f, the effective demand curve facing suppliers is determined as D_f' in Figure 14.7. From here, the analysis proceeds exactly as for a unit tax: The equilibrium is where S_f and D_f' intersect, with the quantity exchanged Q_1, the price received by food producers P_n, and the price paid by consumers P_g. As before, the incidence of the tax is determined by the elasticities of supply and demand.

This analysis is applicable to any number of situations. Suppose that Figure 14.7 were relabeled so that it represented the market for rental housing instead of the food market. Then we could show that the burden of the property tax doesn't depend on whether landlords or tenants pay the property tax. This is counter to the usual perception that landlords bear the burden simply because they write the check.

Taxes on Factors

So far we have discussed taxes on goods, but the analysis can also be applied to factors of production.

The Payroll Tax   Consider the payroll tax used to finance the Social Security system. As noted in Chapter 11, a tax equal to 7.65 percent of workers' earnings

---

[7] Measuring ad valorem tax rates involves a fundamental ambiguity. Is the tax measured as a percentage of the net or gross price? In this example, the tax is 25 percent of the gross price, which is equivalent to a rate of 33 percent of net price. If the price paid by the consumer were $1, the tax paid would be 25 cents, and the price received by producers would be 75 cents. Expressing the 25 cent tax bill as a fraction of 75 cents gives us a 33 percent rate as a proportion of the net price.

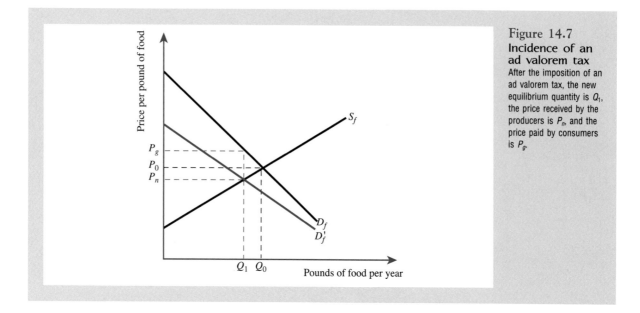

Figure 14.7
Incidence of an ad valorem tax
After the imposition of an ad valorem tax, the new equilibrium quantity is Q_1, the price received by the producers is P_n, and the price paid by consumers is P_g.

must be paid by their employers and a tax at the same rate paid by the workers themselves—a total of 15.3 percent.[8] This division has a long history and is a consequence of our lawmakers' belief that the payroll tax should be shared equally by employers and employees. But the *statutory distinction between workers and bosses is irrelevant.* As suggested earlier, the incidence of this labor tax is determined only by the wedge the tax puts between what employees receive and employers pay.

This point is illustrated in Figure 14.8, where D_L is the demand for labor and S_L is the supply of labor. For purposes of illustration, assume S_L to be perfectly inelastic. Before taxation, the wage is w_0. The ad valorem tax on labor moves the effective demand curve to D_L'. As usual, the distance between D_L' and D_L is the wedge between what is paid for an item and what is received by those who supply it. After the tax is imposed, the wage received by workers falls to w_n. On the other hand, w_g, the price paid by employers, stays at w_0. In this example, despite the statutory division of the tax, the wage rate received by workers falls by exactly the amount of the tax—they bear the entire burden.

Of course, we could have gotten just the opposite result by drawing the supply curve as perfectly elastic. The key point to remember is that nothing about the incidence of a tax can be known without information on the relevant behavioral elasticities. In fact, while estimates of the elasticity of labor supply vary, many economists believe that it is close to zero [Fuchs et al., 1998]. At least in the short run, labor probably bears most of the payroll tax, despite the congressional attempt to split the burden evenly.

Capital Taxation in a Global Economy   The strategy for analyzing a tax on capital is essentially the same as that for analyzing a tax on labor—draw the supply and demand curves, shift or pivot the relevant curve by an amount depending on the tax rate, and see how the after-tax equilibrium compares with the original one. In an economy that is closed to trade, it is reasonable to assume that the demand curve slopes down (firms demand less capital when its price goes up), and that the supply

---

[8] After earnings exceed a certain level, the payroll tax rate falls. See Chapter 11.

Figure 14.8

Incidence of a payroll tax with an inelastic supply of labor

If labor supply is perfectly inelastic, a payroll tax causes the wage received by workers to fall by the exact amount of the tax. Workers therefore bear the entire burden of the tax.

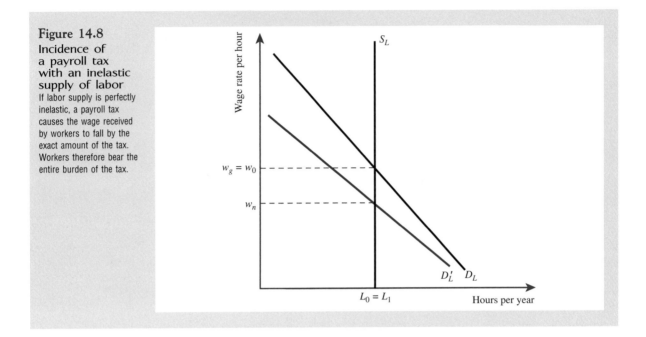

of capital slopes up (people supply more capital—save more—when the return to saving increases).[9] In this case, the owners of capital bear some of the burden of the tax, the precise amount depending on the supply and demand elasticities.

Suppose now that the economy is open and capital is perfectly mobile across countries. In effect, there is a single global market for capital, and if suppliers of capital cannot earn the going world rate of return in a particular country, they will take it out of that country and put it in another. In terms of a supply and demand diagram, the supply of capital to a particular country is perfectly elastic—its citizens can purchase all the capital they want at the going rate of return, but none whatsoever at a lower rate. The implications for the incidence of a tax on capital are striking. As in Figure 14.5, the before-tax price paid by the users of capital rises by exactly the amount of the tax, and the suppliers of capital bear no burden whatsoever. Intuitively, capital simply moves abroad if it has to bear any of the tax; hence, the before-tax rate of return has to rise.

Even in today's highly integrated world economy, capital is not perfectly mobile across countries. Moreover, for a country like the United States whose capital market is large relative to the world market, it is doubtful that the supply curve is perfectly horizontal. Nevertheless, policymakers who ignore globalization will overestimate their ability to place the burden of taxation on owners of capital. To the extent that capital is internationally mobile, taxes on capitalists are shifted to others, and the apparent progressivity of taxes on capital is illusory.

Commodity Taxation without Competition

The assumption of competitive markets has played a major role in our analysis. We now discuss how the results might change under alternative market structures.

---

[9] However, saving need not increase with the rate of return. See Chapter 18.

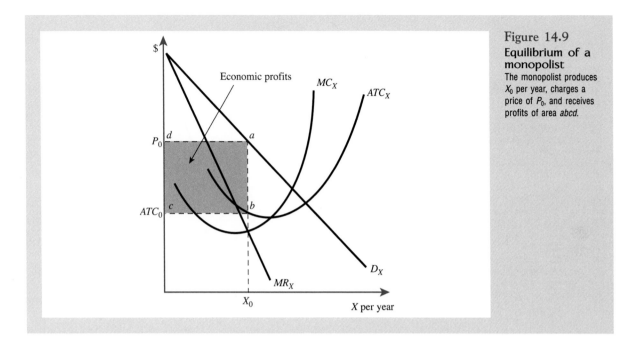

Figure 14.9
Equilibrium of a monopolist
The monopolist produces X_0 per year, charges a price of P_0, and receives profits of area *abcd*.

Monopoly   The polar opposite of competition is monopoly—one seller. Figure 14.9 depicts a monopolist that produces commodity X. Before any taxation, the demand curve facing the monopolist is D_X, and the associated marginal revenue curve is MR_X. The marginal cost curve for the production of X is MC_X, and the average total cost curve, ATC_X. As usual, the condition for profit maximization is that production be carried to the point where marginal revenue equals marginal cost, at output X_0 where the price charged is P_0. Economic profit per unit is the difference between average revenue and average total cost, distance ab. The number of units sold is db. Hence, total profit is ab times db, which is the area of rectangle $abdc$.

Now suppose that a unit tax of u is levied on X. For exactly the same reasons as before, the effective demand curve facing the producer shifts down by a vertical distance equal to u.[10] In Figure 14.10, this demand curve is labeled D_X'. At the same time, the marginal revenue curve facing the firm also shifts down by distance u because the tax reduces the firm's incremental revenue for each unit sold. The new effective marginal revenue curve is labeled MR_X'.

The profit-maximizing output, X_1, is found at the intersection of MR_X' and MC_X. Using output X_1, we find the price received by the monopolist by going up to D_X', the demand curve facing him, and locate price P_n. The price paid by consumers is determined by adding u to P_n, which is shown as price P_g on the diagram. After-tax profit per unit is the difference between the price *received by the monopolist* and average total cost, distance f_g. The number of units sold is if. Therefore, monopoly economic profits after tax are measured by area *fghi*.

What are the effects of the tax? Quantity demanded goes down ($X_1 < X_0$), the price paid by consumers goes up ($P_g > P_0$), and the price received by the monopolist goes down ($P_n < P_0$). Note that monopoly profits are lower under the tax—area *fghi* in

---

[10] Alternatively, we could shift the marginal cost curve *up* by u. The final outcomes are identical.

Figure 14.10
Imposition of a unit tax on a monopolist
The imposition of a unit tax on a monopolistically produced good shifts the effective demand curve and the marginal revenue curve down by the amount of the tax. The tax reduces the equilibrium quantity from X_0 to X_1, increases the price paid by consumers from P_0 to P_g, decreases the price received by the producer from P_0 to P_n, and decreases the monopolist's profits from area *abcd* to area *fghi*.

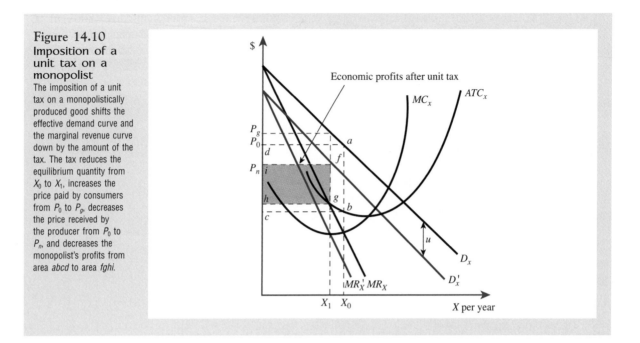

Figure 14.10 is smaller than area *abdc* in Figure 14.9. Despite its market power, a monopolist is generally made worse off by a unit tax on the product it sells. Public debates often assume that a firm with market power can simply pass on all taxes to consumers. This analysis shows that even a completely greedy and grasping monopolist must bear some of the burden. As before, the precise share of the burden borne by consumers depends on the elasticity of the demand schedule.

It is straightforward to repeat the exercise for an ad valorem tax on the monopolist (D_X and MR_X pivot instead of moving down in a parallel fashion); this is left as an exercise for the reader.

Oligopoly   Between the polar extremes of perfect competition and monopoly is the oligopoly market structure in which there are a "few" sellers. Unfortunately, there is no well-developed theory of tax incidence in oligopoly. The reason for this embarrassing fact is simple: Incidence depends primarily on how relative prices change when taxes are imposed, but there is no generally accepted theory of oligopolistic price determination.

Still, we can get a sense of the issues involved by imagining the problem faced by the firms in an oligopolistic market. From the firms' point of view, the ideal situation would be for them to collude and jointly produce the output that maximizes the profits of the entire industry. This output level is referred to as the *cartel solution*. (A cartel is just a group of producers that act together to maximize profits. The international oil cartel OPEC is the most famous example.) The cartel solution requires each firm to cut its output to force up the market price. The problem for the firms is that the cartel solution is very difficult to obtain. Why? Once an agreement about how much each firm should produce is reached, each firm has an incentive to cheat on that agreement—to take advantage of the higher price and produce more than its quota of output. (Again, think about OPEC, and the problems it has in keeping its members from producing "too much" oil.) Consequently, output in an oligopolistic market is typically higher than the cartel solution. The firms would all be better off if there were some mechanism to force all of them to reduce their output.

What happens when this industry's output is subjected to a tax? As is the case both for competition and monopoly, the firms reduce their output. However, unlike the other market structures, this is not necessarily bad for the oligopolistic firms. To be sure, for any given level of before-tax profits, the firms are worse off, because they have to pay the tax. However, as the firms contract their outputs, they move closer to the cartel solution, so their before-tax profits increase. It is theoretically possible for before-tax profits to increase by so much that even after paying the tax, the firms are better off [Delipalla and O'Donnell, 2001]. Of course, it is also possible for the firms to be worse off. One needs more information on just how much the firms cut back their output to obtain a definitive answer.

As economic behavior under oligopoly becomes better understood, improved models of incidence will be developed. In the meantime, most economists feel fairly comfortable in relying on the predictions produced by competitive models, although they realize these are only approximations.

Profits Taxes

So far we have been discussing taxes based on sales. Firms can also be taxed on their **economic profits,** defined as the return to owners of the firm in excess of the opportunity costs of the factors used in production. (Economic profits are also referred to as *supranormal* or *excess* profits.) We now show that for profit-maximizing firms, a tax on economic profits cannot be shifted—it is borne only by the owners of the firm.

Consider first a perfectly competitive firm in short-run equilibrium. The firm's output is determined by the intersection of its marginal cost and marginal revenue schedules. A proportional tax on economic profits changes neither marginal cost nor marginal revenue. Therefore, no firm has the incentive to change its output decision. Because output does not change, neither does the price paid by consumers, so they are no worse off. The tax is completely absorbed by the firms. Here's another way to get to the same result: If the tax rate on economic profits is t_p, the firm's objective is to maximize after-tax profits, $(1 - t_p)\Pi$, where Π is the pretax level of economic profits. But it is just a matter of arithmetic that whatever strategy maximizes Π is identical to the one that maximizes $(1 - t_p)\Pi$. Hence, output and price faced by consumers stay the same, and the firm bears the whole tax.

In long-run competitive equilibrium, a tax on economic profits has no yield, because economic profits are zero—they are all competed away. For a monopolist, there may be economic profits even in the long run. But for the same reasons given in the preceding paragraph, the tax is borne by the owners of the monopoly. If a firm is maximizing profits before the profits tax is imposed, the tax cannot be shifted.[11]

Because they distort no economic decisions, taxes on economic profits might appear to be very attractive policy alternatives. In 2008, for example, certain members of both political parties called for a "profits tax" on oil companies. However,

> **economic profit**
>
> The return to owners of a firm above the opportunity costs of all the factors used in production. Also called *supranormal* or *excess* profit.

---

[11] On the other hand, if the firm is following some other goal, it may raise the price in response to a profits tax. One alternative to profit maximization is revenue maximization; firms try to make their sales as large as possible, subject to the constraint that they earn a "reasonable" rate of return.

profits taxes receive very little support from public finance specialists. The main reason is the tremendous problems in making the theoretical notion of economic profits operational. Economic profits are often computed by examining the rate of return that a firm makes on its capital stock and comparing it to some "basic" rate of return set by the government. Clearly, how the capital stock is measured is important. Should the original cost be used, or the cost of replacing it? And what if the rate of return is high not because of excess profits, but because the enterprise is very risky and investors have to be compensated for this risk? Considerations like these lead to major difficulties in administration and compliance.

Tax Incidence and Capitalization

Several years ago the coastal city of Port Hueneme, California, levied a special tax on beach properties. The tax was determined in part by how close the properties were to the ocean. For owners close to the water, the extra tax was $192 per year. Owners of beachfront property complained vociferously.

This episode leads us to consider the special issues that arise when land is taxed. For these purposes, the distinctive characteristics of land are that it is fixed in supply and it is durable. Suppose the annual rental rate on land is $\$R_0$ this year. It is known that the rental will be $\$R_1$ next year, $\$R_2$ two years from now, and so on. How much should someone be willing to pay for the land? If the market for land is competitive, its price is just equal to the present discounted value of the stream of the rents. Thus, if the interest rate is r, the price of land (P_R) is

$$P_R = \$R_0 + \frac{\$R_1}{1+r} + \frac{\$R_2}{(1+r)^2} + \cdots + \frac{\$R_T}{(1+r)^T} \qquad (14.3)$$

where T is the last year the land yields its services (possibly infinity).

It is announced that a tax of $\$u_0$ will be imposed on land now, $\$u_1$ next year, $\$u_2$ two years from now, and so forth. From Figure 14.4 we know that because land is fixed in supply, the annual rental received by the owner falls by the full amount of the tax. Thus, the landlord's return initially falls to $\$(R_0 - u_0)$, in year 1 to $\$(R_1 - u_1)$, in year 2 to $\$(R_2 - u_2)$, and so on. Prospective purchasers of the land take into account the fact that if they purchase the land, they buy a future stream of tax liabilities as well as a future stream of returns. Therefore, the most a purchaser is willing to pay for the land after the tax is announced (P_R') is

$$P_R' = \$(R_0 - u_0) + \frac{\$(R_1 - u_1)}{1+r} + \frac{\$(R_2 - u_2)}{(1+r)^2} + \cdots + \frac{\$(R_T - u_T)}{(1+r)^T} \qquad (14.4)$$

Comparing Equations (14.4) and (14.3), we see that as a consequence of the tax, the price of land falls by

$$u_0 + \frac{u_1}{1+r} + \frac{u_2}{(1+r)^2} + \cdots + \frac{u_T}{(1+r)^T}$$

Thus, at the time the tax is imposed, the price of the land falls by the present value of *all future tax payments*. This process by which a stream of taxes becomes incorporated into the price of an asset is referred to as **capitalization.**

Because of capitalization, the person who bears the full burden of the tax *forever* is the landlord at the time the tax is levied. To be sure, *future* landlords write checks to the tax authorities, but such payments are not really a "burden" because they just balance the lower price paid at purchase. Capitalization complicates attempts to

capitalization

The process by which a stream of tax liabilities becomes incorporated into the price of an asset.

assess the incidence of a tax on any durable item that is fixed in supply. Knowing the identities of current owners is not sufficient—one must know who the landlords *were* at the time the tax was imposed. It's no wonder the owners of beach property in Port Hueneme were so upset![12]

▶ GENERAL EQUILIBRIUM MODELS

A great attraction of partial equilibrium models is their simplicity—examining only one market at a time is relatively uncomplicated. In some cases, however, ignoring feedback into other markets leads to an incomplete picture of a tax's incidence. Suppose, for example, that the tax rate on cigarettes is increased. To the extent that the demand for cigarettes decreases, so does the demand for tobacco. Farmers who formerly grew tobacco on their land may turn to other crops, perhaps cotton. As the supply of cotton increases, its price falls, harming the individuals who were already producing cotton. Thus, cotton producers end up bearing part of the burden of a cigarette tax.

More generally, when a tax is imposed on a sector that is "large" relative to the economy, looking only at that particular market may not be enough. **General equilibrium analysis** takes into account the ways in which various markets are interrelated.

Another problem with partial equilibrium analysis is that it gives insufficient attention to the question of just who the "producers" of a taxed commodity are. Think again of the cigarette tax and the desire of some policymakers to use it as an instrument to punish "the tobacco industry." Only people can pay taxes, and the producers of tobacco include the shareholders who finance the purchase of machinery, farmers who own the land on which the tobacco is grown, the workers in the factories, and so on. The division of the tax burden among these groups is often important. General equilibrium analysis provides a framework for investigating it.

Before turning to the specifics of general equilibrium analysis, note that the fundamental lesson from partial equilibrium models still holds: Because of relative price adjustments, the statutory incidence of a tax generally tells *nothing* about who really bears its burden.

general equilibrium analysis

The study of how various markets are interrelated.

Tax Equivalence Relations

The idea of dealing with tax incidence in a general equilibrium framework at first appears daunting. After all, thousands of different commodities and inputs are traded in the economy. How can we keep track of all their complicated interrelations? Luckily, for many purposes, useful general equilibrium results can be obtained from models in which there are only two commodities, two factors of production, and no savings. For illustration, call the two commodities food (F) and manufactures (M), and the two factors capital (K) and labor (L). There are nine possible ad valorem taxes in such a model:

t_{KF} = tax on capital used in the production of food

t_{KM} = tax on capital used in the production of manufactures

t_{LF} = tax on labor used in the production of food

t_{LM} = tax on labor used in the production of manufactures

---

[12] When a land tax is anticipated before it is levied, presumably it is borne at least in part by the owner at the time the anticipation becomes widespread. If so, even finding out the identity of the landowner at the time the tax was imposed may not be enough.

t_F = tax on the consumption of food

t_M = tax on consumption of manufactures

t_K = tax on capital in both sectors

t_L = tax on labor in both sectors

t = general income tax

partial factor tax

Tax levied on an input in only some of its uses.

The first four taxes, which are levied on a factor in only some of its uses, are referred to as **partial factor taxes.**

Certain combinations of these taxes are equivalent to others. One of these equivalences is already familiar from the theory of the consumer.[13] Taxes on food (t_F) and manufactures (t_M) at the same rate are equivalent to an income tax (t).[14] To see this, just note that equiproportional taxes on all commodities have the same effect on the consumer's budget constraint as a proportional income tax. Both create a parallel shift inward.

Now consider a proportional tax on both capital (t_K) and labor (t_L). Because in this model all income is derived from either capital or labor, it is a simple matter of arithmetic that taxing both factors at the same rate is also equivalent to an income tax (t).

Perhaps not so obvious is the fact that partial taxes on both capital and labor in the food sector at a given rate ($t_{KF} = t_{LF}$) are equivalent to a tax on food (t_F) at the same rate. Because capital and labor are the only inputs to the production of food, making each of them more expensive by a certain proportion is equivalent to making the food itself more expensive in the same proportion.

More generally, any two sets of taxes that generate the same changes in relative prices have equivalent incidence effects. All the equivalence relations that can be derived using similar logic are summarized in Table 14.2. For a given ad valorem tax rate, the equivalences are shown by reading across the rows or down the columns. To determine the incidence of all three taxes in any row or column, only two have to be analyzed in detail. The third can be determined by addition or subtraction. For example, from the third row, if we know the incidence of taxes on capital and labor, then we also know the incidence of a tax on income.

In the next section, we discuss the incidence of four taxes: a food tax (t_F), an income tax (t), a general tax on labor (t_L), and a partial tax on capital in manufacturing (t_{KM}). With results on these four taxes in hand, the incidence of the other five can be determined by using Table 14.2.

The Harberger Model

Harberger [1974] pioneered the application of general equilibrium models to tax incidence. The principal assumptions of his model are as follows:

1. *Technology.* Firms in each sector use capital and labor to produce their outputs. In each sector, a simultaneous doubling of both inputs leads to a doubling of output, *constant returns to scale.* However, the production technologies may differ across sectors. In general, the production technologies differ with respect to the ease with which capital can be substituted for labor

---

[13] The theory of the consumer is outlined in the appendix at the end of this book.

[14] Note that given the assumption that all income is consumed, an income tax is also equivalent to a tax on consumption expenditure.

Table 14.2 **Tax Equivalence Relations**

t_{KF} and	and	t_{LF} and	are equivalent to	t_F and
t_{KM} are equivalent to	and	t_{LM} are equivalent to	are equivalent to	t_M are equivalent to
t_K	and	t_L	are equivalent to	t

Source: McLure [1971, p. 29].

Any two sets of taxes that generate the same changes in relative prices have equivalent incidence effects. For example, a proportional tax on both capital (t_K) and labor (t_L) is equivalent to an income tax (t).

(the **elasticity of substitution**) and the ratios in which capital and labor are employed. For example, the capital-labor ratio in the production of food is about twice that used in the production of textiles [Congressional Budget Office, 1997]. The industry in which the capital-labor ratio is relatively high is characterized as **capital intensive;** the other is **labor intensive.**

2. *Behavior of factor suppliers.* Suppliers of both capital and labor maximize total returns. Moreover, capital and labor are perfectly mobile—they can freely move across sectors according to the wishes of their owners. Consequently, the net marginal return to capital must be the same in each sector, and so must the net marginal return to labor. Otherwise, it would be possible to reallocate capital and labor in such a way that total net returns could be increased.[15]

3. *Market structure.* Firms are competitive and maximize profits, and all prices (including the wage rate) are perfectly flexible. Therefore, factors are fully employed, and the return paid to each factor of production is the value of its marginal product—the value to the firm of the output produced by the last unit of the input.

4. *Total factor supplies.* The total amounts of capital and labor in the economy are fixed. But, as noted above, both factors are perfectly free to move between sectors.

5. *Consumer preferences.* All consumers have identical preferences. A tax therefore cannot generate any distributional effects by affecting people's uses of income. This assumption allows us to concentrate on the effect of taxes on the sources of income.

6. *Tax incidence framework.* The framework for the analysis is differential tax incidence: We consider the substitution of one tax for another. Therefore, approximately the same amount of income is available before and after the tax, so it is unnecessary to consider how changes in aggregate income may change demand and factor prices.

Clearly, these assumptions are somewhat restrictive, but they simplify the analysis considerably. Later in this chapter, we consider the consequences of dropping some of them. We now employ Harberger's model to analyze several different taxes.

elasticity of substitution

A measure of the ease with which one factor of production can be substituted for another.

capital intensive

An industry in which the ratio of capital to labor inputs is relatively high.

labor intensive

An industry in which the ratio of capital to labor inputs is relatively low.

---

[15] The appendix at the end of this book explains why maximizing behavior results in an allocation in which marginal returns are equal.

Analysis of Various Taxes

A Commodity Tax (t_F)   When a tax on food is imposed, its relative price increases (although not necessarily by the amount of the tax). Consumers therefore substitute manufactures for food. Consequently, less food and more manufactures are produced. As food production falls, some of the capital and labor formerly used in food production are forced to find employment in manufacturing. Because the capital-labor ratios probably differ between the two sectors, the relative prices of capital and labor have to change for manufacturing to be willing to absorb the unemployed factors from food production. For example, assume that food is the capital-intensive sector. (US agriculture does, in fact, use relatively more capital equipment—tractors, combines, and so forth—than many types of manufacturing.) Therefore, relatively large amounts of capital must be absorbed in manufacturing. The only way for all this capital to find employment in the manufacturing sector is for the relative price of capital to fall—including capital already in use in the manufacturing sector. In the new equilibrium, then, *all* capital is relatively worse off, not just capital in the food sector. More generally, a tax on the *output* of a particular sector induces a decline in the relative price of the *input* used intensively in that sector.

To go beyond such qualitative statements, additional information is needed. The greater the elasticity of demand for food, the more dramatic will be the change in consumption from food to manufactures, which ultimately induces a greater decline in the return to capital. The greater the difference in factor proportions between food and manufactures, the greater must be the decrease in capital's price for it to be absorbed into the manufacturing sector. (If the capital-labor ratios for food and manufactured goods were identical, neither factor would suffer relative to the other.) Finally, the harder it is to substitute capital for labor in the production of manufactures, the greater the decline in the rate of return to capital needed to absorb the additional capital.

Thus, on the sources side of the budget, the food tax tends to hurt people who receive a proportionately large share of their incomes from capital. Given that all individuals are identical (assumption 5), there are no interesting effects on the uses side. However, were we to drop this assumption, then clearly those people who consumed proportionately large amounts of food would tend to bear relatively larger burdens. The total incidence of the food tax then depends on both the sources and uses sides. For example, a capitalist who eats a lot of food is worse off on both counts. On the other hand, a laborer who eats a lot of food is better off from the point of view of the sources of income, but worse off on the uses side.

An Income Tax (t)   As already noted, an income tax is equivalent to a set of taxes on capital and labor at the same rate. Since factor supplies are completely fixed (assumption 4), this tax cannot be shifted. It is borne in proportion to people's initial incomes. The intuition behind this result is similar to the analogous case in the partial equilibrium model; since the factors cannot "escape" the tax (by opting out of production), they bear the full burden.

A General Tax on Labor (t_L)   A general tax on labor is a tax on labor in *all* its uses, in the production of both food and manufactures. As a result, there are no incentives to switch labor use between sectors. Further, the assumption of fixed factor supplies implies labor must bear the entire burden.

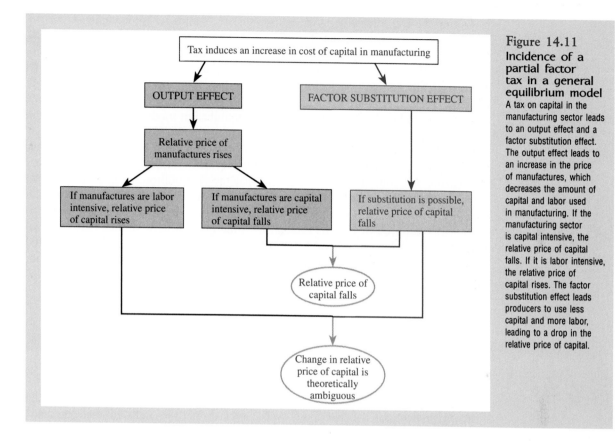

Figure 14.11
Incidence of a partial factor tax in a general equilibrium model
A tax on capital in the manufacturing sector leads to an output effect and a factor substitution effect. The output effect leads to an increase in the price of manufactures, which decreases the amount of capital and labor used in manufacturing. If the manufacturing sector is capital intensive, the relative price of capital falls. If it is labor intensive, the relative price of capital rises. The factor substitution effect leads producers to use less capital and more labor, leading to a drop in the relative price of capital.

A Partial Factor Tax (t_{KM}) When capital used in the manufacturing sector *only* is taxed, there are two initial effects:

1. *Output effect.* The price of manufactures tends to rise, which decreases the quantity demanded by consumers.
2. *Factor substitution effect.* As capital becomes more expensive in the manufacturing sector, producers there use less capital and more labor.

The flowchart in Figure 14.11 traces the consequences of these two effects.

The output effect is described on the left side. As its name suggests, the output effect arises from reducing production in manufacturing. When the price of manufactures increases and demand falls, capital and labor are released from manufacturing and must find employment in the production of food. If the manufacturing sector is labor intensive, then (relatively) large amounts of labor have to be absorbed in the food sector, and the relative price of capital increases. If, on the other hand, the manufacturing sector is capital intensive, the relative price of capital falls. Thus, the output effect is ambiguous with respect to the final effect on the relative prices of capital and labor.

This ambiguity is not present with the factor substitution effect, as depicted in the right-hand side of Figure 14.11. As long as substitution between capital and labor is possible, an increase in the price of capital induces manufacturers to use less capital and more labor, tending to decrease the demand for capital and its relative price.

Putting the two effects together, we see that if manufacturing is capital intensive, both effects work in the same direction, and the relative price of capital must fall. But if the manufacturing sector is labor intensive, the final outcome is theoretically ambiguous. Even though the tax is levied on capital, it can make labor worse off! More generally, as long as factors are mobile between uses, a tax on a given factor in *one* sector ultimately affects the return to *both* factors in *both* sectors. Such insights cannot be obtained with the partial equilibrium models discussed earlier in this chapter.

Much of the applied research on incidence in general equilibrium models has focused on the corporation income tax. Such work assumes that the two sectors are "corporate" and "noncorporate," and that the corporation income tax is an ad valorem tax on capital only on its use in the corporate sector. Given the theoretical ambiguity of the effect of a partial factor tax on the demand for capital, empirical work is required to find its incidence. Although different studies have reached different conclusions, the most typical finding is that much of the tax is shifted to the owners of all capital [President's Advisory Panel on Federal Tax Reform, 2005, p. 34].

Some Qualifications

Changing the assumptions underlying the general equilibrium model affects its implications for tax incidence in the following ways:

Differences in Individuals' Tastes   By assumption 5, all consumers have the same preferences for the two goods. When they do not, tax-induced changes in the distribution of income change aggregate spending decisions and hence relative prices and incomes. Consider, for example, a tax on capital in the corporate sector. As noted above, most analyses suggest that it is largely shifted to the owners of all capital. And because capital tends to be a relatively important source of income for high-income individuals, the tax would appear to be progressive. However, the tax also raises the relative prices of goods produced in capital-intensive industries such as agriculture and petroleum refining, whose outputs (food and gasoline) are purchased in high proportions by families at the low end of the income scale [Fullerton and Rogers, 1997]. Thus, when we allow for differences in uses between high- and low-income families, the tax becomes less progressive than it first appears.

Immobile Factors   By assumption 2, resources are free to flow between sectors, seeking the highest rate of return possible. However, for institutional or technological reasons, some factors may be immobile. For example, if certain land is zoned for residential use, it cannot be used in manufacturing, no matter what the rate of return. Abandoning perfect mobility can dramatically affect the incidence of a tax. For example, earlier we showed that if factors are mobile, the incidence of a partial factor tax is ambiguous, depending on the outcome of several conflicting effects. If the factor is immobile, however, the incidence result is clear-cut: The taxed factor bears the whole burden. Intuitively, this is because the factor cannot "escape" taxation by migrating to the other sector. Note also that because the return to the taxed immobile factor falls by just the amount of the tax, the prices of capital and labor in the untaxed sectors are unchanged, as is the price of the good in the taxed sector.

Table 14.3 **Average Federal Tax Rates and Share of Federal Taxes by Income Quintile (2005)**

Income Category	Average Federal Tax Rate	Share of Federal Taxes
Lowest quintile	4.3%	0.8%
Second quintile	9.9	4.1
Third quintile	14.2	9.3
Fourth quintile	17.4	16.9
Highest quintile	25.5	68.7
All quintiles	20.5	100.0
Top 1%	31.2	27.6

Source: Congressional Budget Office [2007].

According to this applied incidence study, the average federal tax rate ranges from 4.3 percent for households in the lowest quintile to 31.2 percent for households in the top 1 percent of the income distribution. The top one percent pays 27.6 percent of all federal taxes.

Variable Factor Supplies By assumption 4, the total supplies of both factors are fixed. In the long run, however, the supplies of both capital and labor to the economy are variable. Allowing for growth can turn conclusions from the static model completely on their heads. Consider a general factor tax on capital. When the capital stock is fixed, this tax is borne entirely by the capital's owners. In the long run, however, less capital may be supplied due to the tax.[16] To the extent this occurs, the economy's capital-labor ratio decreases, and the return to labor falls. (The wage falls because labor has less capital with which to work, and hence is less productive, other things being the same.) Thus, a general tax on capital can hurt labor.

Because the amount of calendar time that must elapse before the long run is reached may be substantial, short-run effects matter. On the other hand, intelligent policy also requires consideration of the long-run consequences of taxation.

An Applied Incidence Study

The theory of tax incidence has served as a framework for a number of attempts to estimate how the US tax system affects the distribution of income. Table 14.3 reports the findings of a recent study by the Congressional Budget Office [2007]. The study estimates the incidence of all federal taxes. The average tax rate ranges from 4.3 percent for households in the lowest income quintile to 31.2 percent for households in the top 1 percent of the population. This top 1 percent pays 27.6 percent of all federal taxes. These figures suggest that the federal tax system is quite progressive.

However, it should be clear by now that all incidence results depend crucially on the underlying assumptions. This study assumes that there is no shifting of the personal income tax, that payroll taxes are borne by workers, and that commodity taxes are borne by consumers in proportion to their consumption of the taxed items. These assumptions help simplify the problem considerably. But the theory of tax incidence suggests that they are questionable, especially in the long run.

Another limitation of the analysis is that it is based on annual incomes. Using some measure of lifetime income would be more appropriate and could change the

---

[16] However, the supply of capital does not necessarily decrease. See Chapter 18.

results importantly. To see why, we begin by noting that a substantial amount of empirical research suggests people's consumption decisions are more closely related to some lifetime income measure than the value of income in any particular year. Just because a person's income is *temporarily* high or low in a year does not have that great an impact on how much the person consumes.

Assume that the consumption of commodity X is proportional to lifetime income. Assume further that the supply curve for X is horizontal, so that consumers bear the entire burden of any tax on X. Then a tax on X would be proportional with respect to lifetime income. However, in any particular year, some people have incomes that are temporarily higher than their permanent values and some lower. A person with a temporarily high income spends a relatively small proportion of his annual income on X because he does not increase his consumption of X due to the temporary increase in income. Similarly, a person with a temporarily low income devotes a relatively high proportion of her income to good X. In short, based on annual income, good X's budget share appears to fall with income, and a tax on X looks regressive. Consistent with this theory, several investigators have found that incidence results are very sensitive to whether lifetime or annual measures are employed. For example, Hassett, Mathur, and Metcalf [2007] find that a tax on carbon is more regressive with respect to an annual measure of income than a lifetime measure. We conclude that even though studies based on annual income are suggestive, the results should be viewed with some caution.

▶ CONCLUSIONS

We began this chapter with an innocent question: Who bears the burden of a tax? We saw that price changes are the key to finding the burden of a tax, but that price changes depend on a lot of things: market structure, elasticities of supply and demand, mobility of factors of production, and so on. At this stage, an obvious question is: What do we really know?

For taxes that may reasonably be analyzed in isolation, the answer is, "Quite a bit." A partial equilibrium incidence analysis requires only information on the market structure and the shapes of the supply and demand curves. In cases other than a clear-cut monopoly, the competitive market paradigm provides a sensible starting point. Estimates of supply and demand curves can be obtained using the empirical methods discussed in Chapter 2. Incidence analysis is on firm ground.

Even in general equilibrium models, incidence analysis is straightforward for a tax on an immobile factor—the incidence is entirely on the taxed factor. More generally, though, if a tax affects many markets, incidence depends on the reactions of numerous supply and demand curves for goods and inputs. The answers are correspondingly less clear.

Unfortunately, it seems that many important taxes such as the corporate tax fall into the last category. Why is this? It may be for the very reason that the incidence is hard to find. (What are the political chances of a tax that clearly hurts some important group in the population?) Complicated taxes may actually be simpler for a politician because no one is sure who actually ends up paying them.

In any case, the models in this chapter tell us what information is needed to understand the incidence even of very complex taxes. To the extent that this information is currently unavailable, the models serve as a measure of our ignorance. This is not altogether undesirable. As St. Jerome noted, "It is worse still to be ignorant of your ignorance."

Summary

- Statutory incidence is the legal liability for a tax, while economic incidence is the actual burden of the tax. Knowing the legal incidence usually tells us little about economic incidence.

- Economic incidence is determined by the price changes induced by a tax, and depends on individuals' sources and uses of income.

- Depending on the policy being considered, it may be appropriate to examine balanced budget, differential, or absolute incidence.

- In partial equilibrium competitive models, tax incidence depends on the elasticities of supply and demand. The same general approach can be used to study incidence in a monopolized market. For oligopoly, however, there is no single accepted framework for tax analysis.

- Due to capitalization, the burden of future taxes may be borne by *current* owners of an inelastically supplied durable commodity such as land.

- General equilibrium incidence analysis often employs a two-sector, two-factor model. This framework allows for nine possible taxes. Certain combinations of these taxes are equivalent to others.

- In a general equilibrium model, a tax on a single factor in its use only in a particular sector can affect the returns to all factors in all sectors.

- Applied tax incidence studies indicate that the federal tax system is quite progressive. But such studies rest upon possibly problematic assumptions.

Discussion Questions

1. In 2009, it was proposed that the state of Nevada create an entertainment tax that "would require the state's 25 legal brothels to give the state some money on a per-transaction basis" [Friess, 2009]. Discuss the likely incidence of such a tax. Use an appropriate diagram as the basis for your discussion.

2. Consider a society with only two people—one rich and one poor—who have the same utility functions. These utility functions exhibit diminishing marginal utility. Suppose that taxes are set such that the *total* amount of utility that each person loses is the same. Does it follow that the tax will be progressive? Explain.

3. For commodity X, average cost is equal to marginal cost at every level of output. Assuming that the market for X is competitive and the demand curve is linear, analyze the effects when a unit tax of u dollars is imposed. Now analyze the effects of the same tax assuming that the market for X is a monopoly. Discuss the differences.

4. Use a general equilibrium framework to discuss the possible incidence of a tax on cigarettes.

5. In an effort to reduce alcohol consumption, the government is considering a $1 tax on each gallon of liquor sold (the tax is levied on producers). Suppose that the demand curve is $Q^D = 500,000 - 20,000P$ (where Q^D is the number of gallons of liquor demanded and P is the price per gallon), and the supply curve for liquor is $Q^S = 30,000P$ (where Q^S is the number of gallons supplied).

   a. Compute how the tax affects the price paid by consumers and the price received by producers.

   b. How much revenue does the tax raise for the government? How much of the revenue comes from consumers, and how much from producers?

   c. Suppose that the demand for liquor is more elastic for younger drinkers than for older drinkers. Will the liquor tax be more, less, or equally effective at reducing liquor consumption among young drinkers? Explain.

6. Suppose that the demand curve for a particular commodity is $Q^D = a - bP$, where Q^D is the quantity demanded, P is the price, and a and

b are constants. The supply curve for the commodity is $Q^S = c + dP$, where Q^S is quantity supplied and c and d are constants. Find the equilibrium price and output as functions of the constants a, b, c, and d.

Suppose now that a unit tax of u dollars is imposed on the commodity. Show that the new equilibrium is the same regardless of whether the tax is imposed on producers or buyers of the commodity.

7. Suppose that the income tax in a certain nation is computed as a flat rate of 5 percent, but no tax is levied above $50,000 in taxable income. Taxable income, in turn, is computed as the individual's income minus $10,000; that is, everyone gets a $10,000 deduction. What are the marginal and average tax rates for each of the following three workers? (Evaluate the marginal tax rate at each person's current income level.)

 a. A part-time worker with annual income of $9,000.
 b. A retail salesperson with annual income of $45,000.
 c. An advertising executive with annual income of $600,000.

Is the tax progressive, proportional, or regressive with respect to income?

8. Assume that in a given country, tax revenues, T, depend on income, I, according to the formula

$$T = -4,000 + 0.2I$$

Thus, for example, when a household has an income of $50,000, its tax burden is $-4,000 + 0.2 \times 50,000$, or $6,000. Is this a progressive tax schedule? [Hint: Compute average tax rates at several different levels of income.]

Now let's generalize the tax schedule in this problem to:

$$T = a + tI$$

where a and t are numbers. (For example, in the tax schedule above, $a = -4,000$ and $t = 0.2$.) Write down a formula for the average tax rate as a function of the level of income. Show that the tax system is progressive if a is negative, and regressive if a is positive. [Hint: The average tax rate is T/I.]

9. A study by Doyle and Samphantharak [2006] found that the price of gasoline charged at gas stations in Illinois fell 3 percent following a suspension of the 5 percent state gasoline sales tax. Draw a diagram consistent with this finding.

10. In 2007, Venezuelan President Hugo Chavez increased the tax on whiskey, brandy, and cognac by $1.79 per liter and increased the tax on cigarettes by 20 cents per pack. Regarding the liquor tax, one commentator noted, "It's unfair because, in the end, the consumer is the one who pays." Regarding the cigarette tax, another commentator noted, "The Venezuelan is not going to stop . . . smoking" [CNN, 2007]. Diagram models for the liquor and cigarette markets in Venezuela that are consistent with these observations.

11. In 2007, tobacco companies contributed about $4.5 million to campaign against an increase in the state cigarette tax in Oregon [Silverman, 2007]. Under what economic assumptions did it make sense for the companies to do this?

12. During the 2008 presidential campaign, Senator John McCain and Senator Hillary Clinton proposed cutting the federal gasoline tax (which is a unit tax) only during the summer months. Assume that gasoline refiners run near full capacity during the summer, so they are unable to increase supply in the short term. Also assume that the consumers of gasoline have some ability to substitute away from gasoline (for example, by driving fewer miles). If this proposal were implemented, how would the benefit of the tax cut be divided between consumers and suppliers of gasoline? Use a diagram to support your answer.

13. Consider a society with only two people, one who has an income of $200,000 and one who has an income of $20,000. Assume that under the current tax system, the rich person pays $50,000 in taxes and the poor person pays $1,000. Suppose Congress passes a law that cuts the rich person's taxes by $2,000 and the poor person's taxes by $200. Using Equations (14.1) and (14.2), assess whether this tax change increases or decreases progressivity.

Chapter Fifteen

TAXATION AND EFFICIENCY

Waste always makes me angry.

—RHETT BUTLER IN *GONE WITH THE WIND*

Taxes impose a cost on the taxpayer. It is tempting to view the cost as simply the amount of money that he or she hands over to the tax collector. However, an example indicates that this is just part of the story.

Consider Breyer Dazs, a citizen who typically consumes 10 ice cream cones each week, at a price of $1 per cone. The government levies a 25 percent tax on his consumption of ice cream cones, so now Dazs faces a price of $1.25.[1] In response to the price hike, Dazs reduces his ice cream cone consumption to zero, and he spends the $10 per week on other goods and services. Obviously, because Dazs consumes no ice cream cones, the ice cream tax yields zero revenue. Do we want to say that Dazs is unaffected by the tax? The answer is no. Dazs is worse off because the tax has induced him to consume a less desirable bundle of goods than previously. We know that the after-tax bundle is less desirable because, before the tax, Dazs had the option of consuming no ice cream cones. Since he chose to buy 10 cones weekly, this must have been preferred to spending the money on other items. Thus, despite the fact that the tax raised zero revenue, it made Dazs worse off.

A variety of real-world taxes illustrate this point. For example, many cities levy high taxes on airport rental cars as a way of collecting revenues from out-of-towners [Johnson, 2005]. One frequent flyer explained that he stopped flying to Boston to avoid that city"s $10 tax on car rentals, and instead flies through Chicago to Manchester, New Hampshire. Another traveler to Medford, Oregon, stated that he avoids the tax on airport rental cars by instead taking a taxi downtown and renting a car there (where there is no tax). Clearly, while these travelers are not directly paying the tax on airport car rentals, it still makes them worse off.

These examples are a bit extreme. Normally, we expect an increase in price to diminish the quantity demanded but not drive it all the way to zero. Nevertheless, the basic result holds: Because a tax distorts economic decisions, it creates an **excess burden**—a loss of welfare above and beyond the tax revenues collected. Excess burden is sometimes referred to as *welfare cost* or *deadweight loss*.[2] This chapter discusses the theory and measurement of excess burden, and explains its importance for evaluating actual tax systems.

> **excess burden**
>
> A loss of welfare above and beyond taxes collected. Also called *welfare cost* or *deadweight loss*.

---

[1] As emphasized in Chapter 14, the price paid by the consumer generally does not rise by the full amount of the tax. For this example, we assume that the supply curve is horizontal.

[2] See Chapters 6 and 9 for a discussion of the deadweight losses of some expenditure programs.

▶ EXCESS BURDEN DEFINED

Ruth has a fixed income of I dollars, which she spends on only two commodities: barley and corn. The price per pound of barley is P_b and the price per pound of corn is P_c. There are no taxes or "distortions" such as externalities or monopoly in the economy, so the prices of the goods reflect their social marginal costs. For convenience, these social marginal costs are assumed to be constant with respect to output. In Figure 15.1, Ruth's consumption of barley is measured on the horizontal axis and her consumption of corn on the vertical axis. Her budget constraint is line AD, which has slope $-P_b/P_c$ and horizontal intercept I/P_b.[3] Assuming Ruth wants to maximize her utility, she chooses a point like E_1 on indifference curve i, where she consumes B_1 pounds of barley and C_1 pounds of corn.

Now suppose the government levies a tax at a percentage rate of t_b on barley so the price Ruth faces becomes $(1 + t_b)P_b$. (The before-tax price is unchanged because of our assumption of constant marginal social costs.) The tax changes Ruth's budget constraint. It now has a slope of $-[(1 + t_b)P_b/P_c]$ and horizontal intercept $I/[(1 + t_b)P_b]$. This is represented in Figure 15.1 as line AF. (Because the price of corn is still P_c, lines AF and AD have the same vertical intercept.)

Note that at each level of barley consumption, the vertical distance between AD and AF shows Ruth's tax payments measured in corn. To see this, consider an arbitrary quantity of barley B_a on the horizontal axis. Before the tax was imposed, Ruth could have both B_a pounds of barley and C_a pounds of corn. After the tax, however, if she consumed B_a pounds of barley, the most corn she could afford would be C_b pounds. The difference (distance) between C_a and C_b must therefore represent the amount of tax collected by the government measured in pounds of corn. We can convert tax receipts to dollars by multiplying distance C_aC_b by the price per pound of corn, P_c. For convenience, we measure corn in units such that $P_c = 1$. In this case, the distance C_aC_b measures tax receipts in corn *or* dollars.

So far we have not indicated Ruth's choice on her new budget constraint, AF. Figure 15.2 shows that her most preferred bundle is at E_2 on indifference curve ii, where her consumption of barley is B_2, her consumption of corn is C_2, and her tax bill is the associated vertical distance between AD and AF, GE_2. Clearly, Ruth is worse off at E_2 than she was at E_1. However, *any* tax would have put her on a lower indifference curve.[4] The important question is whether the barley tax inflicts a greater utility loss than is necessary to raise revenue GE_2. Alternatively, is there some other way of raising revenue GE_2 that would cause a smaller utility loss to Ruth? If so, the barley tax has an excess burden.

To investigate this issue, we need to find a dollar equivalent of the loss that Ruth suffers by having to move from indifference curve i to ii. One way to measure this is the **equivalent variation**—the amount of income we would have to take away from Ruth (before the barley tax was levied) to induce her to move from i and ii. The equivalent variation measures the loss inflicted by the tax as the size of the reduction in income that would cause the same decrease in utility as the tax.

To depict the equivalent variation graphically, recall that taking away income from an individual leads to a parallel movement inward of her budget line. Hence, to find the equivalent variation, all we have to do is shift AD inward, until it is tangent to

equivalent variation

A change in income that has the same effect on utility as a change in the price of a commodity.

---

[3] The construction of budget constraints and the interpretation of their slopes and intercepts are discussed in the appendix at the end of this book.

[4] This ignores benefits that might be obtained from the expenditures financed by the tax.

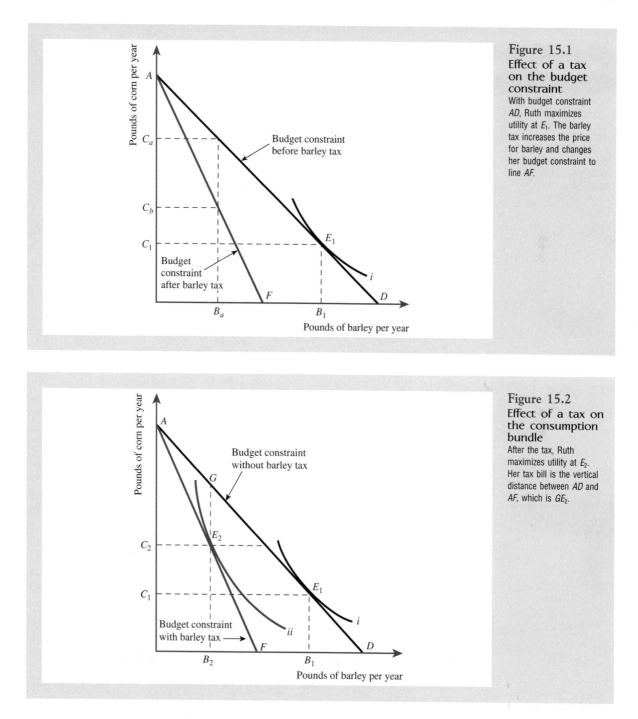

Figure 15.1
Effect of a tax on the budget constraint
With budget constraint *AD*, Ruth maximizes utility at E_1. The barley tax increases the price for barley and changes her budget constraint to line *AF*.

Figure 15.2
Effect of a tax on the consumption bundle
After the tax, Ruth maximizes utility at E_2. Her tax bill is the vertical distance between *AD* and *AF*, which is GE_2.

indifference curve *ii*. The amount by which we have to shift *AD* is the equivalent variation. In Figure 15.3, budget line *HI* is parallel to *AD* and tangent to indifference curve *ii*. Hence, the vertical distance between *AD* and *HI*, ME_3, is the equivalent variation. Ruth is indifferent between losing ME_3 dollars and facing the barley tax.

Note that the equivalent variation ME_3 exceeds the barley tax revenues of GE_2. To see why, just observe that ME_3 equals GN, because both measure the distance

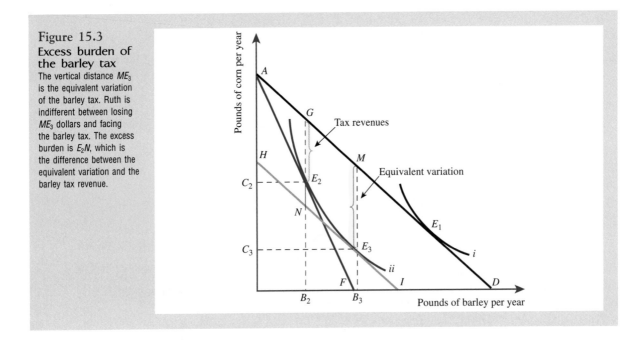

Figure 15.3

Excess burden of the barley tax

The vertical distance ME_3 is the equivalent variation of the barley tax. Ruth is indifferent between losing ME_3 dollars and facing the barley tax. The excess burden is E_2N, which is the difference between the equivalent variation and the barley tax revenue.

between the parallel lines AD and HI. Hence, ME_3 exceeds GE_2 by distance E_2N. This is really quite a remarkable result. It means that the barley tax makes Ruth worse off by an amount that actually exceeds the revenues it generates. In Figure 15.3, the amount by which the loss in welfare (measured by the equivalent variation) exceeds the taxes collected—the excess burden—is distance E_2N.

Does *every* tax entail an excess burden? Define a **lump sum tax** as a certain amount that must be paid regardless of the taxpayer's behavior. If the government levies a $100 lump sum tax on Ruth, there is nothing she can do to avoid paying the $100, other than to leave the country or die. In contrast, the barley tax is not a lump sum tax, because the revenue yield depends on Ruth's barley consumption.

Let us analyze a lump sum tax that leaves Ruth as well off as the barley tax. To begin, we must sketch the associated budget line. It must have two characteristics. First, it must be parallel to AD. (Because a lump sum tax simply takes away money from Ruth, it does not change the relative prices of barley and corn; two budget lines embodying the same price ratio must be parallel.) Second, because of the stipulation that Ruth attain the same utility level as under the barley tax, the budget line must be tangent to indifference curve *ii*.

Budget line HI in Figure 15.3, which is tangent to indifference curve *ii* at point E_3, satisfies both these criteria. If confronted with this budget line, Ruth would consume B_3 pounds of barley and C_3 pounds of corn. The revenue yield of the lump sum tax is the vertical distance between E_3 and the before-tax budget constraint, or distance ME_3. But we showed earlier that ME_3 is also the equivalent variation of the move from indifference curve *i* to *ii*. This comes as no surprise, since a lump sum tax is just a parallel shift of the budget line. Because the revenue yield of a lump sum tax equals its equivalent variation, *a lump sum tax has no excess burden*.

In short, a lump sum tax that leaves Ruth on the *same indifference curve* as the barley tax generates more revenue for the government. Alternatively, if we compared

lump sum tax

A tax whose value is independent of the individual's behavior.

a lump sum tax and a barley tax that raised the *same revenue*, the lump sum tax would leave Ruth on a higher indifference curve.

The skeptical reader may suspect that this result is merely an artifact of the particular way the indifference curves are drawn in Figure 15.3. This is not the case. One can prove that as long as the indifference curves have the usual shape, a tax that changes relative prices generates an excess burden.[5] Alternatively, a tax that changes relative prices is inefficient in the sense that it lowers individual utility more than is necessary to raise a given amount of revenue.

Questions and Answers

The previous section's discussion of excess burden raises some important questions.

If Lump Sum Taxes Are So Efficient, Why Don't Governments Use Them?

Lump sum taxation is an unattractive policy tool for several reasons. Suppose the government announced that every person's tax liability was $2,000 per year. This is a lump sum tax, but most people would consider it unfair because the loss of $2,000 presumably hurts a poor family more than a rich family. In 1990, the government of British Prime Minister Margaret Thatcher implemented a tax that in some ways resembled a lump sum tax. The property tax that had financed local government was replaced by a head tax; in each local jurisdiction the amount depended on that jurisdiction's per capita revenue needs. The tax was lump sum in the sense that a person's tax liability did not vary with the amount of income earned or property owned; it did vary, however, with a person's choice of where to live. The perceived unfairness of that tax was one of the factors that led to Prime Minister Thatcher's downfall in 1990, and it was repealed in 1991 by her successor, Prime Minister John Major.

As a way of producing more equitable results, one might consider making people pay different lump sum taxes based on their incomes. A rich person might be required to pay $20,000 annually, independent of his or her economic decisions, while a poor person would pay only $500. The problem is that people entering the workforce would soon realize that their eventual tax burden depended on their incomes, and adjust their work and savings decisions accordingly. In short, because the amount of income individuals earn is at least in part under their control, the income-based tax is not a lump sum tax.

Ultimately, to achieve an equitable system of lump sum taxes, it would be necessary to base the tax on some underlying "ability" characteristic that measured individuals' *potential* to earn income. In this way, high- and low-potential people could be taxed differently. Because the base is potential, an individual's tax burden would not depend on behavior. Even if such an ability measure existed, however, it would be difficult for it to be observed by the taxing authority. Interestingly, one observable characteristic that has a surprisingly high correlation with income is height—taller people tend to have greater incomes. On this basis, Mankiw and Weinzierl [2007] argue that a tax based on height would be both progressive and efficient—progressive because it would raise a disproportionate amount of money from people with high earnings, and efficient because it would not distort behavior (people cannot change their

---

[5] As noted, this assumes there are no other distortions in the economy. For a proof, see Kaplow [2008b].

height in response to a tax). The argument, of course, is tongue in cheek. Mankiw and Weinzierl are not really advocating a tax system based on height; rather, they make the argument to clarify our thinking about the policy implications of optimal tax theory.

Are There Any Results from Welfare Economics That Would Help Us Understand Why Excess Burdens Arise?

Recall from Chapter 3 that a necessary condition for a Pareto efficient allocation of resources is that the marginal rate of substitution of barley for corn in consumption (MRS_{bc}) equals the marginal rate of transformation of barley for corn in production (MRT_{bc}). Under the barley tax, consumers face a price of barley of $(1 + t_b)P_b$. Therefore, they set

$$MRS_{bc} = \frac{(1+t_b)P_b}{P_c} \tag{15.1}$$

Equation (15.1) is the algebraic representation of the equilibrium point E_2 in Figure 15.3.

Producers make their decisions by setting the marginal rate of transformation equal to the ratio of the prices *they receive*. Even though Ruth pays $(1 + t_b)P_b$ per pound of barley, the barley producers receive only P_b—the difference goes to the tax collector. Hence, profit-maximizing producers set

$$MRT_{bc} = \frac{P_b}{P_c} \tag{15.2}$$

Clearly, as long as t_b is not zero, MRS_{bc} exceeds MRT_{bc}, and the necessary condition for an efficient allocation of resources is violated.

Intuitively, when MRS_{bc} is greater than MRT_{bc}, the marginal utility of substituting barley consumption for corn consumption exceeds the change in production costs necessary to do so. Thus, utility would be raised if such an adjustment were made. However, in the presence of the barley tax there is no *financial* incentive to do so. The excess burden is just a measure of the utility loss. The loss arises because the barley tax creates a wedge between what the consumer pays and what the producer receives. In contrast, under a lump sum tax, the price ratios faced by consumers and producers are equal. There is no wedge, so the necessary conditions for Pareto efficiency are satisfied.

Does an Income Tax Entail an Excess Burden?

The answer is generally yes, but it takes a little thinking to see why. Figure 15.3 showed the imposition of a lump sum tax as a downward parallel movement from AD to HI. This movement could just as well have arisen via a tax that took some proportion of Ruth's income. Like the lump sum tax, an income reduction moves the intercepts of the budget constraint closer to the origin but leaves its slope unchanged. Perhaps, then, lump sum taxation and income taxation are equivalent. If income were fixed, an income tax *would* be a lump sum tax. However, when people's choices affect their incomes, an income tax is *not* generally equivalent to a lump sum tax.

Think of Ruth as consuming *three* commodities, barley, corn, and leisure time, l. Ruth gives up leisure (that is, she supplies labor) to earn income that she spends on barley and corn. In the production sector, Ruth's leisure is an input to the production of the two goods. The rate at which her leisure time can be transformed into barley is MRT_{lb} and into corn MRT_{lc}. Just as a utility-maximizing individual sets the marginal rate of substitution between two commodities equal to their price ratio, the

MRS between leisure and a given commodity is set equal to the ratio of the wage (the price of leisure) and the price of that commodity.

Again appealing to the theory of welfare economics, the necessary conditions for a Pareto efficient allocation of resources in this three-commodity case are

$$MRS_{lb} = MRT_{lb}$$
$$MRS_{lc} = MRT_{lc}$$
$$MRS_{bc} = MRT_{bc}$$

A proportional income tax, which is equivalent to a tax at the same rate on barley and corn, leaves the third equality unchanged, because producers and consumers still face the same *relative* prices for barley and corn. (The tax increases both prices by the same proportion, so their ratio is unchanged.) However, it introduces a tax wedge in the first two conditions. To see why, suppose that Ruth's employer pays her a before-tax wage of w, and the income tax rate is t. Ruth's decisions depend on her after-tax wage, $(1 - t)w$. Hence, she sets $MRS_{lb} = (1 - t)w/P_b$. On the other hand, the producer's decisions are based on the wage rate he or she pays, the before-tax wage, w. Hence, the producer sets $MRT_{lb} = w/P_b$. Consequently, $MRS_{lb} \neq MRT_{lb}$. Similarly, $MRS_{lc} \neq MRT_{lc}$. In contrast, a lump sum tax leaves all three equalities intact. Thus, income and lump sum taxation are generally not equivalent.

The fact that the income tax breaks up two equalities while taxes on barley and corn at different rates break up all three is irrelevant for determining which system is more efficient. Once *any* of the equalities fails to hold, a loss of efficiency results, and the sizes of the welfare losses cannot be compared merely by counting wedges. Rather, the excess burdens associated with each tax regime must be computed and then compared. There is no presumption that income taxation is more efficient than a system of commodity taxes at different rates, which is referred to as *differential commodity taxation*. It *may* be true, but this is an empirical question that cannot be answered on the basis of theory alone.

If the Demand for a Commodity Does Not Change When It Is Taxed, Does This Mean That There Is No Excess Burden?
The intuition behind excess burden is that it results from distorted decisions. If there is no change in the demand for the good being taxed, one might conclude there is no excess burden. This conjecture is examined in Figure 15.4. Naomi, the individual under consideration, begins with the same income as Ruth and faces the same prices and taxes. Hence, her initial budget constraint is AD, and after the barley tax, it is AF. However, unlike Ruth, Naomi does not change her barley consumption after the barley tax; that is, $B_1 = B_2$. The barley tax revenues are E_1E_2. Is there an excess burden? The equivalent variation of the barley tax is RE_3. This exceeds the barley tax revenues of E_1E_2 by E_2S. Hence, even though Naomi's barley consumption is unchanged by the barley tax, it still creates an excess burden of E_2S.

The explanation requires that we distinguish between two types of responses to the barley tax. The movement from E_1 to E_2 is the *uncompensated response*. It shows how consumption changes because of the tax and incorporates effects due to both losing income and the tax-induced change in relative prices. Now, we can imagine decomposing the move from E_1 to E_2 into a move from E_1 to E_3, and then from E_3 to E_2. The movement from E_1 to E_3 shows the effect on consumption of a lump sum tax. This change, called the **income effect,** is due solely to the loss of income because relative prices are unaffected. In effect, then, the movement from E_3 to E_2 is

income effect

The effect of a price change on the quantity demanded due exclusively to the fact that the consumer's income has changed.

Figure 15.4

Excess burden of a tax on a commodity whose ordinary demand curve is perfectly inelastic

Naomi purchases the same amount of barley after the tax as before the tax. Nonetheless, the tax still yields an excess burden of E_2S.

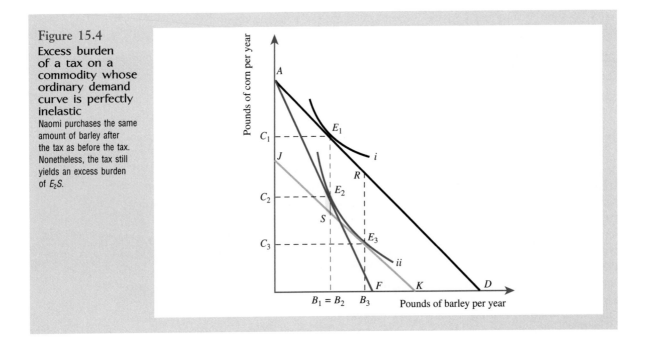

strictly due to the change in relative prices. It is generated by giving Naomi enough income to remain on indifference curve *ii* even as barley's price rises due to the tax. Because Naomi is compensated for the rising price of barley with additional income, the movement from E_3 to E_2 is called the *compensated response*, also sometimes referred to as the **substitution effect.**[6]

The compensated response is the important one for calculating excess burden. Why? By construction, the computation of excess burden involves comparing tax collections at points E_2 and E_3 on indifference curve *ii*. But the movement from E_3 to E_2 along indifference curve *ii* is precisely the compensated response. Note also that it is only in moving from E_3 to E_2 that the marginal rate of substitution is affected. As shown earlier, this change violates the necessary conditions for a Pareto efficient allocation of commodities.

An ordinary demand curve depicts the uncompensated change in the quantity of a commodity demanded when price changes. A **compensated demand curve** shows how the quantity demanded changes when price changes *and* simultaneously income is compensated so that the individual's commodity bundle stays on the same indifference curve. A way of summarizing this discussion is to say that excess burden depends on movements along the compensated rather than the ordinary demand curve.

Although these observations may seem like theoretical nit-picking, they are actually quite important. Policy discussions often focus on whether or not a given tax influences observed behavior, with the assumption that if it does not, no serious efficiency problem is present. For example, some argue that if hours of work do not change when an income tax is imposed, then the tax has no adverse efficiency consequences. We have shown that such a notion is fallacious. A substantial excess burden may be incurred even if the uncompensated response of the taxed commodity is zero.

substitution effect

The tendency of an individual to consume more of one good and less of another because of a decrease in the price of the former relative to the latter.

compensated demand curve

A demand curve that shows how quantity demanded varies with price, holding utility constant.

---

[6] See the appendix at the end of this book for further discussion of income and substitution effects and compensated demand curves.

► EXCESS BURDEN MEASUREMENT WITH DEMAND CURVES

The concept of excess burden can be reinterpreted using (compensated) demand curves. This interpretation relies heavily on the notion of consumer surplus—the difference between what people would be *willing* to pay for a commodity and the amount they actually have to pay. As shown in the appendix at the end of this book, consumer surplus is measured by the area between the demand curve and the horizontal line at the market price. Assume that the compensated demand curve for barley is straight line D_b in Figure 15.5. For convenience, we continue to assume that the social marginal cost of barley is constant at P_b, so that the supply curve is the horizontal line marked S_b.[7] In equilibrium, q_1 pounds of barley are consumed. Consumer surplus, the area between the price and the demand curve, is *aih*.

Again suppose that a tax at percentage rate t_b is levied on barley, so the new price, $(1 + t_b)P_b$, is associated with supply curve S_b'. Supply and demand now intersect at output q_2. Observe the following characteristics of the new equilibrium:

- Consumer surplus falls to the area between the demand curve and S_b', *agf*.
- The revenue yield of the barley tax is rectangle *gfdh*. This is because tax revenues are equal to the product of the number of units purchased (*hd*) and the tax paid on each unit: $(1 + t_b)P_b - P_b = gh$. But *hd* and *gh* are just the base and height, respectively, of rectangle *gfdh*, and hence their product is its area.
- The sum of posttax consumer surplus and tax revenues collected (area *hafd*) is less than the original consumer surplus (*ahi*) by area *fid*. In effect, even if we returned the tax revenues to barley consumers as a lump sum, they would still be worse off by triangle *fid*. The triangle, then, is the excess burden of the tax.

This analysis provides a convenient framework for computing an actual dollar measure of excess burden. The area of triangle *fid* is one-half the product of its base (the tax-induced change in the quantity of barley) and height (the tax per pound). Some simple algebra shows that this product is equivalent to

$$\tfrac{1}{2}\eta P_b q_1 t_b^2 \tag{15.3}$$

where η (Greek *eta*) is the absolute value of the compensated price elasticity of demand for barley.[8] (A proof is provided in Appendix A at the end of the chapter.)

Equation (15.3) has some important implications. First, it indicates that excess burden is higher for a tax applied to a good with a higher compensated price elasticity of demand. A high (absolute) value of η indicates that the compensated quantity demanded is quite sensitive to changes in price. Thus, the presence of η in Equation (15.3) makes intuitive sense—the more the tax distorts the (compensated) consumption

---

[7] The analysis is easily generalized to the case when the supply curve slopes upward. See footnote 8.

[8] The formula is an approximation that holds strictly only for an infinitesimally small tax levied in the absence of any other distortions. When the supply curve is upward sloping rather than horizontal, the excess burden triangle contains some producer surplus as well as consumer surplus. The formula for excess burden then depends on the elasticity of supply as well as the elasticity of demand. In this case, the excess burden is

$$\tfrac{1}{2}\frac{P_b q}{\dfrac{1}{\eta}+\dfrac{1}{\varepsilon}}t_b^2$$

where ε is the elasticity of supply. Note that as ε approaches infinity, this expression collapses to Equation (15.3). This is because an ε of infinity corresponds to a horizontal supply curve as in Figure 15.5.

Figure 15.5

Excess burden of a commodity tax

The tax causes consumer surplus to drop by *gfih*, but raises only *gfdh* in tax revenue. The difference, *fid*, is the excess burden of the tax.

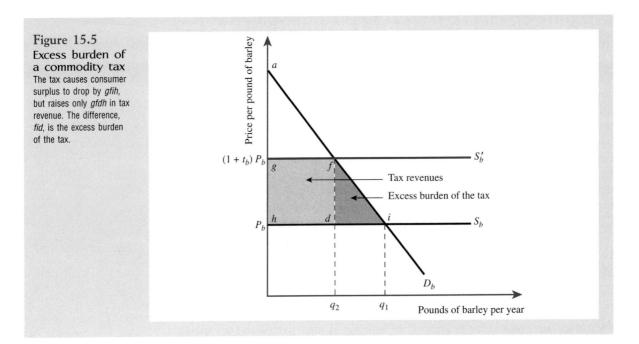

decision, the higher the excess burden. $P_b \times q_1$ is the total revenue expended on barley initially. Its inclusion in the formula shows that the greater the initial expenditure on the taxed commodity, the greater the excess burden.

Equation (15.3) also indicates that it is better to tax many commodities at a lower rate than to tax a few commodities at a higher rate. In other words, a broader tax has less excess burden than a narrow tax. This is because of the presence of t_b^2, which implies that as the tax rate increases, excess burden goes up with its square. Doubling a tax quadruples its excess burden, other things being the same. Therefore, two relatively small taxes will have a smaller excess burden than one large tax that raises the same amount of revenue, other things being the same. Because excess burden increases with the square of the tax rate, the *marginal* excess burden from raising one more dollar of revenue exceeds the *average* excess burden. That is, the incremental excess burden of raising one *more* dollar of revenue exceeds the ratio of total excess burden to total revenues. This fact has important implications for cost-benefit analysis. Suppose, for example, that the average excess burden per dollar of tax revenue is 12 cents, but the marginal excess burden per additional dollar of tax revenue is 27 cents [Jorgenson and Yun, 2001, p. 302]. The social cost of each dollar raised for a given public project is the dollar plus the incremental excess burden of 27 cents. Thus, a public project must produce marginal benefits of more than $1.27 per dollar of explicit cost if it is to improve welfare.

Airline-Ticket Taxation   Let's illustrate Equation (15.3) with a real-world example. Airplane tickets are taxed by the federal government at a rate of 10 percent. What is the excess burden of this tax? The equation tells us that we have to know the price elasticity of demand. According to the survey of Oum et al. [1992], a reasonable estimate is about 1.0. We also need the product of price per ticket and number of tickets sold—airline-ticket revenues. This figure is roughly $107 billion annually [US Bureau of the Census, 2009, p. 658]. Substituting all of this information into

Equation (15.3) tells us that the airline-ticket tax imposes an annual excess burden of $\frac{1}{2} \times 107 \times (0.10)^2$ billion, or \$535 million.

Preexisting Distortions

This analysis has assumed no distortions in the economy other than the tax under consideration. In reality, when a new tax is introduced, there are already other distortions: monopolies, externalities, and preexisting taxes. This complicates the analysis of excess burden.

Suppose that consumers regard gin and rum as substitutes. Suppose further that rum is currently being taxed, creating an excess burden "triangle" as in Figure 15.5. Now the government decides to impose a tax on gin. What is the excess burden of the gin tax? In the gin market, the gin tax creates a wedge between what gin consumers pay and gin producers receive. As usual, this creates an excess burden. But the story is not over. If gin and rum are substitutes, the rise in the consumers' price of gin induced by the gin tax increases the demand for rum. Consequently, the quantity of rum demanded increases. Now, because rum was taxed under the status quo, "too little" of it was being consumed. The increase in rum consumption induced by the gin tax helps move rum consumption back toward its efficient level. There is thus an efficiency gain in the rum market that helps offset the excess burden imposed in the gin market. In theory, the gin tax could actually lower the overall excess burden. This is an example of the **theory of the second best:** In the presence of existing distortions, policies that in isolation would increase efficiency can decrease it and vice versa. (Appendix B at the end of the chapter has a graphical demonstration of this phenomenon.)

theory of the second best

In the presence of existing distortions, policies that in isolation would increase efficiency can decrease it and vice versa.

Thus the efficiency impact of a tax or subsidy cannot be considered in isolation. To the extent that there are other markets with distortions, and the goods in these markets are related (either substitutes or complements), the overall efficiency impact depends on what is going on in all the markets. To compute the overall efficiency impact of a set of taxes and subsidies, it is generally incorrect to calculate separately the excess burdens in each market and then add them up. The aggregate efficiency loss is not equal to the "sum of its parts."

This result can be quite discomfiting because strictly speaking, it means that *every* market in the economy must be studied to assess the efficiency implications of *any* tax or subsidy. In most cases, practitioners simply assume that the amount of interrelatedness between the market of their concern and other markets is sufficiently small that cross-effects can safely be ignored. Although this is clearly a convenient assumption, its reasonableness must be evaluated in each particular case.

The field of environmental economics provides an instance where accounting for preexisting distortions is important. Recall from Chapter 5 that in the presence of an externality, a tax set equal to marginal external cost (a "Pigouvian tax") leads to an efficient outcome. But this result considers only the market in which the externality occurs and ignores efficiency consequences in the labor market. The Pigouvian tax is linked to the labor market because—by raising prices for goods such as energy and transportation—the tax in effect lowers the real wages of workers. Recall that the US income tax system is highly inefficient because it distorts work incentives. Linking these two observations together, it is clear that the Pigouvian tax magnifies the excess burden in the labor market, and this **tax-interaction effect** reduces the overall efficiency of the tax. In light of these labor market effects, it is even possible that a Pigouvian tax can result in an overall decline in efficiency.

tax-interaction effect

The increase in excess burden in the labor market stemming from the reduction in real wages caused by a Pigouvian tax.

double-dividend effect

Using the proceeds from
a Pigouvian tax to reduce
inefficient tax rates.

The inefficiency generated by the tax-interaction effect can be reduced by using the Pigouvian tax revenue to lower inefficient tax rates, such as those associated with the taxation of income. This idea is called the **double-dividend effect.** For example, Metcalf [2007] has proposed that we levy a tax on carbon emissions and use the revenue to reduce payroll taxes. The overall efficiency of a Pigouvian tax with a double-dividend effect would consist of the efficiency gain in the market for the polluting good, the efficiency loss due to the tax-interaction effect in the labor market, and the efficiency gain from using the revenue to lower distorting tax rates.

The Excess Burden of a Subsidy

Commodity subsidies are important components of the fiscal systems of many countries. In effect, a subsidy is just a negative tax, and like a tax, it is associated with an excess burden. To illustrate the calculation of the excess burden of a subsidy, we consider the subsidy for owner-occupied housing provided by the federal government via certain provisions of the personal income tax. (See Chapter 18 for details of the law.) This subsidy is of particular interest because some believe the financial crisis of 2008 and 2009 was caused by people buying too much housing, which may have occurred in part because of the subsidy.

Assume that the demand for owner-occupied housing services is the straight line D_h in Figure 15.6. Supply is horizontal at price P_h, which measures the marginal social cost of producing housing services. Initially, the equilibrium quantity is h_1. Now suppose that the government provides a subsidy of s percent to housing producers. The new price for housing services is then $(1 - s)P_h$ and the associated supply curve is S_h'. The subsidy increases the quantity of housing services consumed to h_2. If the purpose of the subsidy was to increase housing consumption, then it has succeeded. But if its goal was to maximize social welfare, is it an appropriate policy?

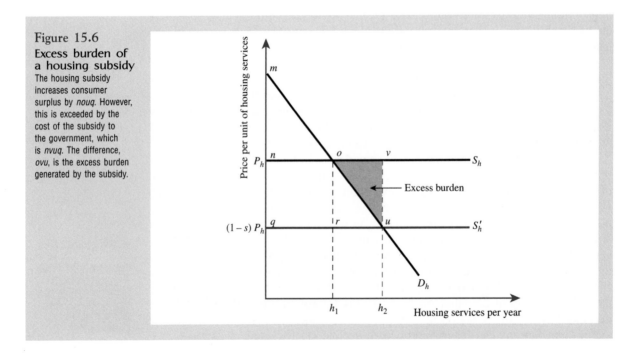

Figure 15.6
Excess burden of a housing subsidy
The housing subsidy increases consumer surplus by *nouq*. However, this is exceeded by the cost of the subsidy to the government, which is *nvuq*. The difference, *ovu*, is the excess burden generated by the subsidy.

Before the subsidy, consumer surplus was area *mno*. After the subsidy, consumer surplus is *mqu*. The benefit to housing consumers is the increase in their surplus, area *nouq*. But at what cost is this benefit obtained? The cost of the subsidy program is the quantity of housing services consumed, *qu*, times the subsidy per unit, *nq*, or rectangle *nvuq*. Thus, the cost of the subsidy actually exceeds the benefit—there is an excess burden equal to the difference between areas *nvuq* and *nouq*, which is the shaded area *ovu*. For someone who owns a $500,000 home, a rough estimate of the excess burden is $1,600 annually.[9]

How can subsidizing a good thing like housing be inefficient? Recall that any point on the demand curve for housing services measures how much people value that particular level of consumption. To the right of h_1, although individuals do derive utility from consuming more housing, its value is less than P_h, the marginal cost to society of providing it. In other words, the subsidy induces people to consume housing services that are valued at less than their cost—hence, the inefficiency.[10]

A very important policy implication follows from this analysis. One often hears proposals to help some group of individuals by subsidizing a commodity that they consume heavily. We have shown that this is an inefficient way to aid people. Less money could make them as well off if it were given to them as a direct grant. In Figure 15.6, people would be indifferent between a housing subsidy program costing *nvuq* and a direct grant of *nouq*, even though the subsidy program costs the government more money.[11] This is one of the reasons many economists prefer direct income transfers to commodity subsidies.

The Excess Burden of Income Taxation

The theory of excess burden applies just as well to inputs as it does to commodities. In Figure 15.7, Jacob's hours of work are plotted on the horizontal axis and his hourly wage on the vertical. Jacob's compensated labor supply curve, which shows the smallest wage that would be required to induce him to work each additional hour, is labeled S_L. Initially, Jacob's wage is w and the associated hours of work L_1. In the same way that consumer surplus is the area between the demand curve and the market price, worker surplus is the area between the supply curve and the market wage rate. When the wage is w, Jacob's surplus is therefore area *adf*.

Now assume that an income tax at a rate t is imposed. The after-tax wage is then $(1 - t)w$, and given supply curve S_L, the quantity of labor supplied falls to L_2 hours. Jacob's surplus after the tax is *agh*, and the government collects revenues equal to *fihg*. The excess burden due to the tax-induced distortion of the work choice is the amount by which Jacob's loss of welfare (*fdhg*) exceeds the tax collected: area *hid* (= *fdhg* − *fihg*). In analogy to Equation (15.3), area *hid* is approximately

$$\tfrac{1}{2}\varepsilon\omega L_1 t^2 \qquad (15.4)$$

where ε is the compensated elasticity of hours of work with respect to the wage.

[9] This figure is based on the assumption that the marginal tax rate is 0.35, the compensated price elasticity is 0.8, the nominal interest rate is 5 percent, the property tax is 2.5 percent of house value, the risk premium for housing investments is 4 percent of house value, and the maintenance and depreciation costs are both 2 percent of house value.

[10] Alternatively, after the subsidy the marginal rate of substitution in consumption depends on $(1 - s)P_h$, while the marginal rate of transformation in production depends on P_h. Hence, the marginal rate of transformation is not equal to the marginal rate of substitution, and the allocation of resources cannot be efficient.

[11] This result is very similar to that obtained when we examined in-kind subsidy programs in Chapter 12. That chapter also discusses why commodity subsidies nevertheless remain politically popular.

THE LIGHTER SIDE OF PUBLIC FINANCE

American Way of Tax*

Humorist Russell Baker never uses the term excess burden in the column reproduced below. Nevertheless, he gives an excellent description of the phenomenon.

NEW YORK—The tax man was very cross about Figg. Figg's way of life did not conform to the way of life several governments wanted Figg to pursue. Nothing inflamed the tax man more than insolent and capricious disdain for governmental desires. He summoned Figg to the temple of taxation.

"What's the idea of living in a rental apartment over a delicatessen in the city, Figg?" he inquired. Figg explained that he liked urban life. In that case, said the tax man, he was raising Figg's city sales and income taxes. "If you want them cut, you'll have to move out to the suburbs," he said.

To satisfy his local government, Figg gave up the city and rented a suburban house. The tax man summoned him back to the temple.

"Figg," he said, "you have made me sore wroth with your way of life. Therefore, I am going to soak you for more federal income taxes." And he squeezed Figg until beads of blood popped out along the seams of Figg's wallet.

"Mercy, good tax man," Figg gasped. "Tell me how to live so that I may please my government, and I shall obey."

The tax man told Figg to quit renting and buy a house. The government wanted everyone to accept large mortgage loans from bankers. If Figg complied, it would cut his taxes.

Figg bought a house, which he did not want, in a suburb where he did not want to live, and he invited his friends and relatives to attend a party celebrating his surrender to a way of life that pleased his government.

The tax man was so furious that he showed up at the party with bloodshot eyes. "I have had enough of this, Figg," he declared. "Your government doesn't want you entertaining friends and relatives. This will cost you plenty."

Figg immediately threw out all his friends and relatives, then asked the tax man what sort of people his government wished him to entertain. "Business associates," said the tax man. "Entertain plenty of business associates, and I shall cut your taxes."

To make the tax man and his government happy, Figg began entertaining people he didn't like in the house he didn't want in the suburb where he didn't want to live.

Then was the tax man enraged indeed. "Figg," he thundered, "I will not cut your taxes for entertaining straw bosses, truck drivers, and pothole fillers."

"Why not?" said Figg. "These are the people I associate with in my business."

"Which is what?" asked the tax man.

"Earning my pay by the sweat of my brow," said Figg.

"Your government is not going to bribe you for performing salaried labor," said the tax man. "Don't you know, you imbecile, that tax rates on salaried income are higher than on any other kind?"

And he taxed the sweat of Figg's brow at a rate that drew exquisite shrieks of agony from Figg and little cries of joy from Washington, which already had more sweated brows than it needed to sustain the federally approved way of life.

"Get into business, or minerals, or international oil," warned the tax man, "or I shall make your taxes as the taxes of 10."

Figg went into business, which he hated, and entertained people he didn't like in the house he didn't want in the suburb where he did not want to live.

At length the tax man summoned Figg for an angry lecture. He demanded to know why Figg had not bought a new plastic factory to replace his old metal and wooden plant. "I hate plastic," said Figg. "Your government is sick and tired of metal, wood, and everything else that smacks of the real stuff, Figg," roared the tax man, seizing Figg's purse. "Your depreciation is all used up."

There was nothing for Figg to do but go to plastic, and the tax man rewarded him with a brand new depreciation schedule plus an investment credit deduction from the bottom line.

* By Russell Baker, *International Herald Tribune*, April 13, 1977, page 14.

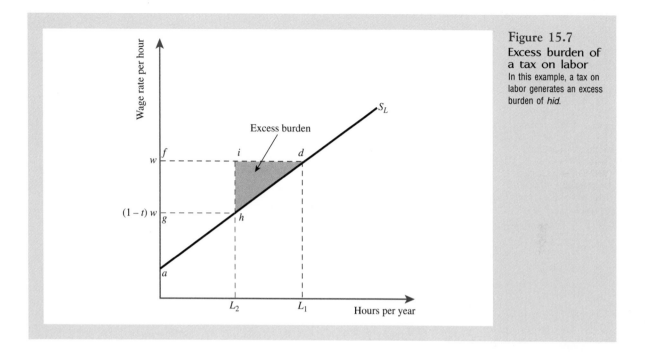

Figure 15.7
Excess burden of a tax on labor
In this example, a tax on labor generates an excess burden of *hid*.

A reasonable estimate of ε for an American male is about 0.2. For illustrative purposes, suppose that before taxation, Jacob works 2,000 hours per year at a wage of $20 per hour. A tax on earnings of 40 percent is then imposed. Substituting these figures into Equation (15.4), the excess burden of the tax is about $640 annually. One way to put this figure into perspective is to note that it is approximately 4 percent of tax revenues. Thus, on average, each dollar of tax collected creates an excess burden of 4 cents.

Of course, wage rates, tax rates, and elasticities vary across members of the population, so different people are subject to different excess burdens. Moreover, the excess burden of taxing labor also depends on tax rates levied on other factors of production. Feldstein [2006a] estimated that an across-the-board increase in personal income tax rates would lead to an excess burden of 76 cents per dollar of revenue. As we show in Chapter 18, however, there is considerable uncertainty about the values of some of the key elasticities. Hence, this particular estimate must be regarded cautiously. Still, it probably provides a good sense of the magnitudes involved.

▶ DIFFERENTIAL TAXATION OF INPUTS

In the income tax example just discussed, we assumed that labor income was taxed at the same rate regardless of where the labor was supplied. But sometimes the tax on an input depends on where it is employed. For instance, because of the corporate income tax, capital used by corporations faces a higher rate than capital used by noncorporate businesses. Another example is the differential taxation of labor in the household and market sectors. If an individual does housework, valuable services

Figure 15.8
The allocation of time between housework and market work
The horizontal distance *OO′* measures the total amount of labor available to society. Individuals allocate labor between housework and market work so that the value of the marginal product of labor is the same in both sectors, which occurs at *H**.

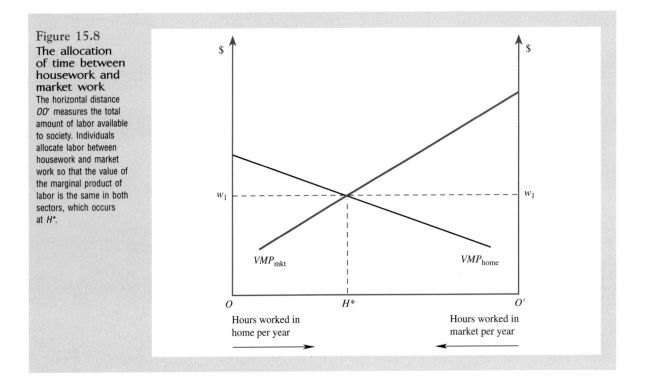

are produced but not taxed.[12] On the other hand, if the same individual works in the market, the services are subject to the income and payroll taxes. The fact that labor is taxed in one sector and untaxed in another distorts people's choices between them.

To measure the efficiency cost, consider Figure 15.8. The horizontal distance OO' measures the total amount of labor available in society. The amount of labor devoted to work in the home is measured by the distance to the right of point O; the amount of labor devoted to work in the market is measured by the distance to the left of point O'. Thus, any point along OO' represents some allocation of labor between the home and the market.

Now, define the *value of marginal product (VMP)* of hours worked in the household sector as the dollar value of the *additional* output produced for each hour worked. The schedule (VMP_{home}) in Figure 15.8 represents the value of the marginal product of household work. It is drawn sloping downward, reflecting the reasonable assumption that as more hours are spent in the home, the incremental value of those hours decreases. This is just a manifestation of the law of diminishing marginal returns. Similarly, VMP_{mkt} shows the value of the marginal product of hours worked in the market sector. (Remember that movements to the left on the horizontal axis represent *increases* in the amount of labor allocated to market work.) Although we expect both schedules to be decreasing with respect to the amount of labor employed

---

[12] The value of housework was expressed nicely by a biblical author who wrote at a time when it was assumed homes were managed only by females. In Proverbs 31, he discusses in detail the many tasks performed by the woman who "looketh well to the ways of her household" (v. 27). His general conclusion is that "her price is far above rubies" (v. 10). Unfortunately, price data on rubies during the biblical era are unavailable.

not the supposed benefits are large enough to justify the costs, intelligent policy requires that excess burden be included in the calculation as a social cost. Moreover, as we see in Chapter 16, excess burden is extremely useful in comparing alternative tax systems. Providing estimates of excess burden is an important task for economists.

Summary

- Taxes generally impose an excess burden—a cost beyond the tax revenue collected.
- Excess burden is caused by tax-induced distortions in behavior. It may be examined using either indifference curves or compensated demand curves.
- Lump sum taxes do not distort behavior but are unattractive as policy tools. Nevertheless, they are an important standard against which to compare the excess burdens of other taxes.
- Excess burden may result even if observed behavior is unaffected, because it is the compensated response to a tax that determines its excess burden.
- When a single tax is imposed, the excess burden is proportional to the compensated elasticity of demand, and to the square of the tax rate.
- Excess burden calculations typically assume no other distortions. If other distortions exist, the incremental excess burden of a new tax depends on its effects in other markets.
- Subsidies also create excess burdens because they encourage people to consume goods valued less than the marginal social cost of production.
- The differential taxation of inputs creates an excess burden. Such inputs are used "too little" in taxed activities and "too much" in untaxed activities.

Discussion Questions

1. Which of the following is likely to impose a large excess burden?
   a. A tax on land.
   b. A tax of 24 percent on the use of cellular phones. (This is the approximate sum of federal and state tax rates in California, New York, and Florida.)
   c. A subsidy for investment in "high-tech" companies.
   d. A tax on soda bought in a cup or glass but not bought in a bottle or can. (Such a tax exists in Chicago.)
   e. A 10-cent tax on a deck of cards that contains no more than 54 cards. (Such a tax exists in Alabama.)
   f. A tax on blueberries. (Such a tax exists in Maine.)

2. Suppose that your neighbor is willing to pay you $100 to do some home repairs for her. You would be willing to do the job for $80, so you strike a deal. Now suppose that the government levies a tax of $25 on all home repair transactions. You pack up your gear and leave your neighbor's home, because it is no longer worthwhile for you to do the job. As a result of your leaving the job, you do not have to pay the $25 tax. Relate this scenario to the concept of excess burden.

3. In 2005, Michigan considered cutting the general sales tax (a tax on most goods at the same rate) and replacing it with a tax on a few products, such as insurance policies. Using Equation (15.3), discuss whether this proposal would increase or decrease efficiency.

4. "In the formula for excess burden given in Equation (15.3), the tax is less than 1. When it is squared, the result is smaller, not bigger. Thus, having t^2 instead of t in the formula makes the tax less important." Comment.

5. In 2008, Michigan adopted a law that gives substantial tax subsidies to moviemakers who film within the state. Use the discussion surrounding Figure 15.9 to assess the efficiency consequences of this subsidy.

6. In 2006, several members of Congress argued for eliminating most of the tax reductions that had been enacted during the previous five years. However, virtually no one was in favor of eliminating the "child tax credit," which cut the taxes of most families by $1,000 per child. One economist argued that keeping the child tax credit "might be good for social purposes, but there's no economic case for it" [Ip, 2006]. Explain what this economist meant using the concept of excess burden.

7. Former Secretary of Labor Robert Reich has advocated for a cap-and-trade program for greenhouse gases. Under Reich's proposal, the government would auction off the permits and distribute the revenues in a lump sum fashion to every adult citizen [Reich, 2008]. What are the implications of this plan for excess burden? If you were interested in reducing excess burden, how would you distribute the revenues?

8. Iran subsidizes gasoline, leading to a price to consumers that is one-fifth the market price [*Economist*, 2007a, pp. 52–53]. Use Figure 15.6 to explain the efficiency implications of this policy.

9. In the United Kingdom, each household that owns a television pays a compulsory levy that is equivalent to $233 per year. The total revenue collected, which is over $7 billion annually, goes to the British Broadcasting Corporation. Do you think that such a tax is likely to have a substantial excess burden relative to the revenues collected?

10. In 2004, Congress voted to subsidize the purchase of capital goods in the manufacturing sector. Nonmanufacturing industries are not eligible for the subsidy. Using the discussion surrounding Figure 15.8, discuss why this subsidy would lead to an inefficient allocation of capital between the manufacturing and nonmanufacturing sectors. (Hint: Reinterpret the horizontal axis as measuring the total amount

of capital in the economy, and the two curves as measuring the value of marginal product of capital in the respective sectors.) Also show on your diagram the amount of the excess burden generated by the manufacturing subsidy.

11. Under the US tax system, capital that is employed in the corporate sector is taxed at a higher rate than capital in the noncorporate sector. This problem will analyze the excess burden of the differential taxation of capital.

Assume that there are two sectors, corporate and noncorporate. The value of marginal product of capital in the corporate sector, VMP_c, is given by $VMP_c = 100 - K_c$, where K_c is the amount of capital in the corporate sector, and the value of the marginal product of capital in the noncorporate sector, K_n, is given by $VMP_n = 80 - 2K_n$, where K_n is the amount of capital in the noncorporate sector. Altogether there are 50 units of capital in society.

a. In the absence of any taxes, how much capital is in the corporate sector and how much in the noncorporate sector? (Hint: Draw a sketch along the lines of Figure 15.9 to organize your thoughts.)

b. Suppose that a unit tax of 6 is levied on capital employed in the corporate sector. After the tax, how much capital is employed in each sector? What is the excess burden of the tax?

12. In an effort to reduce alcohol consumption, the government is considering a $1 tax on each gallon of liquor sold (the tax is levied on producers). Suppose that the supply curve for liquor is upward sloping and its equation is $Q = 30,000P$ (where Q is the number of gallons of liquor and P is the price per gallon). The demand curve for liquor is $Q = 500,000 - 20,000P$.

a. Draw a sketch to illustrate the excess burden of the tax. Next use algebra to calculate the excess burden. Show graphically the excess burden generated by the $1 unit tax. (Hint: Compare the losses of both consumer and producer surplus to tax revenues.)

b. Suppose that each gallon of liquor consumed generates a negative external cost of $0.50. How does this affect the excess burden associated with the unit tax on liquor?

▶ FORMULA FOR EXCESS BURDEN

This appendix shows how the excess burden triangle *fdi* of Figure 15.5 may be written in terms of the compensated demand elasticity. The triangle's area, A, is given by the formula

$$A = \tfrac{1}{2} \times \text{base} \times \text{height} \qquad (15A.1)$$
$$= \tfrac{1}{2} \times (di) \times (fi)$$

fd is just the difference between the gross and net prices (ΔP_b):

$$fd = \Delta P_b = (1 + t_b) \times P_b - P_b = t_b \times P_b \qquad (15A.2)$$

di is the change in the quantity (Δq) induced by the price rise:

$$di = (\Delta q) \qquad (15A.3)$$

Now, note that the definition of the price elasticity, η, is

$$\eta = \frac{\Delta q P_b}{\Delta P_b q}$$

so that

$$\Delta q = \eta \left(\frac{q}{P_b} \right) \Delta P_b \qquad (15A.4)$$

We saw in (15A.2) that $\Delta P_b = t_b \times P_b$, so that (15A.4) yields

$$\Delta q = \eta \times \frac{q}{P_b} \times (t_b P_b) = \eta \times q \times t_b \qquad (15A.5)$$

Finally, recall that $di = \Delta q$ and substitute both (15A.5) and (15A.2) into (15A.1) to obtain

$$A = \tfrac{1}{2}(di)(fd)$$
$$= \tfrac{1}{2}(\eta q t_b) \times (t_b P_b)$$
$$= \tfrac{1}{2} \times \eta \times P_b \times q \times (t_b)^2$$

as in the text.

MULTIPLE TAXES AND THE THEORY OF THE SECOND BEST

This appendix discusses the measurement of excess burden when a tax is imposed in the presence of a preexisting distortion.

In Figure 15.B, we consider two goods, gin and rum, whose demand schedules are D_g and D_r, and whose before-tax prices are P_g and P_r, respectively. (The prices represent marginal social costs and are assumed to be constant.) Rum is currently taxed at a percentage rate t_r, so its price is $(1 + t_r)P_r$. This creates an excess burden in the rum market, triangle *abc*. Now suppose that a tax on gin at rate t_g is introduced, creating a wedge between what gin consumers pay and gin producers receive. This creates an excess burden in the gin market of *efd*. But this is not the end of the story. If gin and rum are substitutes, the increase in the consumers' price of gin induced by the gin tax shifts the demand curve for rum to the right, say to D_r'. Consequently, the quantity of rum demanded increases from r_2 to r_3, distance *cg*. For each bottle of rum purchased between r_2 and r_3, the amount that people pay $[(1 + t_r)P_r]$ exceeds the social cost (P_r) by distance *cb*. Hence, there is a social gain of *cb* per bottle of rum times *cg* bottles, or area *cbhg*.

To summarize: Given that the tax on rum was already in place, the tax on gin creates an excess burden of *efd* in the gin market *and* simultaneously decreases excess burden by *cbhg* in the rum market. If *cbhg* is sufficiently large, the tax can actually reduce overall excess burden. This is an example of the theory of the second best,

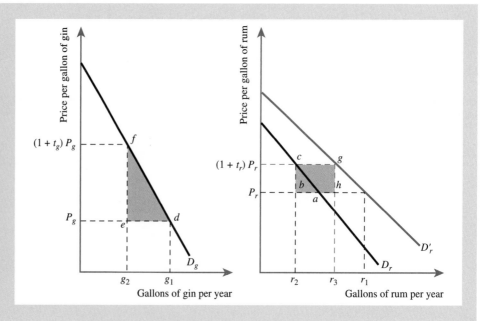

Figure 15.B
Excess burden of a tax in the presence of an existing tax
A tax on gin creates an excess burden of *efd*. The increase in the price of gin shifts the demand curve for rum to the right, because the goods are substitutes. The increase in demand for rum reduces the excess burden associated with the preexisting tax on rum by *cbhg*.

which states that in the presence of existing distortions, policies that in isolation would increase efficiency can decrease it and vice versa.

This discussion is a special case of the result that the excess burden of a *set* of taxes generally depends on the whole set of tax rates, as well as on the degree of substitutability and complementarity among the various commodities. Specifically, suppose that n commodities are subject to taxation. Let P_i be the before-tax price of the ith commodity; t_i the ad valorem tax on the ith commodity; and S_{ij}, the compensated response in the demand of the ith good with respect to a change in the price of the jth good. Then the overall excess burden is

$$-\tfrac{1}{2}\sum_{i=1}^{n}\sum_{j=1}^{n}t_iP_it_jP_jS_{ij}$$

For example, in the two-good case just discussed, where the goods are g and r, the overall excess burden is

$$-\tfrac{1}{2}(t_r^2P_r^2S_{rr}+2t_rP_rt_gP_gS_{rg}+t_g^2P_g^2S_{gg})$$

Chapter Sixteen

Efficient and Equitable Taxation

> *A nation may fall into decay through taxation in two ways. In the first case, when the amount of the taxes exceeds the powers of the nation and is not proportioned to the general wealth. In the second case, when an amount of taxation, proportioned on the whole to the powers of the nation, is viciously distributed.*
>
> —PIETRO VERRI

The US revenue system is under attack. Critics argue that it is inefficient, unfair, and unduly complicated. But when these critics offer proposals for reform, their ideas are generally assailed for the same reasons. How are we to choose? Our goal in this chapter is to establish a set of criteria for evaluating real-world tax systems. We begin by looking at efficiency and distributional considerations that fit squarely within the framework of conventional welfare economics. We then turn to other criteria that do not fit so neatly, but nevertheless have considerable importance and appeal.

▶ OPTIMAL COMMODITY TAXATION

In Florida, wireless phone bills are taxed at a rate of 16.23 percent; most other commodities (except for food, which is exempt) are taxed at a rate of 6 percent. Should wireless phone service be taxed at a higher rate than other things? This is just one example of a very general and very important economic policy question: At what rates should various goods and services be taxed? The purpose of the theory of optimal commodity taxation is to provide a framework for answering this question.

Of course, we can't find the "right" set of taxes without knowing the government's goal. At the outset, we assume that the only goal is to finance the state's expenditures with a minimum of excess burden and without using any lump sum taxes. We return later to issues that arise when distribution as well as efficiency matters.

To begin, consider the situation of Stella, a representative citizen who consumes only two commodities, X and Y, as well as leisure, l. The price of X is P_x, the price of Y is P_y, and the wage rate (which is the price of leisure) is w. The maximum number of hours per year that Stella can work—her **time endowment**—is fixed at $\overline{T}$. Think of $\overline{T}$ as the amount of time left over after sleep. It follows that hours of work are $(\overline{T} - l)$—all time not spent on leisure is devoted to work. Income is the product of the wage rate and hours of work—$w(\overline{T} - l)$. Assuming that Stella

time endowment

The maximum number of hours an individual can work during a given period.

spends her entire income on commodities X and Y (there is no saving), her budget constraint is

$$w(T - l) = P_x X + P_y Y \tag{16.1}$$

The left-hand side gives total earnings, and the right-hand side shows how the earnings are spent.

Equation (16.1) can be rewritten as

$$w\overline{T} = P_x X + P_y Y + wl \tag{16.2}$$

The left-hand side of (16.2) is the value of the time endowment. It shows the income that Stella could earn if she worked every waking hour.

Now suppose that it is possible to tax X, Y, and l at the same ad valorem rate, t. The tax raises the effective price of X to $(1 + t)P_x$, of Y to $(1 + t)P_y$, and of l to $(1 + t)w$. Thus, Stella's after-tax budget constraint is

$$w\overline{T} = (1+t)P_x X + (1+t)P_y Y + (1+t)wl \tag{16.3}$$

Dividing through Equation (16.3) by $(1 + t)$, we have

$$\frac{1}{1+t}w\overline{T} = P_x X + P_y Y + wl \tag{16.4}$$

Comparison of (16.3) and (16.4) points out the following fact: A tax on all commodities *including leisure*, at the same percentage rate, t, is equivalent to reducing the value of the time endowment from $w\overline{T}$ to $[1/(1 + t)] \times w\overline{T}$. For example, a 25 percent tax on X, Y, and l is equivalent to a reduction of the value of the time endowment by 20 percent. However, because w and $\overline{T}$ are fixed, their product, $w\overline{T}$, is also fixed; for any value of the wage rate, an individual cannot change the value of her time endowment. Therefore, a proportional tax on the time endowment is in effect a lump sum tax. From Chapter 15 we know that lump sum taxes have no excess burden. We conclude that a tax at the same rate on all commodities, *including leisure*, is equivalent to a lump sum tax and has no excess burden.

It sounds good, but there is a problem—putting a tax on leisure time is impossible. The only *available* tax instruments are taxes on commodities X and Y. Therefore, *some* excess burden generally is inevitable. The goal of optimal commodity taxation is to select tax rates on X and Y in such a way that the excess burden of raising the required tax revenue is as low as possible. It might seem that the solution to this problem is to tax X and Y at the same rate—so-called **neutral taxation.** We will see that, in general, neutral taxation is *not* efficient.

neutral taxation

Taxing each good at the same rate.

The Ramsey Rule

To raise the revenue with the least excess burden possible, how should the tax rates on X and Y be set? To minimize *overall* excess burden, the *marginal* excess burden of the last dollar of revenue raised from each commodity must be the same. Otherwise, it would be possible to lower overall excess burden by raising the rate on the commodity with the smaller marginal excess burden while lowering the rate on the commodity with the larger marginal excess burden.

To explore the consequences of this typical example of marginal analysis, suppose for simplicity that for our representative consumer, X and Y are unrelated commodities—they are neither substitutes nor complements for each other. Hence,

Figure 16.1

Marginal excess burden

Increasing the unit tax from u_x by one dollar leads to a marginal excess burden of *fbae* and to an increase in tax revenues of *gfih − bae*.

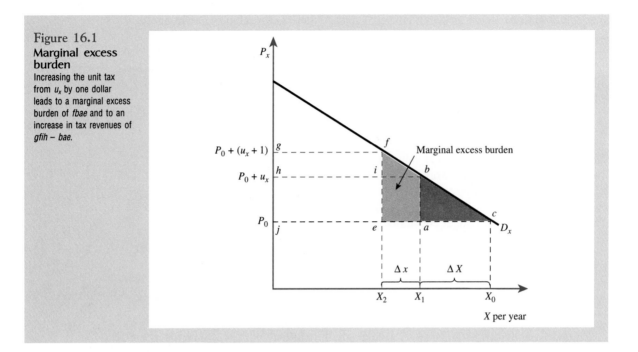

a change in the price of either commodity affects its own demand and not the demand for the other good. Figure 16.1 shows Stella's compensated demand for X, D_x. Assume that she can buy all the X she wants at the price P_0, so the supply curve of X is horizontal.

Suppose that a unit tax of u_x is levied on X, which lowers quantity demanded from X_0 to X_1, ΔX in the figure. As proven in Chapter 15, the excess burden of the tax is the area of triangle *abc*. Now suppose we raise the tax by 1, so it becomes $(u_x + 1)$. The total price is $P_0 + (u_x + 1)$; quantity demanded falls by Δx to X_2; and the associated excess burden is triangle *fec*. The marginal excess burden is the difference between the two triangles, trapezoid *fbae*. The area of the trapezoid is one-half its height (Δx) times the sum of its bases $[u_x + (u_x + 1)]$. Thus, the marginal excess burden is $\frac{1}{2} \Delta x[u_x + (u_x + 1)]$.

With a bit of algebra,[1] we can simplify this expression to obtain that the marginal excess burden is approximately ΔX:

$$\Delta X = \text{marginal excess burden} \qquad (16.5)$$

Recall that excess burden minimization requires information on the marginal excess burden on the *last dollar* of revenue collected. Now that we know the marginal excess burden induced by the tax increase, we must compute the associated increase in revenues. Then all we have to do is divide the marginal excess burden by the change in revenues. By definition, this quotient is the marginal excess burden per incremental dollar of revenue collected.

To compute the change in tax revenues associated with raising the rate from u_x to $(u_x + 1)$, note that when the tax rate is u_x, tax revenues are $u_x X_1$ (the tax per unit times

---

[1] The area of the trapezoid is $\frac{1}{2}\Delta x(2u_x + 1)$ or $\Delta xu_x + (\frac{1}{2})\Delta x$, which we can approximate as Δxu_x because the second term, which corresponds to triangle *fib* is relatively small and can be ignored. Now note that $1/\Delta x$ and $u_x/\Delta X$ are equal because both measure the slope (in absolute value) of D_x. Hence, $\Delta xu_x = \Delta X$, which is the marginal excess burden.

number of units sold). In Figure 16.1, this is rectangle *hbaj*. Similarly, when the tax rate is $(u_x + 1)$, tax revenues are *gfej*. Comparing these two rectangles, we see that when the tax goes up, the government gains area *gfih* but loses *ibae*. Thus, the change in revenues is *gfih − ibae*. Using algebra, this is $X_2 - (X_1 - X_2)u_x$. A bit of mathematical manipulation[2] leads us to the following approximation to the change in tax revenue:

$$X_1 - \Delta X = \text{marginal tax revenue} \tag{16.6}$$

Marginal excess burden per additional dollar of tax revenue is Equation (16.6) divided by (16.5) or

$$\frac{\Delta X}{X_1 - \Delta X}$$

Exactly the same reasoning indicates that if a unit tax of u_y is levied on *Y*, the marginal excess burden per last dollar of revenue is

$$\frac{\Delta Y}{Y_1 - \Delta Y}$$

Because the condition for minimizing overall excess burden is that the marginal excess burden per last dollar of revenue be the same for each commodity, we must set

$$\frac{\Delta X}{X_1 - \Delta X} = \frac{\Delta Y}{Y_1 - \Delta Y}$$

This implies

$$\frac{\Delta X}{X_1} = \frac{\Delta Y}{Y_1}$$

To interpret Equation (16.7), note that the *change* in a variable divided by its *total* value is just the percentage change in the variable. Hence, Equation (16.7) says that *to minimize total excess burden, tax rates should be set so that the percentage reduction in the quantity demanded of each commodity is the same*. This result, called the **Ramsey rule** (after its discoverer, Frank Ramsey [1927]), also holds even for cases when *X*, *Y*, and *l* are related goods—substitutes or complements.

But why should efficient taxation induce equal proportional changes in quantities demanded rather than equal proportional changes in prices? Because excess burden is a consequence of distortions in *quantities*. To minimize total excess burden requires that all these changes be in the same proportion.

A Reinterpretation of the Ramsey Rule

It is useful to explore the relationship between the Ramsey rule and demand elasticities. Let η_x be the compensated elasticity of demand for *X*. Let t_x be the tax rate on *X*, this time expressed as an ad valorem rate rather than a unit tax.[3] Now, by definition of an ad valorem tax, t_x is the percentage increase in the price induced by the tax. Hence, $t_x\eta_x$ is the

Ramsey rule

To minimize total excess burden, tax rates should be set so that the tax-induced percentage reduction in the quantity demanded of each commodity is the same.

[2] Note that the expression for marginal tax revenue is equivalent to $X_2(u_x + 1) - X_1u_x = X_2 + u_x(X_2 - X_1)$. From Figure 16.1, $X_2 = X_1 - \Delta x$. Substituting gives us $X_1 - \Delta x - u_x\Delta x$. But $\Delta x = \Delta X/u_x$ (see previous footnote 1), giving us $X_1 - \Delta X(1 + u_x)/u_x$. Providing that u_x is large relative to 1, this can be approximated as $X_1 - \Delta X$, the expression in the text for marginal tax revenue.

[3] In a competitive market, any unit tax can be represented by a suitably chosen ad valorem tax, and vice versa. For example, suppose a commodity is subject to a unit tax of 5 cents, and the price paid by consumers is 50 cents. Then the resulting excess burden is the same as that associated with an ad valorem tax equal to 10 percent of the after-tax price.

percentage change in the price times the percentage change in quantity demanded when the price increases by 1 percent. This is just the percentage reduction in the demand for X induced by the tax. Defining t_y and η_y analogously, $t_y\eta_y$ is the proportional reduction in Y. The Ramsey rule says that to minimize excess burden, these percentage reductions in quantity demanded must be equal:

$$t_x\eta_x = t_y\eta_y \tag{16.8}$$

Now divide both sides of the equation by $t_y\eta_x$ to obtain

$$\frac{t_x}{t_y} = \frac{\eta_y}{\eta_x} \tag{16.9}$$

inverse elasticity rule

For goods that are unrelated in consumption, efficiency requires that tax rates be inversely proportional to elasticities.

Equation (16.9) is the **inverse elasticity rule:** As long as goods are unrelated in consumption, tax rates should be inversely proportional to elasticities. That is, the higher is η_y relative to η_x, the lower should be t_y relative to t_x.[4] Efficiency does *not* require that all rates be set uniformly.

The intuition behind the inverse elasticity rule is straightforward. Efficient taxes distort decisions as little as possible. The potential for distortion is greater the more elastic the demand for a commodity. Therefore, efficient taxation requires that relatively high rates of taxation be levied on relatively inelastic goods.

Footnote 4

The Corlett-Hague Rule

Corlett and Hague [1953] proved an interesting implication of the Ramsey rule: When there are two commodities, efficient taxation requires taxing the commodity that is complementary to leisure at a relatively high rate. To understand this result intuitively, recall that *if* it were possible to tax leisure, a "first-best" result would be obtainable—revenues could be raised with no excess burden. Although the tax authorities cannot tax leisure, they *can* tax goods that tend to be consumed jointly *with* leisure, indirectly lowering the demand for leisure. If video games are taxed at a very high rate, people buy fewer of them and spend less time at leisure. In effect, then, high taxes on complements to leisure provide an indirect way to "get at" leisure, and, hence, move closer to the perfectly efficient outcome that would be possible if leisure were taxable.

Equity Considerations

At this point you may suspect that efficient tax theory has unpleasant policy implications. For example, the inverse elasticity rule says inelastically demanded goods should be taxed at relatively high rates. Is this fair? Do we really want a tax system that collects the bulk of its revenue from taxes on insulin?

Of course not. Efficiency is only one criterion for evaluating a tax system; fairness is also important. In particular, it is widely agreed that a tax system should

---

[4] A more careful demonstration requires a little calculus. Recall from Equation (15.3) that the excess burdens on commodities X and Y are $\frac{1}{2}\eta_x P_x X t_x^2$ and $\frac{1}{2}\eta_y P_y Y t_y^2$, respectively. Then the total excess burden is $\frac{1}{2}\eta_x P_x X t_x^2 + \frac{1}{2}\eta_y P_y Y t_y^2$. (We can just add up the two expressions because by assumption, X and Y are unrelated.) Now, suppose the required tax revenue is R. Then t_x and t_y must satisfy the relation $P_x X t_x + P_y Y t_y = R$. Our problem is to choose t_x and t_y to minimize $\frac{1}{2}\eta_x P_x X t_x^2 + \frac{1}{2}\eta_y P_y Y t_y^2$ subject to $R - P_x X t_x + P_y Y t_y = 0$. Set up the Lagrangian expression

$$\mathcal{L} = \frac{1}{2}\eta_x P_x X t_x^2 + \frac{1}{2}\eta_y P_y Y t_y^2 + \lambda[R - P_x X t_x - P_y Y t_y]$$

where λ is the Lagrange multiplier. (The method of Lagrangian multipliers is covered in any intermediate calculus book.) Taking $\partial\mathcal{L}/\partial t_x$ yields $\eta_x t_x = \lambda$ and $\partial\mathcal{L}/\partial t_y$ yields $\eta_y t_y = \lambda$. Hence, $\eta_x t_x = \eta_y t_y$, and Equation (16.9) follows immediately.

have **vertical equity:** It should distribute burdens fairly across people with different abilities to pay. The Ramsey rule has been modified to account for the distributional consequences of taxation. Suppose, for example, that the poor spend a greater proportion of their income on commodity X than do the rich, and vice versa for commodity Y. X might be bread, and Y caviar. Suppose further that the social welfare function puts a higher weight on the utilities of the poor than on those of the rich. Then even if X is more inelastically demanded than Y, optimal taxation may require a higher rate of tax on Y than X. True, a high tax rate on Y creates a relatively large excess burden, but it also tends to redistribute income toward the poor. Society may be willing to pay the price of a higher excess burden in return for a more equal distribution of income.

In general, the optimal departure from the Ramsey rule depends on two considerations. First is how much society cares about equality. If society cares only about efficiency—a dollar to one person is the same as a dollar to another, rich or poor—then it may as well strictly follow the Ramsey rule. Second is the extent to which the consumption patterns of the rich and poor differ. If the rich and the poor consume both goods in the same proportion, taxing the goods at different rates cannot affect the distribution of income. Even if society *has* a distributional goal, it cannot be achieved by differential commodity taxation.

vertical equity

Distributing tax burdens fairly across people with different abilities to pay.

Summary

If lump sum taxation were available, taxes could be raised without any excess burden at all. Optimal taxation would need to focus only on distributional issues. Lump sum taxes are not available, however, so the problem is how to raise tax revenue with as small an excess burden as possible. In general, minimizing excess burden requires that taxes be set so that the (compensated) demands for all commodities are reduced in the same proportion. For unrelated goods, this implies that tax rates should be set in inverse proportion to the demand elasticities. However, if society has distributional goals, departures from efficient taxation rules may be appropriate.

Application: Taxation of the Family

Under current federal income tax law, the fundamental unit of income taxation is the family.[5] A husband and wife are taxed on the sum of their incomes. Regardless of whether the wife or the husband earns an extra dollar, it is taxed at the same rate. Is this efficient? In other words, is the family's excess burden minimized by taxing each spouse's income at the same rate?

Imagine the family as a unit whose utility depends on the quantities of three "commodities": total family consumption, husband's hours of work, and wife's hours of work. Family utility increases with family consumption, but decreases with each spouse's hours of work. Each spouse's hours of work depend on his or her wage rate, among other variables. A tax on earnings distorts the work decision, creating an excess burden. (See Chapter 15, Figure 15.7.) How should tax rates be set so the family's excess burden is as small as possible?

Assume for simplicity that the husband's and wife's hours of work are approximately "unrelated goods"—an increase in the husband's wage rate has very little impact on the

---

[5] This section is based on Boskin and Sheshinski [1983].

wife's work decision, and vice versa. This assumption is consistent with much empirical research. Then application of the inverse elasticity rule suggests that a higher tax should be levied on the commodity that is relatively inelastically supplied. To enhance efficiency, whoever's labor supply is relatively inelastic should bear a relatively high tax rate. Numerous econometric studies suggest that husbands' labor supplies are considerably less elastic than wives'. Efficiency could therefore be gained if the current tax law were modified to give husbands higher marginal tax rates than wives.[6]

Again, we emphasize that efficiency is only one consideration in tax design. However, it is interesting that this result is consistent with the claims of some who have argued that on equity grounds, the relative tax rate on the earnings of working wives should be lowered. Chapter 17 contains a discussion of the actual tax treatment of married couples under US law.

▶ OPTIMAL USER FEES

So far we have assumed that all production occurs in the private sector. The government's only problem is to set the tax rates that determine consumer prices. Sometimes, the government itself is the producer of a good or service. In such cases, the government must directly choose a **user fee**—a price paid by users of a good or service provided by the government. As usual, we would like to determine the "best" possible user fee. Analytically, the optimal tax and user fee problems are closely related. In both cases, the government sets the final price paid by consumers. In the optimal tax problem, this is done indirectly by choice of the tax rate, while in the optimal user fee problem, it is done directly.

When should the government choose to produce a good instead of purchasing it from the private sector? Government production may be appropriate when the use of some good or service is subject to continually decreasing average costs—the greater the level of output, the lower the cost per unit. Under such circumstances, it is unlikely that the market for the service is competitive. A single firm can take advantage of economies of scale and supply the entire industry output, at least for a sizable region. This phenomenon is often called **natural monopoly.** Examples are bridges, electricity, and cable television. In some cases, these commodities are produced by the private sector and regulated by the government (electricity); and in others they are produced by the public sector (bridges). Although we study public production here, many of the important insights apply to regulation of private monopolies.

Figure 16.2 measures the output of the natural monopoly, Z, on the horizontal axis, and dollars on the vertical. The average cost schedule is denoted AC_Z. By assumption, it decreases continuously over all relevant ranges of output. Because average cost is decreasing, marginal cost must be less than average. Therefore, the marginal cost curve (MC_Z), which shows the incremental cost of providing each unit of Z, lies below AC_Z. The demand curve for Z is represented by D_Z. The associated marginal revenue curve is MR_Z. It shows the incremental revenue associated with each level of output of Z.

To illustrate why decreasing average costs often lead to public sector production or regulated private sector production, consider what would happen if Z were produced by an unregulated monopolist. A monopolist seeking to maximize profits

---

user fee

A price paid by users of a government-provided good or service.

natural monopoly

A situation in which factors inherent to the production process lead to a single firm supplying the entire industry's output.

---

[6] The important distinction here is not between *husband* and *wife* but between *primary earner* and *secondary earner*. In families where the wife has the lower supply elasticity, efficiency requires that she have the higher tax rate.

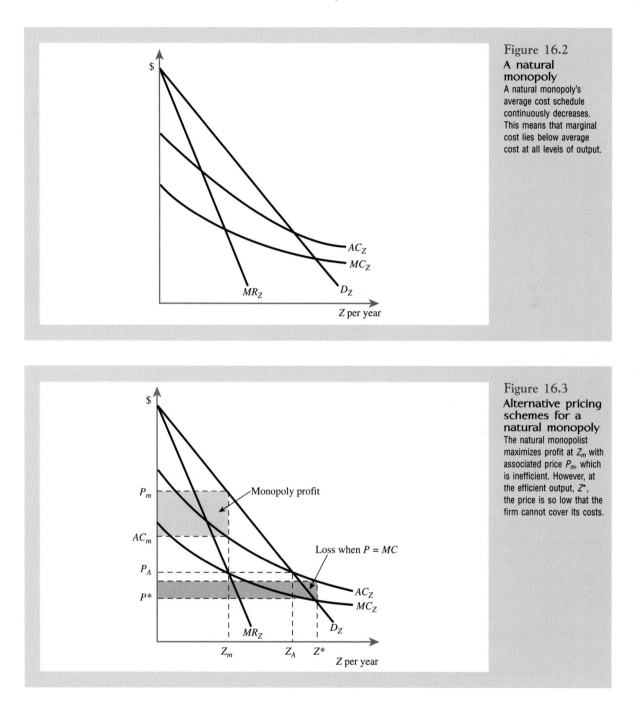

Figure 16.2
A natural monopoly
A natural monopoly's average cost schedule continuously decreases. This means that marginal cost lies below average cost at all levels of output.

Figure 16.3
Alternative pricing schemes for a natural monopoly
The natural monopolist maximizes profit at Z_m with associated price P_m, which is inefficient. However, at the efficient output, Z^*, the price is so low that the firm cannot cover its costs.

produces up to the point that marginal revenue equals marginal cost, output level Z_m in Figure 16.3. The associated price, P_m, is found by going up to the demand curve, D_Z. Monopoly profits are equal to the product of number of units sold times the profit per unit and are represented geometrically by the light-colored rectangle.

Is output Z_m efficient? According to the theory of welfare economics, efficiency requires that price equal marginal cost—the value that people place on the good must equal the incremental cost to society of producing it. At Z_m, price is *greater* than marginal cost. Hence, Z_m is inefficient. This inefficiency plus the fact that society may not approve of the existence of the monopoly profits provide a possible justification for government taking over the production of Z.

The obvious policy prescription seems to be for the government to produce up to the point where price equals marginal cost. In Figure 16.3, the output at which $P = MC$ is denoted Z^*, and the associated price is P^*. There is a problem, however: At output Z^*, the price is less than the average cost. Price P^* is so low that the operation cannot cover its costs, and it suffers losses. The total loss is equal to the product of the number of units sold, Z^*, times the loss per unit, measured as the vertical distance between the demand curve and AC_Z at Z^*. Geometrically, the loss is the darker-colored rectangle in Figure 16.3.

How should the government confront this dilemma? Several solutions have been proposed.

Average Cost Pricing

By definition, when price equals average cost, there are neither profits nor losses—the enterprise just breaks even. The operation no longer has to worry about a deficit. Geometrically, this corresponds to the intersection of the demand and average cost schedules in Figure 16.3, where output is Z_A and price is P_A. However, note that Z_A is less than Z^*. Although average cost pricing leads to more output than at the profit-maximizing level, it still falls short of the efficient amount.

Marginal Cost Pricing with Lump Sum Taxes

Charge $P = MC$, and make up the deficit by levying lump sum taxes. Charging $P = MC$ ensures efficiency in the market for Z; financing the deficit with lump sum taxes on the rest of society guarantees that no new inefficiencies are generated by meeting the deficit. However, there are two problems with this solution:

First, as previously noted, lump sum taxes are generally unavailable. The deficit has to be financed by distorting taxes, such as income or commodity taxes. If so, the distortion due to the tax may more than outweigh the efficiency gain in the market for Z.

Second, there is a widespread belief that fairness requires consumers of a publicly provided service to pay for it—the so-called **benefits-received principle.** If this principle is taken seriously, it is unfair to make up the deficit by general taxation. If the coast guard rescues me from a stormy sea, why should you pay for it?

benefits-received principle

Consumers of a publicly provided service should be the ones who pay for it.

A Ramsey Solution

So far we have been looking at one government enterprise in isolation. Suppose that the government is running *several* enterprises, and as a group they cannot lose money, but any individual enterprise can. Suppose further that the government wants the financing to come from users of the services produced by the enterprises. By how much should the user fee for each service exceed its marginal cost?

Does this question sound familiar? It should, because it is essentially the same as the optimal tax problem. In effect, the difference between the marginal cost and the user fee is just the "tax" that the government levies on the commodity. And just as in the optimal tax problem, the government has to raise a certain amount of revenue—in this case, enough for the group of enterprises to break even. The Ramsey rule gives the answer—set the user fees so that demands for each commodity are reduced proportionately. This analysis, by the way, illustrates one of the nice features of economic theory. Often a framework that is developed to study one problem can be fruitfully applied to another problem that seems to be quite different.

Overview

Of the various possibilities for dealing with natural monopolies, which has the United States chosen? In most cases, both publicly owned and regulated private enterprises have selected average cost pricing. Although average cost pricing is inefficient, it is probably a reasonable compromise. It has the virtue of being fairly simple and adheres to the popular benefits-received principle. Some economists, however, argue that more reliance on Ramsey pricing would be desirable.

▸ OPTIMAL INCOME TAXATION

Thus far, we have assumed that a government can levy taxes on all commodities and inputs. We now turn to the question of how to design systems in which tax liabilities are based on people's incomes. To frame the issue, consider the debate in 2009 when the Obama administration proposed tax increases on families with incomes of more than $250,000. Supporters of the idea argued that it would enhance fairness; opponents said that it was unfair and inefficient. How progressive should the income tax be? As the debate surrounding President Obama's proposal demonstrated, there is hardly a more contentious issue in public finance. Nineteenth-century economist John McCulloch, who opposed progressive taxation, argued that once you abandon proportional taxation, "you are at sea without rudder or compass, and there is no amount of injustice and folly you may not commit." The goal of the theory of optimal income taxation is to provide a rudder, that is, to provide a systematic way for thinking about the "right" trade-off between equity and efficiency.

Edgeworth's Model

At the end of the 19th century, Edgeworth [1959/1897] examined the question of optimal income taxation using a simple model based on the following assumptions.

1. Subject to the revenues required, the goal is to make the sum of individuals' utilities as high as possible. Algebraically, if U_i is the utility of the ith individual and W is social welfare, the tax system should maximize

$$W = U_1 + U_2 + \cdots + U_n \qquad (16.10)$$

   where n is the number of people in the society.

2. Individuals have identical utility functions that depend only on their incomes. These utility functions exhibit diminishing marginal utility of income; as income increases, an individual becomes better off, but at a decreasing rate.

3. The total amount of income available is fixed.

Edgeworth's assumptions are virtually identical to the assumptions behind the optimal income distribution model presented in Chapter 12 under "Rationales for Income Redistribution." There we showed that with these assumptions, maximization of social welfare requires that each person's marginal utility of income be the same. When utility functions are identical, marginal utilities are equal only if incomes are equal. The implications for tax policy are clear: Taxes should be set so that the after-tax distribution of income is as equal as possible. In particular, income should be taken first from the rich because the marginal utility lost is smaller than that of the poor. If the government requires more revenue even after obtaining complete equality, the additional tax burden should be evenly distributed.

Edgeworth's model, then, implies a radically progressive tax structure—incomes are leveled off from the top until complete equality is reached. In effect, marginal tax rates on high-income individuals are 100 percent. However, as stressed in Chapter 12, each of the assumptions underlying this analysis is questionable. In recent decades, economists have investigated how Edgeworth's results change when certain of the assumptions are relaxed.

Modern Studies

One of the most vexing problems with Edgeworth's analysis is the assumption that the total amount of income available to society is fixed. According to this assumption, confiscatory tax rates have no effect on the amount of output produced. More realistically, suppose that individuals' utilities depend not only on income but on leisure as well. Then income taxes distort work decisions and create excess burdens (see Chapter 15). A society with an additive social welfare function thus faces an inescapable dilemma. On the one hand, it desires to allocate the tax burden to equalize the after-tax distribution of income. However, in the process of doing so, it reduces the total amount of real income available. An optimal income tax system—one that maximizes social welfare—must account for the costs (in excess burden) of achieving more equality. In Edgeworth's model, the cost of obtaining more equality is zero, which explains the prescription for a perfectly egalitarian outcome.

How does Edgeworth's result change when work incentives are taken into account? Stern [1987] studied a model similar to Edgeworth's, except that individuals choose between income and leisure. To simplify the analysis, Stern assumed that the tax revenues collected from a person are given by

$$\text{Revenues} = -\alpha + t \times \text{Income} \qquad (16.11)$$

where α and t are positive numbers. For example, suppose that $\alpha = \$3,000$ and $t = 0.25$. Then a person with an income of \$20,000 would have a tax liability of \$2,000 ($= -\$3,000 + 0.25 \times \$20,000$). A person with an income of \$6,000 would have a tax liability of *minus* \$1,500 ($= -\$3,000 + 0.25 \times \$6,000$). Such a person would receive a \$1,500 grant from the government.

In Figure 16.4, we graph Equation (16.11) in a diagram with income measured on the horizontal axis and tax revenues on the vertical. When income is zero, the tax burden is negative—the individual receives a grant from the government of α dollars. Then, for each dollar of income, the individual must pay t dollars to the government. Thus, t is the *marginal* tax rate, the proportion of an additional dollar that must be paid in tax. Because the geometric interpretation of (16.11) is a straight line, it is referred to as a **linear income tax schedule.** In popular discussions, a linear income tax schedule is often called a **flat income tax.** Note that even though the marginal tax rate for a linear tax schedule is constant, the schedule is progressive in the sense that the higher an individual's income, the higher the proportion of income paid in taxes. (See Chapter 14.) Just how progressive depends on the precise values of α and t. Greater values of t are associated with more progressive tax systems. However, at the same time that high values of t lead to more progressiveness, they create larger excess burdens. The optimal income tax problem is to find the "best" combination of α and t—the values that maximize social welfare [Equation (16.10)] subject to the constraint that a given amount of revenue (above the required transfers) be collected.

Stern [1987] finds that allowing for a modest amount of substitution between leisure and income, and with required government revenues equal to about 20 percent of

linear income tax schedule

See *flat income tax.*

flat income tax

A tax schedule for which the marginal tax rate is constant throughout the entire range of incomes.

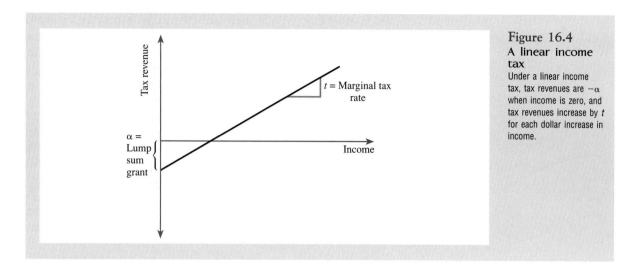

Figure 16.4
A linear income tax
Under a linear income tax, tax revenues are $-\alpha$ when income is zero, and tax revenues increase by t for each dollar increase in income.

income, a value of t of about 19 percent maximizes social welfare.[7] This is considerably less than the value of 100 percent implied by Edgeworth's analysis. Even quite modest incentive effects appear to have important implications for optimal marginal tax rates. Incidentally, Stern's calculated rate is also much smaller than the actual marginal tax rates found in many Western countries. For example, under the US federal personal income tax, the highest statutory marginal income tax rate in 2008 was 35 percent; at times it has been 90 percent.

More generally, Stern showed that the more elastic the supply of labor, the lower the optimal value of t, other things being the same. Intuitively, the cost of redistribution is the excess burden it creates. The more elastic the supply of labor, the greater the excess burden from taxing it. [See Equation (15.4).] More elastic labor supply therefore means a higher cost to redistribution, so that less should be undertaken.

Stern also investigated how alternative social welfare functions affect the results, focusing on the impact of giving different social weights to the utilities of the rich and the poor. In Equation (16.10), more egalitarian preferences are represented by assigning the utilities of poor people higher weights than utilities of the rich. An interesting extreme case is the maximin criterion, according to which the only individual who receives any weight in the social welfare function is the person with the minimum utility (see Chapter 12). Stern found that the maximin criterion calls for a marginal tax rate of about 80 percent. Not surprisingly, if society has extremely egalitarian objectives, high tax rates are called for. Even here, though, the rates fall short of 100 percent.

One limitation of Stern's analysis is that it constrains the income tax system to have only a single marginal tax rate. Gruber and Saez [2002] investigated a more general model that allowed for four marginal tax rates. Their most interesting finding is that people in higher-income brackets should face a *lower* marginal tax rate than people in the lower brackets. The intuition behind the result is that, by lowering the

---

[7] Specifically, the result reported here assumes the elasticity of substitution between leisure and income is 0.6. In Stern's model, this corresponds to a small positive elasticity of labor supply with respect to the net wage, about 0.1.

marginal tax rate on high-income people, they are induced to supply more labor, and the increased tax revenue can be used to lower the tax burdens on low-income individuals. Importantly, although marginal tax rates fall with income, average tax rates rise with income, so the optimal tax system is still progressive. Recently, a canton (state) in Switzerland actually implemented a tax system that imposes lower marginal tax rates on higher earners [Rabushka, 2003].

This cataloging of results may convey a somewhat false sense of precision of what economists really know about the optimal tax system. After all, there are many controversial value judgments behind the additive social welfare that the optimal tax system seeks to maximize. Moreover, as explained in Chapter 18, there is substantial uncertainty about the behavioral elasticities that are crucial to analyzing the trade-off between efficiency and equity. Nevertheless, calculating optimal tax rates under alternative sets of assumptions is extremely informative. The optimal tax literature reveals the implications of alternative ethical and behavioral assumptions, and thus fosters coherent discussions of tax policy.

▶ POLITICS AND THE TIME INCONSISTENCY PROBLEM

Optimal taxation is a purely normative theory. It does not purport to predict what real-world tax systems look like, or to explain how these tax systems emerge. The theory pays little attention to the institutional and political setting in which tax policy is made. Holcombe [2002] argues that in the presence of real-world political institutions, policy recommendations based on optimal tax logic may actually reduce welfare.

Assume that in a certain society, there are three commodities, X, Y, and leisure. Labor is totally fixed in supply, and therefore, income is fixed. Currently, this society levies a tax on X, but its constitution forbids taxing Y. Viewing this situation, a student of optimal tax theory might say something like: "You are running an inefficient tax system. Because labor is totally fixed in supply, you could have no excess burden if you taxed X and Y at equal rates—an income tax. I recommend that you lower the tax on X and impose a tax at the same rate on Y. Set the rates so that the same amount of revenue is collected as before."

Suppose, however, that the citizens suspect that if they allow taxation of Y, their politicians will not lower the tax rate on X. Rather, they will simply take advantage of the opportunity to tax something new to make tax revenues as large as possible. As we saw in Chapter 6, certain theories of the public sector suggest that those who run the government can and will maximize tax revenues despite the wishes of the citizenry. Therefore, by constitutionally precluding the taxation of Y, the citizens may be rationally protecting themselves against an inefficiently large public sector. In other words, if citizens do not trust the government, what looks inefficient through the lens of optimal commodity taxation may be efficient in a larger setting.[8] There is, in fact, some evidence that governments with tax systems that generate large excess burdens tend to grow more slowly than governments with efficient tax systems [Becker and Mulligan, 2003].

---

[8] Winer and Hettich [2004] provide further comparisons between optimal tax theory and an approach that takes politics into account.

Issues relating to these considerations may help explain, in part, the current controversy over the tax treatment of purchases made on the Internet. Proponents of Internet taxation argue that a good purchased in a store is essentially the same commodity as the same good purchased on the Internet. Taxing the former but not the latter distorts consumers' choices between the two modes of purchase, and hence creates an excess burden. Opponents argue that taxing Internet sales would simply fuel increases in the size of the public sector, which is already inefficiently large.

This discussion is related to the **time inconsistency of optimal policy,** which occurs when the government cannot implement an optimal tax policy because the stated policy is inconsistent with the government's incentives over time. Consider a proposal made by the government of Colombia in 2002. To put down a rebellion, a tax of 1.2 percent of the value of their capital would be levied on all individuals and businesses whose assets exceeded the equivalent of $60,000. Importantly, the tax was to be imposed only one time; it would not be repeated in the future. While capitalists presumably would not be pleased to pay the tax, it would appear to have no impact on their current incentives to save for the future. Such a tax is in effect a lump sum levy and therefore fully efficient.

There is a problem, however. The Colombian government has an incentive to renege on its promise that the tax would only be levied once and pull exactly the same trick next year, raising yet more revenue without an excess burden. Thus, the stated tax policy is inconsistent with the government's incentives over time. Even worse, the capitalists realize the government has an incentive to renege. They will change their saving behavior to reflect the expectation that the more they save now, the more they will be taxed next year. Because the expected tax changes behavior, it introduces an inefficiency.

In short, unless the government can *credibly* promise not to renege, it cannot conduct the fully efficient tax policy. To avoid this time inconsistency problem, the government must be able to commit itself to behave in certain ways in the future. How can this be done? One possible approach is to enact constitutional provisions forbidding the government to go back on its promises. However, as long as the government has an underlying incentive to renege, suspicions will remain, frustrating attempts to run an efficient policy. These considerations suggest that the credibility of the political system must be considered before making recommendations based on optimal tax theory.

> **time inconsistency of optimal policy**
>
> **When the government cannot implement an optimal tax policy because the policy is inconsistent with the government's incentives over time, and taxpayers realize this fact.**

▶ OTHER CRITERIA FOR TAX DESIGN

As we have seen, optimal taxation depends on the trade-off between "efficiency" and "fairness." However, the use of these concepts in optimal tax theory does not always correspond closely to lay usage. In the context of optimal tax theory, a fair tax is one that guarantees a socially desirable distribution of the tax burden; an efficient tax is one with a small excess burden. In public discussion, on the other hand, a fair tax is often one that imposes equal liabilities on people who have the same ability to pay, and an efficient tax system is one that keeps down administrative and compliance expenses. These alternative notions of fairness and efficiency in taxation are the subject of this section.

Horizontal Equity

The American humorist Will Rogers once said, "People want *just* taxes more than they want *lower* taxes. They want to know that every man is paying his proportionate share according to his wealth." This criterion for evaluating a tax system is embodied in the economist's notion of **horizontal equity:** People in equal positions should be treated equally. To make horizontal equity an operational idea, one must define "equal positions." Rogers suggests wealth as an index of ability to pay, but income and expenditure might also be used.

Unfortunately, all of these measures represent the *outcomes* of people's decisions and are not really suitable measures of equal position. Consider two individuals, both of whom can earn $10 per hour. Mr. A chooses to work 1,500 hours each year, while Ms. B works 2,200 hours each year. A's income is $15,000 and B's is $22,000, so that in terms of income, A and B are not in "equal positions." In an important sense, however, A and B *are* the same, because their earning capacities are identical—B just happens to work harder. Thus, because work effort is at least to some extent under people's control, two individuals with different incomes may actually be in equal positions. Similar criticism would apply to expenditure or wealth as a criterion for measuring equal positions.

These arguments suggest that the individual's wage *rate* rather than income be considered as a candidate for measuring equal positions, but this idea has problems too. First, investments in human capital—education, on-the-job training, and health care—can influence the wage rate. If Mr. A had to go to college to earn the same wage that Ms. B is able to earn with only a high school degree, is it fair to treat them the same? Second, computing the wage rate requires division of total earnings by hours of work, but the latter is not easy to measure. (How should time spent checking out Facebook be counted?) Indeed, for a given income, it would be worthwhile for a worker to exaggerate hours of work to be able to report a lower wage rate and pay fewer taxes. Presumably, bosses could be induced to collaborate with their employees in return for a share of the tax savings.

As an alternative to measuring equal position either in incomes or wage rates, Feldstein [1976] suggests it be defined in utilities. Hence, the **utility definition of horizontal equity:** (a) If two individuals would be equally well off (have the same utility level) in the absence of taxation, they should also be equally well off if there is taxation; and (b) Taxes should not alter the utility ordering—if A is better off than B before taxation, he should be better off after.

To assess the implications of Feldstein's definition, first assume all individuals have the same preferences, that is, identical utility functions. In this case, individuals who consume the same commodities (including leisure) should pay the same tax, or, equivalently, all individuals should face the same tax schedule. Otherwise, individuals with equal before-tax utility levels would have different after-tax utilities.

Now assume that people have diverse tastes. For example, let there be two types of individuals, Gourmets and Sunbathers. Both groups consume food (which is purchased using income) and leisure, but Gourmets put a relatively high value on food, as do Sunbathers on leisure time. Assume further that before any taxation, Gourmets and Sunbathers have identical utility levels. If the same proportional income tax is imposed on everybody, Gourmets are necessarily made worse off than Sunbathers, because the former need relatively large amounts of income to support their food habits. Thus, even though this income tax is perfectly fair judged by the traditional definition of horizontal equity, it is not fair according to the utility definition. Indeed, as long as tastes for leisure differ, *any* income tax violates the utility definition of horizontal equity.

Of course, the practical difficulties involved in measuring individuals' utilities preclude the possibility of having a utility tax. Nevertheless, the utility definition of horizontal equity has some provocative policy implications. Assume again that all individuals have the same preferences. Then it can be shown that *any* existing tax structure does not violate the utility definition of horizontal equity *if* individuals are free to choose their activities and expenditures.

To see why, suppose that in one type of job a large part of compensation consists of amenities that are not taxable—pleasant offices, access to a swimming pool, and so forth. In another occupation, compensation is exclusively monetary, all of which is subject to income tax. According to the traditional definition, this situation is a violation of horizontal equity, because a person in the job with a lot of amenities has too small a tax burden. But, if both arrangements coexist and individuals are free to choose, then the net after-tax rewards (including amenities) must be the same in both jobs. Why? Suppose that the net after-tax reward is greater in the jobs with amenities. Then individuals migrate to these jobs to take advantage of them. But the increased supply of workers in these jobs depresses their wages. The process continues until the *net* returns are equal. In short, although people in the different occupations pay unequal taxes, there is no horizontal inequity because of adjustments in the *before-tax* wage.

Some suggest that certain tax advantages available only to the rich are sources of horizontal inequity. According to the utility definition, this notion is wrong. If these advantages are open to everyone with high income, and all high-income people have identical tastes, then the advantages may indeed reduce tax progressiveness, but they have no effect whatsoever on horizontal equity.

We are led to a striking conclusion: Given common tastes, a preexisting tax structure cannot involve horizontal inequity. Rather, all horizontal inequities arise from *changes* in tax laws. This is because individuals make commitments based on the existing tax laws that are difficult or impossible to reverse. For example, people may buy larger houses because of the preferred tax treatment for owner-occupied housing. When the tax laws are changed, their welfare goes down, and horizontal equity is violated. As one congressman put it, "It seems unfair to people who have done something in good faith to change the law on them."[9] These observations give new meaning to the dictum, "The only good tax is an old tax."

The fact that tax changes may generate horizontal inequities does not necessarily imply that they should not be undertaken. After all, tax changes may improve efficiency and/or vertical equity. However, the arguments suggest that it might be appropriate to ease the transition to the new tax system. For example, if it is announced that a given tax reform is not to go into effect until a few years subsequent to its passage, people who have based their behavior on the old tax structure will be able to make at least some adjustments to the new regime. The problem of finding fair processes for changing tax regimes—known as **transitional equity**—is very difficult, and not many results are available on the subject.

transitional equity

Fairness in changing tax regimes.

---

[9] See Rosenbaum [1986].

The very conservative implications of the utility definition of horizontal equity should come as no great surprise, because implicit in the definition is the notion that the pretax status quo has special ethical validity. (Otherwise, why be concerned about changes in the ordering of utilities?) However, it is not at all obvious why the status quo deserves to be defended. A more general feature of the utility definition is its focus on the *outcomes* of taxation. In contrast, some have suggested that the essence of horizontal equity is to put constraints on the *rules* that govern the selection of taxes, rather than to provide criteria for judging their effects. Thus, horizontal equity excludes capricious taxes, or taxes based on irrelevant characteristics. For example, we can imagine the government levying special lump sum taxes on people with red hair, or putting very different taxes on angel food and chocolate cakes. The **rule definition of horizontal equity** would presumably exclude such taxes from consideration, even if they had desirable efficiency or distributional effects. In this sense, provisions in the US Constitution that rule out certain kinds of taxes can be interpreted as an attempt to guarantee horizontal equity. (See Chapter 1.)

However, identifying the permissible set of characteristics on which to base taxation is a problem. Most people would agree that religion and race should be irrelevant for purposes of determining tax liability. On the other hand, there is considerable disagreement as to whether or not marital status should influence tax burdens (see Chapter 17). And even with agreement that certain characteristics are legitimate bases for discrimination, the problem of how much discrimination is appropriate still remains. Everyone agrees that serious physical impairment should be taken into account in determining personal tax liability. But how bad must your vision be to qualify for special tax treatment as blind? And by what amount should your tax bill be reduced?

We are forced to conclude that horizontal equity, however defined, is a rather amorphous concept. Yet it has enormous appeal as a principle of tax design. Notions of fairness among equals, regardless of their vagueness, will continue to play an important role in the development of tax policy.

rule definition of horizontal equity

The rules that govern the selection of taxes are more important for judging fairness than the outcomes themselves.

Costs of Running the Tax System

An implicit assumption in the models we have been studying is that collecting taxes involves no costs. This is clearly false. The tax authorities require resources to do their job. Taxpayers incur costs as well, including outlays for accountants and tax lawyers, as well as the value of time spent filling out tax returns and keeping records.

The costs of administering the income tax in the United States are fairly low. For example, the Internal Revenue Service spends only about 44 cents to raise each $100 in taxes. However, the compliance costs of personal income taxation are quite substantial. These compliance costs include the time spent on tax preparation and the cost of such items as professional advice and preparation manuals. Survey evidence suggests that the total compliance cost of the income tax is about 10 percent of revenues [Kaplow, 2008a], or about $122 billion in 2008.

Clearly, the choice of tax and subsidy systems should take account of administrative and compliance costs. Even systems that appear fair and efficient (in the excess burden sense) might be undesirable because they are excessively complicated and expensive to administer. Consider the possibility of taxing household production—housecleaning, child care, and so on. As suggested in Chapter 15, the fact that market work is taxed but housework is not creates a sizable distortion in the allocation of labor. Moreover, taxing differentially on the basis of choice of workplace violates some notions of horizontal equity. Nevertheless, the difficulties involved in valuing household production would create such huge administrative costs that the idea is infeasible.

Unfortunately, administrative problems often receive insufficient attention. A classic case was the federal luxury tax on new jewelry enacted in 1990. The tax applied only to the portion of the price that exceeded $10,000, and only items worn for adornment were subject to the tax. As one commentator noted, the tax was an administrative nightmare: "loose gems and repairs aren't taxed; market value after a major modification is. Thus, . . . you may be taxed if you have gems from your grandma's brooch put in a new setting. But you won't be if you replace a $30,000 diamond lost from a ring; that's a repair."[10] The costs to the Internal Revenue Service of collecting the luxury tax may have exceeded the revenues collected! The tax was finally repealed in 1993.

Obviously, no tax system is costless to administer; the trick is to find the best trade-off between excess burden and administrative costs. For example, administering a sales tax system in which each commodity has its own rate might be very cumbersome, despite the fact that this is the general tack prescribed by the Ramsey rule. Any reductions in excess burden that arise from differentiating the tax rates must be compared to the incremental administrative costs.

Tax Evasion

We now turn to one of the most important problems facing any tax administration—cheating. To begin, one must distinguish between tax avoidance and tax evasion. **Tax avoidance,** which John Maynard Keynes once called "the only intellectual pursuit that carries any reward," is changing your behavior so as to reduce your tax liability. There is nothing illegal about tax avoidance:

> Over and over again courts have said that there is nothing sinister in so arranging one's affairs so as to keep taxes as low as possible. Everybody does so, rich or poor; and all do right, for nobody owes any public duty to pay more than the law demands. . . . To demand more in the name of morals is mere cant [Judge Learned Hand, *Commissioner v. Newman*, 1947].

tax avoidance

Altering behavior in such a way as to reduce your legal tax liability.

POLICY PERSPECTIVE

Architectural Tax Avoidance

People have always been very creative when it comes to avoiding taxes. Consider, for example, the events that transpired in 1696, when King William III of England decided that he needed to raise more money. He couldn't use an income tax, because it was widely viewed as a violation of personal liberty. Instead, he opted for a tax on windows. Because wealthier people have larger houses, and larger houses have more windows, this tax would tend to target the well off. King William may not have anticipated a simple way to avoid the tax—brick up the windows on one's home.

---

[10] See Schmedel [1991].

This centuries old example of tax avoidance is still on display in some houses in England (see top picture below).

Other architectural quirks are also products of tax avoidance. For example, in the 18th century, the government of Brazil levied a tax on *finished* churches. To avoid the tax, some churches at the time were built with one of their towers missing (see bottom picture below). Similarly strange—but predictable—consequences followed from a 17th-century law in Holland, which levied a tax based on the width of one's house: the wider the house, the bigger the tax bill. The people of Amsterdam responded by building houses that were tall, deep, and narrow (see picture on p. 371).

Photo courtesy of Age Fotostock

Photo courtesy of Jonathan Meer.

While these architectural examples may seem whimsical, they illustrate an important truth: people do not react passively to taxation. Rather, they search creatively for ways to avoid or at least reduce their tax burden.

In contrast to tax avoidance, **tax evasion** is failing to pay legally due taxes. If a tax on mushrooms is levied and you sell fewer mushrooms, it is tax avoidance. If you fail to report your sales of mushrooms to the government, it is tax evasion. Tax evasion is not a new problem. Centuries ago Plato observed, "When there is an income tax, the just man will pay more and the unjust less on the same amount of income." In recent years, however, tax evasion has received an especially large amount of public attention. A case that received international notice was that of the actor Wesley Snipes. In 2008, he was found guilty of tax evasion and ordered to pay about $17 million in back taxes plus penalties and interest [Johnston, 2008].

Tax cheating is extremely difficult to measure. The Internal Revenue Service estimates that taxpayers voluntarily pay only about 80 percent of their actual income tax liability. If this estimate is even roughly accurate, it suggests that evasion is a very important issue.

People commit tax fraud in a variety of ways:

- Keep two sets of books to record business transactions. One records the actual business, and the other is shown to the tax authorities. Some evaders use two cash registers.
- Moonlight for cash. Of course, working an extra job is perfectly legal. However, the income received on such jobs is often paid in cash rather than by check. Hence, no legal record exists, and the income is not reported to the tax authorities.
- Underreport income. Failing to report income is a common type of tax evasion. According to the Government Accountability Office, underreporting income is especially prevalent among people with their own businesses [Herman, 2007]. In 2009, US Treasury Secretary Timothy Geithner—who oversees the Internal Revenue

tax evasion

Not paying taxes legally due.

Service—found himself in trouble during his confirmation hearing for failing to pay taxes on some self-employment income.

• Deal in cash. Paying for goods and services with cash and checks made out to "cash" makes it very difficult for the Internal Revenue Service to trace transactions.

At one time, tax evasion was associated with millionaires who hid their capital in Swiss bank accounts. The current image of a tax evader may well be a repairer whose income comes from "unofficial" work not reported for tax purposes, or a parent who evades taxes on wages paid to a baby-sitter. Indeed, people who pay maids, nannies, and other household employees more than roughly $1,500 per year are obligated to pay Social Security taxes for them, yet fewer than 0.25 percent of all households pay this "nanny tax" [Herman, 2004b]. The feeling that "everyone is doing it" is widespread.

We first discuss the positive theory of tax evasion, and then turn to the normative question of how public policy should deal with it.

Positive Analysis of Tax Evasion   Assume Al cares only about maximizing his expected income. He has a given amount of earnings and is trying to choose R, the amount that he hides from the tax authorities. Suppose Al's marginal income tax rate is 0.3; for each dollar shielded from taxable income, his tax bill falls by 30 cents. This is the marginal benefit to him of hiding a dollar of income from the tax authorities. More generally, when Al faces a marginal income tax rate t, the marginal benefit of each dollar concealed is t.

The tax authority does not know Al's true income, but it randomly audits all taxpayers' returns. As a result, there is some probability, ρ, that Al will be audited. (In the United States, only about 0.77 percent of federal income tax returns are audited.) If he is caught cheating, Al pays a penalty that increases with R at an increasing rate. Note that if it were costless to monitor Al every second of every day, opportunities for evasion would not exist. The fact that such monitoring is infeasible is the fundamental source of the problem.

Assuming that Al knows the value of ρ and the penalty schedule, he makes his decision by comparing the marginal costs and benefits of cheating. In Figure 16.5, the

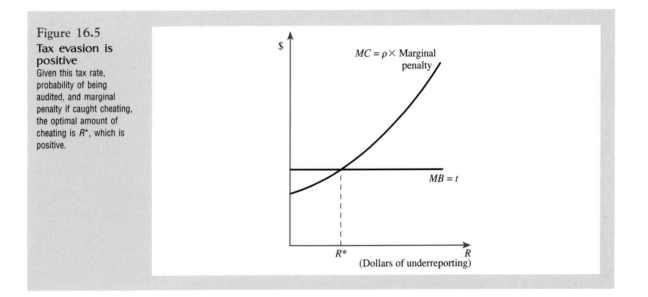

Figure 16.5

Tax evasion is positive

Given this tax rate, probability of being audited, and marginal penalty if caught cheating, the optimal amount of cheating is R^*, which is positive.

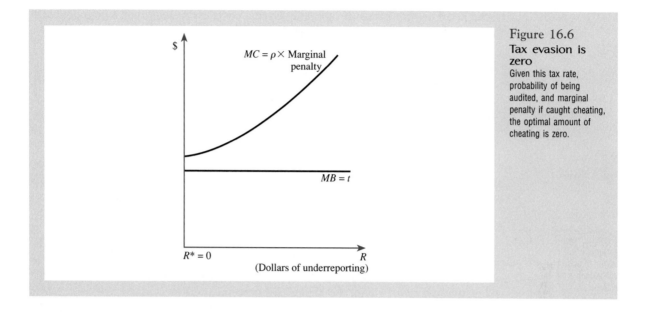

Figure 16.6
Tax evasion is zero
Given this tax rate, probability of being audited, and marginal penalty if caught cheating, the optimal amount of cheating is zero.

amount of income not reported is measured on the horizontal axis, and dollars on the vertical. The marginal benefit (*MB*) for each dollar not reported is *t*, the amount of tax saved. The expected marginal cost (*MC*) is the amount by which the penalty goes up for each dollar of cheating (the marginal penalty) times the probability of detection. For example, if the additional penalty for hiding the thousandth dollar is $1.50 and the probability of detection is 1 in 3, then the *expected* marginal penalty is 50 cents. The "optimal" amount of cheating is where the two schedules cross, at *R**. *R** is optimal in the sense that *on average* it is the policy that maximizes Al's income. In a world of uncertainty, finding the best policy in this "expected value" sense is a reasonable way to proceed. It is possible, of course, that not cheating at all will be optimal. For the individual in Figure 16.6, the marginal cost of cheating exceeds the marginal benefit for all positive values of *R*, so the optimum is equal to zero.

The model predicts that cheating decreases when marginal tax rates go down. This is because a lower value of *t* decreases the marginal benefit of evasion, shifting down the marginal benefit schedule so the intersection with marginal cost occurs at a lower value of *R*. This prediction is consistent with anecdotal evidence. Consider, for example, the case of the Baltic Republic of Estonia, which recently replaced its system of high and increasing marginal tax rates with a flat income tax of 26 percent. The former Prime Minister Mart Laar said that this reform reduced evasion dramatically because "in the real world rich people find a way to avoid high taxes. With a flat tax, they stop worrying about sheltering their income or working in the gray economy" [Tierney, 2006]. The model's prediction is also borne out by econometric studies. For example, Fisman and Wei [2004] find that high tariffs in China lead to substantial tax evasion. According to their estimates, a 1 percent increase in the tax rate on imports induces importers to increase the amount of taxes they evade by 3 percent.

Although this model yields useful insights, it ignores some potentially important considerations.

Psychic Costs of Cheating Simply put, tax evasion may make people feel guilty. One way to model this phenomenon is by adding psychic costs to the marginal cost schedule. For very honest people, the psychic costs are so high they would not cheat even if the expected marginal penalty were zero.

Risk Aversion Figures 16.5 and 16.6 assume people care only about expected income, and that risk per se does not bother them. To the extent that individuals are risk averse, their decisions to engage in what is essentially a gamble may be modified. (Chapter 9 discusses choice under uncertainty.)

Work Choices The model assumes the only decision is how much income to report. The type of job and the amount of before-tax income are taken as given. In reality, the tax system may affect hours of work and job choices. For example, high marginal tax rates might induce people to choose occupations that provide substantial opportunities for evading taxation, the so-called **underground economy.** This includes economic activities that are legal but easy to hide from the tax authorities (home repairs) as well as work that is criminal per se (prostitution, selling drugs). The size of the underground economy is inherently very difficult to measure. The estimates reported by Friedman et al. [2000] place it at 14 percent of Gross Domestic Product in the United States. For Britain, the figure is 7 percent, and for Russia 42 percent. Davis and Henrekson [2004] examined data from a group of developed countries in the 1990s and found that when marginal tax rates increase, so does the probability of participating in the underground sector. This finding is consistent with journalistic reports of what transpired in New York City after cigarette taxes there raised the price per pack to about $7.50. The tax increase fueled a thriving black market in low-tax cigarettes from other states, and the sellers included not only veteran black marketers, "but also amateurs seeking extra income" [Fairclough, 2002, p. B1].

underground economy
Those economic activities that are either illegal, or legal but hidden from tax authorities.

Changing Probabilities of Audit In our simple analysis, the probability of an audit is independent of both the amount evaded and the size of income reported. However, in the United States, audit probabilities depend on occupation and the size of reported income. This complicates the model but does not change its essential aspects.

Clearly, cheating is a more complicated phenomenon than Figures 16.5 and 16.6 suggest. Nevertheless, the model provides us with a useful framework for thinking about the factors that influence evasion decisions. As already suggested, it is difficult to do empirical work on tax evasion. Consequently, it is not known whether high fines or frequent audits are more effective ways of deterring cheating. One tentative result that emerges from several econometric studies is that for most groups a heightened threat of audit increases reported income, but the magnitude of the effect is small [Blumenthal et al., 2001].

Normative Analysis of Tax Evasion
Most public discussions of the underground economy assume that it is a bad thing and that policy should be designed to reduce its size. Although possibly correct, this proposition is worth scrutiny.

An important question in this context is whether or not we care about the welfare of tax evaders. In the jargon of welfare economics, do the utilities of participants in the underground economy belong in the social welfare function? Assume for the moment that they do. Then under certain conditions, the existence of an underground economy raises social welfare. For example, if the supply of labor is more elastic to the underground economy than to the regular economy, optimal tax theory suggests that the former be taxed at a relatively low rate. This is simply an application of the inverse elasticity rule, Equation (16.9). Alternatively, suppose that participants in the underground economy tend to be poorer than those in the regular economy. In fact, many observers believe that the underground economy is a crucial part of life in American inner cities. To the extent society has egalitarian income redistribution objectives, leaving the underground economy intact might be desirable.

Consider now the policy implications when evaders are given no weight in the social welfare function, and the goal is simply to eliminate cheating at the lowest administrative cost possible. Figure 16.5 suggests a straightforward way to accomplish this objective. The expected marginal cost of cheating is the product of the penalty rate and the probability of detection. The probability of detection depends on the amount of resources devoted to tax administration; if the Internal Revenue Service has a big budget, it can catch a lot of cheaters. However, even if the tax authorities have a small budget so that the probability of detection is low, the marginal cost of cheating can still be made arbitrarily high if the penalty is large enough. If only one tax evader were caught each year, but he or she were publicly hanged for the crime, the *expected* cost of tax evasion would deter many people. The fact that such a draconian policy has never been seriously proposed in the United States indicates that existing penalty systems try to incorporate *just retribution*. Contrary to the assumptions of the utilitarian framework, society cares not only about the end result (getting rid of cheaters) but also the processes by which the result is achieved.

▶ OVERVIEW

Traditional analysis of tax systems elucidated several "principles" of tax design: Taxes should have horizontal and vertical equity, be "neutral" with respect to economic incentives, be administratively easy, and so on. Public finance economists have now integrated these somewhat ad hoc guidelines with the principles of welfare economics. The optimal tax literature *derives* the criteria for a good tax using an underlying social welfare function.

On some occasions, optimal tax analysis has corrected previous errors. For example, it may *not* be efficient for all tax rates to be the same (neutral). Furthermore, optimal tax theory has clarified the trade-offs between efficiency and equity in tax design. As a by-product, the various definitions of "equity" have been scrutinized.

The result of this work is not a blueprint for building a tax system, if for no other reason than the economic theory forming the basis for optimal tax theory has its own problems (see Chapter 3). In this context two comments are cogent: (1) Optimal tax theory generally ignores political and social institutions. An "optimal" tax may easily be ruined by politicians or be overly costly to administer. (2) While the optimal tax approach indicates that the concept of horizontal equity is difficult to make operational, the fact remains that *equal treatment of equals* is an appealing ethical concept. Horizontal equity is difficult to integrate with optimal tax theory because of the latter's focus on outcomes rather than processes.

Thus, optimal tax theory has used the tools of welfare economics to add analytical strength to the traditional discussion of tax design. Nevertheless, it is wedded to the utilitarian welfare approach in economics. As such, it is open to criticisms concerning the adequacy of this ethical system.

Summary

- Efficient commodity tax theory shows how to raise a given amount of revenue with a minimum of excess burden.
- The Ramsey rule stipulates that to minimize excess burden, tax rates should be set so that the proportional reduction in the quantity demanded of each good is the same.
- When goods are unrelated in consumption, the Ramsey rule implies that relative tax rates should be inversely related to compensated demand elasticities.
- Choosing optimal user fees for government-produced services is quite similar to choosing optimal taxes.
- Income taxation is a major source of revenue in developed countries. Edgeworth's early study of optimal income taxes indicated that after-tax incomes should be equal. However, when the excess burden of distorting the leisure-income trade-off is included, marginal tax rates of far less than 100 percent are optimal.
- Tax systems may be evaluated by standards other than those of optimal tax theory. Horizontal equity, the costs of administration, incentives for tax evasion, and political constraints all affect the design of tax systems.
- Traditional definitions of horizontal equity rely on income as a measure of "equal position" in society. However, income as conventionally measured is inadequate in this context. The utility definition is more precise, but has radically different policy implications and contains an inherent bias toward the pretax status quo. Other definitions of horizontal equity focus on the rules by which taxes are chosen.
- The costs of running a tax system are ignored in most theoretical analyses. However, administrative and compliance costs affect the choice of tax base, tax rates, and the amount of tax evasion.

Discussion Questions

1. According to estimates by Goolsbee and Petrin [2004], the elasticity of demand for basic cable service is −0.51, and the elasticity of demand for direct broadcast satellites is −7.40. Suppose that a community wants to raise a given amount of revenue by taxing cable service and the use of direct broadcast satellites. If the community's goal is to raise the money as efficiently as possible, what should be the ratio of the cable tax to the satellite tax? Discuss briefly the assumptions behind your calculation.

2. In 2002, the US federal government levied a tax of 3 percent on that part of a car's price exceeding $40,000. [For example, the tax liability on a $50,000 car would be 0.03 × ($50,000 − $40,000), or $300.] Discuss the efficiency, equity, and administrability of this "luxury car tax."

3. "Peter the Great at one time levied a tax upon beards. He held that the beard was a superfluous and useless ornament. The tax is said to have been proportional according to the length of the beard and progressive according to the social position of its possessor" [Groves, 1946, p. 51]. Evaluate Peter's beard tax from the standpoint of optimal tax theory and from the standpoint of horizontal equity.

4. In recent years, farmers in China have been protesting their tax treatment by the government. They have many complaints, including a fee that "is collected for production of 'special products' like nuts, even when none are grown" [Eckholm, 1999, p. A10]. Evaluate this nut tax from the viewpoints of both optimal tax theory and horizontal equity.

5. Suppose that a town is considering a project to install new underground water pipes. Some of the costs are fixed in the sense that they do not increase with an increase in the amount of water consumed. For example, pipes deteriorate over time, independent of the volume of water

flowing through them. Hence, it is impossible to pay for the investment in the pipes by charging consumers an amount based on the marginal cost of the water they consume. Under these circumstances, what might an efficient pricing system look like?

6. In 2008, New York State increased its tax on cigarettes by $1.25 per pack. One commentator noted that "most cigarettes sold [in New York] will actually be trucked up from Virginia or shipped from China, by 'butt-leggers' who can make over $1 million on each tractor-trailer load of smuggled smokes" [Fleenor, 2008]. Use Figure 16.5 to show how this behavior could have been predicted.

7. The government provides patents to pharmaceutical companies that allow them to charge high prices for the drugs they develop for some years. If a company succeeds in developing an effective drug, the patent protection can result in high profits, especially because the marginal cost of drug production is low. Some propose that the government raise revenue by levying a one-time tax on these profits. Would this be an efficient way to raise tax revenue? Include in your answer the concept of the "time inconsistency of optimal policy."

8. Indicate whether each of the following statements is true, false, or uncertain, and explain why:

a. A proportional tax on all commodities including leisure is equivalent to a lump sum tax.

b. Efficiency is maximized when all commodities are taxed at the same rate.

c. Average cost pricing for a natural monopoly allows the enterprise to break even, but the outcome is inefficient.

d. Tom's workplace provides free access to a fitness room; Jerry's does not. Horizontal equity requires that Tom be taxed on the value of having access to the fitness room.

Part Five

THE UNITED STATES
REVENUE SYSTEM

The next five chapters describe and analyze the major sources of revenue in the US fiscal system. This involves some bad news and some good news. The bad news is that it is hard to know just how long the descriptive material will be correct. Despite the fact that there were major changes in the tax system in 1986, 1990, 1993, 1997, 2001, 2003, and 2009, important modifications are under consideration, and more changes are certain to come. The good news is that after seeing the tools of public finance applied to the existing tax institutions, the reader will be able to analyze any new taxes that may arise. Moreover, we discuss some major proposed revisions for each of the existing taxes.

Chapter Seventeen

The Personal Income Tax

It's income tax time again, Americans: time to gather up those receipts, get out those tax forms, sharpen up that pencil, and stab yourself in the aorta.

—DAVE BARRY

adjusted gross income (AGI)

Total income from all taxable sources less certain expenses incurred in earning that income.

taxable income

The amount of income subject to tax.

exemption

When calculating taxable income, an amount per family member that can be subtracted from adjusted gross income.

deductions

Certain expenses that may be subtracted from adjusted gross income in the computation of taxable income.

rate schedule

The tax liability associated with each level of taxable income.

Several years ago, the chairman of the House Ways and Means Committee, Bill Archer, declared that he wanted to "pull the current income tax code out by its roots and throw it away so it can never grow back." The personal income tax that so vexed Representative Archer (and millions of other Americans) is the workhorse of the federal revenue system. In 2008, almost 183 million income tax returns were filed, which generated $1.146 trillion in revenue, about 45 percent of federal revenues [Congressional Budget Office, 2009b]. This chapter discusses problems associated with designing a personal income tax system, the efficiency and equity of the US system, and why so many people want to replace it.

Since its inception in 1913, the income tax code has been revised many times. Our discussion devotes special attention to explaining and evaluating the changes that have been made in recent years.

▶ BASIC STRUCTURE

Americans file an annual tax return that computes their previous year's tax liability. The return is due every April 15. The calculation of tax liability requires a series of steps as summarized in Figure 17.1. The first step is to compute **adjusted gross income (AGI),** defined as total income from all taxable sources less certain expenses (the "above-the-line" deductions) incurred in earning that income. Taxable sources include (but are not limited to) wages, dividends, interest, business and farm profits, rents, royalties, prizes, and even the proceeds from embezzlement.

Not all of AGI is taxed. The second step is to convert AGI to **taxable income**—the amount of income subject to tax. This is done by subtracting various amounts called **exemptions** and **deductions** from AGI. Deductions and exemptions are discussed more carefully later.

The next step is to calculate the amount of tax due by applying the tax rates to the taxable income. A **rate schedule** indicates the tax liability associated with each level of taxable income. Different types of taxpayers face different tax rate schedules. For example, husbands and wives who file tax returns together—joint returns—have different rates than single people. The final step is to subtract tax credits (discussed later) to arrive at the regular tax liability.

Figure 17.1 Computation of federal personal income tax liability
Taxpayers must follow a complicated set of steps to compute their tax liability.

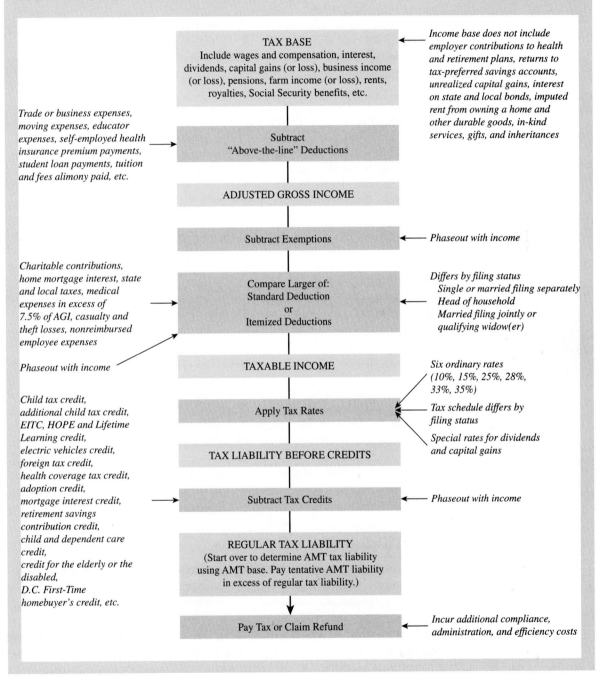

Source: President's Advisory Panel on Federal Tax Reform [2005, p. 24].

For most taxpayers, some tax is withheld out of each paycheck during the year. The amount they actually pay on April 15 is the difference between the tax liability and the accumulated withholding payments. If more has been withheld than is owed, the taxpayer receives a refund.

It sounds pretty straightforward, but in reality, complications arise in every step of the process. We now discuss some of the major problems. If you are interested in the excruciating details, an online searchable version of the tax code is available at www.fourmilab.ch/ustax/ustax.html.

▶ DEFINING INCOME

Clearly, the ability to identify "income" is necessary to operate an income tax. A natural way to begin this section would be to discuss and evaluate the tax code's definition of income. However, the law provides no definition. The constitutional amendment that introduced the tax merely says, "The Congress shall have power to lay and collect taxes on incomes, from whatever source derived." While the tax law does provide examples of income—wages and salaries, rents, dividends, and so on—the words "from whatever source derived" do not really provide a useful standard for deciding whether or not the exclusion of certain items from taxation is appropriate.

Public finance economists have their own traditional standard, the **Haig-Simons (H-S) definition:** Income is the money value of the net increase in an individual's power to consume during a period.[1] This equals the amount actually consumed during the period plus net additions to wealth. Net additions to wealth— saving—must be included in income because they represent an increase in *potential* consumption.

Importantly, the H-S criterion requires the inclusion of *all* sources of potential increases in consumption, regardless of whether the actual consumption takes place, and regardless of the form in which the consumption occurs. The H-S criterion also implies that any decreases in an individual's potential to consume should be subtracted in determining income. An example is expenses that are incurred to earn income. If the gross revenues from Juliet's cigar store are $100,000, but business expenses (such as rent and the cost of the cigars) are $95,000, then Juliet's potential consumption has only increased by $5,000.

Haig-Simons (H-S) definition of income

Money value of the net increase in an individual's power to consume during a period.

Items Included in H-S Income

The H-S definition encompasses those items ordinarily thought of as income: wages and salaries, business profits, rents, royalties, dividends, and interest. However, it also includes certain unconventional items:

Employer Pension Contributions and Insurance Purchases   Pension contributions, even though not made directly to the recipient, represent an increase in the potential to consume. In the same way, even if compensation is paid to an employee in the form of a certain commodity (such as an insurance policy) instead of cash, it is still income.

---

[1] Named after Robert M. Haig and Henry C. Simons, economists who wrote in the first half of the 20th century.

Transfer Payments, Including Social Security Retirement Benefits, Unemployment Compensation, and Welfare   Any receipt, be it from the government or an employer, is income.

Capital Gains   Increases in the value of an asset are referred to as **capital gains,** decreases as **capital losses.** Suppose Brutus owns some shares of Microsoft stock that increase in value from $10,000 to $12,500 over the course of a year. Then he has enjoyed a capital gain of $2,500. This $2,500 represents an increase in potential consumption, and hence, belongs in income.[2] If Brutus sells the Microsoft stock at the end of the year, the capital gain is said to be **realized;** otherwise it is **unrealized.** From the H-S point of view, it is irrelevant whether a capital gain is realized or unrealized. Both represent potential to consume and, hence are income. If Brutus does not sell his Microsoft stock, in effect he chooses to save by reinvesting the capital gain in Microsoft. Because the H-S criterion does not distinguish between different uses of income, the fact that Brutus happens to reinvest is irrelevant. All the arguments for adding in capital gains apply to subtracting capital losses. If Casca's Disney stock decreases in value by $4,200 during a given year, this $4,200 should be subtracted from other sources of income.

> **capital gain (loss)**
>
> An increase (decrease) in the value of an asset.

> **realized capital gain**
>
> A capital gain resulting from the sale of an asset.

> **unrealized capital gain**
>
> A capital gain on an asset not yet sold.

Income in-Kind   Some people receive part or all of their incomes in-kind—in the form of goods and services rather than cash. An example that received much attention in 2009 was that of former Senator Tom Daschle, who had been nominated by President Obama to be Secretary of Health and Human Services. On his previous job, Daschle had received a car and driver for personal use. This in-kind benefit had an estimated worth of $255,000 (which Daschle failed to report as income). Less exotically, farmers provide field hands with food, and corporations such as Google give their employees subsidized lunches or access to company fitness centers. One important form of income in-kind is the annual rental value of owner-occupied homes. A homeowner receives a stream of services from a dwelling. The net monetary value of these services—**imputed rent**—is equal to the rental payments that would have been received had the owner chosen to rent the house out, after subtracting maintenance expenses, taxes, and so on.

In all these cases, from the H-S point of view, it makes no difference whether benefits are received in monetary form or in the form of goods and services. They are all income.

> **imputed rent**
>
> The net monetary value of the services a homeowner receives from a dwelling.

Some Practical and Conceptual Problems

A number of difficulties arise in attempts to use the Haig-Simons criterion as a basis for constructing a tax system.

- Clearly, only income *net of business expenses* increases potential consumption power. But distinguishing between consumption expenditures and costs of obtaining income can be hard. If Calpurnia buys a desk to use while working at home, but the desk is also a beautiful piece of furniture, to what extent is the desk a business expense? What portion of a "three-martini lunch" designed to woo a client is consumption and what portion is business? (According to current law, the answer to the latter question is 50 percent is consumption. Fifty percent of business meal expenses are deductible.)

---

[2] Only the real value of capital gains constitutes income, not gains due merely to inflation. This issue is discussed later.

- Capital gains and losses may be difficult to measure, particularly when they are unrealized. For assets that are traded in active markets, the problem is fairly manageable. Even if Brutus does not sell his Microsoft shares, it is easy to determine their value at any time by consulting the financial section of the newspaper. It is not nearly as simple to measure the capital gain on a piece of art that has appreciated in value.

- Imputed income from durables also presents measurement difficulties. For example, it may be hard to estimate the market rent of a particular owner-occupied dwelling. Similarly, measuring the imputed rental streams generated by other durables such as utility vehicles, compact disc players, and motorboats is not feasible.

- In-kind services are not easy to value. One important example is the income produced by people who do housework rather than participate in the market. These services—housecleaning, cooking, child care, and so forth—are clearly valuable. However, even though markets exist for purchasing these services, it would be difficult to estimate whether a given homemaker's services were equal to the market value.

Evaluating the H-S Criterion

We could list numerous other difficulties involved in implementing the H-S criterion, but the main point is clear. No definition of income can make the administration of an income tax simple and straightforward. Arbitrary decisions about what should be included in income are inevitable. Nevertheless, the Haig-Simons criterion is often regarded as an ideal toward which policymakers should strive: Income should be defined as broadly as is feasible, and all sources of income received by a particular person should be taxed at the same rate.

Why is the H-S criterion so attractive? There are two reasons.

Fairness   Recall the traditional definition of horizontal equity from Chapter 16—people with equal incomes should pay equal taxes. For this dictum to make any sense, the tax base must include *all* sources of income. Otherwise, two people with identical abilities to pay could end up with different tax liabilities.

On the other hand, one can argue that as long as people's abilities to earn income differ, the H-S criterion cannot produce fair outcomes. Suppose that Popeye is endowed with a lot of brains, and Bluto with a lot of brawn. Suppose further that the work done by brawny people is less pleasant than the work done by brainy people. In that case, if Bluto and Popeye have the same *income,* then Popeye has more *utility.* Is it fair to tax them as equals?

Efficiency   Defenders of the criterion argue that it has the virtue of *neutrality*—it treats all forms of income the same, and hence, does not distort the pattern of economic activity. Thus, for example, it is argued that the failure to tax imputed rent from owner-occupied housing leads to excessive investment in housing, other things being the same.

It is doubtless true that many departures from the Haig-Simons criterion create inefficiencies. But it does *not* follow that equal tax rates on all income, regardless of source, would be most efficient. Consider income from rent on unimproved land. The supply of such land is perfectly inelastic, and hence, taxing it at a very high rate would create no excess burden. An efficient tax system would tax the returns to such land at higher rates than other sources of income, and *not* tax all sources at the same rate, as dictated by the H-S criterion. More generally, the optimal tax literature discussed in Chapter 16 suggests that as long as lump sum taxes are ruled out, efficiency is enhanced when relatively high tax rates are imposed on those activities with relatively inelastic supply. "Neutrality," in the sense of equal tax rates on all types of income, generally does *not* minimize excess burden.

Where does this leave us? McLure [2002] points out that we cannot be sanguine about the possibilities for using optimal tax theory as a framework for designing the tax base, noting that optimal tax rules "generally ignore the administrative difficulty of implementation, as well as the fact that a vast amount of information is required to put them into practice." It would be unwise, therefore, to abandon the Haig-Simons criterion altogether. On the other hand, there is no reason to regard the criterion as sacred. Departures from it should be considered on their merits and should not be viewed prima facie as unfair and inefficient.

▶ EXCLUDABLE FORMS OF MONEY INCOME

We have seen that some income sources that would be taxable according to the Haig-Simons criterion are omitted from the tax base for practical reasons. In addition, several forms of income that would be administratively easy to tax are partially or altogether excluded from adjusted gross income.

Interest on State and Local Bonds

The interest earned by individuals on bonds issued by states and localities is not subject to federal tax. From the H-S point of view, this exclusion makes no sense— interest from these bonds is as much an addition to potential consumption as is any other form of income. The exclusion originally followed from the view that it would be unconstitutional for one level of government to levy taxes on the securities issued by another level of government. However, many constitutional experts now believe such taxation would be permissible.

In the absence of legal restrictions, the exclusion of state and local interest might be justified as a powerful tool for helping states and localities to raise revenues. If investors do not have to pay federal tax on interest from state and local bonds, they should be willing to accept a lower before-tax rate of return than they receive on taxable bonds. Suppose Caesar faces a tax rate of 35 percent on additional income, and the rate of return on taxable securities is 15 percent. Then as long as the rate of return on state and local securities exceeds 9.75 percent, Caesar prefers them to taxable securities, other things being the same.[3] More generally, if t is an individual's marginal tax rate and r is the rate of return on taxable securities, he is willing to purchase nontaxable securities as long as their return exceeds $(1 - t)r$. Hence, state and local governments can borrow funds at rates lower than those prevailing on the market. In effect, the revenue forgone by the Treasury subsidizes borrowing by states and localities.

---

[3] In particular, it is assumed the two types of securities are perceived as being equally risky. The demand for assets whose risks differ is discussed in Chapter 18.

Unfortunately, tax-exempt bonds are an expensive way to help state and local governments. To see why, assume there are two taxpayers, Caesar, who faces a 35 percent tax rate on additional income, and Brutus, who faces a 15 percent rate. If the market rate of return on taxable bonds is 15 percent, Caesar's after-tax return is 9.75 percent and Brutus's is 12.75 percent. To induce *both* Caesar and Brutus to buy something other than taxable bonds, the net rate of return must therefore be at least 12.75 percent. Suppose a town issues tax-exempt bonds yielding just slightly more than 12.75 percent, and both Caesar and Brutus purchase the bonds. Some of the tax break is "wasted" on Caesar—he would have been willing to buy the bond at any yield greater than 9.75 percent, yet he receives 12.75 percent.

What is the net effect on government revenues? Suppose that the town borrows $100 from Brutus at the interest rate of 12.75 percent instead of the market rate of 15 percent. This saves the town $2.25 in interest payments. On the other hand, the US Treasury loses $2.25 (= $0.15 \times 15) in income tax revenue. In effect, the Treasury has provided a $2.25 subsidy to the town. Now, if the town borrows $100 from Caesar, it still saves only $2.25. But the Treasury loses $5.25 (= $0.35 \times 15) in tax revenues. Thus, about $3.00 of the tax break is not translated into a gain for the town.

In short, the net effect of tax-exempt bonds is zero only for those investors who are just on the margin of choosing tax-exempt versus taxable securities. For all others, the subsidy to the state and local borrower is outweighed by the revenue lost at the federal level.

Why not eliminate the interest exclusion and subsidize states and localities with direct grants from the federal government? The main reason is political. A direct subsidy to states and localities would be just another item in the federal budget, an item whose existence might be jeopardized by the vagaries of the political climate. Indeed, if the subsidy were made explicit, rather than buried in the tax law, voters might decide it was not worthwhile. Hence, state and local officials have lobbied intensively—and successfully—to maintain this exclusion.

Some Dividends

Under legislation passed in 2003, dividend income is not taxed at the same rate as ordinary income. Rather, it is taxed at a maximal rate of 15 percent. To see the justification for the partial exclusion, note that dividends are paid by corporations, and corporations are subject to a separate tax on their incomes. Hence, in the absence of an exclusion, dividends are taxed twice, once at the individual level and once at the corporate level. The idea behind taxing dividends at a lower rate for individuals is to ameliorate this double taxation to some extent. The issues associated with dividend taxation are discussed further in Chapter 19.

Capital Gains

As we will see later in the chapter, statutory marginal tax rates on ordinary income (for example, wages and interest) go as high as 35 percent. However, the maximum capital gains rate is 15 percent, provided that the asset is held more than one year.[4] Capital gains on assets held less than a year are taxed as ordinary income. Capital losses—decreases in the value of an asset—can be offset against capital gains.

---

[4] Individuals in the lowest tax brackets are taxed at 5 percent on capital gains. As of this writing, the Obama administration is proposing that high-earners be subject to a 20 percent tax on dividends and capital gains.

Suppose Antony realizes a gain of $6,000 on asset *A*, but a loss of $2,000 on asset *B*. Then Antony is treated as if his capital gains are only $4,000. Moreover, capital losses in excess of capital gains (up to a limit of $3,000) can be subtracted from ordinary income. Suppose that in the example just given, asset *B* had lost $8,200. Then Antony could reduce his capital gains liability to zero and still have $2,200 in losses left over. He could reduce his ordinary taxable income by this amount.

In addition to the fact that capital gains are taxed at preferential rates, their treatment departs from the H-S criterion in several important ways.

Only Realizations Taxed   Unless a capital gain is actually realized—the asset is sold—no tax is levied. In effect, the tax on a capital gain is deferred until the gain is realized. The mere ability to postpone taxes may not seem all that important, but its consequences are enormous.[5] Consider Cassius, who purchases an asset for $100,000 that increases in value by 12 percent each year. After the first year, it is worth $100,000 \times (1 + 0.12) = $112,000$. After the second year, it is worth $112,000 \times (1 + 0.12) = $100,000 \times (1 + 0.12)^2 = $125,440$. Similarly, by the end of 20 years, it is worth $100,000 \times (1 + 0.12)^{20} = $964,629$. If the asset is sold at the end of 20 years, Cassius realizes a capital gain of $864,629 (= $964,629 - $100,000$). Assume that the tax rate applied to *realized* capital gains is 15 percent. Then Cassius' tax liability is $129,694 (= $864,629 \times 0.15$), and his net gain (measured in dollars 20 years from now) is $734,935 (= $864,629 - $129,694$).

Now assume that the 15 percent capital gains tax is levied *as the capital gains accrue*, regardless of whether they are realized. At the end of the first year, Cassius has $110,200 [= $100,000 \times (1 + 0.102)$]. (Remember, $1,800 of the $12,000 gain goes to the tax collector, leaving him with only a 10.2 percent gain.) Assuming that the $10,200 after-tax gain is reinvested in the asset, at the end of two years, Cassius has $110,200 \times (1 + 0.102) = $100,000 \times (1.102)^2 = $121,440$. Similarly, by the end of 20 years, he has $100,000 \times (1.102)^{20} = $697,641$. Cassius' after-tax capital gain is $597,641 (= $697,641 - $100,000$). Comparing this to the previous amount of $734,935 makes clear that the seemingly innocent device of letting the gains accrue without tax makes a big difference. This is because the deferral allows the investment to grow geometrically at the before-tax rather than the after-tax rate of interest. In effect, the government gives the investor an interest-free loan on taxes due.

It should now be clear why a favorite slogan among tax accountants is "taxes deferred are taxes saved." Many very complicated tax shelter plans are nothing more than devices for deferring payment of taxes.

Because only realized capital gains are subject to tax, taxpayers who are considering switching or selling capital assets must take into account that doing so will create a tax liability. Consequently, they may be less likely to change their portfolios. This is known as the **lock-in effect,** because the tax system tends to lock investors into their current portfolios. This leads to a misallocation of capital, because it no longer flows to where its return is highest. Several econometric studies have examined the tax treatment of capital gains, and a common finding is that the realization-based system for taxing capital gains does in fact produce a lock-in effect [Ivkovich et al., 2005].

lock-in effect

The disincentive to change portfolios that arises because an individual incurs a tax on realized capital gains.

Gains Not Realized at Death   Capital gains are not taxed at death. Suppose Octavius purchases an asset for $1,000. During Octavius's lifetime, he never sells the asset, and when he dies, it is worth $1,200. Under current US law, the $200 capital

---

[5] At this point, it may be useful to review the discussion of interest compounding from Chapter 8 under "Present Value."

gain is not subject to the income tax when Octavius dies. Moreover, when Octavius Jr. (Octavius's heir) gets around to selling the asset, his computation of capital gains is made as if the purchase price were $1,200, not $1,000. In effect, then, capital gains on assets held to the death of the owner are never subject to the income tax. This provision is whimsically referred to as the *Angel of Death loophole*.

Evaluation of Capital Gains Rules

We conclude that in terms of the Haig-Simons criterion, the tax treatment of capital gains is unsatisfactory. The criterion requires that all capital gains be taxed, whether realized or unrealized. In contrast, the system generally taxes realized gains preferentially, and unrealized capital gains accrue without taxation. If the asset is held until the death of the owner, capital gains escape taxation altogether. While the US tax treatment of capital gains may seem light by the standard of the H-S criterion, it is rather heavy compared to several other countries. In the Netherlands and Germany, for example, capital gains on securities are generally totally exempt from taxation.

The optimal tax literature provides no more justification for preferential treatment of capital gains than the Haig-Simons criterion.[6] However, several rationalizations have been proposed for preferential treatment of this form of capital income. Some argue that capital gains are not regular income, but rather windfalls that occur unexpectedly. Fairness requires that such unexpected gains not create a tax liability. Moreover, because investing requires the sacrifice of abstaining from consumption, it is only fair to reward this sacrifice. However, one could just as well assert that *labor* income should be treated preferentially, because it involves the unpleasantness of work, while those who receive capital gains need only relax and wait for their money to flow in. Ultimately, it is impossible to argue convincingly that production of one source of income or another requires more sacrifice and should therefore be treated preferentially.

Another justification for preferential taxation of capital gains is that it is needed to stimulate capital accumulation and risk taking: "What makes this country's economy so vibrant is its participants' willingness to take chances, innovate, acquire financing, hire new people and break old molds. Every increase in capital gains taxes . . . is a direct tax on this vitality" [Prescott, 2005b, p. A14]. In Chapter 18, we deal at some length with the question of how taxation affects saving and risk-taking incentives. For now, we merely note that although there is some preliminary evidence that decreases in capital gains tax rates induce more individuals to become entrepreneurs [Gompers and Lerner, 1999], it is not clear that special treatment for capital gains does increase saving and risk taking.

Some promote preferential treatment of capital gains because it helps counterbalance inflation's tendency to increase the effective tax rate on capital gains. As we see later, under existing tax rules, inflation does produce an especially heavy burden on capital income. But arbitrarily taxing capital gains at a different rate is not the best solution to this problem.

Finally, we stress that a full picture of the tax treatment of capital income requires taking into account that much of this income is generated by corporations, and corporations are subject to a separate tax system of their own. The overall tax rate on capital income thus depends on the personal *and* corporate rates. We return to this issue in Chapter 19.

---

[6] However, under certain conditions, optimal tax theory suggests that *no* forms of capital income should be taxed. See Chapter 21.

Employer Contributions to Benefit Plans

Employers' contributions to their employees' retirement funds are not subject to tax. Neither does the government tax the interest that accrues on the pension contributions over time. Only when the pension is paid out at retirement are the principal and interest subject to taxation. Similarly, employer contributions to medical insurance plans are not included in income.

As already argued, pensions and health insurance should be counted as income according to the Haig-Simons criterion. Similarly, the interest on pension funds should be taxable as it accrues. However, including such items in the tax base appears to be politically infeasible. In 2008, presidential candidate John McCain recommended scaling back the tax preference for employer-provided health insurance. This proposal gained little public support.

Some Types of Saving

Under certain circumstances, people can save in a variety of tax-favored forms for their retirement or for some other specified purposes. In this section, we list and describe the main plans.

Using an **Individual Retirement Account (IRA),** an individual without a pension at work can deposit up to $5,000 per year in a *qualified account*. (A qualified account includes most of the usual forms of saving: savings accounts, money market funds, etc.) The money so deposited is deductible from adjusted gross income. In addition, single workers with pensions at work can make fully deductible contributions to IRAs. For 2009, the phaseout for these contributions began at $55,000 for single people and $89,000 for married couples. Just as in an employer-managed pension fund, the interest that accrues is untaxed. Tax is due only when the money is paid out at retirement. Penalties are imposed if money is withdrawn early, unless it is spent on certain approved items such as education expenses. In 2006, IRA tax-deductible contributions were $12.5 billion.

Like a conventional IRA, the **Roth IRA** (named after former Senator William Roth) permits a $5,000 per year contribution. The contribution is *not* tax deductible. However, the funds in the account accumulate tax free, and unlike the conventional IRA, there is no tax when the money is withdrawn. In 2009, the phaseout for the Roth IRA began at $105,000 for individuals and $166,000 for couples.

With a **401(k) plan,** named for the section of the Internal Revenue Code that authorizes it, an employee can earmark a portion of his or her salary each year, and no income tax liability is incurred on that portion. The limit on contributions was $16,500 in 2009.

A **Keogh Plan** is available only to self-employed individuals. Such individuals can exclude from taxation 20 percent of their net business income up to a maximum contribution of $49,000. Again, participants are allowed the powerful advantage of tax-free accrual of interest.

An **Education Savings Account** allows eligible families to make a $2,000 per year nondeductible contribution per child; the funds accumulate tax free, and the phaseouts are the same as for the Roth IRA. When the money is withdrawn, it can be used only to pay for qualified higher education expenses of the child.

An important reason for the various tax-favored saving options is to stimulate saving. However, the impact on aggregate saving is unclear. People may merely shuffle around their portfolios, reducing their holdings of some assets and depositing them

Individual Retirement Account (IRA)

For qualified individuals, a savings account in which the contributions are tax deductible and the interest accrues tax free, provided the funds are held until retirement. On withdrawal, both contributions and accrued interest are subject to tax.

Roth IRA

A tax-preferred savings vehicle. Contributions are not tax deductible, but funds accumulate tax free.

401(k) plan

A savings plan under which an employee can earmark a portion of his or her salary each year, with no income tax liability incurred on that portion.

Keogh Plan

A savings plan that allows self-employed individuals to exclude some percentage of their net business income from taxation if the money is deposited into a qualified account.

Education Savings Account

A tax-preferred savings vehicle. Contributions are not tax deductible, but funds accumulate tax free. Funds may be withdrawn to pay for higher education expenses of a child.

into retirement accounts. However, some recent studies favor the view that tax-favored saving options stimulate at least some new saving (see, for example, Benjamin [2003]). In any case, it is clear that the existence of plans for the preferential treatment of retirement saving represents another departure from the H-S criterion. And it is an important departure: About 38 percent of household financial assets are now held in tax-preferred savings accounts.[7]

Even many proponents of tax-favored saving options are dismayed by the complexity associated with the existence of a variety of plans, each with its own eligibility rules, contribution limits, and so on. A number of proposals to simplify the system have been advanced, but none has received much political support.

Gifts and Inheritances

Although gifts and inheritances represent increases in the beneficiaries' potential consumption, these items are not subject to the federal income tax. Instead, separate tax systems cover gifts and estates (see Chapter 21).

▶ EXEMPTIONS AND DEDUCTIONS

In terms of Figure 17.1, we have now completed the computation of adjusted gross income. Once AGI is determined, certain subtractions are made to find taxable income. The two principal subtractions are exemptions and deductions, which we discuss in turn.

Exemptions

A family is allowed an exemption for each of its members. The exemption—$3,650 in 2009—is adjusted annually for inflation. For example, in 2009 a husband and wife with three dependent children could claim five exemptions and subtract $18,250 from AGI. However, exemptions are phased out for people with AGIs above certain levels. For joint returns, personal exemptions are reduced by 2 percentage points for each $2,500 (or fraction thereof) by which AGI exceeds $250,200.[8] Suppose, for example, that our family of five has an AGI of $300,000. Subtracting $250,200 from $300,000, dividing the result by $2,500, and rounding up to the nearest whole number gives us 20. Hence, the family loses 40 percent (= 20 × 2 percent) of its exemptions. Because 40 percent of $18,250 is $7,300, the family can subtract only $10,950 in determining its taxable income. The phaseout is scheduled to be eliminated by 2011.[9]

Why are there exemptions? Some argue that they adjust ability to pay for the presence of children. Raising children involves certain nondiscretionary expenses, and taxable income should be adjusted accordingly. However, as most parents can tell you, if the exemption is really there to compensate for the expenses of child rearing, $3,650 is much too little. Moreover, why should expenses involving children be considered nondiscretionary in the first place? Given the wide availability of contraceptive methods, many would argue that raising children is the result of conscious

---

[7] Computed by authors using data from the Federal Reserve Board's *Flow of Funds Accounts of the United States,* December 11, 2008.

[8] For singles, the beginning of the phaseout range is $166,800. The beginnings for the phaseouts are adjusted annually for inflation.

[9] As of this writing, the Obama administration is proposing that the phaseout be reinstated.

choice. If one couple wishes to spend its money on European vacations while another chooses to raise a family, why should the tax system reward the latter?[10] On the other hand, certain people's religions rule out effective birth-control methods, and for them, children are not a *choice* as the term is conventionally defined.

Exemptions can also be viewed as a method of providing tax relief for low-income families. The higher the exemption, the greater adjusted gross income must be before *any* income tax is due. Consider a family of four with an AGI of $14,600 or less. When this family's $14,600 in exemptions is subtracted from AGI, the family is left with zero taxable income, and hence, no income tax liability. More generally, the greater the exemption level, the greater is the progressivity with respect to average tax rates. This effect is reinforced when exemptions are phased out for high-income families.

Deductions

The other subtraction allowed from AGI is a deduction. There are two kinds: **Itemized deductions** are subtractions for specific expenditures cited in the law. The taxpayer must list each item separately on the tax return and be able to prove (at least in principle) that the expenditures have been made. In lieu of itemizing deductions, the taxpayer can take a **standard deduction,** which is a fixed amount that requires no documentation. Taxpayers can choose whichever deduction minimizes their tax liability.

itemized deduction

A specific type of expenditure that can be subtracted from adjusted gross income in the computation of taxable income.

standard deduction

Subtraction of a fixed amount from adjusted gross income that does not require documentation.

Deductibility and Relative Prices   Before listing itemizable expenditures, let us consider the relationship between deductibility of expenditures on an item and its relative price. Suppose that expenditures on commodity Z are tax deductible. The price of Z is $10 per unit. Suppose further that Cleopatra's marginal tax rate is 35 percent. Then, whenever Cleopatra purchases a unit of Z, it only costs her $6.50. Why? Because expenditures on Z are deductible, purchasing a unit lowers Cleopatra's taxable income by $10. Given a 35 percent marginal tax rate, $10 less of taxable income saves Cleopatra $3.50 in taxes. Hence, her effective price of a unit Z is $10 minus $3.50, or $6.50.

More generally, if the price of Z is P_Z and the individual's marginal tax rate is t, allowing deduction of expenses on Z lowers Z's effective price from P_Z to $(1 - t)P_Z$. This analysis brings out two important facts:

- Because deductibility changes the relative price of the commodity involved, in general, we expect the quantity demanded to change.
- The higher the individual's value of t, the greater the value to her of a given dollar amount of deductions and the lower the effective price of the good.[11]

Itemized Deductions   We now discuss some of the major itemized deductions. The list is far from inclusive; consult any tax guide for further details.

Unreimbursed Medical Expenses That Exceed 7.5 Percent of AGI The justification is that large medical expenses are nondiscretionary and therefore reduce an individual's ability to pay. It is hard to say to what extent health care expenditures are under an

---

[10] If there are positive externalities involved in raising children, then a subsidy might be appropriate (see Chapter 5).
[11] Note that these observations apply more generally to expenditures on any items that are excluded from the tax base, not just deductions. For example, the value of excluding interest from municipal bonds increases with the marginal tax rate, other things being the same. So do the values of fringe benefits such as employer-provided health insurance.

individual's control. A person suffering a heart attack does not have much in the way of choice. On the other hand, people can choose how often to visit their doctors and whether or not to have elective surgery. Moreover, individuals can substitute preventive health care (good diet, exercise, etc.) for formal medical services.

Finally, most people can insure themselves against large medical expenditures (see Chapter 9). Under some insurance plans, the first portion of medical expenses is met entirely by the insured, but after a point, some proportion is paid by the insurance company and the rest by the individual. In effect, by allowing deduction of some medical expenses, the tax system provides a kind of social health care insurance for itemizers. The terms of this "policy" are that the amount the individual pays entirely on his or her own is 7.5 percent of AGI, and after that the Treasury pays a share equal to the marginal tax rate. The pros and cons of providing social health insurance were discussed in Chapters 9 and 10.

State and Local Income and Property Taxes   Under current law, state and local income and property taxes are deductible. In 2008, these deductions amounted to $73.5 billion. [Joint Committee on Taxation, 2008]. State and local sales taxes are *not* deductible.

Supporters of deductibility argue that state and local taxes represent nondiscretionary decreases in ability to pay. An alternative view is that they are simply user fees. A person pays state and local taxes in return for benefits such as public schools and police protection. Some people choose to live in jurisdictions that provide a lot of such services, and they pay relatively high amounts of tax; others opt for low-service, low-tax jurisdictions. To the extent this description is accurate, there is no particular reason to allow deductibility of state and local taxes.

On the other hand, if state and local taxes are not user fees, it may be appropriate to regard them as decreases in ability to pay.[12] Unfortunately, determining what proportion of state and local taxes are user fees is difficult.

This deduction can also be considered a way to help state and local governments finance themselves. For people who itemize on their federal tax returns, the deduction lowers the effective cost of state and local tax payments. This may increase political support for tax increases at the state and local levels. Why isn't a more direct method of subsidy used? As was true for the interest exemption for state and local bonds, political considerations are an important part of the explanation. A subsidy hidden in the tax code may be easier to maintain than an explicit subsidy.

Certain Interest Expenses   Some payments of interest are deductible and others are not:

- Interest paid on consumer debt such as credit card charges and car loans is *not* deductible.
- Certain individuals who have paid interest on qualified education loans may deduct up to $2,500 for such interest expenses.[13] This deduction is available even to taxpayers who do not itemize.
- Deductions for interest on debt incurred to purchase financial assets cannot exceed the amount of income from these assets. Suppose, for example, that your investment

---

[12] But not necessarily! If the taxes are capitalized into the value of property, the current owners may not be bearing any of their burden. (See Chapter 14.)

[13] The deduction is phased out starting at an AGI of $145,000 for couples.

income was $10,000, but the associated interest expenses were $25,000. All you can deduct on your tax return is $10,000. The remaining $15,000 cannot be used to shelter other sources of income from taxation.

- Interest on home mortgages is subject to special treatment. Mortgage interest for the purchase of up to two residences is deductible, up to a limit of the interest on a $1 million purchase or improvement. Also deductible is interest on a *home equity loan*—a loan for which the home serves as collateral and whose proceeds can be used to finance any purchase (except securities that generate tax-free income). For example, one can obtain a home equity loan and use the money to buy a car. In effect, then, the law allows homeowners to deduct interest on consumer loans, but denies this privilege to renters. There is, in fact, evidence that some consumers shuffle consumer debt into mortgage debt to take advantage of this provision [Maki, 2001]. However, deductible interest on home equity loans is limited to the interest on $100,000 of debt.

Do these rules make sense in terms of the Haig-Simons criterion? For a business investment, it is pretty clear that interest should be deductible. It is a cost of doing business, and hence should not be subject to income tax. The treatment of consumer interest is more controversial. Some argue that it is perfectly appropriate to deduct consumer interest payments because they represent decreases in an individual's potential consumption. Others argue that interest on consumer loans should be regarded merely as a higher price one pays to obtain a commodity sooner than would otherwise be possible. Whatever view is taken, it is hard to justify a system that makes the opportunity to deduct consumer interest depend arbitrarily on one's status as a homeowner.

Tax Arbitrage The deductibility of interest together with the exemption of certain types of capital income from taxation can lead to lucrative opportunities for smart investors. Assume that Caesar, who has a 35 percent tax rate, can borrow all the money he wants from the bank at a rate of 15 percent. Assuming that Caesar satisfies the criteria for deductibility of interest, for every dollar of interest paid, his tax bill falls by 35 cents. Hence, Caesar's effective borrowing rate is only 9.75 percent. Suppose that the going rate of return on tax-exempt state and local bonds is 11 percent. Then Caesar can borrow from the bank at an effective rate of 9.75 percent and lend to states and localities at 11 percent. The tax system appears to have created a "money machine" that can be cranked to generate infinite amounts of income. The process of taking advantage of such opportunities is referred to as *tax arbitrage*.

This example overstates the potential returns to tax arbitrage, because in real-world capital markets, people cannot borrow arbitrarily large sums of money. Moreover, competition among those who engage in tax arbitrage tends to reduce the return to that activity. For example, as more and more arbitrageurs buy municipal bonds, their rate of return goes down. If everyone had a 35 percent marginal tax rate, in equilibrium we would expect the return on municipals to fall until it was exactly 65 percent of the rate on taxable bonds. At that point, there would be no net advantage to owning municipals. Still, some opportunities for gain are present. The tax authorities realized this many years ago and made it illegal to deduct interest from loans whose proceeds are used to purchase tax-exempt bonds. But it is not easy to prove that someone is breaking this rule. Given that money can be used for many different purposes, how can it be proved that a given loan was "for" municipal bond purchases rather than for some other purpose? This very simple scam illustrates some important general lessons:

- Interest deductibility in conjunction with preferential treatment of certain capital income can create major money-making opportunities. This is one reason why countries such as Canada do not allow the deductibility of mortgage interest.
- High-income individuals are particularly likely to benefit from these opportunities because they tend to face relatively high tax rates and to have good access to borrowing.
- The tax authorities can certainly declare various tax arbitrage schemes to be illegal, but it is hard to enforce these rules. Moreover, clever lawyers and accountants are always on the lookout for new tax arbitrage opportunities. The Internal Revenue Service is usually right behind them trying to plug the loopholes. In the process, many inefficient investments are made, and a lot of resources are spent on tax avoidance and tax administration.

Charitable Contributions   Individuals can deduct the value of contributions made to religious, charitable, educational, scientific, or literary organizations. Gifts of property are deductible, but personal services are not. In most cases, total charitable deductions cannot exceed 50 percent of adjusted gross income. In 2007, individuals recorded charitable deductions of nearly $200 billion.

Some argue that charitable donations constitute a reduction in taxable capacity and, hence, should be excluded from taxable income. However, as long as the contributions are voluntary, this argument is unconvincing. If people don't receive as much satisfaction from charity as from their own consumption, why make the donations in the first place? Probably the best way to understand the presence of the deduction is as an attempt by the government to encourage charitable giving.

Has the deduction succeeded in doing so? The deductibility provision changes an individual's "price" for a dollar's worth of charity from $1 to $(1 - t)$, where t is the taxpayer's marginal tax rate. The effectiveness of the deduction in encouraging giving therefore depends on the price elasticity of demand for charitable contributions. If the price elasticity is zero, charitable giving is unaffected. The deduction is just a bonus for those who would give anyway. If the price elasticity exceeds zero, then giving is encouraged.

Many econometric studies have estimated the elasticity of charitable giving with respect to its after-tax price. Typically, a regression is estimated in which the dependent variable is the amount of charitable donations, and the explanatory variables are (1) the "price" of charitable donations (one minus the marginal tax rate); (2) income; and (3) personal characteristics of individuals that might influence their decisions to give, such as age and marital status. Recent studies suggest that the price elasticity of demand for donations is less than 1, perhaps around 0.7 [Bakija and Heim, 2008]. If correct, this figure suggests that the deduction has a substantial effect on giving. Consider an individual with a marginal tax rate of 35 percent. The deductibility of charitable donations lowers the price of giving from $1 to 65 cents, a reduction of 35 percent. With an elasticity of 0.7, this increases charitable donations by 24.5 percent. Note, however, that with an elasticity less than 1, the amount that giving increases is less than the revenue that the Treasury loses.

The deduction is controversial apart from its effectiveness in stimulating donations. Opponents argue that allowing deduction of contributions to churches and synagogues constitutes a violation of the principle of separation of church and state. On the other hand, proponents believe that in the absence of the deduction, many institutions now funded privately would be forced to scale back their activities or close. The current decentralized system stimulates a variety of activities and, hence, promotes the goal of a pluralistic society.

Deductions and Complexity   Every deduction requires rules to determine which expenditures qualify and which do not. Designing such rules is difficult, even for such apparently straightforward deductions as medical expenditures. Consider the case of a severely obese woman who lost more than 100 pounds and developed "a mass of loose-hanging skin which spanned the width of her abdomen and spilled over onto her upper thighs." She had surgery to correct the problem and deducted the expense. The Internal Revenue Service disallowed the deduction, saying that it was cosmetic. But the Tax Court ruled for the woman, saying that the sagging skin was an aftereffect of the disease [Herman, 2002, p. A1].

The charitable deduction provides more examples. Donations to fraternities and sororities are not deductible. Donations to universities are deductible. What's the proper treatment of a gift to a university that is to be used for constructing a facility for holding sorority meetings? (Under current law, it is deductible.) Or consider the deductibility of wild game that is hunted and then donated to natural history museums. How should such contributions be valued for tax purposes? Currently, these trophies are frequently appraised at many times their market value, leading to big tax deductions for wealthy hunters [Kaufman, 2005].

The fact that itemized deductions increase complexity does not necessarily mean that they are a bad thing. However, complexity is a factor that needs to be taken into account when assessing the costs and benefits of any particular deduction.

Deductions versus Credits   As already noted, the higher an individual's marginal tax rate, the greater the value of a deduction of a given dollar amount. In contrast, a **tax credit** is a subtraction from tax liability (*not* taxable income), and hence, its value is independent of the individual's marginal tax rate. A tax credit of $100 reduces tax liability by $100 whether an individual's tax rate is 15 percent or 35 percent. Subtracting tax credits is the last stage in computing one's tax liability. (See Figure 17.1.)

tax credit
A subtraction from tax liability (as opposed to a subtraction from taxable income).

Current law allows a variety of tax credits. A family receives a $1,000 per child tax credit.[14] Credits are also allowed for some college expenses. For example, for the first two years of college, there is a credit of up to $1,800 per student, known as the Hope credit.[15] There is also a Lifetime Learning credit of up to $2,000 per tax return for all years of college. Legislation passed in 2009 created the Making Work Pay credit, which is a refundable credit equal to the lesser of 6.2 percent of a person's earned income or $400 ($800 for married couples).[16] All of these credits are subject to phaseouts. In terms of dollars involved, the most important tax credit is the earned income tax credit that was described in Chapter 13.

---

[14] For married couples, the credit is phased out starting at an AGI of $110,000. For singles, it is phased out starting at an AGI of $75,000.

[15] Legislation passed in 2009 raised the limit on the tax credit to $2,500 and made the credit available for four years of college. The legislation adopts these changes for 2009 and 2010 only.

[16] The 2009 law created this credit for only two years. As of this writing, the Obama administration is proposing to make the Making Work Pay credit permanent.

Some argue that deductions and exemptions should be converted into credits. For example, the deduction of mortgage interest payments could be changed to a credit for some percentage of the value of interest paid. With a 20 percent interest credit, individuals could subtract from their tax bills an amount equal to one-fifth of their interest payments. Proponents of credits argue that they are fairer than deductions. Under a regime of tax deductions, a poor person (with a low marginal tax rate) benefits less than a rich person (with a high marginal tax rate) even if they both have identical interest expenses. With a credit, the dollar benefit is the same.

The choice between deductions and credits should depend at least in part on the purpose of the exclusion. If the motivation is to correct for the fact that a given expenditure reduces ability to pay, a deduction is appropriate. If the purpose is mainly to encourage certain behavior, it is unclear whether credits or deductions are superior. A credit reduces the effective price of the favored good by the *same* percentage for all individuals; a deduction decreases the price by *different* percentages for different people. If people's elasticities of demand differ, it may make sense to present them with different effective prices. For example, it is ineffective to give *any* subsidy to someone whose elasticity of demand for the favored good is zero.

Itemized Deduction Phaseout Otherwise allowable itemized deductions are reduced by 1 percent of the amount by which AGI exceeds $159,950. However, the reduction cannot be more than 80 percent of the total of itemized deductions.[17] Consider, for example, a family with an AGI of $200,000, mortgage interest of $15,000, and local property taxes of $5,000. In the absence of the phaseout, the family would be allowed to deduct $20,000. Because AGI exceeds $159,950 by $40,050, its itemized deduction must be reduced by $801 (= $40,050 × 0.02). Hence, only $19,199 of deductions are allowed.

The Standard Deduction Itemized deductions are listed separately on the individual's tax return, and in principle each one requires documentation (such as receipts) to prove that the expenditure was indeed made. All this record-keeping increases the administrative cost of the system. To simplify tax returns, the standard deduction was introduced in 1944. It is a fixed amount available to all taxpayers. Each household can choose between taking the standard deduction or itemizing, depending on which offers the greater advantage. The standard deduction in 2009 was $11,400 for joint filers and $5,700 for singles.[18] The standard deduction is adjusted annually for inflation. About 63 percent of tax returns now use the standard deduction.

Impact on the Tax Base

How does the presence of exemptions and deductions influence the size of the tax base? In 2006, AGI was about $7.4 trillion. After completing all the subtractions from AGI, taxable income was only $5.5 trillion, a reduction of about 26 percent. Hence, deductions and exemptions are large relative to the size of the potential tax base.

---

[17] In computing the 80 percent maximum, medical expenses and investment interest are excluded. The threshold is adjusted annually for inflation.

[18] A joint filer who is elderly (over 65) or blind is entitled to a $1,100 deduction above the standard deduction.

Tax Expenditures

Failure to include a particular item in the tax base results in a loss to the Treasury. Suppose that as a consequence of not taxing item *Z*, the Treasury loses $1 billion. Compare this to a situation in which the government simply hands over $1 billion of general revenues to purchasers of item *Z*. In a sense, these activities are equivalent as both subsidize purchases of *Z*. It just so happens that one transaction occurs on the expenditure side of the budget and the other on the revenue side. The former is a **tax expenditure,** a revenue loss caused by the exclusion of some item from the tax base. The list of tax expenditures has about 140 items. Estimates of the total revenue loss from tax expenditures for 2008 exceed $1 trillion [Joint Committee on Taxation, 2008].

> **tax expenditure**
>
> **A loss of tax revenue because some item is excluded from the tax base.**

The law requires that an annual tax expenditure budget be compiled by the Congressional Budget Office. A major intent of the law is to raise public consciousness of the symmetry between a *direct* subsidy for an activity via an expenditure and an *implicit* subsidy through the tax system. However, the notion of a tax expenditure budget has been subject to several criticisms.

First, a serious technical problem arises in the way the computations are made. It is assumed that in the absence of a deduction for a given item, all the expenditures currently made on it would flow into taxable income. Given that people probably adjust their behavior in response to changes in the tax system, this is not a good assumption, so the tax expenditure estimates may be quite far off the mark.

Second, the tax expenditure budget is simply a list of items exempt from taxation. However, to characterize an item as exempt, you must first have some kind of criterion for deciding what ought to be included. As we have seen, no rigorous set of principles exists for determining what belongs in income. One person's loophole is someone else's appropriate adjustment of the tax base. Hence, considerable arbitrariness is inevitably involved in deciding what to include in the tax expenditure budget.

Finally, the tax expenditure concept has been attacked on philosophical grounds:

> [L]urking behind the concept of the tax expenditure is a more sinister premise, which is a point not just about national accounting practices but about political philosophy and political economics. It is the subtle disposition to think of all income as virtual state property, and forbearance to tax away every last penny of it as itself a tax expenditure [Fried, 1995, p. C7].

Defenders of the tax expenditure concept argue that the concept does not really carry this ideological baggage. It is merely an attempt to force recognition of the fact that the tax system is a major method for subsidizing various activities. Moreover, the fact that the estimates are not exact does not mean that they are useless for assessing the implications of tax policy.

Why are tax expenditures so popular? Part of the reason is probably political: "In this age of fiscal austerity, new spending programs are a tough sell in Congress. But if the same initiatives are dressed up as tax cuts they look much more palatable" [Stevenson, 1997, p. E1].

The Simplicity Issue

The income tax law has been complicated for a long time. President Franklin Roosevelt did not even bother to read a major piece of his administration's tax legislation, the Revenue Act of 1942. Roosevelt observed that it "might as well have been written in a foreign language" [Samuelson, 1986]. By 1986, the set of instructions for filing the basic personal tax return (Form 1040) was 48 pages long. There were 28 possible schedules to fill out.

The desire to simplify the tax system was one of the driving forces behind a major piece of legislation passed in 1986, the **Tax Reform Act of 1986 (TRA86).** TRA86 raised the standard deduction, so that fewer families now need to itemize their returns and keep extensive records of various transactions. In addition, TRA86 raised the personal exemption substantially. This simplifies life for the low-income families who now do not have to file at all because they have no tax liability. (However, such families may have to file a relatively simple return if they require a refund on tax withholding.) On the other hand, TRA86 made certain rules, such as those pertaining to the deductibility of interest, more complicated than they were before.

To the extent that any simplification was achieved in 1986, the gains have been lost since then. Legislation enacted in the early 1990s brought us the exemption and itemized deduction phaseouts and rules that allowed capital gains tax breaks on stock in some types of companies but not in others. But the floodgates really broke in 1997, with provisions that were described as "mind-numbing" and "a nightmare of complexity." The 1997 law introduced several new kinds of IRAs with complicated rules governing who could use them. It also made reporting capital gains more difficult by applying different rates to assets held for different lengths of time. Additional tax credits have been introduced since 1997, each of which is subject to phaseouts, making it harder for taxpayers to determine whether they qualified and to what extent.

According to a recent poll, one-third of Americans find that completing the annual tax return is more onerous than making large tax payments. Further, more than two-thirds of taxpayers incorrectly answer basic questions on their returns [President's Advisory Panel on Federal Tax Reform, 2005, pp. 2–3]. Since 1986 there have been over 15,000 changes to the tax code. By 2008 the Form 1040 instructions were up to 161 pages, and the Internal Revenue Code contained nearly 3,700,000 words. In an article entitled "The Tax Maze Begins Here," a journalist noted, "People with doctoral degrees and even some tax lawyers and accountants say they find themselves stumped" when it comes to filling out today's tax returns [Johnston 2000, p. BU1]. The following cartoon reflects the prevailing view that the system is complex and virtually incomprehensible.

Recent years have presented a new type of complexity to taxpayers. Tax laws enacted in 2001, 2003, and 2009 contained a variety of "sunsetting" provisions. Such provisions require a given change in the tax law to expire at a specific date in the future. For example, tax legislation passed in 2001 reduced marginal tax rates, but stipulated that in 2011 they would revert back to their levels in 2000. There was considerable uncertainty about whether Congress would actually allow such an increase to take place, which complicated the lives of taxpayers who were trying to do financial planning.

▶ RATE STRUCTURE

With respect to Figure 17.1, we are now at the point of determining the tax rate that is applied to taxable income. A bracket system is used to define tax rates. The taxable income scale is divided into segments, and the law specifies the marginal tax rate that applies to income in that segment. Actually, there are four different rate schedules, one each for married couples who file together (joint returns), married people who

---

Tax Reform Act of 1986 (TRA86)

Tax legislation that eliminated a number of itemized deductions and other tax preferences, and lowered marginal tax rates for many taxpayers.

© 2003 Thaves/Dist. by NEA, Inc. Reprinted with permission from Tom Thaves.

file separately, unmarried people, and single people who are heads of households. (A head of household maintains a home that includes a dependent.)

When the federal income tax was introduced in 1913, the bracket rates ranged from 1 percent to 7 percent. As late as 1939, half the taxpayers faced marginal rates below 4 percent. With the advent of World War II, rates went up substantially. In 1945, the lowest bracket rate was 23 percent, and the highest 94 percent. Rates eventually came down after the war. By the mid-1980s, there were 14 brackets, with marginal tax rates ranging from 11 percent to 50 percent. The Tax Reform Act of 1986 was a drastic change in the rate structure. The number of brackets was reduced to two, and the maximum statutory rate was set at only 28 percent. Rates crept back up in the 1990s; this trend was reversed by the 2001 tax act, which included a phased reduction in rates over the period 2001–2010. For example, prior to the 2001 legislation, the top marginal tax rate was 39.6 percent; it is currently 35 percent.[19] The tax rate schedules for single and joint returns in 2009 are given in Table 17.1.

Table 17.1 **Official Statutory Tax Rate Schedule (2009)**

Single Returns		Joint Returns	
Taxable Income	**Marginal Tax Rate**	**Taxable Income**	**Marginal Tax Rate**
$0–$8,350	10%	$0–$16,700	10%
$8,351–$33,950	15	$16,701–$67,900	15
$33,951–$82,250	25	$67,901–$137,050	25
$82,251–$171,550	28	$137,051–$208,850	28
$171,551–$372,950	33	$208,851–$372,950	33
$372,951 and over	35	$372,951 and over	35

Source: http://www.irs.gov.

Under current law, statutory marginal tax rates range from 10 percent to 35 percent.

---

[19] Under current law, the reduction in marginal tax rates is set to be reversed in 2011. As of this writing, the Obama administration is proposing to allow the reinstatement of the 36 and 39.6 tax brackets for high-earners.

Unfortunately, these official statutory marginal tax rates do not necessarily correspond to effective marginal tax rates. The phaseouts of various deductions and credits discussed earlier can lead to higher marginal tax rates than those in the table. Consider, for example, an individual in the itemized deduction phaseout range. When he earns another dollar, there is a direct increase in his tax liability in an amount dictated by the rate for his tax bracket. In addition, there is an indirect effect triggered by the fact that his deductions go down, so his taxable income goes up. The result is an effective marginal tax rate that exceeds the statutory rate. Similar stories apply to the phaseout of personal exemptions, IRA deductions, the child tax credit, the education tax credit, and so on. (See Discussion Question 10 at the end of the chapter for further details.) At the bottom of the income scale, marginal tax rates can be negative because the earned income tax credit (EITC) subsidizes wages (see Chapter 13). However, within the EITC phaseout range, actual rates exceed statutory rates substantially.

Effective versus Statutory Rates

Now is a good time to recall the distinction between statutory and effective tax rates. In this section, we have been discussing the former, the legal rates established by the law. In general, these differ from effective tax rates for at least three reasons:

- Because the tax system treats certain types of income preferentially, taxable income may be considerably lower than some more comprehensive measures of income. The fact that tax rates rise rapidly with taxable income does not by itself tell us much about how taxes vary with comprehensive income.

- Even in the absence of loopholes, the link between statutory and effective tax rates is weak. As Chapter 14 emphasized, taxes can be shifted, so income taxes need not be borne by the people who pay the money to the government. The economic incidence of the income tax is determined by market responses when the tax is levied, and the true pattern of the burden is not known.

- The tax system imposes decreases in utility that exceed revenue collections. Excess burdens arise because taxes distort behavior away from patterns that otherwise would have occurred (see Chapter 15). Similarly, the costs of compliance with the tax code, in taxpayers' own time as well as explicit payments to accountants and lawyers, must be considered.

In this connection, note that contrary to the impression sometimes received in popular discussions, items like tax-exempt bonds do not, in general, allow the rich to escape entirely the burden of taxation. Consider again Caesar, whose marginal tax rate is 35 percent, and who can buy taxable assets that pay a return of 15 percent. Suppose that the going rate on municipal bonds is 11 percent. We expect that other things being the same, Caesar will buy municipals because their 11 percent return exceeds the after-tax return of 9.75 percent on taxable securities. To be sure, Caesar writes no check to the government. But the tax system nevertheless makes him worse off, because in its absence, he would have been able to make a return of 15 percent. In general, the rate of return on tax-preferred items tends to fall by an amount that reflects the tax advantage. Because of this tendency, high-income individuals face higher tax rates on their capital income than their tax bills would suggest. They are taxed *implicitly* in the form of lower rates of return.

Thus, statutory rates alone probably tell us little about the progressiveness of the current system. Conceivably, a statute with lower marginal tax rates but a broader base would lead to a system with incidence as progressive as that of the current system, and perhaps even more so. At the same time, a system with lower marginal tax rates would reduce excess burden and perhaps lower tax evasion. Such considerations have prompted a number of proposals to restructure the income tax dramatically. One plan that has received a lot of attention is the flat income tax.[20] A flat income tax has two attributes:

- It applies the same rate of tax to everyone and to each component of income.
- It allows computation of the tax base with no deductions from total income except personal exemptions and strictly defined business expenses.

Assuming that a certain amount of tax revenue must be collected, the key trade-off under a flat income tax is between the size of the personal exemption and the marginal tax rate. A higher exemption may be desirable to secure relief for those at the bottom of the income schedule and to increase progressiveness (with respect to average tax rates). But a higher exemption means that a higher marginal tax rate must be applied to maintain revenues. A tax rate of roughly 16 percent together with a personal exemption at the current level would satisfy the revenue requirements.[21]

Proponents of the flat income tax claim that lowering marginal tax rates would reduce both the excess burden of the tax system and the incentive to cheat. Moreover, the simplicity gained would lower administrative costs and improve taxpayer morale. And all of this could be achieved without a serious cost in equity because, as just noted, the flat income tax can be made quite progressive by suitable choice of the exemption level.

Opponents of the flat income tax believe that it would probably redistribute more of the tax burden from the rich to the middle classes. It is hard to evaluate this claim because of the usual difficulties involved in doing tax incidence analysis (see Chapter 14). Critics also note that the whole range of conceptual and administrative problems involved in defining income will not disappear merely by declaring that business expenses are to be "strictly defined." As pointed out earlier, there will *never* be a simple income tax code.

Altig et al.'s [2001] analysis of a flat income tax lends support to the positions of both the proponents and opponents. They studied a very extreme variant—no deductions or exemptions of any kind, just a flat rate on total income—and found that this flat tax would substantially improve efficiency, increasing the long-run level of output by about 5 percent. However, the reform would hurt low-income individuals, who benefit from low effective rates under the status quo.

The notion of a flat income tax enjoyed some popularity in the 1980s, and one way to think of the Tax Reform Act of 1986 is as a movement in that direction—it lowered the statutory maximum rate from 50 percent to 28 percent and broadened the base by disallowing certain deductions (such as those for state and local sales taxes), and by including all realized capital gains in AGI. However, as noted, high-end rates have increased in recent years; capital gains are again taxed preferentially; and the new IRAs and tax credits have blown new holes in the tax base. The political momentum currently appears to be away from a flat income tax.

---

[20] Another, quite different reform, a *flat consumption tax*, has been proposed by several politicians such as former presidential candidate Steve Forbes. It is explained in Chapter 21.

[21] Authors' calculation. It does not take into account behavioral responses to the change.

▶ TAXES AND INFLATION

The personal exemption, the standard deduction, the minimum and maximum dollar amounts for each tax rate bracket, the earned income credit, and the thresholds for the deduction and exemption phaseouts are adjusted annually to offset the effects of inflation. The purpose of this process, referred to as **tax indexing,** is to remove automatically the influence of inflation upon real tax liabilities. This section discusses motivations for tax indexing and whether the US system of indexing is adequate.

How Inflation Can Affect Taxes

Economists customarily distinguish between "anticipated" and "unanticipated" inflation. The latter is generally viewed as being worse for efficiency, because it does not allow people to adjust their behavior optimally to price level changes. However, with an unindexed income tax system, even perfectly anticipated inflation causes distortions.

The best understood distortion is the phenomenon known as **bracket creep.** Suppose that Gertrude's earnings and the price level both increase at the same rate over time. Then Gertrude's **real income** (the amount of actual purchasing power) is unchanged. However, an unindexed tax system is based on her **nominal income**—the number of dollars received. As nominal income increases, Gertrude is pushed into tax brackets with higher marginal tax rates. Hence, the proportion of income that is taxed increases despite the fact that real income stays the same. Even individuals who are not pushed into a higher bracket find more of their incomes taxed at the highest rate to which they are subject. Inflation brings about an automatic increase in real tax burdens without any legislative action.

Another effect of inflation occurs when exemptions and the standard deduction are set in nominal terms. In an unindexed system, increases in the price level decrease their real value. Again, inflation increases the effective tax rate.

It turns out, however, that even with a simple proportional income tax without exemptions or deductions, inflation distorts tax burdens. To be sure, under such a system, general inflation does not affect the real tax burden on wage and salary incomes. If a worker's earnings during a year double, so do his taxes, and there are no real effects. But inflation changes the real tax burden on *capital* income.

Suppose Calpurnia buys an asset for $5,000. Three years later, she sells it for $10,000. Suppose further that during the three years, the general price level doubled. In real terms, selling the asset nets Calpurnia zero. However, capital gains liabilities are based on the difference between the *nominal* selling and buying prices. Hence, Calpurnia incurs a tax liability on $5,000 of illusory capital gains. In short, because the inflationary component of capital gains is subject to tax, the real tax burden depends on the inflation rate.

Those who receive taxable interest income are similarly affected. Suppose that the **nominal interest rate** (the rate observed in the market) is 16 percent. Suppose further that the anticipated rate of inflation is 12 percent. Then for someone who lends at the 16 percent nominal rate, the **real interest rate** is only 4 percent, because that is the percentage by which the lender's real purchasing power increases. However, taxes are levied on nominal, not real, interest payments. Hence, tax must be paid on receipts that represent no gain in real income.

---

tax indexing

Automatically adjusting the tax schedule to compensate for inflation so that an individual's real tax burden is independent of inflation.

---

bracket creep

When an increase in an individual's nominal income pushes the individual into a higher tax bracket despite the fact that his or her real income is unchanged. See also tax indexing.

---

real income

A measure of income that accounts for changes in the general price level.

---

nominal income

Income measured in terms of current prices.

---

nominal interest rate

The interest rate observed in the market.

---

real interest rate

The nominal interest rate corrected for changes in the level of prices by subtracting the expected inflation rate.

Let us consider this argument algebraically. Call the nominal interest rate i. Then the after-tax nominal return to lending for an individual with a marginal tax rate of t is $(1 - t)i$. To find the real after-tax rate of return, we must subtract the expected rate of inflation, π. Hence, the real after-tax rate of return r is

$$r = (1 - t)i - \pi \qquad (17.1)$$

Suppose $t = 25$ percent, $i = 16$ percent, and $\pi = 10$ percent. Then although the nominal interest rate is 16 percent, the real after-tax return is only 2 percent.

Now suppose for simplicity that any increase in the expected rate of inflation increases the nominal interest rate by the same amount; if inflation increases by 4 percentage points, the nominal interest rate increases by 4 percentage points. One might guess that the two increases would cancel out, leaving the real after-tax rate of return unchanged at 2 percent. But Equation (17.1) contradicts this prediction. If π goes from 10 percent to 14 percent and i goes from 16 percent to 20 percent, then with t equal to 25 percent, r decreases to 1 percent. Inflation, even though it is perfectly anticipated, is not "neutral." This is a direct consequence of the fact that nominal rather than real interest payments are taxed.

So far we have been considering the issue from the point of view of lenders. Things are just the opposite for borrowers. In the absence of taxes, the real rate paid by borrowers is the nominal rate minus the anticipated inflation rate. However, assuming the taxpayer satisfies certain criteria, the tax law allows deductibility of nominal interest payments from taxable income. Thus, debtors can subtract from taxable income payments that represent no decrease in their real incomes. Inflation decreases the tax burden on borrowers.

Coping with the Tax/Inflation Problem

As inflation rates began to increase in the late 1960s, people became acutely aware of the fact that inflation leads to unlegislated increases in the real income tax burden. The initial response was to mitigate these effects by a series of ad hoc reductions in statutory rates. Half a dozen such tax cuts were enacted between 1969 and 1981, and they were partially successful in undoing some effects of inflation.

Nevertheless, the process was unpopular. Each tax cut offset inflation only for a short time. After a while, it became necessary to make more changes. The whole business increased public cynicism about the tax-setting process. Many citizens learned that the tax "reductions" about which their legislators boasted were nothing of the kind when measured in *real* terms. Lenin is alleged to have said, "The way to crush the bourgeoisie is to grind them between the millstones of taxation and inflation." Although the interaction of taxes and inflation in the United States had not created quite such drastic effects, it had certainly produced serious distortions.

In 1981, dissatisfaction with the ad hoc approach led to the enactment of legislation requiring indexing of certain parts of the tax code. Currently the personal exemption, standard deduction, bracket widths, and earned income tax credit are all indexed. These provisions have effectively ended bracket creep. However, no moves have been made in the direction of indexing capital income. This is due in part to the administrative complexity such a statute would entail. For example, as suggested earlier, increases in inflation generate real gains for debtors, because the real value of the amounts they have to repay decreases. In a fully indexed system, such gains would have to be measured and taxed, a task that would certainly be complex.

Should indexing be maintained? Opponents of indexing argue that a system of periodic ad hoc adjustments is a good thing because it allows the legislature to examine and revise other aspects of the tax code that may need changing.[22] Proponents of indexing argue that reducing the opportunities for revising the tax code may itself be a benefit, because the tax law should be stable and predictable. Moreover, fewer opportunities to change the law also mean fewer chances for legislative mischief. The most important argument of those who favor indexing is that it eliminates unlegislated increases in real tax rates. They believe that allowing the real tax schedule to be changed systematically by a nonlegislative process is antithetical to democratic values.

Proponents of indexing also note that its repeal would have a disproportionately large effect on the tax liabilities of low-income families. For example, high-income families lose some or all of the advantage of personal exemptions because of the exemption phaseout. Hence, if the exemption were no longer indexed, their taxes would not be affected at all, but the real tax liabilities of lower-income individuals would increase. Similarly, higher-income families are more likely to itemize than take the standard deduction, so eliminating its indexation would tend to affect mostly low-income families.

▶ THE ALTERNATIVE MINIMUM TAX

alternative minimum tax (AMT)

The tax liability calculated by an alternative set of rules designed to force individuals with high levels of preference income to incur at least some tax liability.

As noted earlier, certain types of income such as interest on state and local bonds are treated preferentially by the tax system. This makes it possible for some high-income households to have little or no tax liability. In 1969 the secretary of the Treasury set off a political firestorm when he announced that 155 individuals with incomes above $200,000 had paid no federal income tax several years earlier. The **alternative minimum tax (AMT),** enacted in 1969 and modified several times since then, was an attempt to ensure that rich people who benefited from various tax shelters paid at least some tax.

The AMT is essentially a shadow tax system with its own rules for computing the tax base and its own rate schedule. The first step in the computation is to take regular taxable income and add to it items called *AMT preferences*. These items include (but are not limited to) personal exemptions, the standard deduction, and itemized deductions for state taxes. The next step is to subtract the AMT exemption—in 2009 it was $69,950 for married couples and $46,200 for single individuals.[23] This gives us *alternative minimum tax income (AMTI)*. The exemption is the same regardless of the number of dependents, and is phased out for high-income individuals. AMTI is subject to rates of 26 percent on the first $175,000 and 28 percent on the rest. Importantly, unlike the ordinary income tax, neither the exemption nor the brackets are adjusted for inflation.

---

[22] We have been dealing with this debate from a microeconomic standpoint. People also disagree about the macroeconomic consequences of indexing. Opponents argue that it removes an important tool for conducting macroeconomic policy. For example, if more fiscal restraint is needed during an inflationary period, this is automatically generated by increases in tax revenues. In contrast, voting tax increases and/or expenditure cuts takes time. On the other hand, indexing proponents argue that the automatic rise in federal revenues may simply encourage legislators to spend more, and hence have no stabilizing effect. Indeed, they argue that a nonindexed system creates incentives for legislators to pursue inflationary policies, because these policies tend to increase the real quantity of resources available to the public sector.

[23] These exemption amounts are temporary extensions. They are set to revert to lower amounts unless new legislation is forthcoming.

The tax liability computed by applying this relatively flat rate schedule to AMTI is called *tentative AMT*. To complete the process, compare tentative AMT with tax liability under the regular income tax. If tentative AMT is greater than regular income tax liability, the difference is the taxpayer's AMT, and the taxpayer must pay AMT on top of his regular income tax.

We noted at the outset that the original purpose of the AMT was to catch high-income individuals who were sheltering most or all of their income. It was never intended to be a mass tax. Yet under current law, by 2015 about 32 million taxpayers will be on the AMT, and the cost of repealing the AMT is greater than the cost of repealing the regular income tax! [Burman et al., 2007]. Why is this happening? To understand the reason, recall that the AMT kicks in only when tax liability under the AMT is greater than tax liability under the regular income tax. Hence, anything that reduces tax liability under the regular tax relative to the AMT tends to increase the number of AMT taxpayers. In this context, two facts are relevant. First, the AMT is not adjusted for inflation, and the ordinary income tax generally is. Hence, the AMT is subject to bracket creep, and over time even moderate rates of inflation raise AMT relative to ordinary tax liabilities. Second, the 2001 tax law cut the regular income tax without making any substantial changes in the AMT. By itself, this change will account for almost a doubling of the number of AMT taxpayers by 2010.

Should we care that the AMT is becoming a mass tax? The answer is that we should, because it is bad tax policy from virtually every perspective. From the point of view of fairness, the AMT exemption preferences—personal exemptions, standard deduction, and itemized deductions for state taxes—are of greatest importance to middle-income taxpayers. As the AMT grows in importance, these are the taxpayers who are adversely affected, not the very rich. From the point of view of efficiency, recall from Chapter 15 that the excess burden of an income tax varies with the square of the marginal tax rate. The minimum rate under the AMT is 26 percent, considerably higher than the regular income tax rates of many families that will be thrown into the AMT. Finally, the AMT is notoriously complicated. One of the main problems is that the only way to find out if you have to pay the AMT is to go through the entire laborious AMT calculation. Thus, even families that ultimately don't have to pay the tax still have to fill out the AMT return, adding substantially to the burden of tax compliance. At the same time, many families that are required to pay the AMT don't ever realize it: According to the Treasury Department, about 226,000 income-tax returns filed in 2006 failed to include the AMT when appropriate [Herman, 2008].

In short, the US income tax system is heading for a train wreck by the end of the decade. Most observers believe that Congress will act to avert the wreck, although it is not clear how, given that repealing the AMT would reduce tax revenues by more than repealing the regular income tax. There are a number of possibilities: The exemption and brackets could be indexed for inflation, the exemption could be raised, or the AMT could be eliminated altogether. Abstracting from the revenue costs, outright repeal has considerable attraction. If Congress doesn't want people to benefit from certain preferences, it makes more sense simply to eliminate those preferences from the regular income tax rather than invent a whole new tax system to get at them. In short, the AMT is another demonstration of the income tax system's lack of coherence. As former Senator Bill Bradley trenchantly put it, "A minimum tax is an admission of failure. It demonstrates not only that the system is broke, but also that Congress doesn't have the guts to fix it."

▶ CHOICE OF UNIT AND THE MARRIAGE TAX

We have discussed at length problems that arise in defining income for tax purposes. Yet, even very careful definitions of income give little guidance with respect to choosing *who* should be taxed on the income. Should each person be taxed separately on his or her own income? Or should individuals who live together in a family unit be taxed on their joint incomes? In this section, we discuss some of the issues surrounding this controversial issue.[24]

Background

To begin, consider the following three principles:

1. The income tax should embody increasing marginal tax rates.
2. Families with equal incomes should, other things being the same, pay equal taxes.
3. Two individuals' tax burdens should not change when they marry; the tax system should be **marriage neutral.**

marriage neutral

Individuals' tax liabilities are independent of their marital status.

The second and third principles are a bit controversial, but it is probably fair to say they are broadly accepted as desirable features of a tax system. While agreement on the first principle is weaker, increasing marginal tax rates seem to have wide political support.

Despite the appeal of these principles, a problem arises when it comes to implementing them: In general, *no tax system can adhere to all three simultaneously.* This point is made easily with an arithmetic example. Consider the following simple progressive tax schedule: A taxable unit pays in tax 10 percent of all income up to $6,000, and 50 percent of all income in excess of $6,000. The first two columns of Table 17.2 show the incomes and tax liabilities of four individuals, Lucy, Ricky, Fred, and Ethel. [For example, Ricky's tax liability is $12,100 (= 0.10 × $6,000 + 0.50 × $23,000).] Now assume that romances develop—Lucy marries Ricky, and Ethel marries Fred. In the absence of joint filing, the tax liability of each individual is unchanged. However,

Table 17.2   Tax Liabilities under a Hypothetical Tax System

	Individual Income	Individual Tax	Family Tax with Individual Filing	Joint Income	Joint Tax
Lucy	$ 1,000	$ 100 ⎫	$12,200	$30,000	$12,600
Ricky	29,000	12,100 ⎭			
Ethel	15,000	5,100 ⎫	10,200	30,000	12,600
Fred	15,000	5,100 ⎭			

If the income tax is levied on individuals, then Lucy and Ricky pay higher taxes as a family than do Ethel and Fred, violating the principle that families with equal incomes should pay equal taxes. If instead the family is the taxable unit, then the two families pay the same tax, but tax burdens depend on marital status.

---

[24] For further details see the references in Carasso and Steuerle [2002].

"And do you promise to love, honor, and cherish each other, and to pay the United States government more in taxes as a married couple than you would have paid if you had just continued living together?" © The New Yorker Collection 1993 Arnie Levin from cartoonbank.com. All Rights Reserved.

two families with the same income ($30,000) pay different amounts of tax. (The Lucy-Rickys pay $12,200, while the Ethel-Freds pay only $10,200, as noted in the third column.) Suppose instead that the law views the family as the taxable unit, so that the tax schedule applies to joint income. In this case, the two families pay equal amounts of tax, but now tax burdens have been changed by marriage. Of course, the actual change in the tax burden depends on the difference between the tax schedules applied to individual and joint returns. This example has assumed for simplicity that the schedule remains unchanged. But it does make the main point: Given increasing marginal tax rates, we cannot have both principles 2 and 3.

What choice has the United States made? Over time, the choice has changed. Before 1948, the taxable unit was the individual, and principle 2 was violated. In 1948, the family became the taxable unit, and simultaneously **income splitting** was introduced. Under income splitting, a family with, for example, an income of $50,000 is taxed as if it were two individuals with incomes of $25,000. Clearly, with increasing marginal tax rates, this can be a major advantage. Note also that under such a regime, an unmarried person with a given income finds her tax liability reduced substantially if she marries a person with little or no income. Indeed, under the 1948 law, it was possible for an individual's tax liability to fall drastically when she married—a violation of principle 3.

income splitting

Using the arithmetic average of family income to determine each family member's taxable income, regardless of whose income it is.

The differential between a single person's tax liability and that of a married couple with the same income was so large that Congress created a new schedule for unmarried people in 1969. Under this schedule, a single person's tax liability could never be more than 20 percent higher than the tax liability of a married couple with the same taxable income. (Under the old regime, differentials of up to 40 percent were possible.)

Unfortunately, this decrease in the single-married differential was purchased at the price of a violation of principle 3 in the opposite direction: It was now possible for persons' tax liabilities to increase when they married. In effect, the personal income tax levied a tax on marriage. In 1981, Congress attempted to reduce the "marriage tax" by introducing a new deduction for two-earner married couples. Two-earner families received a deduction equal to 10 percent of the lower-earning spouse's wage income, but no more than $3,000. However, the two-earner deduction was eliminated by TRA86. It was deemed to be unnecessary because lower marginal tax rates reduced the importance of the "marriage tax."

Whatever the merits of this argument, marginal tax rates increased substantially after 1986, and marriage taxes grew along with them. The 2001 tax law reduced the marriage tax by expanding the standard deduction for married couples only and increasing the width of the 15 percent bracket, again for married couples only. According to Carasso and Steuerle's [2002] calculations, the 2001 law considerably reduced marriage penalties for most married households. However, marriage penalties still exist, and they tend to be highest when both spouses have similar earnings.

Analyzing the Marriage Tax

The economist surveying this scene is likely to ask the usual two questions—is it equitable and is it efficient? Much of the public debate focuses on the equity issue: Is it fairer to tax individuals or families? One argument favoring the family is that it allows a fairer treatment of nonlabor income (dividends, interest, profits). There are fears that with individual filing, high-earning spouses would transfer property to their mates to lower family tax bills (so-called bedchamber transfers of property). It is difficult to predict the extent to which this would take place. The view implicit in these fears is that property rights within families are irrelevant. However, given current high rates of divorce, turning property over to a spouse just for tax purposes may be a risky strategy, and there is no strong evidence that such transfers would occur in massive amounts.

The family can also be defended as the appropriate unit of taxation on a more philosophical level. As the late John Cardinal O'Connor put it, "Marriage matters supremely to every person and every institution in our society" [Allen, 1998, p. A1]. However, opponents of family-based taxation argue that it leads to serious conceptual problems, if for no other reason than it is hard to determine just what constitutes a family. For example, if married couples are taxed on their joint income, should the same approach be applied to two brothers who share a home or a daughter who takes care of an elderly father? Must the relationship be defined by blood or marriage so that, for example, same-sex couples or members of a commune are excluded?

Clearly, beliefs concerning the choice of the fairest taxable unit are influenced by value judgments and by attitudes toward the role of the family in society. The debate continues to be lively. Indeed, family-based income taxation has recently been subjected to legal challenge. A man filed a suit in federal Tax Court arguing that he was entitled to file a joint return with another man with whom he had an "economic partnership." The judge ruled that the use of marriage as a criterion for determining tax liability is "constitutionally valid" [Herman, 2000, p. A1].

When we turn to the efficiency aspects of the problem, one question is whether the marriage tax distorts individuals' behavior. The tax system changes the "price of marriage," and anecdotes about postponed marriage, divorce, or separation for tax reasons are common. From a statistical point of view, however, it is hard to make a very strong case that the marriage tax substantially distorts decisions related to marriage. Alm and Whittington [2003] find a negative relationship between the likelihood that a cohabiting couple marries and the size of their subsequent marriage penalty, but the magnitude of the effect is very small.

An efficiency concern that is easier to document surrounds the impact of joint filing on labor supply decisions. Chapter 16 stated that because married women tend to have more elastic labor supply schedules than their husbands, efficient taxation requires taxing wives at a lower rate. Under joint filing, both spouses face identical marginal tax rates on their last dollars of income. Hence, joint filing is inefficient.

It is hard to imagine Congress implementing separate income tax schedules for wives and husbands. This does not mean, however, that it is impossible to make family taxation more efficient. One possible reform would be simply to eliminate joint filing and have all people file as individuals. This would not only enhance efficiency, but it would also be more marriage neutral than the current system. A number of other nations, including Canada, have opted for this approach.[25]

Unfortunately, individual filing would lead to a violation of principle 2: equal taxation of families with equal incomes. This brings us back to where we started. No tax system can satisfy all three criteria, so society must decide which have the highest priority.

▶ TREATMENT OF INTERNATIONAL INCOME

We now turn to the tax treatment of individual income that is earned abroad. Such income is potentially of interest to the tax authorities of the citizen's home and host governments. US law recognizes the principle that the host country has the primary right to tax income earned within its borders. At the same time, the United States adheres to the notion that an American citizen, wherever he or she earns money, has a tax obligation to the native land. To avoid double taxation of foreign source income, the United States taxes income earned abroad, but allows a credit for tax paid to foreign governments.[26] Suppose that Ophelia's US tax liability on her income earned in Germany is $7,000, and she had paid $5,500 in German income taxes. Then Ophelia can take a $5,500 credit on her US tax return, so she need pay only $1,500 to the Internal Revenue Service. A US citizen's total tax liability, then, is based on *global* income.

Global versus Territorial Systems   The philosophical premise of the US system is that equity in taxation is defined on a citizenship basis. If you are a US citizen, your total tax liability should be roughly independent of whether you earn

---

[25] However, in the Canadian system, the primary income earner in a household can receive a nonrefundable tax credit for a spouse who has earned little or no income.

[26] The credit cannot exceed what the US tax on the foreign income would have been.

global system

A system under which an individual is taxed on income whether it is earned in the home country or abroad.

territorial system

A system under which an individual earning income in a foreign country owes taxes only to the host government.

your income at home or abroad. We refer to this as a **global system.** In contrast, virtually every other country adheres to a **territorial system**—a citizen earning income abroad need pay tax only to the host government. Which system is better? It is hard to say which is superior on either equity or efficiency grounds. We now expand on the problem.

Equity John, a citizen of the United Kingdom, and Sam, a US citizen, both work in Hong Kong and have identical incomes. Because the United Kingdom has a territorial system, John pays tax only to Hong Kong. Sam, on the other hand, also owes money to the United States (provided that his US tax bill is higher than his Hong Kong tax payment). Thus, Sam pays more tax than John, even though they have the same income. Although a global system produces equal treatment for citizens of the same country, it can lead to different treatments for citizens of different countries. Should horizontal equity be defined on a national or world basis? Each principle has some merit, but in general, no system of international tax coordination can satisfy both.

Efficiency A global system may distort international production decisions. Suppose that American firms operating abroad have to pay the US income tax for their American employees. Dutch firms, which operate under the territorial system, have no analogous obligation. Other things being the same, then, the US companies may end up paying more for their labor, and hence be at a cost disadvantage.[27] Dutch firms could conceivably win more contracts than the American firms, even if the latter are more technologically efficient.

On the other hand, a territorial system can distort a different decision—where people locate. Citizens of a given country may find their decision to work abroad influenced by the fact that their tax liability depends on where they live. Under a global regime, you cannot escape your country's tax collector unless you change citizenship. Hence, there is less incentive to relocate just for tax purposes.

Thus, the global system may distort production decisions, and the territorial system residential decisions. It is hard to know which distortion creates a larger efficiency cost.

▶ STATE INCOME TAXES

The role of individual income taxes in state revenue systems has been growing rapidly.[28] In 1960, 12.2 percent of state tax collections were from individual income taxes; by 2005, the figure was 34 percent [US Bureau of the Census, 2009, p. 278]. Presently, 34 states and the District of Columbia have broad-based individual income taxes that include wages. Two additional states tax interest and dividends, but not wages.

State income taxes tend to be similar in structure to the federal tax. The tax base is found by subtracting various deductions and exemptions from gross income, and tax liability is determined by associating a marginal tax rate with each of several income brackets. The marginal rates are much lower than those of the federal system.

---

[27] This assumes (a) the incidence of the US tax falls on employers rather than employees, and (b) American companies cannot respond simply by hiring foreign workers. The validity of assumption (a) depends on the elasticity of supply of US workers to US firms abroad. To the extent the supply curve is not horizontal, employees bear part of the tax. (See Chapter 14.)

[28] Income taxes are generally not of much importance for local governments, although in some of the larger cities, they play a significant role.

Among the states that levied income taxes in 2009, the highest bracket rates were mostly in the 8 to 10 percent range. (The maximum was 10.3 percent in California.) The states differ considerably with respect to rules governing deductions and exemptions. Some rule out practically all deductions, while others follow rules similar to the federal system.

It is important not to neglect the effect of state income taxes when assessing overall marginal tax rates. The marginal tax rate facing a Californian in the highest tax bracket is 35 percent from the federal tax and then another 10.3 percent from the California income tax, or a total of 45.3 percent. If the individual itemizes her deductions and subtracts state and local taxes, the effect is muted a bit, but the fact is that the cumulative marginal tax rates in high-tax states approach 50 percent.

▶ POLITICS AND TAX REFORM

Our discussion of the income tax has revealed a number of features that are hard to justify on the basis of either efficiency or equity. A natural question is why is improving the tax system so difficult? One reason is that in many cases, even fairly disinterested experts disagree about what direction reform should take. For example, we noted earlier that despite a consensus among economists that differentially taxing various types of capital income is undesirable, there is dispute about how this should be remedied. What one person views as a reform can be perceived by another as a turn for the worse.

Another difficulty is that attempts to change specific provisions encounter fierce political opposition from those whom the changes will hurt. State government officials, for example, lobby ferociously whenever proposals to limit the deductibility of state income taxes are floated. Chapter 6 discussed some theories suggesting that in the presence of special-interest groups, the political process can lead to inefficient expenditure patterns. The same theories might explain the difficulties involved in attempts to improve the tax system.

Organized lobbies are not the only impediments to reform. In many cases, once a tax provision is introduced, ordinary people modify their behavior on its basis and are likely to lose a lot if it is changed. For example, many families purchase larger houses than they otherwise would because mortgage interest and property taxes are deductible. Presumably, if these provisions were eliminated, housing values would fall. Homeowners would not take this lying down. Certain notions of horizontal equity suggest it is unfair to change provisions that have caused people to make decisions that are costly to reverse (see Chapter 16).

In any case, the history since 1986 suggests that a tax system with relatively low rates and a broad base is not stable politically. What are the prospects for a return to the principles of TRA86? Many observers believe that to the extent there are future changes in the tax law, the tendency will be to build additional preferences into the tax code, eroding the tax base and complicating the system further. As Congressman Charles Rangel quipped, critics of the status quo like to "talk about pulling the tax code up by the roots, but every year, they just add more fertilizer to it." This is because a stable and simple tax code is not in the interest of politicians: A major function of the tax system is "enabling legislators (and presidents) to raise campaign funds by inserting or removing loopholes in our present obscenely complicated code" [Friedman, 1998]. We conclude that one cannot be optimistic about the possibilities for improvement.

Note that all of our discussion of reform of the status quo has assumed that we would continue to use income as the tax base. Some observers have argued that any tax system based on income is bound to be seriously flawed. Chapter 21 discusses this radical critique of the income tax and its implications for tax policy.

Summary

- Computing federal individual income tax liability has three major steps: measuring total income (adjusted gross income), converting total income to taxable income, and calculating taxes due.

- A traditional benchmark measure of income is the Haig-Simons definition: Income during a given period is the net change in the individual's power to consume.

- Implementation of the Haig-Simons criterion is confounded by several difficulties: (1) Income must be measured net of the expenses of earning it. (2) Unrealized capital gains and the imputed income from durable goods are not easily gauged. (3) It is difficult to measure the value of in-kind receipts.

- Critics of the Haig-Simons criterion argue that it guarantees neither fair nor efficient outcomes.

- The US income tax base excludes (1) interest on state and local bonds, (2) employer contributions to pension and medical plans, (3) gifts and inheritances.

- Exemptions are fixed amounts per family member. Exemptions are subtracted from adjusted gross income (AGI) and phased out at high-income levels.

- Deductions are either standard or itemized. A standard deduction reduces taxable income by a fixed amount.

- Itemized deductions are permitted for expenditures on particular goods and services. They are phased out at high-income levels. Itemized deductions change after-tax relative prices, which often affects economic behavior.

- Major itemized deductions in the US tax code include (1) unreimbursed medical expenses in excess of 7.5 percent of AGI, (2) state and local income and property taxes, (3) certain interest expenses, (4) charitable contributions.

- Tax expenditures are the revenues forgone due to preferential tax treatment.

- The final step in determining tax liability is to apply a schedule of rates to taxable income. Because of various phaseouts, the actual statutory marginal tax rates exceed the official rates.

- The alternative minimum tax (AMT) was designed to make sure that high-income taxpayers who heavily utilize tax shelters would pay at least some federal income tax. However, due to certain structural flaws, it could soon be the tax system confronting millions of middle-class Americans.

- Bracket widths, personal exemptions, the standard deduction, and the earned income credit are now indexed against inflation. However, there are no provisions to correct for inflation's effect on the taxation of capital income.

- No system of family taxation can simultaneously achieve increasing marginal tax rates, marriage neutrality, and equal taxes for families with equal incomes. Under current law, joint tax liabilities may increase or decrease upon marriage, depending on the couple's circumstances.

- The United States follows a global system with respect to the tax treatment of income earned in other countries. The total amount of tax due is supposed to be roughly independent of whether the income is earned at home or abroad.

- Income tax systems are important as revenue raisers for the states. State income taxes have lower rates than the federal system and vary widely in their exact provisions.

Discussion Questions

1. Under current law, if your capital losses exceed your capital gains, you can deduct as much as $3,000 of losses against other forms of income. In the wake of massive declines in the stock market, in 2009 Senator Orrin Hatch suggested that figure be increased. Evaluate this proposal from the viewpoint of the Haig-Simons criterion. That is, would the proposal lead to an income tax base that is closer to or farther from the Haig-Simons ideal than the status quo?

2. In 2007, Bahram Akradi, the chairman of a firm called Life Time Fitness, received $31,777 from the company for his home cell-phone plan, wireless card, and Internet connectivity. According to the Haig-Simons definition of income, how should this benefit be treated for tax purposes? What difficulty do you see in devising a consistent system for determining whether such benefits should be taxable?

*3. Singh, who has a federal personal income tax rate of 28 percent, holds an oil stock that appreciates in value by 10 percent each year. He bought the stock one year ago. Singh's stockbroker now wants him to switch the oil stock for a gold stock that is equally risky. Singh has decided that if he holds on to the oil stock, he will keep it only one more year and then sell it. If he sells the oil stock now, he will invest all the (after-tax) proceeds of the sale in the gold stock and then sell the gold stock one year from now. What is the minimum rate of return the gold stock must pay for Singh to make the switch? Relate your answer to the lock-in effect.

*Difficult

4. The 2009 tax law included the Making Work Pay tax credit, which is a refundable tax credit equal to the lesser of 6.2 percent of a person's earned income or $400 ($800 for married couples). The credit phases out between $75,000 and $95,000 of adjusted gross income ($150,000 and $190,000 for married couples). How does this tax credit influence effective marginal tax rates in the phaseout range?

5. Li's marginal tax rate is 35 percent, and he itemizes his tax deductions. How much is a $500 deduction worth to him? How much is a $500 tax credit worth to him?

6. Suppose that a typical taxpayer has a marginal personal income tax rate of 35 percent. The nominal interest rate is 13 percent, and the expected inflation rate is 8 percent.
   a. What is the real after-tax rate of interest?
   b. Suppose that the expected inflation rate increases by 3 percentage points to 11 percent, and the nominal interest rate increases by the same amount. What happens to the real after-tax rate of return?
   *c. If the inflation rate increases as in part b, by how much would the nominal interest rate have to increase to keep the real after-tax interest rate at the same level as in part a? Can you generalize your answer using an algebraic formula?

*Difficult

7. In 2009, President Obama proposed limiting the rate at which itemized deductions can reduce tax liability to 28 percent. What would this do to the price of charitable donations for an itemizing taxpayer in the 35 percent tax bracket? If the price elasticity of demand for donations is 1.0, how would this affect charitable donations by itemizers?

8. In 2009, President Obama proposed an increase in the tax rates on dividends and capital gains. Would these changes make sense in terms of the Haig-Simons definition of income? What effects do you think these changes will have on behavior?

9. Suppose that Kentucky decides to subject interest earned by its residents from out-of-state municipal bonds to the state income tax, but to exempt from state income taxes any interest earned from Kentucky municipal bonds. What effect will this have on the before-tax interest rate paid by Kentucky municipal bonds? Does the Kentucky Treasury lose more or less tax revenue than the interest savings to its residents? What effect will this have on the net earnings for people in Illinois who own Kentucky municipal bonds?

10. The purpose of this problem is to determine how effective marginal tax rates are affected by the itemized deduction and personal exemption phaseouts.

a. Consider a family of four whose AGI places it in the exemption phaseout range, and whose taxable income places it in the 35 percent tax bracket.

i. In the absence of the phaseout, how much are the family's exemptions?

ii. Now suppose the family's income increases by $2,500. Given a 35 percent bracket, by how much does its tax liability increase?

iii. By how much does the increase in income reduce the family's exemptions? By how much does this increase the family's taxable income?

iv. By how much does the increase in taxable income increase their tax liability, given that they are in the 35 percent bracket?

v. Combine your answers from parts ii and iv to find the effective marginal tax rate. (Divide the change in tax liability by the $2,500 change in income.)

b. Now consider a different family whose AGI places it in the deduction phaseout range, and the family itemizes its tax deductions. Suppose the family receives another $100 of before-tax income.

i. Assuming a 35 percent marginal tax rate, what is the change in tax liability?

ii. What happens to the family's allowable itemized deductions and taxable income?

iii. How does the change in taxable income affect the family's tax liability?

iv. What is the family's effective marginal tax rate?

11. You will need a calculator for this problem. Sanchez earns $4,000, and she wants to save it for retirement, which is 10 years away. She can either save it in a taxable account or put it into a Roth IRA. Suppose that Sanchez can receive an annual rate of return of 8 percent and her marginal tax rate is 25 percent. By the time she reaches retirement, how much money would she have in either option? [Note: Sanchez has to pay tax on the $4,000, so she cannot put the full amount either into the taxable account or the Roth IRA.]

Chapter Eighteen

Personal Taxation and Behavior

If you are out to describe the truth, leave elegance to the tailor.

—ALBERT EINSTEIN

During the 1980s, the top statutory marginal income tax rate in the United States fell from 70 percent to 28 percent. During the 1990s, it went back up to 39.6 percent, but in 2001 it was reduced to 35 percent. The most recent reductions in tax rates are set to expire. Some believe that these cuts should be made permanent, and others say that we should revert back to higher rates. Central to the debate is the question of how taxes affect economic behavior. Those who favor lower taxes argue that high income taxes are bad for incentives to work, save, and take risks:

> People respond to incentives. You don't make economic policy for nations, you make it for people. . . . [Y]ou can't expect an economy to grow when people don't have the incentive to work, or when entrepreneurs lack the incentive to take a chance [Prescott, 2005a, p. A10].

The proponents of higher taxes respond that such objections are exaggerated. Taxes are like the weather: People talk about them a lot, but don't do anything about them.

Economists are just as interested in this issue as politicians. The theory of taxation tells us, after all, that both the incidence and efficiency of a tax system depend on how it affects behavior. As shown in Chapter 17, the income tax affects incentives for myriad decisions—everything from the purchase of medical services to the amount of charitable donations. We focus on four particularly important topics that have been studied intensively—the effects of taxation on labor supply, saving, housing consumption, and portfolio decisions.

► LABOR SUPPLY

In 2007, about 146 million Americans worked an average of about 34 hours per week and received total compensation of roughly $7.8 trillion, approximately 64 percent of national income [*Economic Report of the President, 2009*, pp. 316, 327, 340]. How labor supply is determined and whether taxes affect it are the issues to which we now turn.

Figure 18.1
Utility-maximizing choice of leisure and income
This individual maximizes utility at point E_1, where he works FT hours and earns OG.

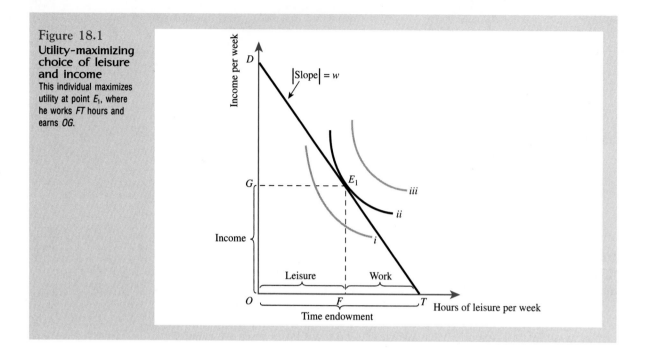

Theoretical Considerations

Hercules is deciding how much of his time to devote each week to work and how much to leisure. Chapter 13 showed how to analyze this choice graphically. To review the main points from that discussion:

time endowment

The maximum number of hours an individual can work during a given period.

- The number of hours available for market work and nonmarket uses ("leisure") is referred to as the **time endowment.** In Figure 18.1, it is distance OT on the horizontal axis. Assuming that all time not spent on leisure is devoted to market work, any point on the horizontal axis simultaneously indicates hours of leisure and hours of work.
- The budget constraint shows the combinations of leisure and income available to an individual given his or her wage rate. If Hercules's wage rate is $\$w$ per hour, then his budget constraint is a straight line whose slope in absolute value is w. In Figure 18.1, this is represented by line TD.
- The point on the budget constraint that is chosen depends on the individual's tastes. Assume that preferences for leisure and income can be represented by normal, convex-to-the-origin indifference curves. Three such curves are labeled i, ii, and iii in Figure 18.1. Hercules maximizes utility at point E_1, where he devotes OF hours to leisure, works FT hours, and earns income OG.

We are now in a position to analyze the effects of taxation. Suppose that the government levies a tax on earnings at rate t. The tax reduces the reward for working an hour from $\$w$ to $\$(1 - t)w$. When Hercules consumes an hour of leisure, he now gives up only $\$(1 - t)w$, not $\$w$. In effect, the tax reduces the opportunity cost of an hour of leisure. In Figure 18.2, the budget constraint facing Hercules is no longer TD. Rather, it is the flatter line, TH, whose slope in absolute value is $(1 - t)w$. The original income-leisure choice, E_1, is no longer attainable. Hercules must choose a

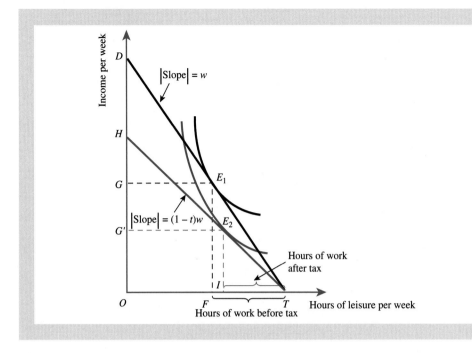

Figure 18.2

Proportional income tax decreasing hours of labor supplied

A tax on earnings at rate t reduces the opportunity cost of leisure and rotates the budget constraint to *TH*. For this individual, the substitution effect dominates the income effect—the tax decreases hours of work from *FT* to *IT*. After-tax income is *OG'*.

point somewhere along the after-tax budget constraint *TH*. In Figure 18.2, this is E_2, where he consumes *OI* hours of leisure, works *IT* hours, and has an after-tax income of *OG'*. The tax lowers Hercules's labor supply from *FT* hours to *IT* hours.

Can we therefore conclude that a "rational" individual *always* reduces labor supply in response to a proportional tax? To answer this question, consider Poseidon, who faces exactly the same before- and after-tax budget constraints as Hercules, and who chooses to work the same number of hours (*FT*) before imposition of the tax. As indicated in Figure 18.3, when Poseidon is taxed, he *increases* his hours of work from *FT* to *JT*. This is not "irrational." Depending on a person's tastes, he may want to work more, less, or the same amount after a tax is imposed.

The source of the ambiguity is the conflict between two effects generated by the tax, the **substitution effect** and the **income effect.** When the tax reduces the take-home wage, the opportunity cost of leisure goes down, and there is a tendency to substitute leisure for work. This is the substitution effect, and it tends to decrease labor supply. At the same time, for any number of hours worked, the tax reduces the individual's income. Assuming that leisure is a normal good, for any number of hours worked, this loss in income reduces the consumption of leisure, other things being the same. But a decrease in leisure means an increase in work. The income effect therefore tends to induce an individual to work more. Thus, the two effects work in opposite directions. It is simply impossible to know on the basis of theory alone whether the income effect or substitution effect dominates. For Hercules, shown in Figure 18.2, the substitution effect dominates. For Poseidon, shown in Figure 18.3, the income effect is more important. For a more general discussion of income and substitution effects, see the appendix at the end of this book.

The analysis of a progressive tax is very similar to that of a proportional tax. Suppose that Hercules is now confronted with increasing marginal tax rates: t_1 on his first $5,000 of earnings, t_2 on his second $5,000 of earnings, and t_3 on all income above $10,000. (Note the similarity to the US income tax, which assigns a marginal

substitution effect

The tendency of an individual to consume more of one good and less of another because of a decrease in the price of the former relative to the latter.

income effect

The effect of a price change on the quantity demanded due exclusively to the fact that the consumer's income has changed.

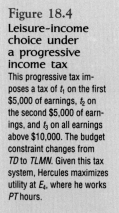

Figure 18.3
Proportional income tax increasing hours of labor supplied
For this individual, the income effect dominates the substitution effect—the tax increases work from *FT* to *JT* hours. After-tax income is *OK*.

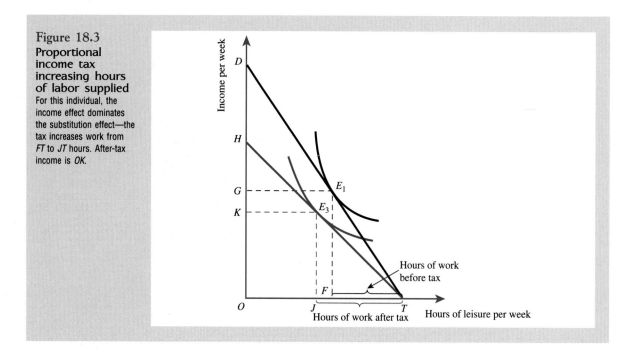

Figure 18.4
Leisure-income choice under a progressive income tax
This progressive tax imposes a tax of t_1 on the first $5,000 of earnings, t_2 on the second $5,000 of earnings, and t_3 on all earnings above $10,000. The budget constraint changes from *TD* to *TLMN*. Given this tax system, Hercules maximizes utility at E_4, where he works *PT* hours.

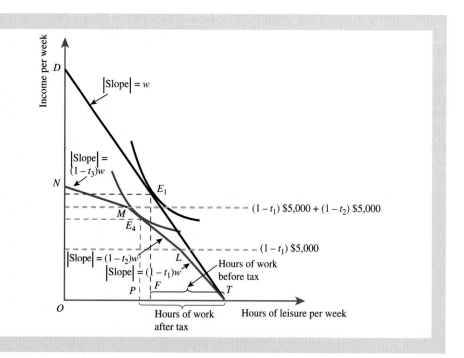

tax rate to each income bracket.) Again, the before-tax budget line is *TD*, which is depicted in Figure 18.4. After tax, the budget constraint is the kinked line *TLMN*. Up to $5,000 of before-tax income, the opportunity cost of an hour of leisure is $(1 - t_1)w$, which is the slope (in absolute value) of segment *TL*. At point *L*, Hercules's income is $(1 - t_1) \times \$5,000$. On segment *ML* the absolute value of the slope is $(1 - t_2)w$. *ML* is flatter than *TL* because t_2 is greater than t_1. At point *M*, after-tax income is $(1 - t_1) \times \$5,000 + (1 - t_2) \times \$5,000$; this is after-tax income at point L plus the increment to income after receiving an additional \$5,000 that is taxed at rate t_2. Finally, on segment MN the slope is $(1 - t_3)w$, which is even flatter. Depending on his preferences, Hercules can end up anywhere on $TLMN$. In Figure 18.4, he maximizes utility at E_4 where he works PT hours.

EMPIRICAL EVIDENCE
How Does Labor Supply Respond to Taxes?

Knowing the elasticity of labor supply with respect to the after-tax wage is critical for assessing the impact of taxes on work effort. If labor supply is very elastic, then an increase in the tax rate substantially reduces hours of work. If it is inelastic, then hours of work don't change very much. Indeed, our theoretical analysis indicates that it's even possible for a tax on earnings to increase hours of work. Only empirical work can resolve this theoretical ambiguity.

Eissa [2001] used a quasi-experimental analysis to estimate the elasticity of labor supply for one particularly important group of workers, married women. The Tax Reform Act of 1986 (TRA86) reduced the top marginal tax rate by 44 percent, but reduced marginal tax rates at the lower end of the distribution by much less. Recall from Chapter 17 that a married person's marginal tax rate depends on total family income, including the earnings of his or her spouse. In effect, then, TRA86 generated a natural experiment in which the treatment group consisted of women married to very high earners (who saw a substantial drop in their tax rates) and the control group consisted of women married to moderate earners (who experienced little or no reduction in their tax rates). Eissa found that after TRA86 went into effect, the women in the treatment group did in fact increase their hours of work relative to the women in the control group. Using a difference-in-differences approach, she estimated a labor supply elasticity of 0.8. In terms of our theoretical model, this implies that for married women, the substitution effect of an increase in after-tax wages dominates the income effect.

Taken as a whole, the empirical literature suggests the following:

- For males between the ages of roughly 20 and 60, the effect of changes in the net wage on hours of work is small in absolute value and is often statistically insignificant. An elasticity of about 0.05 seems a sensible estimate.

- The hours of work and labor force participation decisions of married women seem to be quite sensitive to changes in the net wage, although the degree of responsiveness has become smaller over time. A reasonable estimate of their labor supply elasticity would be about 0.4 [Blau and Kahn, 2005].

Some Caveats

The theoretical and empirical results just described are certainly more useful than the uninformed guesses often heard in political debates. Nevertheless, we should be aware of some important qualifications.

Demand-Side Considerations   The preceding analyses ignore effects that changes in the supply of labor might have on the demand side of the market. Suppose that taxes on married women were lowered in such a way that their net wages increased by 10 percent. With a labor supply elasticity of 0.4, their hours of work would increase by 4 percent. If firms could absorb all of these hours at the new net wage, that would be the end of the story. More typically, such an increase in labor supply lowers the *before*-tax wage. This mitigates the original increase in the *after*-tax wage, so that the final increase in hours of work is less than originally guessed.

The situation becomes even more complicated when we realize major changes in work decisions could influence consumption patterns in other markets. For example, if married women increased their hours of work, the demand for child care would probably increase. To the extent this raised the price of child care, it might discourage some parents of small children from working, at least in the short run. Clearly, it is complicated to do a "general equilibrium" analysis that traces through the implications for all markets. Most investigators are willing to assume that the first-round effects are a reasonable approximation to the final result.

Individual versus Group Effects   Our focus has been on how much an individual works under alternative tax regimes. It is difficult to use such results to predict how the total hours of work supplied by a *group* of workers will change. When the tax schedule changes, incentives change differently for different people. For example, in a move from a proportional to a progressive tax, low-income workers may find themselves facing lower marginal tax rates while just the opposite is true for those with high incomes. The labor supplies of the two groups might move in opposite directions, making the overall outcome difficult to predict. A further complication is that the labor supply elasticity might vary by income level.

Human Capital   The number of hours worked annually is an important and interesting indicator of labor supply. But the effective amount of labor supplied by an individual depends on more than the number of hours elapsed at the workplace. A highly educated, healthy, well-motivated worker presumably is more productive than a counterpart who lacks these qualities, even if they both work the same number of hours. Some have expressed fears that taxes induce people to invest too little in the acquisition of skills. Economic theory yields surprising insights into how taxes might affect the accumulation of **human capital**—investments that people make in themselves to increase their productivity.

human capital

The investments that individuals make in education, training, and health care that raise their productive capacity.

Consider Hera, who is contemplating entering an on-the-job training program. Suppose that over her lifetime, the program increases Hera's earnings by an amount whose present value is B. However, participation in the program reduces the time currently available to Hera for income-producing activity, which costs her C in forgone wages. If she is sensible, Hera makes her decision using the investment criterion described in Chapter 8 and enters the program only if the benefits exceed the costs:

$$B - C > 0 \qquad (18.1)$$

Now suppose that Hera's earnings are taxed at a proportional rate t. The tax takes away some of the higher wages earned by virtue of participation in the training program. One might guess that the tax therefore lowers the likelihood of her participation. This reasoning is misleading. To see why, assume for the moment that after the tax Hera continues to work the same number of hours as she did before. The tax does indeed reduce the training program's benefits from B to $(1 - t)B$. But at the same time, it reduces the costs. Recall that the costs of the program are the forgone wages. Because these wages would have been taxed, Hera gives up not C, but only $(1 - t)C$. The decision to enter the program is based on whether after-tax benefits exceed after-tax costs:

$$(1 - t)B - (1 - t)C = (1 - t)(B - C) > 0 \qquad (18.2)$$

A glance at Equation (18.2) indicates that it is exactly equivalent to (18.1). Any combination of benefits and costs that was acceptable before the earnings tax is acceptable afterward. In this model, a proportional earnings tax reduces benefits and cost in the same proportion and therefore has no effect on human capital investment.

A key assumption here is that labor supply is constant after the tax is imposed. Suppose instead that Hera increases her supply of labor. (The income effect dominates.) In this case, the tax leads to an increase in human capital accumulation. In effect, labor supply is the utilization rate of the human capital investment. The more hours a person works, the greater the payoff to an increase in the wage rate from a given human capital investment. Therefore, if the tax induces more work, it makes human capital investments more attractive, other things being the same. Conversely, if the substitution effect predominates so that labor supply decreases, human capital accumulation is discouraged.

This simple model ignores several considerations:

- The returns to a human capital investment cannot be known with certainty. As shown later in this chapter, risky returns complicate the analysis of taxation.

- Some human capital investments involve costs other than forgone earnings. College tuition, which is not tax deductible, is an obvious example.

- Other aspects of the tax system can affect human capital investments. For example, increased taxes on the returns to physical investments (for example, interest and dividends) tend to increase human capital investment. In effect, one can view physical and human capital as two alternative investment vehicles; increasing the tax on one enhances the relative attractiveness of the other.

- Equation (18.2) assumes a proportional tax. When the tax system is progressive, the benefits and costs of human capital investments may be taxed at different rates.

However, complicating the model by taking such considerations into account just confirms the basic result—from a theoretical point of view, the effect of earnings taxation on human capital accumulation is ambiguous. Unfortunately, little empirical work on this important question is available.

The Compensation Package

The basic theory of labor supply assumes that the hourly wage is the only reward for working. In reality, employers often offer employees a compensation package that includes not only wages but also health benefits, pensions, "perks" such as access to a company car, in-house sports facilities, and so on. As we noted in Chapter 17, most of the nonwage component of compensation is not taxed. When marginal tax rates fall, the relative attractiveness of untaxed forms of income declines, and vice versa. Hence, changes in taxes might affect the composition of the compensation package. Some evidence exists that this is the case. For example, according to Gruber and Lettau [2004], for each 10 percent rise in the tax subsidy to health insurance, the number of firms offering insurance coverage increases by about 3 percent.

Figure 18.5
Tax rates, hours of work, and tax revenue
Given labor supply curve S_L, tax revenues first increase, and then decrease, as the tax rate increases.

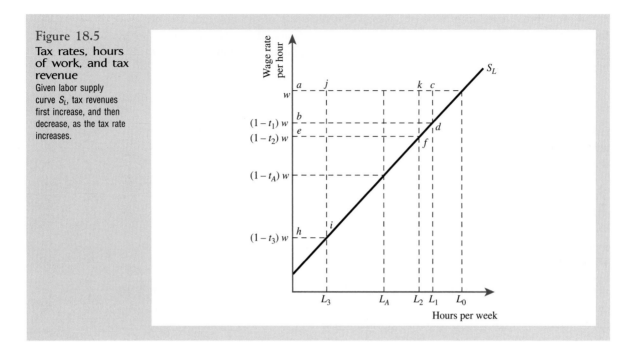

The Expenditure Side
The standard analysis of labor supply and taxation ignores the disposition of the tax receipts. However, at least some of the revenues are used to purchase public goods, the availability of which can affect work decisions. If the tax money is used to provide recreational facilities such as national parks, we expect the demand for leisure to increase, other things being the same. On the other hand, expenditure on child care facilities for working parents might increase labor supply. Ideally, we should examine the labor supply consequences of the entire budget, not just the tax side. For example, Rogerson [2007] observes that even though tax rates are higher in Scandinavian countries than in the rest of Europe, labor supply is also higher. He argues that the reason is that Scandinavian governments spend relatively more on items such as family services.

Labor Supply and Tax Revenues
So far, our emphasis has been on finding the labor supply associated with any given tax regime. We now explore the related issue of how tax collections vary with the tax rate.

Consider the supply curve of labor S_L depicted in Figure 18.5. It shows the optimal amount of work for each after-tax wage, other things being the same. As it is drawn, hours of work increase with the net wage—the substitution effect dominates. The before-tax wage, w, is associated with L_0 hours of work. Obviously, since the tax rate is zero, no revenue is collected. Now suppose a proportional tax at rate t_1 is imposed. The net wage is $(1 - t_1)w$, and labor supply is L_1 hours. Tax collections are equal to the tax per hour worked (*ab*) times the number of hours worked (*ac*), or rectangle *abdc*. Similar reasoning indicates that if the tax rate were raised to t_2, tax revenues would be *eakf*. Area *eakf* exceeds *abdc*—a higher tax rate leads to greater revenue collections. Do government revenues always increase when the tax rate goes up? No. For example, at tax rate t_3, revenues *haji* are less than those at the lower

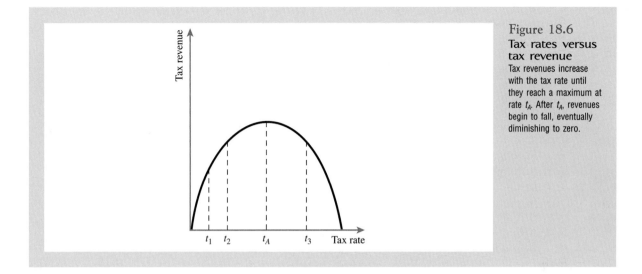

Figure 18.6
Tax rates versus tax revenue
Tax revenues increase with the tax rate until they reach a maximum at rate t_A. After t_A, revenues begin to fall, eventually diminishing to zero.

rate t_2. Although the tax collected *per hour* is very high at t_3, the number of hours falls so much that the product of the tax rate and hours is fairly low. Indeed, as the tax rate approaches 100 percent, people stop working altogether and tax revenues fall to zero.

All of this is summarized compactly in Figure 18.6, which shows the tax rate on the horizontal axis and tax revenue on the vertical. At very low tax rates, revenue collections are low. As tax rates increase, revenues increase, reaching a maximum at rate t_A. For rates exceeding t_A, revenues begin to fall, eventually diminishing to zero. Note that it would be absurd for the government to impose any tax rate exceeding t_A, because tax rates could be reduced without the government losing any revenue.

Hard as it may be to believe, Figure 18.6 is at the center of an ongoing political controversy. This is largely due to the well-publicized assertion by economist Arthur B. Laffer [1979] that the United States operates to the right of t_A. In the popular press, the tax rate–tax revenue relationship is known as the **Laffer curve.** The notion that tax rate reductions create no revenue losses was an important tenet of the supply-side economics espoused by the Reagan administration, and it continues to play an important role in policy debates. For example, in the 2008 presidential election, Senator John McCain said, "Tax cuts, . . . , as we all know, increase revenues."

The popular debate surrounding the Laffer curve has been confused and confusing. A few points are worth making:

Laffer curve

A graph of the tax rate–tax revenue relationship.

- In our simple model, whether tax revenues rise or fall when the tax rate changes is determined by the extent to which changes in hours worked offset the change in the tax rate. This is precisely the issue of the elasticity of labor supply investigated by public finance economists. Hence, the shape of a Laffer curve is determined by the elasticity of labor with respect to the net wage.

- Some critics of supply-side economics argue that the very idea that tax rate reductions can lead to increased revenue is absurd. However, the discussion surrounding Figure 18.6 suggests that in principle, lower tax rates can indeed lead to higher revenue collections.

- It is therefore an empirical question whether or not the economy is actually operating to the right of t_A. As noted earlier, the consensus among economists who have studied taxes and labor supply is that the overall elasticities are modest in size. It is safe to conclude that the economy is not operating to the right of t_A. General tax rate reductions are unlikely to be self-financing in the sense of unleashing so much labor supply that tax revenues do not fall. However, some economists have estimated that European countries are actually quite close to the peak of the Laffer curve [Uhlig and Trabandt, 2006.]

- Changes in labor supply are not the only way in which increased tax rates can affect tax revenues. As noted, people can substitute nontaxable forms of income for wages when tax rates go up, so that even with a fixed supply of labor, tax revenues can fall. In the same way, people (especially those with high incomes) can substitute nontaxable forms of capital income such as municipal bond interest for taxable forms of capital income. Or individuals may cheat more when tax rates increase. Based on a survey of the literature, Feldstein [2008a] concludes that tax rates have a substantial impact on taxable income. For middle- and high-income taxpayers, he estimates that the elasticity of taxable income with respect to the tax rate is about 0.5. This estimate implies, for example, that reducing the marginal tax rate on a typical high-income individual from 40 percent to 30 percent would increase her taxable income by more than 12 percent. Thus, the decrease in revenue would be less than if there were no behavioral response. On the other hand, the tax decrease would not be self-financing.

- Even if tax revenues fail to increase when tax rates fall, it does not mean that tax rate reduction is necessarily undesirable. As emphasized in previous chapters, determination of the optimal tax system depends on a wide array of social and economic considerations. Those who believe that the government sector is too large would presumably be quite happy to see tax revenues reduced.

▶ SAVING

A second type of behavior that may be affected by taxation is saving. Most modern analysis of saving decisions is based on the **life-cycle model,** which was introduced in Chapter 11 and says that individuals' consumption and saving decisions during a given year are the result of a planning process that considers their lifetime economic circumstances. The amount you save each year depends not only on your income that year but also on the income that you expect in the future and the income you received in the past. This section uses the life-cycle model to explore the impact of taxes on saving decisions.

life-cycle model

The theory that individuals' consumption and saving's decisions during a given year are based on a planning process that considers lifetime circumstances.

Consider Scrooge, who expects to live two periods: "now" (period 0) and the "future" (period 1). Scrooge has an income of I_0 dollars now and knows that his income will be I_1 dollars in the future. (Think of "now" as "working years," when I_0 is labor earnings; and the "future" as retirement years, when I_1 is fixed pension income.) His problem is to decide how much to consume in each period. When Scrooge decides how much to consume, he simultaneously decides how much to save or borrow. If his consumption this period exceeds his current income, he must borrow. If his consumption is less than current income, he saves.

The first step in analyzing the saving decision is to depict the possible combinations of present consumption (c_0) and future consumption (c_1) available to Scrooge—his intertemporal budget constraint. In Chapter 11, we made the following observations about the intertemporal budget constraint:

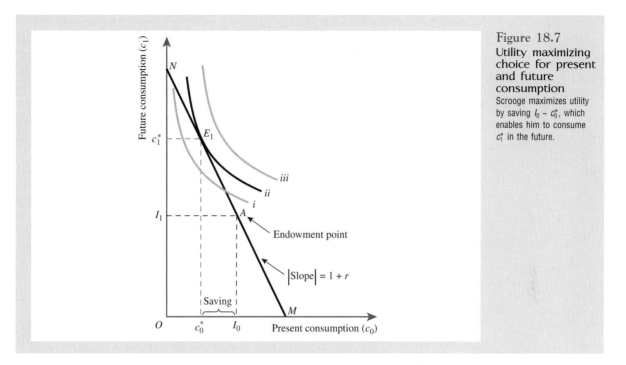

Figure 18.7
Utility maximizing choice for present and future consumption
Scrooge maximizes utility by saving $I_0 - c_0^*$, which enables him to consume c_1^* in the future.

- One option available to Scrooge is to consume all his income just as it comes in—to consume I_0 in the present and I_1 in the future. This bundle is called the endowment point. The intertemporal budget constraint must pass through the endowment point.

- Provided that the individual can borrow and lend at an interest rate of r, the constraint is a straight line whose slope in absolute value is $1 + r$.[1]

Scrooge's budget constraint is drawn as MN in Figure 18.7; note that it runs through the endowment point, A. To determine the choice along MN, we introduce Scrooge's preferences between future and present consumption, which are represented by conventionally shaped indifference curves in Figure 18.7. Under the reasonable assumption that more consumption is preferred to less consumption, curves farther to the northeast represent higher levels of utility.

Subject to budget constraint MN, Scrooge maximizes utility at point E_1, where he consumes c_0^* in the present and c_1^* in the future. With this information, it is easy to find how much Scrooge saves. Because present income, I_0, exceeds present consumption, c_0^*, then by definition the difference, $I_0 - c_0^*$, is saving.

Of course, this does not prove that it is always rational to save. If the highest feasible indifference curve had been tangent to the budget line below point A, present consumption would have exceeded I_0, and Scrooge would have borrowed. Although the following analysis of taxation assumes Scrooge is a saver, the same techniques can be applied if he is a borrower.

---

[1] To represent the budget line algebraically, note that the fundamental constraint facing Scrooge is that the present value of his consumption equals the present value of his income. (See Chapter 8 for an explanation of present value.) The present value of his consumption is $c_0 + c_1/(1 + r)$, while the present value of his income stream is $I_0 + I_1/(1 + r)$. Thus, his selection of c_0 and c_1 must satisfy $c_0 + c_1/(1 + r) = I_0 + I_1/(1 + r)$. The reader can verify that viewed as a function of c_0 and c_1, this is a straight line whose slope is $-(1 + r)$ and that passes through the point (I_0, I_1).

We now consider how the amount of saving changes when a proportional tax on interest income is introduced.[2] In this context, it is important to specify whether payments of interest by borrowers are deductible from taxable income. Before the Tax Reform Act of 1986, interest payments generally were deductible. Under current law, however, it is not safe to assume that a particular taxpayer is allowed to deduct interest payments. It depends, among other things, on whether he or she is a homeowner. (See Chapter 17 for details.) We therefore analyze the effect on saving both with and without deductibility.

Case I: Deductible Interest Payments and Taxable Interest Receipts

How does the budget line in Figure 18.7 change when interest is subject to a proportional tax at rate t, and interest payments by borrowers are deductible? Figure 18.8 reproduces the before-tax constraint MN from Figure 18.7. The first thing to note is that the after-tax budget constraint must also pass through the endowment point (I_0, I_1), because interest tax or no interest tax, Scrooge always has the option of neither borrowing nor lending.

Next, observe that the tax reduces the rate of interest received by savers from r to $(1 - t)r$. Therefore, the opportunity cost of consuming a dollar in the present is only $[1 + (1 - t)r]$ dollars in the future. At the same time, for each dollar of interest Scrooge pays, he can deduct \$1 from taxable income. This is worth \$$t$ to him in lower taxes. Hence, the effective rate that has to be paid for borrowing is $(1 - t)r$. Therefore, the cost of increasing current consumption by one dollar, in terms of future consumption, is only $[1 + (1 - t)r]$ dollars. Together, these facts imply that the after-tax budget line has a slope (in absolute value) of $[1 + (1 - t)r]$.

The budget line that passes through (I_0, I_1) and has a slope of $[1 + (1 - t)r]$ is PQ in Figure 18.8. As long as the tax rate is positive, it is flatter than the pretax budget line MN.

To complete the analysis, we draw in indifference curves. The new optimum is at E^t, where present consumption is c_0^t, and future consumption is c_1^t. As before, saving is the difference between present consumption and present income, distance $c_0^t I_0$. Note that $c_0^t I_0$ is less than $c_0^* I_0$, the before-tax amount that was saved. The interest tax thus lowers saving by distance $c_0^* c_0^t$.

However, saving does not always fall. For a counterexample, consider Figure 18.9. The before- and after-tax budget lines are identical to their counterparts in Figure 18.8, as is the before-tax equilibrium at point E_1. But the new tangency occurs at point $\tilde{E}$, to the left of E_1. Consumption in the present is $\tilde{c}_0$, and in the future, $\tilde{c}_1$. In this case, a tax on interest actually increases saving, from $c_0^* I_0$ to $\tilde{c}_0^* I_0$. Thus, depending on the individual's preferences, taxing interest can either increase or decrease saving.

The ambiguity arises because of the conflict between two different effects. On one hand, taxing interest reduces the opportunity cost of present consumption, which tends to increase c_0 and lower saving. This is the substitution effect, which comes about because the tax changes the price of c_0 in terms of c_1. On the other hand, the fact that interest is being taxed makes it harder for a lender to achieve any future consumption goal. This is the income effect, which arises because the tax lowers real income. If present consumption is a normal good, a decrease in income lowers c_0,

---

[2] We could consider an *income* tax that includes wages as well as interest, but this would complicate matters without adding any important insights.

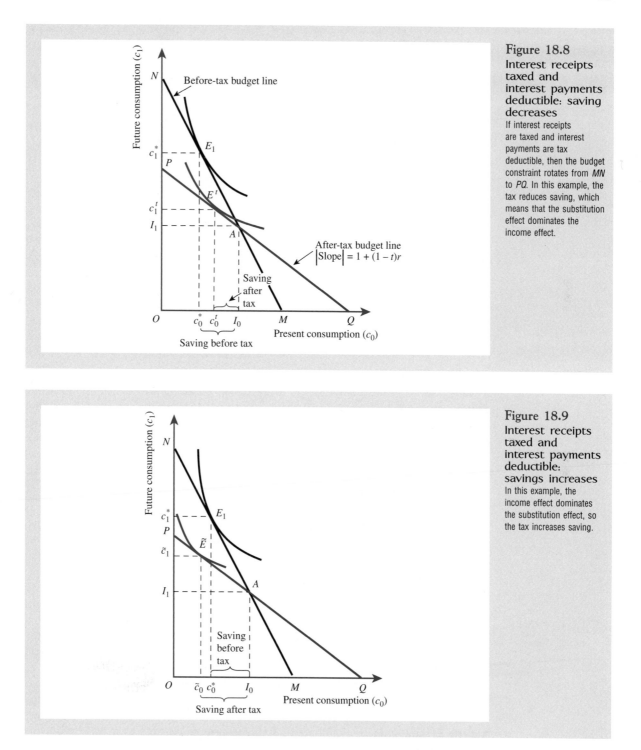

Figure 18.8
Interest receipts taxed and interest payments deductible: saving decreases
If interest receipts are taxed and interest payments are tax deductible, then the budget constraint rotates from MN to PQ. In this example, the tax reduces saving, which means that the substitution effect dominates the income effect.

Figure 18.9
Interest receipts taxed and interest payments deductible: savings increases
In this example, the income effect dominates the substitution effect, so the tax increases saving.

and hence raises saving. Just as in the case of labor supply, whether the substitution or income effect dominates cannot be known on the basis of theory alone.

If the notion that a rational person might actually increase her saving in response to an increased tax on interest seems bizarre to you, consider the extreme case of

Figure 18.10
Interest receipts taxed and interest payments nondeductible
If interest receipts are taxed, but interest payments are not tax deductible, then the budget constraint changes from *MN* to *PAM*.

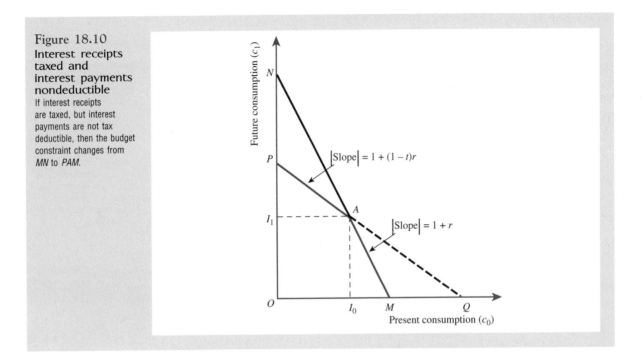

a "target saver," whose only goal is to have a given amount of consumption in the future—no more and no less. (Perhaps she wants to save just enough to pay her children's future college tuition.) If the tax rate goes up, then the only way for her to reach her target is to increase saving, and vice versa. Thus, for the target saver, saving and the after-tax interest rate move in opposite directions.

Case II: Nondeductible Interest Payments and Taxable Interest Receipts

We now consider how the budget constraint changes when interest is taxed at rate t, but borrowers cannot deduct interest payments from taxable income. Figure 18.10 reproduces the before-tax budget constraint MN from Figure 18.7. As was true for Case I, the after-tax budget constraint must include the endowment point (I_0, I_1). Now, starting at the endowment point, suppose Scrooge decides to save \$1, that is, move \$1 to the left of point A. Because interest is taxed, this allows him to increase his consumption next period by $[1 + (1 - t)r]$ dollars. *To the left of point A, then, the opportunity cost of increasing present consumption by \$1 is* $[1 + (1 - t)r]$ dollars of future consumption. Therefore, the absolute value of the slope of the budget constraint to the left of point A is $[1 + (1 - t)r]$. This coincides with segment PA of the after-tax budget constraint in Figure 18.9.

Now suppose that starting at the endowment point, Scrooge decides to borrow \$1, that is, move \$1 to the right of point A. Because interest is nondeductible, the tax system does not affect the cost of borrowing. Thus, the cost to Scrooge of borrowing the \$1 now is $(1 + r)$ dollars of future consumption, just as it was before the interest tax. Hence, *to the right of point A the opportunity cost of increasing present consumption by a dollar is* $(1 + r)$ dollars. This coincides with segment AM of the before-tax budget constraint MN.

Putting all this together, we see that when interest receipts are taxable but interest payments are nondeductible, the intertemporal budget constraint has a kink at the endowment point. To the left of the endowment point, the absolute value of the slope is $[1 + (1 - t)r]$; to the right, it is $(1 + r)$. What is the impact on saving? If Scrooge was a borrower before the tax was imposed, he is not affected. That is, if Scrooge maximized utility along segment AM before the tax was imposed, he also does so after. On the other hand, if Scrooge was a saver before the tax, his choice between present and future consumption must change, because points on segment NA are no longer available to him. However, just as in the discussion surrounding Figures 18.8 and 18.9, we cannot predict whether Scrooge will save more or less. It depends on the relative strengths of the income and substitution effects.

Some Additional Considerations   This simple two-period model ignores some important real-world complications:

- The analysis, as usual, is couched in real terms—it is the *real* net rate of return that governs behavior. As was emphasized in Chapter 8, care must be taken to correct the *nominal* rates of return observed in the market for inflation.

- In the model there is one asset for saving, and the returns to saving are taxed at a single rate. In reality, there are numerous assets, each with its own before-tax rate of return. Moreover, as observed in Chapter 17, the returns to different assets are taxed at different rates. It is therefore an oversimplification to speak of how changes in "the" after-tax rate of return influence saving.

- The model focuses only on private saving. For many purposes, the important variable is *social saving*, defined as the sum of government and private saving. For example, if the government were to save a sufficiently high proportion of tax receipts from an interest tax, social saving could go up even if private saving decreased.

- Some investigators have questioned the validity of the life-cycle model itself. The life-cycle hypothesis posits that people are forward looking; critics argue that a more realistic assumption is that people are myopic. The life-cycle model also assumes that people can borrow and lend freely at the going rate of interest; critics point out that many people are not able to borrow. Of course, neither the proponents of the life-cycle view nor its detractors need be 100 percent correct. At any given time, some families' saving behavior may be explained by the model, while others' saving behavior may be myopic or constrained.

Despite the controversies surrounding the life-cycle hypothesis, most economists are willing to accept it as a pretty good approximation to reality.

EMPIRICAL EVIDENCE

The Effect of Taxation on Saving

The basic result of our theoretical analysis is that the effect of taxation on individual saving is ambiguous and must therefore be assessed with empirical research. To do so, researchers have generally been forced to rely on observational studies in which the quantity of saving is the dependent variable and the independent variables are the after-tax rate of return to saving, disposable income, and other variables that might plausibly affect saving. If the coefficient on the rate of return is positive, the conclusion is that increases in taxes depress saving, and vice versa.

Unfortunately, this approach faces many challenges. For example, it is likely that changes in the rate of return are correlated with changes in people's expectations about future economic conditions, which are not easy to measure. However, changes in expected economic conditions could very well exert an independent effect on the amount people save. Hence, any relationship in the data between saving and the after-tax rate of return might be driven by expectations about future economic activity, and not really tell us anything about the impact of taxes.

Another problem with observational studies relates to the measurement of the rate of return variable. People are motivated by the *real* rate of return, not the *nominal* rate of return. Computing the real market return therefore requires subtracting the *expected* inflation rate from the observed nominal market rate. Presumably, people's expectations are based on past experience plus anticipation of the future, but no one knows exactly how expectations are formed. Studies using alternative methods for computing expected inflation rates can come to different conclusions.

These and other problems have prevented economists from reaching a firm consensus on how taxes affect saving. Given these caveats, the research presented by the Joint Committee on Taxation [2005] suggests that a reasonable estimate of the long-run savings elasticity is about 0.29.

Tax-Preferred Savings Accounts

As noted in Chapter 17, certain taxpayers are allowed to save in a variety of tax-preferred savings accounts. Although Keogh accounts, 401(k) plans, and the traditional Individual Retirement Accounts (IRAs) differ in their details, they share certain key attributes: The funds deposited into them accumulate at the before-tax rate of interest, and the maximum amounts that can be deposited in any given year are limited by law. A perennial issue in tax policy debates is whether the contribution limits should be increased: Should people be allowed to save more in tax-preferred accounts?

The central question in debates over such proposals is whether contributions to these accounts represent new saving, or whether people simply deposit money that otherwise would have been saved in some other form. Different investigators have come to very different conclusions on this issue. The basic problem is that it is hard to determine whether differences in people's saving behavior are due to differences in tastes or due to the presence of tax-preferred saving accounts. Suppose, for example, that over time we observe that some people increase both their tax-preferred assets and their other assets. One investigator might say, "This proves that tax-preferred accounts represent new saving, because tax preferred assets grew without diminishing other assets." Another investigator could respond, "Nope. All that is going on is that these people have a strong taste for saving, and over time they increase their holdings of all kinds of assets." While the empirical literature is mixed, a study by Benjamin [2003] suggests that tax-favored saving options stimulate at least some new saving.

The discussion so far has assumed that the administrative details of tax-preferred savings accounts are irrelevant. Consider two possible scenarios. In the first, your boss says that she will set up a 401(k) account for you. [Recall from Chapter 17 that a 401(k) plan is a kind of tax-preferred savings account similar to a traditional IRA.] All you have to do is fill out a form requesting her to do so. In the second scenario, your boss says that she will set up a 401(k) account for you unless you fill out a form requesting her not to do so. Conventional economic theory suggests that the outcomes in the two scenarios should be identical—you figure out whether or not you want the 401(k) and make your decision. The default option is irrelevant. However, work by Beshears et al. [2006] suggests that the way in which the options are presented has a major effect. In one company, for example, when eligible employees were automatically enrolled in a 401(k) plan, participation after three months was 35 percentage points higher than when employees had to ask to be included in the plan. After two years, participation was 25 percentage points higher under automatic enrollment compared to requested enrollment. Thus, defaults appear to exert an important effect on saving behavior, and this should be taken into account in the design of saving incentives. More generally, these results suggest that to understand saving behavior, it may be necessary to go beyond conventional economic models and take into account insights from psychology that are often ignored by economists.

Taxes and the Capital Shortage

The taxation of capital income is a major political issue. Much of the debate centers on the proposition that by discouraging saving, the tax system has led to a *capital shortage*—insufficient capital to meet our national "needs."

A major problem with this line of reasoning is that, as we have just shown, it is not at all obvious that taxation reduces the supply of saving. Let us assume, for the sake of argument, that saving indeed declines because of taxes. Nevertheless, as long as the capital market is competitive, a decrease in saving does not create a gap between the demand for investment funds and their supply. Instead, the interest rate adjusts to equate quantities supplied and demanded. However, it is true that the new equilibrium will, other things being equal, involve a lower rate of investment, possibly leading to lower productivity growth.

But to look only at these issues is misleading. Taxation of *any* factor may reduce the equilibrium quantity. The important efficiency question is whether taxation of capital income leads to larger excess burdens than other ways of raising tax revenues. We defer to Chapter 21 a discussion of whether economic efficiency would be enhanced if taxes on capital were eliminated. In the meantime, we note that there is no reason a high rate of investment alone is a desirable objective. In a utilitarian framework, at least, capital accumulation is a means of enhancing individual welfare, not an end in itself.

Finally, the entire argument that saving incentives can increase the capital stock rests on the premise that investment in the economy depends on its own rate of saving: All national saving is channeled into national investment. This is true in an economy that is closed to international trade. In an open economy, however, domestic saving can be invested abroad. This means that tax policy designed to stimulate saving may not lead to more domestic investment. To the extent that saving flows freely across national boundaries to whatever investment opportunities seem most attractive, the ability of tax policy to stimulate investment through saving is greatly diminished.

Empirical studies indicate that countries with high domestic saving tend to have high domestic investment, and vice versa. While the data are open to other interpretations, this suggests that saving may not flow into and out of the economy as freely as one would expect in a completely integrated world capital market [Kho et al., 2006]. As long as saving and domestic investment are correlated, tax policy that affects saving can generally be expected to affect investment. The size of the effect, however, is smaller than one would find in a totally closed economy.

▶ HOUSING DECISIONS

When people talk of a capital shortage, they are usually concerned with the amount of capital available to businesses for producing goods. Another very important form of capital is owner-occupied housing. A tax code can have little impact on the overall level of saving yet still significantly affect the allocation of saving across different types of investment. This section discusses how the tax code favors investment in housing. This issue is of particular importance given that some believe that the financial crisis that began in 2008 was caused, in part, by tax-induced overinvestment in housing.

The effects of the income tax on housing investment can best be illustrated with an example. Macbeth owns a house and decides to rent it out. What is his net income? He receives rent from his tenants, but also has to incur some operating expenses such as making repairs. Call R his rent less these operating expenses. Suppose that Macbeth took out a mortgage to buy the house, and his yearly interest payments are I. These interest payments are a business expense, and need to be subtracted from R to find net income. Finally, suppose that the house increases in value during the course of the year by ΔV. This is a capital gain, which is also a component of income. (If the house goes down in value, then ΔV is negative; i.e., a capital loss reduces income.) Putting all of this together, Macbeth's net income as a landlord, R_{net}, is

$$R_{net} = R - I + \Delta V$$

Under a tax system based on conventional Haig-Simons principles, R_{net} is added into Macbeth's taxable income.

Now suppose that instead of renting the house, Macbeth and his wife move into it themselves. By virtue of living in the house, they receive a benefit equal to the market rental value of the house, while still incurring the operating expenses and mortgage interest payments and getting the capital gain. That is, they receive an *imputed* net rent on the home equal to R_{net}. Whether they live in the house or not, they receive a net benefit of R_{net}; the only difference is that when they rent out the house they explicitly receive the rent in cash, while if they live in the house they effectively pay it to themselves. But implicit or not, it is still income, and under a Haig-Simons income tax, it should be taxed. However, under US law, the implicit rent that people receive on their homes is not included in the tax base, and for most households, housing capital gains are exempt from taxation.[3] By excluding imputed rent from homeownership from the tax base, the tax system in effect subsidizes owner-occupied housing.

Recall from Chapter 17 that homeowners who itemize their deductions can deduct mortgage interest and property tax payments on their tax returns. These deductions lowered tax revenues by about $92 billion in 2008 [Joint Committee on Taxation, 2008]. However, the deductibility of mortgage interest and property taxes is not the fundamental source of the subsidy to homeownership. Indeed, if imputed rent were included in the tax base, then mortgage interest and property taxes would be legitimate deductions, because they would be construed as expenses of earning this

---

[3] The law provides a $250,000 exclusion on the capital gain on the sale of a principal residence ($500,000 in the case of a joint return).

rental income. The basic issue is the failure to include imputed rent in the tax base in the first place.

By excluding net imputed rent from taxation, in effect the tax code lowers the price of owning a home and increases the demand for owner-occupied housing. Based on calculations in Poterba and Sinai [2008], eliminating the exclusion of net imputed rent from taxation would increase the cost of owner-occupied housing by about 12.5 percent for middle-income families. Assuming that the long-run price elasticity of demand for housing is about −1.0, this would induce a 12.5 percent decrease in the quantity consumed.

The implicit subsidy affects not only how much housing people purchase but also whether they become owners or renters in the first place. At the end of World War II, 48 percent of US households resided in owner-occupied housing; the figure is now about 68 percent [US Department of Housing and Urban Development and US Department of Commerce, 2008]. Over this period, many taxpayers were moving into higher tax brackets, enhancing the attractiveness of the implicit subsidy to owner occupation. Of course, other factors were changing that might have influenced housing patterns; for example, incomes rose considerably. However, a variety of studies indicate that tax considerations have played an important part in the growth of homeownership [Gervais, 2002].

Proposals for Change

In Chapter 5 under "Positive Externalities," we discussed the pros and cons of providing a subsidy for owner-occupied housing. The point made there was that from an externality point of view, the subsidy does not have strong support. Although there is some evidence that homeowners are more likely than renters to take care of their property, to garden, and so on, the positive externalities of living near homeowners are not large enough to justify the subsidy [Glaeser and Shapiro, 2003]. However, it is unclear whether homeownership really does generate positive externalities. As noted by economist James Poterba, "There's a pervasive problem in trying to sort out whether there is something intrinsic about homeownership that causes these externalities or whether the people that become homeowners are the kind of people that generate these externalities" [quoted in Porter, 2005].

Further, the subsidy's value increases with income—73 percent of the tax expenditures associated with the deduction of mortgage interest go to households whose incomes exceed $100,000 [Joint Committee on Taxation, 2008, p. 76]. Hence, one can hardly claim that it equalizes the income distribution. The subsidy is also concentrated geographically—California homeowners receive between 19 and 22 percent of the gross benefits of the aggregate tax preference [Sinai and Gyourko, 2004]. In addition, some argue that the tax advantages for homeownership provided incentives for families to take on risky mortgages, thus contributing to the housing and financial crisis of 2008 and 2009. In light of these facts, a number of proposals have been made to reform the federal tax treatment of housing. Probably the most radical change would be to include net imputed rent in taxable income. Such a move might create administrative problems, because the authorities would have to determine the potential market rental value of each house. Nevertheless, a portion of imputed rental income is taxed in some European countries, such as Belgium and The Netherlands.

Taxing imputed rent does not appear politically feasible. Homeowners are more likely to perceive their houses as endless drains on their financial resources than as revenue producers. It would not be easy to convince homeowners—who comprise more than half the electorate—that taxing imputed rental income is a good idea.

Several reform proposals have focused on reducing the value of mortgage interest and property tax deductions to upper-income individuals. One possibility would be simply to disallow these deductions. While elimination of the property tax deduction has appeared on the legislative agenda in the past, it has never come anywhere near being enacted. Further, no serious politician has even whispered about completely removing the mortgage interest subsidy.

An alternative to eliminating the property tax and mortgage interest deductions would be to put upper limits on the dollar amounts that can be deducted. Another possibility, which was recommended by the President's Advisory Panel on Federal Tax Reform [2005], would be to convert the mortgage interest deduction into a credit: Each homeowner would be allowed to subtract 15 percent of mortgage interest payments from tax liability. While a deduction has a greater value to a household the higher its marginal tax rate, with a credit those with higher marginal tax rates would not enjoy an advantage, other things being the same. For example, under the current system, a person who pays $1,000 in mortgage interest reduces his tax liability by $350 if he is in the 35 percent tax bracket, while a person in the 10 percent bracket with the same mortgage payment reduces his tax liability by only $100. Replacing the deduction with a 15 percent credit means that both these individuals would reduce their tax liability by the same amount, $150. This proposal has not received support from either political party. However, in 2009, President Obama proposed limiting the value of deductions for high-earners: Those in the 33 percent tax bracket or higher would only receive a 28 percent deduction.

Evaluating these proposals is difficult because it is not clear what their objectives are and what other policy instruments are assumed to be available. For example, if a more equal income distribution is the goal, why bother with changing from deductions to credits? It would make more sense just to adjust the rate schedule appropriately.

Finally, we note that much of the debate over the tax treatment of housing implicitly assumes that full taxation of imputed rent would be the most efficient solution. Recall from the theory of optimal taxation (Chapter 16) that if lump sum taxes are excluded, the efficiency-maximizing set of tax rates is generally a function of the elasticities of demand and supply for all commodities. Only in very special cases do we expect efficiency to require equal rates for all sources of income. On the other hand, it is also highly improbable that the efficient tax rate on imputed rental income is zero. Determining the appropriate rate is an important topic for further research.

▶ PORTFOLIO COMPOSITION

Taxes may affect not only the total amount of wealth that people accumulate but the assets in which that wealth is held as well. A popular argument is that low taxes (especially on capital gains) encourage investment in risky assets. As an editorial in the *Wall Street Journal* [2001, p. A18] argued, "high marginal tax rates . . . discourage incentives . . . to take risks." This proposition seems plausible. Why take a chance on a risky investment if your gains are going to be grabbed by the tax collector? However, the problem is considerably more complicated than this line of argument suggests.

Most modern theoretical work on the relationship between taxes and portfolio composition is based on the path-breaking analysis of Tobin [1958]. In Tobin's model, individuals make their decisions about whether to invest in an asset on the basis of two characteristics—the expected return on the asset, and how risky that return is. Other things being the same, investors prefer assets that are expected to yield high returns. At the same time, investors dislike risk; other things being the same, investors prefer safer assets.

Suppose there are two assets. The first is perfectly safe but it yields a zero rate of return. (Imagine holding money in a world with no inflation.) The second is a bond that *on average* yields a positive rate of return, but it is risky—there is some chance that the price will go down, in which case the investor incurs a loss.

The investor can adjust the return and risk on the entire portfolio by holding different combinations of the two assets. In one extreme case he or she could hold only the safe asset—there is no return, but no risk. On the other hand, the investor could hold only the risky asset—his or her expected return rises, but so does the risk involved. The typical investor holds a combination of both the risky and safe assets to suit tastes concerning risk and return.

Now assume a proportional tax is levied on the return to capital assets. Assume also the tax allows for **full loss offset**—individuals can deduct all losses from taxable income. (To some extent, this reflects actual practice in the United States; see Chapter 17.) Because the safe asset has a yield of zero, the tax has no effect on its rate of return—the return is still zero. In contrast, the risky asset has a positive expected rate of return, which is lowered by the presence of the tax. The tax seems to reduce the attractiveness of the risky asset compared to the safe asset.

However, at the same time that the tax lowers the return to the risky asset, it lowers its riskiness as well. Why? In effect, introduction of the tax turns the government into the investor's silent partner. If the investor wins (in the sense of receiving a positive return), the government shares in the gain. But because of the loss-offset provision, if the individual loses, the government also shares in the loss. Suppose, for example, that an individual loses $100 on an investment. If the tax rate is 35 percent, by subtracting $100 from taxable income, she lowers her tax bill by $35. Even though the investment lost $100, the investor loses only $65. In short, introduction of the tax tightens the dispersion of returns—the highs are less high and the lows are less low—and hence, reduces the risk. Thus, although the tax makes the risky asset *less* attractive by reducing its expected return, it simultaneously makes it *more* attractive by decreasing its risk. If the second effect dominates, taxation can on balance make the risky asset more desirable.

Resolving this ambiguity econometrically is very difficult. A major problem is that it is hard to obtain reliable information on just which assets people hold. Individuals may not accurately report their holdings to survey takers because they are not sure of the true values at any point in time. Alternatively, people might purposely misrepresent their asset positions because of fears that the information will be reported to the tax authorities. In one study using a fairly reliable data set, Poterba and Samwick [2003] found that other things (including total wealth) being the same, people in higher tax brackets have a higher probability of holding common stock, which is quite risky. This finding lends at least tentative support to the notion that taxation increases risk taking. But the issue is far from resolved.

full loss offset

Allowing individuals to deduct from taxable income all losses on capital assets.

▶ A NOTE ON POLITICS AND ELASTICITIES

Despite much investigation, the effect of income taxation on several important kinds of behavior is not known for sure. Different experts are therefore likely to give policymakers different pieces of advice. In this situation, it is almost inevitable that policymakers will adopt those behavioral assumptions that are most consistent with their goals. Although it is dangerous to generalize, liberals tend to believe that behavior is not very responsive to the tax system, while conservatives take the opposite view. Liberals assume low elasticities because they can raise large amounts of money for public sector activity without having to worry too much about charges that they are "killing the goose that laid the golden egg." In contrast, conservatives assume high elasticities because this limits the volume of taxes that can be collected before serious efficiency costs are imposed on the economy. Thus, when journalists, politicians, and economists make assertions about how taxes affect incentives, one should evaluate their claims in light of what their hidden agendas might be.

Summary

- The US personal income tax affects many economic decisions, including labor supply, saving, residential housing consumption, and portfolio choice. Analysis of the behavioral effects of taxation is among the most contentious of all areas of public policy.

- Econometric studies of labor supply indicate prime age males vary their hours only slightly, if at all, in response to tax changes, while hours of married women are more sensitive to variations in the after-tax wage rate.

- Earnings taxes can increase, decrease, or leave unchanged the amount of human capital investments. The outcome depends in part on how taxes affect hours of work.

- The effect of tax rates on tax revenues depends on the responsiveness of labor supply to changes in tax rates and on the extent of substitution between taxable and nontaxable forms of income.

- The effect of taxes on saving may be analyzed using the life-cycle model, which assumes that people's annual consumption and saving decisions are influenced by their lifetime resources. Taxing interest income lowers the opportunity cost of present consumption and thereby creates incentives to lower saving. However, such a tax reduces total lifetime resources, which tends to reduce present consumption, that is, increase saving. The net effect on saving is an empirical question.

- Econometric studies of saving behavior have foundered on both conceptual and practical difficulties. As a result, there is no firm consensus of opinion on the effects of taxation on saving.

- The personal income tax excludes the imputed rent from owner-occupied housing from taxation. This increases both the percentage of those choosing to own their homes and the quantity of owner-occupied housing.

- The theoretical effects of taxation on portfolio composition are ambiguous. Taxes reduce the expected return on a risky asset but also lessen its riskiness. The net effect of these conflicting tendencies has not been empirically resolved.

Discussion Questions

1. Most economists believe that a reduction in all statutory federal income tax rates in the United States would be unlikely to generate an increase in tax revenues. However, a recent study suggests that this might not be the case for the tax systems in certain cities [see Haughwout et al., 2004]. Why might a reduction in tax rates be more likely to increase revenues at the city level rather than the federal level?

2. Suppose that individuals view their loss of income from income taxes as offset by the benefits of public services purchased with the

revenues. How are their labor supply decisions affected? (Hint: Decompose the change in hours worked into income and substitution effects.)

3. Under current law, employer-provided health care benefits are excluded from taxation. Use an indifference curve analysis to model the impact of eliminating the exclusion upon the amount of health care benefits. (Hint: Think of an individual as consuming two commodities, "health care benefits" and "all other goods.")

4. During the 2008 presidential campaign, Senator Obama proposed eliminating the income tax for all seniors earning less than $50,000. Seniors making above this threshold would still be subject to the income tax, which could potentially mean a tax liability of thousands of dollars. Sketch a budget constraint in a leisure-income diagram that is consistent with this proposal. If this proposal were adopted, what would happen to the labor supply for seniors?

5. According to Feldstein [2008b], "only about 10% to 20%" of a one-time tax rebate provided to taxpayers in 2008 was spent immediately. Using the life-cycle model of Figure 18.7, explain why this result could have been predicted. (Hint: Think about how a one-time rebate affects the endowment point and budget constraint in Figure 18.7. Contrast this to how a permanent rebate affects the endowment point and budget constraint.)

6. According to Nobel laureate Ed Prescott, "increasing tax rates [in Europe] will not increase revenue" [Prescott, 2004b]. What assumptions must hold in order for this statement to be correct?

7. In the face of reduced interest rates, one financial columnist gave the following advice: "To compensate for such modest returns, aim to save even more every month" [Clements, 2003]. Use the life-cycle model to evaluate whether a rational person would follow this advice. If

so, what does it imply about the shape of the individual's supply curve of saving?

8. One of your authors received the following message in an e-mail from a student: "An individual who owns the house he lives in forgoes receiving rent from a tenant. This forgone rent represents an opportunity cost to the homeowner and therefore should not be taxed based on the Haig-Simons definition of income." Evaluate this statement.

9. Recall from Chapter 13 that the earned income tax credit (EITC) provides a credit to low-income individuals, with the size of the subsidy first increasing, and then decreasing, with the level of earnings. One pundit suggested a "family-friendly" change in the tax law, under which the EITC would be replaced with a large increase in the child tax credit, which reduces tax liability a certain amount for each child in the household. Show how this change would affect the budget constraint facing a low-income household. How would labor supply be affected?

10. In an economy, the supply curve of labor, S, is given by

$$S = -100 + 200w_n$$

where w_n is the after-tax wage rate. Assume that the before-tax wage rate is fixed at 10.

a. Write a formula for tax revenues as a function of the tax rate, and sketch the function in a diagram with the tax rate on the horizontal axis and tax revenues on the vertical axis. [Hint: Note that $w_n = (1 - t)10$, where t is the tax rate, and that tax revenues are the product of hours worked, the gross wage, and the tax rate.] Suppose that the government currently imposes a tax rate of 70 percent. What advice would you give it?

b. Try this problem if you know some calculus: At what tax rate are tax revenues maximized in this economy?

THE CORPORATION TAX

I'll probably kick myself for having said this, but when are we going to have the courage to point out that in our tax structure, the corporation tax is very hard to justify?

—PRESIDENT RONALD W. REAGAN

In 2007, about $7 trillion—or 51 percent of the Gross Domestic Product—originated in nonfinancial corporations [*Economic Report of the President, 2009*, p. 302]. A **corporation** is a form of business organization in which ownership is usually represented by transferable stock certificates. The stockholders have *limited liability* for the acts of the corporation. This means that their liability to the creditors of the corporation is limited to the amount they have invested.

Corporations are independent legal entities and as such are often referred to as artificial legal persons. A corporation may make contracts, hold property, incur debt, sue, and be sued. And just like any other person, a corporation must pay tax on its income. Corporation income tax revenues account for about 14 percent of federal tax collections [*Economic Report of the President, 2009*, p. 379]. This chapter explains the structure of the federal corporation income tax and analyzes its effects on the allocation of resources.

corporation

A state-chartered form of business organization, usually with limited liability for shareholders (owners) and an independent legal status.

▶ WHY TAX CORPORATIONS?

Let's begin by addressing the question raised in President Reagan's quotation above: Does it make sense to have a special tax system for corporations in the first place? To be sure, from a *legal* point of view, corporations are people. But from an economic standpoint, this notion makes no sense. As we stressed in Chapter 14, only real people can pay a tax. If so, why should corporate activity be subject to a special tax? Why not just tax the incomes of the corporation *owners* via the personal income tax?

A number of justifications for a separate corporation tax have been proposed: First, contrary to the view just stated, corporations—especially very big ones—really are distinct entities. Large corporations have thousands of stockholders, and the managers of such corporations are controlled only very loosely, if at all, by the stockholders-owners. Most economists would certainly agree that ownership and control are separated in large corporations, and this creates important problems for understanding how corporations function. Nevertheless, it does not follow that the corporation should be taxed as a separate entity.

A second justification for corporate taxation is that the corporation receives a number of special privileges from society, the most important of which is limited liability of the stockholders. The corporation tax can be viewed as a user fee for this benefit. However, there is no reason to believe that the revenues paid approximate the benefits received. In any case, why should we regard laws that permit an efficient way for individuals to aggregate their capital as being a benefit that requires a payment? Laws that allow other kinds of contracts are not viewed in this way.

Finally, the corporation tax protects the integrity of the personal income tax. Suppose that Karl's share of the earnings of a corporation during a given year is $10,000. According to the economist's standard convention for defining income, this $10,000 is income whether the money happens to be retained by the corporation or paid out to Karl. If the $10,000 is paid out, it is taxed in an amount that depends on his personal income tax rate. In the absence of a corporation tax, the $10,000 creates no tax liability if it is retained by the corporation. Hence, unless corporation income is taxed, Karl can reduce his tax liability by accumulating income within the corporation. Of course, the money will be taxed when it is eventually paid out, but in the meantime, the full $10,000 grows at the before-tax rate of interest. Remember from Chapter 17, taxes deferred are taxes saved.

It is certainly true that not taxing corporate income creates opportunities for personal tax avoidance. But a special tax on corporations is not the only way to include earnings accumulated in corporations. We discuss an alternative method many economists view as superior at the end of this chapter.

▶ STRUCTURE

The corporate tax rate structure is graduated. The lowest bracket is 15 percent, and the highest bracket, which begins at $10 million of taxable income, is 35 percent.[1] Most corporate income is taxed at the 35 percent rate, so for our purposes, the system can safely be presented as a flat rate of 35 percent. This rate is low by historical standards. Before the Tax Reform Act of 1986, it was 46 percent. The act lowered the rate to 34 percent, and it was raised a point in 1993.

However, as in the case of the personal income tax, the statutory rate by itself gives relatively little information about the effective burden. We must know which deductions from before-tax corporate income are allowed. Accordingly, we now discuss the rules for defining taxable corporate income.[2]

Employee Compensation Deducted

As we saw in Chapter 17, a fundamental principle in defining personal income is that income should be measured net of the expenses incurred in earning it. The same logic applies to the measurement of corporate income. One important business expense is labor, and compensation paid to workers (wages and benefits) is excluded from taxable income.

Interest, but Not Dividends, Deducted

When corporations borrow, interest payments to lenders are excluded from taxable income. Again, the justification is that business costs should be deductible. However, when firms finance their activities by issuing stock, the dividends paid to

---

[1] In certain ranges, the effective marginal tax rate may exceed 35 percent.

[2] Note also that many of these rules apply to noncorporate businesses. Also, a corporate alternative minimum tax applies in certain cases.

the stockholders are *not* deductible from corporate earnings. We discuss the consequences of this asymmetry later.

Depreciation Deducted

Suppose that during a given year the XYZ Corporation makes two purchases: (1) $1,000 worth of stationery, which is used up within the year; and (2) a $1,000 air conditioner, which will last for 10 years. How should these two items be treated for purposes of determining XYZ's taxable income? The stationery case is fairly straightforward. Because it is entirely consumed within the year of its purchase, its entire value should be deductible from that year's corporate income, and the tax law does in fact allow such a deduction. The air conditioner is more complicated because it is a durable good. When the air conditioner is purchased, the transaction is merely an exchange of assets—the firm gives up cash in exchange for the air conditioner. The purchase of the asset *per se* is not an economic cost. However, as the air conditioner is used, it is subject to wear and tear, which decreases its value. This decrease in value, called **economic depreciation,** is an economic cost to the firm.

It follows that during the first year of the air conditioner's life, a consistent definition of income requires that only the economic depreciation experienced that year be subtracted from the firm's before-tax income. Similarly, the economic depreciation of the machine during its second year of use should be deductible from that year's gross income, and so on for as long as the machine is in service.

It is a lot easier to state this principle than to apply it. In practice, the tax authorities do not know exactly how much a given investment asset depreciates each year, or even what its useful life is. The tax law has rules that indicate for each type of asset what proportion of its acquisition value can be depreciated each year, and over how many years depreciation can be taken—the **tax life** of the asset. These rules often fail to reflect true economic depreciation. For example, there is some evidence that personal computers depreciate in value more rapidly than allowed by the tax rules [Doms et al., 2004].

economic depreciation

The extent to which an asset decreases in value during a period of time.

tax life

The number of years an asset can be depreciated.

Calculating the Value of Depreciation Allowances
How much is it worth to a firm to be able to depreciate an asset? Assume that the tax life of the $1,000 air conditioner is 10 years, and a firm is allowed to depreciate one-tenth of the machine's value each year. How much is this stream of depreciation allowances worth to the XYZ Corporation?

At the end of the first year, XYZ is permitted to subtract one-tenth of the acquisition value, or $100, from its taxable income. With a corporation income tax rate of 35 percent, this $100 deduction saves the firm $35. Note, however, that XYZ receives this benefit a year after the machine is purchased. The present value of the $35 is found by dividing it by $(1 + r)$, where r is the opportunity cost of funds to the firm. (See Chapter 8 if you need to review present value.)

At the end of the second year, XYZ is again entitled to subtract $100 from taxable income, which generates a saving of $35 that year. Because this saving comes two years in the future, its present value is $35/(1 + r)^2$. Similarly, the present value of depreciation taken during the third year is $35/(1 + r)^3$, during the fourth year, $35/(1 + r)^4$, and so on. The present value of the entire stream of depreciation allowances is

$$\frac{\$35}{1+r} + \frac{\$35}{(1+r)^2} + \frac{\$35}{(1+r)^3} + \cdots + \frac{\$35}{(1+r)^{10}}$$

For example, if $r = 10$ percent, this expression is equal to $215.10. In effect, then, the depreciation allowances lower the price of the air conditioner after taxes from $1,000 to $784.90 (= $1,000 − $215.10). Intuitively, the effective price is below the acquisition price because the purchase leads to a stream of tax savings in the future.

More generally, suppose that the tax law allows a firm to depreciate a given asset over T years, and the proportion of the asset that can be written off against taxable income in the nth year is $D(n)$. The $D(n)$ terms sum to 1, meaning that the tax law eventually allows the entire purchase price of the asset to be written off. [In the preceding example, T was 10, and $D(n)$ was equal to $\frac{1}{10}$ every year. Some depreciation schemes, however, allow $D(n)$ to vary by year.] Consider the purchase of an investment asset that costs $1. The amount that can be depreciated at the end of the first year is $D(1)$ dollars, the value of which to the firm is $\theta \times D(1)$ dollars, where θ is the corporation tax rate. [Because the asset costs $1, $D(1)$ is a fraction.] Similarly, the value to the firm of the allowances in the second year is $\theta \times D(2)$. The present value of all the tax savings generated by the depreciation allowances from a $1 purchase, which we denote ψ, is

$$\psi = \frac{\theta \times D(1)}{1+r} + \frac{\theta \times D(2)}{(1+r)^2} + \cdots + \frac{\theta \times D(T)}{(1+r)^T} \qquad (19.1)$$

Because ψ is the tax saving for one dollar of expenditure, it follows that if the acquisition price of an asset is q, the presence of depreciation allowances lowers the effective price to $(1 - \psi)q$. For example, a value of $\psi = 0.25$ indicates that for each dollar spent on an asset, 25 cents worth of tax savings are produced. Hence, if the machine cost $1,000 ($q = $1,000$), the effective price is only 75 percent of the purchase price, or $750.

Equation (19.1) suggests that the tax savings from depreciation depend critically on the value of T and the function $D(n)$. In particular, the tax benefits are greater: (1) The shorter the time period over which the machine is written off—the lower is T; and (2) The greater the proportion of the machine's value that is written off at the beginning of its life—the larger the value of $D(n)$ when n is small. Schemes that allow firms to write off assets faster than true economic depreciation are referred to as **accelerated depreciation.** An extreme possibility is to allow the firm to deduct from taxable income the asset's full cost at the time of acquisition. This is referred to as **expensing.**

accelerated depreciation

Allowing firms to take depreciation allowances faster than true economic depreciation.

Under current law, every depreciable asset is assigned one of eight possible tax lives (that is, values of T). The tax lives vary from 3 to 39 years. For example, certain racehorses are three-year property; most computers and business equipment are in the five-year class, while most nonresidential structures have a tax life of 31½ years. Generally, tax lives are shorter than actual useful lives. This has potential consequences for corporate investment behavior, which we discuss later.

expensing

Deducting the entire value of an asset in the computation of taxable income.

Intangible Assets: Take Me Out to the Ballgame   Our discussion of depreciation has assumed that the asset involved is tangible, like a printer or a truck. Similar issues arise in the context of intangible assets. Suppose that a company spends money on an advertising campaign. The campaign is expected to increase sales over a period of years. One can think of the advertising as an asset that is producing a stream of revenues over time, just like a machine. By analogy, then, the firm should be allowed to deduct only the depreciation of the advertising "asset" each year. Determining the appropriate depreciation schedules for such assets is a major headache for tax administrators.

A good example relates to the acquisition of baseball franchises. If you buy a baseball team, part of what you are buying is the contracts of the players. The tax authorities have ruled that the component of the acquisition cost that is attributable to player contracts is a depreciable asset, and can be depreciated (straight-line) over a five-year period. On the other hand, other components of the value of the franchise, such as television contracts, are not depreciable. Predictably, club owners are locked in perpetual battle with the Internal Revenue Service over the value of the player-component of acquisition costs—the owners want a large proportion of the cost allocated to player contracts while the IRS wants a small proportion. In addition, the IRS notes that most other intangibles are depreciated over a 15-year period rather than the 5 years for player contracts, and wants baseball treated like other businesses. These disputes take place in an environment in which it is difficult to determine the merits of the various arguments. In short, intractable complexities are involved in administering depreciation rules. However, dealing with depreciation is unavoidable with a tax based on income.

Investment Tax Credit

investment tax credit (ITC)

A reduction in tax liability equal to some portion of the purchase price of an asset.

Before 1986, the tax code included an **investment tax credit (ITC),** which permitted a firm to subtract some portion of the purchase price of an asset from its tax liability at the time the asset was acquired. If an air conditioner cost $1,000, and if the XYZ firm was allowed an investment tax credit of 10 percent, the purchase of an air conditioner lowered XYZ's tax bill by $100. The effective price of the air conditioner (before depreciation allowances) was thus $900. More generally, if the investment tax credit was k and the acquisition price was q, the effective price of the asset was $(1 - k)q$. In contrast to depreciation allowances, the value to the firm of an ITC did not depend on the corporate income tax rate. This was because the credit was subtracted from tax liability rather than taxable income. In the early 1980s, the credit for equipment was 6 or 10 percent (depending on its tax life).

The Tax Reform Act of 1986 eliminated the investment tax credit. However, a 2009 law introduced investment tax credits for investments in advanced energy technologies. Thus, k is now equal to zero for most, but not all, investments.

Treatment of Dividends versus Retained Earnings

So far we have been focusing on taxes directly payable by the corporation. For many purposes, however, the important issue is not the corporation's tax liability per se, but rather the total tax rate on income generated in the corporate sector. Understanding how the corporate and personal tax structures interact is important.

Corporate profits may either be retained by the firm or paid to stockholders in the form of dividends. Dividends paid are *not* deductible from corporation income and hence are subject to the corporation income tax. Further, until recently, dividends received by stockholders were treated as ordinary income and taxed at the individual's marginal income tax rate. In effect, then, such payments were taxed twice—once at the corporation level and again when distributed to the shareholder. Some movement in the direction of removing this **double taxation** of dividends was included in legislation passed in 2003, which set a maximal rate of 15 percent on dividends received at the individual level.

double taxation

Taxing corporate income first at the corporate level, and again when it is distributed to shareholders.

To assess the tax consequences to the stockholder of retained earnings is a bit more complicated. Suppose that XYZ retains $1 of earnings. To the extent that the stock market accurately values firms, the fact that the firm now has one more dollar causes the value of XYZ stock to increase by $1. But as we saw in Chapter 17, income generated by increases in the value of stock—capital gain—is treated preferentially for tax purposes. This is because the gain received by a typical XYZ stockholder is not taxed until it is realized, and even then the rate is relatively low. The tax system thus creates incentives for firms to retain earnings rather than pay them out as dividends.

Effective Tax Rate on Corporate Capital

We began this section by noting the statutory tax rate on capital income in the US corporate sector is currently 35 percent. Clearly, it would be most surprising if this were the effective rate as well. At the corporate level, computing the effective rate requires considering the effects of interest deductibility, depreciation allowances, and inflation. Moreover, as just noted, corporate income in the form of dividends and realized capital gains is also taxed at the personal level. Allowing for all these considerations, Djankov et al. [2008] estimate the effective tax rate on corporate capital income to be 32.0 percent. Compared to other developed nations, the United States is at the high end of the distribution, but not an extreme outlier. For example, the same study estimates that the effective rate in the United Kingdom is 21.4, in Germany 23.6, and in Japan 31.60.

Of course, any such calculation requires assumptions on items such as the appropriate choice of discount rate [r of Equation (19.1)], the expected rate of inflation, the extent of true economic depreciation, and so forth. Moreover, as we will see in the next section, the effective burden of the corporate tax depends in part on how investments are financed—by borrowing, issuing stock, or using internal funds. Investigators using other assumptions might generate somewhat different effective tax rates. It is unlikely, however, that alternative methods would much modify the difference between statutory and effective marginal tax rates.

▶ INCIDENCE AND EXCESS BURDEN

Understanding tax rules and computing effective tax rates is only the first step in analyzing the corporation tax. We still must determine who ultimately bears the burden of the tax and measure the costs of any inefficiencies it induces. The economic consequences of the corporation tax are among the most controversial subjects in public finance. An important reason for the controversy is disagreement with respect to just what kind of tax it is. We can identify several views.

A Tax on Corporate Capital

Recall from our discussion of the structure of the corporation tax that the firm is not allowed to deduct from taxable income the opportunity cost of capital supplied by shareholders. Since the opportunity cost of capital is included in the tax base, it appears reasonable to view the corporation tax as a tax on capital used in the corporate sector. In the classification scheme developed in Chapter 14, the corporation tax is a partial factor tax. This is the view that predominates in most writing on the subject.

In a model that examines effects in all markets ("general equilibrium"), the tax on corporate capital leads to a migration of capital from the corporate sector until after-tax rates of return are equal throughout the economy. Evidence that the corporation tax does indeed lead to less economic activity being undertaken by corporations is provided by Goolsbee [2004], who notes that in states with relatively high corporation income tax rates, the number of firms doing business as corporations is relatively low, other things being the same. As capital moves to the noncorporate sector, the rate of return to capital there is depressed so that ultimately *all* owners of capital, not just those in the corporate sector, are affected. The reallocation of capital between the two sectors also affects the return to labor. The extent to which capital and labor bear the ultimate burden of the tax depends on the technologies used in production in each of the sectors, as well as the structure of consumers' demands for corporate and noncorporate goods. In their survey of public finance economists, Fuchs et al. [1998] found that virtually all of them believe that the burden of the corporate income tax is shared by both capital and labor, "but there is significant disagreement about the precise division."

Turning now to efficiency aspects of the problem, we discussed computation of the excess burden of a partial factor tax in Chapter 15. By inducing less capital accumulation in the corporate sector than otherwise would have been the case, the corporation tax diverts capital from its most productive uses and creates an excess burden. According to the estimates of Jorgenson and Yun [2001, p. 302], the excess burden of the corporation tax is very high, about 24 percent of the revenues collected.

A Tax on Economic Profits

An alternative view is that the corporation tax is a tax on economic profits. This view is based on the observation that the tax base is determined by subtracting costs of production from gross corporate income, leaving only "profits." As we explained in Chapter 14, analyzing the incidence of a tax on economic profits is straightforward. As long as a firm maximizes economic profits, a tax on them induces no adjustments in firm behavior—all decisions regarding prices and production are unchanged. Hence, there is no way to shift the tax, and it is borne by the owners of the firm at the time the tax is levied. Moreover, by virtue of the fact that the tax leaves behavior unchanged, it generates no misallocation of resources. Hence, the excess burden is zero.

Modeling the corporation tax as a simple tax on economic profits is almost certainly wrong. The base of a pure profits tax is computed by subtracting from gross earnings the value of *all* inputs *including* the opportunity cost of the inputs supplied by the owners. As noted earlier, no such deduction for the capital supplied by shareholders is allowed, so the base of the tax includes elements other than economic profits.

Nevertheless, there are circumstances under which the corporation tax is *equivalent* to an economic profits tax. Stiglitz [1973] showed that under certain conditions, as long as the corporation is allowed to deduct interest payments made to its creditors, the corporation tax amounts to a tax on economic profits.

To understand the reasoning behind this result, consider a firm that is contemplating the purchase of a machine costing $1. Suppose the before-tax value of the output produced by the machine is known with certainty to be G dollars. Suppose also that the firm finances the purchase with debt—it borrows $1 and must pay an interest charge of r dollars. In the absence of any taxes, the firm buys the machine if the net return (total revenue minus depreciation minus interest) is positive. Algebraically, the firm purchases the machine if

$$G - r > 0 \tag{19.2}$$

Now assume that a corporation tax with the following features is levied: (1) Net income is taxed at rate θ; and (2) Net income is computed by subtracting interest costs from total revenue. What is the effect on the firm's decision? Clearly, the firm must choose on the basis of the *after*-tax profitability of the project. In light of feature 2, the firm's taxable income is $G - r$. Given feature 1, the project therefore creates a tax liability of $\theta(G - r)$, so the after-tax profit on the project is $(1 - \theta)(G - r)$. The firm undertakes the project only if the after-tax profit is positive, that is, if

$$(1 - \theta)(G - r) > 0 \qquad (19.3)$$

Now note that any project that passes the after-tax criterion (19.3) also satisfies the before-tax criterion (19.2). [Just divide Equation (19.3) through by $(1 - \theta)$ to get Equation (19.2).] Hence, the tax leaves the firm's investment decision unchanged— anything it would have done before the tax, it will do after. The owners of the firm continue to behave exactly as they did before the tax; they simply lose some of their profit on the investment to the government. In this sense the tax is equivalent to an economic profits tax. And like an economic profits tax, its incidence is on the owners of the firm, and it creates no excess burden.

This conclusion depends critically on the underlying assumptions, and these can easily be questioned. Recall that the argument assumes that firms finance their additional projects by borrowing. There are several reasons why they might instead raise money by selling shares or using retained earnings. For example, firms may face constraints in the capital market and be unable to borrow all they want. Alternatively, if a firm is uncertain about the project's return, it might be reluctant to finance the project by borrowing. If things go wrong, the greater a firm's debt, the higher the probability of bankruptcy, other things being the same.

Hence, Stiglitz's main contribution is not the conclusion that the corporate tax has no excess burden. Rather, the key insight is that the impact of the corporation tax depends in an important way on the structure of corporate finance.

▶ EFFECTS ON BEHAVIOR

This section discusses three important types of decisions that the corporation tax can affect: (1) The total amount of physical investment (equipment and structures) to undertake; (2) The kinds of physical assets to purchase; and (3) The way to finance these investments. In a sense, it is artificial to discuss these decisions separately because presumably the firm makes them simultaneously. However, we discuss them separately for expositional ease.

Total Physical Investment

A firm's net investment during a given period is the increase in physical assets during that time. The main policy question is whether features such as accelerated depreciation and the investment tax credit stimulate investment demand. The question is important. For example, when Congress made depreciation allowances more generous in 2009, the goal was to increase investment. Opponents asserted that it would not have much effect. Who was right?

The answer depends in part on your view of how corporations make their investment decisions. Many different models have been proposed, and there is no agreement on which is the best.[3] We discuss three investment models that have received substantial attention.

---

[3] See Chirinko [2002] for a discussion of various models.

Accelerator Model   Suppose the ratio of capital to output in production is fixed. For example, production of every unit of output requires three units of capital. Then for each unit increase in output, the firm must increase its capital stock—invest—three units of capital. Thus, the main determinant of the amount of investment is changes in the level of output demanded.

This theory, sometimes referred to as the accelerator model, implies that depreciation allowances and ITCs are basically *irrelevant* when it comes to influencing physical investment. It is only the quantity of output that influences the amount of investment, because technology dictates the ratio in which capital and output must be used. In other words, tax benefits for capital may make capital cheaper, but in the accelerator model this does not matter, because the demand for capital does not depend on its price.

Neoclassical Model   A less extreme view of the investment process is that the ratio of capital to output is not technologically fixed. Rather, the firm can choose among alternative technologies. But how does it choose? According to Jorgenson's [1963] neoclassical model, a key variable is the firm's **user cost of capital**—the cost the firm incurs as a consequence of owning an asset. As we show later, the user cost of capital includes both the opportunity cost of forgoing other investments and direct costs such as depreciation and taxes. The user cost of capital indicates the rate of return a project must attain to be profitable. For example, if the user cost of capital on a project is 15 percent, a firm undertakes the project only if its rate of return exceeds 15 percent. The higher the user cost of capital, the lower is the number of profitable projects, and the lower the firm's desired stock of capital. In the neoclassical model, when the cost of capital increases, firms choose less capital-intensive technologies, and vice versa. To the extent that tax policy reduces the cost of capital, it can increase the amount of capital that firms desire and, hence, increase investment.

All of this leaves open two important questions: (1) How do changes in the tax system affect the user cost of capital? and (2) Just how sensitive is investment to changes in the user cost of capital? We discuss these questions in turn.

The User Cost of Capital   Consider Leona, an entrepreneur who can lend her money and receive an after-tax rate of return of 10 percent. Leona is the sole stockholder in a corporation that runs a chain of hotels. Because she can always earn 10 percent simply by lending in the capital market, she will not make any investment in the hotel that yields less than that amount. Assume that Leona is considering the acquisition of a vacuum cleaner that would experience economic depreciation of 2 percent annually. Ignoring taxes for the moment, the user cost of capital for the vacuum cleaner would be 12 percent, because the vacuum cleaner would have to generate a 12 percent return to earn Leona the 10 percent return that she could receive simply by lending her money. Algebraically, if r is the after-tax rate of return and δ is the economic rate of depreciation, the user cost of capital is $(r + \delta)$. If the vacuum cleaner cannot earn $(r + \delta)$ (or 12 percent) after taxes, there is no reason to purchase it.

Now assume that the corporate tax rate is 35 percent, that Leona's marginal tax rate on dividends is 15 percent, and that all of the corporation's earnings are paid out to Leona as dividends. Then if the corporation earns \$1, a corporation tax of \$0.35 (= 0.35 × \$1) is due, leaving \$0.65 available to distribute to Leona. When Leona receives the \$0.65 as dividends, she pays individual tax at a rate of 15 percent, leading to a tax liability of \$0.098 (= 0.15 × \$0.65), which leaves her with \$0.552. Algebraically, if θ is the corporate tax rate and t is the individual tax rate on dividend income, the after-tax return from \$1 of corporate profits is $(1 - \theta) \times (1 - t)$.

user cost of capital

The opportunity cost to a firm of owning a piece of capital.

How do these taxes affect the cost of capital? We have to find a before-tax return such that, after the corporate and individual income taxes, Leona receives 12 percent. Calling the user cost of capital C, then C must be the solution to the equation $(1 - 0.35) \times (1 - 0.15) \times C = 12$ percent, or $C = 21.7$ percent. Thus, Leona is unwilling to purchase the vacuum cleaner unless its before-tax return is 21.7 percent or greater. Using our algebraic notation, the user cost of capital is the value of C that solves the equation $(1 - \theta) \times (1 - t) \times C = (r + \delta)$, or

$$C = \frac{r + \delta}{(1 - \theta) \times (1 - t)} \tag{19.4}$$

So far, we have shown how corporate and individual tax rates increase the user cost of capital. However, other provisions in the tax code such as accelerated depreciation lower the cost of capital. In Equation (19.1), we defined ψ as the present value of the depreciation allowances that flow from a \$1 investment. Suppose that ψ for the vacuum cleaner is 0.25. In effect, then, depreciation allowances reduce the cost of acquiring the vacuum cleaner by one-fourth, and hence lower by one-fourth the before-tax return that the firm has to earn to attain any given after-tax return. In our example, instead of having to earn 21.7 percent, the vacuum cleaner now only has to earn 16.3 percent $[21.7 \times (1 - 0.25)]$. Algebraically, depreciation allowances lower the cost of capital by a factor of $(1 - \psi)$. Similarly, we showed that an investment tax credit at rate k reduces the cost of a \$1 acquisition to $(1 - k)$ dollars. In the presence of both depreciation allowances and an investment tax credit, the cost of capital falls by a factor of $(1 - \psi - k)$.[4] Thus, the expression for C in Equation (19.4) must be multiplied by $(1 - \psi - k)$ to adjust for accelerated depreciation and investment tax credits:

$$C = \frac{(r + \delta) \times (1 - \psi - k)}{(1 - \theta) \times (1 - t)} \tag{19.5}$$

Equation (19.5) summarizes how the corporate tax system influences the firm's user cost of capital. By taxing corporate income, the tax makes capital investment more expensive, other things being the same. However, depreciation allowances and ITCs tend to lower the user cost. Any change in the corporation tax system influences some combination of θ, ψ, and k, and hence changes the user cost of capital.

Effect of User Cost on Investment Once we know how the tax system affects the user cost of capital, the next step is to determine how changes in the user cost influence investment. If the accelerator model is correct, even drastic reductions in the user cost have no impact on investment. On the other hand, if investment responds to the user cost of capital, depreciation allowances and ITCs can be powerful tools for influencing investment. While there are differences in the literature, an elasticity of investment with respect to the user cost of 0.4 is plausible [Chirinko, 2002].

An important implicit assumption in this discussion is that the before-tax price of capital goods is not affected by tax-induced changes in the user cost of capital. If, for example, firms start purchasing more capital goods in response to the introduction of an investment tax credit, this does not increase the price of capital goods. In more technical terms, the supply curve of capital goods is perfectly horizontal. However, Goolsbee [2003] found that the introduction of an investment tax credit increases the relative wages of workers who produce capital goods, which would tend to increase the price of capital goods. Hence, some of the increase in investment induced by the credit is dampened by an increase in the before-tax price of capital goods.

---

[4] This assumes the basis used to compute depreciation allowances is not reduced when the firm takes the ITC.

Finally, we must remember that the United States is, to a large extent, an open economy. If the tax code makes investment in the United States more attractive to foreigners, saving from abroad can finance investment in this country. The consequence for tax policy toward investment is the flip side of the relationship we saw in Chapter 18 between tax policy and saving: The possibility of domestic saving flowing out of the country makes it harder to stimulate domestic investment indirectly by manipulating saving, but the possibility of attracting foreign capital makes it easier to stimulate investment through direct manipulation of the user cost of capital.

cash flow

The difference between revenues and expenditures.

Cash Flow Model   If you ask people in business what determines their investment decisions, they likely will mention **cash flow**—the difference between revenues and expenditures for inputs. The more money that is on hand, the greater the capacity for investment. In contrast, cash flow is irrelevant in the neoclassical investment model. In that model, internal funds and borrowed money both have the same opportunity cost—the going rate of return in the economy. Further, the firm can borrow as much money at the going rate of return as it wishes. Under these conditions, if the return on producing a new kind of computer chip exceeds the opportunity cost, the firm will make the chip, whether it has to borrow the money or use internal sources.

A critical assumption behind the neoclassical story is that the cost to the firm of internal and external funds is the same. Many economists believe that this is a bad assumption. To see why, suppose that the managers of the firm have better information about the prospects for the computer chip than the potential lenders do. In particular, the lenders may view the project as being more uncertain than management and so charge a very high interest rate on the loan. Or they might not be willing to lend any money at all. Thus, the cost of internal funds is lower than the cost of external funds, so the amount of investment depends on the volume of these internal funds, the cash flow.

There does indeed seem to be a statistical relationship between cash flow and investment [Stein, 2003]. However, the interpretation of this finding is not clear—do firms invest because their cash flow is high, or do successful firms have both high cash flow and investment? In any case, if the cash flow theory is correct, it has major implications for the impact of taxes on investment behavior. For example, in the neoclassical model, a lump sum tax on the corporation has no effect on investment. In contrast, in a cash flow model, investment falls. Currently, cash flow models are an active subject of research.

Types of Asset

The tax system affects the types of assets purchased by firms as well as the total volume of investment. For example, the system encourages the purchase of assets that receive relatively generous depreciation allowances. Gravelle [2004] computed the effective marginal tax rates on various types of assets and found that structures were taxed slightly more heavily than equipment.

Corporate Finance

In addition to "real" decisions concerning physical investment, the owners of a firm must determine how to finance the firm's operations and whether to distribute or retain profits. We now discuss the effects of taxes on these financial decisions.

Why Do Firms Pay Dividends?   Profits earned by a corporation may be either distributed to shareholders in the form of dividends or retained by the company. If we assume that (1) outcomes of all investments are known in advance with certainty and (2) there are no taxes, then the owners of a firm are indifferent between a dollar of dividends and a dollar of retained earnings. Provided that the stock market accurately reflects the firm's value, $1 of retained earnings increases the value of the firm's stock by $1. This $1 capital gain is as much income as a $1 dividend receipt. Under the previous assumptions, then, stockholders do not care whether profits are distributed.

Of course, in reality, considerable uncertainty surrounds the outcomes of investment decisions, and corporate income *is* subject to a variety of taxes. As already noted, when dividends are paid out, the shareholder incurs a tax liability, while retained earnings generate no concurrent tax liability. True, the retention creates a capital gain for the stockholder, but no tax is due until the gain is realized.

On the basis of these observations, it appears that paying dividends is more or less equivalent to giving away money to the tax collector, and we would expect firms to retain virtually all of their earnings. Surprise! In a typical year, almost 66 percent of after-tax corporate profits are paid out as dividends [*Economic Report of the President, 2009*, p. 389]. This phenomenon is a puzzle for students of corporate finance.

One possible explanation is that dividend payments signal the firm's financial strength. If investors perceive firms that regularly pay dividends as "solid," then paying dividends enhances the value of the firms' shares. In the same way, a firm that reduces its dividend payments may be perceived as being in financial straits. However, although it is conceivable that the owners of a firm would be willing to pay some extra taxes to provide a positive signal to potential shareholders, it is hard to imagine that the benefits gained are worth the huge sums sacrificed.

Another explanation centers on the fact that not all investors have the same marginal tax rate. In particular, untaxed institutions (such as pension funds and universities) face a rate of zero. Those with low marginal tax rates would tend to put a relatively high valuation on dividends, and it may be that some firms "specialize" in attracting these investors by paying out dividends. This is referred to as a **clientele effect,** because firms set their financial policies to cater to different clienteles. Econometric studies of the clientele effect are hindered by the lack of data on just who owns shares in what firms. However, there is some evidence that mutual funds, whose shareholders are taxable, tend to hold stocks with low-dividend yields, while untaxed institutions show no preference between low- and high-dividend stocks [Graham, 2003].

clientele effect

Firms structure their financial policies to meet different clienteles' needs. Those with low dividend payments attract shareholders with high marginal tax rates, and vice versa.

Effect of Taxes on Dividend Policy   Because the tax system appears to bias firms against paying dividends (although it by no means discourages them completely), the natural question is how corporate financial policy would change if the tax treatment of dividends vis-à-vis retained earnings were modified. Suppose that for whatever reasons, firms want to pay some dividends as well as retain earnings. One factor that determines the desired amount of retained earnings is the opportunity cost in terms of after-tax dividends paid to stockholders. For example, if there were no taxes, the opportunity cost of $1 of retained earnings would be $1 of dividends. On the other hand, if the stockholder faces a 15 percent marginal income tax rate on dividends, the opportunity cost of retaining a dollar in the firm is only 85 cents of dividends.[5] In effect, then, the current tax system lowers the opportunity cost of retained earnings.

---

[5] A more careful calculation would take into account the effective capital gains tax liability that is eventually generated by the retention. This is ignored for purposes of illustration.

EMPIRICAL EVIDENCE

The Effect of Dividend Taxes on Dividend Payments

Economic theory suggests that dividend payments should increase when the opportunity cost of retained earnings increases. In 2003, the top tax rate paid on dividends earned by individuals was lowered dramatically, from 35 percent to only 15 percent. This sharp decline in the tax rate presents an opportunity to estimate credibly how responsive dividend payments are to their tax treatment.

Using data spanning over 20 years, Chetty and Saez [2004] found that dividend payments surged immediately following the tax cut. The number of corporations paying dividends increased, reversing two decades of decline, and corporations that historically had already been paying dividends raised their payouts significantly. In order to rule out other causes for the increase in dividends, they showed that dividends did not increase for corporations whose largest shareholders were nontaxable institutions. They concluded that the tax cut led to an increase in dividends of about 20 percent. Putting this finding together with other data, they calculated that the elasticity of dividend payments with respect to the marginal tax rate on dividend income is about −0.5. It appears, then, that the tax system does indeed affect corporate retained earnings.

Some argue that a tax-induced bias against paying dividends is desirable because increasing retained earnings makes more money available for investment. Now, it is true that retained earnings represent saving. However, it may be that shareholders take corporate saving into consideration when making their personal financial decisions. Specifically, if owners of the firm perceive that the corporation is saving a dollar on their behalf, they may simply reduce their personal saving by that amount. Thus, although the composition of overall saving has changed, its total amount is just the same as before the retention. There is indeed some econometric evidence that personal and corporate saving are somewhat offsetting [Poterba, 1991]. This analysis illustrates once again the pitfalls of viewing the corporation as a separate person with an existence apart from the stockholders.

Debt versus Equity Finance   Another important financial decision for a corporation is how to raise money. The firm has basically two options. It can borrow money (issue debt). The firm must pay interest on its debt, and inability to meet the interest payments or repay the principal may have serious consequences. A firm can also issue shares of stock (equity), and stockholders may receive dividends on their shares.

Recall that under the US tax system, corporations may deduct payments of interest from taxable income, but are not allowed to deduct dividends. The tax law therefore builds in a bias toward debt financing. Indeed, we might wonder why firms do not use debt financing exclusively. Part of the answer lies in the uncertainty that firms face. There is always some possibility of a very bad outcome and bankruptcy. The more a firm borrows, the higher its debt payments, and the greater the probability of bankruptcy, other things being the same. Heavy reliance on debt finance has in fact led some major corporations to declare bankruptcy, including K-Mart, Enron, and WorldCom. Some argue that by encouraging the use of debt, the tax system has the undesirable effect of increasing probabilities of bankruptcy above levels that otherwise would have prevailed.

That said, it is difficult to estimate precisely the impact that the tax system has on the debt-equity choice. In one econometric study, Gordon and Lee [2001] note that if taxes affect debt-equity ratios, then corporations with lower tax rates should use less debt, other things being the same. This is because the advantage of being able to deduct interest from corporate taxable income is less when the tax rate is lower. Gordon and Lee's analysis of US firms is consistent with this hypothesis. They find that lowering the corporate rate by 10 percentage points lowers the percentage of the firm's assets financed by debt by 4 percent.

▶ STATE CORPORATION TAXES

Almost all the states levy their own corporation income taxes, and corporate tax revenues account for about 12 percent of total state and local revenues [*Economic Report of the President, 2009*, p. 385]. Like state personal income taxes, state corporate tax systems differ substantially with respect to rate structures and rules for defining taxable income.

All of the complications that arise in analyzing the incidence and efficiency effects of the federal corporation income tax also bedevil attempts to understand the state systems. The variation in rates across state lines gives rise to a set of even more intractable questions. If a given state levies a corporation tax, how much of the burden is exported to citizens of other states? How is the portion that is not exported shared by the residents of the state?

Preliminary answers to these questions may be obtained by applying the theory of tax incidence (Chapter 14). Recall the general intuitive proposition that immobile factors of production are more likely to end up bearing a tax than mobile factors, other things being the same. This means, for example, that if capital is easier to move to another state than labor, the incidence of a state corporation tax tends to fall on labor. Thus, analyzing a system of varying corporate tax rates requires that the effects of interstate mobility be added to the already formidable list of factors that come into play when studying the federal corporation tax. Research on this issue is at a formative stage.

▶ TAXATION OF MULTINATIONAL CORPORATIONS

American firms do a substantial amount of investment abroad. In 2007, the value of the stock of assets directly invested in foreign countries was over $17 trillion [*Economic Report of the President, 2009*, p. 407]. The tax treatment of foreign source income is of increasing importance.

US multinational corporations are subject to tax at the standard rate on their global taxable income, including income earned abroad. A credit is then allowed for foreign taxes paid. The credit cannot exceed the amount that would have been owed under US tax law. Suppose, for example, that a US corporation earns $100 in a foreign country with a 15 percent tax rate. The corporation pays $15 to the foreign country. In the absence of the foreign tax credit, it would owe $35 to the US Treasury (because the US corporate tax rate is 35 percent). However, the firm can take a $15 credit against the $35 liability, and needs to pay the United States only $20.

In 2003, corporations filing a US tax return claimed $50 billion in foreign tax credits, reducing their tax liability by 33.5 percent [Singmaster, 2007, p. 225].

A number of considerations complicate the taxation of foreign source corporate income.

Subsidiary Status   Taxation of the income from a foreign enterprise can be deferred if the operation is a **subsidiary.** (A foreign subsidiary is a company owned by a US corporation but incorporated abroad and, hence, a separate corporation from a legal point of view.) Profits earned by a subsidiary are taxed only if returned **(repatriated)** to the parent company as dividends. Thus, for as long as the subsidiary exists, earnings retained abroad can be kept out of reach of the US tax system. It is hard to say how much tax revenue is lost because of deferral. Given the credit system, the answer depends on the tax rate levied abroad. If all foreign countries have tax rates greater than that of the United States, no additional tax revenue is gained by this country. However, to the extent that a foreign country taxes corporate income less heavily than does the United States, deferral makes the country attractive to US firms as a "tax haven."[6]

Income Allocation   It is often difficult to know how much of a multinational firm's total income to allocate to its operations in a given country. The procedure now used for allocating income between domestic and foreign operations is the **arm's length system.** Essentially the domestic and foreign operations are treated as separate enterprises doing business independently ("at arm's length"). The taxable profits of each entity are computed as its own sales minus its own costs.

The problem is that it is not always clear how to allocate costs to various locations, and this can lead to major opportunities for tax avoidance. To see why, consider a multinational firm that owns a patent for a gene-splicing process. One of the subsidiaries owns the patent, and the other subsidiaries pay royalties to it for the privilege of using the process. The company has an incentive to assign the patent to one of its subsidiaries in a low-tax country, so that the royalties received from the other subsidiaries will be taxed at a relatively low rate. At the same time, it wants the subsidiaries that use the patent to be in relatively high-tax countries—high tax rates mean that the value of the deductions associated with the royalty payments is maximized. Indeed, since the transaction is entirely internal to the company, it will set the royalty payment to be as large as possible in order to maximize the tax benefit of this arrangement. And if there is no active market for the rights to the patent outside the company, then the tax authorities have little basis for deciding whether or not the royalty payment is excessive.

This is called the **transfer-pricing** problem, because it refers to the price that one part of the company uses for transferring resources to another. Given that it is essentially arbitrary how costs for many items are assigned to various subsidiaries, multinational corporations and the tax authorities are constantly at odds over whether

---

subsidiary

A company owned by one corporation but chartered separately from the parent corporation.

repatriate

To return the earnings of a subsidiary to its parent company.

arm's length system

A method of calculating taxes for multinational corporations by treating transactions between domestic and foreign operations as if they were separate enterprises.

transfer price

The price that one subsidiary charges another for some input.

---

[6] A few countries such as the Bahamas have intentionally structured their laws to allow US firms to abuse the tax system. There are some provisions to limit the tax savings from these true tax havens, but they have not had much impact.

the companies have done their transfer pricing appropriately. This has become one of the most complicated areas of tax law.

Evaluation

An evaluation of the US tax treatment of multinational firms requires a careful statement of the policy goal. One possible objective is to maximize worldwide income; another is to maximize national income. A system that is optimal given one goal may not be optimal given another.

Maximization of World Income   The maximization of world income requires that the before-tax rate of return on the last dollar invested in each country—the marginal rate of return—be the same.[7] To see why, imagine a situation in which marginal returns are not equal. Then one can increase world income simply by taking capital from a country where its marginal return is low and moving it to one where the marginal return is high.[8] Algebraically, if r_{US} is the marginal rate of return in the United States and r_f is the marginal rate of return in a given foreign country, then worldwide efficiency requires

$$r_f = r_{US} \tag{19.6}$$

What kind of tax system induces profit-maximizing firms to allocate their capital so that the outcome is consistent with Equation (19.6)? The answer hinges on the fact that investors make their decisions on the basis of after-tax returns. They therefore allocate their capital across countries so that the after-tax marginal return in each country is equal. If t_{US} is the US tax rate and t_f is the foreign tax rate, a firm allocates its capital so that

$$(1 - t_f)r_f = (1 - t_{US})r_{US} \tag{19.7}$$

Condition (19.7) tells us that efficiency is attained if and only if t_f equals t_{US}. Intuitively, if we want capital allocated efficiently from a global standpoint, capital must be taxed at the same rate wherever it is located.

The policy implication seems to be that if the United States cares about maximizing world income, it should devise a system that makes its firms' tax liabilities independent of their location. A *full* credit against foreign taxes paid would do the trick. However, as already noted, the US system allows a tax credit *only* up to the amount that US tax on the foreign earnings would have been.

Why is the credit limited? Our model implicitly assumes the behavior of foreign governments is independent of US government actions. Suppose the United States announces it will pursue a policy of allowing a full foreign tax credit to its multinational firms. Then foreign governments have an incentive to raise their own tax rates on US corporations virtually without limit. Doing so will not drive out the foreign countries' American firms, because the tax liability for their domestic operations is reduced by a dollar for every dollar foreign taxes are increased.[9] Essentially, the program turns into a transfer from the United States to foreign treasuries. Limiting the credit is an obvious way to prevent this from happening.

---

[7] As usual, we refer here to rates of return after differences in risk are taken into account.

[8] For further discussion of this principle, see the appendix at the end of this book.

[9] The amount the foreign government can extract in this way is limited to the firm's tax liability to the United States on its domestic operations. Suppose the firm's tax liability on its US operations is $1,000. If the foreign government levies a tax of $1,000, under a full credit, the firm's US tax liability is zero. If the foreign government raises the tax to $1,001, the firm's domestic tax liability cannot be reduced any further (because there is no negative income tax for corporations).

Maximization of National Income   At the outset, we noted the importance of defining the objectives of tax policy on foreign source corporate income. Some argue that tax policy should maximize not world income, but national income. We must exercise care in defining national income here. It is the sum of *before*-tax domestically produced income and foreign source income *after* foreign taxes are paid. This is because taxes paid by US firms to the US government, although not available to the firms themselves, are still part of US income. Thus, domestic income is counted before tax. However, taxes paid to foreign governments are not available to US citizens, so foreign income is counted after tax.

National income maximization requires a different condition than Equation (19.6). The difference arises because marginal rates of return must now be measured from the US point of view. According to the US perspective, the marginal rate of return abroad is $(1 - t_f)r_f$—foreign taxes represent a cost from the US point of view and hence are excluded in valuing the rate of return. The marginal return on investments in the United States is measured at the before-tax rate, r_{US}. Hence, maximization of national income requires

$$(1 - t_f)r_f = r_{US} \qquad (19.8)$$

A comparison with Equation (19.6) suggests that under a regime of world income maximization, investments are made abroad until $r_f = r_{US}$, while if national income maximization is the goal, foreign investment is carried to the point where $r_f = r_{US}/(1 - t_f)$. In other words, if national income maximization is the goal, the before-tax marginal rate of return on foreign investment is higher than it would be if global income maximization were the goal. [As long as t_f is less than 1, $r_{US} < r_{US}/(1 - t_f)$.] But under the reasonable assumption that the marginal return to investment decreases with the amount of investment, a higher before-tax rate of return means less investment. In short, from a national point of view, world income maximization results in "too much" investment abroad.

What kind of tax system induces American firms to allocate their capital so that Equation (19.8) is satisfied? Suppose that, contrary to the US system, multinational firms are allowed to *deduct* foreign tax payments from their US taxable income. (For example, a firm with domestic income of $1,000 and foreign taxes of $200 would have a US taxable income of $800.) Given that foreign tax payments are deductible, a firm's overseas return of r_f increases its taxable US income by $r_f(1 - t_f)$. Therefore, after US taxes, the return on the foreign investment is $r_f(1 - t_f)(1 - t_{US})$. At the same time, the after-tax return on investments in the United States is $r_{US}(1 - t_{US})$. Assuming that the investors equalize after-tax marginal returns at home and abroad,

$$r_f(1 - t_f)(1 - t_{US}) = r_{US}(1 - t_{US}) \qquad (19.9)$$

Clearly, Equations (19.8) and (19.9) are equivalent. [Just divide both sides of (19.9) by $(1 - t_{US})$.] Because Equation (19.8) is the condition for national income maximization, this implies that deduction of foreign tax payments leads to a pattern of investment that maximizes US income.

Such reasoning has led to some political support for replacing the foreign-tax credit with a deduction. One important problem with the case for deductions is that the analysis assumes the capital-exporting country can impose the tax rate that maximizes its income, while the capital-importing foreign countries passively keep their own tax rates constant. Suppose, to the contrary, that the capital-exporting country takes into account the possibility that changes in its tax rate may induce changes in the host countries' tax rates. The United States might believe, for example, that if it lowers its tax rate on capital invested abroad, host governments will do the same. In this case, it may be worthwhile for the United States to tax preferentially income earned abroad. Of course, host governments might choose to raise their tax rates when the US rate goes down. The point is that with interdependent behavior, the national income-maximizing tax system generally does not consist of a simple deduction for foreign taxes paid. The effective tax rate on foreign source income can be either larger or smaller than that associated with deductibility. Just as in the strictly domestic context, optimal tax theory shows that simple rules of thumb for tax policy do not necessarily achieve a given goal.

Finally, we note that our normative analysis of international taxation rests on the positive assumption that firms take into account after-tax rates of return when deciding in which countries to invest. Desai et al. [2003] examined the amount of foreign direct investment in European countries, and estimated that a 10 percent higher tax rate is associated with 7.7 percent less investment from abroad, other things being the same. This evidence suggests that the assumption that firms respond to after-tax rates of return is reasonable.

▶ CORPORATION TAX REFORM

We observed earlier that if corporate income were untaxed, individuals could avoid personal income taxes by accumulating income within corporations. Evidently, this would lead to serious equity and efficiency problems. The US response has been to construct a system that taxes corporate income twice: first at the corporate level, where the statutory tax rate is currently 35 percent, and again at the personal level, where distributions of dividends are currently taxed at a maximum statutory rate of 15 percent.

A number of proposals have been made to integrate personal and corporate income taxes into a single system. We now discuss two of them, full integration and dividend relief.

Full Integration

The most radical approach is the **partnership method,** sometimes referred to as **full integration.** Under this approach, all earnings of the corporation during a given year, whether they are distributed or not, are attributed to stockholders just as if the corporation were a partnership. Each shareholder is then liable for personal income tax on his share of the earnings. Thus, if Karl owns 2 percent of the shares of Microsoft, each year his taxable income includes 2 percent of Microsoft's taxable earnings. The corporation tax as a separate entity is eliminated.

The debate in the United States over the partnership method has focused on several issues:

Nature of the Corporation   Those who favor full integration emphasize that a corporation is, in effect, merely a conduit for transmitting earnings to shareholders. It makes more sense to tax the people who receive the income than the institution that happens to pass it along. Those who oppose full integration argue that in large

partnership method

Each stockholder incurs a tax liability on his or her share of the earnings of a corporation, whether or not the earnings are distributed.

full integration

See *partnership method.*

modern corporations, it is ridiculous to think of the shareholders as partners, and that the corporation is best regarded as a separate entity.

Administrative Feasibility   Opponents of full integration stress the administrative difficulties that it would create. How are corporate earnings imputed to individuals who hold stock for less than a year? Would shareholders be allowed to deduct the firm's operating losses from their personal taxable income? Proponents of full integration argue that a certain number of fairly arbitrary decisions must be made to administer any complicated tax system. The administrative problems here are no worse than those in other parts of the tax code and can probably be dealt with satisfactorily.

Effects on Efficiency   Those who favor integration point out that the current corporate tax system imposes large excess burdens on the economy, many of which would be eliminated or at least lessened under full integration. The economy would benefit from four types of efficiency gains:

- The misallocation of resources between the corporate and noncorporate sectors would be eliminated.
- To the extent that integration lowered the rate of taxation on the return to capital, tax-induced distortions in savings decisions would be reduced.
- Integration would remove the incentives for "excessive" retained earnings that characterize the current system. Firms with substantial retained earnings are not forced to convince investors to finance new projects. Without the discipline that comes from having to persuade outsiders that projects are worthwhile, such firms may invest inefficiently. For example, some observers believe that Microsoft's ill-advised entry into cable television would not have occurred if it had not had huge amounts of cash (about $40 billion!) on hand [*Economist,* 2003].
- Integration would remove the present system's bias toward debt financing because there would be no separate corporate tax base from which to deduct payments of interest. High ratios of debt to equity increase the probability of bankruptcy. This increased risk and the actual bankruptcies that do occur lower welfare without any concomitant gain to society.

Although it is difficult to determine the value of all these efficiency gains, some estimates suggest that they are quite high. Jorgenson and Yun [2001] found that the present value of the lifetime efficiency gain from full integration would be more than $250 billion.

Opponents of full integration point out that given all the uncertainties concerning the operation of the corporation tax, the supposed efficiency gains may not exist at all. For example, as discussed earlier, to the extent that Stiglitz's view of the tax as equivalent to a levy on pure profits is correct, the tax induces no distortion between the corporate and noncorporate sectors. Similarly, there is no solid evidence that corporations invest internal funds less efficiently than those raised externally.

Effects on Saving   Some argue that full integration would lower the effective tax rate on capital and therefore lead to more saving. As we saw in Chapter 18, this is a non sequitur. Theoretically, the volume of saving may increase, decrease, or stay the same when the tax rate on capital income decreases. Econometric work has not yet provided a definitive answer.

Effect on the Distribution of Income   If the efficiency arguments in favor of full integration are correct, then in principle, all taxpayers could benefit if it were instituted. Still, people in different groups would be affected differently. For example, stockholders with relatively high personal income tax rates would tend to gain less from integration than those with low personal income tax rates. At the same time, integration would tend to benefit those individuals who receive a relatively large share of their incomes from capital. Taking these effects together, there may be a roughly U-shaped pattern to the distribution of benefits of integration—people at the high and low ends of the income distribution gain somewhat more than those in the middle.[10]

Overview   Clearly, there is considerable uncertainty surrounding the likely impact of full integration. This simply reflects our imperfect knowledge of the workings of the current system of corporate taxation. There is by no means unanimous agreement that introducing the partnership method would be a good thing. However, on the basis of the existing and admittedly imperfect evidence, many economists have concluded that both efficiency and equity would be enhanced if the personal and corporate taxes were integrated.

Dividend Relief

A less extreme approach to integration has at its starting point the notion that the source of many of the problems with the status quo is that dividends are taxed twice, once at the corporation level and again at the individual level. The idea of dividend relief is to eliminate double taxation while still maintaining the corporation tax as a separate system. There are basically two approaches. One is to allow the corporation to deduct dividends paid to stockholders just as it now deducts interest payments to bondholders. The advantage of this scheme is that it removes the asymmetric tax treatment of debt and equity. Further, dividends end up getting taxed at the individual's marginal tax rate, which makes sense from the standpoint of the Haig-Simons definition of income.

An alternative approach is simply to exclude dividends from taxation at the individual level. Under this approach, dividends are taxed only once, but at the corporation rate rather than the individual rate. From an efficiency point of view, this approach is probably less satisfactory than a corporate dividend deduction—there remains some non-neutrality in the treatment of debt and equity. But it likely enhances efficiency relative to the status quo, and is relatively easy to administer. As mentioned earlier, legislation passed in 2003 moved in the direction of a dividend exclusion, by lowering the tax rate applied to dividends at the individual level. Prior to 2003, they were taxed as ordinary income; since 2003 they have been taxed at the capital gains rate at a maximum statutory rate of 15 percent. However, at the time of this writing, President Obama is proposing to increase the rate to 20 percent for high-income families.

---

[10] See, for example, Fullerton and Rogers [1997].

Summary

- Corporations are subject to a separate federal income tax. The tax accounts for about 10 percent of all federal revenues.

- Before applying the 35 percent tax rate, firms may deduct employee compensation, interest payments, and depreciation allowances. These are meant to measure the cost of producing revenue. Dividends, the cost of acquiring equity funds, are not deductible. However, dividends are taxed preferentially at the individual level.

- Investment tax credits (ITCs) are deducted from the firm's tax bill when particular physical capital assets are purchased. Today, the ITC applies only to a few types of investments.

- The corporate tax has been viewed either as an economic profits tax or as a partial factor tax. In the former case, the tax is borne entirely by owners of firms, while in the latter the incidence depends on capital mobility between sectors, substitutability of factors of production, the structure of consumer demand, and the sensitivity of capital accumulation to the net rate of return.

- The effect of the corporate tax system on physical investment depends on (1) its effect on the user cost of capital, and (2) the sensitivity of investment to changes in the user cost.

- In the accelerator model, investment depends only on output, making the user cost irrelevant. The neoclassical model assumes that capital demand depends on the user cost. In the cash flow model, internal funds play a key role in determining investment.

- In the neoclassical investment model, the user cost of capital (C) is

$$C = \frac{(r + \delta) \times (1 - \psi - k)}{(1 - \theta) \times (1 - t)}$$

where r is the after-tax interest rate, δ the economic depreciation rate, θ the corporation tax rate, k the ITC, and ψ the present value of depreciation allowances per dollar.

- Estimates of the effect of the user cost on investment vary greatly, but most recent research suggests that there is some responsiveness.

- Due to the double taxation of dividends, it is puzzling that firms pay them. Dividends may serve as a signal of the firm's financial strength, or be used to cater to particular clienteles.

- Interest deductibility provides a strong incentive for debt finance. However, increasing the proportion of debt may lead to larger bankruptcy costs.

- Most states have corporate income taxes. The possibilities for tax exporting and interstate mobility of factors of production complicate analysis of these taxes.

- US multinational corporations are allowed tax credits for taxes paid to foreign governments. Complications arise due to tax deferral using foreign subsidiaries and opportunities for tax avoidance via transfer pricing.

- One possible corporate tax reform is full integration of the corporate and personal income taxes. Owners of stock would be taxed on their share of corporate income as if they were partners. The corporation tax as a separate entity would cease to exist.

- Another approach to integration is dividend relief, in which dividends are taxed only once, either by allowing a deduction at the corporate level or an exclusion at the individual level.

Discussion Questions

1. Caterpillar Inc.'s CEO, Jim Owen, noted, "Sitting on a big wad of cash doesn't make any sense whatsoever for shareholders [because] it tends to promote bad practice among management. . . . You've got more [cash] than you know what to do with, and you think you're so damned good you can buy anything and make it better" [Brat and Gruley, 2007]. If this view is correct, what does it imply about the efficiency consequences of the corporate tax treatment of dividends versus retained earnings?

2. An economist recently advocated for "abolishing [the corporate tax] outright" [Reinhardt, 2007]. What problem might such a proposal create? [Hint: Consider the interactions between the personal income tax and the corporate tax.]

3. Under US law, depreciation allowances are based on the original cost of acquiring the asset. No account is taken for the effects of inflation on the price level over time.

    a. How does inflation affect the real value of depreciation allowances? Organize your answer around Equation (19.1).

    b. When inflation increases, what is the impact on the user cost of capital? Organize your answer around Equation (19.5).

    c. Suggest a policy that could undo the effects of inflation from part b.

4. Clausing [2007] found that corporate tax revenues rise and then fall with increases in the corporate tax rate. She also found that "smaller, more open economies have lower revenue-maximizing tax rates than do larger or more closed economies." Explain what might account for this result.

5. Several years ago, RJR Nabisco incurred $2 million in costs for package design—the physical construction of a package and its graphic design. Nabisco wanted to deduct the entire $2 million in the year it was spent; the Internal Revenue Service insisted that the $2 million be treated like a capital expenditure and depreciated over time. Eventually, the Tax Court sided with Nabisco.

    a. Explain carefully why Nabisco would prefer to have the $2 million treated as a current expense rather than a capital expenditure.

    b. Do you agree with the ruling of the Tax Court?

6. During the 2008 presidential campaign, Senator John McCain proposed lowering the corporate tax rate from 35 percent to 25 percent. Evaluate the effect of this proposal on efficiency, equity, and the amount of investment.

7. A letter to the editor of the *Wall Street Journal* made the following claim: "The tax code's most regressive and unfair individual tax is—guess what?—the corporate income tax! All products and services purchased by individual taxpayers and the poor must be priced to pay for the federal income taxes of all the companies involved in the production/distribution/retail chain. So not only does the corporate income tax impose an unseen, incremental 40% tax burden on the vast majority of individual taxpayers, it also reduces the buying power of those too poor to pay income taxes" [Christy, 2006, p. A17]. Discuss the assumptions about the nature of the corporation tax implied by this statement, using the tax equivalence relationships provided in Table 14.2.

8. In 2009, President Obama proposed increasing the dividend tax rate from 15 percent to 20 percent for high-earners. How would this proposal affect the user cost of capital?

9. Legislation passed in 2009 allowed businesses to immediately write off 50 percent of the cost of depreciable assets acquired within the year. Explain how this would affect the user cost of capital and how it would affect business investment.

10. During the wave of corporate accounting scandals in 2001, it was revealed that Enron had raised money using a special financial instrument that had been developed by the investment banking firm of Goldman Sachs & Company. The financial instrument, called a MIPS (Monthly Income Preferred Shares),

"was designed in such a way that it could be called debt or equity, as needed. For the tax man, it resembled a loan. . . . For shareholders and rating agencies . . . it resembled equity" [McKinnon and Hitt, 2002]. Explain why using such a financial instrument would be attractive to a corporation (or at least a corporation managed by people who weren't overly concerned with ethical issues).

11. The ABC corporation is contemplating purchasing a new computer system that would yield a before-tax return of 30 percent. The system would depreciate at a rate of 1 percent a year. The after-tax interest rate is 8 percent, the corporation tax rate is 35 percent, and a typical shareholder of ABC has a marginal tax rate of 30 percent. Assume for simplicity that there are no depreciation allowances or investment tax credits. Do you expect ABC to buy the new computer system? Explain your answer. [Hint: Use Equation (19.4).]

DEFICIT FINANCE

"Generational theft." That's how critics characterized President Obama's 2009 budget proposal when they learned that it contemplated a budget deficit of $1.7 trillion, or 12.4 percent of Gross Domestic Product [US Office of Management and Budget, 2009, p. 114]. Contentious debates over the deficit are nothing new—the issue has dominated discussions of economic policy for years. This chapter discusses problems in measuring the size of the deficit, who bears its burden, and when it is a suitable way to finance government expenditures.

▶ HOW BIG IS THE DEBT?

We need a few definitions to begin our discussion. The **deficit** during a time period is the excess of spending over revenues; if revenues exceed expenditures, there is a **surplus.** That seems simple enough until we recall from Chapter 1 that the federal government does not include all its activities in its official budget. Under current rules, for example, revenues and expenditures associated with Social Security are off-budget. Despite this legal distinction, a proper measure of the extent of government borrowing requires that all revenues and expenditures be taken into account. Hence, it is useful to consider the sum of the **on-budget deficit (or surplus)** (which considers only on-budget activity) and the **off-budget deficit (or surplus)** (which takes into account only off-budget activity) to arrive at the total deficit or surplus. For example, in 2008, the on-budget deficit was $638 billion, but adding in a $183 billion off-budget surplus gave a total deficit of $455 billion [Congressional Budget Office, 2009a, p. 15].

Figure 20.1 shows total federal deficits (i.e., including off-budget revenues and expenditures) from 1965 to 2008. To put these figures in perspective, we also show their size relative to Gross Domestic Product (GDP). The budget was in surplus from 1998 through 2001, but deficits have generally been the rule.

One must distinguish between the concepts of deficit and debt. The **debt** at a given time is the sum of all past budget deficits. That is, the debt is the cumulative excess of past spending over past receipts. Thus, in a year with a deficit, the debt goes up; in a year with a surplus, the debt goes down. In the jargon of economics, the debt is a "stock variable" (measured at a point in time), while deficits and surpluses are "flow variables" (measured during a period of time). As reported in official government statistics, the federal debt at the end of 2008 was about $5.8

deficit

The excess of expenditures over revenues during a period of time.

surplus

The excess of revenues over spending during a period of time.

on-budget deficit

The deficit resulting from on-budget expenditures and revenues.

off-budget deficit

The deficit resulting from off-budget expenditures and revenues.

debt

The total amount owed at a given point in time; the sum of all past deficits.

Figure 20.1   Federal government deficits and surpluses (1965–2008)
For most of the past 40 years, the budget has been in deficit. In 2008, the deficit was $455 billion, which was 3.2 percent of Gross Domestic Product.

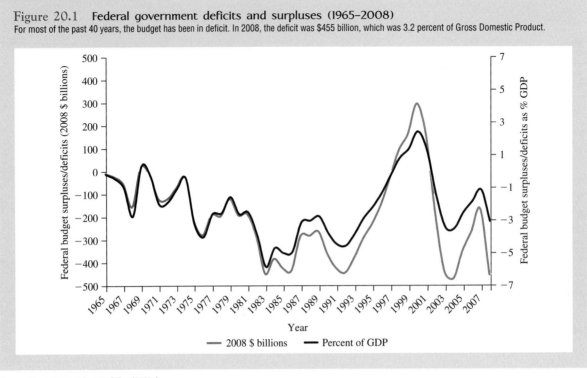

Source: Congressional Budget Office [2009a].

trillion, a number so large that it is hard to comprehend. As the humorist Russell Baker [1985] observed, "Like the light year, the trillion is an abstruse philosophical idea that can interest only persons with a morbid interest in mathematics. This explains why most people go limp with boredom when told that the national debt will soon be $2 trillion, or $20 trillion, or $200 trillion. The incomprehensible is incomprehensible, no matter how you number it."

Despite Baker's warning, let us try to put the debt in perspective, again by comparing it to GDP. The 2008 federal debt of $5.8 trillion was about 41 percent of that year's GDP—41 cents of every dollar produced would have been required to liquidate the debt. Figure 20.2 reports the federal government debt from 1965 through 2008.

Just like a private borrower, the government must pay interest to its lenders. In 2008, interest payments were $249 billion, or 8.4 percent of federal outlays [Congressional Budget Office, 2009a, p. 16].

Interpreting Deficit, Surplus, and Debt Numbers

It is hard to overestimate the political importance of numbers of the sort reported in Figures 20.1 and 20.2. Public officials and journalists focus on them almost exclusively when assessing the state of public finance. In 2009, for example, there were fierce debates over the possible consequences of anticipated deficits stemming from President Obama's budget proposals. It is quite likely, though, that the figures that formed the basis for this and other debates about deficits were not economically meaningful. In this section we explain why.

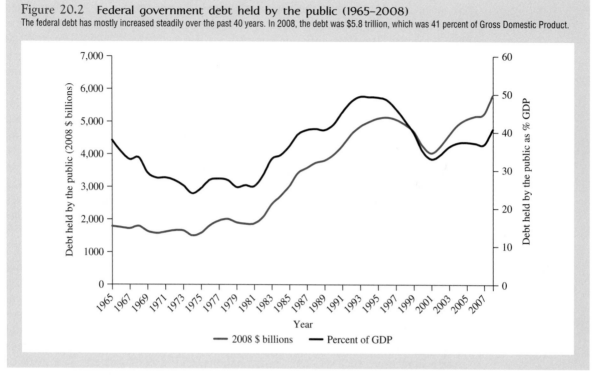

Figure 20.2 Federal government debt held by the public (1965–2008)

The federal debt has mostly increased steadily over the past 40 years. In 2008, the debt was $5.8 trillion, which was 41 percent of Gross Domestic Product.

Source: Congressional Budget Office [2009a].

Government Debt Held by the Federal Reserve Bank   In the course of conducting its monetary operations, the Federal Reserve Bank purchases US government securities.[1] Its holdings in 2007 were $780 billion [*Economic Report of the President, 2009*, p. 380]. Because statutorily the Federal Reserve Bank is an independent agency, its holdings are counted as debt held by the public; the amount of debt held by nongovernmental agencies is more relevant for most purposes.

State and Local Government Debt   Although we often think of debt as a federal government issue, state and local governments borrow as well. In 2005, state and local debt outstanding was $2.1 trillion [US Bureau of the Census, 2009, p. 265]. The federal figure for that year was $4.6 trillion; the sum of the two numbers is relevant if we wish to assess the pressure that government as a whole has exerted on credit markets.

Effects of Inflation   Standard calculations of the deficit view taxes as the only source of government revenue. However, when the government is a debtor and the price level changes, changes in the real value of the debt may be an important source of revenue. To see why, suppose that at the beginning of the year you owe a

---

[1] Some agencies of the federal government lend to the Treasury, but unlike the Federal Reserve Bank, their holdings are not included in figures on debt held by the public.

creditor $1,000, and the sum does not have to be repaid until the end of the year. Suppose further that over the course of the year, prices rise by 10 percent. Then the dollars you use to repay your creditor are worth 10 percent less than those you borrowed. In effect, inflation has reduced the real value of your debt by $100 (10 percent of $1,000). Alternatively, your real income has increased by $100 as a consequence of inflation. Of course, at the same time, your creditor's real income has fallen by $100.[2]

Let us apply this logic to an analysis of the federal deficit in 2008. At the beginning of fiscal year 2008, the federal government's outstanding debt was about $5.0 trillion. During 2008, the rate of inflation was about 3.8 percent. Hence, inflation reduced the real value of the federal debt by $190 billion (= $5.0 trillion $\times$ 0.038). In effect, this is as much a receipt for the government as any conventional tax. If we take this "inflation tax" into account, the conventionally measured deficit of $455 billion is reduced to $265 billion. However, the government's accounting procedures do not allow the inclusion of gains due to inflationary erosion of the debt. This induces a tendency to overestimate the size of the real deficit.

Capital versus Current Accounting   The federal government lumps together all expenditures that are legally required to be included in the budget. There is no attempt to distinguish between *current spending* and *capital spending*. Current spending refers to expenditures for services that are consumed within the year— upkeep at the Washington Monument or salaries for marines, for example. Capital spending, in contrast, refers to expenditures for durable items that yield services over a long time, such as dams, radar stations, and aircraft carriers. The stock of federally financed physical capital is about $2.4 trillion, of which approximately $785 billion is related to national defense [US Office of Management and Budget, 2008, p. 66].

In contrast to federal government practice, both US businesses and many state and local governments generally keep separate budgets for current and capital expenditure. Maintaining a separate capital budget provides a more accurate picture of an organization's financial status. Why? Purchasing a durable asset does not generally represent a "loss." It is only a trade of one asset (money) for another (the durable). Hence, the asset does not contribute to an organization's deficit. Of course, as the capital asset is used, it wears out (depreciation), and this *does* constitute a loss. Thus, standard accounting procedures require that only the annual depreciation of durable assets be included in the current budget, not their entire purchase price.

The idea of the federal government adopting capital budgeting is controversial. Proponents of capital budgeting note that its absence can lead to inefficient programs [Bassetto and Sargent, 2006] and sometimes even bizarre governmental decisions. For example, politicians can hold "yard sales" in which they sell off government assets to the private sector and claim that they are reducing the deficit. Part of the Bush administration's deficit reduction plan, for example, was to sell a large number of nondefense federal buildings. As we pointed out in Chapter 4, there may be good reasons for selling such assets, but they have nothing to do with reducing the real budget deficit. They simply represent the government trading one asset for the other.

---

[2] If the inflation is anticipated by borrowers and lenders, one expects the interest rate charged to be increased to take inflation into account. This phenomenon was discussed in Chapter 17.

However, under the current accounting system, the proceeds of such sales are treated as equivalent to tax revenues, and so count toward reducing the deficit.

A final argument in favor of capital budgeting is that it reminds people that borrowing is not necessarily a bad thing. Just as a prudent household may go into debt to purchase capital assets like a house or a car, a prudent government can borrow to finance the purchase of long-lived assets.

Opponents of capital budgeting point out that, for governments, it is particularly difficult to distinguish between current and capital expenditure. Are educational and job-training programs a current expense, or an investment in human capital that will yield future returns? Is a missile an investment (because it will last a long time), or a current expenditure (because it is not reusable)? Such ambiguities could lead to political mischief, with every proponent of a new spending program claiming it was an investment and therefore belonged in the capital budget. In fact, advocates of transfer programs such as food stamps often promote them as "investments," because enhancing the diets of the poor today increases their future productivity. Critics assert that classifying transfer payments as investments renders meaningless the distinction between capital and current spending.

Tangible Assets   Suppose that a family owns tangible assets (yachts, houses, Rembrandts) worth $15 million, owes the local bank $25,000 for credit card charges, and has no other assets or liabilities. It would be pretty silly to characterize the family's overall position as being $25,000 in debt. All assets and liabilities must be considered to assess overall financial position.

The federal government has not only massive financial liabilities (as depicted in Figure 20.2), but vast tangible assets as well. These include residential and nonresidential buildings, equipment, gold, and mineral rights. However, public discussion focuses almost entirely on the government's financial liabilities, and not its tangible assets. Some have argued that the omission of tangibles leads to a highly misleading picture of the government's financial position.

Implicit Obligations   A bond is simply a promise to make certain payments of money in the future. The present value of these payments is the amount by which the bond contributes to the debt. But bonds are not the only method that the federal government uses to promise money in the future. It can do so by legislation. A prominent example is Social Security, which promises benefits to future retirees that must be paid out of future tax revenues. The precise value is hard to calculate, but estimates of Social Security's unfunded future liability range around $14 trillion. Medicare's Hospital Insurance program similarly imposes future obligations on the government; their present value is about $22 trillion. In addition, federal legislation promises retirement benefits to civilian and military employees. Federal pension liabilities are about $4.7 trillion [US Office of Management and Budget, 2008, p. 185].

Of course, legislative promises and official debt are not exactly equivalent. Their legal status is quite different; explicit forms of debt represent legal commitments, while Social Security and Medicare payments can be reduced by legislative action, at least in principle. Nevertheless, political support for these programs is strong, and it would be surprising to see the government substantially renege on these promises. On this basis, a number of economists have argued that the present value of promised Social Security, Medicare, and other entitlement benefits should be included in the national debt.

Summing Up

How big is the national debt? The answer depends on which assets and liabilities are included in the calculation, and how they are valued. As in other similar situations, the "correct" answer depends on your purposes. For example, if the goal is to obtain some sense of all the obligations that have to be met by future taxpayers, then measures including implicit obligations like Social Security are appropriate. But if the purpose is to assess the effect of fiscal policy on credit markets (discussed later), then it is more suitable to use conventional deficit measures that include only official liabilities. Considerable caution must be exercised in interpreting figures on debts, deficits, and surpluses.

▶ THE BURDEN OF THE DEBT

Practically everyone agrees that reducing the national debt would be a good thing. But why should we care about the national debt, and whether it is increasing or decreasing? It's a tough question, and answering it requires hard thinking about the costs of debt finance and who bears them.

We begin by noting that future generations either have to retire the debt, or else refinance it. (Refinancing simply means borrowing new money to pay existing creditors.) In either case, there is a transfer from future taxpayers to bondholders because even if the debt is refinanced, interest payments must be made to the new bondholders. It would appear, then, that future generations must bear the burden of the debt. Humorist Dave Barry expressed this view by comparing the debt to "going to a fancy restaurant and ordering everything on the menu, secure in the knowledge that, when the bill comes, you'll be dead" [Barry, 2004].

But the theory of incidence (Chapter 14) tells us to be suspicious of this line of reasoning. Merely because the legal burden is on future generations does not mean that they bear the real burden. Just as in the case of tax incidence, the chain of events set in motion when borrowing occurs can make the economic incidence quite different from the statutory incidence. As with other incidence problems, the answer depends on the assumptions made about economic behavior.

Lerner's View

internal debt

The amount that a government owes to its own citizens.

Assume the government borrows from its own citizens—the obligation is an **internal debt.** According to Lerner [1948], an internal debt creates no burden for the future generation. Members of the future generation simply owe it to each other. When the debt is paid off, there is a transfer of income from one group of citizens (those who do not hold bonds) to another (bondholders). However, the future generation as a whole is no worse off in the sense that its consumption level is the same as it would have been. As an 18th-century writer named Melon put it, the "right hand owes to the left" [Musgrave, 1985, p. 49].

external debt

The amount a government owes to foreigners.

The story is quite different when a country borrows from abroad to finance current expenditure. This is referred to as an **external debt.** In the United States, about 54 percent of the privately held federal debt is held by foreign investors, so this is a consequential issue [*Economic Report of the President, 2009*, p. 388]. Suppose that the money borrowed from overseas is used to finance current consumption. In this case, the future generation certainly bears a burden, because its consumption level is reduced by an amount equal to the loan plus the accrued interest that must be sent

Table 20.1 **Overlapping Generations Model**

	The Period 2010–2030		
	Young	**Middle-Aged**	**Old**
(1) Income	$ 12,000	$ 12,000	$12,000
(2) Government borrowing	−6,000	−6,000	
(3) Government-provided consumption	4,000	4,000	4,000
		The Year 2030	
	Young	**Middle-Aged**	**Old**
(4) Government raises taxes to pay back the debt	$−4,000	$−4,000	$−4,000
(5) Government pays back the debt		+6,000	+6,000

This overlapping generations model shows how government borrowing can transfer income from the young generation to the old generation.

to foreign lenders.[3] If, on the other hand, the loan is used to finance capital accumulation, the outcome depends on the project's productivity. If the marginal return on the investment is greater than the marginal cost of funds obtained abroad, the combination of the debt and capital expenditure actually makes the future generation better off. To the extent that the project's return is less than the marginal cost, the future generation is worse off.

The view that an internally held debt does not burden future generations dominated the economics profession in the 1940s and 1950s. Economists now believe that things are considerably more complicated.

An Overlapping Generations Model

In Lerner's model, a "generation" consists of everyone who is alive at a given time. A more sensible way to define a generation is everyone who was born at about the same time. Using this definition, at any given time several generations coexist simultaneously, a phenomenon that is central to an **overlapping generations model.** Analysis of a simple overlapping generations model shows how the burden of a debt can be transferred across generations.

Assume that the population consists of equal numbers of young, middle-aged, and old people. Each generation is 20 years long, and each person has a fixed income of $12,000 over the 20-year period. There is no private saving—everyone consumes their entire income. This situation is expected to continue forever. Income levels for three representative people for the period 2010 to 2030 are depicted in row 1 of Table 20.1.

Now assume that the government decides to borrow $12,000 to finance public consumption. The loan is to be repaid in the year 2030. Only the young and the

overlapping generations model

A model that takes into account the fact that several different generations coexist simultaneously.

---

[3] If the loan is refinanced, only the interest must be paid.

middle-aged are willing to lend to the government—the old are unwilling because they will not be around in 20 years to obtain repayment. Assume that half the lending is done by the young and half by the middle-aged, so that consumption of each person is reduced by $6,000 during the period 2010 to 2030. This fact is recorded in row 2 of Table 20.1. However, with the money obtained from the loan, the government provides an equal amount of consumption for all—each person receives $4,000. This is noted in line 3.

Time passes, and the year 2030 arrives. The generation that was old in 2010 has departed from the scene. The formerly middle-aged are now old, the young are now middle-aged, and a new young generation has been born. The government has to raise $12,000 to pay off the debt. It does so by levying a tax of $4,000 on each person. This is recorded in line 4. With the tax receipts in hand, the government can pay back its debt holders, the now middle-aged and old (row 5). (We assume for simplicity that the rate of interest is zero, so all the government has to pay back is the principal. Introducing a positive rate of interest would not change the substantive result and means there is no need to discount future consumption to find its present value.)

The following results now emerge from Table 20.1:

1. As a consequence of the debt and accompanying tax policies, the generation that was old in 2010 to 2030 has a lifetime consumption level $4,000 higher than it otherwise would have enjoyed.

2. Those who were young and middle-aged in 2010 to 2030 are no better or worse off from the point of view of lifetime consumption.

3. The young generation in 2030 has a lifetime consumption stream that is $4,000 lower than it would have been in the absence of the debt and accompanying fiscal policies.

In effect, $4,000 has been transferred from the young of 2030 to the old of 2010. To be sure, the debt repayment in 2030 involves a transfer between people who are alive at the time, but the young are at the short end of the transfer because they have to contribute to repaying a debt from which they never benefited. Note also that the internal-external distinction that was key in Lerner's model is irrelevant here; even though the debt is all internal, it creates a burden for the future generation.

The model in Table 20.1 suggests a natural framework for comparing across generations the burdens (and benefits) of government fiscal policies. This framework, called **generational accounting,** involves the following steps. First, take a representative person in each generation and compute the present value of all taxes she pays to the government. Next, compute the present value of all transfers received from the government, including Social Security, Medicare, and so on. The difference between the present value of the taxes and the transfers is the "net tax" paid by a member of that generation. By comparing the net taxes paid by different generations, one can get a sense of how government policy redistributes income across generations.

Most calculations using this framework suggest that current generations benefit at the expense of future generations. Kotlikoff [2002] estimates that, if current policies remain in place, future generations will face a lifetime net tax rate that is 41.6 percent higher than that facing people born today. Of course, such calculations rest heavily on assumptions about future tax rates, interest rates, and so on. Further, they do not allow for the possibility that individuals in a given generation may care about their descendants as well as themselves (see below). Thus, the main contribution of the generational accounts framework is to focus our attention on the lifetime (rather

generational accounting

Method for measuring the consequences of government fiscal policy that takes into account the present value of all taxes and benefits received by members of each generation.

than annual) consequences of government fiscal policies. The specific net tax rates must be taken with a grain of salt.

Neoclassical Model

The intergenerational models discussed so far assume that the taxes levied to pay off the debt affect neither work nor saving behavior. If taxes distort these decisions, real costs are imposed on the economy.

We have also ignored the potentially important effect of debt finance on capital formation. The neoclassical model of the debt stresses that when the government initiates a project, whether financed by taxes or borrowing, resources are removed from the private sector. One usually assumes that when tax finance is used, most of the resources removed come at the expense of consumption. On the other hand, when the government borrows, it competes for funds with individuals and firms who want the money for their own investment projects. If so, debt has most of its effect on private investment. To the extent that these assumptions are correct, debt finance leaves the future generation with a smaller capital stock, all other things equal. Its members therefore are less productive and have smaller real incomes than otherwise would have been the case. Thus, the debt imposes a burden on future generations through its impact on capital formation. (Note, however, that one of the things that is held equal here is the public sector capital stock. As suggested earlier, to the extent that the public sector undertakes productive investment with the resources it extracts from the private sector, the total capital stock increases.)

The assumption that government borrowing reduces private investment plays a key role in the neoclassical analysis. It is referred to as the **crowding out hypothesis**— when the public sector draws on the pool of resources available for investment, private investment gets crowded out. Crowding out results from changes in the interest rate. When the government increases its demand for credit, the interest rate, which is just the price of credit, goes up. But if the interest rate increases, private investment becomes more expensive and less of it is undertaken.[4]

Expressed this way, it would appear relatively straightforward to test the crowding out hypothesis. Just examine the historical relationship between the interest rate and government deficits (as a proportion of Gross Domestic Product). A positive correlation between the two variables would support the crowding out hypothesis. The question of how deficits affect interest rates has been a hot political topic. For example, some opponents of the Obama administration's budget proposals, which included substantial increases in debt, argued that they would lead to a rise in interest rates.

Unfortunately, resolving this controversy is complicated because other variables also affect interest rates. For example, during a recession, investment decreases and hence the interest rate falls. At the same time, slack business conditions lead to smaller tax collections, which increases the deficit, all other things equal. Hence, the data may show an inverse relationship between interest rates and deficits, although this says nothing one way or the other about crowding out. This occurred during the recession of 2008 and 2009, when interest rates were very low even though deficits had increased dramatically. As usual, the problem is to sort out the *independent* effect

> **crowding out hypothesis**
>
> **Government borrowing decreases private investment by raising the market interest rate.**

---

[4] When capital is internationally mobile, the debt-induced increase in the interest rate leads to an inflow of funds from abroad. This increases the demand for dollars, causing the dollar to appreciate, which increases the relative price of American exports. Hence, net exports are crowded out rather than domestic investment. In the US economy, some of both domestic investment and exports are likely crowded out.

of deficits on interest rates, and as we showed in Chapter 2, this kind of problem can be quite difficult. Several decades of intensive econometric work on this issue have failed to lead to conclusive results. A reasonable estimate based on recent studies is an increase in the federal deficit amounting to 1 percent of GDP raises interest rates by about 0.3 percentage points [Congressional Budget Office, 2005b, p. 4].

Despite the murkiness of the econometric evidence, the theoretical case for at least partial crowding out is so strong that most economists agree that large deficits cause some reduction in the capital stock.[5] However, the precise size of this reduction, and hence the decrease in welfare for future generations, is not known with any precision. One estimate is that a $1 increase in the budget deficit results in a 36 cent decrease in domestic investment [Congressional Budget Office, 2008a]. If this estimate is correct, it suggests that deficit spending has had a negative, but not disastrous, impact on the economy.

Ricardian Model

Our discussion so far has ignored the potential importance of individuals' intentional transfers across generations. Barro [1974] has argued that when the government borrows, members of the "old" generation realize that their heirs will be made worse off. Suppose further that the old care about the welfare of their descendants and therefore do not want their descendants' consumption levels reduced. What can the old do about this? One possibility is simply to increase their bequests by an amount sufficient to pay the extra taxes that will be due in the future. The result is that nothing really changes. Each generation consumes exactly the same amount as before the government borrowed. In terms of the model in Table 20.1, the old generation in 2010 saves $4,000 to give to the young of 2030 so that the consumption of each generation is unchanged.

In effect, then, private individuals undo the intergenerational effects of government debt policy so that tax and debt finance are essentially equivalent. This view, that the form of government finance is irrelevant, is often referred to as the Ricardian model because its antecedents appeared in the work of the 19th-century British economist David Ricardo. (However, Ricardo was skeptical about the theory that now bears his name.)

Barro's provocative hypothesis on the irrelevance of government fiscal policy has been the subject of much debate. Some reject the idea as being based on incredible assumptions, such as people understanding precisely how current deficits will lead to future tax burdens. Indeed, as emphasized earlier in this chapter, it isn't even clear how big the debt is! Another criticism is that people are not as farsighted as supposed in the model.

On the other hand, one could argue that the ultimate test of the theory is not the plausibility of its assumptions, but whether or not its predictions are confirmed by the data. Skeptics note that in the early 1980s, there was a huge increase in federal deficits. If the Ricardian model were correct, one would have expected private saving to increase commensurately. However, private saving (relative to net national product) actually fell. While this finding is suggestive, it is not conclusive because factors other than the deficit affect the saving rate. A number of econometric studies have

---

[5] To the extent that higher interest rates attract foreign investment, less crowding out occurs. However, the burden on future generations is roughly unchanged because of the interest they must pay to foreigners.

analyzed the relationship between budget deficits and saving. (See Congressional Budget Office [2005b].) The evidence is rather mixed, and the Ricardian model has both critics and adherents among professional economists.

Overview

The burden of the debt is essentially a tax incidence problem in an intergenerational setting. Like many other incidence problems, the burden of the debt is hard to pin down. First, it is not obvious how burden should be defined. One possibility is to measure it in terms of the lifetime consumption possibilities of a group of people about the same age. Another is in terms of the consumption available to all people alive at a given time. Even when we settle on a definition, the existence of a burden depends on the answers to several questions: Is the debt internal or external? How are various economic decisions affected by debt policy? What kind of projects are financed by the debt? Empirical examination of some of these decisions has been attempted, but so far no consensus has emerged.

▶ TO TAX OR TO BORROW?

During her campaign to be the 2008 presidential candidate of the Democratic Party, then-Senator Hillary Clinton was asked if she would support a tax to help finance the wars in Iraq and Afghanistan. She responded with an unequivocal no. This touched off a debate about whether it was appropriate to leave future generations responsible for funding current wars. The choice between debt and taxes is one of the most fundamental questions in the field of public finance. Armed with the results of our discussion of the burden of the debt, we are in a good position to evaluate several approaches to answering the question.

Benefits-Received Principle

This normative principle states that the beneficiaries of a government program should have to pay for it. Thus, to the extent that the program creates benefits for future generations, it is appropriate to shift the burden to future generations via debt finance. A possible example is borrowing to pay for schools that benefit students by increasing their future earnings.

Intergenerational Equity

Suppose that due to technological progress, our grandchildren will be richer than we are. If it makes sense to transfer income from rich to poor people within a generation, why shouldn't we transfer income from rich to poor generations? Of course, if future generations are expected to be poorer than we are (due, say, to increases in prices of certain natural resources), then this logic leads to just the opposite conclusion.

Efficiency Considerations

From an efficiency standpoint, the question is whether debt or tax finance generates a higher excess burden. The key to analyzing this question is to realize that *every* increase in government spending must ultimately be financed by an increase in taxes. The choice between tax and debt finance is just a choice between the timing of the

Figure 20.3
The relationship between tax rate and excess burden
Excess burden increases with the square of the tax rate.

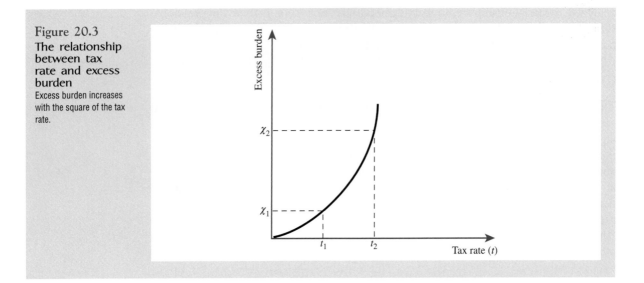

taxes. With tax finance, one large payment is made at the time the expenditure is undertaken. With debt finance, many small payments are made over time to finance the interest due on the debt. The present values of the tax collections must be the same in both cases.

If the present values of tax collections for the two methods are the same, is there any reason to prefer one or the other on efficiency grounds? Assume for simplicity that all revenues to finance the debt are raised by a tax on labor income. As shown in Chapter 15 [Equation (15.4)], such a tax distorts labor supply decisions, creating an excess burden of

$$\tfrac{1}{2}\epsilon wLt^2$$

where ϵ is the compensated elasticity of hours of work with respect to the wage, w is the before-tax wage, L is hours worked, and t is the ad valorem tax rate. Note that excess burden increases with the *square* of the tax rate—when the tax rate doubles, the excess burden quadruples. Thus, from the excess burden point of view, two small taxes are preferred to one big tax.

This point is illustrated in Figure 20.3, which depicts the quadratic relationship between excess burden and the tax rate. The excess burden associated with the low tax rate, t_1, is X_1, and the excess burden associated with the higher rate, t_2, is X_2. From an efficiency standpoint, it is better to be taxed twice at rate t_1, than once at rate t_2. The implication is that debt finance, which results in a series of relatively small tax rates, is superior to tax finance on efficiency grounds.

This argument ignores an important consideration—to the extent the increase in debt reduces the capital stock, it creates an additional excess burden.[6] Thus, while debt finance may be more efficient from the point of view of labor supply choices, it will be less efficient from the point of view of capital allocation decisions. A priori it is unclear which effect is more important, so we cannot know whether debt or tax finance is more efficient.

---

[6] More precisely, an additional excess burden is created if the capital stock starts out below the optimal level because of, for example, capital income taxes (see Feldstein [1985, p. 234]).

Thus, "crowding out," which was so important in our discussion of the intergenerational burden of the debt, is also central to the efficiency issue. Recall that according to the Ricardian model, there is no crowding out. Thus, taxes distort only labor supply choices, and debt finance is unambiguously superior on efficiency grounds. However, to the extent that crowding out occurs, tax finance becomes more attractive. Clearly, because the empirical evidence on crowding out is inconclusive, we cannot know for sure the relative efficiency merits of debt versus tax finance.

Macroeconomic Considerations

Thus far, we have made our usual assumption that all resources are fully employed. Recall from Chapter 8 that this implies that government spending diverts resources from the private sector, and thus imposes costs on society (which should be compared to the benefits of the government expenditure). This framework is appropriate for characterizing long-run tendencies in the economy. However, when the economy is not operating at its full potential, then government spending can draw upon unemployed labor and capital and help return the economy to full employment. To the extent this is the case, deficit finance can be desirable because of the low opportunity cost of the resources diverted from the private sector. This approach is sometimes referred to as **functional finance**—use taxes and deficits to keep aggregate demand at the right level, and don't worry about balancing the budget per se.

> **Functional Finance**
>
> Using fiscal policy to keep aggregate demand at the desired level, regardless of the impact on deficits.

There is considerable controversy over functional finance, in part based on disagreements over the extent to which government spending actually puts to work resources that otherwise would have been unemployed. While a thorough discussion of the relevant aspects of macroeconomics would take us much too far afield, a couple of points are worth making:

- If Barro's intergenerational altruism model is correct, people can undo the effects of government debt policy. Government cannot stabilize the economy.[7]
- There is a lot of uncertainty regarding just how long it takes for changes in fiscal policy to become translated into changes in employment. But successful unemployment policy requires that the timing be right. Otherwise, one might end up stimulating the economy when it is no longer required, perhaps contributing to inflation. This timing issue played an important role in the 2009 debate over the fiscal stimulus package that was proposed by the Obama administration.

Moral and Political Considerations

Some have suggested that the decision between tax and debt finance is a moral issue. As President Thomas Jefferson put it in 1813, "I trust that . . . we shall all consider ourselves unauthorized to saddle posterity with our debts, and morally bound to pay them ourselves." Morality requires self-restraint; deficits are indicative of a lack of restraint; therefore, deficits are immoral. The implicit assumption that debt is immoral is a feature of political debates.

As emphasized throughout this text, ethical issues are critical in the formulation of public policy, so arguments that deficits are immoral deserve serious consideration.

---

[7] More precisely, *anticipated* changes in policy have no impact. Unanticipated changes may have an effect, because by definition, people cannot change their behavior to counteract them.

One should note, however, that this *normative* view seems to rest heavily on the unproven *positive* hypothesis that the burden of the debt is shifted to future generations. Moreover, it is not clear why this particular normative view is superior to, for example, the benefits-received principle, which implies that sometimes borrowing is the morally right thing to do.

Another argument against deficit spending is political. As noted in Chapter 6, some believe that the political process tends to underestimate the costs of government spending and to overestimate the benefits. The discipline of a balanced budget may produce a more careful weighing of benefits and costs, thus preventing the public sector from growing beyond its optimal size.

However, some who think that government spends too much have a different viewpoint, arguing that deficits may serve as an effective brake on government spending. According to Nobel laureate Milton Friedman [2003, p. A10], the conventional view is that the level of government spending is fixed, regardless of whether there is a deficit or not. If that is true, then raising taxes can eliminate the deficit. But Friedman argues that a better model is that spending is not fixed—if the government gets more money in taxes, it will simply spend the money. "What is predetermined is not spending but the politically tolerable deficit. Raise taxes by enough to eliminate the existing deficit and spending will go up to restore the tolerable deficit." A better strategy for restraining government is cutting taxes. "Resulting deficits will be an effective . . . restraint on the spending propensities of the executive branch and the legislature." As emphasized in Chapter 6, it is very difficult to assess the validity of theories of government spending. Indeed, other researchers find that tax cuts do not lead to lower government spending [Romer and Romer, 2007]. In any case, this issue reminds us of the importance of considering the political environment when making policy recommendations.

▶ OVERVIEW

The national debt is an emotional and difficult subject. The analysis of this chapter brings the following perspectives to bear on the debate:

- The size of the deficit during a given year depends on one's accounting conventions. This fact underscores the arbitrariness of any number that purports to be *the* deficit, *the* surplus, or *the* debt.
- The consequences of deficits and surpluses, while potentially important, are hard to measure. And even if we knew exactly what the effects were, the implications for the conduct of debt policy would still depend on ethical views concerning the intergenerational distribution of income.

In light of all these considerations, it makes little sense to evaluate the economic operation of the public sector solely on the basis of the size of the official deficit or surplus. A deficit is not necessarily bad, and a surplus is not necessarily good. More important is whether the levels of government services are optimal, particularly considering the costs of securing the resources required to provide these services. A lively debate over the spending and financing activities of government is important in a democracy. The consequences of deficit versus other forms of finance are important and worthy of public consideration. Nevertheless, the tendency of both liberals and conservatives to evaluate the state of public finance solely on the basis of the deficit tends to obscure and confuse the debate.

Summary

- Borrowing is an important method of government finance. The deficit during a period of time is the excess of spending over revenues; the surplus is the excess of revenues over spending; the debt as of a given point in time is the algebraic sum of past deficits and surpluses.

- Official figures regarding the size of federal government deficits, surpluses, and debts must be viewed with caution for several reasons:

  State and local governments also have large amounts of debt outstanding.

  Inflation erodes the real value of the debt; the official deficit or surplus does not reflect this fact.

  The federal government does not distinguish between capital and current expenditure. However, attempts to design a capital budget for the federal government could founder on both conceptual and political problems.

  Tangible assets owned by the government should be taken into account, as should the government's implicit obligations (such as promises to pay Social Security and Medicare benefits).

- Whether or not the burden of debt is borne by future generations is controversial. One view is that an internal debt creates no net burden for the future generation because it is simply an intragenerational transfer. However, in an overlapping generations model, debt finance can produce a real burden on future generations.

- The burden of the debt also depends on whether debt finance crowds out private investment. If it does, future generations have a smaller capital stock and, hence, lower real incomes, all other things equal. In a Ricardian model, voluntary transfers across generations undo the effects of debt policy, so that crowding out does not occur.

- Several factors influence whether a given government expenditure should be financed by taxes or debt. The benefits-received principle suggests that if the project will benefit future generations, then having them pay for it via loan finance is appropriate. Also, if future generations are expected to be richer than the present one, some principles of equity suggest that it is fair to burden them.

- From an efficiency standpoint, one must compare the excess burdens of tax and debt finance. If there is no crowding out, debt finance has less of an excess burden, because a series of small tax increases generates a smaller excess burden than one large tax increase. However, if crowding out occurs, this conclusion may be reversed.

Discussion Questions

1. How would each of the following events affect the national debt as it is currently measured?

   a. The government borrows to finance a Memorial Day parade.

   b. The Statue of Liberty is sold to a group of private entrepreneurs.

   c. A law is passed promising free medical care to every child under five years of age.

   d. The government levies a tax of $100 on Lynne this year, and promises to pay her $105 next year.

   e. The government borrows $100 from Lynne this year, and pays back the $100 with 5 percent interest next year.

   If you were designing an accounting system for the government, how would you treat each of these items?

2. In 2004, the German government considered selling publicly owned gold in order to reduce its budget deficit. Do you think this is a sensible approach to reducing the German deficit? Explain.

3. According to Schick [2002, p. 46], "The arrival of a surplus [in the late 1990s] triggered a spending frenzy that vitiated the discretionary spending caps established by the 1990 Budget Enforcement Act and made a mockery of the BEA requirement that increased spending be offset by cuts in other spending or by revenue increases." Discuss the relationship of this episode to Milton Friedman's approach to thinking about the relationship between deficits and government spending.

4. Suppose that the compensated elasticity of labor supply with respect to the wage is zero. On efficiency grounds, what are the consequences for the optimal choice between debt and tax finance for a temporary increase in government spending?

5. In 2009, Virginia Congressman Eric Cantor said that the debt "will be put onto future generations." Under what conditions is Representative Cantor's comment correct?

6. In his 2009 budget proposal, President Obama wrote, "Unfortunately, we are also inheriting the worst economic crisis since the Great Depression—which will force us to increase deficit spending temporarily as we try to jump-start economic growth." Under what conditions is it sensible to use a deficit to finance government spending?

Chapter Twenty-One

FUNDAMENTAL TAX REFORM: TAXES ON CONSUMPTION AND WEALTH

> *But when the impositions are laid upon those things which men consume, every man payeth equally for what he useth: nor is the common wealth defrauded by the luxurious waste of private men.*
>
> —THOMAS HOBBES

There is substantial dissatisfaction with the federal personal and corporate income tax systems. As a bipartisan presidential panel on tax reform noted, "If you were to start from scratch, the current tax code would provide a guide on what to avoid. . . . [W]e have a tax code that distorts basic economic decisions, sets up incentives for unwise or unproductive investments, and induces people to work less, save less, and borrow more. By some estimates, this economic waste may be as much as $1 trillion dollars each year" [President's Advisory Panel on Federal Tax Reform, 2005, p. 1].

We discussed some options for improving the personal income and corporation taxes in Chapters 17 and 19, respectively. In this chapter we analyze a more fundamental reform of the tax system—changing the base of the system from income to consumption. With a consumption tax, the tax base is the value (or quantity) of commodities sold to a person for *actual* consumption, while for an income tax, the base is the change in *potential* consumption.

There is a rich economic literature on the pros and cons of replacing the income tax with a consumption tax. One controversial issue that arises with a consumption tax is what to do about people who have large incomes and consume little, thereby paying little in taxes and accumulating large amounts of wealth, which can then be passed on to their heirs. We therefore devote part of this chapter to analyzing the current and proposed tax treatment of wealth, particularly of bequests.

▶ EFFICIENCY AND EQUITY OF PERSONAL CONSUMPTION TAXES

Advocates for replacing the income tax with a consumption tax argue that efficiency, equity, and administrative simplicity would be enhanced. Defenders of the income tax argue that the case for a personal consumption tax is seriously flawed. We now discuss the controversy.

Efficiency Issues

The efficiency of a consumption tax versus an income tax can be examined using the life-cycle model of consumption and saving discussed in Chapters 11 and 18. In that model, an individual's labor supply each period is fixed. The two commodities she purchases are present consumption, c_0, and future consumption, c_1. If r is the interest rate, every additional dollar of consumption today means that the individual's future consumption is reduced by $(1 + r)$. Hence, the relative price of c_0—its opportunity cost—is $(1 + r)$.

Consider now the case of Juliet, on whom a 30 percent income tax is levied. Assuming that the tax allows for the deductibility of interest payments, how does this affect the relative price of c_0?[1] If Juliet saves a dollar and it earns a return of r, the government taxes away 30 percent of the return, leaving her only $0.70 \times r$. If she borrows a dollar, the interest payments are deductible, so the cost of borrowing is reduced to $0.70 \times r$. In short, the income tax reduces the relative price of present consumption from $(1 + r)$ to $(1 + 0.70r)$. A wedge is inserted between the amount a borrower pays and a lender receives. As we showed in Chapter 15, tax wedges create excess burdens. We conclude that an income tax generates an excess burden.

Now consider a consumption tax that raises the same amount of revenue as the income tax. The key thing to note is that with the consumption tax the market rate of return available to Juliet is unchanged. This is because receiving interest income by itself does not create a tax liability. Hence, after the consumption tax, the relative price of c_0 is still $(1 + r)$. Unlike the income tax, there is no tax wedge and, hence, no excess burden. This neutral treatment of saving is frequently cited as the key advantage of a consumption tax. As Lazear and Poterba [2006, p. 4] write, "By eliminating the favored treatment of present consumption over future consumption that results from the taxation of saving in an income tax, a consumption tax removes the disincentive to save."

While the consumption tax, unlike the income tax, leaves unchanged the rate at which Juliet can trade off consumption between the two periods, in general, it *does* distort the rate at which she can trade off leisure against consumption. Recall from Chapter 15 that even a tax at the same rate on every commodity distorts the choice between leisure and each of the taxed commodities, so it is not clear that taxing all commodities at the same rate is efficient. The key insight is that the consumption tax distorts the choice between consumption and leisure. To see why, suppose that Juliet has a wage of $5 per hour. Suppose further that the price of the good she consumes is $1 per unit. Then for each hour of leisure she gives up, Juliet can get 5 units of consumption goods. Now suppose that a consumption tax of 25 percent is levied, so the price of the consumption good increases to $1.25. Now Juliet can only get 4 units of the consumption good for each hour of leisure she gives up (because $5/1.25 = 4$). Hence, the consumption tax distorts the decision between leisure and consumption.

In short, while an income tax distorts the saving decision and a consumption tax does not, both taxes distort the labor supply decision. One cannot simply conclude that a consumption tax is preferable because it only distorts one market instead of two. Rather, both systems induce an efficiency cost, and only empirical work can determine which tax's cost is smaller. Nonetheless, most studies indicate that given

---

[1] As stressed in Chapters 17 and 18, not all taxpayers can deduct payments of interest. Discussion Question 7 at the end of the chapter examines how the analysis is modified when interest is not deductible.

what is known about labor supply and saving behavior, a consumption tax creates a smaller excess burden than an income tax, even when labor supply distortions created by both taxes are taken into account. (See, for example, Feldstein [2006a].)

Equity Issues

Progressiveness   The conventional view is that consumption taxes are regressive. As the Washington organization Citizens for Tax Justice put it, with a consumption tax, "Wealthy people are taxed at a far lower rate than middle-income families. Why? Because higher-income people spend a smaller proportion of their income."[2]

This line of reasoning has three problems. First, it looks at the tax as a proportion of *annual* income. In the absence of severe credit market restrictions, *lifetime* income is more relevant, and there is reasonably strong evidence that people consume about the same proportion of their lifetime income in a given year. Second, and perhaps more fundamentally, the conventional view ignores the theory of tax incidence by assuming that taxes on a good are borne entirely by the consumers of that good. As emphasized in Chapter 14, however, a commodity tax generally is shifted in a way that depends on the supply and demand responses when the tax is imposed. The effect of consumption taxes on the distribution of income is an open question. Finally, it is incorrect to assume that all consumption taxes result in the same level of statutory progressivity. As we show below, some consumption tax prototypes allow the tax burden to depend on the particular family's characteristics, so the rate schedule can be made as progressive as desired.

Ability to Pay   Opponents of a consumption tax argue that *actual* consumption is merely one component of *potential* consumption. It is the power to consume, not necessarily its exercise, that is relevant. They point out that under a consumption tax, a miserly millionaire might have a smaller tax liability than a much poorer person. A possible response is that it is fairer to tax an individual according to what he or she "takes out" of the economic system, in the form of consumption, than what he or she "contributes" to society, as measured by income. As Thomas Hobbes said in the 17th century:

> For what reason is there, that he which laboureth much, and sparing the fruit of his labour, consumeth little, should be more charged, than he that liveth idly, getteth little, and spendeth all he gets; seeing the one hath no more protection from the commonwealth than the other [1963/1651, p. 303].

From this point of view, if the miserly millionaire chooses not to consume very much, that is all to the good, because the resources he or she saves become available to society for capital accumulation. This view is humorously expressed by Steven Landsburg in the text box on the following page.

A related question is whether or not an income tax results in double taxation of interest income. Some argue that an income tax is unfair because it taxes capital income twice: once when the original income is earned, and again when the investment produces a return. However, the logic of income taxation impels that the return to saving be taxed. Whether or not this is fair depends, as usual, on value judgments.

---

[2] Citizens for Tax Justice, "The Loophole Lobbyists vs. The People," Washington, DC, undated.

THE LIGHTER SIDE OF PUBLIC FINANCE

"What I Like about Scrooge"

Economist Steven Landsburg makes the case for replacing the income tax with a consumption tax on the grounds that misers help society.

Here's what I like about Ebenezer Scrooge: His meager lodgings were dark because darkness is cheap, and barely heated because coal is not free. His dinner was gruel, which he prepared himself. Scrooge paid no man to wait on him.

Scrooge has been called ungenerous. I say that's a bum rap. What could be more generous than keeping your lamps unlit and your plate unfilled, leaving more fuel for others to burn and more food for others to eat? Who is a more benevolent neighbor than the man who employs no servants, freeing them to wait on someone else?

Oh, it might be slightly more complicated than that. Maybe when Scrooge demands less coal for his fire, less coal ends up being mined. But that's fine, too. Instead of digging coal for Scrooge, some would-be miner is now free to perform some other service for himself or someone else.

Dickens tells us that the Lord Mayor, in the stronghold of the mighty Mansion House, gave orders to his 50 cooks and butlers to keep Christmas as a Lord Mayor's household should—presumably for a houseful of guests who lavishly praised his generosity. The bricks, mortar, and labor that built the Mansion House might otherwise have built housing for hundreds; Scrooge, by living in three sparse rooms, deprived no man of a home. By employing no cooks or butlers, he ensured that cooks and butlers were available to some other household where guests reveled in ignorance of their debt to Ebenezer Scrooge.

In this whole world, there is nobody more generous than the miser—the man who *could* deplete the world's resources but chooses not to. The only difference between miserliness and philanthropy is that the philanthropist serves a favored few while the miser spreads his largess far and wide.

If you build a house and refuse to buy a house, the rest of the world is one house richer. If you earn a dollar and refuse to spend a dollar, the rest of the world is one dollar richer—because you produced a dollar's worth of goods and didn't consume them.

Who exactly gets those goods? That depends on how you save. Put a dollar in the bank and you'll bid down the interest rate by just enough so someone somewhere can afford an extra dollar's worth of vacation or home improvement. Put a dollar in your mattress and (by effectively reducing the money supply) you'll drive down prices by just enough so someone somewhere can have an extra dollar's worth of coffee with his dinner. Scrooge, no doubt a canny investor, lent his money at interest. His less conventional namesake Scrooge McDuck filled a vault with dollar bills to roll around in. No matter. Ebenezer Scrooge lowered interest rates. Scrooge McDuck lowered prices. Each Scrooge enriched his neighbors as much as any Lord Mayor who invited the town in for a Christmas meal.

Saving *is* philanthropy, and—because this is both the Christmas season and the season of tax reform—it's worth mentioning that the tax system should recognize as much. If there's a tax deduction for charitable giving, there should be a tax deduction for saving. What you earn and don't spend is your contribution to the world, and it's equally a contribution whether you give it away or squirrel it away.

Of course, there's always the threat that some meddling ghosts will come along and convince you to deplete your savings, at which point it makes sense (insofar as the taxation of income ever makes sense) to start taxing you. Which is exactly what individual retirement accounts are all about: They shield your earnings from taxation for as long as you save (that is, for as long as you let others enjoy the fruits of your labor), but no longer.

Great artists are sometimes unaware of the deepest meanings in their own creations. Though Dickens might not have recognized it, the primary moral of *A Christmas Carol* is that there should be no limit on IRA contributions. This is quite independent of all the other reasons why the tax system should encourage saving (e.g., the salutary effects on economic growth).

If Christmas is the season of selflessness, then surely one of the great symbols of Christmas should be Ebenezer Scrooge—the old Scrooge, not the reformed one. It's taxes, not misers, that need reforming.

Annual versus Lifetime Equity   Events that influence a person's economic position for only a very short time do not provide an adequate basis for determining ability to pay. Indeed, some have argued that ideally tax liabilities should be related to lifetime income. Proponents of a consumption tax point out that an annual income tax generates tax burdens that can differ quite substantially even for people who have the same lifetime wealth.

To see why, consider Mr. Grasshopper and Ms. Ant, both of whom live for two periods. Let's assume there's an income tax of 50 percent and that the interest rate is 10 percent. Suppose Grasshopper and Ant both earn $1,000 this period and no income next period. Suppose also that Grasshopper decides to consume all of his after-tax income while Ant decides to save it all for future consumption. Grasshopper pays $500 in taxes this period, consumes the remaining $500, and pays no taxes next period. Ant, however, pays $500 in taxes on her earnings this period, saves the remaining $500, and then pays taxes of $25 (= 0.50 × 0.10 × $500) next period on interest earned. With an after-tax interest rate of 5 percent, this $25 next period is worth about $24 in present value. Therefore, an income tax leads to a higher tax burden for the saver ($524) compared to the spender ($500). If, instead, there were a consumption tax of 50 percent, then Grasshopper would pay $500 in taxes this period and no taxes next period. Ant would pay no taxes this period but would pay $550 (= 0.50 × 1.10 × $1,000) in taxes next period. But with an interest rate of 10 percent, $550 next period is equal to exactly $500 today in present value (see Chapter 8). Therefore, under the consumption tax, individuals with the same lifetime income pay the same lifetime taxes (in present value terms).

We can present this result more formally. Assume that in the present, Grasshopper and Ant have identical fixed labor incomes of I_0, and in the future, they both have labor incomes of zero. (The assumption of zero second-period income is made solely for convenience.) Grasshopper chooses to consume heavily early in life because he is unconcerned about his retirement years. Ant chooses to consume most of her wealth later in life, because she wants a lavish retirement.

Define Ant's present consumption in the presence of a proportional income tax as c_0^A, and Grasshopper's as c_0^G. By assumption, $c_0^G > c_0^A$. Ant's future income before tax is the interest she earns on her savings: $r(I_0 - c_0^A)$. Similarly, Grasshopper's future income before tax is $r(I_0 - c_0^G)$.

Now, if the proportional income tax rate is t, in the present Ant and Grasshopper have identical tax liabilities of tI_0. However, in the future, Ant's tax liability is $tr(I_0 - c_0^A)$, while Grasshopper's is $tr(I_0 - c_0^G)$. Because $c_0^G > c_0^A$, Ant's future tax liability is higher. Solely because Ant has a greater taste for saving than Grasshopper, her lifetime tax burden (the discounted sum of taxes in the two periods) is greater than Grasshopper's.

In contrast, under a proportional consumption tax, lifetime tax burdens are *independent* of tastes for saving, other things being the same.[3] To prove this, just write down the equation for each taxpayer's budget constraint. Because all of Ant's non-capital income (I_0) comes in the present, its present value is simply I_0. Now, the present value of lifetime consumption must equal the present value of lifetime income. Hence, Ant's consumption pattern must satisfy the relation

$$I_0 = c_0^A + \frac{c_1^A}{1+r} \qquad (21.1)$$

---

[3] However, when marginal tax rates depend on the level of consumption, this may not be the case.

Similarly, Grasshopper is constrained by

$$I_0 = c_0^G + \frac{c_1^G}{1+r} \tag{21.2}$$

Equations (21.1) and (21.2) say simply that the lifetime value of income must equal the lifetime value of consumption.

If the proportional consumption tax rate is t_c, Ant's tax liability in the first period is $t_c c_0^A$; her tax liability in the second period is $t_c c_1^A$; and the present value of her lifetime consumption tax liability, R_c^A, is

$$R_c^A = t_c c_0^A + \frac{t_c c_1^A}{1+r} \tag{21.3}$$

Similarly, Grasshopper's lifetime tax liability is

$$R_c^G = t_c c_0^G + \frac{t_c c_1^G}{1+r} \tag{21.4}$$

By comparing Equations (21.3) and (21.1), we see that Ant's lifetime tax liability is equal to $t_c I_0$. [Just multiply Equation (21.1) through by t_c.] Similarly, Equations (21.2) and (21.4) indicate that Grasshopper's lifetime tax liability is also $t_c I_0$. We conclude that under a proportional consumption tax, two people with identical lifetime incomes always pay identical lifetime taxes (where lifetime is interpreted in the present value sense). This stands in stark contrast to a proportional income tax, where the pattern of lifetime consumption influences lifetime tax burdens.

A related argument in favor of the consumption tax centers on the fact that income tends to fluctuate more than consumption. In years when income is unusually low, individuals may draw on their savings or borrow to smooth out fluctuations in their consumption levels. Annual consumption is likely to be a better reflection of lifetime circumstances than annual income.

Opponents of consumption taxation question whether a lifetime point of view is really appropriate. There is too much economic and political uncertainty for a lifetime perspective to be realistic. Moreover, the consumption smoothing described in the lifetime arguments requires that individuals be able to save and borrow freely at the going rate of interest. Given that individuals often face constraints on the amounts they can borrow, it is not clear how relevant the lifetime arguments are. Although a considerable body of empirical work suggests the life-cycle model is a useful analytical framework (see Browning and Crossley [2001]), this argument still deserves some consideration. Finally, under the consumption tax two people with identical lifetime incomes will *not* pay identical lifetime taxes if one of them bequeaths his accumulated wealth upon death. This leads to a discussion of the appropriate tax on accumulated wealth, which we discuss later in the chapter.

Having discussed the efficiency and equity implications of a consumption tax, we turn now to investigating four different ways in which a consumption tax can be administered: a retail sales tax, a value-added tax (VAT), the Hall-Rabushka flat tax, and the cash-flow tax.

▶ RETAIL SALES TAX

general sales tax

A tax levied at the same rate on the purchase of all commodities.

In the United States today, when we think about a consumption tax, normally it's the retail sales taxes levied by most states on purchases of a wide variety of commodities (see Table 21.1). A **general sales tax** imposes the same tax rate on the purchase of all commodities. In the United States, state sales taxes that cover a wide variety of

Table 21.1   **State and Local Sales Tax Revenues by Source**
($ billions)

Source	State	Local
General sales tax	$226.7	$55.5
Motor fuel	35.7	1.3
Alcoholic beverages	4.9	0.4
Tobacco	14.5	0.5
Public utilities	11.4	12.2
Percent of own-source revenue from sales taxes	34.5%	10.3%

Source: US Bureau of the Census. [2008c]. Figures are for 2005–2006.

Sales taxes are important revenue sources for state and local governments. They account for 34.5 percent of state governments' revenues and 10.3 percent of local governments' revenues.

goods are often given the label *general*. This is something of a misnomer, however, because even states that tax most goods exempt the sales of virtually all services from taxation.

A **selective sales tax,** also referred to as an **excise tax,** or a **differential commodity tax,** is levied at different rates on the purchase of different commodities. (Some of those rates can be zero.)[4]

Sales taxes generally take one of two forms: A **unit tax** is a given amount for each unit purchased. For example, if you target practice or hunt with a bow and arrow, you pay a federal unit tax of 39 cents per arrow. In contrast, an **ad valorem tax** is computed as a percentage of the value of the purchase. For example, the federal excise tax rate on bows is 11 percent.

The federal government levies no general sales tax. It does tax motor fuel, alcoholic beverages, tobacco, and a few other commodities, but these taxes account for less than 10 percent of federal revenues. As Table 21.1 indicates, sales taxes are particularly important in the revenue systems of state governments. Forty-five states plus the District of Columbia have general sales taxes, with rates that vary from 2.9 to 7.25 percent. Most of the states exempt food from tax, and virtually all exempt prescription drugs. In about half the states, municipalities and counties levy their own general sales taxes.

Rationalizations

Perhaps the main attraction of sales taxes is ease of administration. The sales tax is collected from sellers at the retail level. Relative to an income tax, fewer individuals need to be monitored by the tax authorities. This is not to say that administration of a sales tax is without complications. Many difficulties arise because it is unclear whether a given transaction creates a tax liability. In California, "snacks" were once subject to a special sales tax while "food" was not. What is a snack and what is food?

selective sales tax

See *excise tax.*

excise tax

A tax levied on the purchase of a particular commodity.

differential commodity tax

See *excise tax.*

unit tax

A tax levied as a fixed amount per unit of commodity purchased.

ad valorem tax

A tax computed as a percentage of the purchase value

---

[4] Another type of sales tax is a *use tax*—a sales tax that residents of a given state must pay on purchases made in other states. The purpose of a use tax is to prevent individuals from avoiding sales taxes by making purchases out of state. Historically, use taxes have yielded very little revenue. However, some states are becoming more aggressive in their collection techniques, so use taxes may become more important in the future.

Under the law, Ritz crackers and wrapped slices of pie were subject to the snack tax, while soda crackers and a slice of pie served on a plate were not. The confusion of this law contributed to its repeal. Some states determine whether a juice is a nontaxable food by a formula based on the amount of actual fruit in the juice. The point is that defining the base for a sales tax requires arbitrary distinctions, just like the personal and corporate income taxes. Moreover, as is true for other taxes, tax evasion can be a real problem. A case that received a lot of attention recently was that of the former chairman of Tyco International, Dennis Kozlowski, who was indicted for evading New York City sales taxes on millions of dollars of artwork that he purchased there. (He pretended that the art was being shipped to his office in New Hampshire, which has no sales tax.) A less exotic but more significant example is provided by Canada, which several years ago cut its high taxes on cigarettes after concluding that smuggling was creating unacceptable demands on law enforcement agencies.

Despite such stories, most observers believe that, at present levels, compliance with state-level retail taxes is quite good. We return later to the issue of administrative problems that might be encountered with a national retail sales tax.

Efficiency and Distributional Implications of State Sales Taxes

A critical issue in the design of a retail sales tax is whether or not different rates should be applied to different commodities. In an optimal tax framework, the key question is what role can differential commodity taxes play given that an income tax is already in place? If the income tax is designed optimally, then under fairly reasonable conditions, social welfare cannot be improved by levying differential commodity taxes.[5] However, if for some reason the income tax is not optimal, differential commodity taxes can improve welfare. For example, if society has egalitarian goals, social welfare can be improved by taxing luxury goods at relatively high rates.

A related question is how to set the rates, given a decision to have differential commodity taxes. Obviously, the answer depends on the government's objectives. If the goal is to collect a specified amount of revenue as efficiently as possible, tax rates should be set so that the compensated demand for each commodity is reduced in the same proportion (see Chapter 16). When the demand for each good depends only on its own price, this is equivalent to the rule that tax rates be inversely related to compensated price elasticities of demand. Tax goods with inelastic demands at relatively high rates, and tax goods with elastic demands at relatively low rates. Efficiency does not require the same tax rate for each commodity.

If the government cares about equity as well as efficiency, optimal tax theory requires departures from the inverse elasticity rule. As noted in Chapter 16, if price-inelastic commodities make up a high proportion of the budgets of the poor, governments with egalitarian objectives should tax such goods lightly or not at all. This may help explain why so many states do not tax food, even though they tax other commodities.

Within the conventional welfare economics framework, another justification for differential sales taxes is the presence of externalities. If consumption of a commodity

---

[5] Suppose the utility function of each individual is a function of his or her consumption of leisure and a set of other commodities. Then as long as the marginal rate of substitution between any two commodities is independent of the amount of leisure, differential commodity taxation cannot improve social welfare in the presence of an optimal earnings tax.

generates costs not included in its price, then efficiency requires a tax on the use of that good (see Chapter 5). High tax rates on tobacco—state plus federal rates now average over $2 per pack—are sometimes rationalized in this way. Smokers impose costs on others by polluting the atmosphere, so a tax on tobacco may enhance economic efficiency.

In some cases, sales taxes can be viewed as substitutes for user fees. For example, with current technology, it is difficult to charge motorists a fee for every mile driven, even though driving creates costs in terms of road damage, congestion, and so on. Because the amount of road use is related to gasoline consumption, road use can be taxed indirectly by putting a tax on gasoline. Of course, the correspondence is far from perfect: Some cars are more fuel efficient than others, and some do more damage than others. Still, an approximately correct user fee may be more efficient than none at all.

Several other rationalizations for differential sales taxes lie outside the framework of conventional economics. Taxes can be set higher for certain commodities (such as alcohol or tobacco) that are regarded as "sinful." Such commodities are the opposite of "merit goods" (see Chapter 3), which are viewed as being good per se. In both cases, the government is essentially imposing its preferences on those of the citizenry.

While a sales tax that is uniform across all commodities is almost certainly not efficient, the information required to determine fully efficient taxes is not presently available (and perhaps never will be). Therefore, uniform tax rates might not be a bad approach. This is particularly the case if departures from uniformity open the door to tax rate differentiation based on political rather than equity or efficiency considerations.

A National Retail Sales Tax?

Is a retail sales tax a desirable means of replacing our current tax system with a consumption tax? Several legislators have indeed proposed exchanging all existing federal taxes for a national retail sales tax, which they refer to as the "Fair Tax." As one proponent stated, compared to our current system, a retail sales tax is "much more easily monitored by the states, [and] you don't have to be a citizen nor declare how you got the money. If you spend it, we collect at the time. How simple is that?" [Alsenz, 2007].

As already noted, compliance is in fact not much of a problem with current state sales taxes. But as also noted, the rates associated with those systems are relatively low, in the range of 3 to 7 percent. According to the Department of the Treasury, in order to raise as much revenue as the federal personal income, a federal retail tax rate of about *34 percent* would be required [Bartlett, 2007]. And at high rates, a retail sales tax becomes extremely difficult to enforce since it "collects all the money from what is, for compliance purposes, the weakest link in the production and distribution chain—retail. Consumers have no incentive to make sure retailers are paying their sales tax, and retailers have no incentive to pay aside from the threat of audit" [Slemrod and Bakija, 2004]. We know from the theory of tax evasion (Chapter 16) that the benefit to cheating depends on the size of the tax rate. With the relatively low sales tax rates now in existence, the benefit is apparently not high enough to make it worthwhile to cheat extensively. But according to the Department of the Treasury, noncompliance with a sales tax means that the rate would need to be raised from 34 percent to 49 percent in order to maintain the same revenue as the current income tax. Hence, a national retail sales tax loses some of its allure as a tax reform option.

▶ VALUE-ADDED TAX

Can one structure a sales tax that has better compliance properties than a retail sales tax? To think about this issue, note that goods are typically produced in several stages. Consider a simple model of bread production.[6] The farmer grows wheat and sells it to a miller who turns it into flour. The miller sells the flour to a baker who transforms it into bread. The bread is purchased by a grocer who sells it to consumers. A hypothetical numerical example is provided in Table 21.2. Column 1 shows the purchases made by the producer at each stage of production, and column 2 shows the sales value at each stage. For example, the miller pays $400 to the farmer for wheat, and sells the processed wheat to the baker for $700. The **value added** at each stage of production is the difference between the firm's sales and the purchased material inputs used in production. The baker paid $700 for the wheat and sold the bread for $950, so his value added is $250. The value added at each stage of production is computed by subtracting purchases from sales, shown in column 3.[7]

A **value-added tax (VAT)** is a percentage tax on value added applied at each stage of production. For example, if the rate of the VAT is 20 percent, the grocer would pay $10, which is 20 percent of $50. Column 4 shows the amount of VAT liability at each stage of production. The total revenue created by the VAT is found by summing the amounts paid at each stage, and equals $200.

The identical result could have been generated by levying a 20 percent tax at the retail level, that is, by a tax of 20 percent on the value of sales made to consumers by the grocer. *In essence, then, a VAT is just an alternative method for collecting a retail sales tax.*

Implementation Issues

Although the United States has never had a national VAT, this tax is popular in Europe. The European experience indicates that certain administrative decisions have a major impact on a VAT's ultimate economic effects.

The first is how purchases of investment assets by firms are treated in the computation of value added. The practice in Europe is to treat an investment good like any other material input. Its full value is subtracted from sales, despite the fact that

> **value added**
>
> The difference between sales and the cost of purchased material inputs.

> **value-added tax (VAT)**
>
> A percentage tax on value added at each stage of production.

Table 21.2   **Implementation of a Value-Added Tax (VAT)**

Producer	Purchases	Sales	Value Added	VAT at 20 Percent Rate
Farmer	$ 0	$ 400	$ 400	$ 80
Miller	400	700	300	60
Baker	700	950	250	50
Grocer	950	1,000	50	10
Total	$2,050	$3,050	$1,000	$200

A valued-added tax is a percentage tax applied to the difference between the firm's sales and the purchased material inputs at each stage of production.

---

[6] For a detailed description of how value-added taxes work, see Cnossen [2001].

[7] By definition, value added must equal the sum of factor payments made by the producer: wages, interest, rent, and economic profits.

it is durable. This is referred to as a **consumption-type VAT** because the tax base excludes investment and involves only consumption.

Second, a collection procedure must be devised. European countries use the **invoice method,** which can be illustrated in the hypothetical example in Table 21.2. Each firm is liable for tax on the basis of its total sales, but it can claim the taxes already paid by its suppliers as a credit against this liability. For example, the baker is liable for taxes on his $950 in sales, giving him a tax obligation of $190 (= 0.20 × $950). However, he can claim a credit of $140 (the sum of taxes paid by the farmer and the miller), leaving him a net obligation of $50. The catch is that the credit is allowed only if supported by invoices provided by the baker and the miller. This system provides an incentive for the producers to police themselves against tax evasion. Whatever taxes the farmer and miller evade must be paid by the baker, so the baker will only do business with firms that provide proper invoices. The invoice method cannot eliminate evasion completely. For example, producers can collude to falsify invoices. Nevertheless, compliance is better than it would be under a national retail sales tax.

Finally, a rate structure is needed. In our simple example, all commodities are taxed at the same rate. In Europe, commodities are taxed differentially. Food and health care products are taxed at low rates, presumably because of equity considerations. For reasons of administrative feasibility, some countries exempt very small firms. Banking and finance institutions escape taxation because they tend to provide services in kind; therefore, it is difficult to compute value added. The consumption of services generated by owner-occupied housing is exempt from tax for the same reasons that it is usually exempted from income taxation (see Chapter 18).

Nonuniform taxation increases administrative complexity, especially when firms produce multiple outputs, some of which are taxable and some of which are not. But the system can work, as evidenced by the European experience. For the United States, then, the question is not whether a national VAT is feasible, but whether it would be better than the status quo.

A VAT for the United States?

The VATs suggested for the United States are usually of the European consumption type, and hence essentially general sales taxes. Therefore, the arguments regarding the pros and cons of sales taxes made earlier in this chapter are applicable. The fundamental problem is the same for both types of taxes: Attempts to obtain additional equity by exempting various goods may increase the excess burden of the tax system as a whole and create administrative complexity.

More generally, the desirability of a national VAT can be determined only if we know what tax (or taxes) it would replace, how the revenues would be spent, and so forth. For example, many public finance economists believe that the corporation income tax is undesirable in practically all respects and would be happy to see a VAT replace it, other things being the same. However, they would probably have much greater reservations about replacing the personal income tax with a VAT. Altig et al. [2001] analyzed the impact of replacing the existing US tax system with a comprehensive proportional consumption tax like a VAT, and found that in the long run, it would increase income by about 9 percent. This result, however, depends importantly on assumptions about the responsiveness of saving to changes in the income tax. As noted in Chapter 18, this is a controversial issue, so this particular figure must be regarded with some caution.

---

consumption-type VAT

Capital investments are subtracted from sales in the computation of the value added.

---

invoice method

Each firm is liable for taxes on total sales but can claim the taxes already paid by suppliers as a credit against this liability, provided this tax payment is verified by invoices from suppliers.

In addition, we must consider the political implications of introducing a VAT. Once it is in place, each percentage point increase in a comprehensive VAT would yield roughly $50 billion in tax revenues [Congressional Research Service, 2006]. In a world where political institutions accurately reflect citizens' wishes, this observation may not be very significant. But for those who believe that the government's actions may not advance the interests of the public (see Chapter 6), the revenue potential of a VAT is frightening. Some fear that the VAT might be used to sneak by an increase in the size of the government sector:

> Because it would be collected by business enterprises, VAT would be concealed in the total price the consumer paid and hence not perceived as a direct tax burden. That is its advantage to legislators—and its major defect to the taxpayers [Friedman, 1980, p. 90].

Indeed, in virtually all countries with a VAT, the rate has increased over time. For example, in the nations of the European Union, when the VAT was introduced, the average rate was 13.9 percent; it is now 19.4 percent, an increase of almost 40 percent [Cnossen, 2001, p. 485]. At the same time, the share of Gross Domestic Product devoted to taxes in these countries has increased. Indeed, Becker and Mulligan [2003] show that the greater the number of years a country has had a VAT, the larger its government. Of course, this does not prove that the VAT was responsible for a larger government sector. On the other hand, one would not expect to be successful in assuaging the fears just expressed by appealing to the experience of other countries with the VAT.

Finally, it is important to consider the international implications of a VAT, because some VAT proponents have argued that the tax would enhance America's trade position vis-à-vis its competitors. This notion rests on the fact that according to the World Trade Organization (WTO), which regulates international trade practices, a VAT can be rebated on a country's exports and levied on imports. In contrast, personal and corporate income taxes cannot be rebated. Since a VAT can be rebated while income taxes cannot, some have argued that US international competitiveness would be enhanced if the United States adopted a VAT and simultaneously reduced the role of income taxation. For example, former Speaker of the House Dennis Hastert [2004] argued that the US tax system creates a competitive disadvantage compared to countries with a VAT because "our widgets have a tax burden. Their widgets don't." Therefore, "for us to return capital and jobs to the United States, we're going to have to change our present tax system and adopt a flat tax, a national sales tax, an ad valorem tax, or a VAT."

To analyze this argument, consider each part separately: introduction of a VAT, and then reduction in personal and corporate income taxes. Imposing a VAT would tend to increase the relative prices of the taxed goods by an amount determined by the relevant supply and demand elasticities. However, all that rebating the VAT at the border does is undo the price increase generated by the tax. If you put an extra weight on a horse and then remove it, the horse does not run any faster.

Turning now to the second part of the plan, would reducing corporate and personal income taxes reduce the relative prices of American exports? Again, the answer depends on the incidence of these taxes, and it is not at all obvious. For example, if the market for labor is competitive and its supply is perfectly inelastic, producers' wage costs are unchanged when personal income taxes are reduced. The entire benefit of the tax reduction goes to workers (see Chapter 14). In this case, prices may not change at all. More generally, of course, prices might fall, but no evidence suggests that the reduction would be very large.

In short, there is no reason to believe that adoption of a VAT would dramatically improve the US trade position. Of course, this fact by itself does not mean that a

"Thanks for my pocket money Dad. But you forgot to add 17.5% v.a.t." © Kes. Reprinted with permission from www.CartoonStock.com.

VAT would be a bad thing. As noted already, VATs have both advantages and disadvantages. But they are not a panacea for US trade imbalances.

▶ HALL-RABUSHKA FLAT TAX

A distinguishing feature of both the retail sales tax and the VAT is that the legal incidence falls upon businesses. Consumers make no explicit payments to the government (although they bear a share of the economic incidence). However, much of the recent interest in consumption taxes has centered on *personal* consumption taxes that require individuals to file tax returns and write checks to the government. Unlike the retail sales tax or the VAT, these systems allow individuals' tax liabilities to depend on their personal circumstances.

The best known of these proposals is the one put forward by Hall and Rabushka (H&R) [1995], which they call a *flat tax*. A version of the H&R proposal was the centerpiece of 2000 presidential candidate Steve Forbes's campaign, and was also endorsed by Rudy Giuliani during his run for the 2008 Republican presidential nomination. The H&R proposal has two tax-collecting vehicles, a business tax and an individual compensation tax. The coordinated use of these two instruments allows the government to levy a progressive tax.

The calculation of the business tax base begins with a computation like that of a consumption-type VAT—sales less purchases from other firms. The key difference is that the firm also deducts payments to its workers. Firms then pay a flat rate of tax on the final amount.

The base for the individual tax is the wage payments received by individuals. No capital income is taxed at the individual level. In principle, any tax schedule could be applied to this base—the tax rate could be flat or increasing, and an exemption might or might not be allowed. H&R propose only one rate (19 percent), and it is the same as the rate that applies to cash flow at the business level. H&R build progressivity into the system by allowing an exemption of $25,000 (for a family of four). No other deductions are allowed. This is what permits the rate to be so low.

At this point you might be wondering why the H&R tax is a consumption tax. To see why, consider a VAT that taxes all goods and services at the same rate, say, 19 percent. As shown above, this is economically equivalent to a 19 percent retail sales tax. Now consider an H&R-type flat tax that taxes both individuals and firms at 19 percent and that has no exemptions or deductions at the personal level. Recall that under the VAT, the firm's tax base is sales minus purchases from other firms. Wage payments are not deductible. In effect, then, wage payments are subject to a 19 percent tax. Under the H&R tax, wage payments are deductible at the firm level, but they are taxed at the individual level. The amount of tax is exactly the same as under a VAT; all that changes is the point of collection for part of the tax. The personal exemption simply builds some progressivity into the system. In short, except for the exemption, the H&R flat tax is essentially equivalent to a VAT or a retail sales tax. Hence, for all intents and purposes, any results pertaining to the economic effects of one apply to all.

▶ CASH-FLOW TAX

Another personal consumption tax is the cash-flow tax. Under this variant, each household files a return reporting its consumption expenditures during the year. Just as under the personal income tax, various exemptions and deductions can be taken to allow for special circumstances such as extraordinary medical expenses. Each individual's tax bill is then determined by applying a rate schedule to the adjusted amount of consumption.

From an administrative point of view, the big question is how do the taxpayers compute their annual consumption? The most sensible approach is to measure consumption on a *cash-flow basis*, meaning that it would be calculated simply as the difference between all cash receipts and saving. To keep track of saving, qualified accounts would be established at savings banks, security brokerage houses, and other types of financial institutions. Funds that were certified by these institutions as having been deposited in qualified accounts would be exempt from tax. Most of the record-keeping responsibility would be met by these institutions and would not involve more paperwork than exists already. As long as capital gains and interest from such accounts were retained, they would not be taxed. For some taxpayers, such qualified accounts already exist in the forms of 401(k) plans and conventional Individual Retirement Accounts (see Chapter 17). One way to look at a cash-flow tax is simply as an expansion of the opportunities to invest in such accounts. However, many analysts believe that the record-keeping requirements associated with a cash-flow tax would make it very difficult administratively.

▶ INCOME VERSUS CONSUMPTION TAXATION

We have now discussed four prototypes for a broad-based consumption tax: a retail sales tax, a VAT, the Hall-Rabushka flat tax, and the cash-flow tax. They differ substantially in how they are administered, but their economic effects are basically the same, because they are just different ways of taxing the same base, consumption. With this discussion as background, we now catalog some other advantages and disadvantages of consumption taxation relative to income taxation and also note a few problems that are common to both.

Advantages of a Consumption Tax

Proponents of consumption taxation point to several advantages of these systems.

No Need to Measure Capital Gains and Depreciation   Some of the most vexing problems with taxing income arise from difficulties in measuring additions to wealth. For example, it requires calculation of capital gains and losses even on those assets not sold during the year, a task so difficult that it is not even attempted under the current system. Similarly, for those who have income produced by capital equipment, additions to wealth must be lowered by the amount the equipment depreciates during the year. As noted in Chapter 19, we know very little about actual depreciation patterns. Under a consumption tax, all such problems disappear because additions to wealth per se are no longer part of the tax base.

Fewer Problems with Inflation   In the presence of a nonindexed income tax, inflation creates important distortions. Some of these are caused by a progressive rate structure, but some would occur even if the tax were proportional. These distortions occur because computing capital income requires the use of figures from years that have different price levels. For example, if an asset is sold, calculation of the capital gain or loss requires subtracting the value in the year of purchase from its value in the current year. In general, part of the change in value is due to inflation, so individuals are taxed on gains that do not reflect increases in real income. As noted in Chapter 17, setting up an appropriate scheme for indexing income generated by investments is complicated and has not been attempted in the United States.

In contrast, under a consumption tax, calculation of the tax base involves only current-year transactions. Therefore, distortions associated with inflation are much less of a problem.

No Need for Separate Corporation Tax   Some consumption tax variants would allow removal of the corporation income tax, at least in theory. Recall from Chapter 19 that one of the main justifications of the corporation tax is to get at income that people accumulate in corporations. If accumulation per se were no longer part of the personal income tax base, this would not be necessary. Elimination of the corporation tax would probably enhance efficiency.

Advocates of consumption taxation stress that adoption would not be as radical a move as first appearances might suggest. In some respects, the present system already looks very much like a consumption tax:

- For some taxpayers, income is exempt from taxation when it is saved in certain forms such as 401(k) plans and IRAs.
- Unrealized capital gains on financial assets are untaxed, as are virtually all capital gains on housing.
- Realized capital gains are free of all taxation at the death of the owner.
- Accelerated depreciation reduces the amount of investment purchases included in the tax base.

In light of these considerations, characterizing the status quo as an income tax is a serious misnomer; it is more a hybrid between income and consumption taxation. Indeed, as discussed in the Policy Perspective below, one prominent approach to tax reform is to maintain the hybrid structure, but move it more toward a consumption tax.

POLICY PERSPECTIVE

President's Advisory Panel on Federal Tax Reform

The last systematic government attempt to consider tax reform was the 2005 report by the President's Advisory Panel on Federal Tax Reform. This bipartisan panel recommended making the US tax system "simpler, fairer, and more conducive to economic growth" [p. xiii]. The panel considered proposals for a consumption tax (including a flat tax, national retail sales tax, and a value-added tax), but instead it recommended two hybrid options.

The two reform options—known as the Simplified Income Tax (SIT) plan and the Growth and Investment Tax (GIT) plan—have some common features. Among other things, they would both (a) eliminate the individual and corporate alternative minimum tax; (b) replace the existing standard deduction, personal exemption, earned income tax credit, and child tax credit with a simplified "family credit" and "work credit"; (c) replace the mortgage interest deduction with a tax credit equal to 15 percent of mortgage interest paid, up to a limit; (d) reduce the tax preference for employer-sponsored health insurance; and (e) eliminate the deductibility of state and local taxes. Both plans would also reduce the number of tax brackets and the maximum marginal tax rate to 33 percent under SIT and 30 percent under GIT.

The panel emphasized, "An income tax reduces the return to saving because it taxes the income that saving generates. . . . The tax on savings therefore operates like a penalty for those who choose to save" [pp. 89–90]. In order to reduce the disincentive to save, both proposed options create three savings plans (Save at Work, Save for Retirement, and Save for Family) that would increase the allowable amount of tax-free savings for retirement, health, education, and housing. Adopting these savings plans would represent an important step toward a consumption base, because the allowable amounts are sufficiently large that many American families would never be taxed on their capital income. Both plans would also reduce the double taxation on corporate earnings, another move that would reduce the effective tax rate on capital income. The GIT plan takes additional moves toward a consumption tax by, among other things, allowing businesses to expense their investments immediately, by lowering tax rates on businesses, and by imposing a single, low tax rate on dividends, interest, and capital gains.

The panel's report discusses many of the issues discussed in the tax chapters in this textbook. It also acknowledges the political economy implications discussed in Chapter 6 by admitting, "Many stand waiting to defend their breaks, deductions, and loopholes, and to defeat our efforts. That is part of the legislative process." Indeed, to date there have been no congressional proposals to implement either of the panel's reform options.

Disadvantages of a Consumption Tax

Critics of a personal consumption tax note a number of disadvantages:

Administrative Problems   Opponents of a consumption tax argue that it would be complicated to administer. Consider, for example, the business level tax of the H&R proposal. The tax base excludes investment expenditures. However, distinguishing consumption commodities from investment expenditures is not always simple, particularly for small businesses. (Is a desk purchased for use at home consumption or investment?) Of course, a similar problem exists under the income tax. But the incentives for avoidance and evasion are stronger under the H&R tax, because firms deduct the entire value of the investment item, while under the income tax, generally only a portion can be deducted. (Recall the discussion of depreciation allowances from Chapter 19.)

Transitional Issues   Introduction of a consumption tax could create serious transitional problems. Individuals who had accumulated wealth for future consumption under the existing income tax system would suffer during the transition period. The interest, dividends, and realized capital gains that they received during their working years were subject to the personal income tax. A reasonable expectation for such people is that when they decided to consume their wealth (say, at retirement), their consumption would not be subject to new taxes. If a consumption tax were suddenly introduced, however, these expectations would be disappointed.

This observation, by the way, puts the distributional consequences of moving to a consumption tax in a new light. Introduction of such a tax would be accompanied, in effect, by a one-time tax on existing wealth. Because wealth is unequally distributed, this would have a progressive impact on the distribution of income. Such a one-time tax on wealth does not affect saving or leisure decisions, and thus imposes no excess burden. Nonetheless, fairness would seem to require that the elderly be compensated for the losses they incur during the transition. Consumption tax advocates have proposed a number of rules for alleviating transitional problems (see Bradford [1998]). But the more special rules there are, the more complicated and inefficient the system becomes.

Gifts and Bequests   The discussion surrounding Equations (21.1) through (21.4) demonstrated that in a simple life-cycle model, a proportional consumption tax is equivalent to a tax on lifetime income. Contrary to the assumptions of the life-cycle model, some people set aside part of their lifetime income for gifts and bequests. How should such transfers be treated under a consumption tax? One view is that there is no need to tax gifts and bequests until they are consumed by their recipients. An alternative position is that gifts and bequests should be treated as consumption on the part of the donor. Hence, gifts and bequests should be taxed at the time the transfer is made. Proponents of this view point out that it would not be politically viable to institute a tax system that allowed substantial amounts of wealth to accumulate free of tax, and then failed to tax it on transfer. However, as explained later, major conceptual and practical problems are involved in taxing transfers of wealth.

Problems with Both Systems

Even the most enthusiastic proponents of the consumption tax recognize that its adoption would not usher in an era of tax nirvana. Several of the most intractable problems inherent in the income tax system would also plague any consumption tax. These include, but are not limited to:

- Defining consumption itself. (For example, are health care expenditures part of consumption, or should they be deductible?)
- Choosing the unit of taxation and determining an appropriate rate structure.
- Valuing fringe benefits of various occupations. (For example, if a job gives a person access to the company swimming pool, should the consumption benefits be taxed? If so, how can they be valued?)
- Determining a method for averaging across time if the schedule has increasing marginal tax rates.
- Taxing production that occurs in the home.
- Discouraging incentives to avoid taxes by participating in the underground economy.

Finally, we emphasize that it is not fair to compare an *ideal* consumption tax to the *actual* income tax. Historically, special interests have persuaded politicians to tax certain types of income preferentially. Adoption of a consumption tax could hardly be expected to eliminate political corruption of the tax structure. One pessimistic economist suggested, "I find the choice between the consumption base and the income base an almost sterile debate; we do not tax all income now, and were we to adopt a consumption tax system, we would end up exempting as much consumption from the tax base as we do income now."[8] It is hard to predict whether a real-world consumption tax would be better than the current system.

▸ WEALTH TAXES

As mentioned earlier, one objection to a consumption tax is that it allows a person who saves a lot over his lifetime to avoid paying taxes if he passes on his accumulated wealth as gifts or bequests to others. While some believe there is no need to tax such transfers until they are consumed by their recipients, others argue that it is inappropriate to allow substantial amounts of wealth to accumulate free of tax. Other justifications for taxing wealth include:

Wealth taxes help to correct certain (inevitable) problems that arise in the administration of an income tax. Recall that *all* capital gains, realized or not, belong in the tax base of a comprehensive income tax. In practice, it is often impossible to tax unrealized capital gains. By taxing the wealth of which these gains become a part, perhaps this situation can be remedied. Now, it is true that wealth at a given point in time includes the sum of capital gains and losses from all earlier years. However, there is no reason to believe that the yield from an annual wealth tax approximates the revenues that would have been generated by full annual taxation of unrealized capital gains.

The higher an individual's wealth, the greater his or her ability to pay, other things—including income—being the same. Therefore, wealthy individuals should pay higher taxes. Suppose that a miser has accumulated a huge hoard of gold that yields no income. Should she be taxed on the value of the hoard?

---

[8] Emil Sunley quoted in Makin [1985, p. 20].

Some believe that as long as the miser was subject to the income tax while the hoard was accumulating, it should not be taxed again. Others would argue that the gold per se generates utility and should be subject to tax. Perhaps the major problem in the ability-to-pay argument is that even rich people have a substantial component of their wealth in *human* capital—their stock of education, skills, and so on. However, there is no way to value human capital except by reference to the income it yields. This logic points us back to income as the appropriate base.

Wealth taxation reduces the concentration of wealth, which is desirable socially and politically. As we saw in Chapter 12, although it is difficult to measure income precisely, the best estimates suggest the distribution of income in the United States is quite unequal. The quality of data on wealth is even lower. What information there is suggests that the distribution of wealth is very unequal. One survey indicated that the top 1 percent of the wealth distribution owned 38 percent of the total [Wolff, 2001]. The desirability of such inequality turns on a complicated set of ethical issues quite similar to those discussed in Chapter 12 in connection with the distribution of income. A related concern is that a highly concentrated distribution of wealth leads to corruption of democratic political processes. Skeptics respond that if concentration of power is the issue, then there is no justification for taxing accretions of wealth of $1 million, $10 million, or even $50 million. As Stein [1997] notes, "It takes a lot more money than that to generate power in the US today." Stein further observes that there are sources of influence other than money: "Oprah Winfrey ha[s] more power than any megarich person today." Should Oprah face a special tax because she is powerful?

Wealth taxes are payments for benefits that wealth holders receive from government. As President Theodore Roosevelt said, "The man of great wealth owes a peculiar obligation to the State because he derives special advantages from the mere existence of government." One might argue, for example, that a major goal of defense spending is to protect (from foreign enemies) our existing wealth. If so, perhaps a wealth tax is a just method for financing defense. In addition, government makes certain expenditures that are likely to benefit wealth holders especially. If the state builds and maintains a road that goes by my store, then it confers a benefit on me for which I should pay. Although the notion of basing taxes on benefits has some appeal, it is not clear that any feasible wealth tax can achieve this goal. A lawyer arguing the case for taxing property asked rhetorically, "[I]sn't it true that one with twice as much house receives twice as much benefit from . . . police and fire services rendered to property?" [Hagman, 1978, p. 42]. Contrary to what he apparently believed, the answer is "probably not." The value to a given household of most services provided by local government depends on factors other than house size. For example, the value of education depends on the number of children. Even the value of fire and police services depends on how much furniture is in the house and how much insurance protection has been purchased. If benefit taxation is the goal, a system of user fees for public services would be more appropriate than a wealth tax.

To summarize, wealth taxes—whether as an add on to an income tax system or to a consumption tax system—have been rationalized on both ability-to-pay and benefit grounds. Both sets of arguments are very controversial.

By far the most important wealth tax in the United States is the property tax, which is particularly crucial to the operations of local governments. Accordingly, we postpone our discussion of the property tax until Chapter 22, in which we discuss subnational units of government, and instead focus here on taxes on gifts and bequests.

▶ ESTATE AND GIFT TAXES

The federal government levies wealth taxes against estates and gifts. These taxes are levied at irregular intervals on the occurrence of certain events—the estate tax on the death of the wealth holder (decedent), and the gift tax when property is transferred between the living (inter vivos). Both federal and some state governments levy taxes on gifts and estates. At neither level are the taxes very important as revenue raisers. Estate and gift taxes account for only about 1 percent of federal tax revenues [*Economic Report of the President, 2009*, p. 380]. The legal incidence of the federal tax does not touch the lives of most citizens. Fewer than 1 percent of all decedents have estates that are subject to the tax. Some have suggested that the role of estate and gift taxes should be expanded. However, as noted later, legislation passed in 2001 phased out the estate tax (frequently referred to by its opponents as the *death tax*) over a decade. The arguments for and against estate and gift taxes are explored in this section.

Rationales

The following issues have been raised in the debate over the desirability of estate taxes:

Payment for Services   Some argue that the government protects property rights and oversees the transfer of property from the decedent to his or her heirs. As compensation for providing these services, the state is entitled to a share of the estate. Those who oppose the estate tax believe that providing such services is a fundamental right that does not have to be paid for. As actress Whoopi Goldberg put it, "I don't want to get taxed just because I died. I just don't think it's right." Moreover, it seems arbitrary to pick out property transfers as special objects of taxation. If Moe spends $10,000 on a trip to Europe, Curly spends $10,000 on his daughter's college education, and Larry leaves $10,000 to his son, why should Larry face a special tax?

Reversion of Property to Society   Proponents of the estate tax claim that ultimately, all property belongs to society as a whole. During an individual's lifetime, society permits her to dispose of the property she has managed to accumulate as she wishes. But at death, the property reverts to society, which can dispose of it at will. In this view, although people may be entitled to what they earn, their descendants hold no compelling ethical claim to it. Recall from Chapter 12 that many controversial value judgments lie behind such assertions. Opponents believe that it is fundamentally wrong to argue that a person holds wealth only at the pleasure of "society," or that "society" ever has any valid claim on personal wealth.

Incentives   The most famous statement of the theme that estate taxes are good for incentives is Andrew Carnegie's: "The parent who leaves his son enormous wealth generally deadens the talents and energies of the son, and tempts him to lead a less useful and less worthy life than he otherwise would." By taxing away estates, the government can prevent this from happening. There is some evidence that Carnegie's conjecture about the labor supply effects of inheritances is correct. In their econometric study of the behavior of a group of individuals who received large inheritances, Holtz-Eakin et al. [1993] found that the higher the inheritance, the less likely that the recipient continued to work after receiving it.

Nevertheless, the incentive problem is more complicated than suggested by Carnegie, because we must take into account the donor's behavior, not just the recipient's. Consider Lear, an individual who is motivated to work hard during his lifetime to leave a big estate to his daughters. The presence of an estate tax might discourage Lear's work effort. ("Why should I work hard if my wealth is going to the tax collector instead of my daughters?") On the other hand, with an estate tax, a greater amount of wealth has to be accumulated to leave a given after-tax bequest. Thus, the presence of an estate tax might induce Lear to work harder to maintain the net value of his estate. Consequently, the impact of an estate tax on a donor's work effort is logically indeterminate.[9] Even if Carnegie were right that the estate tax leads potential heirs to work more, it might also generate incentives for donors to work less. Theory alone does not tell us which tendency dominates. Similarly, we cannot predict how an estate tax affects the donor's saving behavior. It is easy to describe scenarios in which he saves less and in which he saves more.

The estate tax can affect not only the amount of wealth transferred across generations but also the form in which the transfers occur. A tax on bequests of physical capital creates incentives to transmit wealth in the form of human capital. Thus, instead of giving each daughter $80,000 worth of stocks and bonds, Lear might spend $80,000 on each of their college educations. An estate tax could thus lead to overinvestment in human capital.

Kopczuk and Slemrod [2001] examined estate tax returns filed between 1916 and 1996 to assess the effect of estate tax rates on reported estates. They found a negative relationship between the magnitude of the tax rate that prevailed 10 years before death and the size of the estate, which suggests that increases in the tax rate reduce wealth accumulation. A rough calculation based on their estimates suggests that overall wealth accumulation would rise by 1.5 percent if the tax were eliminated. While this finding is provocative, Kopczuk and Slemrod emphasize that it must be regarded with caution because it is not clear how best to calculate the lifetime estate tax rate that is relevant. Presumably, the rate is determined in part by expectations of what the rate will be when the individual dies, but it is not clear how such expectations are formed. Nevertheless, this result suggests that the incentive effects of the estate tax may be substantial.

Relation to Personal Income Tax   Estate and gift taxation is necessary, it can be argued, because receipts of gifts and inheritances are excluded from the recipient's personal income tax base. A natural response to this observation is to ask why gifts and estates are not included in adjusted gross income. After all, they constitute additions to potential consumption, and by the conventional definition are therefore income to the recipient. However, there has always been a strong aversion to including inheritances and gifts in the income tax base. Such receipts simply are not perceived as being in the same class as those from wages and interest. It is not

---

[9] The ambiguity arises because of the familiar conflict between substitution and income effects (see Chapter 18).

necessarily the case, though, that the estate and gift tax is the best remedy for this omission. We discuss a possible alternative later.

Income Distribution   An estate tax is a valuable tool for creating a more equal distribution of income. As William Gates Sr. (the father of the Microsoft billionaire) argued, an estate tax is needed for "protecting our democracy from a further buildup of hereditary wealth" [Gates and Collins, 2002]. Let us leave aside the normative question of whether or not the government ought to pursue a more equal income distribution and consider the positive issue of whether or not an effective system of estate taxation is likely to achieve this goal. Certainly the prevailing assumption is that it would: "From its beginning the estate tax was viewed as a counterweight to an undue concentration of wealth" [Gale and Slemrod, 2000, p. 931]. However, there are several reasons why taxing bequests might backfire and create a less equal distribution of income.

- If the estate tax reduces saving, there will be less capital. This leads to a lower real wage for labor, and under certain conditions, a smaller share of income going to labor.[10] To the extent that capital income is more unequally distributed than labor income, the effect is to increase inequality.
- *Within* a generation, it is likely that most individuals transfer wealth only to others who are worse off than they are. Such transfers clearly tend to enhance equality. Reducing such voluntary transfers could well lead to more inequality.
- Suppose that parents whose earnings capacities are much higher than average produce children whose earnings capacities are closer to the average level. (This phenomenon is known as *regression toward the mean*.) Well-off parents, who wish to compensate their children for their lesser earnings capacity by making bequests, tend to decrease inequality *across* generations. Conversely, reducing such transfers increases intergenerational inequality.

A related concern is that the focus of policy should be the inequality of consumption rather than the inequality of wealth. To the extent that the estate tax encourages rich people to spend more money while they are alive, then it worsens consumption inequality. We conclude that, from a theoretical point of view, the effect of estate taxation on inequality is ambiguous. Empirical research has not settled whether the equality-increasing or equality-decreasing effect dominates.

Provisions

Gift taxation and estate taxation are inextricably bound. Suppose that estates are taxed and gifts are not. If Lear desires to pass his wealth on to his daughters and knows it will be taxed at his death, then he can avoid tax by making the transfer as a gift *inter vivos*. Similar opportunities would arise if there were a gift tax but no estate tax. Since 1976, the gift and estate taxes in the United States have been integrated and are officially referred to as the **unified transfer tax.**

The unified transfer tax is similar in basic structure to the personal income tax. After the gross estate is calculated, various deductions and exemptions are subtracted,

unified transfer tax

A tax in which amounts transferred as gifts and bequests are jointly taken into account.

---

[10] When the wage rate decreases, the quantity of labor demanded increases. Thus, what happens to labor income—the product of the wage and the quantity demanded—depends on the elasticity of demand for labor. This in turn depends on the ease with which capital may be substituted for labor (the elasticity of substitution of capital for labor).

leaving the taxable estate. The tax liability is determined by applying a progressive rate schedule to the taxable estate.

Computing the Taxable Base   The **gross estate** consists of all property owned by the decedent at the time of death, including real property, stocks, bonds, and insurance policies. It also includes gifts made during the decedent's lifetime. To find the **taxable estate,** deductions are allowed for funeral expenses, costs of settling the estate (lawyers' fees), and any outstanding debts of the estate. Gifts to charity are deductible without limit.

The following deductions are available:

- In 2009, each estate was allowed a lifetime exemption of $3.5 million. No federal estate tax is levied on estates that are less than the lifetime exemption. The exemption is not indexed for inflation.
- All qualified transfers to spouses—by gift or bequest—are deductible in arriving at the taxable base. Thus, the estate of a multimillionaire who leaves $2 million to her children and the rest to her husband bears no tax liability. Because of the spousal deduction, most married couples do not pay any estate tax until both spouses have died.
- In 2009, each individual was qualified for an annual gift exclusion of $13,000 per recipient. (The recipient need not be a relative.) Consider a family with three children. Each year Mom can give $13,000 to each child, as can Dad. Together, then, the couple can give their three children annually $78,000 tax free. Interestingly, there is some evidence that wealthy people do not fully exploit the tax advantages of distributing wealth before death. Why? There is a story about a rich man who gave each of his children $1 million when they reached the age of 21. When asked why he did so, the millionaire explained that he wanted his children to be able to tell him to "go to hell"—to have total financial independence. It appears that most people would just as soon *not* have their children be able to tell them to go to hell. These people therefore keep control of their wealth as long as possible, even at the cost of a larger-than-necessary tax liability.

Rate Structure   The taxable base is subject to increasing marginal tax rates. For 2009, the maximum rate was 45 percent. It is hard to say whether or not this rate is efficient. As usual, the answer depends on the responsiveness of behavior to changes in the tax rate. But as indicated earlier, little is known about how economic decisions are affected by estate and gift taxes.

gross estate

All property owned by the decedent at the time of death.

taxable estate

The gross estate less deductions for costs of settling the estate, outstanding debts of the estate, and charitable contributions.

POLICY PERSPECTIVE

Death of the Estate Tax?

The estate tax has been the source of much controversy. Legislation passed in 2001 moved toward eliminating the tax by gradually increasing the lifetime exemption from $675,000 in 2001 to $3.5 million in 2009. It also reduced the highest rate from 55 percent in 2001 to 45 percent by 2007. Then, according to the 2001 legislation, in 2010 the estate tax is eliminated. However, like other provisions of the 2001 tax law, the estate tax provisions were set to expire at the end of 2010, meaning a return to the 2001 estate tax levels in 2011. According to this law, if your rich great-aunt dies on December 31, 2010, no tax will be levied on her estate, but if she dies on January 1, 2011, after an exemption of $675,000, her estate will be subject to marginal rates up to 55 percent. This bizarre situation leads to the thought that deaths might be timed to avoid the estate tax. Yes, it sounds weird, but there is actually some evidence from Australia that suggests that some deaths were timed to accord with the elimination of the Australian inheritance tax [Gans and Leigh, 2006]. As of this writing, President Obama is proposing to keep the 2009 exemption level ($3.5 million) and tax rate (45 percent) indefinitely.

Special Problems   A number of difficulties arise in the administration of an estate and gift tax.

Jointly Held Property Suppose a husband and wife own property together. For purposes of estate taxation, should this be considered one estate or two? We discussed the philosophical problems concerning whether the family or the individual should be the unit of taxation in Chapter 17 under "Choice of Unit and the Marriage Tax," so there is no need to do so again here. Under current federal law, half of the value of jointly held property is now included in the gross estate of the first spouse to die, regardless of the relative extent to which the spouses contributed to the accumulation of the property.[11]

Closely Held Businesses Suppose Lear wants to bequeath his business, which is the only asset he owns, to his daughters. Because there is no cash in Lear's estate, the daughters may have to sell the business to pay the estate tax due. To reduce the likelihood of such an event, the law allows the estate taxes on closely held businesses to be paid off over as long as 14 years, at favorable rates of interest. Moreover, in computing the gross estate, qualified family farms and businesses are valued at less than their fair market value. Such provisions reflect a value judgment that it is socially desirable per se to have the same family control a given business for several generations. They also reflect the political power of the owners of small businesses.

Avoidance Strategies An implicit goal of the estate tax is to tax wealth at least once a generation. However, people can avoid the tax in a number of ways. Many of them involve setting up *trusts*, which are arrangements whereby a person or institution known as a trustee holds legal title to assets with the obligation to use them for the benefit of another party. As an example of the use of trusts for estate tax avoidance, consider the problem facing parents who own life insurance policies naming their children as beneficiaries. The proceeds from insurance policies are included in the parents' gross estate. However, parents can establish an **insurance trust** and assign the insurance policy to the trust. Since the parents no longer own the policy, it is out of their estate, and their children receive the full benefit of the life insurance.

Another relatively simple and popular technique involves granting one's heirs shares of stock in a closely held corporation. Specifically, suppose that Mickey incorporates his business and owns all the stock. During his lifetime, Mickey makes gifts of a substantial portion of the stock—but less than half—to his heirs, Morty

insurance trust

A trust that is the legal owner of a life insurance policy. It allows the beneficiaries of the policy to avoid the estate tax.

---

[11] More precisely, this rule holds for joint property owned with *right of survivorship*, meaning that on the death of one owner, the property automatically passes to the other owner.

and Ferdy. If the transfers occur relatively early in the life of the business, the shares are not worth very much, so little if any gift tax liability is incurred. Because Mickey owns the majority of the firm's stock, he stays in charge of the company and effectively controls the value of the transferred shares. If Mickey's firm prospers, by the time he dies, Morty's and Ferdy's shares may be extremely valuable. Mickey has thus managed to transfer substantial wealth to his heirs and shield the transfer from the gift and estate tax. What about the shares that Mickey still owns at death? Other more complicated techniques are available to shelter them.

In short, many methods are available for making intergenerational transfers of wealth without bearing any taxes and without losing effective control of the property during your life. Many of these avoidance techniques are complicated and expensive. As noted in a report by the congressional Joint Economic Committee, estate tax liabilities "depend on the skill of the estate planner, rather than on capacity to pay" [Joint Economic Committee, 2006, p. 34]. In effect, the only people who pay the tax are those who neglect to do the appropriate planning. However, even in cases where the tax generates no revenues, it may create excess burdens and/or compliance costs for people who modify their behavior to avoid it.

Reforming Estate and Gift Taxes

For those who wish to expand the role of estate and gift taxes, the most straightforward approach would be to lower the lifetime exemption. However, if the estate tax is ever to play an important part in the revenue system, methods for dealing with avoidance via trusts and other such instruments must be devised.

Some tax theorists propose integrating the estate and gift tax system into the personal income tax. Gifts and inheritances would be taxed as income to the recipients. As noted earlier, such receipts are income and, according to the Haig-Simons definition of income, should therefore be included in adjusted gross income. To account for the fact that income in this form tends to be "lumpy," some form of averaging would have to be devised.

There is, however, popular resistance to taxing gifts and inheritances as ordinary income. A different method of moving the focus of estate and gift taxation from the donor to the recipient is an **accessions tax,** under which each individual is taxed on total lifetime acquisitions from inheritances and gifts. The rate schedule could be made progressive and include an exemption, if so desired. The attraction of such a scheme is that it relates tax liabilities to the recipient's ability to pay rather than to the estate. Administrative difficulties would arise from the need for taxpayers to keep records of all sizable gifts and estates. But if it is ever decided to tax wealth transfers more aggressively, an accessions tax deserves serious consideration. On the other hand, for those who object to the taxation of wealth transfers on philosophical or economic grounds, the best reform of the estate tax is the one scheduled for 2010: Abolish it.

accessions tax

A tax levied on an individual's total lifetime acquisitions from inheritances and gifts.

▶ PROSPECTS FOR FUNDAMENTAL TAX REFORM

Our discussion of the consumption tax has revealed a number of advantages and disadvantages. Advocates of the consumption tax argue that the current system is complicated, inefficient, and unfair and thus in need of broad reform. Opponents basically agree with the assessment of the current system, but argue that a consumption tax would inevitably suffer from similar problems and would introduce problems of its own.

What are the prospects of fundamental tax reform? Even those in favor of such reform concede that the obstacles are formidable. However, attempts to make broad changes in the tax system might be more likely to succeed than attempts to modify specific provisions on a piecemeal basis. If *everyone's* ox is being gored, people are less apt to fight for their particular loopholes. The experience of the last major tax reform in 1986 lends some support to this viewpoint. One reason it passed was that on certain key votes, its supporters were able to package it as an all-or-nothing proposition. They argued that one had to accept the whole set of changes or no changes at all. It is noteworthy, however, that even with a very popular president and extremely powerful congressional leaders behind the bill, it nearly died several times.

The conditions for politically successful tax reform are nicely summarized by Edward Lazear and James Poterba, two members of the President's Advisory Panel on Federal Tax Reform:

> If reform proposals are dissected by politicians in an attempt to promote provisions that reduce their constituents' tax liabilities while excising those that might lead to higher taxes, then reform will inevitably fail. But if reform proposals are viewed instead as a collection of provisions that taken together leave most families in a position not very different from their current one, while also shifting the tax system toward a structure that will promote long-term economic growth and reduce the burden of tax compliance, then these proposals can command broad popular support and even enthusiasm. Genuine tax reform is a difficult process that requires commitment to the goal of creating a more efficient, simpler, and fairer tax system [Lazear and Poterba, 2006, p. 7].

An alternative approach is suggested by humorist Dave Barry:

> We put the entire Congress on an island. All the food on this island is locked inside a vault, which can be opened only by an ordinary American taxpayer named Bob. Every day, the congresspersons are given a section of the Tax Code, which they must rewrite so that Bob can understand it. If he can, he lets them eat that day; if he can't he doesn't. Or, he can give them food either way. It doesn't matter. The main thing is, we never let them off the island [Barry, 2003].

Summary

- Proponents of personal consumption taxes argue that they eliminate double taxation of interest income, promote lifetime equity, tax individuals on the basis of the amount of economic resources they use, may be adjusted to achieve any desired level of progressiveness, and are administratively superior to an income tax.

- Opponents of consumption taxes point out difficult transition problems, argue that income better measures ability to pay, that they are administratively burdensome, and that in the absence of appropriate taxes on gifts and bequests, they would lead to excessive concentration of wealth.

- Consumption taxes are typically viewed as regressive. However, this view is based on calculations involving annual rather than lifetime income, and assumes that the incidence of the tax falls on the purchaser.

- Four consumption tax prototypes are a retail sales tax, a value-added tax, the Hall-Rabushka flat tax, and a cash-flow tax. Their administrative attributes differ substantially; but their economic effects are basically the same.

- General sales and excise taxes are important revenue sources at the state and local levels.

- A major attraction of sales taxes is ease of administration, at least when the rates are not too high. Some sales taxes can be justified as correctives for externalities or as substitutes for user fees.

- The value-added tax (VAT) is popular in Europe but is not used in the United States. The VAT is levied on the difference between sales revenue and cost of purchased commodity inputs.

- Personal consumption taxes allow an individual's tax liability to depend upon his or her personal circumstances. One example is the Hall-Rabushka flat tax, which taxes the difference between firms' revenues and expenditures for inputs at a flat rate and applies the same rate to individuals' wages. Progressivity is built into the system by means of a personal exemption. Another example is the cash-flow tax, which taxes each individual on his or her annual consumption expenditures.

- Proponents of wealth taxes believe that they permit the taxation of unrealized capital gains that escape the income tax, reduce the concentration of wealth, and compensate for benefits received by wealth holders. Some also argue that wealth is a good index of ability to pay and should, therefore, be subject to tax.

- Estate and gift taxes are levied on the value of wealth transfers, either from a decedent or from another living individual. Neither is a major revenue source at any level of government. Little is known about the incentive effects or incidence of estate and gift taxes.

- Major proposals for reform of estate and gift taxes are either to incorporate these transfers in the personal income tax system or to institute an accessions tax (a tax based on total lifetime gifts and bequests received). Opponents of the estate tax argue for abolishing it.

Discussion Questions

1. Zach lives two periods. He earns $10,000 in the first period and nothing in the second period. The rate of return is 10 percent, and there is an income tax (applied to labor and interest earnings) of 50 percent. Zach decides to save half of his first period earnings, which he consumes (along with interest earned) in the second period.

   a. What is Zach's income tax liability each period? What is the present value of his lifetime tax payments?

   b. Suppose that a consumption tax of 50 percent replaces the income tax in the second period (after Zach has made his saving decision). How much does he pay in taxes the second period? What is the present value of his lifetime tax payments? Compare your answer to the present value of lifetime tax payments in part a, and explain the relevance of the comparison to transitional problems in moving to a consumption tax.

2. According to a *New York Times* columnist, "The estate tax affects a surprisingly small number of

people. In 2003, . . . just 1.25 percent of all deaths resulted in taxable estates, with most of them paying relatively little" [Norris, 2005, p. C1]. Is counting the number of taxable estates and the amount of tax revenue collected a good way to assess the burden of the estate tax?

3. Discuss carefully the following quotation: "It is reasonable to assume . . . that business can pass along the full value of the [value-added] tax to final consumers. But if [it is assumed that] businesses have the power to raise prices a dollar for each dollar they pay in value-added taxes, then it should also [be] assume[d] businesses can similarly raise prices against every dollar they now pay in payroll and corporate income taxes" [Cockburn and Pollin, 1992, p. A15].

4. An interesting set of tax questions came up in 1998 when baseball stars Mark McGwire and Sammy Sosa were getting close to breaking the record for the number of home runs during a single season. Assume for this discussion that the home run ball that broke the record would be worth $1 million. In each case below, what

are the tax consequences for the fan who catches the ball?

a. The fan gives the ball back to the player who hit it.

b. The fan keeps the ball and holds onto it until he dies.

c. The fan gives the ball to a charity, and the charity sells the ball for a profit.

d. The fan sells the ball immediately.

e. The fan sells the ball after holding it a year.

5. In 2007, two members of Congress submitted the *Fair Tax Act*, which would replace the income, estate, payroll, and corporation taxes with a flat retail sales tax on goods and services. According to a supporter of an earlier version of the Fair Tax [Vessalla, 2001], the proposal has the following virtues:

a. "What you earn is what you keep."

b. "Investment and savings would soar."

c. "There is no evading the Fair Tax."

Evaluate each of these claims.

6. In January 2003, Professor David Bradford told a *New York Times* reporter that a consumption tax discourages work effort. Shortly thereafter, he received the following e-mail: "Since when is a tax on consumption a disincentive to work? This sort of specious reasoning ran amok in this article. I laughed as I saw it was labeled 'Economic Analysis.'" Who was correct, Professor Bradford or his correspondent? Justify your answer using either an arithmetic or algebraic argument. [Hint: Bradford was right.]

7. Rich lives two periods. His earnings in the present are 100; in the future they are 75.6. The interest rate is 8 percent.

a. Suppose that Rich's earnings are subject to a 25 percent tax. Suppose also that interest earnings are taxed at the same rate and interest paid is tax deductible. Using our life-cycle model, show that this tax generates an excess burden. (Hint: How does the tax change the intertemporal budget constraint?)

b. Suppose now that interest payments are not tax deductible. Does this tax generate an excess burden if Rich is a borrower?

c. Now assume the tax in part *a* is scrapped in favor of a consumption tax. What consumption tax rate would yield the same tax revenue? Does this tax distort the choice between present and future consumption?

d. Now assume the consumption tax in part *c* is instituted, but the deduction of interest payments remains. Does this tax distort the choice between present and future consumption?

8. Amy and Shirley both live two periods. Both have earnings of 1,000 in the present and zero in the future. The interest rate is 8 percent. Suppose that they are each subject to an income tax, and Amy's first period consumption is 200 while Shirley's is 300. Who has the higher lifetime tax burden? Under a proportional consumption tax, how would their lifetime tax burdens compare?

9. Suppose that Aviva can earn supplemental income by working overtime. She intends to use any income she earns to buy shares of stock in a corporation, with the intention of leaving the shares to her children in her will. She is 60 years old and expects to live 25 more years. Aviva faces the following marginal tax rates: a 35 percent combined income and payroll tax, a 35 percent corporate tax paid by the firm whose stock she buys, a 15 percent tax on the dividends earned (there are no capital gains), and a 45 percent tax on her estate when she dies. If the before-tax return on the stock is 7 percent, how much will Aviva's children get on every dollar Aviva earns in supplemental income? How does this compare to their gain if there were no taxes?

Part Six

MULTIGOVERNMENT PUBLIC FINANCE

Sometimes it is useful to think of public finance decisions as being made by a single government. In the United States, however, an astounding number of entities have the power to tax and spend. There are more than 89,000 governmental jurisdictions: 1 federal, 50 state, 3,033 county, 19,492 municipal, 16,519 township, 13,051 school district, and 37,381 special district [US Bureau of the Census, 2009, p. 259]. The interaction of state, local, and federal governments plays a crucial role in US public finance. In Chapter 22 we examine the fiscal issues that arise in federal systems.

Public Finance in a Federal System

> *Texans can run Texas.*
>
> —GEORGE W. BUSH

In 2002, Congress passed the No Child Left Behind Act of 2001 (NCLB). NCLB shifted oversight of the educational system from local school districts and states toward the national government. Under NCLB, each state must test students from third through eighth grade and must issue report cards comparing the scores obtained in each school. Schools that do not show adequate progress in their scores must allow students to transfer to other schools, at the school district's expense. NCLB also requires that teachers either have a college degree in each field they teach or demonstrate they are qualified by passing an exam.[1]

The law's passage contributed to an ongoing controversy about the role of the federal government in education. Opponents of NCLB argue that setting educational standards and determining teacher qualifications are best left to local school districts and the states. They believe that the federal government simply doesn't know enough about local conditions to make sensible regulations governing education. For example, many officials in rural states say that some of their schools must rely on a single person teaching a number of subjects, so it is impossible for them to fulfill NCLB's requirement that teachers have a degree in each subject they teach. Allowing students to transfer from low-performing schools also presents problems in rural areas. Enforcing this law in some parts of Alaska would require flying students 164 miles across the Bering Sea [Dillon, 2003]. Opponents of the NCLB also complain that it is unfair for them to have to raise state and local taxes to comply with federal mandates. Defenders of NCLB claim that education is a national issue and therefore federal oversight is necessary and appropriate.

This debate highlights several enduring questions that surround the operation of the US system of public finance:

- Is decentralized government desirable?
- If so, which levels of government should decide on different policies?
- Are locally raised taxes a good way to pay for the services provided by state and local governments? Or should the money come from the federal government?

---

[1] For a discussion of other aspects of the NCLB, see Chapter 7.

These are important issues in the United States, where the appropriate division of power among the various levels of government has been a matter of controversy since the nation's founding. The issues are of equal consequence to China, which is considering whether or not to devolve power to provincial governments, and to European nations, which are currently deciding which economic policymaking functions will be surrendered to the European Union. This chapter examines the normative and positive aspects of public finance in a federal system.

▶ BACKGROUND

A **federal system** consists of different levels of government that provide public goods and services and have some scope for making decisions. The subject of **fiscal federalism** examines the functions undertaken by different levels of government and how the different levels of government interact with each other. One federal system is more centralized than another when more of its decision-making powers are in the hands of authorities with a larger jurisdiction. The most common measure of the extent to which a system is centralized is the **centralization ratio,** the proportion of total direct government expenditures made by the central government. ("Direct" government expenditure comprises all expenditure except transfers made to other governmental units.) Centralization ratios vary widely across nations. In France, it is 81 percent; in Canada, 43 percent; and in the United States, 46 percent.[2]

Figure 22.1 shows that the US centralization ratio has increased since the early part of the 20th century, although the movement upward has not been steady. However, the centralization ratio is by no means a foolproof indicator. For example, states and localities make expenditures for computers in public libraries, but some of the money comes in the form of grants from the federal government. The Child Online Protection Act requires that libraries install software to screen against obscene materials; libraries that do not comply lose their grants. Most libraries comply. Who is really in charge? The point is that if local and state government spending behavior is constrained by the central government, the centralization ratio underestimates the true extent of centralization in the system. In fact, a substantial amount of state and local spending is dictated by the federal government. The federal government simply mandates that the subfederal government provide certain services, but without a corresponding increase in financial support.

A number of important activities are mostly in the hands of state and local governments, including education and public safety. On the other hand, the federal government has the entire responsibility for defense and Social Security. And all three levels of government spend substantial amounts of money on public welfare. Is this division of powers in the US fiscal system sensible? Before providing an answer, we need to discuss the special features associated with local government.

federal system

Consists of different levels of government that provide public goods and services and have some scope for making decisions.

fiscal federalism

The field that examines the functions undertaken by different levels of government and how the different levels of government interact with each other.

centralization ratio

The proportion of total direct government expenditures made by the central government.

---

[2] Computed from Fisman and Gatti [2002, p. 340], except see Figure 22.1 for the United States.

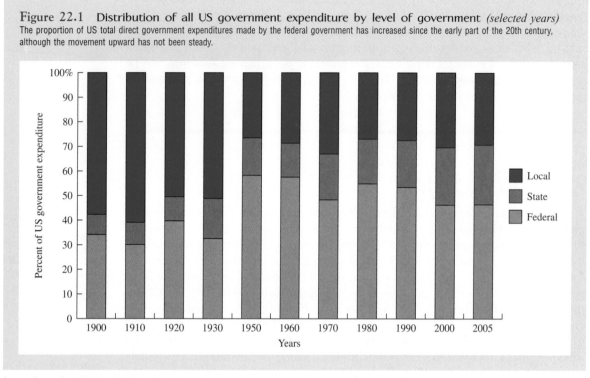

Figure 22.1 Distribution of all US government expenditure by level of government *(selected years)*
The proportion of US total direct government expenditures made by the federal government has increased since the early part of the 20th century, although the movement upward has not been steady.

Source: Figures for 1900 through 1980 are from Pommerehne [1977]. Figures after 1980 are computed from various editions of the US Bureau of the Census, *Statistical Abstracts of the United States.*

▶ COMMUNITY FORMATION

To understand the appropriate fiscal roles for local jurisdictions, we examine why communities are formed. In this context, it is useful to think of a community as a **club**—a voluntary association of people who band together to share some kind of benefit. This section develops a theory of clubs and uses it to explain how the size of a community and its provision of public goods are determined.

Consider a group of people who wish to band together to purchase land for a public park. For simplicity, assume that all members of the group have identical tastes and that they intend to share equally the use of the park and its costs. The "community" can costlessly exclude all nonmembers, and it operates with no transaction costs. Given the assumption of identical tastes, we need to consider only the desires of a representative member. Two decisions must be made: how large a park to acquire and how many members to have in the community.

Assuming that it wants to maximize the welfare of its citizens, how does the community decide? Consider first the relationship between the total cost per member and the number of members, *given* that a certain size park is selected. Clearly, the larger the community, the more people there are to shoulder the expense of the park, and the smaller the required contribution per member. If the per capita cost continually decreases with membership size, why not simply invite as many people as possible to join? The problem is that as more people join the community, the park becomes congested. The marginal congestion cost measures the dollar cost of the incremental congestion created by each new member. We assume that marginal

club

A voluntary association of people who band together to finance and share some kind of benefit.

congestion cost increases with the number of members. *The community should expand its membership until the marginal decrease in the membership fee just equals the per-person marginal increase in congestion costs.*

Now turn to the flip side of the problem: For any given number of members in the community, how big should the park be? A bigger park yields greater benefits, although like most goods, we assume it is subject to diminishing marginal utility. The per-member marginal cost of increased park acreage is just the price of the extra land divided by the number of members sharing its cost. *Acreage should be increased to the point where each member's marginal benefit just equals the per-member marginal cost.*

We can now put together these two pieces of the picture to describe an optimal community or club. The optimal community is one in which the number of members and the level of services simultaneously satisfy the condition that the marginal cost equal the corresponding marginal benefit. Although this club model is very simple, it highlights the crucial aspects of the community-formation process. Specifically, it suggests how community size depends on the type of public goods the people want to consume, the extent to which these goods are subject to crowding, and the costs of obtaining them, among other things.

How close is the analogy between a club and a real-world community? In many cases, it is closer than you might think. Over 50 million Americans live in areas governed by neighborhood associations [Tierney, 2005, p. A27]. These "gated communities" decide how many members they will have, how many security guards to hire, whether to construct golf courses and communal swimming pools, and so forth. Nevertheless, in most cases, viewing communities as clubs leaves unanswered several important questions that are relevant for understanding local public finance:

- How are the public services to be financed? A country club can charge a membership fee, but a town normally levies taxes to pay for public goods.
- A club (or gated community) can exclude nonmembers and so eliminate the free rider problem. How can towns achieve this end?
- When people throughout the country organize themselves into many different clubs (communities), is the overall allocation of public goods equitable and efficient?

These questions are taken up in the next section.

▶ THE TIEBOUT MODEL

"Love it or leave it." When people who oppose US federal government policy are given this advice, it is about as constructive as telling them to "drop dead." Only in extreme cases do we expect people to leave their country because of government policy.[3] Because of the large pecuniary and psychic costs of emigrating, a more realistic option is to stay home and try to change the policy. On the other hand, most citizens are not as strongly attached to their local communities. If you dislike the policies being followed in Skokie, Illinois, the easiest thing to do may be to move a few miles away to Evanston. This section discusses the relationship among intercommunity mobility, voluntary community formation, and the efficient provision of public goods.

Chapter 4 examined the idea that markets generally fail to provide public goods efficiently. The root of the problem is that the market does not force individuals to

---

[3] For example, in the 1960s, some young men left the country to evade military service in Vietnam.

reveal their true preferences for public goods. Everyone has an incentive to be a free rider. The usual conclusion is that some kind of government intervention is required.

In an important article, Tiebout [1956] (rhymes with "me too") argued that the ability of individuals to move among jurisdictions produces a market-like solution to the local public goods problem. As the cartoon suggests, individuals vote with their feet and locate in the community that offers the bundle of public services and taxes they like best. Much as Jones satisfies her demand for private goods by purchasing them on the market, she satisfies her demand for public services by the appropriate selection of a community in which to live, and pays taxes for the services. In equilibrium, people distribute themselves across communities on the basis of their demands for public services. Each individual receives her desired level of public services and cannot be made better off by moving (or else she would). Hence, the equilibrium is Pareto efficient, and government action is not required to achieve efficiency.

Tiebout's Assumptions

Tiebout's provocative assertion that a quasi-market process can solve the public goods problem has stimulated a lot of research. Much of it has been directed toward finding a precise set of sufficient conditions under which the ability of citizens to vote with their feet leads to efficient public goods provision. The key conditions follow.[4]

Government activities generate no externalities. As noted later, spillover effects among communities can lead to inefficiencies.

Individuals are completely mobile. Each person can travel costlessly to a jurisdiction whose public services are best for him. The location of his place of employment puts no restriction on where he resides and does not affect his income.

People have perfect information with respect to each community's public services and taxes.

---

[4] Not all of these conditions were included in Tiebout's original article.

There are enough different communities so that each individual can find one with public services meeting her demands.

The cost per unit of public services is constant, so that if the quantity of public services doubles, the total cost also doubles. In addition, if the number of residents doubles, the quantity of the public service provided must double. To see why these conditions are required for a Tiebout equilibrium to be efficient, imagine instead that the cost per unit of public services fell as the scale of provision increased. In that case, there would be scale economies of which independently operating communities might fail to take advantage.

This assumption makes the public service essentially a publicly provided private good. "Pure" public goods (such as national defense) do not satisfy this assumption. However, many local public services such as education and garbage collection fit this description reasonably well.

Public services are financed by a proportional property tax. The tax rate can vary across communities.[5]

*Communities can enact **exclusionary zoning laws**—statutes that prohibit certain uses of land.* Specifically, they can require that all houses be of some minimum size. To see why this assumption is crucial, recall that in Tiebout equilibrium, communities are segregated on the basis of their members' demands for public goods. If income is positively correlated with the demand for public services, community segregation by income results. In high-income communities, the *level* of property values tends to be high, and, hence, the community can finance a given amount of public spending with a relatively low property tax *rate*. Low-income families have an incentive to move into rich communities and build relatively small houses. Because of the low tax rate, low-income families have relatively small tax liabilities, but nevertheless enjoy the high level of public service provision. As more low-income families get the idea and move in, the tax base per family in the community falls. Tax rates must be increased to finance the expanded level of public services required to serve the increased population.

exclusionary zoning laws

Statutes that prohibit certain uses of land.

Since we assume perfect mobility, the rich have no reason to put up with this. They just move to another community. But what stops the poor from following them? In the absence of constraints on mobility, nothing. Clearly, a game of musical suburbs can develop in a Tiebout model. Exclusionary zoning prevents this phenomenon and thus maintains a stable Pareto efficient equilibrium.

Tiebout and the Real World

The Tiebout model is clearly not an exact description of the real world. People are not perfectly mobile; there are not enough communities to provide each family with a bundle of services that suits it perfectly; and so on. Moreover, contrary to the model's implication, we observe many communities with massive income differences and, hence, presumably different desired levels of public service provision. Just consider any major city.

However, we should not dismiss the Tiebout mechanism too hastily. There is a lot of mobility in the American economy. A persistent pattern is that in any given

---

[5] Tiebout [1956] assumed finance by head taxes. The more realistic assumption of property taxation is from Hamilton [1975].

year, about 17 percent of Americans have different residences than they had the year before [US Bureau of the Census, 2009, p. 36]. Moreover, most metropolitan areas allow a wide range of choice with respect to type of community. Within a 20-mile radius of a large American city, one can often choose to locate among several hundred suburbs. Certainly, casual observation suggests that across suburbs there is considerable residential segregation by income, that exclusionary zoning is practiced widely, and that service levels differ (even when incomes are similar).

There have been several formal empirical tests of the Tiebout hypothesis. One type of study looks at whether the values of local public services and taxes are capitalized into local property values. The idea is that if people move in response to local packages of taxes and public services, differences in these packages should be reflected in property values. A community with better public services should have higher property values, other things (including taxes) being the same. These capitalization studies are discussed later in this chapter in the context of property taxation. As noted there, capitalization does appear to be a widespread phenomenon. Another type of study examines whether changes in the levels of local public goods lead to migration across jurisdictions. For example, Banzhaf and Walsh [2008] find evidence that people migrate between communities as local air quality changes. They conclude that "households do appear to vote with their feet in response to changes in public goods." These results suggest that, at least in some settings, the Tiebout model is a good depiction of reality.

▶ OPTIMAL FEDERALISM

Now that we have an idea of how to characterize local governments, we return to our earlier question. What is the optimal allocation of economic responsibilities among levels of government in a federal system? Let us first briefly consider macroeconomic functions. Most economists agree that spending and taxing decisions intended to affect the levels of unemployment and inflation should be made by the central government. No state or local government is large enough to affect the overall level of economic activity. It would not make sense, for example, for each locality to issue its own money supply and pursue an independent monetary policy.

With respect to the microeconomic activities of enhancing efficiency and equity, there is considerably more controversy. Posed within the framework of welfare economics, the question is whether a centralized or decentralized system is more likely to maximize social welfare. For simplicity, most of our discussion assumes just two levels of government, "central" and "local." No important insights are lost with this assumption.

Disadvantages of a Decentralized System

Consider a country composed of a group of small communities. Each community government makes decisions to maximize a social welfare function depending only on the utilities of its members—outsiders do not count.[6] How do the results compare to those that would emerge from maximizing a national social welfare function that took into account all citizens' utilities? We consider efficiency and then equity issues.

Efficiency Issues   A system of decentralized governments might lead to an inefficient allocation of resources for several reasons.

---

[6] We ignore for now the questions of how the social welfare function is determined and whether the people who run the government actually try to maximize it (see Chapters 3 and 6).

Externalities A public good with benefits that accrue only to members of a particular community is called a **local public good.** For example, the public library in Austin, Texas, has little effect on the welfare of people in Ann Arbor, Michigan. However, the activities undertaken by one community can sometimes affect the well-being of people in other communities. If one town provides good public education for its children and some of them eventually emigrate, then other communities may benefit from having a better-educated workforce. Towns can affect each other negatively as well. Victoria, British Columbia, dumps its raw sewage into the sea; some of the waste makes its way to Seattle, Washington, whose citizens don't like it one bit. In short, communities impose externalities (both positive and negative) on each other. If each community cares only about its own members, these externalities are overlooked. Hence, according to the standard argument (see Chapter 5), resources are allocated inefficiently.

local public good

A public good that benefits only the members of a particular community.

Scale Economies in Provision of Public Goods For certain public services, the cost per person falls as the number of users increases. For example, the more people who use a public library, the lower the cost per user. If each community sets up its own library, costs per user are higher than necessary. A central jurisdiction, on the other hand, could build one library, allowing people to benefit from the scale economies.

Of course, various activities are subject to different scale economies. The optimal scale for library services might differ from that for fire protection. And both surely differ from the optimal scale for national defense. This observation, incidentally, helps rationalize a system of overlapping jurisdictions—each jurisdiction can handle those services with scale economies that are appropriate for the jurisdiction's size.

On the other hand, consolidation is not the only way for communities to take advantage of scale economies. Some New Jersey communities jointly run their school systems and libraries, taking advantage of scale economies yet still retaining their independence. Alternatively, in California, some towns contract out to other governments or to the private sector for the provision of certain public goods and services. These arrangements weaken the link between the jurisdiction's decisions over how much of a publicly provided good to consume and how much to produce.

Inefficient Tax Systems Roughly speaking, efficient taxation requires that inelastically demanded or supplied goods be taxed at relatively high rates, and vice versa. (See Chapter 16.) Suppose that the supply of capital to the entire country is fixed, but capital is highly mobile across subfederal jurisdictions. Each jurisdiction realizes that if it levies a substantial tax on capital, the capital will simply move elsewhere, thus making the jurisdiction worse off. In such a situation, a rational jurisdiction taxes capital very lightly, or even subsidizes it. One example is Connecticut, which since 2006 has offered film producers a 30 percent tax credit. Over a two-year period, the tax credit attracted over 66 feature films, television shows, and commercials [Foderaro, 2008]. More generally, Chirinko and Wilson [2006] found that over the last 40 years, state investment tax incentives have become increasingly large and increasingly common.

In reality, of course, the total capital stock is not fixed in supply. Nor is it known just how responsive firms' locational decisions are to differences in local tax rates, although there is some statistical evidence that employment growth in a jurisdiction is inversely correlated with its tax rates on businesses [Mark et al., 2000]. But the basic point remains: Taxes levied by decentralized communities are unlikely to be efficient from a national standpoint. Instead, communities are likely to select taxes on the basis of whether they can be exported to outsiders. For example, if a community has the only coal mine in the country, we expect that the incidence of a locally imposed tax on coal will fall largely on coal users outside the community.[7] A coal tax would be a good idea from the community's point of view, but not necessarily from the nation's.[8]

An important implication of tax shifting is that communities may purchase too many local public goods. Efficiency requires that local public goods be purchased up to the point where their marginal social benefit equals marginal social cost. If communities can shift some of the burden to other jurisdictions, the community's perceived marginal cost is less than marginal social cost. When communities set marginal social benefit equal to the perceived marginal cost, the result is an inefficiently large amount of local public goods.

Scale Economies in Tax Collection Individual communities may not be able to take advantage of scale economies in the collection of taxes. Each community has to devote resources to tax administration, and savings may be obtained by having a joint taxing authority. Why not split the costs of a single computer to keep track of tax returns, rather than have each community purchase its own? Of course, some of these economies might be achieved just by cooperation among the jurisdictions, without actual consolidation taking place. In some states, for example, taxes levied by cities are collected by state revenue departments.

Equity Issues

Maximizing social welfare may require income transfers to the poor. Suppose that the pattern of taxes and expenditures in a particular community is favorable to its low-income members. If there are no barriers to movement between communities, we expect an in-migration of the poor from the rest of the country. As the poor population increases, so does the cost of the redistributive fiscal policy. At the same time, the town's upper-income people may decide to exit. Why should they pay high taxes for the poor when they can move to another community with a more advantageous fiscal structure? Thus, the demands on the community's tax base increase while its size decreases. Eventually the redistributive program has to be abandoned.

This argument relies heavily on the notion that people's decisions to locate in a given jurisdiction are influenced by the available tax-welfare package. There is some anecdotal support for this proposition. In the 1990s, California lawmakers were sufficiently concerned about welfare-induced migration to their state that they restricted new migrants, for their first year in the state, to the welfare benefits of the states from which they had moved. However, the Supreme Court declared such laws to be unconstitutional in 1999.

Some evidence along these lines is provided by Feldstein and Wrobel [1998] who note that if high-income individuals can avoid unfavorable tax conditions by migrating to states with lower tax rates, then employers in high-tax states will have to pay higher before-tax wages in order to keep their workers. The net effect is no change in the distribution of income. Feldstein and Wrobel find that, in fact, when states raise their tax rates, before-tax wages soon increase. The interpretation of this finding is

---

[7] As usual, a precise answer to the incidence question requires information on market structure, elasticity of demand, and the structure of costs. See Chapter 14.

[8] Coal-producing states such as Montana have tried to export their tax burdens to the rest of the country.

a bit tricky; it might be the case that causation runs in the other direction—states whose citizens have experienced wage increases vote for more progressive tax systems. In any case, the result suggests that caution is required when decentralized jurisdictions attempt to undertake income redistribution.

Advantages of a Decentralized System

Tailoring Outputs to Local Tastes   Some people want their children's high schools to have extensive athletic programs; others believe this is unnecessary. Some people enjoy parks; others do not. A centralized government tends to provide the same level of public services throughout the country, regardless of the fact that people's tastes differ. As de Tocqueville observed, "In great centralized nations the legislator is obliged to give a character of uniformity to the laws, which does not always suit the diversity of customs and of districts." Clearly, it is inefficient to provide individuals with more or less of a public good than they desire if the quantity they receive can be more closely tailored to their preferences. Under a decentralized system, individuals with similar tastes for public goods group together, so communities provide the types and quantities of public goods desired by their inhabitants. (Remember the "club" view of communities.)

A closely related notion is that a local government's greater proximity to the people makes it more responsive to citizens' preferences than central government.[9] This is especially likely to be the case in a large country where the costs of obtaining and processing information on everybody's tastes are substantial. The chief executive of McDonald's once said, "You can't manage 25,000 restaurants in a centralized way. Many decisions need to be decided closer to the marketplace" [Barboza 1999]. A federal system applies the same principle to government.

This logic suggests that the more preferences vary within an area, the greater the benefits to decentralized decision making within that area. To examine whether this notion has any predictive power, Strumpf and Oberholzer-Gee [2002] examined how states differ with respect to which level of government regulates the sale of liquor. People of different religious backgrounds differ about whether liquor should be prohibited. Therefore, the theory of federalism suggests that states with more religious diversity should be more likely to decentralize control over regulatory policy toward alcohol, other things being the same. They found support for this hypothesis—local control increases with variation of preferences within the state.

The logic of federalism also suggests that economic regulations enacted at the national level may not make sense in every community. For example, we showed in Chapter 5 that it does not make sense for environmental regulations to be uniform throughout the country. The marginal costs and benefits of pollution abatement depend on population density, weather patterns, and so on. To the extent that officials in a given jurisdiction have better information about specific issues relating to their area than the federal government, it makes sense to give them some latitude in determining regulatory policy. In the United States, the states can opt to take responsibility for implementing and enforcing some federal environmental policies. There is some evidence that states that take advantage of this option are more stringent than the federal government in enforcing the regulations [Sigman, 2003].

---

[9] However, if one believes that the preferences of members of some communities are wrong, this advantage turns into a disadvantage. For example, a community might decide to legalize slavery. Determining the circumstances under which the central government should be able to overrule state and local governments is a difficult political and ethical issue.

Fostering Intergovernment Competition   In many contexts, government managers lack incentives to produce at minimum feasible cost (see Chapter 6). Managers of private firms who fail to minimize costs are eventually driven out of business. In contrast, government managers can continue to muddle along. However, if citizens can choose among communities, then substantial mismanagement may cause citizens simply to move away. This threat may create incentives for government managers to produce more efficiently and be more responsive to their citizens. In this context, it is interesting to note that some evidence suggests that the more decentralized a country's fiscal system, the less corrupt its government is likely to be, other things being the same [Fisman and Gatti, 2002].

Experimentation and Innovation in Locally Provided Goods and Services   For many policy questions, no one knows what the right answer is, or even whether a single solution is best in all situations. One way to find out is to let each community choose its own way, and then compare the results. A system of diverse governments enhances the chances that new solutions to problems will be sought. As Supreme Court Justice Louis Brandeis once observed, "It is one of the happy incidents of the Federal system that a single courageous state may, if its citizens choose, serve as a laboratory, and try moral, social, and economic experiments without risk to the rest of the country."

From all appearances, Brandeis's laboratories are busily at work:

- Item: Sacramento, California, has adopted "smart-growth" city planning principles to reduce fuel consumption and air pollution. For example, the city has "clustered the places where people live more closely with the businesses where they work and shop" [Campoy, 2008].

- Item: In 2006, Massachusetts introduced an individual health insurance mandate, along with subsidies for the purchase of insurance, in an attempt to achieve universal health care coverage within the state (see Chapter 10).

- Item: To provide elderly people the option of home care rather than institutional care, Vermont adopted a system that pays family members to care for aging relatives [Lagnado, 2006].

Historically, some programs that began as experiments at the state level eventually became federal policy. During the Great Depression, for example, the designers of Social Security took advantage of the experience of several states that had earlier instituted social insurance programs.

Implications

The foregoing discussion makes it clear that a purely decentralized system cannot be expected to maximize social welfare. Efficiency requires that commodities with spillovers that affect the entire country—national public goods like defense—be provided at the national level. On the other hand, local public goods should be provided locally. As Dave Cieslewicz, the mayor of Madison, Wisconsin, put it when people in his town were debating whether to take a stand on the conflict between Israelis and Palestinians: "I got elected to get the garbage picked up and get the streets plowed, [not to] act on matters of international policy" [Napolitano, 2004].

This leaves us with the in-between case of community activities that create spillover effects that are not national in scope. One possible solution is to put all the communities that affect each other under a single regional government. In theory, this government would take into account the welfare of all its citizens, and so internalize the externalities. However, a larger governmental jurisdiction may be less responsive to local differences in tastes.

An alternative method for dealing with externalities is a system of Pigouvian taxes and subsidies. Chapter 5 shows that the government can enhance efficiency by taxing activities that create negative externalities and subsidizing activities that create positive externalities. We can imagine the central government using similar devices to influence the decisions of local governments. For example, if primary and secondary education create benefits that go beyond the boundaries of a jurisdiction, the central government can provide communities with educational subsidies. Local autonomy is maintained, yet the externality is corrected. We see later that some federal grants to communities roughly follow this model.

Our theory suggests a fairly clean division of responsibility for public good provision—local public goods by localities, and national public goods by the central government. In practice, there is considerable interplay between levels of government. For example, most law enforcement agents are state and local officials. Yet many of their actions are governed by federal criminal law, which "has grown explosively as Congress has taken stands against such offenses as carjacking and church burning, disrupting a rodeo and damaging a livestock facility" [Derthick, 2000, p. 27]. Given that localities might act inappropriately in the absence of such regulations, their presence may improve welfare. However, some believe the system of federal regulation over subfederal governmental units has become so complicated that it is hard to determine which level of government has responsibility for what. This might help explain the inadequate response to Hurricane Katrina in 2005: Confusion over the roles that each level of government should play led to a lack of coordination that delayed critical services.

Proposals have been made to reform the US federal system along the lines suggested by the theory of optimal federalism, but they have not been enacted. The political failure of such proposals is probably well explained by Representative Barney Frank of Massachusetts, who observed, "99.9 percent of Congress clearly prefer that the issue be decided at that level of government which will decide the issue the way they like" [Clymer, 1997, p. 6].

If a division of responsibilities is appropriate from an efficiency standpoint, does the same hold for income distribution? Most economists believe the mobility considerations discussed earlier rule out relying heavily on local governments to achieve distributional aims. An individual jurisdiction that attempts to do so is likely to find itself in financial trouble. This may be one of the reasons why New York City often is under fiscal stress. In fact, the great bulk of spending for income maintenance in the United States is done at the federal level. Social Security, Supplemental Security Income, food stamps, and the earned income credit are all federal programs. Although the 1996 welfare reform (discussed in Chapter 13) gave the states some new responsibilities in this area, the amount of money involved is relatively minor compared to that spent by the federal programs.

Public Education in a Federal System

A useful way to apply the theory of optimal federalism is to employ it to analyze education, one of the most important items in the budgets of state and local governments.[10] Total government spending on education in 2005 was over $835 billion. Of this, the federal government spent 17 percent, state governments 23 percent, and other governments the rest. Education accounts for about 18 percent of direct expenditures at the state level and about 38 percent of local spending [US Bureau of the Census, 2009, pp. 141, 266]. Nine out of ten American children are educated in public schools.

Does this pattern of spending on education by the different levels of government conform to our views of optimal federalism? One argument for the decentralized provision of a good is that it can be tailored to local tastes. Because many parents hold strong views about their children's education and these views differ across communities, the leading role played by local governments in providing education makes sense. One could, of course, allow local discretion over school policy while providing funding from state or federal levels of government. Politically, however, it may be difficult to maintain control of the schools if the financing comes from some other level of government—he who pays the piper, calls the tune. In California, for example, a substantial amount of public funding comes from the state government. The public schools are subject to a 9,000-page state education code, which tells them which textbooks to buy, how to teach phonics, and that their cafeterias must have full-service kitchens, among other things [Kronholz, 2000, p. A10].

Local governments raise money for education primarily through property taxation; there are wide variations in the amount of property wealth available to school districts. Variations in the property tax base can be associated with huge differences in funding for school districts. In 2006, for example, among California school districts with at least 10,000 students, per-pupil spending was 11 times higher in the weathiest district than in the poorest district [US Bureau of the Census, 2008d]. An egalitarian view of educational spending would call for funding from a level of government that could redistribute resources across local boundaries, regardless of its possible effects on local autonomy. As we see later in this chapter, intergovernmental grants are an important part of education finance.

Federal funding for education is centered in two areas: At the elementary and secondary levels, Department of Education funding goes primarily to programs serving disadvantaged ($14.7 billion in 2006) and special education ($11.8 billion in 2006) children [US Bureau of the Census, 2009, p. 141]. This is consistent with the observation that redistribution is hard to carry out at the local level. In higher education, a great deal of federal spending is directed toward research. The information forthcoming from research is a public good, and we have seen that centralized provision or subsidization of public goods can avoid the free rider problem that might arise at the local level.

One should note, however, that the federal role in education does not stop with funding. A vast body of federal law and regulation governs public education. Federal legislation covers such diverse topics as teacher training, libraries, standards for handicapped students, and sex education. States whose practices do not follow the rules may lose federal funds. Thus, although the system of American education finance seems broadly consistent with the basic tenets of optimal federalism, the division of decision making is not as clear as the theory would suggest.

---

[10] The more fundamental question of whether government should be involved in providing education in the first place is discussed in Chapter 7.

▶ PROPERTY TAX

In 2005, property taxes in the United States were $336 billion, about $11.3 billion of which were collected by the states and $324.6 billion by localities [US Bureau of the Census, 2009, p. 266]. There is no federal property tax. Although it is not as important as many other taxes when viewed from a national perspective, the property tax plays a key role in local public finance—it accounts for about 72 percent of local governments' tax revenues.

An individual's property tax liability is the product of the tax rate and the property's **assessed value**—the value the jurisdiction assigns to the property. In most cases, jurisdictions attempt to make assessed values correspond to market values.[11] However, if a piece of property has not been sold recently, the tax collector does not know its market value and must therefore make an estimate, perhaps based on the market values of comparable properties that have been sold recently.

Market and assessed values diverge to an extent that depends on the accuracy of the jurisdiction's estimating procedure. The ratio of the assessed value to market value is called the **assessment ratio.** If all properties have the same statutory rate and the same assessment ratio, their effective tax rates are the same. Suppose, however, that assessment ratios differ across properties. Ophelia and Hamlet both own properties worth $100,000. Ophelia's property is assessed at $100,000 and Hamlet's at $80,000. Clearly, even if they face the same statutory rate (say, 2 percent), Ophelia's effective rate of 2 percent (= $2,000/$100,000) is higher than Hamlet's 1.6 percent (= $1,600/$100,000). In fact, many communities do a very poor job of assessing values so that properties with the same statutory rate face drastically different effective rates.

To analyze the property tax, at the outset one must realize that in the United States, literally thousands of jurisdictions operate their property tax systems more or less independently. No jurisdiction includes a comprehensive measure of wealth in its tax base, but there are major differences with respect to just what types of property are excludable and what rates are applied. Religious and nonprofit institutions make "voluntary" contributions in lieu of taxes for property owned. Some communities tax new business plants preferentially, presumably to attract more commercial activity. Few areas tax personal wealth other than homes so that items such as cars, jewels, and stocks and bonds are usually exempt. Typically, structures and the land on which they are built are subject to tax. But, as Table 22.1 demonstrates, the effective rates differ substantially across jurisdictions.

Thus, although we continue to describe the subject matter of this section as "the" property tax, it should now be clear that there is no such thing. The variety of property taxes is crucial to assessing the economic effects of the system as a whole.

assessed value

The value a jurisdiction assigns to a property for tax purposes.

assessment ratio

The ratio of a property's assessed value to its market value.

Incidence and Efficiency Effects

The question of who ultimately bears the burden of the property tax is controversial. We discuss three different views and then try to reconcile them.

Traditional View: Property Tax as an Excise Tax   The traditional view is that the property tax is an excise tax that falls on land and structures. Incidence of the tax

---

[11] However, sometimes certain types of property are systematically assessed at lower rates than others. For example, many states have special assessment rates for farm property.

Table 22.1   Residential Property Tax Rates *(selected cities)*

City	Effective Tax Rate
Newark	2.03%
Detroit	2.01
Atlanta	1.75
New Orleans	1.75
Chicago	1.58
Charlotte	1.20
Los Angeles	1.10
New York	0.66

Source: US Bureau of the Census [2009, p. 276]. Figures are for 2006.

Effective property tax rates differ substantially across jurisdictions.

is determined by the shapes of the relevant supply and demand schedules as explained in Chapter 14. The shapes of the schedules are different for land and structures.

Land As long as the amount of land is fixed, its supply curve is perfectly vertical, and landowners bear the entire burden of a tax levied on it. Intuitively, because its quantity is fixed, land cannot "escape" the tax. This is illustrated in Figure 22.2. $S_{\mathscr{L}}$ is the supply of land. Before the tax, the demand curve is $D_{\mathscr{L}}$, and the equilibrium rental value of land is $P_0^{\mathscr{L}}$. The imposition of an ad valorem tax on land pivots the demand curve. The after-tax demand curve is $D_{\mathscr{L}}'$. The rent received by suppliers of land (landowners), $P_n^{\mathscr{L}}$, is found at the intersection of the supply curve with $D_{\mathscr{L}}'$. We find the rent paid by the users of land by adding the tax per acre of land to $P_n^{\mathscr{L}}$, giving $P_g^{\mathscr{L}}$. As expected, the rent paid by the users of the land is unchanged

Figure 22.2
Incidence of a tax on land
The supply curve for land is perfectly inelastic, so landowners bear the entire burden of a tax on land.

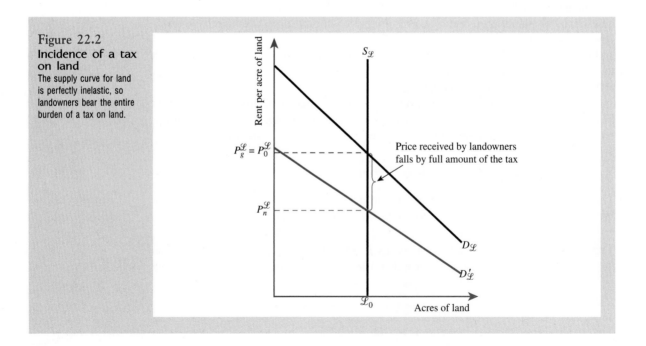

$(P_0^{\mathscr{L}} = P_g^{\mathscr{L}})$; the rent received by landowners falls by the full amount of the tax. Landowners bear the entire burden of the tax.

As discussed in Chapter 14, under certain circumstances the tax is capitalized into the value of the land. Prospective land purchasers take into account the fact that if they buy the land, they also buy a future stream of tax liabilities. This lowers the amount they are willing to pay for the land. Therefore, the landlord, when the tax is levied, bears the tax for all time. To be sure, future landlords write checks to the tax authorities, but such payments are not really a burden because they just balance the lower price paid at purchase. Capitalization complicates attempts to assess the incidence of the land tax. Knowing the identities of current owners is not sufficient; we must know who the landlords *were* at the time the tax was imposed.

To the extent that land is *not* fixed in supply, the preceding analysis requires modification. For example, the supply of urban land can be extended at the fringes of urban areas that are adjacent to farmland. Similarly, the supply can be increased if landfills or reclamation of wasteland is feasible. In such cases, the tax on land is borne both by landlords and the users of land, in proportions that depend on the elasticities of demand and supply. But a vertical supply curve for land is usually a good approximation of reality.

Structures To understand the traditional view of the tax on structures, we begin by considering the national market for capital. Capital can be used for many purposes: construction of structures, equipment for manufacturing, public sector projects like dams, and so forth. At any given time, capital has some price that rations it among alternative uses. According to the traditional view, in the long run, the construction industry can obtain all the capital it demands at the market price. Thus, the supply curve of structures is perfectly horizontal.

The market for structures under these conditions is depicted in Figure 22.3. Before the tax, the demand for structures by tenants is D_B, and the supply curve, S_B, is

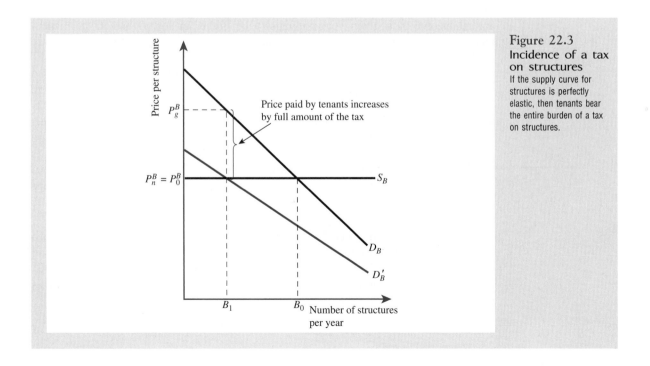

Figure 22.3
Incidence of a tax on structures
If the supply curve for structures is perfectly elastic, then tenants bear the entire burden of a tax on structures.

horizontal at the going price, P_0^B. At price P_0^B the quantity exchanged is B_0. On imposition of the tax, the demand curve pivots to D_B', just as the demand for land pivoted in Figure 22.2. But the outcome is totally different. The price received by the suppliers of structures, P_n^B, is the same as the price before the tax was imposed ($P_n^B = P_0^B$). Demanders of structures pay a price, P_g^B, which exceeds the original price, P_0^B, by precisely the amount of the tax. Hence, the burden is shifted entirely to tenants. This result, of course, follows from the assumption of a horizontal supply curve. Intuitively, horizontal supply means capital will leave the housing sector if it does not receive a return of at least P_0^B. But if the price received by the suppliers of capital cannot fall, tenants must bear the entire tax.

Summary and Implications of the Traditional View The tax on land falls on landowners (or, more precisely, the landowners at the time the tax is levied); the tax on structures is passed on to tenants. Therefore, the land part of the property tax is borne by people in proportion to the amount of rental income they receive, and the structures part of the tax is borne by people in proportion to the amount of housing they consume. It follows that the impact of the land part of the tax on progressiveness hinges on whether or not the share of income from land ownership tends to rise with income. There is fairly widespread agreement that it does, so this part of the tax is progressive. Similarly, the progressiveness of the tax on structures depends critically on whether the proportion of income devoted to housing rises or falls as income increases. If it falls, then the structures part of the tax is regressive, and vice versa.

An enormous amount of econometric work has focused on how housing expenditures actually do respond to changes in income. The ability to reach a consensus has been impeded by disagreement over which concept of income to use. Some investigators use *yearly* income. They tend to find that the proportion of income devoted to housing falls as income increases, suggesting that the tax is regressive. Other investigators believe that some measure of *permanent* income is more relevant to understanding housing decisions. According to this view, the fact that a family's annual income in a given year happens to be higher or lower than its permanent income has little impact on that year's housing consumption. Housing decisions are made in the context of the family's long-run prospects, not yearly variations.

Of course, if permanent income is the appropriate variable, then one must find some way to estimate it. One approach is to define permanent income as the average of several years' annual incomes. Housing expenditures turn out to be more responsive to changes in permanent income than to changes in annual income. Indeed, although the evidence is mixed, a reasonable conclusion is that housing consumption is roughly proportional to permanent income. Hence, the structures part of the tax is probably neither regressive nor progressive. Unfortunately, analyses based on annual income, which suggest the tax is regressive, generally dominate public discussions of the tax.

The New View: Property Tax as a Capital Tax   The traditional view uses a standard partial equilibrium framework. As we noted in Chapter 14, although partial equilibrium analysis is often useful, it may produce misleading results for taxes that are large relative to the economy. The so-called new view of the property tax takes a general equilibrium perspective and leads to some surprising conclusions.[12]

---

[12] See Zodrow [2007] for details.

According to the new view, it is best to think of the property tax as a general wealth tax with some assets taxed below the average rate and some taxed above. Both the average level of the tax and the deviations from that average have to be analyzed.

General Tax Effect Assume for the moment that the property tax can be approximated as a uniform tax on all capital. Then the property tax is just a general factor tax on capital. Assume further that the supply of capital to the economy is fixed. As shown in Chapter 14, when a factor is fixed in supply, it bears the full burden of a general tax levied on it. Hence, the property tax falls entirely on owners of capital. And since the proportion of income from capital tends to rise with income, a tax on capital tends to be progressive. Thus, the property tax is progressive, a conclusion that turns the traditional view exactly on its head!

Excise Tax Effects As noted earlier, the property tax is emphatically not a uniform tax. Rates vary according to the type of property and the jurisdiction in which it is located. Hence, the property tax is a set of excise taxes on capital. According to the new view, capital tends to migrate from areas where it faces a high tax rate to those where the rate is low. In a process reminiscent of the Harberger model presented in Chapter 14, as capital migrates into low-tax-rate areas, its before-tax rate of return there is bid down. At the same time, the before-tax rate of return in high-tax areas increases as capital leaves. The process continues until after-tax rates of return are equal throughout the economy. In general, as capital moves, returns to other factors of production also change. The impact on the other factors depends in part on their mobility. Land, which is perfectly immobile, cannot shift the tax. (In this conclusion, at least, the new and old views agree.) Similarly, the least-mobile types of capital are most likely to bear the tax. The ultimate incidence depends on how production is organized, the structure of consumer demand, and the extent to which various factors are mobile.

Long-Run Effects Our discussion of the general tax effect of the property tax assumed the amount of capital available to the economy is fixed. However, in the long run, the supply of capital may depend on the tax rate. If the property tax decreases the supply of capital, the productivity of labor, and hence the real wage, falls. If the tax increases capital accumulation, just the opposite occurs.

Summary of the New View The property tax is a general tax on capital with some types of capital taxed at rates above the average, others below. The general effect of the tax is to lower the return to capital, which tends to be progressive in its impact on the income distribution. The differentials in tax rates create excise effects, which tend to hurt immobile factors in highly taxed jurisdictions. The adjustment process set in motion by these excise effects is very complicated, and not much is known about their effects on progressiveness. Neither can much be said concerning the importance of long-term effects created by changes in the size of the capital stock. If the excise and long-run effects do not counter the general effect too strongly, the overall impact of the property tax is progressive.

Property Tax as a User Fee

The discussion so far has ignored the fact that communities use property taxes to purchase public services such as education and police protection. In the Tiebout model, the property tax is just the cost of purchasing public services, and each individual buys exactly the amount he or she desires. Thus, the property tax is really not a tax at all; it is more like a user fee for public services. This view has three important implications:

- The notion of the *incidence of the property tax* is meaningless because the levy is not a tax in the normal sense of the word.
- The property tax creates no excess burden. Because it is merely the fee for public services, it does not distort the housing market any more than the price of any other commodity.
- By allowing the deduction of property tax payments, the federal income tax in effect subsidizes the consumption of local public services for individuals who itemize on their tax returns. As long as the demand for local public services slopes downward, the deduction increases the size of the local public sector desired by itemizers, other things being the same [Metcalf, 2008].

As noted earlier, the link between property taxes and services received is often tenuous, so we should not take the notion of the property tax as a user fee too literally. Nevertheless, this line of reasoning has interesting implications. For example, if people care about the public services they receive, we expect the depressing effects of high property taxes on housing values to be counteracted by the public services financed by these taxes. In a classic paper, Oates [1969] constructed an econometric model of property value determination. In his model, the value of homes in a community depends positively on the quality of public services in the community and negatively on the tax rate, other things being the same. Of course, across communities, factors that influence house prices do differ. These include physical characteristics of the houses, such as number of rooms, and characteristics of the communities themselves, such as distance from an urban center. These factors must be considered when trying to sort out the effects of property taxes and local public goods on property values. Oates used multiple regression analysis to do so.

Oates's regression results suggest that increases in the property tax rate decrease housing values, while increases in per-pupil expenditures increase housing values. Moreover, the parameter values implied that the increase in property values created by expanding school expenditures approximately offset the decrease generated by the property taxes raised to finance them. These results need to be interpreted with caution. For one thing, expenditure per pupil may not be an adequate measure of local public services. Localities provide many public services other than education, such as police protection, parks, and libraries. Furthermore, even if education were the only local public good, expenditure per pupil might not be a good measure of educational quality. It is possible, for example, that expenditures in a given community are high because the community has to pay a lot for its teachers, its schools are not administered efficiently, or its students are particularly difficult to educate.

Subsequent to Oates's study, many other investigators have examined the relationships among property values, property taxes, and local public goods using data from different geographical areas and employing different sets of explanatory variables. Although the results are a bit mixed, Oates's general conclusion seems to be valid—property taxes and the value of local public services are capitalized into housing prices. (See, for example, Weimer and Wolkoff [2001].) Thus, if two communities have the same level of public services, but the first has higher taxes than the second (perhaps because its cost of providing the services is greater), we expect the first to have lower property values, other things being the same. More generally, these results imply that to understand how well off members of a community are, we cannot look at property tax rates in isolation. Government services and property values must also be considered.

Reconciling the Three Views   The three views of the property tax are not mutually exclusive. Each may be valid in different contexts. If, for example, we want to find the consequences of eliminating all property taxes and replacing them with a national sales tax, the "new view" is appropriate because a change that affects all communities requires a general equilibrium framework. On the other hand, if a given community is considering lowering its property tax rate and making up the revenue loss from a local sales tax, the "traditional view" offers the most insight. This is because a single community is so small relative to the economy that its supply of capital is essentially perfectly horizontal, and Figure 22.3 applies. Finally, when taxes and benefits are jointly changed and people are sufficiently mobile to be able to pick and choose communities, the "user fee view" is useful.

Why Do People Hate the Property Tax So Much?

On June 7, 1978, the voters of California approved a statewide property tax limitation initiative known as Proposition 13. Its key provisions were (1) to put a 1 percent ceiling on the property tax rate that any locality could impose, (2) to limit the assessed value of property to its 1975 value,[13] and (3) to forbid state and local governments to impose any additional property taxes without approval by a two-thirds majority local vote. Proposition 13 began a movement to limit the property tax that is still going strong today. Public opinion polls regularly indicate that people dislike the property tax even more than the federal income tax.

Why is the property tax so unpopular? Several explanations have been advanced:

Because housing market transactions typically occur infrequently, the property tax must be levied on an estimated value. To the extent that this valuation is done incompetently (or corruptly), the tax is perceived as unfair.

The property tax is highly visible. Under the federal income and payroll taxes, payments are withheld from workers' paychecks, and the employer sends the proceeds to the government. In contrast, the property tax is often paid directly by the taxpayer. Moreover, the payments are due on a quarterly or an annual basis, so each payment comes as a large shock. It is hard to know how seriously to take this argument. Even taxpayers who are somehow oblivious to the fact that federal income and payroll taxes are withheld during the year receive a pointed reminder of how much they have paid every April. There may be enough rage in that one month to last a whole year.

The property tax is perceived as being regressive. This perception is due partly to the continued dominance of the "traditional view" of the property tax in public debate. It is reinforced by the fact that some property owners, particularly the elderly, do not have enough cash to make property tax payments and may therefore be forced to sell their homes. Some states have responded to this phenomenon by introducing **circuit breakers** that provide benefits to taxpayers

circuit breakers

Transfers to individuals based on the excess of residential property tax payments over some specified portion of income.

---

[13] For property transferred after 1975, the assessed value was defined as the market value at which the transaction took place.

(usually in the form of a refund on state income taxes) that depend on the excess of residential property tax payments over some specified proportion of income. A better solution would be to defer tax payments until the time when the property is transferred.

Taxpayers may dislike other taxes as much as the property tax, but they feel powerless to do anything about the others. It is relatively easy to take aim at the property tax, which is levied locally. Residents of Canaan, New York, demonstrated this fact when they sued the local assessor after their property tax bills more than doubled within 10 years [Smith, 2005]. In contrast, mounting a drive against the federal income tax is very difficult, if for no other reason than a national campaign would be necessary and hence involve large coordination costs.

In light of the widespread hostility toward the tax, it is natural to ask whether it can be improved. A very modest proposal is to improve assessment procedures. The use of computers and modern valuation techniques can make assessments more uniform. Compared to the current system of differing effective tax rates within a jurisdiction, uniform tax rates would probably enhance efficiency. The equity issues are more complicated. Superficially, it seems a violation of horizontal equity for two people with identical properties to pay different taxes on them. However, the phenomenon of capitalization requires that we distinguish carefully between the owners at the time the tax is levied and the current owners. A property with an unduly high tax rate will sell for a lower price, other things being the same. Thus, a high tax rate does not necessarily make an individual who buys the property *after* the tax is imposed worse off. Indeed, equalizing assessment ratios could generate a whole new set of horizontal inequities.

personal net worth tax

A tax based on the difference between the market value of all the taxpayer's assets and liabilities.

A more ambitious reform of the property tax would be to convert it into a **personal net worth tax,** whose base is the difference between the market value of all the taxpayer's assets and liabilities. An advantage of such a system over a property tax is that by allowing for deduction of liabilities, it provides a better index of ability to pay. Moreover, because it is a personal tax, exemptions can be built into the system and the rates can be varied to attain the desired degree of progressivity.

A personal net worth tax is a kind of general wealth tax, and we discussed the administrative and economic issues associated with wealth taxation in Chapter 21. In the context of property tax reform, it is particularly important to note that because individuals can have assets and liabilities in different jurisdictions, a net worth tax would undoubtedly have to be administered by the federal government. This brings us to what many people consider to be the main justification for the current system of property taxation. Whatever its flaws, the property tax can be administered locally without any help from the federal or state governments. Hence, it provides local government with considerable fiscal autonomy. According to this view, elimination of the property tax would ultimately destroy the economic independence of local units of government.

California's experience after Proposition 13 is consistent with this notion. Because Proposition 13 limited the ability of communities to raise money via property taxes, that measure increased the importance of state revenues, and this appears to have shifted power over education policy from the localities to the state government. Similarly, Cheung [2008] found that Proposition 13 also led to a shift toward homeowners' associations, which are private institutions that have authority to tax, provide public services, and enforce regulations on their members. Thus, the political role of the property tax needs to be taken seriously in any discussion of its reform.

▶ INTERGOVERNMENTAL GRANTS

As already noted, federal grants are a very important source of revenue to states and localities. Grants from one level of government to another are the main method for changing fiscal resources within a federal system. Table 22.2 indicates that between 1960 and 2007, grants from the federal government increased both in real terms and as a proportion of total federal outlays.[14] Grants as a percentage of state and local expenditures have also increased. The importance of grants as an element in local public finance is particularly striking. Grants from federal and state government are about 35 percent of total local general revenues [US Bureau of the Census, 2009, p. 266]. Grants help finance activities that run practically the entire gamut of government functions, everything from food inspection to rural community fire protection.

Why have intergovernmental transfers grown so much over the long run? This question is closely related to why government spending in general has increased. As we saw in Chapter 6, the answer is far from clear. One explanation for the growth of grants emphasizes that over the last several decades, the demand for the types of services traditionally provided by the state and local sector—education, transportation, and police protection—has been growing rapidly. However, the state and local revenue structures, which are based mainly on sales and property taxes, have not provided the means to keep pace with the growth of desired expenditures. In contrast, federal tax revenues have grown automatically over time, largely due to the progressive nature of the federal personal income tax and, until the advent of indexing in the mid-1980s, inflation. Hence, there is a "mismatch" between where tax money is collected and where it is demanded. Grants from the central government to states and localities provide a way of correcting this mismatch.

Table 22.2	**Relation of Federal Grants-in-Aid to Federal and State and Local Expenditures** *(selected fiscal years)*		
Year	**Total Grants (billions of 2007 dollars)***	**Grants as a Percent of Total Federal Outlays**	**Grants as a Percent of State and Local Expenditures**
1960	$ 23	4.61%	10.0%
1970	84	9.6	17.1
1980	160	12.3	21.9
1990	164	8.9	15.2
2000	296	13.3	19.5
2007	379	13.1	19.9

*Amounts are converted to 2007 dollars using the GDP deflator.

Source: Computed from *Economic Report of the President, 2009* [pp. 377, 381].

Between 1960 and 2007, grants from the federal government increased in real terms, as a percent of total federal outlays, and as a percent of state and local expenditures.

---

[14] In addition to explicit grants, the federal government subsidizes states and localities by exempting from taxation the interest on state and local bonds and allowing the deductibility of state/local income and property taxes. In 2008, tax expenditures for the interest exclusion were $19 billion; for tax deductibility, $48 billion [Joint Committee on Taxation, 2008, p. 59].

The mismatch theory is unsatisfying because it fails to explain why states and localities cannot raise their tax *rates* to keep up with increases in the demand for local public goods and services. As noted in the next section, we probably have to turn to political considerations to explain the pattern of intergovernmental grants.

Types of Grants

A grant's structure influences its economic impact. There are basically two types, conditional and unconditional, which we discuss in turn.

categorical grants

Grants for which the donor specifies how the funds can be used.

Conditional Grants   These are sometimes called **categorical grants.** The donor specifies, to some extent, the purposes for which the recipient can use the funds. The vast majority of federal grants are earmarked for specific purposes, and the rules for spending the money are often spelled out in minute detail. For example, the federal government gives grants to states to establish anti–drunk driving programs. The terms of the law specify everything from the percent of blood-alcohol concentration that constitutes intoxication to how soon an offender's driver's license must be taken away after he or she is convicted. Such restrictions are not atypical.

There are several types of conditional grants.

Matching Grants For every dollar given by the donor to support a particular activity, a certain sum must be expended by the recipient. For example, a grant might stipulate that whenever a community spends a dollar on education, the federal government will contribute a dollar as well.

The standard theory of rational choice can help us analyze matching grants. In Figure 22.4, the horizontal axis measures the quantity of local government output, G, consumed by the residents of the town of Smallville. The vertical axis measures

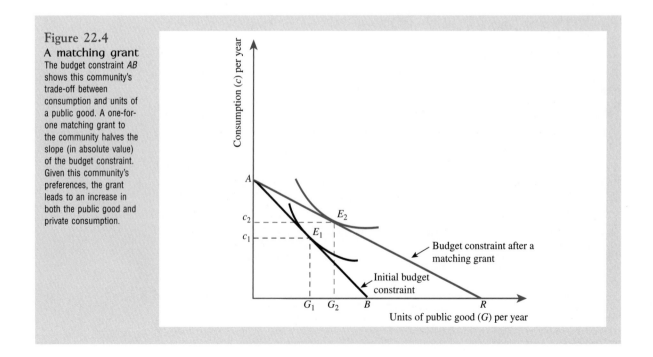

Figure 22.4
A matching grant
The budget constraint AB shows this community's trade-off between consumption and units of a public good. A one-for-one matching grant to the community halves the slope (in absolute value) of the budget constraint. Given this community's preferences, the grant leads to an increase in both the public good and private consumption.

Smallville's total consumption, c. Assume for simplicity that units of G and c are defined so the price of one unit of each is \$1. Hence, assuming no saving, c is equal to after-tax income. With these assumptions, Smallville's budget constraint between c and G is a straight line (AB in Figure 22.4) whose slope in absolute value is one.[15] The unitary slope indicates that for each dollar Smallville is willing to spend, it can obtain one unit of public good.

Suppose that Smallville's preferences for G and c can be represented by a set of conventionally shaped indifference curves.[16] Then if the town seeks to maximize its utility subject to the budget constraint, it chooses point E_1, where public good consumption is G_1 and community after-tax income is c_1.

Now suppose that a one-for-one matching grant regime is instituted. When Smallville gives up \$1 of income, it can obtain *\$2* worth of G—one of its own dollars and one from the federal government. The slope (in absolute value) of Smallville's budget line therefore becomes one-half. In effect, the matching grant halves the price of G. It is an ad valorem subsidy on consumption of the public good. The new budget line is drawn in Figure 22.4 as AR.

Smallville now consumes G_2 public goods and has c_2 available for private consumption. Note that not only is G_2 greater than G_1 but c_2 is also greater than c_1. Smallville uses part of the grant to buy more of the public good and part to reduce its tax burden. It would be possible, of course, to draw the indifference curves so that c_2 equals c_1, or even so that c_2 is less than c_1. Nevertheless, it is a distinct possibility that part of the grant meant to stimulate public consumption will be used not to buy more G but to obtain tax relief. In an extreme case, the community's indifference curves might be such that $G_2 = G_1$—the community consumes the same amount of the public good and uses the entire grant to reduce taxes. Thus, theory alone cannot indicate how a matching grant affects a community's expenditure on a public good. It depends on the responsiveness of demand to changes in price. Economists have therefore conducted statistical studies of how the demands for various public goods vary with their prices. According to the literature surveyed by Fisher and Papke [2000], the price elasticity of demand for education lies between 0.15 and 0.50.

A matching grant is a sensible way to correct for the presence of a positive externality. As explained in Chapter 5, when an individual or a firm generates a positive externality at the margin, an appropriate subsidy can enhance efficiency. The same logic applies to a community. Of course, all the problems that arise in implementing the subsidy scheme are still present. In particular, the central government has to be able to measure the actual size of the externality. In this context, it is interesting to note that many federal grant programs are very difficult to rationalize using efficiency criteria. The high matching rates (often 80 to 90 percent) are much greater than reasonable estimates of the externalities generated by the subsidized state and local activities [Oates, 1999, p. 1129]. In fact, the literature surveyed by Borck and Owings [2003] suggests that political rather than efficiency considerations predominate in the distribution of governmental grants. For example, more money tends to go to states that have representatives on important congressional committees.

---

[15] Details on the construction of budget constraints are provided in the appendix at the end of this book. This model ignores the deduction of state and local property taxes in the federal income tax system. If taxpayers itemize deductions and the marginal federal income tax rate is t, the absolute value of the slope of AB is $(1 - t)$.

[16] Of course, this supposition ignores all the problems—and perhaps the impossibility—of preference aggregation raised in Chapter 6. We return to this issue later.

Figure 22.5
A closed-ended matching grant
A closed-ended matching grant puts a limit on how much the central government will contribute. This leads to the kinked budget constraint, *ADF*. Given this community's preferences, the new equilibrium results in more consumption of the public good than without the grant, but less than under the open-ended matching grant.

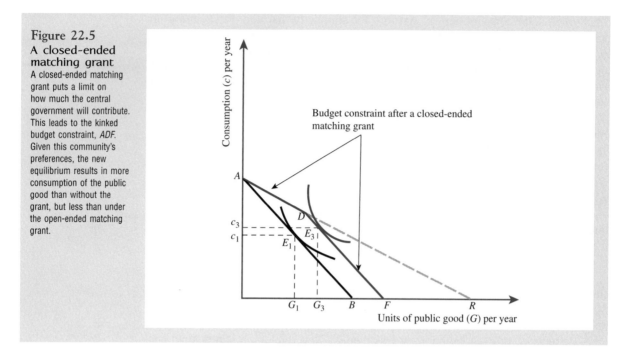

Matching Closed-Ended Grant The cost to the donor of a matching grant ultimately depends on the recipient's behavior. If Smallville increases its consumption of G substantially, the central government's contributions will be quite large, and vice versa. To put a ceiling on the cost, the donor may specify some maximum amount that it will contribute. Such a closed-ended matching grant is illustrated in Figure 22.5. As before, prior to the grant, Smallville's budget line is AB, and the equilibrium is at point E_1. With the closed-ended matching grant, the budget constraint is the kinked line segment ADF. Segment AD's slope is minus one-half, reflecting the one-for-one matching provision. But after some point D, the donor no longer matches dollar for dollar. Smallville's opportunity cost of a unit of government spending again becomes $1, which is reflected in the slope of segment DF.

The new equilibrium at E_3 involves more consumption of G than under the status quo, but less than under the open-ended matching grant. The fact that the grant runs out limits its ability to stimulate expenditure on the public good. However, in some cases the closed-endedness can be irrelevant. If desired community consumption of G involves an expenditure below the ceiling, the presence of the ceiling is irrelevant. In graphical terms, if the new tangency had been along segment AD of Figure 22.5, it would not matter that points along DR were not available. Baker et al. [1999] conducted an interesting study of the impact of moving from an open-ended to a closed-ended matching grant system in Canada. Before the 1990s, for every dollar a Canadian province spent on welfare programs, the central government matched the dollar. In order to contain costs, in 1990 the central government converted the program to a closed-ended system in three of the ten provinces. Consistent with the story in Figure 22.5, spending in the three affected provinces fell relative to the others.

Nonmatching Grant Here the donor gives a fixed sum of money with the stipulation that it be spent on the public good. Figure 22.6 depicts a nonmatching grant to buy

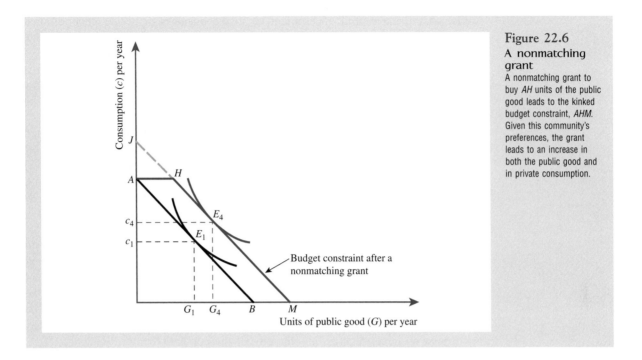

Figure 22.6
A nonmatching grant
A nonmatching grant to buy *AH* units of the public good leads to the kinked budget constraint, *AHM*. Given this community's preferences, the grant leads to an increase in both the public good and in private consumption.

AH units of *G*. At each level of community income, Smallville can now buy *AH* more units of the public good than it did before. Thus, the new budget constraint is found by adding a horizontal distance *AH* to the original budget constraint *AB*. The result is the kinked line *AHM*.

Smallville maximizes utility at point E_4. Note that although public good consumption goes up from G_1 to G_4, the difference between the two is less than the amount of the grant, *AH*. Smallville has followed the stipulation that it spend the entire grant on *G*, *but* at the same time, it has reduced its own expenditures for the public good. If the donor expected expenditures to be increased by exactly *AH*, then Smallville's reaction frustrates these hopes. It turns out that the situation depicted in Figure 22.6 is a good description of reality. Communities often use some portion of nonmatching conditional grant money to reduce their own taxes. According to one estimate, for example, for each dollar of education aid received by a community, local taxes go down by 30 to 70 cents [Fisher and Papke, 2000, p. 157].

Unconditional Grants   Observe from Figure 22.6 that budget line *AHM* looks almost as if it were created by giving the community an unrestricted lump sum grant of *AH* dollars. Such unconditional grants are sometimes referred to as **revenue sharing.** An unconditional grant would have led to a budget line *JM*, which is just segment *MH* extended to the vertical axis. Smallville happens to behave exactly the same way facing constraint *AHM* as it would have if it had faced *JM*. In this particular case, then, *the conditional grant could just as well have been an unrestricted lump sum grant.* Intuitively, as long as the community wants to consume at least an amount of the public good equal to the grant, the fact that the grant is conditional is irrelevant. In contrast, if the community wanted to consume less of the public good than *AH* (if the highest indifference curves were tangent somewhere along *JM* to the left of *H*), then the conditional nature of the grant would actually affect behavior.

revenue sharing

A grant from the federal government to a state or locality that places no restrictions on the use of funds.

Why should the central government be in the business of giving unconditional grants to states and localities? The usual response is that such grants can equalize the income distribution. The validity of this argument is unclear. Even if a goal of public policy is to help poor people, it does not follow that the best way to do so is to help poor communities. After all, the chances are that a community with a low average income has some relatively rich members and vice versa. If the goal is to help the poor, why not give them the money directly?

One possible explanation is that the central government is particularly concerned that the poor consume a greater quantity of the publicly provided good. An important example is education. This is a kind of commodity egalitarianism (Chapter 12) applied to the output of the public sector. However, as we just demonstrated, with unconditional grants we cannot know for sure that all the money will ultimately be spent on the favored good. (Indeed, the same is also true for conditional grants.)

Measuring Need   In any case, a redistributive grant program requires the donor to determine which communities "need" money and in what amounts. Federal allocations are based on complicated formulas established by Congress. The amount of grant money received by a state depends on such factors as per capita income, the size of its urban population, and the amount of its state income tax collections. The allocations to localities are functions of such conventional economic factors and may also depend on items such as the ethnicity of the population.

An important factor in determining how much a community receives from the federal government is its **tax effort,** normally defined as the ratio of tax collections to tax capacity. The idea is that communities that try hard to raise taxes but still cannot finance a very high level of public services are worthy of receiving a grant. Unfortunately, this and related measures may yield little or no information about a community's true effort. Suppose that Smallville is in a position to export its tax burden in the sense that the incidence of any taxes it levies falls on outsiders. Then a high tax rate tells us nothing about how much the members of the community are sacrificing.

More fundamentally, the tax effort approach may be rendered totally meaningless because of the phenomenon of capitalization. Consider two towns, Sodom and Gomorrah. They are identical except for the fact that Sodom has a brook providing water at essentially zero cost. In Gomorrah, on the other hand, it is necessary to dig a well and pump the water.

Gomorrah levies a property tax to finance the water pump. If there is a tax in Gomorrah and none in Sodom, and the communities are otherwise identical, why should anyone live in Gomorrah? As people migrate to Sodom, property values increase there (and decrease in Gomorrah) until there is no net advantage to living in either community. In short, property values are higher in Sodom to reflect the presence of the brook.

For reasons discussed previously, we do not expect the advantage to be necessarily 100 percent capitalized into Sodom's property values. Nevertheless, capitalization compensates at least partially for the differences between the towns. Just because Gomorrah levies a tax does *not* mean it is "trying harder" than Sodom, because the Sodomites have already paid for their water by a higher price for living there. We conclude that conventional measures of tax effort may not be very meaningful.

The Flypaper Effect

Our community indifference curve analysis begs a fundamental question: *Whose* indifference curves are they? According to median voter theory (Chapter 6), the

tax effort

The ratio of tax collections to tax capacity.

preferences are those of the community's median voter. Bureaucrats and elected officials play a passive role in implementing the median voter's wishes.

A straightforward implication of the median voter rule is that a $1 increase in community income has exactly the same impact on public spending as receipt of a $1 unconditional grant. In terms of Figure 22.6, both events generate identical parallel outward shifts of the initial budget line. If the budget line changes are identical, the changes in public spending must also be identical.

A considerable amount of econometric work has been done on the determinants of local public spending. (See Inman [2008] for a review.) Contrary to what one might expect, virtually all studies conclude that a dollar received by the community in the form of a grant results in *greater* public spending than a dollar increase in community income. Roughly speaking, the estimates suggest that a dollar received as a grant generates 40 cents of public spending, while an additional dollar of private income increases public spending by only 10 cents. This phenomenon has been dubbed the **flypaper effect,** because the money seems to stick in the sector where it initially hits.

Some explanations of the flypaper effect focus on the role of bureaucrats. Recall from Chapter 6 that some argue that bureaucrats seek to maximize the sizes of their budgets. As budget maximizers, the bureaucrats have no incentive to inform citizens about the community's true level of grant funding. By concealing this information, the bureaucrats may trick citizens into voting for a higher level of funding than would otherwise have been the case. According to this view, the flypaper effect occurs because citizens are unaware of the true budget constraint.

Intergovernmental Grants for Education

In 1971, the court case of *Serrano v. Priest* ushered in a new era in education finance. The California Supreme Court ruled that disparities in property wealth across school districts led to unconstitutionally disparate school quality when local property taxation was exclusively relied on for school finance. Since then, courts have struck down similar financing schemes in more than a dozen states. In response, states have assumed an increasingly large role in financing elementary and secondary education. States use two basic kinds of grants to support local schools: **Foundation aid** seeks to ensure a minimum level of expenditure per pupil, regardless of local property wealth. **District power equalization (DPE) grants** ensure that the revenue raised by the local property tax rate corresponds to what would be raised if the district's property wealth per pupil did not fall below a guaranteed level.

From our standpoint, the key thing about these grants is that they represent a centralization of school finance. Instead of a system in which each locality funds its own schools via the property tax, the state raises the money via an income tax, and transfers resources to poorer districts through one mechanism or another.

Is this a sensible way to improve the educational attainment of children from disadvantaged backgrounds? The threshold question is whether higher expenditures lead to better education. After all, we are ultimately concerned with educational outcomes for students, not educational expenditures per se. We discussed this issue in Chapter 7 and concluded that, according to the econometric evidence, it is not at all clear that more spending leads to better outcomes.

A second issue relates to the impact of centralized financing on voters' support for public education. Recall that in the Tiebout model, people choose their communities on the basis of their demands for education (and other public services) and pay for this education via the property tax. Centralized finance eliminates the link

flypaper effect

A dollar received by the community in the form of a grant to its government results in greater public spending than a dollar increase in community income.

foundation aid

Grant designed to ensure a minimum level of expenditure.

district power equalization (DPE) grant

Grant to local government to raise local revenue to a level that would be achieved if the local property tax base were at a certain hypothetical level.

between what people pay for their children's education and what they receive, perhaps weakening voter support for public education as a whole. On this basis, some have argued that reforming the finance of education might actually lead to a drop in spending on education. However, Murray et al. [1998] find that in states with court-mandated reform, spending in low-income districts increased while spending in high-income districts remained the same, leading to an overall increase in education expenditures.

▶ OVERVIEW

At the beginning of this chapter we posed some questions concerning federal systems: Is decentralized decision making desirable? How should responsibilities be allocated? How should local governments finance themselves? Our answers suggest that federalism is a sensible system. Allowing local communities to make their own decisions very likely enhances efficiency in the provision of local public goods. However, efficiency and equity are also likely to require a significant economic role for a central government. In particular, a system in which only local resources are used to finance local public goods is viewed by many as inequitable.

While our focus has naturally been on economic issues, questions of power and politics are never far beneath the surface in discussions of federalism. The dispersion of economic power is generally associated with the dispersion of political power. How should power be allocated? Is your image of subfederal government a racist governor keeping black students out of the state university, or a town hall meeting in which citizens democratically make collective decisions? When you think of the central government, do you picture an uncaring and remote bureaucrat imposing bothersome regulations, or a justice department lawyer working to guarantee the civil rights of all citizens? The different images coexist in our minds, creating conflicting feelings about the proper distribution of governmental power.

Summary

- In a federal system, different governments provide different services to overlapping jurisdictions.
- The club model of community formation indicates that community size and quantity of public goods depend on tastes for public goods, costs of providing public services, and the costs of crowding.
- The Tiebout model emphasizes the roles of mobility, property taxes, and zoning rules in local public finance. Under certain conditions, "voting with the feet"—moving to one's preferred community—results in a Pareto efficient allocation of public goods.

- Disadvantages of decentralization are inter-community externalities, forgone scale economies in the provision of public goods, inefficient taxation, and lack of ability to redistribute income.
- Advantages of decentralization are the ability to alter the mix of public services to suit local tastes, the beneficial effects of competition among local governments, and the potential for low-cost experimentation at the subfederal level.
- Local responsibility for education can be justified on the basis of different tastes across communities. However, some federal involvement

in the distribution of resources available for education may be appropriate.

- Property taxes are an important revenue source for state and local governments. The "traditional view" of the property tax is that it is an excise tax on land and structures. The "new view" is that the property tax is a general tax on all capital with rates that vary across jurisdictions and different types of capital. The "user fee view" regards property taxes as payment for local public services.

- The property tax is very unpopular. Perhaps its main advantage in the context of a federal system is that it can be administered locally.

- Grants may be either conditional (categorical) or unconditional (lump sum). Each type of grant embodies different incentives for local governments. The final mix of increased expenditure versus lower local taxes depends on the preferences dictating local choices.

- Empirical studies of intergovernmental grants indicate a *flypaper effect*—an increase in grant money induces greater spending on public goods than does an equivalent increase in local income. One possible explanation is that bureaucrats exploit citizens' incomplete information about the community budget constraint.

Discussion Questions

1. Both state and federal governments have regulations with respect to the amount of information that pharmaceutical companies have to provide about the health risks of their products. A case brought before the Supreme Court in 2008 centered on whether a company could be sued if it had complied with the federal regulations but not a particular state's regulations. Using the theory of fiscal federalism as a framework, discuss whether federal or state governments should set consumer-safety regulations.

2. According to Hines and Summers [2009], globalization increases the mobility of capital and labor across countries. Consequently, taxes on these inputs create substantial excess burdens. Hines and Summers suggest that countries should enter into agreements to limit these inefficiencies by standardizing their tax rates. Use the Tiebout model as a framework for addressing the efficiency implications of this proposal.

3. Are you dissatisfied with your government? Then you might be interested in the notion of "seasteading." The idea is to use refitted oil rigs to create permanent dwelling places at sea. The floating islands would be outside any territories claimed by any country and would thus have their own sovereignty. How does this idea relate to the Tiebout model?

4. In California, property values are reassessed only after a sale has taken place. For properties that have not been sold in the past year, the law allows only a small increase in the assessed value. Consequently, someone who purchased his home many years ago likely has a lower property tax bill than someone who purchased an identical home recently. Does this violate horizontal equity? In your answer, carefully define all key concepts.

5. Illustrate the following circumstances using community indifference curves and the local government budget constraint:

    a. An unconditional grant increases both the quantity of public goods purchased and local taxes.

    b. A matching grant leaves provision of the public good unchanged.

    c. A closed-ended matching grant has the same impact as a conditional nonmatching grant.

    d. A closed-ended matching grant leaves local taxes unchanged.

6. Suppose that your state receives a nonmatching grant from the federal government that is targeted to education spending. What does economic theory suggest would be the impact of this grant on education spending and on private consumption in your state? What does the

flypaper effect suggest will happen to education spending in your state relative to an equivalent increase in private income?

7. A number of states have debated whether to institute lotteries. One argument used to great effect by lottery proponents is that lottery revenues will be devoted to education.

   Sketch a state's budget constraint between "education" and "expenditures on all other commodities." Show how the introduction of revenues from a lottery affects the budget constraint. Draw an indifference map, and show how education expenditures compare before and after the lottery. According to your diagram, do education expenditures increase by the full amount of the lottery revenues? Why would it be difficult to determine whether the government was keeping its promise to spend all the lottery revenues on education?

8. Assume that the towns of Belmont and Lexington have different demand curves for firefighters and can hire firefighters at the same constant marginal cost. Suppose that historically their state government has required the two towns to hire the same number of firefighters, but the state has recently decentralized decision making. Show that the gain in welfare from decentralization is greater the more inelastic the communities' demand curves, other things being the same.

9. Heal [2001, p. 1] notes that when Frederick Law Olmsted, the designer of New York City's Central Park, was asked how the city could pay for the park, "he responded that its presence would raise property values and the extra tax revenues would easily repay the construction costs. History shows that was correct." This episode illustrates best which of the three views of the nature of the local property tax?

10. The federal government subsidizes state spending on welfare, thus changing the effective price to states of welfare spending. According to Baicker [2005], the elasticity of state spending on benefits per recipient is 0.38. Suppose that the federal government matches state welfare spending on a one-for-one basis, and then changes to a two-for-one basis. How would you expect state welfare spending to change?

SOME BASIC MICROECONOMICS

> *We are living in a material world.*
>
> — MADONNA

Certain tools of microeconomics are used throughout the text. We briefly review them in this appendix. Readers who have taken an introductory course in microeconomics will likely find this review sufficient to refresh their memories. Those confronting the material for the first time may want to consult one of the standard introductory texts. The subjects covered are demand and supply, consumer choice, marginal analysis, and consumer and producer surplus.

▶ DEMAND AND SUPPLY

Within a recent two-year period, the price per pound of coffee beans dropped from 95 cents to 45 cents. Coffee producers were distressed, but coffee consumers were pleased. Why did the price fall so much? The demand and supply model provides a framework for thinking about how the price and output of a commodity are determined in a competitive market. We discuss in turn the determinants of demand, supply, and their interaction.

Demand

Which factors influence people's decisions to consume certain goods? Continuing with our coffee example, a bit of introspection suggests that the following factors affect the amount that people want to consume during a given time period:

1. **Price.** We expect that as the price goes up, the quantity demanded goes down.
2. **Income.** Changes in income affect people's consumption opportunities. It is hard to say a priori, however, what effect such changes have on consumption of a given good. Perhaps people purchase more coffee when their incomes go up. On the other hand, it may be that as incomes increase, people consume less coffee, perhaps spending their money on cognac instead. If an increase in income increases the demand (other things being the same), the good is called a **normal good.** If an increase in income decreases demand (other things being the same), the good is called an **inferior good.**
3. **Prices of related goods.** Suppose the price of tea goes up. If people can substitute coffee for tea, this increase in the price of tea increases the amount of coffee people wish to consume. Now suppose the price of cream goes up. If people consume coffee and cream together, this tends to decrease the amount of coffee consumed. Goods like tea and coffee are called **substitutes;** goods like coffee and cream are called **complements.**

---

normal good

A good for which demand increases as income increases and demand decreases as income decreases, other things being the same.

inferior good

A good whose demand decreases as income increases.

substitutes

Two goods are substitutes if an increase in the price of one good leads to increased consumption of the other good.

complements

Two goods are complements if an increase in the price of one good leads to decreased consumption of the other good.

4. **Tastes.** The extent to which people "like" a good affects the amount they demand. Not much coffee is demanded by Mormons because their religion prohibits it. Often, it is realistic to assume that consumers' tastes stay the same over time, but not always. For example, when some scientists claimed that coffee might cause birth defects, many pregnant women dropped the beverage.

We see, then, that a wide variety of things can affect demand. However, it is often useful to focus on the relationship between the quantity of a commodity demanded and its price. Suppose that we fix income, the prices of related goods, and tastes. We can imagine varying the price of coffee and seeing how the quantity demanded changes under the assumption that the other relevant variables stay at their fixed values. A **demand schedule** (or **demand curve**) is the relation between the market price of a good and its quantity demanded during a given time period, other things being the same. (Economists often use the Latin for "other things being the same," *ceteris paribus*.)

A hypothetical demand schedule for coffee is represented graphically by curve D_c in Figure A.1. The horizontal axis measures pounds of coffee per year in a particular market, and the price per pound is measured on the vertical. Thus, for example, if the price is $2.29 per pound, people are willing to consume 750 pounds; when the price is only $1.38, they are willing to consume 1,225 pounds. The downward slope of the demand schedule reflects the reasonable assumption that when the price goes up, the quantity demanded goes down.

The demand curve can also be interpreted as an approximate schedule of "willingness to pay," because it shows the maximum price that people would pay for a given quantity. For example, when people purchase 750 pounds per year, they value it at $2.29 per pound. At any price more than $2.29, they would not willingly consume 750 pounds per year. If for some reason people were able to obtain 750 pounds at a price less than $2.29, this would in some sense be a "bargain."

As already stressed, the demand curve is drawn on the assumption that all other variables that might affect quantity demanded do not change. What happens if one of them does? Suppose, for example, that the price of tea increases, and as a consequence, people want to buy more coffee. In Figure A.2, we reproduce schedule D_c from Figure A.1 (before the increase). Due to the increase in the price of tea, at *each price* of coffee people are willing to purchase more coffee than they did previously. In effect, then, an increase in the price of tea shifts each point on D_c to the right. The collection of new points is D_c'. Because D_c' shows how much people are willing to consume at each price (*ceteris paribus*), it is by definition the demand curve.

More generally, a change in any variable that influences the demand for a good—except its own price—shifts the demand curve.[1] (A change in a good's own price induces a movement *along* the demand curve.)

Supply

Now consider the factors that determine the quantity of a commodity that firms supply to the market. We will continue using coffee as our example.

1. **Price.** It is often reasonable to assume that the higher the price per pound of coffee, the greater the quantity profit-maximizing firms are willing to supply.
2. **Price of inputs.** Coffee producers employ inputs to produce coffee—labor, land, and fertilizer. If their input costs go up, the amount of coffee that they can profitably supply at any given price goes down.

---

[1] There is no need, incidentally, for D_c' to be parallel to D_c. In general, this will not be the case.

demand schedule

The relation between the price of a good and the quantity demanded, *ceteris paribus*.

demand curve

A graph of the demand schedule.

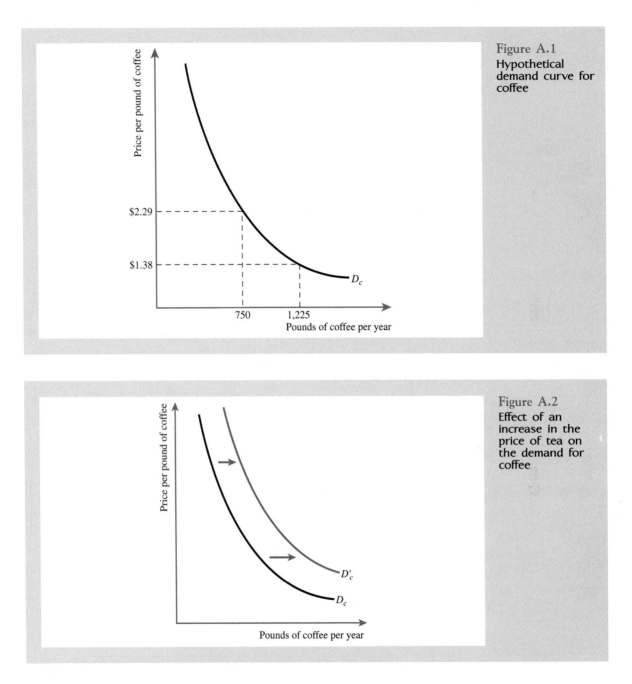

Figure A.1
Hypothetical demand curve for coffee

Figure A.2
Effect of an increase in the price of tea on the demand for coffee

3. **Conditions of production.** The most important factor here is the state of technology. If there is a technological improvement in coffee production, the supply increases. Other variables also affect production conditions. For agricultural goods, weather is important. Several years ago, for example, flooding in Latin America seriously reduced the coffee crop.

   As with the demand curve, we focus on the relationship between the quantity of a commodity supplied and its price, holding the other variables at fixed levels. The **supply schedule** is the relation between market prices and the amount of a good that

supply schedule

The relation between market price of a good and the quantity that producers are willing to supply, *ceteris paribus*.

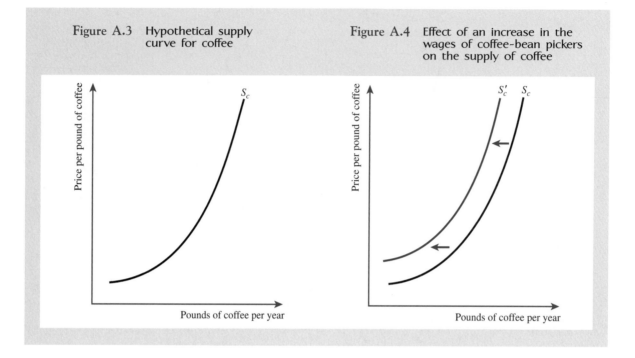

Figure A.3   Hypothetical supply curve for coffee

Figure A.4   Effect of an increase in the wages of coffee-bean pickers on the supply of coffee

producers are willing to supply during a given time period, *ceteris paribus*. A supply schedule for coffee is depicted as S_c in Figure A.3. Its upward slope reflects the assumption that the higher the price, the greater the quantity supplied, *ceteris paribus*.

When any variable that influences supply (other than the commodity's own price) changes, the supply schedule shifts. Suppose, for example, that the wage rate for coffee-bean pickers increases. This increase reduces the amount of coffee that firms are willing to supply at any given price. The supply curve therefore shifts to the left. As depicted in Figure A.4, the new supply curve is S'_c. More generally, when any variable other than the commodity's own price changes, the supply curve shifts. (A change in the commodity's price induces a movement along the supply curve.)

Equilibrium

The demand and supply curves provide answers to a set of hypothetical questions: *If* the price of coffee is $2 per pound, how much are consumers willing to purchase? *If* the price is $1.75 per pound, how much are firms willing to supply? Neither schedule by itself tells us the actual price and quantity. But taken together, they do.

In Figure A.5 we superimpose demand schedule D_c from Figure A.1 on supply schedule S_c from Figure A.3. We want to find the price and output at which there is an **equilibrium**—a situation that tends to be maintained unless there is an underlying change in the system. Suppose the price is P_1 dollars per pound. At this price, the quantity demanded is Q_1^D and the quantity supplied is Q_1^S. Price P_1 cannot be maintained, because firms want to supply more coffee than consumers are willing to purchase. This excess supply tends to push the price down, as suggested by the arrows.

Now consider price P_2. At this price, the quantity of coffee demanded, Q_2^D, exceeds the quantity supplied, Q_2^S. Because there is excess demand for coffee, we expect the price to rise.

equilibrium

A situation that tends to be maintained unless there is an underlying change in the system.

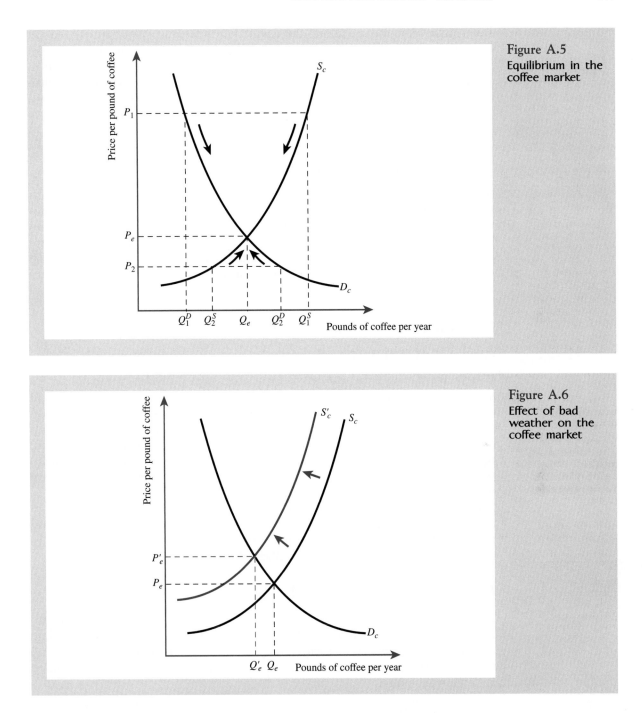

Figure A.5
Equilibrium in the coffee market

Figure A.6
Effect of bad weather on the coffee market

Similar reasoning suggests that any price at which the quantity supplied and quantity demanded are unequal cannot be an equilibrium. In Figure A.5, quantity demanded equals quantity supplied at price P_e. The associated output level is Q_e pounds per year. Unless something else in the system changes, this price and output combination continues year after year. It is an equilibrium.

Suppose something else does change. For example, the weather turns bad, ruining a considerable portion of the coffee crop. In Figure A.6, D_c and S_c are reproduced from Figure A.5, and as before, the equilibrium price and output are P_e and Q_e, respectively. Because of the weather change, the supply curve shifts to the left, say, to S'_c. Given the new supply curve, P_e is no longer the equilibrium price. Rather, equilibrium is at the intersection of D_c and S'_c, at price P'_e and output Q'_e. Note that, as one might expect, the crop disaster leads to a higher price and smaller output— $P'_e > P_e$ and $Q'_e < Q_e$. More generally, a change in any variable that affects supply or demand creates a new equilibrium combination of price and quantity.

Supply and Demand for Inputs

Supply and demand can also be used to investigate the markets for inputs into the production process. (Inputs are sometimes referred to as *factors of production*.) For example, we could label the horizontal axis in Figure A.5 "number of hours worked per year" and the vertical axis "wage rate per hour." Then the schedules would represent the supply and demand for labor, and the market would determine wages and employment. Similarly, supply and demand analysis can be applied to the markets for capital and for land.

Measuring the Shapes of Supply and Demand Curves

price elasticity of demand	
The absolute value of the percentage change in quantity demanded divided by the percentage change in price.	

Clearly, the market price and output for a given item depend substantially on the shapes of its demand and supply curves. Conventionally, the shape of the demand curve is measured by the **price elasticity of demand:** the absolute value of the percentage change in quantity demanded divided by the percentage change in price.[2] If a 10 percent increase in price leads to a 2 percent decrease in quantity demanded, the price elasticity of demand is 0.2. An important special case is when the quantity demanded does not change at all with a price increase. Then the demand curve is vertical and elasticity is zero. At the other extreme, when the demand curve is horizontal, then even a small change in price leads to a huge change in quantity demanded. By convention, this is referred to as an infinitely elastic demand curve. Similarly, the **price elasticity of supply** is defined as the percentage change in quantity supplied divided by the percentage change in price.

price elasticity of supply	
The absolute value of the percentage change in quantity supplied divided by the percentage change in price.	

▶ THEORY OF CHOICE

The fundamental problem of economics is that resources available to people are limited relative to their wants. The theory of choice shows how people make sensible decisions in the presence of such scarcity. In this section we develop a graphical representation of consumer tastes and show how these tastes can best be gratified with a limited budget.

Tastes

We assume that an individual derives satisfaction from the consumption of commodities. In this context, the notion of *commodities* should be interpreted very broadly. It includes not only items such as food, cars, and compact disc players but

---

[2] The elasticity need not be constant all along the demand curve.

"It's true that more is not necessarily better, Edward, but it frequently is." © The New Yorker
Collection 1985 Charles Saxon from cartoonbank.com. All Rights Reserved.

also less tangible things like leisure time, clean air, and so forth. Economists use
the slightly archaic word **utility** as a synonym for satisfaction. Consider Oscar who
consumes only two commodities, marshmallows and donuts. (Using mathematical
methods, all the results for the two-good case can be shown to apply to situations
in which there are many commodities.) Assume further that for all feasible quantities of marshmallows and donuts, Oscar is never satiated—more consumption of
either commodity always produces some increase in his utility. Like the father in
the cartoon, economists believe that under most circumstances, this assumption is
pretty realistic.

In Figure A.7, the horizontal axis measures the number of donuts consumed each
day, and the vertical axis shows daily marshmallow consumption. Thus, each point
in the quadrant represents some bundle of marshmallows and donuts. For example,
point *a* represents a bundle with seven marshmallows and five donuts.

Because Oscar's utility depends only on his consumption of marshmallows and
donuts, we can also associate with each point in the quadrant a certain level of utility.
For example, if seven marshmallows and five donuts create 100 "utils" of happiness,
then point *a* is associated with 100 "utils."

Some commodity bundles create more utility than point *a*, and others less. Consider point *b* in Figure A.7, which has both more marshmallows and donuts than
point *a*. Since satiation is ruled out, *b* must yield higher utility than *a*. Bundle *f* has
more donuts than *a* and no fewer marshmallows, and is also preferred to *a*. Indeed,
any point to the northeast of *a* is preferred to *a*.

utility

The amount of
satisfaction a person
derives from consuming
a particular bundle of
commodities.

Figure A.7
Ranking
alternative
bundles

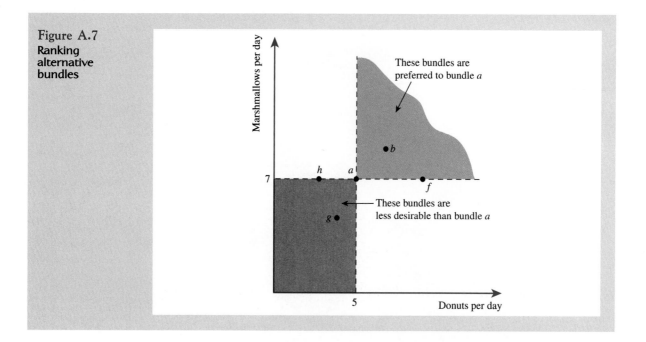

Similar reasoning suggests that bundle *a* is preferred to bundle *g*, because *g* has fewer marshmallows and donuts than *a*. Point *h* is also less desirable than *a*, because although it has the same number of marshmallows as *a*, it has fewer donuts. Point *a* is preferred to any point southwest of it.

We have identified some bundles that yield more utility than *a* and some that yield less. Can we find some bundles that produce just the same amount of utility? Presumably there are such bundles, but we need more information about the individual to find out which they are. Consider Figure A.8, which reproduces point *a* from Figure A.7. Imagine that we pose the following question to Oscar: "You are now consuming seven marshmallows and five donuts. If I take away one of your donuts, how many marshmallows do I need to give you to make you just as satisfied as you were initially?" Suppose that after thinking a while, Oscar (honestly) answers that he would require two more marshmallows. Then by definition, the bundle consisting of four donuts and nine marshmallows yields the same amount of utility as *a*. This bundle is denoted *i* in Figure A.8.

We could find another bundle of equal utility by asking: "Starting again at point *a*, suppose I take away one marshmallow. How many more donuts must I give you to keep you as well off as you originally were?" Assume the answer is two donuts. Then the bundle with six marshmallows and seven donuts, denoted *j* in Figure A.8, must also yield the same amount of utility as bundle *a*.

We could go on like this indefinitely—start at point *a*, take away various amounts of one commodity, find out the amount of the other commodity required for compensation, and record the results on Figure A.8. The outcome is curve U_0, which shows all points that yield the same amount of utility. U_0 is referred to as an **indifference curve,** because it shows all consumption bundles among which the individual is indifferent.

By definition, the *slope* of a curve is the change in the value of the variable measured on the vertical axis divided by the change in the variable measured on the horizontal—the "rise over the run." The slope of an indifference curve has an

indifference curve

The locus of consumption bundles that yields the same total utility.

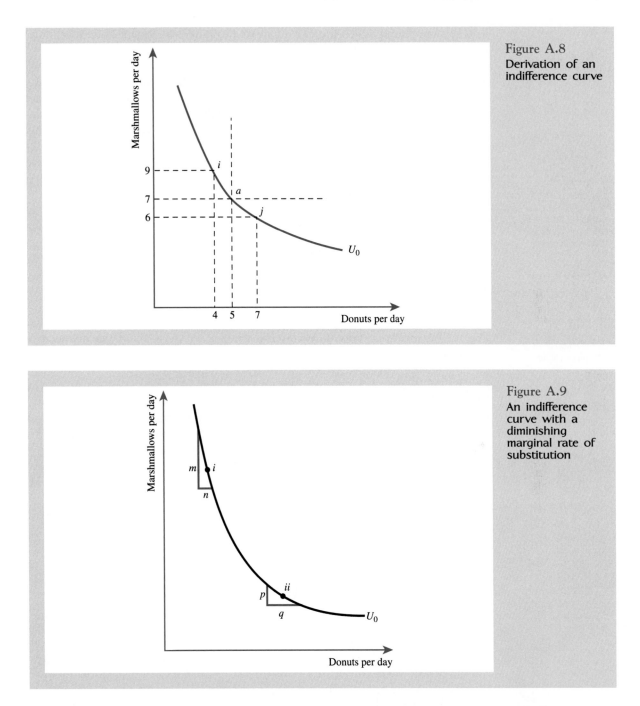

Figure A.8
Derivation of an indifference curve

Figure A.9
An indifference curve with a diminishing marginal rate of substitution

important economic interpretation. It shows the rate at which the individual is willing to trade one good for another. For example, in Figure A.9, around point i, the slope of the indifference curve is $-m/n$. But by definition of an indifference curve, n is just the amount of donuts that Oscar is willing to substitute for sacrificing m marshmallows. For this reason, the absolute value of the slope of the indifference curve is referred to as the **marginal rate of substitution** of donuts for marshmallows, abbreviated MRS_{dm}. As noted later, *marginal* means *additional* or *incremental*. The indifference curve's slope shows the *marginal* rate of substitution because it

marginal rate of substitution

The rate at which an individual is willing to trade one good for another; it is the absolute value of the slope of an indifference curve.

indicates the rate at which the individual would be willing to substitute marshmallows for an *additional* donut.

The marginal rate of substitution in Figure A.9 declines as we move down along the indifference curve. For example, around point *ii*, MRS_{dm} is p/q, which is clearly smaller than m/n. This makes intuitive sense. Around point *i*, Oscar has a lot of marshmallows relative to donuts and is therefore willing to give up quite a few marshmallows in return for an additional donut—hence a high MRS_{dm}. On the other hand, around point *ii*, Oscar has a lot of donuts relative to marshmallows, so he is unwilling to sacrifice a lot of marshmallows in return for yet another donut. The decline of MRS_{dm} as we move down along the indifference curve is called a **diminishing marginal rate of substitution.**

Recall that our construction of indifference curve U_0 used bundle *a* as a starting point. But point *a* was chosen arbitrarily, and we could just as well have started at any other point in the quadrant. In Figure A.10, if we start with point *b* and proceed in the same way, we generate indifference curve U_1. Or starting at point *k*, we generate indifference curve U_2. Note that any point on U_2 represents a higher level of utility than any point on U_1, which in turn, is preferred to any point on U_0. If Oscar wants to maximize his utility, he tries to reach the highest indifference curve that he can.

The entire collection of indifference curves is referred to as the **indifference map.** The indifference map tells us everything there is to know about the individual's preferences.

diminishing marginal rate of substitution

The marginal rate of substitution falls as we move down along an indifference curve.

indifference map

The collection of all indifference curves.

Budget Constraint

Basic Setup   Suppose that marshmallows (M) cost 3 cents apiece, donuts (D) cost 6 cents, and Oscar's weekly income is 60 cents. What options does Oscar have? His purchases must satisfy the equation

$$3 \times M + 6 \times D = 60 \tag{A.1}$$

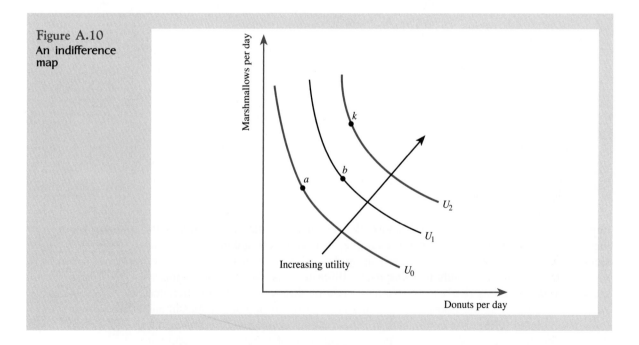

Figure A.10
An indifference map

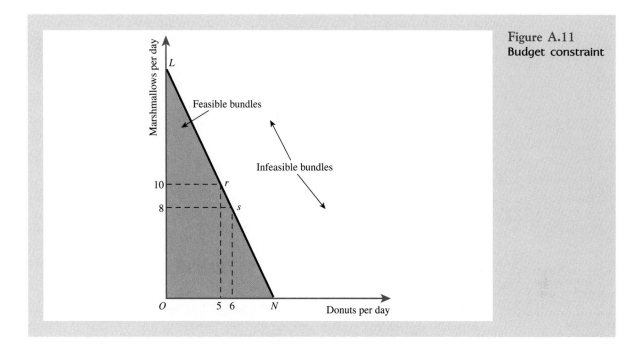

Figure A.11
Budget constraint

In words, expenditures on marshmallows ($3 \times M$) plus expenditures on donuts ($6 \times D$) must equal income (60).[3] Thus, for example, if $M = 10$, then to satisfy Equation (A.1), D must equal 5 ($3 \times 10 + 6 \times 5 = 60$). Alternatively, if $M = 8$, then D must equal 6 ($3 \times 8 + 6 \times 6 = 60$).

Let us represent Equation (A.1) graphically. The usual way is to graph a number of points that satisfy the equation. This is straightforward once we recall from basic algebra that (A.1) is just the equation of a straight line. Given two points on the line, the rest of the line is determined by connecting them. In Figure A.11, point r represents 10 marshmallows and 5 donuts, and point s represents 8 marshmallows and 6 donuts. Therefore, the line associated with Equation (A.1) is LN, which passes through these points. By construction, *any* combination of marshmallows and donuts that lies along LN satisfies Equation (A.1). Line LN is known as the **budget constraint** or the **budget line.** Any point on or below LN (the shaded area) is feasible because it involves an expenditure less than or equal to income. Any point above LN is impossible because it involves an expenditure greater than income.

Two aspects of line LN are worth noting. First, the horizontal and vertical intercepts of the line have economic interpretations. By definition, the vertical intercept is the point associated with $D = 0$. At this point, Oscar spends all his 60 cents on marshmallows, buying 20 ($= 60 \div 3$) of them. Hence, distance OL is 20. Similarly, at point N, Oscar consumes zero marshmallows, but he can afford a binge consisting of 10 ($= 60 \div 6$) donuts. Distance ON is therefore 10. In short, the vertical and horizontal intercepts represent bundles in which Oscar consumes only one of the commodities.

The slope also has an economic interpretation. To calculate the slope, recall that the "rise" (OL) is 20 and the "run" (ON) is 10, so the slope (in absolute value) is 2.

budget constraint

The representation of the bundles among which a consumer may choose, given his income and the prices he faces.

---

[3] If Oscar is a utility maximizer, he will not throw away any of his income.

Note that 2 is the ratio of the price of donuts (6 cents) to the price of marshmallows (3 cents). This is no accident. The absolute value of the slope of the budget line indicates the rate at which the market permits an individual to substitute marshmallows for donuts. Because the price of donuts is twice the price of marshmallows, Oscar can trade two marshmallows for each donut.

To generalize this discussion, suppose that the price per marshmallow is P_m, the price per donut is P_d, and income is I. Then in analogy to Equation (A.1), the budget constraint is

$$P_m M + P_d D = I \qquad\qquad (A.2)$$

If M is measured on the vertical axis and D on the horizontal, the vertical intercept is I/P_m and the horizontal intercept is I/P_d. The slope of the budget constraint, in absolute value, is P_d/P_m. A common mistake is to assume that because M is measured on the vertical axis, the absolute value of the slope of the budget constraint is P_m/P_d. To see that this is wrong just divide the rise (I/P_m) by the run (I/P_d): (I/P_m) ÷ (I/P_d) = P_d/P_m. Intuitively, P_d must be in the numerator because its ratio to P_m shows the rate at which the market permits one to trade M for D.

Changes in Prices and Income   The budget line shows Oscar's consumption opportunities given his current income and the prevailing prices. What if any of these change? Return to the case where $P_m = 3$, $P_d = 6$, and $I = 60$. The associated budget line, $3M + 6D = 60$, is drawn as LN in Figure A.12. Now suppose that Oscar's income falls to 30. Substituting into Equation (A.2), the new budget line is $3M + 6D = 30$. To graph this equation, note that the vertical intercept is 10 and the horizontal intercept is 5. Denoting these two points in Figure A.12 as R and S, respectively, and recalling that two points determine a line, we find that the new budget constraint is RS. The slope of RS in absolute value is 2, just like that of LN.

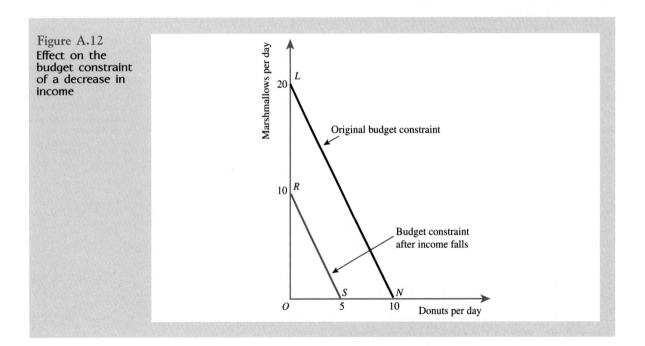

Figure A.12
Effect on the budget constraint of a decrease in income

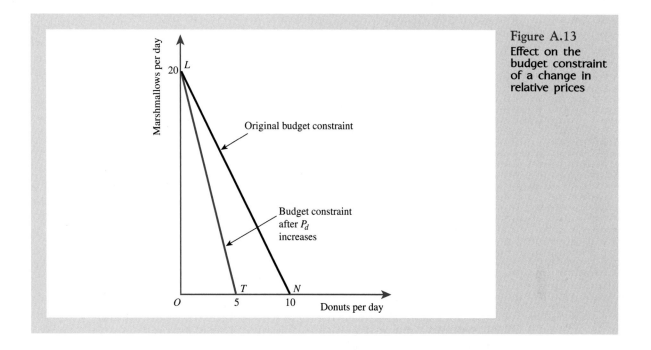

Figure A.13
Effect on the budget constraint of a change in relative prices

This is because the relative prices of donuts and marshmallows have not changed. A change in income, *ceteris paribus,* induces a parallel shift in the budget line. If income decreases, the constraint shifts in; if income increases, it shifts out.

Return again to the original constraint, $3M + 6D = 60$, which is reproduced in Figure A.13 as LN. Suppose that the price of D increases to 12, but everything else stays the same. Then, by Equation (A.2), the budget constraint is $3M + 12D = 60$. To graph this new constraint, we begin by noting that it has a vertical intercept of 20, which is the same as that of LN. Because the price of M has stayed the same, if Oscar spends all his money only on M, then he can buy just as much as he did before. The horizontal intercept, however, is changed. It is now at five donuts ($= 60 \div 12$), a point denoted T in Figure A.13. The new budget constraint is then LT. The slope of LT in absolute value is 4 ($= 20 \div 5$), reflecting the fact that the market now allows each individual to trade four marshmallows per donut.

More generally, when the price of one commodity changes, *ceteris paribus*, the budget line pivots along the axis of the good whose price changes. If the price goes up, the line pivots in; if the price goes down, the line pivots out.

Equilibrium The indifference map shows what Oscar *wants* to do; the budget constraint shows what he *can* do. To find out what Oscar *actually* does, they must be put together.

In Figure A.14, we superimpose the indifference map from Figure A.10 onto budget line LN from Figure A.11. The problem is to find the combination of M and D that maximizes Oscar's utility subject to the constraint that he cannot spend more than his income.

Consider first bundle i on U_2. This bundle is ruled out, because it is above LN. Oscar might like to be on indifference curve U_2, but he simply cannot afford it. Next consider point ii, which is certainly feasible, because it lies below the budget constraint. But it cannot be optimal, because Oscar is not spending his whole income.

Figure A.14
Utility maximization subject to a budget constraint

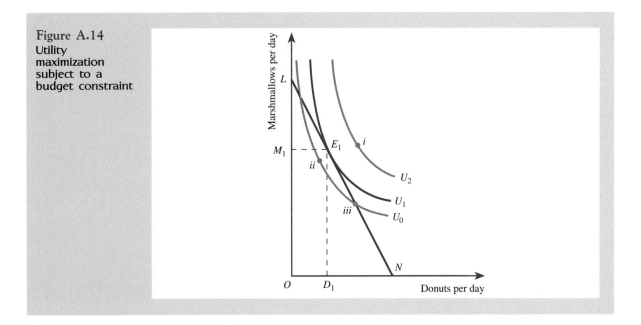

In effect, at bundle *ii*, he just throws away money that could have been spent on more marshmallows and/or donuts.

What about point *iii*? It is feasible, and Oscar is not throwing away any income. Yet he can still do better in the sense of putting himself on a higher indifference curve. Consider point E_1, where Oscar consumes D_1 donuts and M_1 marshmallows. Because it lies on LN, it is feasible. Moreover, it is more desirable than bundle *iii*, because E_1 lies on U_1, which is above U_0. Indeed, no point on LN touches an indifference curve that is higher than U_1. Therefore, the bundle consisting of M_1 and D_1 maximizes Oscar's utility subject to budget constraint LN. E_1 is an equilibrium because unless something else changes, Oscar continues to consume M_1 marshmallows and D_1 donuts day after day.

Note that at the equilibrium, indifference curve U_1 just barely touches the budget line. Intuitively, this is because Oscar is trying to achieve the very highest indifference curve he can while still keeping on LN. In more technical language, line LN is *tangent* to curve U_1 at point E_1. This means that at point E_1 the slope of U_1 is equal to the slope of LN.

This observation suggests an equation to characterize the utility-maximizing bundle. Recall that by definition, the slope of the indifference curve (in absolute value) is the marginal rate of substitution of donuts for marshmallows, MRS_{dm}. The slope of the budget line (in absolute value) is P_d/P_m. But we just showed that at equilibrium, the two slopes are equal, or

$$MRS_{dm} = \frac{P_d}{P_m} \tag{A.3}$$

Equation (A.3) is a necessary condition for utility maximization.[4] That is, if the consumption bundle is not consistent with Equation (A.3), then Oscar could do better by

---

[4] The equation holds only if some of each commodity is consumed. If the consumption of some commodity is zero, then a related inequality needs to be satisfied.

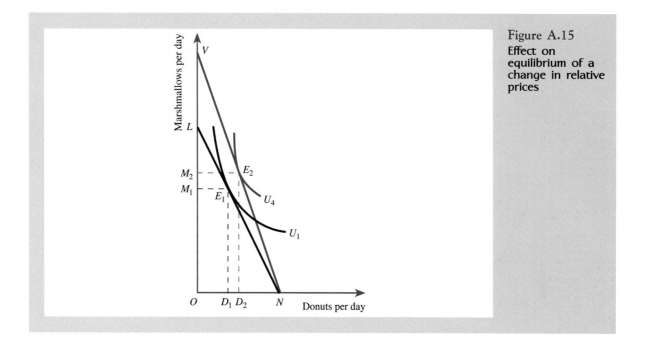

Figure A.15
Effect on equilibrium of a change in relative prices

reallocating his income between the two commodities. Intuitively, MRS_{dm} is the rate at which Oscar is willing to trade M for D, while P_d/P_m is the rate at which the market allows Oscar to trade M for D. At equilibrium, these two rates must be equal.

Now suppose that the price of marshmallows falls. Figure A.15 reproduces the equilibrium point E_1 from Figure A.14. As we showed earlier, when a price changes (*ceteris paribus*) the budget line pivots along the axis of the good whose price has changed. Because P_m falls, the budget line LN pivots around N to a higher point on the vertical axis. The new budget line is VN. Given that Oscar now faces budget line VN, E_1 is no longer an equilibrium. The fall in P_m creates new opportunities for Oscar, and as a utility maximizer, he takes advantage of them. Specifically, subject to budget line VN, Oscar maximizes utility at point E_2, where he consumes M_2 marshmallows and D_2 donuts.

At the new equilibrium, more of both D and M are consumed than at the old equilibrium ($D_2 > D_1$ and $M_2 > M_1$). The price decrease in marshmallows allows Oscar to purchase more marshmallows and still have money left to purchase more donuts. While this is common, it need not always be the case. The change depends on the tastes of the particular individual. Suppose that Bert faces exactly the same prices as Oscar and also has the same income. Bert's indifference map and budget constraints are depicted in Figure A.16. Bert's donut consumption is totally unchanged by the decrease in the price of marshmallows. On the other hand, Ernie's preferences, depicted in Figure A.17, are such that a fall in P_m leaves the amount of marshmallows the same, and only the amount of donuts increases. Thus, we require information about the individual's indifference map to predict just how he or she will respond to a change in relative prices.

More generally, a change in prices and/or income leads to a new budget constraint. The individual then *reoptimizes*—finds the point that maximizes utility subject to the new budget constraint. This usually involves the selection of a new commodity

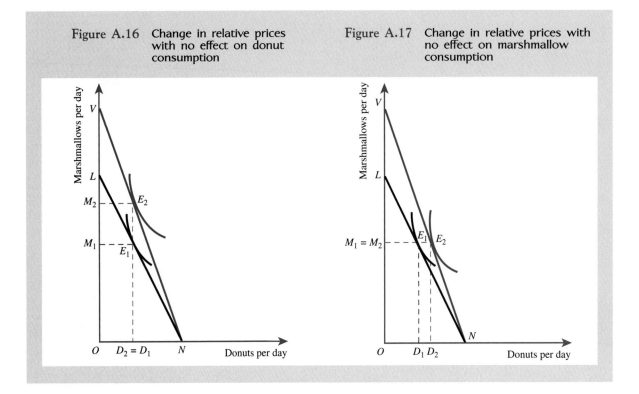

Figure A.16   Change in relative prices with no effect on donut consumption

Figure A.17   Change in relative prices with no effect on marshmallow consumption

bundle, but without information on the individual's tastes, one cannot know for sure exactly what the new bundle looks like. We do know, however, that as long as the individual is a utility maximizer, the new bundle satisfies the condition that the price ratio equal the marginal rate of substitution.

Derivation of Demand Curves

There is a simple connection between the theory of consumer choice and individual demand curves. Recall from Figure A.15 that at the original price of marshmallows—call it P_m^1—Oscar consumed M_1 marshmallows. When the price fell to P_m^2, Oscar increased his marshmallow consumption to M_2. This pair of points may be plotted as in Figure A.18.

Repeating this experiment for various prices of marshmallows, we find the quantity of marshmallows demanded at each price, holding fixed money income, the price of donuts, and tastes. By definition, this is the demand curve for marshmallows, shown as D_m in Figure A.18. Thus, we can derive the demand curve from the underlying indifference map.

Substitution and Income Effects

Figure A.19 depicts the situation of Grover, who initially faces budget constraint WN, and maximizes utility at point E_1 on indifference curve i, where he consumes D_1 donuts. Suppose now that the price of donuts increases. Grover's budget constraint pivots from WN to WZ, and at the new equilibrium, point E_2 on indifference curve ii, he consumes D_2 donuts.

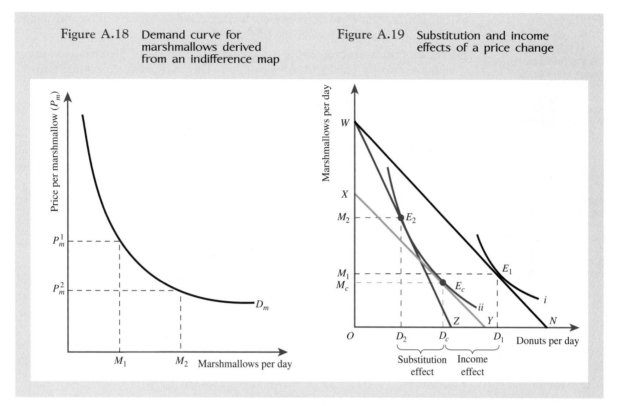

Figure A.18 Demand curve for marshmallows derived from an indifference map

Figure A.19 Substitution and income effects of a price change

Just for hypothetical purposes, suppose that at the new equilibrium E_2, the price of donuts falls back to its initial level, but that *simultaneously,* Grover's income is adjusted so that he is kept on indifference curve *ii*. If this hypothetical adjustment were made, what budget constraint would Grover face? Suppose we call this budget constraint *XY*. We know that *XY* must satisfy two conditions:

- Because Grover is kept on indifference curve *ii*, *XY* must be tangent to indifference curve *ii*.

- The slope (in absolute value) must be equal to the ratio of the original price of donuts to the price of marshmallows. This is because of the stipulation that the price of donuts equals its original value. Recall, however, that the slope of *WN* is the ratio of the original price of donuts to the price of marshmallows. Hence, *XY* must have the same slope as *WN*; that is, it must be parallel to *WN*.

In Figure A.19, *XY* is drawn to satisfy these two conditions—the line is parallel to *WN* and is tangent to indifference curve *ii*. If Grover were confronted with constraint *XY*, he would maximize utility at point E_c, where his consumption of donuts is D_c.

Why is this hypothetical budget line of any interest? Because drawing line *XY* helps us break down the effect of the change in the price of donuts into two components, the first from E_1 to E_c and the second from E_c to E_2.

1. The movement from E_1 to E_c is generated by the parallel shift of *WN* down to *XY*. But recall from Figure A.12 that such parallel movements are associated with changes in income, holding relative prices constant. Hence, the

income effect

The effect of a price change on the quantity demanded due exclusively to the fact that the consumer's income has changed.

movement from E_1 to E_c is essentially induced by a change in income and is called the **income effect** of the price change.

2. The movement from E_c to E_2 is a consequence purely of the change in the relative price of donuts to marshmallows. This movement shows that Grover substitutes marshmallows for donuts when donuts become more expensive. Hence, the movement from E_c to E_2 is called the **substitution effect.** Because the movement from E_c to E_2 involves compensating income (in the sense of changing income to stay on the same indifference curve), the movement from E_c to E_2 is sometimes called the compensated response to a change in price. If we wish to keep utility at the level represented by indifference curve *ii*, we measure the substitution effect by moving along *ii*. If, alternatively, we had wanted to keep utility at the level enjoyed along indifference curve *i*, we could have measured the substitution effect along indifference curve *i* instead. In any case, the compensated response to a price change shows how the price change affects quantity demanded when income is simultaneously altered so that the level of utility is constant.

substitution effect

The tendency of an individual to consume more of one good and less of another because of a decrease in the price of the former relative to the latter.

Intuitively, when the price of donuts increases two things happen:

*   The increase in price reduces the individual's real income—his or her ability to afford commodities. When income goes down, the quantity purchased generally changes, even without any change in relative prices. This is the income effect.
*   The increase in the price of donuts makes donuts less attractive relative to marshmallows, inducing the substitution effect.

Any change in prices can be broken down into an income effect and a substitution effect.

We could repeat the exercise depicted in Figure A.19 for any change in the price of marshmallows. Suppose that for each price, we find the compensated quantity of donuts demanded and make a plot with price on the vertical axis and donuts on the horizontal. This plot is called the **compensated demand curve** for donuts. The ordinary demand curve discussed at the beginning of this appendix shows how quantity demanded varies with price, holding the level of *money income* fixed. In contrast, the compensated demand curve shows how quantity demanded varies with price, holding the level of *utility* fixed.

compensated demand curve

A demand curve that shows how quantity demanded varies with price, holding utility constant.

marginal

Incremental, additional.

▶ MARGINAL ANALYSIS

In economics, the word **marginal** usually means *additional* or *incremental*. Suppose, for example, the annual total benefit per citizen of a 50-mile road is $42, and the annual total benefit of a 51-mile road is $43.50. Then the marginal benefit of the 51st mile is $1.50 ($43.50 − $42.00). Similarly, if the annual total cost per person of maintaining a 50-mile road is $38, and the total cost of a 51-mile road is $40, then the marginal cost of the 51st mile is $2.

Economists focus a lot of attention on marginal quantities because they usually convey the information required for rational decision making. Suppose that the government is deciding whether to construct the 51st mile. The key question is whether the *marginal* benefit is at least as great as the *marginal* cost. In our example, the marginal cost is $2 while the marginal benefit is only $1.50. Does it make sense to spend $2 to create $1.50 worth of benefits? The answer is no, and the extra mile should not be built. Note that basing the decision on total benefits and costs would

Table A.1 **Total Profit**		
Tons of Fertilizer	Wheat	Corn
0	$ 0	$ 0
1	100	325
2	150	385
3	170	415
4	175	435
5	177	441
6	178	444

Table A.2 **Marginal Profit**		
Tons of Fertilizer	Wheat	Corn
1	$100	$325
2	50	60
3	20	30
4	5	20
5	2	6
6	1	3

have led to the wrong answer. The total cost per person of the 51-mile road ($40) is less than the total benefit ($43.50). Still, it is not sensible to build the 51st mile. An activity should be pursued only if its marginal benefit is at least as large as its marginal cost.[5]

Another example of marginal analysis: Farmer McGregor has two fields. The first is planted in wheat and the second in corn. McGregor has seven tons of fertilizer to distribute between the two fields and wants to allocate the fertilizer so that his total profits are as high as possible. The relationship between the amount of fertilizer and *total* profitability for each crop is depicted in Table A.1. For example, if six tons of fertilizer were devoted to wheat and one ton to corn, total profits would be $503 (= $178 + $325).

To find the optimal allocation of fertilizer between the fields, it helps to compute the marginal contribution to profits made by each ton of fertilizer. The first ton in the wheat field increases profits from $0 to $100, so the marginal contribution is $100. The second ton increases profits from $100 to $150, so its marginal contribution is $50. The complete set of computations for both crops is recorded in Table A.2.

Suppose that McGregor puts two tons of fertilizer on the wheat field and five tons on the cornfield. Is he maximizing profits? To answer this question, we must determine whether any other allocation would lead to higher total profits. Suppose that one ton of fertilizer were removed from the cornfield and devoted instead to wheat. Removing the fertilizer from the cornfield lowers profits there by $6. But at the same time, profits from the wheat field increase by $20 (the marginal profit associated with the third ton of fertilizer in the wheat field). Farmer McGregor would therefore be $14 richer on balance. Clearly, it is not sensible for McGregor to put two tons of fertilizer on the wheat field and five tons on the corn, because he can do better (by $14) with three tons devoted to wheat and four to corn.

Is this latter allocation optimal? To answer, note that at this allocation, the marginal profit of fertilizer in each field is equal to $20. When the marginal profitability of fertilizer is the same in each field, there is *no way* that fertilizer can be reallocated between fields to increase total profit. In other words, total profits are maximized when the marginal profit in each field is the same. If you don't believe it, try to find an allocation of the seven tons of fertilizer that leads to a total profit higher than the $605 ($170 + $435) associated with the allocation at which the marginal profits are equal.

---

[5] If the marginal cost of an action just equals its marginal benefit, one is indifferent between taking the action and not taking it.

Figure A.20
Measuring
consumer surplus

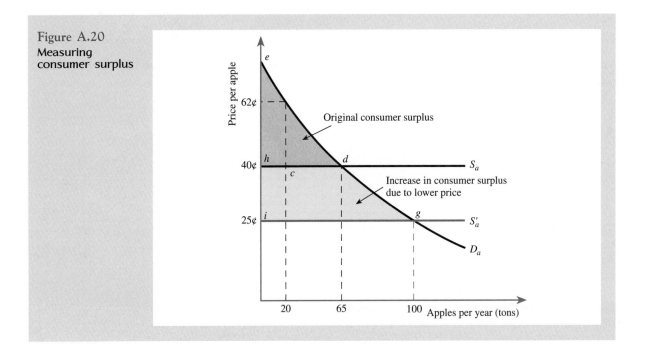

In general, if resources are distributed across several activities, maximization of *total* returns requires that *marginal* returns in each activity be equal.[6]

▶ CONSUMER AND PRODUCER SURPLUS

Our supply and demand model tells us how prices change in response to changes in the underlying economic environment. It is often useful to be able to put a dollar value on how such price changes affect people's welfare. Suppose, for example, that initially the price of apples is 40¢ per apple, but then it falls to 25¢. Clearly, apple consumers are better off because of the change. But by just how much are they better off? *Consumer surplus* is a tool for obtaining a dollar measure.

Consumer Surplus

To begin our discussion of consumer surplus, consider the demand curve for apples, D_a, depicted in Figure A.20. Assume consumers can obtain all the apples they demand at the going market price, 40¢. Then the supply curve for apples, S_a, is a horizontal line at this price. According to the diagram, the associated quantity demanded is 65 tons.

Suppose now that more land is brought into apple production, and the supply curve shifts to S'_a. At the new equilibrium, the price falls to 25¢, and apple consumption increases to 100 tons. How much better off are consumers? Another way

---

[6] More precisely, this result requires that the marginal returns be diminishing, as they are in Table A.2. In most applications, this is a reasonable assumption.

of stating this question is, "How much would consumers be willing to pay for the privilege of consuming 100 tons of apples at 25¢ per apple rather than 65 tons of apples at 40¢?"

To provide an answer, begin by recalling that the demand curve shows the *maximum* amount that individuals *would* be willing to pay for each apple they consume. Consider some arbitrary quantity of apples, say, 20 tons. The most people would be willing to pay for the 20th ton is the vertical distance up to the demand curve, 62¢. Initially, consumers in fact had to pay only 40¢ per apple. In a sense then, on their purchase of the 20th ton, consumers enjoyed a surplus of 22¢. The amount by which the sum that individuals would have been *willing* to pay exceeds the sum they *actually* have to pay is called the **consumer surplus.**

Of course, the same exercise could be repeated at any quantity, not just at 20 tons. When the price is 40¢ per apple, the consumer surplus at each output level equals the distance between the demand curve and the horizontal line at 40¢. Summing the surpluses for each apple purchased, we find that the total consumer surplus when the price is 40¢ is the area *ehd*. More generally, *consumer surplus is measured by the area under the demand curve and above a horizontal line at the market price.*

When the price falls to 25¢, consumer surplus is still the area under the demand curve and above a horizontal line at the going price; because the price is now 25¢, the relevant area is *eig*. Consumer surplus therefore increases by the difference between areas *eig* and *ehd*, area *higd*. Thus, the area behind the demand curve between the two prices measures the value to consumers of being able to purchase apples at the lower price.

To implement this procedure for a real-world problem, an investigator needs to know the shape of the demand curve. Generally, this can be obtained by using one or more of the tools of positive analysis discussed in Chapter 2. Hence, consumer surplus is a very practical tool for measuring the changes in welfare induced by changes in the economic environment.

A caveat that may be important under some circumstances: The area under an ordinary demand curve provides only an approximation to the true value of the change in consumer welfare. This is because as price changes, so do people's real incomes, and this may change the value that they place on additions to their income (the marginal utility of income). However, Willig [1976] has shown that measuring consumer surplus by the area under the ordinary demand curve is likely to be a pretty good approximation in most cases, and this approach is used widely in applied work.[7]

> **consumer surplus**
>
> The amount by which consumers' willingness to pay for a commodity exceeds the sum they actually have to pay.

Producer Surplus

In analogy to consumer surplus, we can define **producer surplus** as the amount of income individuals receive in excess of what they would require to supply a given number of units of a factor. To measure producer surplus, consider Jacob's labor supply curve (*S*), which is represented in Figure A.21. Each point on the labor supply curve shows the wage rate required to coax Jacob into supplying the associated number of hours of work. Hence, the distance between any point on the labor supply curve and the wage rate is the difference between the minimum payment that

> **producer surplus**
>
> The amount that producers receive in payment in excess of what they would require to supply a given quantity of a commodity.

---

[7] Alternatively, one can compute welfare changes using areas under a *compensated demand curve,* which is defined earlier in this appendix.

Figure A.21
Measuring
producer surplus

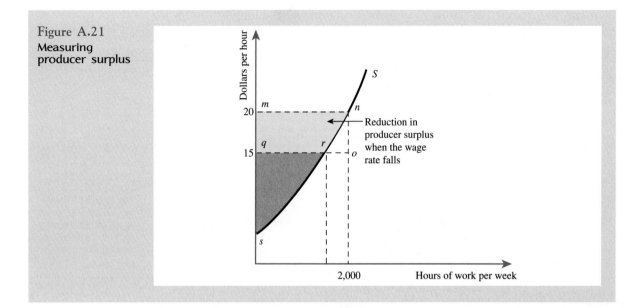

Jacob needs to receive for that hour of work and the amount he actually receives (the wage rate). Thus, *the area above the supply curve and below the wage rate is the producer surplus.*

To strengthen your understanding of producer surplus, imagine that initially Jacob works 2,000 hours per year at a wage of $20 per hour, but then his wage falls to $15 per hour. How much worse off is he? One possible answer is: "He was working 2,000 hours and is now earning $5 less per hour, so he is worse off by $10,000." This corresponds to area *mqon* in Figure A.21. However, producer surplus analysis tells us that this answer is incorrect. Before the wage cut, Jacob's surplus is area *msn*. When the wage rate falls to $15, his surplus falls to *qsr*. Hence, Jacob's loss from the wage cut is area *mqrn*. This is less than the naive answer of *mqon*. Intuitively, the naive answer overstates the loss in welfare because it ignores the fact that when a person's wage falls, he can substitute leisure for consumption. While the increased consumption of leisure certainly does not fully compensate for the wage decrease, it does have some value.

401(k) plan A savings plan under which an employee can earmark a portion of his or her salary each year, with no income tax liability incurred on that portion.

Accelerated depreciation Allowing firms to take depreciation allowances faster than true economic depreciation.

Accessions tax A tax levied on an individual's total lifetime acquisitions from inheritances and gifts.

Actuarially fair insurance premium An insurance premium for a given time period set equal to the expected payout for the same time period.

Actuarially fair return An insurance plan that on average pays out the same amount that it receives in contributions.

Ad valorem tax A tax computed as a percentage of the purchase value

Additive social welfare function An equation defining social welfare as the sum of individuals' utilities.

Add-on accounts Personal accounts that are funded from workers' resources rather than by diverting money from the payroll tax.

Adjusted gross income (AGI) Total income from all taxable sources less certain expenses incurred in earning that income.

Adverse selection The phenomenon under which the uninformed side of a deal gets exactly the wrong people trading with it (that is, it gets an adverse selection of the informed parties).

Agenda manipulation The process of organizing the order in which votes are taken to ensure a favorable outcome.

Aid to Families with Dependent Children (AFDC) Program of cash transfers from 1935 to 1996. Anyone whose income was below a particular level and met certain other conditions was entitled to a cash benefit indefinitely.

Alternative minimum tax (AMT) The tax liability calculated by an alternative set of rules designed to force individuals with high levels of preference income to incur at least some tax liability.

Annuity Insurance plan that charges a premium and then pays a sum of money at some regular interval for as long as the policyholder lives.

Arm's length system A method of calculating taxes for multinational corporations by treating transactions between domestic and foreign operations as if they were separate enterprises.

Assessed value The value a jurisdiction assigns to a property for tax purposes.

Assessment ratio The ratio of a property's assessed value to its market value.

Asymmetric information A situation in which one party engaged in an economic transaction has better information about the good or service traded than the other party.

Average indexed monthly earnings (AIME) The top 35 years of wages in covered employment, indexed each year for average wage growth. The AIME is used to compute an individual's Social Security benefit.

Average tax rate Ratio of taxes paid to income.

Benefit-cost ratio The ratio of the present value of a stream of benefits to the present value of a stream of costs for a project.

Benefits-received principle Consumers of a publicly provided service should be the ones who pay for it.

Bequest effect Theory that people may save more in order to finance a larger bequest to children in order to offset the intergenerational redistribution of income caused by Social Security.

Biased estimate An estimate that conflates the true causal impact with the impact of outside factors.

Bracket creep When an increase in an individual's nominal income pushes the individual into a higher tax bracket despite the fact that his or her real income is unchanged. See also tax indexing.

Budget constraint The representation of the bundles among which a consumer may choose, given his income and the prices he faces.

Budget line See *budget constraint*.

Cap-and-trade A policy of granting permits to pollute, with the number of permits set at the desired pollution level, and allowing polluters to trade the permits.

Capital gain (loss) An increase (decrease) in the value of an asset.

Capital intensive An industry in which the ratio of capital to labor inputs is relatively high.

Capitalization The process by which a stream of tax liabilities becomes incorporated into the price of an asset.

Capitation-based reimbursement A system in which health care providers receive annual payments for each patient in their care, regardless of services actually used by that patient.

Cartel An arrangement under which suppliers band together to restrict output and raise price.

Carve-out accounts Personal accounts that are funded by diverting payroll tax revenues away from the traditional Social Security system.

Cash flow The difference between revenues and expenditures.

Catastrophic insurance policy   An insurance policy that has a high deductible and generous coverage for high medical costs.

Categorical grants   Grants for which the donor specifies how the funds can be used.

Centralization ratio   The proportion of total direct government expenditures made by the central government.

Certainty equivalent   The value of an uncertain project measured in terms of how much certain income an individual would be willing to give up for the set of uncertain outcomes generated by the project.

Charter schools   Public schools that operate under special state government charters. Within limits established by their charters, these schools can experiment with a variety of approaches to education and have some independence in making spending and hiring decisions.

Circuit breakers   Transfers to individuals based on the excess of residential property tax payments over some specified portion of income.

Clientele effect   Firms structure their financial policies to meet different clienteles' needs. Those with low dividend payments attract shareholders with high marginal tax rates, and vice versa.

Club   A voluntary association of people who band together to finance and share some kind of benefit.

Coase theorem   Provided that transaction costs are negligible, an efficient solution to an externality problem is achieved as long as someone is assigned property rights, independent of who is assigned those rights.

Coinsurance   A percentage of the cost of a medical service that the insured must pay.

Command-and-control regulations   Policies that require a given amount of pollution reduction with limited or no flexibility with respect to how it may be achieved.

Commodity egalitarianism   The idea that some commodities ought to be made available to everybody.

Community rating   The practice of charging uniform insurance premiums for people in different risk categories within a community, thus resulting in low-risk people subsidizing high-risk people.

Compensated demand curve   A demand curve that shows how quantity demanded varies with price, holding utility constant.

Complements   Two goods are complements if an increase in the price of one good leads to decreased consumption of the other good.

Congestion pricing   A tax levied on driving equal to the marginal congestion costs imposed on other drivers.

Consumer surplus   The amount by which consumers' willingness to pay for a commodity exceeds the sum they actually have to pay.

Consumption smoothing   Reducing consumption in high-earning years in order to increase consumption in low-earning years.

Consumption-type VAT   Capital investments are subtracted from sales in the computation of the value added.

Contract curve   The locus of all Pareto efficient points.

Control group   The comparison group of individuals who are not subject to the intervention being studied.

Copayment   A fixed amount paid by the insured for a medical service.

Corporation   A state-chartered form of business organization, usually with limited liability for shareholders (owners) and an independent legal status.

Correlation   A measure of the extent to which two events move together.

Cost effective   A policy that achieves a given outcome at the lowest cost possible.

Cost-based reimbursement   A system under which health care providers receive payment for all services required.

Cost-benefit analysis   A set of procedures based on welfare economics for guiding public expenditure decisions.

Cost-effectiveness analysis   Comparing the costs of the various alternatives that attain similar benefits to determine which one is the cheapest.

Counterfactual   The outcome for people in the treatment group had they not been treated.

Cross-sectional data   Data that contain information on entities at a given point in time.

Crowd out   When public provision of a good substitutes for private provision of the good.

Crowding out hypothesis   Government borrowing decreases private investment by raising the market interest rate.

Cycling   When paired majority voting on more than two possibilities goes on indefinitely without a conclusion ever being reached.

Deadweight loss   The pure waste created when the marginal benefit of a commodity differs from its marginal cost.

Debt   The total amount owed at a given point in time; the sum of all past deficits.

Deductible   The fixed amount of expenditures that must be incurred by the insured within a year before the insured is eligible to receive insurance compensation.

Deductions   Certain expenses that may be subtracted from adjusted gross income in the computation of taxable income.

Deficit   The excess of expenditures over revenues during a period of time.

Demand curve   A graph of the demand schedule.

Demand schedule   The relation between the price of a good and the quantity demanded, *ceteris paribus*.

Dependency ratio   The ratio of Social Security beneficiaries to covered workers.

Diagnosis related groups   Classification system used to determine prospective compensation payments in the Medicare Hospital Insurance program.

Difference-in-difference analysis   An analysis that compares changes over time in an outcome of the treatment group to changes over the same time period in the outcome of the control group.

Differential commodity tax   See *excise tax*.

Diminishing marginal rate of substitution   The marginal rate of substitution falls as we move down along an indifference curve.

Discount factor   The number by which an amount of future income must be divided to compute its present value. If the interest rate is r and the income is receivable T periods in the future, the discount factor is $(1 + r)^T$.

Discount rate   The rate of interest used to compute present value.

District power equalization (DPE) grant   Grant to local government to raise local revenue to a level that would be achieved if the local property tax base were at a certain hypothetical level.

Double taxation   Taxing corporate income first at the corporate level, and again when it is distributed to shareholders.

Double-dividend effect   Using the proceeds from a Pigouvian tax to reduce inefficient tax rates.

Double-peaked preferences   If, as a voter moves away from his or her most preferred outcome, utility goes down, but then goes back up again.

Earned income tax credit (EITC)   A tax credit for low-income individuals.

Econometrics   The statistical tools for analyzing economic data.

Economic depreciation   The extent to which an asset decreases in value during a period of time.

Economic incidence   The change in the distribution of real income induced by a tax.

Economic profit   The return to owners of a firm above the opportunity costs of all the factors used in production. Also called supranormal or excess profit.

Edgeworth Box   A device used to depict the distribution of goods in a two good–two person world.

Education Savings Account   A tax-preferred savings vehicle. Contributions are not tax deductible, but funds accumulate tax free. Funds may be withdrawn to pay for higher education expenses of a child.

Elasticity of substitution   A measure of the ease with which one factor of production can be substituted for another.

Emissions fee   A tax levied on each unit of pollution.

Endowment point   The consumption bundle that is available if an individual neither borrows nor saves.

Entitlement programs   Programs whose expenditures are determined by the number of people who qualify, rather than pre-set budget allocations.

Equilibrium   A situation that tends to be maintained unless there is an underlying change in the system.

Equivalent variation   A change in income that has the same effect on utility as a change in the price of a commodity.

Excess burden   A loss of welfare above and beyond taxes collected. Also called welfare cost or deadweight loss.

Excise tax   A tax levied on the purchase of a particular commodity.

Exclusionary zoning laws   Statutes that prohibit certain uses of land.

Exemption   When calculating taxable income, an amount per family member that can be subtracted from adjusted gross income.

Expected utility   The average utility over all possible uncertain outcomes, calculated by weighting the utility for each outcome by its probability of occurring.

Expected value   The average value over all possible uncertain outcomes, with each outcome weighted by its probability of occurring.

Expenditure incidence   The impact of government expenditures on the distribution of real income.

Expensing   Deducting the entire value of an asset in the computation of taxable income.

Experience rating   The practice of charging different insurance premiums based on the existing risk of the insurance buyers.

Experimental study   An empirical study in which individuals are randomly assigned to the treatment and control groups.

External debt   The amount a government owes to foreigners.

Externality   A cost or benefit that occurs when the activity of one entity directly affects the welfare of another in a way that is outside the market mechanism.

Federal system   Consists of different levels of government that provide public goods and services and have some scope for making decisions.

Fee for service   See *cost-based reimbursement*.

Fiscal federalism The field that examines the functions undertaken by different levels of government and how the different levels of government interact with each other.

Flat income tax A tax schedule for which the marginal tax rate is constant throughout the entire range of incomes.

Flat-of-the-curve medicine The notion that at a certain point, the additional health gains of greater spending on health care are relatively limited.

Flypaper effect A dollar received by the community in the form of a grant to its government results in greater public spending than a dollar increase in community income.

Foundation aid Grant designed to ensure a minimum level of expenditure.

Free rider The incentive to let other people pay for a public good while you enjoy the benefits.

Full integration See *partnership method*.

Full loss offset Allowing individuals to deduct from taxable income all losses on capital assets.

Fully funded A pension system in which an individual's benefits are paid out of deposits that have been made during his or her working life, plus accumulated interest.

Functional distribution of income The way income is distributed among people when they are classified according to the inputs they supply to the production process (for example, landlords, capitalists, laborers).

Functional finance Using fiscal policy to keep aggregate demand at the desired level, regardless of the impact on deficits.

General equilibrium analysis The study of how various markets are interrelated.

General sales tax A tax levied at the same rate on the purchase of all commodities.

Generational accounting Method for measuring the consequences of government fiscal policy that takes into account the present value of all taxes and benefits received by members of each generation.

Global system A system under which an individual is taxed on income whether it is earned in the home country or abroad.

Gross estate All property owned by the decedent at the time of death.

Haig-Simons (H-S) definition of income Money value of the net increase in an individual's power to consume during a period.

Health Maintenance Organization Organization that offers comprehensive health care from an established network of providers, often using capitation-based reimbursement.

Health Savings Accounts (HSAs) A type of insurance plan in which a person has a catastrophic insurance policy, and the person or the person's employer puts money in an account that can be used to pay for out-of-pocket medical expenses. The contributions to the account are tax deductible.

Hicks-Kaldor criterion A project should be undertaken if it has a positive net present value, regardless of the distributional consequences.

Horizontal equity People in equal positions should be treated equally.

Horizontal summation The process of creating a market demand curve by summing the quantities demanded by each individual at every price.

Hospital insurance Part A component of Medicare that covers inpatient medical care and is funded through a payroll tax.

Hot spots Localized concentrations of emissions.

Human capital The investments that individuals make in education, training, and health care that raise their productive capacity.

Impure public good A good that is rival and/or excludable to some extent.

Imputed rent The net monetary value of the services a homeowner receives from a dwelling.

Incentive-based regulations Policies that provide polluters with financial incentives to reduce pollution.

Income effect The effect of a price change on the quantity demanded due exclusively to the fact that the consumer's income has changed.

Income splitting Using the arithmetic average of family income to determine each family member's taxable income, regardless of whose income it is.

Independence of irrelevant alternatives Society's ranking of two different projects depends only on individuals' rankings of the two projects, not on how individuals rank the two projects relative to other alternatives.

Indifference curve The locus of consumption bundles that yields the same total utility.

Indifference map The collection of all indifference curves.

Individual Retirement Account (IRA) For qualified individuals, a savings account in which the contributions are tax deductible and the interest accrues tax free, provided the funds are held until retirement. On withdrawal, both contributions and accrued interest are subject to tax.

Inferior good A good whose demand decreases as income increases.

In-kind transfer Payments from the government to individuals in the form of commodities or services rather than cash.

Instrumental variables analysis An analysis that relies on finding some variable that affects entry into the treatment group, but in itself is not correlated with the outcome variable.

Insurance premium Money paid to an insurance company in exchange for compensation if a specified adverse event occurs.

Insurance trust A trust that is the legal owner of a life insurance policy. It allows the beneficiaries of the policy to avoid the estate tax.

Internal debt The amount that a government owes to its own citizens.

Internal rate of return The discount rate that would make a project's net present value zero.

Intertemporal budget constraint The set of feasible consumption levels across time.

Inverse elasticity rule For goods that are unrelated in consumption, efficiency requires that tax rates be inversely proportional to elasticities.

Investment tax credit (ITC) A reduction in tax liability equal to some portion of the purchase price of an asset.

Invoice method Each firm is liable for taxes on total sales but can claim the taxes already paid by suppliers as a credit against this liability, provided this tax payment is verified by invoices from suppliers.

Itemized deduction A specific type of expenditure that can be subtracted from adjusted gross income in the computation of taxable income.

Job lock The tendency for workers to remain in their job in order to keep their employer-provided health insurance coverage.

Keogh Plan A savings plan that allows self-employed individuals to exclude some percentage of their net business income from taxation if the money is deposited into a qualified account.

Labor intensive An industry in which the ratio of capital to labor inputs is relatively low.

Laffer curve A graph of the tax rate–tax revenue relationship.

Life-cycle model The theory that individuals' consumption and savings decisions during a given year are based on a planning process that considers lifetime circumstances.

Lindahl prices The tax share an individual must pay per unit of public good.

Linear income tax schedule See *flat income tax*.

Loading fee The difference between the premium an insurance company charges and the actuarially fair premium level.

Local public good A public good that benefits only the members of a particular community.

Lock-in effect The disincentive to change portfolios that arises because an individual incurs a tax on realized capital gains.

Logrolling The trading of votes to obtain passage of a package of legislative proposals.

Lump sum tax A tax whose value is independent of the individual's behavior.

Majority voting rule One more than half of the voters must favor a measure for it to be approved.

Managed care Any of a variety of health care arrangements in which prices are kept down by supply-side control of services offered and prices charged.

Marginal Incremental, additional.

Marginal cost The incremental cost of producing one more unit of output.

Marginal rate of substitution The rate at which an individual is willing to trade one good for another; it is the absolute value of the slope of an indifference curve.

Marginal rate of transformation The rate at which the economy can transform one good into another good; it is the absolute value of the slope of the production possibilities frontier.

Marginal tax rate The proportion of the last dollar of income taxed by the government.

Marriage neutral Individuals' tax liabilities are independent of their marital status.

Maximin criterion Social welfare depends on the utility of the individual who has the minimum utility in the society.

Means-tested A spending program whose benefits flow only to those whose financial resources fall below a certain level.

Median voter The voter whose preferences lie in the middle of the set of all voters' preferences; half the voters want more of the item selected and half want less.

Median voter theorem As long as all preferences are single peaked and several other conditions are satisfied, the outcome of majority voting reflects the preferences of the median voter.

Medicaid Federal- and state-financed health insurance policy for the poor.

Medicare Federally funded government program that provides health insurance to people aged 65 and over and to the disabled.

Merit good A commodity that ought to be provided even if people do not demand it.

Monopoly A market with only one seller of a good.

Moral hazard When obtaining insurance against an adverse outcome leads to changes in behavior that increase the likelihood of the outcome.

Natural monopoly A situation in which factors inherent to the production process lead to a single firm supplying the entire industry's output.

Neutral taxation Taxing each good at the same rate.

Nominal amounts Amounts of money that are valued according to the price levels that exist in the years that the amounts are received.

Nominal income Income measured in terms of current prices.

Nominal interest rate The interest rate observed in the market.

Normal good A good for which demand increases as income increases and demand decreases as income decreases, other things being the same.

Normal retirement age Age at which an individual qualifies for full Social Security retirement benefits. Historically, it was 65, but is now gradually being increased to 67.

Observational study An empirical study that relies on observed data that are not obtained from an experimental setting.

Off-budget deficit The deficit resulting from off-budget expenditures and revenues.

Off-budget items Federal expenditures and revenues that are excluded by law from budget totals.

On-budget deficit The deficit resulting from on-budget expenditures and revenues.

Original position An imaginary situation in which people have no knowledge of what their economic status in society will be.

Overlapping generations model A model that takes into account the fact that several different generations coexist simultaneously.

Panel data Data that contain information on individual entities at different points of time.

Pareto efficient An allocation of resources such that no person can be made better off without making another person worse off.

Pareto improvement A reallocation of resources that makes at least one person better off without making anyone else worse off.

Partial equilibrium models Models that study only one market and ignore possible spillover effects in other markets.

Partial factor tax Tax levied on an input in only some of its uses.

Partnership method Each stockholder incurs a tax liability on his or her share of the earnings of a corporation, whether or not the earnings are distributed.

Pay-as-you-go (unfunded) A pension system in which benefits paid to current retirees come from payments made by current workers.

Peak A point on the graph of an individual's preferences at which all the neighboring points have lower utility.

Perfect price discrimination When a producer charges each person the maximum he or she is willing to pay for the good.

Performance standard A command-and-control regulation that sets an emissions goal for each individual polluter and allows some flexibility in meeting the goal.

Personal accounts Retirement savings accounts managed by individuals as part of a Social Security privatization plan. They are also known as "individual accounts" or "personal savings accounts."

Personal net worth tax A tax based on the difference between the market value of all the taxpayer's assets and liabilities.

Pigouvian tax A tax levied on each unit of an externality-generator's output in an amount equal to the marginal damage at the efficient level of output.

Point-of-service plan Similar to PPO, yet also assigns each enrollee a primary care provider to serve as a gatekeeper.

Political economy The field that applies economic principles to the analysis of political decision making.

Poverty line A fixed level of real income considered enough to provide a minimally adequate standard of living.

Preferred Provider Organization Organization that provides health care from providers who accept lower fees for access to the network and that give incentives to enrollees to obtain services from within the network of providers.

Present value The value today of a given amount of money to be paid or received in the future.

Present value criteria Rules for evaluating projects stating that (1) only projects with positive net present value should be carried out; and (2) of two mutually exclusive projects, the preferred project is the one with the higher net present value.

Price elasticity of demand The absolute value of the percentage change in quantity demanded divided by the percentage change in price.

Price elasticity of supply The absolute value of the percentage change in quantity supplied divided by the percentage change in price.

Primary insurance amount (PIA) The basic Social Security benefit payable to a worker who retires at the normal retirement age or becomes disabled.

Private good A commodity that is rival and excludable in consumption.

Privatization The process of turning services that are supplied by the government over to the private sector for provision and/or productions.

Producer surplus The amount that producers receive in payment in excess of what they would require to supply a given quantity of a commodity.

Production possibilities curve A graph that shows the maximum quantity of one output that can be produced, given the amount of the other output.

Progressive A tax system under which an individual's average tax rate increases with income.

Proportional A tax system under which an individual's average tax rate is the same at each level of income.

Prospective payment system Payment system, currently used by the Medicare Hospital Insurance program, in which the compensation level is set prior to the time that care is given.

Public economics See *public finance*.

Public finance The field of economics that analyzes government taxation and spending.

Public good A good that is nonrival and nonexcludable in consumption.

Public sector economics See *public finance*.

Publicly provided private goods Rival and excludable commodities that are provided by governments.

Pure public good A commodity that is nonrival and nonexcludable in consumption.

Quasi-experimental study An observational study that relies on circumstances outside of the researcher's control to mimic random assignment.

Ramsey rule To minimize total excess burden, tax rates should be set so that the tax-induced percentage reduction in the quantity demanded of each commodity is the same.

Rate schedule The tax liability associated with each level of taxable income.

Real amounts Amounts of money adjusted for changes in the general price level.

Real income A measure of income that accounts for changes in the general price level.

Real interest rate The nominal interest rate corrected for changes in the level of prices by subtracting the expected inflation rate.

Realized capital gain A capital gain resulting from the sale of an asset.

Regression line The line that provides the best fit through a scatter of data points.

Regression-discontinuity analysis An analysis that relies on a strict cut-off criterion for eligibility of the intervention under study in order to approximate an experimental design.

Regressive A tax system under which an individual's average tax rate decreases with income.

Regulatory budget An annual statement of the costs imposed on the economy by government regulations. (Currently, there is no such budget.)

Rent-seeking Using the government to obtain higher than normal returns ("rents").

Repatriate To return the earnings of a subsidiary to its parent company.

Replacement ratio The ratio of average Social Security benefits to average covered wages.

Resource-based relative value scale system Set of values based on time and effort of physician labor used to determine physicians' fees in the supplementary medical insurance component of Medicare.

Retirement effect To the extent that Social Security induces people to retire earlier, people may save more in order to finance a longer retirement.

Retrospective payment system Payment system, originally used by the Medicare Hospital Insurance program, in which compensation is paid after the care is completed and thus provides little incentive to economize on costs.

Revenue sharing A grant from the federal government to a state or locality that places no restrictions on the use of funds.

Risk aversion A preference for paying more than the actuarially fair premium in order to guarantee compensation if an adverse event occurs.

Risk premium The amount above the actuarially fair premium that a risk-averse person is willing to pay to guarantee compensation if an adverse event occurs.

Risk smoothing Paying money in order to guarantee a certain level of consumption should an adverse event occur.

Roth IRA A tax-preferred savings vehicle. Contributions are not tax deductible, but funds accumulate tax free.

Rule definition of horizontal equity The rules that govern the selection of taxes are more important for judging fairness than the outcomes themselves.

Safety valve price Within a cap-and-trade system, a price set by government at which polluters can purchase additional permits beyond the cap.

School accountability A system of monitoring the performance of schools through standardized tests and either issuing "report cards" on the schools' test performances or linking financial incentives to the test outcomes.

School voucher A voucher given to a family to help pay for tuition at any qualified school. The school redeems the voucher for cash.

Selective sales tax See *excise tax*.

Shadow price The underlying social marginal cost of a good.

Single-peaked preferences Utility consistently falls as a voter moves away from his or her most preferred outcome.

Size distribution of income The way that total income is distributed across income classes.

Social insurance programs Government programs that provide insurance to protect against adverse events.

Social rate of discount The rate at which society is willing to trade off present consumption for future consumption.

Social Security Trust Fund A fund in which Social Security surpluses are accumulated for the purpose of paying out benefits in the future.

Social Security wealth The present value of one's expected Social Security benefits minus expected payroll taxes paid.

Social welfare function A function reflecting society's views on how the utilities of its members affect the well-being of society as a whole.

Standard deduction Subtraction of a fixed amount from adjusted gross income that does not require documentation.

Standard error A statistical measure of how much an estimated regression coefficient might vary from its true value.

State Children's Health Insurance Program (SCHIP) Program that expanded Medicaid eligibility to some children with family incomes above Medicaid limits.

Statutory incidence Indicates who is legally responsible for a tax.

Subsidiary A company owned by one corporation but chartered separately from the parent corporation.

Substitutes Two goods are substitutes if an increase in the price of one good leads to increased consumption of the other good.

Substitution effect The tendency of an individual to consume more of one good and less of another because of a decrease in the price of the former relative to the latter.

Supplemental Security Income (SSI) A welfare program that provides a minimum income guarantee for the aged and disabled.

Supplementary medical insurance Part B component of Medicare that covers physician services and medical services rendered outside the hospital and is funded by a monthly premium and by general revenues.

Supply schedule The relation between market price of a good and the quantity that producers are willing to supply, *ceteris paribus*.

Surplus The excess of revenues over spending during a period of time.

Sustainable solvency Expected present values of revenues and expenditures are equal into the indefinite future.

Tax avoidance Altering behavior in such a way as to reduce your legal tax liability.

Tax credit A subtraction from tax liability (as opposed to a subtraction from taxable income).

Tax effort The ratio of tax collections to tax capacity.

Tax evasion Not paying taxes legally due.

Tax expenditure A loss of tax revenue because some item is excluded from the tax base.

Tax indexing Automatically adjusting the tax schedule to compensate for inflation so that an individual's real tax burden is independent of inflation.

Tax-interaction effect The increase in excess burden in the labor market stemming from the reduction in real wages caused by a Pigouvian tax.

Tax life The number of years an asset can be depreciated.

Tax Reform Act of 1986 (TRA86) Tax legislation that eliminated a number of itemized deductions and other tax preferences, and lowered marginal tax rates for many taxpayers.

Tax shifting The difference between statutory incidence and economic incidence.

Tax wedge The tax-induced difference between the price paid by consumers and the price received by producers.

Taxable estate The gross estate less deductions for costs of settling the estate, outstanding debts of the estate, and charitable contributions.

Taxable income The amount of income subject to tax.

Technology standard A type of command-and-control regulation that requires firms to use a particular technology to reduce their pollution.

Temporary Assistance for Needy Families (TANF) Welfare program passed in 1996 under which payments to recipients are available only on a temporary and provisional basis.

Territorial system A system under which an individual earning income in a foreign country owes taxes only to the host government.

Theory of the second best In the presence of existing distortions, policies that in isolation would increase efficiency can decrease it, and vice versa.

Third-party payment Payment for services by someone other than the consumer.

Time endowment The maximum number of hours an individual can work during a given period.

Time inconsistency of optimal policy When the government cannot implement an optimal tax policy because the policy is inconsistent with the government's incentives over time, and taxpayers realize this fact.

Time-series data　Data that contain information on an entity at different points in time.

Transfer price　The price that one subsidiary charges another for some input.

Transitional equity　Fairness in changing tax regimes.

Treatment group　The group of individuals who are subject to the intervention being studied.

Underground economy　Those economic activities that are either illegal, or legal but hidden from tax authorities.

Unified budget　The document that includes all the federal government's revenues and expenditures.

Unified transfer tax　A tax in which amounts transferred as gifts and bequests are jointly taken into account.

Unit tax　A tax levied as a fixed amount per unit of commodity purchased.

Unrealized capital gain　A capital gain on an asset not yet sold.

User cost of capital　The opportunity cost to a firm of owning a piece of capital.

User fee　A price paid by users of a government-provided good or service.

Utilitarian social welfare function　An equation stating that social welfare depends on individuals' utilities.

Utility　The amount of satisfaction a person derives from consuming a particular bundle of commodities.

Utility definition of horizontal equity　A method of classifying people of "equal positions" in terms of their utility levels.

Utility possibilities curve　A graph showing the maximum amount of one person's utility given each level of utility attained by the other person.

Value added　The difference between sales and the cost of purchased material inputs.

Value-added tax (VAT)　A percentage tax on value added at each stage of production.

Vertical equity　Distributing tax burdens fairly across people with different abilities to pay.

Vertical summation　The process of creating an aggregate demand curve for a public good by adding the prices each individual is willing to pay for a given quantity of the good.

Voting paradox　With majority voting, community preferences can be inconsistent even though each individual's preferences are consistent.

Wealth substitution effect　The crowding out of private savings due to the existence of Social Security.

Welfare economics　The branch of economic theory concerned with the social desirability of alternative economic states.

Workfare　Able-bodied individuals who qualify for income support receive it only if they agree to participate in a work-related activity.

Aaronson, Daniel, Lisa Barrow, and William Sander. 2003. "Teachers and Student Achievement in the Chicago Public High Schools." Working Paper 2002-28, Federal Reserve Bank of Chicago.

Aboulafia, Richard. 2006. "The Airbus Debacle." *Wall Street Journal* (June 20, 2006): p. A20.

Acemoglu, Daron, Simon Johnson, James A. Robinson, and Pierre Yared. 2005. "From Education to Democracy?" Working Paper No. 11204. Cambridge, MA: National Bureau of Economic Research.

Ackerman, Frank and Lisa Heinzerling. 2004. *Priceless: On Knowing the Price of Everything and the Value of Nothing.* New York: New Press.

Alesina, Alberto and Eliana La Ferrara. 2005. "Preferences for Redistribution in the Land of Opportunities." *Journal of Public Economics* 89(5-6): 897–931.

Allen, Mike. 1998. "Cardinal Sees Marriage Harm in Partners Bill." *New York Times* (May 25, 1998): p. A1.

Alm, James and Leslie A. Whittington. 2003. "Shacking Up or Shelling Out: Income Taxes, Marriage, and Cohabitation." *Review of Economics of the Household* 1(3): 169–186.

Alsenz, Joe. 2007. "Letter to the Editor." *Wall Street Journal* (December 10, 2007): p. A17.

Altig, David, Alan J. Auerbach, Laurence J. Kotlikoff, Kent A. Smetters, and Jan Walliser. 2001. "Simulating Fundamental Tax Reform in the United States." *American Economic Review* 91: 574–595.

Anders, George and Ron Winslow. 1997. "HMOs' Woes Reflect Conflicting Demands of American Public." *Wall Street Journal* (December 22, 1997).

Anderson, Gary M., Dennis Halcoussis, Linda Johnston, and Anton D. Lowenberg. 2000. "Regulatory Barriers to Entry in the Healthcare Industry: The Case of Alternative Medicine." *The Quarterly Review of Economics and Business* 40: 485–502.

Armitage-Smith, George. 1907. *Principles and Methods of Taxation.* London: John Murray.

Arrow, Kenneth J. 1951. *Social Choice and Individual Values.* New York: Wiley.

Atkinson, Anthony B. and Joseph E. Stiglitz. 1980. *Lectures on Public Economics.* New York: McGraw-Hill.

Attanasio, Orazio P. and Agar Brugiavini. 2003. "Social Security and Households' Saving." *Quarterly Journal of Economics* 118(3): 1075–1120.

Attanasio, Orazio P. and Susann Rohwedder. 2003. "Pension Wealth and Household Saving: Evidence from Pension Reforms in the United Kingdom." *American Economic Review* 93(5): 1499–1521.

Auerbach, Alan J. 2008. "Federal Budget Rules: The US Experience." Working Paper No. 14288. Cambridge, MA: National Bureau of Economic Research.

Baicker, Katherine. 2005. "Extensive or Intensive Generosity? The Price and Income Effects of Federal Grants." *Review of Economics and Statistics* 87(2).

Baicker, Katherine, William Dow, and Jonathan Wolfson. 2006. "Health Savings Accounts: Implications for Health Spending." *National Tax Journal* 59(3): 463–476.

Baicker, Katherine and Helen Levy. 2007. "Employer Health Insurance Mandates and the Risk of Unemployment." Working Paper No. 13528. Cambridge, MA: National Bureau of Economic Research.

Baker, Michael, A., Abigail Payne, and Michael Smart. 1999. "An Empirical Study of Matching Grants: The 'Cap on CPA'." *Journal of Public Economics* 72: 269–288.

Baker, Russell. 1985. "Reagan Revises Dirksen." *New York Times* (October 2, 1985): p. A27.

Bakija, Jon and Bradley T. Heim. 2008. "How Does Charitable Giving Respond to Incentives and Income? Dynamic Panel Estimates Accounting for Predictable Changes in Taxation." Working Paper No. 14237. Cambridge, MA: National Bureau of Economic Research.

Banzhaf, H. Spencer and Randall P. Walsh. 2008. "Do People Vote with Their Feet? An Empirical Test of Tiebout's Mechanism." *American Economic Review* 98(3): 843–863.

Barboza, David. 1999. "Pluralism under Golden Arches." *New York Times* (February 12, 1999): p. C1.

Barro, Robert J. 1974. "Are Government Bonds Net Wealth?" *Journal of Political Economy* 82: 1095–1117.

Barry, Dave. 2003. "Want a Little Something EGTRRA?" *The Miami Herald* (April 6, 2003).

Barry, Dave. 2004. "Federal Deficit: Meet the Other White Meat." *Miami Herald* (March 7, 2004).

Bartlett, Bruce. 2007. "Fair Tax, Flawed Tax." *Wall Street Journal* (August 27, 2007): p. A7.

Bassetto, Marco and Thomas Sargent. 2006. "Politics and Efficiency of Separating Capital and Ordinary Government Budgets." *Quarterly Journal of Economics* 121(4).

Bauman, Kurt J. 1999. "Shifting Family Definitions: The Effect of Cohabitation and Other Household Relationships on Measures of Poverty." *Demography* 36(3): 315–325.

Baumol, William J. 1976. "Book Reviews—Economics and Clean Water." *Yale Law Journal* 85(3): 441–446.

Baumol, William J. and Hilda Baumol. 1981. "Book Review." *Journal of Political Economy* 89(2): 425–428.

Bazelon, Coleman and Kent Smetters. 1999. "Discounting Inside the Washington, D.C. Beltway." *Journal of Economic Perspectives* 13(4): 213–228.

Becker, Gary S. and Casey B. Mulligan. 2003. "Deadweight Costs and the Size of Government." *Journal of Law and Economics* 46(2): 293–340.

Benjamin, Daniel J. 2003. "Does 401(k) Eligibility Increase Saving? Evidence from Propensity Score Subclassification." *Journal of Public Economics* 87(5-6): 1259–1290.

Beshears, John, James J. Choi, David Laibson, and Brigitte C. Madrian. 2006. "The Importance of Default Options for Retirement Savings Outcomes: Evidence from the United States." Working Paper No. 12009. Cambridge, MA: National Bureau of Economic Research.

Biggs, Andrew G. 2008. "The Social Security Earnings Test: The Tax That Wasn't." AEI Tax Policy Outlook (July 2008).

Blair, Douglas H. and Robert A. Pollak. 1983. "Rational Collective Choice." *Scientific American* 249(2): 88–95.

Blank, Rebecca. 2002. "Evaluating Welfare Reform in the United States." *Journal of Economic Literature* 40: 1105–1166.

Blank, Rebecca. 2005. "On Overview of Welfare-to-Work Efforts." *CESifo DICE Report* 3(2): 3–7.

Blank, Rebecca. 2006. "Was Welfare Reform Successful?" *The Economists' Voice* 3(4): www.bepress.com/ev/vol3/iss4/art2.

Blau, Francine D. and Lawrence M. Kahn. 2005. "Changes in the Labor Supply Behavior of Married Women: 1980–2000." Working Paper No. 11230. Cambridge, MA: National Bureau of Economic Research.

Blume-Kohout, Margaret E. and Neeraj Sood. 2008. "The Impact of Medicare Part D on Pharmaceutical R&D." Working Paper No. 13857. Cambridge, MA: National Bureau of Economic Research.

Blumenthal, Marsha, Charles Christian, and Joel Slemrod. 2001. "Taxpayer Response to an Increased Probability of Audit: Evidence from a Controlled Experiment in Minnesota." *Journal of Public Economics* 79(3): 455–483.

Boardman, Anthony E., David H. Greenberg, Aidan R. Vining, and David L. Weimer. 2006. *Cost Benefit Analysis: Concepts and Practice*, 3rd edition. Upper Saddle River, NJ: Pearson Prentice Hall.

Borck, Rainald and Stephanie Owings. 2003. "The Political Economy of Intergovernmental Grants." *Regional Science and Urban Economics* 33: 139–156.

Boskin, Michael J., Ellen R. Dulberger, Robert J. Gordon, Zvi Griliches, and Dale W. Jorgenson. 1998. "Consumer Prices, the Consumer Price Index, and the Cost of Living." *Journal of Economic Perspectives* 12(1): 3–26.

Boskin, Michael and Eytan Sheshinski. 1983. "Optimal Treatment of the Family: Married Couples." *Journal of Public Economics* 20: 281–297.

Bradford, David F. 1998. "Transition To and Tax Rate Flexibility in a Cash-Flow Type Tax." In James Poterba (ed.), *Tax Policy and the Economy* 12. Cambridge, MA: The MIT Press: 151–172.

Brat, Ilan and Bryan Gruley. 2007. "Global Trade Galvanizes Caterpillar." *Wall Street Journal* (February 26, 2007): p. B1.

Brody, Jane E. 2006. "To Lower Risk on Jogging Trail, Get Off the Couch." *New York Times* (June 20, 2006): Personal Health Section, p. 7.

Brown, Margaret E., Andrew B. Bindman, and Nicole Lurie. 1998. "Monitoring the Consequences of Uninsurance: A Review of the Methodologies." *Medical Care Research and Review* 55(2): 177–210.

Browning, Edgar K. 2002. "The Case Against Income Redistribution." *Public Finance Review* 30: 509–530.

Browning, Martin and Thomas F. Crossley. 2001. "The Life-Cycle Model of Consumption and Saving." *Journal of Economic Perspectives* 15: 3–22.

Buchanan, James M. 1960. "Social Choice, Democracy, and Free Markets." In *Fiscal Theory and Political Economy—Selected Essays*, James M. Buchanan (ed.). Chapel Hill: University of North Carolina Press: 75–89.

Buchanan, James M. 1995. "Clarifying Confusion about the Balanced Budget Amendment." *National Tax Journal* 48: 347–356.

Bureau of Labor Statistics. 2008. *Employment & Earnings* 55(12): (December 2008).

Burke, Vee. 2006. "Cash and Noncash Benefits for Persons with Limited Income: Eligibility Rules, Recipient and Expenditure Data, FY2002–04." Congressional Research Service. Washington, DC.

Burman, Leonard E., William G. Gale, Greg Leiserson, and Jeffrey Rohaly. 2007. "The AMT: What's Wrong and How to Fix It." *National Tax Journal* 60: 385–406.

Burman, Leonard E., Bowen Garrett, and Surachai Khitatrakun. 2008. "The Tax Code, Employer-Sponsored Insurance, and the Distribution of Tax Subsidies." In *Using Taxes to Reform Health Insurance: Pitfalls and Promises*, Henry J. Aaron and Leonard E.Burman (eds.). Brookings Institution Press, pp. 36–56.

Burtraw, Dallas. 2002. "Book Review." *Regional Science and Urban Economics* 32: 139–144.

Butler, Stuart M. 1992. "Creating a National Health System through Tax Reform." *National Tax Association—Proceedings of the Eighty-fifth Annual Conference.*

Cameron, Stephen V. and James J. Heckman. 2001. "The Dynamics of Educational Attainment for Blacks, Hispanics, and Whites." *Journal of Political Economy* 109(3): 455–499.

Campoy, Ana. 2008. "With Gas Over $4, Cities Explore Whether It's Smart to Be Dense." *Wall Street Journal* (July 7, 2008): p. A1.

Carasso, Adam and C. Eugene Steuerle. 2002. "How Marriage Penalties Change under the 2001 Tax Bill." Discussion Paper No. 2. Washington, DC: Urban-Brookings Tax Policy Center.

Card, David. 1999. "The Causal Effect of Education on Earnings." *Handbook of Labor Economics Volume 3A*, Orley Ashenfelter and David Card (eds.). Elsevier Science.

Card, David and Alan B. Krueger. 1996. "School Resources and Student Outcomes: An Overview of the Literature and New Evidence from North and South Carolina." *Journal of Economic Perspectives* 10(4): 31–50.

Card, David and Lara D. Shore-Sheppard. 2004. "Using Discontinuous Eligibility Rules to Identify the Effects of the Federal Medicaid Expansions on Low-Income Children." *Review of Economics and Statistics* 86(3): 752–766.

Cardon, James H. and Igal Hendel. 2002. "Asymmetric Information in Health Insurance: Evidence from the National Medical Expenditure Survey." *RAND Journal of Economics* 32(3): 408–427.

Cawley, John and Tomas Philipson. 1999. "An Empirical Examination of Information Barriers to Trade in Insurance." *American Economic Review* 89(4): 827–846.

Centers for Medicare and Medicaid Services (CMS). 2002. "Managed Care Trends." http://cms.hhs.gov/medicaid/managedcare/trends02.pdf.

Centers for Medicare and Medicaid Services (CMS). 2008a. *CMS Statistics 2008*. Department of Health and Human Services.

Centers for Medicare and Medicaid Services (CMS). 2008b. *Medicare Trustees Report*. Department of Health and Human Services.

Centers for Medicare and Medicaid Services (CMS). 2008c. *National Health Expenditure Data*. Department of Health and Human Services.

Chamberlain, Andrew and Gerald Prante. 2007. "Who Pays Taxes and Who Receives Government Spending? An Analysis of Federal, State and Local Tax and Spending Distributions, 1991–2004." Tax Foundation Working Paper No. 1.

Chay, Kenneth Y. and Michael Greenstone. 2003. "The Impact of Air Pollution on Infant Mortality: Evidence from Geographic Variation in Pollution Shocks Induced by a Recession." *Quarterly Journal of Economics* 118(3): 1121–1167.

Chay, Kenneth Y. and Michael Greenstone. 2005. "Does Air Quality Matter? Evidence from the Housing Market." *Journal of Political Economy* 113(2): 376–424.

Chetty, Raj and Emmanuel Saez. 2004. "Dividend Taxes and Corporate Behavior: Evidence from the 2003 Dividend Tax Cut." Working Paper No. 10841. Cambridge, MA: National Bureau of Economic Research.

Cheung, Ron. 2008. "The Effect of Property Tax Limitations on Residential Private Governments: The Case of Proposition 13." *National Tax Journal* 61(1): 35–56.

Chiappori, Pierre-Andre and Bernard Salanié. 2000. "Testing for Asymmetric Information in Insurance Markets." *Journal of Political Economy* 108(1): 56–78.

Chirinko, Robert S. 2002. "Corporate Taxation, Capital Formation, and the Substitution Elasticity between Labor and Capital." *National Tax Journal* 40: 339–355.

Chirinko, Robert S. and Daniel J. Wilson. 2006. "State Investment Tax Incentives: What Are the Facts?" Federal Reserve Bank of San Francisco Working Paper No. 2006-49.

Chivers, C. J. 2004. "Cash vs. Benefits: Efficiency, or Assault on Russia's Soul?" *New York Times* (June 18, 2004): p. A3.

Christy, George C. 2006. "The Most Poisonous Tax for America's Economy." *Wall Street Journal*, Letter to the Editor (May 5, 2006): p. A17.

Cinyabuguma, Matthias, Talbot Page, and Louis Putterman. 2005. "Cooperation Under the Threat of Expulsion in a Public Goods Experiment." *Journal of Public Economics* 89: 1421–1435.

City of Clinton v. Cedar Rapids and Missouri River RR. Co. 1868. 24 Iowa 475.

Clausing, Kimberly. 2007. "Corporate Tax Revenues in OECD Countries." *International Tax and Public Finance* 14(2): 115–134.

Clements, Jonathan. 2003. "Why the Rising Market Is a Bummer: Practically Everything's Overpriced." *Wall Street Journal* (October 8, 2003): p. D1.

Clymer, Adam. 1997. "Switching Sides on States' Rights." *New York Times* (June 1, 1997): Section 4, pp. 1, 6.

CNN. 2007. "The Price of Vice Increases in Venezuela" (October 15, 2007).

Cnossen, Sijbren. 2001. "Tax Policy in the European Union—A Review of Issues and Options," *FinanzArchiv* 58: 466–558.

Coase, Ronald H. 1960. "The Problem of Social Cost." *Journal of Law and Economics* 3(1): 1–44.

Coase, Ronald H. 1974. "The Lighthouse in Economics." *Journal of Law and Economics* 17(2): 357–376.

Cockburn, Alexander and Robert Pollin. 1992. "Why the Left Should Support the Flat Tax." *Wall Street Journal* (April 2, 1992): p. A15.

Coleman, James S., Ernest Q. Campbell, Carol F. Hobson, James M. McPartland, Alexander M. Mood, Frederic D. Weinfield, and Robert L. York. 1966. *Equality of Educational Opportunity*. Washington, DC: US Office of Education.

Commonwealth Fund. 2007. *2007 Health Policy Survey in Seven Countries*.

Congressional Budget Office (CBO). 1997. *The Economic Effects of Comprehensive Tax Reform*. Washington, DC: US Government Printing Office.

Congressional Budget Office (CBO). July 1998. *Social Security and Private Saving: A Review of the Empirical Evidence*. Washington, DC: US Government Printing Office.

Congressional Budget Office (CBO). March 2004a. *Administrative Costs of Private Accounts in Social Security*. Washington, DC: US Government Printing Office.

Congressional Budget Office (CBO). 2004b. "Fuel Economy Standards Versus a Gasoline Tax." *Economic and Budget Issue Brief*, March 9, 2004.

Congressional Budget Office (CBO). December 2005a. *Global Population Aging in the 21st Century and Its Economic Implications*. Washington, DC: US Government Printing Office.

Congressional Budget Office (CBO). 2005b. "Long-Term Economic Effects of Chronically Large Federal Deficits." *Economic and Budget Issue Brief* (October 13, 2005).

Congressional Budget Office (CBO). 2006. "Is Social Security Progressive?" *Economic and Budget Issue Brief* (December 15, 2006).

Congressional Budget Office (CBO). 2007. *Historical Effective Tax Rates: 1979 to 2005*. Washington, DC: US Government Printing Office.

Congressional Budget Office. 2008a. *The Long-Term Economic Effects of Some Alternative Budget Policies: Appendix C* (May 19, 2008).

Congressional Budget Office. 2008b. *Policy Options for Reducing CO_2 Emissions*. Washington, DC: US Government Printing Office.

Congressional Budget Office (CBO). 2009a. *The Budget and Economic Outlook: Fiscal Years 2009 to 2019*.

Congressional Budget Office (CBO). 2009b. *Historical Budget Data* (January 2009).

Congressional Research Service. 2006. "Value-Added Tax: A New US Revenue Source?" *CRS Report to Congress* (August 22, 2006).

Cooper, Christopher. 2007. "In Katrina's Wake: Where Is the Money?" *Wall Street Journal* (January 27, 2007): p. A1.

Corlett, W. J. and D. C. Hague. 1953. "Complementarity and the Excess Burden of Taxation." *Review of Economic Studies* 21: 21–30.

Crane, Mark W. 2005. "The Impact of Regulatory Costs on Small Firms," Small Business Administration: www.sba.gov/advo/research/rs264tot.pdf.

Currie, Janet. 2004. "The Take Up of Social Benefits." Working Paper No. 10488. Cambridge, MA: National Bureau of Economic Research.

Currie, Janet and Jonathan Gruber. 1996. "Health Insurance Eligibility, Utilization of Medical Care, and Child Health." *Quarterly Journal of Economics* 111(2): 431–466.

Cushing, Matthew J. and Mary G. McGarvey. 2003. "The Efficiency of Race- and Gender-Targeted Income Transfers." *Public Finance Review* 31(5): 455–486.

Cushman, John H., Jr. 1997. "E.P.A. Head Adamant on Clean Air Rules." *New York Times* (June 1, 1997): p. A1.

Cutler, David M. 2002. "Health Care and the Public Sector." In *Handbook of Public Economics*, Volume 4, Alan J. Auerbach and Martin Feldstein (eds.). Amsterdam: North Holland.

Cutler, David M. 2003. "Employee Costs and the Decline in Health Insurance Coverage." In *Frontiers in Health Policy Research*, Volume 6. David Cutler and Alan Garber (eds.). Cambridge, MA: MIT Press, 2003.

Cutler, David M. 2004. *Your Money or Your Life: Strong Medicine for America's Health Care System.* New York: Oxford University Press.

Cutler, David M. 2007. "The Lifetime Costs and Benefits of Medical Technology." Working Paper No. 13478. Cambridge, MA: National Bureau of Economic Research.

Cutler, David M. and Srikanth Kadiyala. 2001. "The Economics of Better Health: The Case of Cardiovascular Disease." Mimeo.

Cutler, David M. and Mark McClellan. 2001. "Is Technological Change in Medicine Worth It?" *Health Affairs* 20(5): September–October 2001.

Cutler, David M. and Sarah J. Reber. 1998. "Paying for Health Insurance: The Trade-Off between Competition and Adverse Selection." *Quarterly Journal of Economics* 113(2): 433–466.

Davis, Stephen J. and Magnus Henrekson. 2004. "Tax Effects on Work Activity, Industry Mix and Shadow Economy Size." Working Paper No. 10509. Cambridge, MA: National Bureau of Economic Research.

Davis, Susan. 2008. "Obama Tilts Toward Center, Irking Some Activists." *Wall Street Journal* (June 24, 2008): p. A8.

Deaton, Angus and Christina Paxson. 2001. "Mortality, Income, and Income Inequality Over Time in Britain and the United States." Working Paper No. 8534. Cambridge, MA: National Bureau of Economic Research.

Dee, Thomas S. 1999. "State Alcohol Policies, Teen Drinking and Traffic Fatalities." *Journal of Public Economics* 72: 289–315.

Delipalla, Sofia and Owen O'Donnell. 2001. "Estimating Tax Incidence, Market Power, and Market Conduct: The European Cigarette Industry." *International Journal of Industrial Organization* 19(6): 885–908.

Derthick, Martha. 2000. "American Federalism—Half-Full or Half-Empty." Volume 18, *Brookings Review*: 24–28.

Desai, Mihir, C. Fritz Foley, and James Hines Jr. 2003. "Chains of Ownership, Regional Tax Competition, and Foreign Direct Investment." In *Foreign Direct Investment in the Real and Financial Sector of Industrial Countries.* Heinz Hermann and Robert Lipsey (eds.). Heidelberg: Springer Verlag: 61–98.

Dewenter, Kathryn and Paul H. Malatesta. 2001. "State-owned and Privately Owned Firms: An Empirical Analysis of Profitability, Leverage, and Labor Intensity." *American Economic Review* 91: 320–334.

Diamond, Peter A. and Jonathan Gruber. 1999. "Social Security and Retirement in the United States." In *Social Security and Retirement Around the World.* Jonathan Gruber and David A. Wise (eds.). Chicago: University of Chicago Press.

Diamond, Peter A. and Peter R. Orszag. 2005. "Saving Social Security." *Journal of Economic Perspectives* 19(2): 11–32.

Dillon, Sam. 2003. "New Federal Law May Leave Many Rural Teachers Behind." *New York Times* (June 23, 2003): p. A1.

Djankov, Simeon, Tim Ganser, Caralee McLiesh, Rita Ramalho, and Andrei Shleifer. 2008. "The Effect of Corporate Taxes on Investment and Entrepreneurship." Working Paper No. 13756. Cambridge, MA: National Bureau of Economic Research.

Doms, Mark E., Wendy E. Dunn, Stephen D. Oliner, and Daniel E. Sichel. 2004. "How Fast Do Personal Computers Depreciate? Concepts and New Estimates." *Tax Policy and the Economy* 18: 37–79.

Doyle, Joseph J., Jr. and Krislert Samphantharak. 2006. "$2.00 Gas! Studying the Effects of a Gas Tax Moratorium." Working Paper No. 12266. Cambridge, MA: National Bureau of Economic Research.

Duggan, Mark G. 2004. "Does Contracting Out Increase the Efficiency of Government Programs? Evidence from Medicaid HMOs." *Journal of Public Economics* 88(12): 2549–2572.

Dugger, Celia A. 2001. "In India's Capital, a Prayer for the Belching Buses." *New York Times* (September 28, 2001): p. A3.

Eberstadt, Nicholas. 2005. "Broken Yardstick." *New York Times* (September 9, 2005): p. A25.

Eckholm, Erik. 1999. "Rising Farmers' Protests Meet Violence in China." *New York Times* (February 1, 1999): p. A10.

Economic Report of the President, 2003. Washington, DC: US Government Printing Office, 2003.

Economic Report of the President, 2004. Washington, DC: US Government Printing Office, 2004.

Economic Report of the President, 2009. Washington, DC: US Government Printing Office, 2009.

Economist. 2003. "The Dividend Puzzle" (January 11, 2003): pp. 53–54.

Economist. 2007a. "All Hands to the Pump" (March 24, 2007): pp. 52–53.

Economist. 2007b. "Gently Does It" (July 28, 2007): p. 27.

Economist. 2007c. "Going Up or Down?" (June 9, 2007): pp. 49–50.

Economist. 2007d. "The Hunt for the Odourless Pig" (November 24, 2007): p. 36.

Economist. 2007e. "Schools Unchained" (September 6, 2007): pp. 14–15.

Economist. 2007f. "Vote for Me, Dimwit" (June 16, 2007): p. 42.

Economist. 2008. "A Harvest of Disgrace" (May 24, 2008): pp. 46–48.

Edgeworth, F. Y. 1959/1897. "The Pure Theory of Taxation." Reprinted in *Readings in the Economics of Taxation.* Richard A. Musgrave and Carl S. Shoup (eds.). Homewood, IL: Irwin: 258–296.

Eissa, Nada. 2001. "Taxation and Labor Supply of Married Women: The Tax Reform Act of 1986 as a Natural Experiment." Working Paper No. 5023. Cambridge, MA: National Bureau of Economic Research.

Eissa, Nada and Hilary Hoynes. 2006. "Behavioral Responses to Taxes: Lessons from the EITC and Labor Supply." In *Tax Policy and the Economy*, James Poterba (ed.). 20: 73–110.

Engelhardt, Gary V. and Jonathan Gruber. 2004. "Social Security and the Evolution of Elderly Poverty." Working Paper 10466. Cambridge, MA: National Bureau of Economic Research.

Fairclough, Gordon. 2002. "Pssst! Wanna Cheap Smoke?" *Wall Street Journal* (December 27, 2002): p. B1.

Fattah, Hassan M. 2006. "First Time Out, Kuwaiti Women Become a Political Force." *New York Times* (June 26, 2006): p. A3.

Feldstein, Martin. 1974. "Social Security, Induced Retirement, and Aggregate Capital Accumulation." *Journal of Political Economy* 82(5): 905–926.

Feldstein, Martin. 1976. "On the Theory of Tax Reform." *Journal of Public Economics* 6: 77–104.

Feldstein, Martin. 1982. "Inflation, Tax Rules, and Investment: Some Econometric Evidence." *Econometrica* 50(4): 825–862.

Feldstein, Martin. 1985. "Debt and Taxes in the Theory of Public Finance." *Journal of Public Economics* 28(2): 233–246.

Feldstein, Martin. 1996. "Social Security and Saving: New Time Series Evidence." *National Tax Journal* 49: 151–164.

Feldstein, Martin. 2005. "Rethinking Social Insurance." *American Economic Review* 95(1): 1–24.

Feldstein, Martin. 2006a. "The Effect of Taxes on Efficiency and Growth." Working Paper No. 12201. Cambridge, MA: National Bureau of Economic Research.

Feldstein, Martin. 2006b. "Tradeable Gasoline Rights." *Wall Street Journal* (June 5, 2006): p. A10.

Feldstein, Martin. 2008a. "Effects of Taxes on Economic Behavior." Working Paper No. 13745. Cambridge, MA: National Bureau of Economic Research.

Feldstein, Martin. 2008b. "The Tax Rebate Was a Flop: Obama's Stimulus Plan Won't Work Either." *Wall Street Journal* (August 7, 2008): p. A15.

Feldstein, Martin and Andrew Samwick. 2002. "Potential Paths of Social Security Reform." In *Tax Policy and Economy 2002,* Volume 16. James Poterba (ed.). Cambridge: MIT Press: 181–224.

Feldstein, Martin and Marian Vaillant Wrobel. 1998. "Can State Taxes Redistribute Income?" *Journal of Public Economics* 68: 369–396.

Figlio, David N. 2005. "Testing Crime and Punishment." Working Paper No. 11194. Cambridge, MA: National Bureau of Economic Research.

Figlio, David N. and Lawrence Kenny. 2006. "Individual Teacher Incentives and Student Perfomance." Working Paper No. 12627. Cambridge, MA: National Bureau of Economic Research.

Finkelstein, Amy. 2004. "Minimum Standards, Insurance Regulation and Adverse Selection: Evidence from the Medigap Market." *Journal of Public Economics* 88(12): 2515–2547.

Finkelstein, Amy. 2005. "The Aggregate Effects of Health Insurance: Evidence from the Introduction of Medicare." Working Paper No. 11619. Cambridge, MA: National Bureau of Economic Research.

Finkelstein, Amy and Robin McKnight. 2005. "What Did Medicare Do (and Was It Worth It)?" Working Paper No. 11609. Cambridge, MA: National Bureau of Economic Research.

Fisher Ronald C. and Leslie E. Papke. 2000. "Local Government Responses to Education Grants." *National Tax Journal* 53: 153–168

Fisman, Raymond and Roberta Gatti. 2002. "Decentralization and Corruption: Evidence across Countries." *Journal of Public Economics* 83: 325–346.

Fisman, Raymond and Shang-Jin Wei. 2004. "Tax Rates and Tax Evasion: Evidence from 'Missing Imports' in China." *Journal of Political Economy* 112(2): 471–500.

Fleenor, Patrick. 2008. "Cigarette Taxes Are Fueling Organized Crime." *Wall Street Journal* (May 7, 2008): p. A17.

Foderaro, Lisa W. 2008. "Gone with the Cash: Films Go for the Best Tax Breaks." *New York Times* (March 29, 2008): p. B1.

Fogel, Robert W. 2004. *The Escape from Hunger and Premature Death, 1700–2100: Europe, America, and the Third World.* Cambridge, England: Cambridge University Press.

Folland, Sherman, Allen Goodman and Miron Stano. 2006. *Economics of Health and Health Care*, 5th edition. Upper Saddle River, NJ: Prentice Hall.

Freedman, David A. 1991. "Statistical Models and Shoe Leather." *Sociological Methodology* 21: 291–313.

Freeman, A. Myrick III. 2002. "Environmental Policy Since Earth Day I: What Have We Gained?" *Journal of Economic Perspectives* 16: 125–146.

Fried, Charles. 1995. "Whose Money Is It?" *Washington Post* (January 1, 1995): p. C7.

Friedman, Eric, Simon Johnson, Daniel Kaufmann, and Pablo Zoido-Lobaton. 2000. "Dodging the Grabbing Hand: The Determinants of Unofficial Activity in 69 Countries." *Journal of Public Economics* 76: 495–520.

Friedman, Milton. 1980. "Our New Hidden Taxes." *Newsweek* (April 14, 1980): p. 90.

Friedman, Milton. 1998. "Let's Revamp the Tax Code—But How?" *Wall Street Journal* (April 15, 1998): p. A22.

Friedman, Milton. 2003. "What Every American Wants." *Wall Street Journal* (January 15, 2003): p. A10.

Friess, Steve. 2009. "Nevada Brothels Want to Pay Tax, but State Says No." *International Herald Tribune* (January 26, 2009).

Fuchs, Victor. 2000. "An Economist's View of Health Care Reform." *New York Times* (May 2, 2000): pp. F6–F7.

Fuchs, Victor R., Alan B. Krueger, and James M. Poterba. 1998. "Economists' Views about Parameters, Values, and Policies: Survey Results in Labor and Public Economics." *Journal of Economic Literature* 36(3): 1387–1425.

Fullerton, Don and Diane Lim Rogers. 1997. "Neglected Effects on the Uses Side: Even a Uniform Tax Would Change Relative Goods Prices." *American Economic Review* 87: 120–125.

Gale, William G. and Joel B. Slemrod. 2000. "A Matter of Life and Death: Reassessing the Estate and Gift Tax." *Tax Notes* (August 14, 2000): 927–932.

Gallagher, L. Jerome, Megan Gallagher, Kevin Perese, Susan Schreiber, and Keith Watson. 1998. "One Year after Welfare Reform: A Description of State Temporary Assistance for Needy

Families (TANF) Decisions as of October 1997." Washington, DC: The Urban Institute.

Gans, Joshua S. and Andrew Leigh. 2006. "Did the Death of Australian Inheritance Taxes Affect Deaths?" *The B.E. Journal of Economic Analysis & Policy* 6(1): Article 23.

Gates, William H., Sr. and Chuck Collins. 2002. "Tax the Wealthy." *The American Prospect* 13 (June 17, 2002) [www.prospect.org/print/V13/11/index.html].

Gayer, Ted. 2000. "Neighborhood Demographics and the Distribution of Hazardous Waste Risks: An Instrumental Variables Estimation." *Journal of Regulatory Economics* 17(2): 131–155.

Gayer, Ted and John K. Horowitz. 2006. "Market-based Approaches to Environmental Regulation." *Foundations in Trends in Microeconomics* 1(4): 201–326.

Gentleman, Amelia. 2006. "India's Vultures Fall Prey to a Drug in the Cattle They Feed On." *New York Times* (March 28, 2006): p. A4.

Gerber, Alan, Dean S. Karlan, and Daniel Bergan. 2006. "Does the Media Matter? A Field Experiment Measuring the Effect of Newspapers on Voting Behavior and Political Opinions." *Yale Economic Applications and Policy Discussion Paper*, No. 12.

Gervais, Martin. 2002. "Housing Taxation and Capital Accumulation." *Journal of Monetary Economics* 49: 1461–1489.

Glaeser, Edward L. 2005. "Inequality." Working Paper No. 11511. Cambridge, MA: National Bureau of Economic Research.

Glaeser, Edward L., Giacomo A. M. Ponzetto, and Andrei Shleifer. 2006. "Why Does Democracy Need Education?" Working Paper No. 12128. Cambridge, MA: National Bureau of Economic Research.

Glaeser, Edward L., Jose A Scheinkman, and Andrei Shleifer. 2003. "The Injustice of Inequality." *Journal of Monetary Economics*. Carnegie-Rochester Series on Public Policy.

Glaeser, Edward L. and Jesse M. Shapiro. 2003. "The Benefits of the Home Mortgage Interest Deduction." *Tax Policy and the Economy* 17: 37–82.

Glaeser, Edward L. and Andrei Shleifer. 2005. "The Curley Effect: The Economics of Shaping the Electorate." *Journal of Law, Economics, and Organizations* 21: 1–19.

Goklany, Indur. 1999. *Clearing the Air: The Real Story of the War on Air Pollution*. Washington, DC: Cato Institute.

Gompers, Paul A. and Josh Lerner. 1999. "What Drives Venture Capital Fundraising?" Working Paper No. 6906. Cambridge, MA: National Bureau of Economic Research.

Goolsbee, Austan. 1998. "Does Government R&D Policy Mainly Benefit Scientists and Engineers?" *American Economic Review* 88: 298–302.

Goolsbee, Austan. 2003. "Investment Tax Subsidies and the Wages of Capital Goods Workers: To the Workers Go the Spoils?" *National Tax Journal* LVI: 153–166.

Goolsbee, Austan. 2004. "The Impact and Inefficiency of the Corporate Income Tax: Evidence from State Organizational Form Data." *Journal of Public Economics* 88(11): 2283–2299.

Goolsbee, Austan and Amil Petrin. 2004. "The Consumer Gains from Direct Broadcast Satellites and the Competition with Cable Television." *Econometrica* 72(2): 351–381.

Gordon, Roger H. and Young Lee. 2001. "Do Taxes Affect Corporate Debt Policy? Evidence from US Corporate Tax Return Data." *Journal of Public Economics* 8: 195–224.

Gottschalk, Peter and Enrico Spolaore. 2002. "On the Evaluation of Economic Mobility." *Review of Economic Studies* 69(1): 191–208.

Government Accountability Office. 2007. "Vulnerabilities Exposed through Covert Testing of TSA's Passenger Screening Process" (November 15, 2007): GAO-08-48T.

Graham, John R. 2003. "Taxes and Corporate Finance: A Review." *Review of Financial Studies* 16: 1074–1128.

Gravelle, Jane G. 2004. "The Corporate Tax: Where Has It Been and Where Is It Going?" *National Tax Journal* LVII(4): 903–923.

Griffin, Michael. 2007. "The Real Reasons We Explore Space." *Air & Space Magazine* (July 1, 2007).

Grogger, Jeffrey. 2003. "The Effects of Time Limits and Other Policy Changes on Welfare Use, Work, and Income among Female-Headed Families." *Review of Economics and Statistics* 85(2): 394–408.

Groves, Harold M. 1946. *Financing Government*. New York: Henry Holt.

Groves, Theodore and Martin Loeb. 1975. "Incentives and Public Inputs." *Journal of Public Economics* 4(3): 211–226.

Gruber, Jonathan and Michael Lettau. 2004. "How Elastic Is the Firm's Demand for Health Insurance?" *Journal of Public Economics* 88(7): 1273–1294.

Gruber, Jonathan and Emmanuel Saez. 2002. "The Elasticity of Taxable Income: Evidence and Implications." *Journal of Public Economics* 84: 1–33.

Gruber, Jonathan and Kosali Simon. 2007. "Crowd-out Ten Years Later: Have Recent Public Insurance Expansions Crowded Out Private Health Insurance?" Working Paper No. 12858. Cambridge, MA: National Bureau of Economic Research.

Gruber, Jonathan and David Wise (eds). 2004. *Social Security Programs and Retirement around the World*. Chicago: University of Chicago Press.

Guryan, Jonathan. 2003. "Does Money Matter? Estimates from Education Finance Reform in Massachusetts." Working Paper No. 8269. Cambridge, MA: National Bureau of Economic Research.

Hadley, Jack and John Holahan. 2004. "The Cost of Care for the Uninsured: What Do We Spend, Who Pays, and What Would Full Coverage Add to Medical Spending?" Issue Update for Kaiser Commission on Medicaid and the Uninsured.

Hagman, Donald C. 1978. "Proposition 13: A Prostitution of Conservative Principles." *Tax Review* 39(9): 39–42.

Hahn, Robert W. 1984. "Market Power and Transferable Property Rights." *Quarterly Journal of Economics* 99(4): 753–765.

Hahn, Robert W. and Patrick M. Dudley. 2007. "How Well Does the US Government Do Benefit-Cost Analysis?" *Review of Environmental Economics and Policy* 1(2): 192–211.

Hall, Robert E. and Alvin Rabushka. 1995. *The Flat Tax,* 2nd ed. Stanford, CA: Hoover Institution Press.

Hamilton, Bruce. 1975. "Zoning and Property Taxation in a System of Local Governments." *Urban Studies* 12: 205–211.

Hanushek, Eric A. 2002. "Publicly Provided Education." In *Handbook of Public Economics.* Alan J. Auerbach and Martin

Feldstein (eds.). Amsterdam: Elsevier: 2045–2141. (Also: Working Paper No. 02138. Cambridge, MA: National Bureau of Economic Research.)

Hanushek, Eric A. and Margaret E. Raymond. 2005. "Does School Accountability Lead to Improved Student Performance?" *Journal of Policy Analysis and Management* 24(2): 297–327.

Hanushek, Eric A., Steven G. Rivkin, and John F. Kain. 2005. "Teachers, Schools, and Academic Achievement." *Econometrica* 73: 417–458.

Harberger, Arnold C. 1974. "The Incidence of the Corporation Income Tax." In *Taxation and Welfare*. Arnold C Harberger (ed.). Boston: Little, Brown.

Harford, Tim. 2006. *The Undercover Economist*. Oxford: Oxford University Press.

Hart, Oliver, Andrei Shleifer, and Robert W. Vishny. 1997. "The Proper Scope of Government: Theory and an Application to Prisons." *Quarterly Journal of Economics* 112(4): 1127–1161.

Hassett, Kevin A., Aparna Mathur, and Gilbert E. Metcalf. 2007. "The Incidence of a US Carbon Tax: A Lifetime and Regional Analysis." Working Paper No. 13554. Cambridge, MA: National Bureau of Economic Research.

Hastert, Dennis. 2004. *Speaker: Lessons from Forty Years in Coaching and Politics*. New York: Regnery Publishing, Inc.

Hastings, Justine S. and Jeffrey M. Weinstein. 2007. "No Child Left Behind: Estimating the Impact on Choices and Student Outcomes." Working Paper No. 13009. Cambridge, MA: National Bureau of Economic Research.

Haughwout, Andrew, Robert Inman, Steven Craig, and Thomas Luce. 2004. "Local Revenue Hills: Evidence and Lessons from Four US Cities." *Review of Economics and Statistics* 86(2): 570–585.

Heal, Geoffrey. 2001. "Bundling Public and Private Goods: Are Development and Conservation Necessarily in Conflict?" Working Paper. New York: Columbia Business School.

Heal, Geoffrey. 2003. "Bundling Biodiversity." *European Economic Association* 1(2–3): 553–560.

Heckman, James J. 1999. "Policies to Foster Human Capital." Working Paper No. 7288. Cambridge, MA: National Bureau of Economic Research.

Heckman, James J. 2000. "Policies to Foster Human Capital." *Research in Economics* 54(1): 3–36.

Heckman, James J. 2008. "Schools, Skills, and Synapses." Working Paper No. 14064. Cambridge, MA: National Bureau of Economic Research.

Henderson, James M. and Richard E. Quandt. 1980. *Microeconomic Theory: A Mathematical Approach*, 3rd edition. New York: McGraw-Hill.

Herbert, Bob. 1995. "Safety? Too Costly." *New York Times* (April 19, 1995): p. A23.

Herman, Tom. 2000. "Tax Report." *Wall Street Journal* (July 19, 2000): p. A1.

Herman, Tom. 2002. "Tax Report." *Wall Street Journal* (February 20, 2002): p. A1.

Herman, Tom. 2004a. "Tax Bill Revises Key Deduction; Though Corporations Are Focus, Measure Also Benefits Many Individuals; Impact Giving." *Wall Street Journal* (October 12, 2004): p. D1.

Herman, Tom. 2004b. "Tax Report: Many Filers Ignore Nanny Tax, Expecting Not to Get Caught." *Wall Street Journal* (December 15, 2004): p. D2.

Herman, Tom. 2007. "Sole Proprietors' Face Tax Scrutiny." *Wall Street Journal* (August 22, 2007): p. D3.

Herman, Tom. 2008. "How AMT Confuses Taxpayers." *Wall Street Journal* (August 13, 2008): p. D2.

Hertz, Tom. 2006. *Understanding Mobility in America*. Center for American Progress.

Hines, James R. Jr and Lawrence H. Summers. 2009. "How Globalization Affects Tax Design." Working Paper No. 14664. Cambridge, MA: National Bureau of Economic Research.

Hitler, Adolf. 1971/1925. *Mein Kampf* (translated by Ralph Manheim). Boston: Houghton Mifflin.

Hobbes, Thomas. 1963/1651. *Leviathan*. New York: Meridian Books.

Holcombe, Randall G. 2002. "The Ramsey Rule Reconsidered." *Public Finance Review* 30: 562–578.

Holsey, Cheryl M. and Thomas E. Borcherding. 1997. "Why Does Government's Share of National Income Grow? An Assessment of the Recent Literature on the US Experience." In *Perspectives on Public Choice*. D. Mueller (ed.). Cambridge, England: Cambridge University Press.

Holt, Stephen D. 2005. "Making Work *Really* Pay: Income Support and Marginal Effective Tax Rates Among Low-Income Working Households."

Holtz-Eakin, Douglas, David Joulfaian, and Harvey S. Rosen. 1993. "The Carnegie Conjecture: Some Empirical Evidence." *Quarterly Journal of Economics* 108(2): 413–435.

Hotz, V. Joseph, Charles H. Mullin, and John Karl Scholz. 2006. "Examining the Effect of the Earned Income Tax Credit on the Labor Market Participation of Families on Welfare." Working Paper No. 11968. Cambridge, MA: National Bureau of Economic Research.

Hotz, V. Joseph and John Karl Scholz. 2003. "The Earned Income Tax Credit." In *Means-Tested Transfer Programs in the US*. Robert A. Moffitt (ed.). Chicago: University of Chicago Press.

Howell, William G. and Paul E. Peterson. 2002. *The Education Gap: Vouchers and Urban Schools*. Washington, DC: Brookings Institution Press.

Hoxby, Caroline. 2000. "The Effects of Class Size on Student Achievement: New Evidence from Population Variation." *Quarterly Journal of Economics* 115(4): 1239–1285.

Hoxby, Caroline. 2002a. "The Cost of Accountability." Working Paper No. 8855. Cambridge, MA: National Bureau of Economic Research.

Hoxby, Caroline. 2002b. "School Choice and School Accountability (Or Could School Choice Be a Tide That Lifts All Boats?)" Working Paper No. 8873. Cambridge, MA: National Bureau of Economic Research.

Hoxby, Caroline. 2004. "School Choice and School Competition: Evidence from the United States." *Swedish Economic Policy Review* 10(2).

Hoxby, Caroline and Jonah E. Rockoff. 2004. "The Impact of Charter Schools on Student Achievement." Working Paper. Harvard Institute of Economic Research.

Hoynes, Hilary, Marianne Page, and Ann Stevens. 2006. "Poverty in America: Trends and Explanations." *Journal of Economic Perspectives* 20(1): 47–68.

Hurd, Michael D. 1990. "Research on the Elderly: Economic Status, Retirement, and Consumption and Savings." *Journal of Economic Literature* 28(2): 565–637.

Husted, Thomas A. and Lawrence W. Kenny. 1997. "The Effect of the Expansion of the Voting Franchise on the Size of Government." *Journal of Political Economy* 105: 54–82.

Inman, Robert P. 2008. "The Flypaper Effect." Working Paper No. 14579. Cambridge, MA: National Bureau of Economic Research.

Intergovernmental Panel on Climate Change. 2007. *Climate Change 2007: Synthesis Report, Summary for Policymakers*: Geneva, Switzerland.

Ip, Greg. 2006. "The Thorny Question about Tax Increases Concerns Economic Risks over the Long Term." *Wall Street Journal* (November 7, 2006): p. A2.

Ivkovich, Zoran, James M. Poterba, and Scott J. Weisbenner. 2005. "Tax-Motivated Trading by Individual Investors." *American Economic Review* 95(5): 1605–1630.

Jacob, Brian A. 2005. "Accountability, Incentives and Behavior: The Impact of High-Stakes Testing in the Chicago Public Schools." *Journal of Public Economics* 89: 761–796.

Jacob, Brian A. and Lars Lefgren. 2004. "Remedial Education and Student Achievement: A Regression-Discontinuity Analysis." *Review of Economics and Statistics* 86(1): 226–244.

Jacob, Brian A. and Steven D. Levitt. 2003. "Rotten Apples: An Investigation of the Prevalence and Predictors of Teacher Cheating." *Quarterly Journal of Economics* 118(3): 834–877.

Jamison, Eliot A., Dean T. Jamison, and Eric A. Hanushek. 2006. "The Effects of Education Quality on Income Growth and Mortality Decline." Working Paper No. 12652. Cambridge, MA: National Bureau of Economic Research.

Jepsen, Christopher and Steven Rivkin. 2002. "What Is the Tradeoff Between Smaller Classes and Teacher Quality?" Working Paper No. 9205. Cambridge, MA: National Bureau of Economic Research.

Johansen, Leif. 1977. "The Theory of Public Goods: Misplaced Emphasis?" *Journal of Public Economics* 7(1): 147–152.

Johnson, Avery. 2005. "Travelers Hit with Slew of New Taxes on Rental Cars." *Wall Street Journal* (November 9, 2005): p. D1.

Johnson, Paul. 1983. *Modern Times*. New York: Harper & Row.

Johnston, David Cay. 2000. "The Tax Maze Begins Here. No, Here. No . . ." *New York Times* (February 27, 2000): p. BU1.

Johnston, David Clay. 2008. "Wesley Snipes Cleared on Serious Tax Charges." *Wall Street Journal* (February 2, 2008): p. C1.

Joint Committee on Taxation. 2005. *Macroeconomic Analysis of Various Proposals to Provide $50 Billion in Tax Relief* (March 1, 2005): JCX-4-05.

Joint Committee on Taxation. 2008. *Estimates of Federal Tax Expenditures for Fiscal Years 2008–2012*. Washington, DC: US Government Printing Office, October 31, 2008.

Joint Economic Committee. 2006. "Report of the Joint Economic Committee on the 2006 Economic Report of the President." December 8, 2006.

Jorgenson, Dale W. 1963. "Capital Theory and Investment Behavior." *American Economic Review* 53(2): 247–259.

Jorgenson, Dale W. 1998. "Did We Lose the War on Poverty?" *Journal of Economic Perspectives* 12: 79–96.

Jorgenson, Dale W. and Kun-Young Yun. 2001. *Investment, Volume 3, Lifting the Burden: Tax Reform, the Cost of Capital, and US Economic Growth*. Cambridge, MA: MIT Press.

Kaestner, Robert, Neeraj Kaushal, and Garrett Van Ryzin. 2003. "Migration Consequences of Welfare Reform." *Journal of Urban Economics* 53(3): 357–379.

Kahn, Joseph. 2001. "Equality at Trade Talks: No Country Gets a Vote." *New York Times* (November 12, 2001): p. A3.

Kaiser Family Foundation. 2008. *Employer Health Benefits 2008 Annual Survey*.

Kane, Thomas J. 1998. *The Price of Admissions—Rethinking How Americans Pay for College*. Washington, DC: Brookings Institution Press.

Kaplow, Louis. 2008a. "Taxation," in *Handbook of Law and Economics*, Volume 1, A. Mitchell Polinsky and Steven Shavell, (eds.). Elsevier. Amsterdam.

Kaplow, Louis. 2008b. *The Theory of Taxation and Public Economics*. Princeton, NJ: Princeton University Press.

Kaufman, Marc. 2005. "Big-Game Hunting Brings Big Tax Breaks." *Washington Post* (April 5, 2005): p. D1.

Kaushal, Neeraj, Qin Gao, and Jane Waldfogel. 2006. "Welfare Reform and Family Expenditures: How are Single Mothers Adapting to the New Welfare and Work Regime?" Working Paper No. 12624. Cambridge, MA: National Bureau of Economic Research.

Keller, Bill. 1994. "Same Old Bureaucracy Serves New South Africa." *New York Times* (June 4, 1994): p. A1.

Keynes, John Maynard. 1965/1936. *The General Theory of Employment, Interest, and Money*. New York: Harcourt Brace and World.

Kho, Bon-Chan, Rene M. Stulz, and Francis E. Warnock. 2006. "Financial Globalization, Governance, and the Evolution of the Home Bias." Working Paper No. 12389. Cambridge, MA: National Bureau of Economic Research.

Kinzer, Stephen. 1996. "At 25, the Hippies' 'Free City' Isn't So Carefree." *New York Times* (May 16, 1996): p. A3.

Kleiner, Morris M. and Robert T. Kudrle. 2000. "Does Regulation Affect Economic Outcomes? The Case of Dentistry." *Journal of Law and Economics* 43: 547–582.

Kling, Jeffery R., Jeffrey B. Liebman, and Lawrence F. Katz. 2007. "Experimental Analysis of Neighborhood Effects." *Econometrica* 75:1(2007): pp: 83–119.

Kolata, Gina. 2003. "Patients in Florida Lining Up for All That Medicare Covers." *New York Times* (September 13, 2003): p. A1.

Kopczuk, Wojciech and Joel Slemrod. 2001. "The Impact of the Estate Tax on the Wealth Accumulation and Avoidance Behavior of Donors." In *Rethinking Estate and Gift Taxation*. W. Gale, J. R. Hines, Jr., and J. Slemrod (eds.). Brookings Institution Press: 299–343.

Kotlikoff, Lawrence J. 2002. "Generational Policy." In *Handbook of Public Economics*, Volume 4. Alan J. Auerbach and Martin Feldstein (eds.). Amsterdam: North Holland.

Krauss, Clifford. 2003. "Long Lines Mar Canada's Low-Cost Health Care." *New York Times* (February 13, 2003): p. A3.

Kristol, Irving. 1997. "Income Inequality Without Class Conflict." *Wall Street Journal* (December 18, 1997): p. A22.

Kronholz, Jane. 2000. "A Superintendent Is Entrepreneurial about Charters." *Wall Street Journal* (April 11, 2000): p. A10.

Krueger, Alan B. 1999. "Experimental Estimates of Education Production Functions." *Quarterly Journal of Economics* 114(2): 497–532.

Krueger, Alan B. and Diane M. Whitmore. 2001. "The Effect of Attending a Small Class in the Early Grades on College-Test Taking and Middle School Test Results: Evidence from Project STAR." *Economic Journal* 111: 1–28.

Krueger, Alan B. and Pei Zhu. 2004. "Another Look at the New York City School Voucher Experiment." *American Behavioral Scientist* 47(5): 658–698.

Krugman, Paul. 2001. "The Public Interest." *New York Times* (October 10, 2001): p. A19.

Krugman, Paul. 2006a. "First, Do More Harm." *New York Times* (January 16, 2006).

Krugman, Paul. 2006b. "Outsourcer in Chief." *New York Times* (December 11, 2006): p. A27.

Kulish, Nicholas. 2008. "$1.85 Fee to See a Doctor? Some Say It's Too Much." *New York Times* (May 27, 2008): p. A9.

Ladd, Helen F. 2002. "School Vouchers: A Critical View." *Journal of Economic Perspectives* 16(4): 3–24.

Laffer, Arthur B. 1979. "Statement Prepared for the Joint Economic Committee, May 20." Reprinted in *The Economics of the Tax Revolt: A Reader*. Arthur B. Laffer and Jan P. Seymour (eds.). New York: Harcourt Brace Jovanovich: 75–79.

Lagnado, Lucette. 2006. "Seniors in Vermont Are Finding They Can Go Home Again." *Wall Street Journal* (October 23, 2006); p. A1.

Landsburg, Steven E. 2004. "What I Like about Scrooge." *Slate* (December 9, 2004).

Lazear, Edward P. and James M. Poterba. 2006. "Reforming Taxes to Promote Economic Growth." *The Economists' Voice* 3(1): Article 3.

Lee, Chulhee. 2005. "Rising Family Income Inequality in the United States, 1968–2000: Impacts of Changing Labor Supply, Wages, and Family Structure." Working Paper No. 11836. Cambridge, MA: National Bureau of Economic Research.

Lee, Jaekyung. 2001. "School Reform Initiatives as Balancing Acts: Policy Variation and Educational Convergence among Japan, Korea, England and the United States." *Education Policy Analysis Archives* 9(13). http://epaa.asu.edu/epaa/v9n13.html.

Leimer, Dean R. and Selig D. Lesnoy. 1982. "Social Security and Private Saving: New Time Series Evidence." *Journal of Political Economy* 90(3): 606–629.

Lerner, A. P. 1948. "The Burden of the National Debt." In *Income, Employment, and Public Policy: Essays in Honor of Alvin H Hansen*. L. A. Metzler et al. (eds.). New York: W. W. Norton.

Levin, Jonathan and Barry Nalebuff. 1995. "An Introduction to Vote-Counting Schemes." *Journal of Economic Perspectives* 9: 3–26.

Levit, Katherine R., Cathy A. Cowan, Helen C. Lazenby, et al. 1994. "National Health Spending Trends, 1960–1993." *Health Affairs* 13(5): 14–31.

Levy, Helen and David Meltzer. 2004. "What Do We Really Know about Whether Health Insurance Affects Health?" In *Health Policy and the Uninsured*. Catherine G. McLaughlin (ed.). Washington, DC: The Urban Institute Press.

Liebman, Jeffrey. 2001. "Redistribution in the Current US Social Security System." Working Paper No. 8625. Cambridge, MA: National Bureau of Economic Research.

Liebman, Jeffrey, Maya MacGuineas, and Andrew Samwick. 2005. "Nonpartisan Social Security Reform Plan."

Lindahl, Erik. 1958/1919. "Just Taxation—A Positive Solution." In *Classics in the Theory of Public Finance*. R. A. Musgrave and A. T. Peacock (eds.). New York: St. Martin's Press.

Liptak, Adam. 2007. "A Deal for the Public: If You Win, You Lose." *New York Times* (July 9, 2007): p. A10.

Lott, John R. 1999. "Public Schooling, Indoctrination, and Totalitarianism." *Journal of Political Economy* Volume 107(6)(2): S127–S157.

Ludwig, Jens and Deborah A. Phillips. 2007. "The Benefits and Costs of Head Start." Working Paper No. 12973. Cambridge, MA: National Bureau of Economic Research.

Luhnow, David. 2008. "Nationalism, Crony Capitalism May Thwart Mexico in Boosting Oil Production." *Wall Street Journal* (March 31, 2008): p. A2.

Lurie, Nicole, N. B. Ward, Martin F. Shapiro, C. Gallego, R. Vaghaiwalla, and Robert H. Brook. 1986. "Termination of Medi-Cal Benefits: A Follow-up Study One Year Later." *New England Journal of Medicine* 314(19): 1266–1268.

Lyall, Sarah. 2003. "Europe Weighs the Unthinkable: High College Fees." *New York Times* (December 25, 2003): p. A3.

Madrian, Brigitte C. 2006. "The US Health Care System and Labor Markets." Working Paper No. 11980. Cambridge, MA: National Bureau of Economic Research.

Maki, Dean M. 2001. "Household Debt and the Tax Reform Act of 1986." *American Economic Review* 91: 305–319.

Makin, John H., ed. 1985. *Real Tax Reform—Replacing the Income Tax.* Washington, DC: American Enterprise Institute for Public Policy Research.

Mankiw, Gregory N. and Matthew Weinzierl. 2007. "The Optimal Taxation of Height: A Case Study of Utilitarian Income Redistribution." Harvard Working Paper.

Mark, Stephen T., Therese J. McGuire, and Leslie E. Papke. 2000. "The Influence of Taxes on Employment and Population Growth: Evidence from the Washington, D.C. Metropolitan Area." *National Tax Journal* 53: pp. 105–124.

Marsh, Bill. 2007. "Putting a Price on the Priceless: One Life." *New York Times* (September 9, 2007): p. wk4.

McClellan, Mark and Jonathan Skinner. 2005. "The Incidence of Medicare." *Journal of Public Economics,* 90(1–2), pp: 257–276 (2006).

McKinnon, John D. and Greg Hitt. 2002. "How Treasury Lost in Battle to Quash a Dubious Security." *Wall Street Journal* (February 4, 2002): p. A1.

McLure, Charles E., Jr. 1971. "The Theory of Tax Incidence with Imperfect Factor Mobility." *Finanzarchiv* 30.

McLure, Charles E., Jr. 2002. "Thinking Straight about the Taxation of Electronic Commerce: Tax Principles, Compliance Problems, and Nexus." In *Tax Policy and the Economy,* Volume 16. James M Poterba (ed.). Cambridge, MA: MIT Press.

Metcalf, Gilbert E. 2007. "A Green Employment Tax Swap: Using a Carbon Tax to Finance Payroll Tax Relief." The Brookings Institution and World Resources Institute.

Metcalf, Gilbert E. 2008. "Assessing the Federal Deduction for State and Local Tax Payments." Working Paper No. 14023. Cambridge, MA: National Bureau of Economic Research.

Meyer, Bruce D. and Wallace K. C. Mok. 2007. "Quasi-experimental Evidence on the Effects of Unemployment Insurance from New York State." Working Paper No. 12865. Cambridge, MA: National Bureau of Economic Research.

Meyer, Bruce D. and Dan T. Rosenbaum. 2001. "Welfare, the Earned Income Tax Credit, and the Labor Supply of Single Mothers." *Quarterly Journal of Economics* 116: 1063–1114.

Meyer, Bruce D. and James X. Sullivan. 2007. "Further Results on Measuring the Well-Being of the Poor Using Income and Consumption." Working Paper No. 13413. Cambridge, MA: National Bureau of Economic Research.

Miller, Henry J. 1997. "Gore Remakes Economics in His Own Image." *Wall Street Journal* (May 13, 1997): p. A22.

Miller, John J. 2007. "Should Libraries' Target Audience be Cheapskates with Mass-Market Tastes?" *Wall Street Journal* (January 3, 2007): p. D9.

Millward, David. 2006. "Is This the End of the Road for Traffic Lights?" *The Telegraph* (November 4, 2006).

Mishan, E. J. 1971. "The Post-War Literature on Externalities: An Interpretative Essay." *Journal of Economic Literature* 9: 1–28.

Modigliani, Franco. 1986. "Life Cycle, Individual Thrift and the Wealth of Nations." *American Economic Review* 76(3): 297–313.

Moffitt, Robert A. 2003. "The Temporary Assistance for Needy Families Program." In *Means-Tested Transfer Programs in the US.* Robert A. Moffitt (ed.). Chicago: University of Chicago Press.

Munnell, Alicia, H. 1999. "Reforming Social Security: The Case Against Individual Accounts." *National Tax Journal,* vol. LII, no. 4: 783–802.

Murphy, Kevin M. and Robert Topel. 2000. "Medical Research–What's It Worth?" *The Milken Institute Review,* First Quarter, 23–30.

Murray, Charles. 2006. *In Our Hands: A Plan to Replace the Welfare State.* Washington, DC: AEI Press.

Murray, Sheila E., William N. Evans, and Robert M. Schwab. 1998. "Education-Finance Reform and the Distribution of Education Resources." *American Economic Review* 88: 789–812.

Musgrave, Richard A. 1959. *The Theory of Public Finance.* New York: McGraw-Hill.

Musgrave, Richard A. 1985. "A Brief History of Fiscal Doctrine." In *Handbook of Public Economics,* Vol. 1. Alan Auerbach and Martin S Feldstein (eds.). Amsterdam: North-Holland.

Napolitano, Jo. 2004. "Proposal to Adopt a Palestinian City as a 'Sister' Creates a Family Feud for Madison." *New York Times* (May 29, 2004): p. A10.

Nataraj, Sita and John B. Shoven. 2004. "Has the Unified Budget Undermined the Federal Government Trust Funds?" Working Paper No. 10953. Cambridge, MA: National Bureau of Economic Research.

Newhouse, Joseph P. 1992. "Medical Care Costs: How Much Welfare Loss?" *Journal of Economic Perspectives* 6(3): 3–22.

Newhouse, Joseph P. 2001. "Medical Care Price Indices: Problems and Opportunities; The Chung-Hua Lectures." Working Paper No. 8168. Cambridge, MA: National Bureau of Economic Research.

Newhouse, Joseph P. and the Insurance Experiment Group. 1993. *Free for All? Lessons from the RAND Health Insurance Experiment.* Cambridge, MA: Harvard University Press.

Nicol v. Ames. 1899. 173 US 509, 515.

Niskanen, William A., Jr. 1971. *Bureaucracy and Representative Government.* Chicago: Aldine.

Nordhaus, William D. 2008. *A Question of Balance: Weighing the Options on Global Warming Policies.* New Haven, CT: Yale University Press.

Norris, Floyd. 2005. "How to Assure the Very Rich Stay That Way." *New York Times* (September 9, 2005): p. C1.

Nozick, Robert. 1974. *Anarchy, State, and Utopia.* Oxford: Basil Blackwell.

Oates, Wallace E. 1969. "The Effects of Property Taxes and Local Spending on Property Values: An Empirical Study of Tax Capitalization and the Tiebout Hypothesis." *Journal of Political Economy* 77: 957–971.

Oates, Wallace E. 1999. "An Essay on Fiscal Federalism." *Journal of Economic Literature* 37: 1120–1149.

Office of Family Assistance. 2006. *Temporary Assistance to Needy Families: Seventh Annual Report to Congress.*

Olsen, Edgar O. 2003. "Housing Programs for Low-Income Households." In *Means Tested Transfer Programs in the US.* Robert A. Moffitt (ed.). Chicago: University of Chicago Press.

O'Neill, June E. and Dave M. O'Neill. 2007. "Health Status, Health Care, and Inequality: Canada vs. the US." *Forum for Health Economics and Policy* 10(1).

Organization for Economic Cooperation and Development (OECD). 2004. *Learning for Tomorrow's World: First Results from the OECD Programme for International Student Assessment (PISA) 2003.*

Organization for Economic Cooperation and Development (OECD). 2007a. Center for Educational Research and Innovation. *Education at a Glance.*

Organization for Economic Cooperation and Development (OECD). 2007b. *National Accounts of the OECD Countries— Volume IV: General Government Accounts.* Paris, France. http://stats.oecd.org.

Organization for Economic Cooperation and Development (OECD). 2008a. *OECD Economic Outlook* (December 2008): Paris, France.

Organization for Economic Cooperation and Development (OECD). 2008b. *OECD Health Data.* Paris, France.

Oum, Tae Hoon, W. G. Waters, and Jong-Say Yong. 1992. "Concepts of Price Elasticities of Transport Demand and Recent Empirical Estimates: An Interpretative Survey." *Journal of Transport Economics and Policy* 26: 139–154.

Parry, Ian W. H., Margaret Walls, and Winson Harrington. 2007. "Automobile Externalities and Policies." *Journal of Economic Literature* 45(2): 373–399.

Passell, Peter. "Lend to Any Student." *New York Times* (April 1, 1985): p. A20.

Pauly, Mark and Bradley Herring. 1999. *Pooling Health Insurance Risks.* Washington, DC: AEI Press.

Peltzman, Sam. 1975. "The Effects of Automobile Safety Regulation." *Journal of Political Economy* 83(4): 677–725.

Peltzman, Sam. 1997. "Class Size and Earnings." *Journal of Economic Perspectives* 11(4): 225–226.

Persson, Torsten and Guida Tabellini. 1999. "Political Economics and Public Finance." Working Paper No. 7097. Cambridge, MA: National Bureau of Economic Research.

Phelps, Charles E. 2003. *Health Economics*, 3rd edition. Boston: Addison Wesley.

Phi Delta Kappa/Gallup. 2005. "The Annual Gallup Poll of the Public's Attitudes toward the Public Schools, 1974–2004." Gallup Polling, Gallup.

Pommerehne, Werner. 1977. "Quantitative Aspects of Federalism: A Study of Six Countries." In *The Political Economy of Fiscal Federalism*. Wallace Oates (ed.). Lexington, MA: DC Heath, pp. 275–355.

Porter, Eduardo. 2005. "Buy a Home, and Drag Society Down." *New York Times* (November 13, 2005): p. WK3.

Portney, Paul R. 2000. "Air Pollution Policy." In *Public Policies for Environmental Protection*, 2nd edition. Paul R. Portney and Robert N. Stavins (eds.). Washington, DC: Resources for the Future.

Poterba, James M. 1991. "Dividends, Capital Gains, and the Corporate Veil: Evidence from Britain, Canada, and the United States." In *National Saving and Economic Performance.* Douglas B Bernheim and John B Shoven (eds.). Chicago: University of Chicago Press: 49–71.

Poterba, James M. and Andrew Samwick. 2003. "Taxation and Household Portfolio Composition: US Evidence from the 1980s and 1990s." *Journal of Public Economics* 87: 5–38.

Poterba, James M. and Todd Sinai. 2008. "Tax Expenditures for Owner-Occupied Housing: Deductions for Property Taxes and Mortgage Interest and the Exclusion of Imputed Rental Income." *American Economic Review* 98(2): 84–89.

Pozen, Robert, Sylvester J. Schieber, and John B. Shoven. 2004. "Improving Social Security's Progressivity and Solvency with Hybrid Indexing." *American Economic Review* 94(2): 187–191.

Prescott, Edward C. 2004a. "It's Irrational to Save." *Wall Street Journal* (December 29, 2004): p. A8.

Prescott, Edward C. 2004b. "Why Do Americans Work So Much More Than Europeans?" Working Paper No. 10316. Cambridge, MA: National Bureau of Economic Research.

Prescott, Edward C. 2005a. "Even Europeans Will Respond to Incentives." *Wall Street Journal* (August 2, 2005): p. A10.

Prescott, Edward C. 2005b. "Stop Messing with Federal Tax Rates." *Wall Street Journal* (December 20, 2005): p. A14.

President's Advisory Panel on Federal Tax Reform. 2005. *Simple, Fair, and Pro-Growth: Proposals to Fix America's Tax System* (November 1, 2005). Washington, DC: US Government Printing Office.

Rabushka, Alvin. 2003. "Could a Degressive Tax Be Better Than a Flat Tax?" *The Daily Report*, The Hoover Institution.

Ramsey, Frank P. 1927. "A Contribution to the Theory of Taxation." *Economic Journal* 37: 47–61.

Rawls, John. 1971. *A Theory of Justice.* Cambridge, MA: Harvard University Press.

Reich, Robert B. 2008. "How about a Cap-and-Trade Dividend?" *Wall Street Journal* (June 4, 2008): p. A21.

Reinhardt, Uwe. 2007. "Letter to the Editor." *Wall Street Journal* (December 7, 2007).

Riedl, Brian M. 2002. "Agriculture Lobby Wins Big in New Farm Bill." *Heritage Foundation Backgrounder*, No. 1534, April 9, 2002.

Rogerson, Richard. 2007. "Taxation and Market Work: Is Scandinavia an Outlier?" Working Paper No. 12890. Cambridge, MA: National Bureau of Economic Research.

Romer, Christina D. and David H. Romer. 2007. "Do Tax Cuts Starve the Beast: The Effect of Tax Changes on Government Spending." Working Paper No. 13548. Cambridge, MA: National Bureau of Economic Research.

Rosenbaum, David E. 1986. "Big Changes Loom in Final Tax Bill, Lawmakers Agree." *New York Times* (May 26, 1986): p. C1.

Rosenberg, Debra. 2002. "Medicare's Foundation Is Crumbling." *Newsweek* (December 9, 2002): p. 11.

Ross, Gilbert L. 1999. "Price of Alarmism." *New York Times* (September 2, 1999): p. A26.

Rouse, Cecilia E. 1998. "Private School Vouchers and Student Achievement: An Evaluation of the Milwaukee Parental Choice Program." *Quarterly Journal of Economics* 113(2): 553–602.

Rouse, Cecilia E., Jane Hannaway, Dan Goldhaber, and David N. Figlio. 2007. "Feeling the Florida Heat? How Low-Performing Schools Respond to Voucher and Accountability Pressure." Working Paper No. 13681. Cambridge, MA: National Bureau of Economic Research.

Samuelson, Paul A. 1955. "The Pure Theory of Public Expenditure." *Review of Economics and Statistics* 36: 387–389.

Samuelson, Robert J. 1986. "The True Tax Burden." *Newsweek* (April 21, 1986): p. 68.

Sanbonmatsu, Lisa, Jeffrey R. Kling, Greg J. Duncan, and Jeanne Brooks-Gunn. 2006. "Neighborhoods and Academic Achievement: Results from the Moving to Opportunity Experiment." *Journal of Human Resources,* 41(4): 649–691.

Santerre, Rexford E. and Stephen P. Neun. 2004. *Health Economics: Theories, Insights, and Industry Studies*, 3rd edition. Cincinnati, OH: Thomson South-Western.

Schick, Allen. 2002. "The Deficit That Didn't Just Happen." *The Brookings Review* (Spring): 45–46.

Schmedel, Scott R. 1991. "Tax Report." *Wall Street Journal* (January 9, 1991): p. A1.

Schultze, Charles L. 1995. "The Balanced Budget Amendment: Needed? Effective? Efficient?" *National Tax Journal* 48: 317–328.

Sen, Amartya. 1999. "The Possibility of Social Choice." *American Economic Review* 89: 349–378.

Sheshinski, Eytan and Luis Felipe Lopez-Calva. 1999. "Privatization and Its Benefits: Theory and Evidence." Working Paper. Cambridge, MA: Harvard Institute for International Development.

Shleifer, Andrei. 1998. "State versus Private Ownership." *Journal of Economic Perspectives* 12(4): 133–150.

Shoven, John B. and Sita N. Slavov. 2006. "Political Risk Versus Market Risk in Social Security." Working Paper No. 12135. Cambridge, MA: National Bureau of Economic Research.

Sigman, Hilary. 2003. "Letting States Do the Dirty Work: State Responsibility for Federal Environmental Regulation." *National Tax Journal* 56: 107–122.

Silverman, Julia. 2007. "Tobacco Ads Paying Off in Oregon." *Associated Press* (October 2, 2007).

Sinai, Todd and Joseph Gyourko. 2004. "The (Un)changing Geographical Distribution of Housing Tax Benefits: 1980 to 2000." *Tax Policy and the Economy* 18: 165–208.

Sinai, Todd and Joel Waldfogel. 2002. "Do Low-Income Housing Subsidies Increase Housing Consumption?" Working Paper No. 8709. Cambridge, MA: National Bureau of Economic Research.

Singmaster, Robert. 2007. "Corporate Foreign Tax Credit, 2003." *Internal Revenue Service Statistics of Income Bulletin.*

Skinner, Jonathan, Elliott Fisher, and John E. Wennberg. 2005. "The Efficiency of Medicare." In *Analyses in the Economics of Aging*, David Wise (ed.). Chicago: University of Chicago Press.

Slemrod, Joel and Jon Bakija. 2004. *Taxing Ourselves,* 3rd ed. Cambridge, MA: MIT Press.

Smith, Adam. 1977/1776. *The Wealth of Nations*. London: J.M. Dent and Sons.

Smith, Ray A. 2005. "Homeowners Revolt Against Tax Assessors." *Wall Street Journal* (January 25, 2005): p. D1.

Snow, John. 1855. *On the Mode of Communication of Cholera.* London: John Churchill, New Burlington Street, England.

Social Security Administration. April 2008. *Annual Statistical Supplement to the Social Security Bulletin, 2007*. Washington, DC.

Social Security Trustees. 2008. *The 2008 Annual Report of the Board of Trustees of the Federal Old-Age and Survivors Insurance and Disability Insurance Trust Funds*. Washington, DC: US Government Printing Office.

Stavins, Robert N. 2003. "Experience with Market-based Environmental Policy Instruments." In *The Handbook of Environmental Economics*, Volume 1. Karl-Goran Maler and Jeffrey R. Vincent (eds.). Amsterdam: North Holland.

Stein, Herbert. 1996. "The Income Inequality Debate." *Wall Street Journal* (May 1, 1996): p. A14.

Stein, Herbert. 1997. "Death *and* Taxes." *Wall Street Journal* (July 3, 1997): p. A10.

Stein, Jeremy C. 2003. "Agency, Information and Corporate Investment." In *Handbook of the Economics of Finance,* Vol. 1A. G. M. Constantinides, M. Harris, and R. M. Stulz (eds.). Amsterdam: North-Holland.

Stern, Nicholas. 1987. "The Theory of Optimal Commodity and Income Taxation: An Introduction." In *The Theory of Taxation for Developing Countries*. David Newbery and Nicholas Stern (eds.). New York: Oxford University Press: 22–59.

Stern, Nicholas. 2006. *The Economics of Climate Change*. Cambridge, UK: Cambridge University Press.

Steuerle, C. Eugene and Jon M. Bakija. 1994. *Retooling Social Security for the 21st Century: Right and Wrong Approaches to Reform.* Washington DC: The Urban Institute.

Stevenson, Richard W. 1997. "The Secret Language of Social Engineering." *New York Times* (July 6, 1997): p. E1.

Stiglitz, Joseph E. 1973. "Taxation, Corporate Financial Policy, and the Cost of Capital." *Journal of Public Economics* 2: 1–34.

Stone, Lawrence. 1977. *The Family, Sex, and Marriage in England, 1500–1800*. New York: Harper & Row.

Strumpf, Koleman S. and Felix Oberholzer-Gee. 2002. "Endogenous Policy Decentralization: Testing the Central Tenet of Economic Federalism." *Journal of Political Economy* 110: 1–36.

Stuckart, Wilhem and Hans Globke. 1968. "Civil Rights and the Natural Inequality of Man." In *Nazi Culture*. Georget L. Morse (ed.). New York: Universal Library.

Sugg, Ike C. 1996. "Selling Hunting Rights Saves Animals." *Wall Street Journal* (July 23, 1996): p. A22.

Taheri, Amir. 2003. "Shiite Schism." *Wall Street Journal* (April 7, 2003).

Tideman, T. Nicolaus and Gordon Tullock. 1976. "A New and Superior Process for Making Social Choices." *Journal of Political Economy* 84: 1145–1160.

Tiebout, Charles. 1956. "A Pure Theory of Local Expenditures." *Journal of Political Economy* 64: 416–424.

Tierney, John. 2001. "Is a US Force the Safest Bet for Airports?" *New York Times* (October 16, 2001): p. D1.

Tierney, John. 2005. "The Mansion Wars." *New York Times* (November 15, 2005): p. A27.

Tierney, John. 2006. "New Europe's Boomtown." *New York Times* (September 5, 2006): p. A23.

Tobin, James. 1958. "Liquidity Preference as Attitude toward Risk." *Review of Economic Studies* 25: 65–86.

Tomsho, Robert. 2001. "Fund-Raising Drive for Schools Leaves Manchester Disunited." *Wall Street Journal* (February 7, 2001): p. A1.

Transport for London. 2007. "Central London Congestion Charging: Impacts Monitoring." Fifth Annual Report.

Tresch, Richard W. 2002. *Public Finance: A Normative Theory*, 2nd edition. New York: Academic Press.

Tucker, Robert C., ed. 1978. *The Marx-Engels Reader*, 2nd edition. New York. W.W. Norton.

Uchitelle, Louis. 2001. "Now, Uncle Sam Wants You." *New York Times* (November 25, 2001): p. WK3.

Uhlig, Harald and Mathias Trabandt. 2006. "How Far Are We from the Slippery Slope? The Laffer Curve Revisited." Working Paper 5657. Center for Economic Policy Research.

US Bureau of the Census. 2007. *The Effect of Government Taxes and Transfers on Income and Poverty in the United States: 2005*. March 2007.

US Bureau of the Census. 2008a. *Current Population Reports: Income, Poverty and Health Insurance Coverage in the United States: 2007:* www.census.gov/prod/2008pubs/p60-235.pdf.

US Bureau of the Census. 2008b. *Current Population Survey: Annual Social and Economic Supplements:* www.census.gov/hhes/www/income/histinc/h02AR.html.

US Bureau of the Census. 2008c. "Federal, State, and Local Governments: State and Local Government Finances." www.census.gov/govs/www/estimate.html.

US Bureau of the Census. 2008d. *Public Education Finances: 2006.*

US Bureau of the Census. 2009. *Statistical Abstract of the United States: 2008*, 128th edition. Washington, DC: www.census.gov/statab/www/.

US Centers for Disease Control and Prevention. 2005. *Health, United States, 2005.* National Center for Health Statistics.

US Department of Agriculture. 2008. *Characteristics of Food Stamp Households: Fiscal Year 2007.* Food Stamp Program. Report No. FNS-03-030-TMN.

US Department of Education. 2007a. *Digest of Education Statistics, 2007.* http://nces.ed.gov/programs/digest/d07.

US Department of Education. 2007b. *National Assessment of Educational Progress (NAEP).* Institute of Education Sciences, National Center for Education Statistics.

US Department of Health and Human Services. 2008. *Administration for Children and Families, Caseload Data 2007.*

US Department of Housing and Urban Development and US Department of Commerce. 2008. *American Housing Survey for the United States: 2007.*

US Department of Labor. 2008. "Unemployment Insurance Data Summary." *Employment and Training Division.*

US Office of Management and Budget (OMB). 2003. *Circular A-4, Regulatory Analysis.* www.whitehouse.gov/omb/circulars/a004/a-4.pdf.

US Office of Management and Budget (OMB). 2008. *Analytical Perspectives: Budget of the United States Government, Fiscal Year 2009.* Washington, DC: US Government Printing Office.

US Office of Management and Budget (OMB). 2009. *A New Era of Responsibility: Renewing America's Promise.* US Government Printing Office. Washington, DC.

Vessella, Tom. 2001. "How about This for a Tax Plan: Eliminate the IRS." *The Princeton Tory*: 17–18.

Viscusi, W. Kip. 1992. *Fatal Tradeoffs: Public and Private Responsibilities for Risk.* New York: Oxford University Press.

Viscusi, W. Kip. 2006. "The Value of Life." In *The New Palgrave Dictionary of Economics*, 2nd edition. Steven Durlauf and Lawrence Blume (eds.). London: Macmillan.

Viscusi, W. Kip and Joseph E. Aldy. 2003. "The Value of a Statistical Life: A Critical Review of Market Estimates throughout the World." *Journal of Risk and Uncertainty* 27(1): 5–76.

Viscusi, W. Kip and Ted Gayer. 2005. "Quantifying and Valuing Environmental Health Risks." In *Handbook of Environmental Economics*, Volume 2. Karl-Goran Maler and Jeffrey R. Vincent (eds.). Elsevier. Amsterdam.

von Wartburg, Markus and William G. Waters II. 2004. "Congestion Externalities and the Value of Travel Time Savings." In *Towards Estimating the Social and Environmental Costs of Transport in Canada: A Report for Transport Canada.* Anming Zhang, Anthony E. Boardman, David Gillen, and William G. Waters II (eds.). Vancouver, Canada: Centre for Transportation Studies, University of British Columbia.

Wall Street Journal. 2001. "Non-Stop Taxes." (April 19, 2001): p. A18.

Wall Street Journal. 2008. "Conrad's Gift." (March 7, 2008): p. A14.

Weimer, David L. and Michael J. Wolkoff. 2001. "School Performance and Housing Values: Using Non-Contiguous District and Incorporation Boundaries to Identify School Effects." *National Tax Journal* 54: 231–254.

Weitzman, Martin L. 1974. "Prices vs. Quantities." *Review of Economic Studies* 41(4): 477–491.

Weitzman, Martin L. 2007. "A Review of the Stern Review on the Economics of Climate Change." *Journal of Economic Literature* 45(3): 703–724.

White, Bobby. 2008. "California Balks at Paying Billions to Improve Prison Hospitals." *Wall Street Journal* (July 21, 2008): p. A3.

Whitmore, Diane. 2002. "What Are Food Stamps Worth?" Industrial Relations Section Working Paper No. 468. Princeton, NJ: Princeton University.

Willig, Robert. 1976. "Consumer Surplus without Apology." *American Economic Review* 66(4): 589–597.

Wilson, James Q. 1994. "A New Approach to Welfare Reform: Humility." *Wall Street Journal* (December 29, 1994): p. A10.

Wilson, James Q. 2000. "Pork Is Kosher under Our Constitution." *Wall Street Journal* (February 15, 2000): p. A26.

Winer, Stanley and Walter Hettich. 2004. "The Political Economy of Taxation: Positive and Normative Analysis When Collective Choice Matters." In *The Encyclopedia of Public Choice.* C. Rowley and F. Schneider (eds.). Kluwer Academic.

Wolff, Edward N. 2001. "Recent Trends in Wealth Ownership, 1983–1998." In *Assets for the Poor: The Benefits of Spreading Asset Ownership.* Thomas M. Shapiro and Edward N. Wolff (eds.). Russell Sage Press: 34–73.

Woodbury, Stephen A. and Robert G. Spiegelman. 1987. "Bonuses to Workers and Employers to Reduce Unemployment: Randomized Trials in Illinois." *American Economic Review* 77(4): 513–530.

Wooldridge, Jeffrey M. 2009. *Introductory Econometrics*, 4th edition. Cincinnati, OH: South-Western College Publishing.

You, Jong-sung and Sanjeev Khagram. 2004. "Inequality and Corruption." Hauser Center for Nonprofit Organizations Working Paper No. 22. Kennedy School of Government Working Paper Series: RWP04-001.

Zimmerman, Jonathan. 2007. "Letter to the Editor." *New York Times* (March 24, 2007).

Zodrow, George R. 2007. "The Property Tax Incidence Debate and the Mix of State and Local Finance of Local Public Expenditures." *CESifo Economic Studies* 53(4): 495–521.

Name Index

Page numbers followed by an *n* indicate notes.

A

Aaronson, D., 143*n*
Aboulafia, R., 69
Acemoglu, D., 137
Ackerman, F., 167
Akradi, Bahram, 413
Aldy, J. E., 167*n*
Alesina, A., 267
Allen, M., 408
Alm, J., 409
Alsenz, J., 485
Altig, D., 401, 487
Anders, G., 225
Anderson, G. M., 196
Archer, B., 380
Armitage-Smith, G., 301
Arrow, K. J., 116
Atkinson, A. B., 113*n*
Attanasio, O. P., 245, 245*n*
Auerbach, A. J., 131, 401, 487
Austen, Jane, 255

B

Baicker, K., 221, 222, 536
Baker, M. A., 530
Baker, Russell, 342, 462
Bakija, J., 394, 485
Banzhaf, H. S., 512
Barboza, D., 515
Barro, R. J., 470
Barrow, L., 143*n*
Barry, D., 380, 502
Bartlett, B., 485
Bassetto, M., 464
Bauman, K. J., 261
Baumol, H., 49
Baumol, W. J., 49, 100
Bazelon, C., 162
Becker, G. S., 364, 488
Benjamin, D. J., 390, 430
Bergan, D., 126
Beshears, J., 431
Biggs, A. G., 234
Bindman, A, B., 198
Blair, D. H., 116*n*
Blank, R., 282–285, 295
Blau, F. D., 421
Blume-Kohout, M. E., 202
Blumenthal, M., 374
Boardman, A. E., 152*n*, 163*n*
Borcherding, T. E., 128
Borck, R., 529
Boskin, M. J., 249, 357*n*
Bradford, D. F., 493, 504
Bradley, B., 405
Brandeis, Louis, 516

Brat, I., 459
Brody, J. E., 32
Brook, R. H., 198
Brooks-Gunn, J., 294
Brown, M. E., 198
Browning, E. K., 267, 297
Browning, M., 482
Brugiavini, A., 245
Buchanan, J. M., 117, 132*n*
Buckley, Christopher, 248
Burger, Warren, 346
Burke, V., 276*n*
Burman, L. E., 207, 405
Burtraw, D., 101
Bush, George H. W., 174
Bush, George W., 18, 148, 168, 180, 227, 296, 506
Butler, Rhett, 329
Butler, S. M., 221

C

Calderon, Felipe, 70
Cameron, S. V., 139
Campbell, E. Q., 142
Campoy, A., 516
Cantor, Eric, 476
Carasso, A., 406*n*, 408
Card, D., 145, 171, 172, 218
Carnegie, Andrew, 496–499
Cawley, J., 189*n*
Chamberlain, A., 269
Chavez, Hugo, 14, 328
Chay, K. Y., 79, 80
Chetty, R., 450
Cheung, R., 526
Chiappori, P.-A., 189*n*, 254
Chirinko, R. S., 445*n*, 447
Chivers, C. J., 274
Choi, J. J., 431
Christian, C., 374
Christy, G. C., 459
Cieslewicz, Dave, 516
Cinyabuguma, M., 64*n*
Clausing, K., 459
Clay, Henry, 4, 120
Clements, J., 437
Clinton, Hillary Rodham, 328, 471
Clinton, William Jefferson (Bill), 7, 33, 63, 174, 235
Clymer, A., 517
Cnossen, S., 488
Coase, R. H., 63, 82
Cockburn, A., 503
Colbert, Jean Baptiste, 301
Coleman, J. S., 142
Collins, C., 498
Cooper, Katrina, 66

Corlett, W. J., 356
Craig, S., 436
Crane, M. W., 8
Crossen, S., 486*n*
Crossley, T. F., 482
Currie, J., 220, 292
Cushing, M. J., 264
Cushman, J. H., Jr., 174
Cutler, D. M., 189, 197, 200, 201, 210

D

Daschle, Tom, 383
Davis, S. J., 119, 374
Dee, T. S., 28
Delipalla, S., 317
Derthick, M., 517
de Tocqueville, Alexis, 515
Dewenter, K., 68
Diamond, P. A., 246, 248
Dillon, S., 506
Director, Aaron, 129*n*
Disraeli, Benjamin, 117, 205
Djankov, S., 443
Doms, M. E., 440
Dow, W., 222
Doyle, J., Jr., 328
Dudley, P. M., 174
Duggan, M. G., 218
Dulberger, E. R., 249
Duncan, G. J., 294
Dunn, W. E., 440

E

Eberstadt, N., 260
Edgeworth, F. Y., 35*n*, 361, 362
Einstein, Albert, 415
Eisenhower, Dwight, 200
Eissa, N., 419
Engelhardt, G. V., 231
Engels, Friedrich, 41*n*
Evans, W. N., 534

F

Fairclough, G., 374
Fattah, H. M., 134
Faulkner, William, 70
Feldman, M., 265
Feldstein, M., 31, 106, 222, 245, 253, 343, 424, 437, 472*n*, 479, 514–517
Figlio, D. N., 143, 148, 149
Finkelstein, A., 198, 215, 216, 226
Fisher, E., 216
Fisher, R. C., 529, 531

Subject Index

Page numbers followed by an *n* indicate notes.